Mr. Cheap's Chicago

Bargains, factory outlets, off-price stores, deep discount stores, cheap eats, cheap places to stay, and cheap fun things to do.

Mark Waldstein

BOB ADAMS, INC.
Holbrook, Massachusetts

Published by Bob Adams, Inc.
260 Center Street, Holbrook, MA 02343

ISBN: 1-55850-291-2

Printed in the United States of America

A   B   C   D   E   F   G   H   I   J

Library of Congress Cataloging-in-Publication Data
Waldstein, Mark.
Mr. Cheap's Chicago : bargains, factory outlets, off-price stores, deep discount stores,
cheap eats, cheap places to stay, and cheap fun things to do / Mark Waldstein.
p.   cm.
Includes index.
ISBN: 1-55850-291-2 : $8.95
1. Chicago (Ill.)—Guidebooks. 2. Shopping—Illinois—Chicago—Guidebooks.
3. Restaurants—Illinois—Chicago—Guidebooks. 4. Bed and breakfast accommodations—
Illinois—Chicago—Guidebooks. 5. Hotels—Illinois—Chicago—Guidebooks. 6. Outlet
stores—Illinois—Chicago—Guidebooks. I. Title. II. Title: Mister Cheap's Chicago
F548.18.W32   1994
917.73'110443—dc20   93-43271
                                                                  CIP

*This book is available at quantity discounts for bulk purchases.
For information, call 1-800-872-5627.*

ACKNOWLEDGEMENTS

A project of this enormity cannot possibly be done alone. First of all,
I want to thank my publisher, Bob Adams, and my agent, Doe Coover, for
working together to pave the way for this series. I'm extremely grateful to my
two assistants, Erica and Tami (better known as the Cheapettes), for plunging
so bravely into the wacky world of Mr. Cheap. Also on the publishing side, a
special thank you to Alina Stankiewicz, whose hard work got us on the map
while her bubbly nature made it fun.
Thanks also to Ann Burger, whose warmth and hospitality could make
any city feel like home. Long-time friend, part-time chauffeur and full-time
wunderkind Mark D'Arienzo, along with wife Laurie, were of invaluable
support and comradeship. And, for all the fun...er, research help, thanks to
Katherine Wahl and Doug Thurman, Vince Mahler and Julie Eudeikis, Karen
Tarjan and Steve Herson, Gayle and Bob Jacobs, and Isabelle Liss.
Further thank-yous go to Neil and Janet Jorgensen, the Dickman fam-
ily, Sharon and Curt Zimmerman, Deanne England, Kristin Morris, Chrystina
Hanson, Mary Jacob and Denise Alban-Kern.

CONTENTS

ENTERTAINMENT

RESTAURANTS

A FEW (CAREFULLY CHOSEN) WORDS
FROM MR. CHEAP

About this "cheap" business. I'll admit, there are more elegant ways to put the idea.

Lots of folks want to save money, especially in these tough times. When it comes to low *prices*, few people know as many good places as I do. But, strictly speaking, that doesn't make these stores and restaurants "cheap." Nor does it make anyone who uses this book a "cheapskate." I think *thrifty* would be a better word. Or perhaps *frugal*.

After all, a cheap person, in my mind, is someone who has plenty of money to burn, and refuses to touch it; a thrifty person would probably spend the cash if he or she had it—especially for something of good value. Most of us fall into the latter category, don't we?

Anyway, everyone loves a bargain, and it's my pleasure to pass these hints along. This idea grew out of my own personal experience, from years of living on the financial edge as a "starving artist." My background is in theater and writing; and as most people know, actors don't make any money even with steady work. I learned to live "cheaply" out of necessity, and developed my first book (*Mr. Cheap's Boston*) as a way to put this knowledge to good use, helping out folks in similar straits. That book wound up on the *Boston Globe* bestseller list; *Mr. Cheap's New York* followed. Suddenly, I discovered myself on a mission!

There is, by now, a research technique behind these books, but "cheaping" is hardly an exact science. Prices change all the time. Stores come and go. Restaurants change their menus. Now, you won't find the exact same items on the shelves tomorrow that I found during my travels; but the descriptions in this book are sure to help you track down just about anything you may be looking for, at the lowest possible price.

A few words of caution: "You gets what you pays for." It's been said many times, and it's generally true. With new merchandise in particular, prices are always discounted for a reason. It may be that the item is simply a leftover from last year, yet still perfectly good; in other cases, if the price is low, the quality may not be far behind. I have tried to point out, wherever I could, items that are cheap because they are less well made, or because they are irregular or damaged. Even these "IR" goods may be useful to the reader who only needs them to last for a short time—students furnishing a dorm room, for example—or to shoppers who happen to be handy with a hammer, or a needle and thread. Sometimes, the *truly* cheap is all you need.

I expect to hear from readers who insist I've left out their favorite diner, or some resale boutique they love. To these fellow bargain hunters, I say, Mr. C can't be *everywhere*; but please do pass along the information, and I'll be happy to scout them out for our next edition. The address is:

Mr. Cheap
c/o Bob Adams, Inc.
260 Center St.
Holbrook, MA 02343

So, get ready to use the book—but be careful how you use the name! As you can see, "cheap" can mean many things. And when you tell someone that you paid only $45 for your designer outfit, nobody will be laughing. They'll just want to know how you did it.

On to the goodies!

Mark Waldstein
a.k.a. Mr. Cheap

SHOPPING

The hundreds of stores in this section are all places which will save you money in some way. They actually cover a broad spectrum of discount shopping, from the latest designer clothing to thrift shops, new furniture to used, major brands to second-rate imitations. Mr. Cheap wants to cover it all, giving his readers as many options as possible for saving cash.

Whenever possible, Mr. C points out *why* an item is marked down—whether it's discontinued, second-quality (imperfect), or just plain cheap stuff. Thus informed, it's up to you to decide which stores and merchandise are for you.

The prices quoted, again, are based upon items Mr. C found at the time of his research. You shouldn't expect to find the same items, at the same prices, when you shop; the prices are just examples which are similar to what you may find. Even if they've gone up, the descriptions herein should help you compare one place against another.

Many stores which sell several kinds of merchandise have been cross-referenced for you, appearing in each appropriate chapter; but remember to consult "Discount Department Stores" and "Flea Markets and Emporia" for many of the same items which have their own chapters. Similarly, the "General Markets" portion of the "Food Shops" chapter gives you more places to look for individual kinds of foods.

Go to it!

APPLIANCES

There are lots of places to save money on appliances and electronics in Chicago. Some, unfortunately, are as far below repute as they are below retail. With merchandise that is imported from foreign countries, there is a greater possibility of shady deals, or inferior quality. Mr. C says this not out of any kind of prejudice, but because he wants you to be careful.

One of the best ways to protect yourself, if you have doubts as to *any* store's reliability, is to ask about their guarantee policy; make sure the item you want carries an American warranty. Since some stores deal directly with manufacturers in the Far East, their merchandise may carry a foreign warranty instead. Even for identical products, a foreign warranty can make repairs a hassle—unless you don't mind paying the postage to Japan. Remember, you are perfectly within your rights to inquire about this in the store.

Appliance Recycle
- 1854 N. Besley Court, Chicago; (312) 384-1471

This may be Mr. Cheap's favorite find in all of Chicago. It was certainly a most dramatic discovery, worthy of no one less than Dr. Livingstone, of deepest Africa fame. For, tucked away in a ghost town of a tiny industrial side street off of Elston, Dr. Liv—er, Mr. C found himself knocking on a nondescript, tightly locked door which did bear the correct address (and nothing else). After a few moments with no answer, he concluded that any business here must have long since gone. But, as Mr. C began to walk away, he heard someone call out, "You looking for appliances?" And sure enough, from the building's loading dock, a man was waving him over.

Inside, the sight was overwhelming. Appliance Recycle has filled two floors of a cavernous warehouse with a sea of used refrigerators, stoves, washers, and dryers. Where do they come from? Stores which take them as trade-ins for new models, and then sell them off to places like this—only you've never seen any such reseller

as large as this one. Most of the stock comes from Sears stores, all over the country. AR's crackerjack team goes to work, rehabbing each appliance into perfect working order; they back this up with a 30-day warranty on parts and labor, just in case there's a problem they've missed.

So, you can get a Frigidaire side-by-side refrigerator/freezer, originally selling for $1200, for a cool $575—or a 20-cubic foot Kenmore side-by-side for just $350, with a crushed ice dispenser built into the front. Since so many of the models come from Sears, Kenmore is the most frequently seen brand here. Washing machines and dryers each sell for around $150 and up; electric ranges range from $125 to about $375, depending on size. Any of these may easily be half the price of a new model, or less—and you can even do trade-ins right here. There is some room, in fact, for a bit of good old-fashioned haggling—it's worth a try. Could a setting like this possibly offer any other kind of shopping?

Delivery service is available; the guys here are extremely friendly and laid-back. Appliance Recycle is open

Mondays through Fridays from 7:00 a.m. to 4:00 p.m., and Saturdays from 9-2. The only approach, by the way, is to go south from Cortland Street, between Elston and Ashland. Look for the loading dock on your right. Good luck.

Aronson Furniture and Appliances

- 3939 N. Ashland Ave., Chicago; (312) 871-6900
- 5657 W. Belmont Ave., Chicago; (312) 889-0312
- 1379 N. Milwaukee Ave., Chicago; (312) 235-9000
- 4630 S. Ashland Ave., Chicago; (312) 376-3401
- 3401 W. 47th St., Chicago; (312) 376-3400
- 2301 W. 95th St., Chicago; (312) 445-1888
- River Oaks West Shopping Center, Calumet City; (708) 891-1700

Since 1940, Aronson has been offering mid-range brands in all kinds of major goods for the home. Over the years, it has grown into one of Chicago's high-volume retailers, yet it hasn't lost sight of its own humble beginnings. As you can see above, it maintains branches in all parts of the city, north and south; this is the kind of place for regular folks who need to stretch the budget, but want good value for their money. Prices here can range from 30% to 60% off retail for furniture, appliances, and even jewelry.

In the appliances department, Mr. C noted that most major items—such as washers and dryers by Amana, and gas ranges by Admiral—are priced about $100 below retail. A Frigidaire 20-cubic foot side-by-side refrigerator/freezer was seen for $969, well below its $1165 list price. And an Emerson Quiet Cool air conditioner was reduced from $599 to $499.

Aronson's stores are open seven days a week, including weekday evenings. They also offer very flexible credit plans—as one person here put it, "If people see something they like, we'll give them every chance to buy it."

But wait—there's more! Aronson also has two clearance centers, the **Aronson Bargain Warehouses,** located at 2440 N. Milwaukee Ave., telephone (312) 276-2066, and 8530 S. Cottage Grove Ave., telephone (312) 873-8999. At these cavernous, no-frills places, you can find incredible savings on leftovers, closeouts, and slightly-damaged floor models. You never know what will turn up here, but there is sure to be a vast selection of sofas selling for as little as $120, bedroom sets as low as $200, refrigerators under $300, and color televisions from $166, plus lamps, chairs and lots more. Everything is sold "as is," of course, with all sales final.

Broadway Vacuum Company

- 5240 N. Clark St., Chicago; (312) 784-0814

You can really clean up here, saving money by purchasing an ultra-cheap used or repaired vacuum cleaner. It's educational, too, listening all the while to the talk shows that the owner plays on the television in the fix-it room.

There are only a couple dozen or so vacuums on display in this tiny repair shop/store, and they're not what you'd call recent models; but they work fine. A Eureka upright was seen here selling for $48.50, and a Hoover for $59.50; most in the store don't go much above this price range.

The selection seems mostly to be Hoovers, but since they fix whatever they can find, you may spot other brands such as Regina, Kenmore, Electrolux, and more. BVC also sells bags to go with your "new" vacuum, and if anything should go wrong with it, you know they'll be familiar with it—inside and out.

Edward Don & Company Outlet

- 2525 N. Elston Ave., Chicago; (312) 489-7739.

One of several super outlets on this stretch of Elston, Edward Don is not to be missed. It's a restaurant supply house that's open to the public, with lots to see for your kitchen and dining rooms. The back room here is full

9

MR. CHEAP'S PICKS
Appliances

✔ **Appliance Recycle**—A veritable sea of reconditioned refrigerators, still-cooking stoves, and scrubbed-up washers, all at a fraction of their original prices.

✔ **Aronson's Bargain Warehouse**—Floor models and overstocks at leftover prices.

✔ **J & D Whirlpool and Bath Outlet**—Cheap Jacuzzis? You bet.

✔ **Modern Overseas Appliances**—One of the many cheap import shops along Devon. Check everything carefully, and don't be afraid to haggle.

of discontinued and close-out kitchen supplies and appliances, while the front area offers a wide range of their regularly-priced kitchen accessories.

The appliance selection is limited, but you can find some real deals. Mr. C noticed a Mirro 22-quart stockpot selling for $22 up front; that back room, however, is the true bargain bonanza. Here, you may grab a closeout on a 30-cup Regal coffee-maker for $44, or a discontinued, brand-new Eureka vacuum—industrial grade—an amazing bargain at $95.

The store is open Mondays through Fridays from 10:00 a.m. to 6:00 p.m., Saturdays from 9-5, and Sundays from 11-4.

J & D Whirlpool and Bath Outlet
• 2730 N. Elston Ave., Chicago; (312) 252-6886
• 2745 N. Harlem Ave., Chicago; (312) 622-5420

Here's another no-frills setting, for appliances which are anything but. If you've always wanted a Jacuzzi, but found them somewhat out of reach, try looking here. In fact, says co-owner Douglas Denning, this store sells "everything for the bathroom but tile," not to mention kitchen cabinets and sinks as well. The selection here is not large; there may only be four or five of a particular item on hand, each one a different model. But then, new stuff arrives all the time. The stock comes directly from the manufacturers—these are items which may have a slight blemish and cannot be sold at full price, but are in perfect working order. J & D does these manufacturers a favor by selling them off at discount.

For example, a hot tub by Aquatic, with a DuPont Lucite finish, was recently on sale for $1,500—marked down from a retail price of $2,200. Why? It had a slight scratch, evidently made at the factory. Honestly, you couldn't see it unless you knew exactly where to look. Another hot tub was reduced from $1,700 to $1,200; there were several of these, completely unmarred. They were simply discontinued models.

Among the other items seen here recently were Pace kitchen cabinets, Bertch cultured marble sink tops, Kohler toilets and tubs, as well as mirrors and vanity sinks. One Kohler tub was marked down from an original $2,500 to a soothing $600. Second-quality sink tops were reduced from $80 to $50 each. Lots of landlords and contractors shop here, checking in frequently just to see what may have come in. Suffice it to say, with the hot tubs in particular, most items don't hang around here for long.

JP's Super Store
• 2425 W. Devon Ave., Chicago; (312) 761-4422

JP's is a mish-mash of merchandise in a gigantic, no-frills (read: cardboard boxes all over the floor) set-up. You'll find some great brand names here as well as some mystery manufacturers. Like so many of the importers along this stretch of Devon, they offer a little bit of everything from small appliances to stereo and video.

Appliances may be the best bet here. Mr. C saw an Osterizer blender for $39.99; and a two-slice toaster by Oster for just $24.99. Among the other items on display were a large roast-sized Hamilton Beach toaster oven/broiler for $70, and a Black and Decker Series 200 steam iron for $26.99.

You can also get cheap luggage, in brands like Royal and Continental. You wouldn't want that gorilla in the TV commercials to get his mitts on these, but they will get you through your next vacation or two.

A word of warning: Do watch your step as you wander around the warehouse. With lots of stray boxes lying around on the floor, to say you can really trip over a bargain here is true in more ways than one. JP's is open from 10:30 a.m to 7:30 p.m., seven days a week.

Modern Overseas Appliances
- 2334 W. Devon Ave., Chicago; (312) 761-7665

One of the many international-flavored electronics stores along Devon, Modern Overseas stocks a typical assortment of appliances, electronics, and—fitting right in—cosmetics, watches, and pens. Among the bargains you may find here are such items as a Panasonic microwave oven for $160; a Eureka upright vacuum cleaner, with light, for $60; a Norelco rechargeable triple-head rotary shaver for $40; and a Black and Decker steam iron for $17.99. Plus VCRs, camcorders, televisions, stereo components, and much more. As with all of these shops, do be careful to get units that are intended for use at American voltage levels (110 or 120 volts); many items are built to foreign standards, which will not work in this country. The store is open seven days a week, from 11:00 a.m. to 8:00 p.m.

Across the street is another, slightly larger shop selling much the same stuff: **International Video and Electronics**, at 2355 W. Devon Avenue, telephone (312) 338-9033. At both shops, by the way, you may want to try your hand at negotiating the prices down a bit. The language barrier can make it tough, but all of these places are competing with each other. You can always find another store to try.

Nelson Brothers
- 2750 W. Grand Ave., Chicago; (312) 235-3414
- 4840 N. Broadway, Chicago; (312) 561-3900
- 6250 S. Cottage Grove Ave., Chicago; (312) 324-6551
- 6535 S. Halsted St., Chicago; (312) 487-2123

And other suburban locations
The "sales counselors," as they're dubbed here at Nelson Brothers, could use a little help themselves; when asked, two of them began arguing over where their store's other branches were located. If you can put up with this, give the store a shot for mid-quality furniture in traditional American and Euro-modern styles, as well as brand-name appliances and home furnishing accessories.

Appliance prices are good, if not always spectacular; a Speed Queen large capacity, heavy duty washer was seen for $549. Microwave ovens, stoves and dishwashers are also available, and certainly worth checking out in your search. Open seven days a week.

Plass
- 2019 W. Irving Park Rd., Chicago; (312) 868-0100

And many other suburban locations
For more than fifty years, Plass has been saving folks money on big-ticket kitchen appliances, specializing in built-in units for home and commercial use. Unlike many of its suburban locations, which also carry televisions and other electronics, this in-town branch stays in the kitchen only. They carry just about all the major brands, including Amana, Tappan, Maytag, Caloric, Frigidaire, Kelvinator, and many others. If you're in the market for a new dishwasher, refrigerator, gas range, built-in oven, or the like, this is a place you should cer-

tainly check out. Plass claims, in fact, that it will beat any price on an identical item found elsewhere for less—before or after your purchase here. Delivery and removal of old appliances are both available. Plass is open from 9 a.m. to 5 p.m. on weekdays, from 9-4 on Saturdays, and closed on Sundays.

Southwest Furniture and Appliance
- 2934 N. Milwaukee Ave., Chicago; (312) 227-4224
- 3239 S. Halsted St., Chicago; (312) 567-9752

Southwest specializes in repairing and selling used appliances, as well as new furniture. The South Halsted store fixes more appliances and also sells more, so they're the better bet for a good selection on washers, ovens and refrigerators—but either place can save you lots of dough.

Need to furnish a kitchen, cheap, and don't mind used-car-lot plastic flags flying overhead? An almond-covered used Hot Point refrigerator is $129 here; a General Electric fridge in lovely avocado is $159. It's scratched, but nothing a few magnets couldn't cover. The main thing, after all, is that the inside works.

Meanwhile, not everything is necessarily scuffed up. Mr. C found an impressively clean Magic Chef gas stove for $159. These appliances, as well as the used dishwashers, all leave the store with a 30-day warranty; the store also accepts trade-ins.

Southwest Furniture and Appliance is open Mondays through Saturdays from 10-7, and 11-5 on Sundays.

BEDS AND MATTRESSES

The Bedding Experts
- 1871 N. Clybourn Ave., Chicago; (312) 528-9000
- 3145 N. Halsted St., Chicago; (312) 871-3636
- 4851 N. Western Ave., Chicago; (312) 728-7121
- 3101 N. Central Ave., Chicago; (312) 622-0155
- 4445 N. Pulaski Rd., Chicago; (312) 604-8200
- 5689 S. Archer Ave, Chicago; (312) 585-2300

And many other suburban locations. The Experts are one of, if not *the* biggest, mattress chains in all of Chicagoland. At their frequent sales, you may find Sealy twin-size mattresses and box springs selling for as little as $43 apiece; queen sets for $173; and kings for $273 a set. These prices may be up to 60% or more off retail.

Bed frames are also a good deal here, like a metal frame daybed for $148, bunk beds from $188 and a queen or king-size black iron bed frame for $598.

Because Bedding Experts is such a large company, they can promise delivery within 24 hours; and all advertised items are guaranteed to be in stock. They also have a 60-day price guarantee on every item in stock; if you find your mattress cheaper somewhere else within two months, with proof, they'll refund you the difference. And that's the difference here.

Bed Mart
- 3135 N. Clark St., Chicago; (312) 477-1701
- 1747 N. Sheffield Ave., Chicago; (312) 335-3336
- 1807 Central St., Evanston; (708) 864-3401

And many other suburban locations. Okay, so the name isn't the most exciting you've ever heard. But Bed Mart's high-volume business will help you get a mattress at a reasonable price, and that's something to jump up and down about (not on the beds, please). In fact, they claim they will beat any other price on a particular model, or you get the bed for free (?!).

Bed Mart carries famous brand names like Sealy, Serta, Simmons, and Stearns and Foster. During a recent special, they were offering a queen-size Serta Classic set for $368, including the box spring and frame. Individual Simmons pieces started at $47 twin, $87 full. And Simmons Beautyrest mattresses, retail priced at $429 in full size, were on sale here for $179.

You can finance your purchase for ninety days, and next-day delivery is promised. The stores are open daily 10:30 to 9, Saturdays 10 to 5 and Sundays 11 to 5.

"The Bedpost"
(Heller Brothers Bedding)
- 2828 W. 48th Place, Chicago; (312) 376-9520

You could lose some sleep trying to find this South Side factory, but once you get there, the $$$ you'll save will bring you plenty of zzzzz's. When you think about buying "factory direct," *this* is the kind of place you're picturing. Co-owner Larry Heller took Mr. C on a tour of the whole operation, in fact, showing how he and his brothers make their mattresses from start to finish; that's how proud and confident he is of the high quality here. Every one is made individually, almost entirely by hand, using only small machinery; cranking 'em out at high speed would not be the Heller Brothers' way. Yet, because you can order and purchase directly from this no-frills showroom, you save big over famous name brands at fancier stores. "All of the cost goes into quality," says Larry.

They make a wide range of bedding, including custom orders for school dorms and hospitals. Of course, if you've spent any time in either sort of place, you'd hardly call that a good recommendation. How about this: When Oprah bought herself an antique four-poster, she asked these fellas to design a mattress to fit its unique specifications. They also make the beds for the Chicago Fire Department—and you *know* those guys need some good sleep.

Where were we? Oh yes...wide range of bedding. You have quite a choice of densities and firmness, from simple foam fillings to the strongest-gauge inner springs. They will even use "polysteel" springs to make super-firm mattresses for heavy people that will really last. Speaking of which, all of the mattresses are fully warrantied; some for as much as ten or twenty years.

So, how much for these resplendent resting places? Mattresses made with inner springs, not foam, start from just $49 in twin size. "Good" quality sets kick in at about $100 each piece, perhaps half of what you'd pay for name brands. And you can get a "Premium" full-size set for about $200, with queen-size sets from $275. If you only need a mattress, you can have one for about 60% of the price per set.

Delivery is available, though not free. The Bedpost is open weekdays from 8 a.m. to 3 p.m., and Saturday mornings from 8-11. Closed on Sundays.

Furniture Connection
- 3128 N. Broadway (2nd Floor), Chicago; (312) 281-7411

Upstairs from one of Mr. C's literary haunts, Barbara's Bookstore, is this large and attractive shop selling contemporary furniture and bedding at good discounts. There are some traditional looks too, but you'll probably want to go for the trendy Euro and Far East styles. Prices can be as much as 40% below retail, especially during special promotions.

Furniture Connection also sells name-brand mattresses at everyday discounts of 25% to 50% off retail. These start as low as $43 for a firm twin mattress or boxspring; in full size, each piece is $57. They go up through several grades, all the way to "Ultra pillow top super plush," in which queen sets are $569 and king sets are $769, top o' the line. These fancier models include a frame, and delivery, at no extra charge.

The store is open weekdays from 10 a.m. to 8 p.m., Saturdays from 10-5, and Sundays from 11-5.

MR. CHEAP'S PICKS
Beds and Mattressses

✔ **The Bedpost**—This South Side factory makes high-quality mattresses and sells direct-to-you.

✔ **Furniture Liquidation Centers**—Good quality, inexpensive bed frames, bunk beds, and more.

✔ **Verlo Mattress Factory Stores**—Among the very best in selection, prices and low pressure selling.

Furniture Liquidation Center
- 5923 N. Clark St., Chicago; (312) 275-5888
- 2600 W. 79th St., Chicago; (312) 778-8727

This large, rambling showroom is absolutely jam-packed with closeouts taken directly from national manufacturers in furniture for the living room, dining room, and bedroom, along with mattress sets and decorative items. The materials range from chintzy to solid, and styles range from elegantly traditional to brightly modern; there's plenty to see in everything.

Class up your bedroom with a cherry wood set by V.B. Williams, including a queen-size headboard, triple-dresser, hutch, mirror, and armoire. It should sell for over $3,000 at fancier stores, but here, it's only $2,100. Again, at the other end of the spectrum, FLC has things like bunk beds from $39 (Mr. C liked a handsome one with a dark pine frame, reduced from $399 to $249). They also have closeouts on Sealy mattress sets.

To add some spice to these rooms, there are table lamps, floor lamps, and framed prints of every size, shape and color scheme. The salesmen are friendly, and financing is also available. Furniture Liquidation Center just opened its South Side location in the spring of '93. Formerly a lumberyard, this branch is even bigger than the Uptown store, and similarly crammed with bargains. Open seven days a week; daily from 10 a.m. to 8 p.m., and Sundays from 11-5.

Gaines Furniture Outlet
- 4944 W. 73rd St., Chicago; (708) 496-0355

Newly relocated into a giant warehouse just below Midway Airport, this South Side store buys out factory overstocks and second-quality merchandise, and resells them at super-cheap prices. Wouldya believe a four-piece bedroom set, including headboard, bed frame, mirror, and dresser, for $145? Well, believe it—though, before we go on, Mr. C should point out that this is one of those instances where "you gets what you pays for." Naturally, you're not going to find too many major brand names at these prices. Much of this stock is made from cheap wood, or that pressed-chips-and-veneer material. But hey, this may be all you need.

Gaines also sells mattresses and bed frames; Mr. C found a white lacquered brass daybed frame (no mattress) for a mere $38. Mattresses themselves sell for as little as $12 per twin-size piece; even at this price, these are innerspring mattresses, not foam. You do have to buy them in sets, though. Better models range from $49 per piece in full size, for example, up to $89 per piece; even king size only goes up to $109 per piece. These carry limited warranties of up to twenty years.

Gaines is open until 8 p.m. on weekdays, and until 6 p.m. on Saturdays and Sundays.

Marjen Furniture
- 2707 N. Halsted St., Chicago; (312) 929-0008
- 8121 N. Milwaukee Ave., Niles; (708) 966-1088

First of all, a point of order. Within Chicago City Limits, there are two stores called Marjen. Both sell inexpensive furniture and bedding. And, although they were once related to each other, both are now separate businesses. Be not confused!

This Marjen specializes in Sealy mattresses. A queen-size Sealy superfirm mattress, box spring and frame set was seen for $450; queen sets start as low as $245, for "real" mattresses (i.e., "no foam"). Lesser-quality mattresses can be had for a mere $49 and up, in twin size. And Marjen claims they can bring their beds to your door in only an hour(!).

Open weekdays from 10:30 a.m. to 8 p.m., Saturdays 10:30-5:00, Sundays 11:00-5:00.

Mar-Jen Furniture

- 1536 W. Devon Ave., Chicago; (312) 338-6636

Okay, here's the other Mar-jen (note the spelling difference, too). This uptown competitor focuses more on low- to mid-range price and quality, in a wider variety of furniture for all rooms in the house.

In bedding, the names found here include Spring Air, Englander, King Koil, and Serta. On sale, some of these sell for a remarkably cheap $39 per piece (twin size). These do fall, of course, into the "you gets what you pays for" category. A few notches up, Mr. C found a queen-size Spring Air Golden Unipedic set, with an original retail price of $650, selling for just $299. This deal included a free bedframe, delivery, setup, and removal of your old bed.

Futons start as low as $99, with a variety of convertible frames available. A black metal version, with futon, was recently on sale for $218. Daybeds start at $99 complete. And bedroom furniture sets may be found for under $400, including a dresser, mirror, nightstand, and headboard to go with traditional mattress sets.

Mar-jen offers free delivery to any part of the city, north or south. Free layaway plans are available, too. They're open from 10:30 a.m. until 7 or 8 p.m. on weeknights, 10-6 on Saturdays, 11-5 on Sundays.

Mattress World

- 3509 S. Halsted St., Chicago; (312) 376-5396
- 6630 S. Pulaski Rd., Chicago; (312) 767-4170
- 1838 W. 95th St., Chicago; (312) 238-8090
- 2340 N. Clybourn Ave., Chicago; (312) 348-4455

And many other suburban locations
This local chain offers good discounts on closeouts from such major manufacturers as Sealy, Spring Air, and Restonic. They specialize in mattresses and boxsprings, but also offer a limited selection of brass frames, headboards, and the like. A daybed by Spring Air, for instance, was seen for $279; it had an all-brass frame with a white lacquer finish.

But again, it's the mattresses themselves which have the best deals and selection. A recent sale featured basic Sealy models starting as low as $39 per piece in twin size, and $69 per piece in full size. Posturepedic models started at $99 per twin piece and $139 full; queen and king sizes, available in sets only, were $349 and $449 respectively. All prices include your choice of a free frame or free delivery, and they'll take away your old mattress, if you wish. Mattress World also offers discounts on multiple sets, and a one-year price guarantee on everything they sell. Their newest store, on Clybourn, is their first venture onto the North Side; all branches are open weekdays from 11 a.m. to 8 p.m., Saturdays from 11-5, and Sundays from 1-5.

Verlo Mattress Factory Stores

- 241 W. North Ave., Chicago; (312) 266-1144
- 7128 W. Grand Ave., Chicago; (312) 622-1600

And many other suburban locations.
The West Town and Old Town locations of these two stores may not place them in the best of neighborhoods, but for the selection, service and prices, this may be *the* place to get a mattress and bedframe in Chicagoland. The salespeople are low-pressure because the merchandise

sells itself very well—most of their business is done by referral from satisfied customers, a fact that also allows them to advertise less than other mattress companies in town. And since the mattresses are made right at the Grand Avenue location, the customer can take advantage of no freight costs. All of these factors result in savings that can be passed on to the customers.

Mr. C likes how each mattress is displayed with a cross-section of its inside, so you know exactly how the springs and cushioning are arranged in different styles and different firmnesses. Custom-made mattresses can also be ordered.

Many models have a 15-year warranty included in the price. An added bonus is that the handles on the mattresses pull out for easy moving; and there is minimum settling because Verlo only uses high-grade materials for its cushioning.

The "Excellence" model is $179 each full piece, or $438 for a queen set. The "Supreme" style is $169 for each twin piece, $219 for each full piece, or $538 a queen and $718 a king set. "Magic Nite" is only $69 for each twin piece and $348 for the entire king set—yet, even this budget model carries a six year warranty.

The Verlo salesmen will be happy to explain how their mattresses have springs of differing tightness throughout the bed. On the edge, they're looser, while the middle third has tighter springs for more support, so that some of these mattresses may never need to be rotated.

Bedframes, while not made in the Verlo factories, are shipped direct and are also great buys. A goldtone metal daybed frame for a twin mattress, for example, was only $129.99.

The store also offers occasional specials, such as free pillows, bed frames, or mattress pads with a purchase. You'll rest assured knowing that Verlo provides free local delivery, free removal and disposal of old mattresses, and free 90-day financing on purchases.

BOOKS

You can save extra money on books by shopping for *used* items. Chicago is blessed with enough of these to give the hungriest bookworm indigestion; several are mixed into the listings below. Save even more by bringing in books that you no longer want. Most stores will give you a choice of cash or in-store credit; you'll usually get a higher figure by choosing the credit. It's a good, cheap way to check out new authors—and to keep your library lean.

Aspidistra Bookshop
- 2630 N. Clark St., Chicago; (312) 549-3129

Not only is Aspidistra difficult to pronounce, but the books themselves are only kinda-sorta organized. Let's just say that all titles beginning with the letter G are in the "G" section; good luck from there, since the alphabetizing ends at that point. The man at the cash register was seemingly oblivious to the surrounding disorder, but this casual atmosphere is refreshingly different from the snooty formalities of many other retail bookstores.

We'll forgive Aspidistra, of course, because the store's precariously-tall shelves are so densely packed with paperbacks by almost any author you can name. Just watch your step on the snags in the 1960's vintage carpeting!

The photography section is especially vast in this store; and their first editions must certainly make great investments if you can afford to shell out the cash. A first edition of Maya Angelou's *I Know Why the Caged Bird Sings* costs $30.

Meanwhile, all you not-so-big spenders, don't despair. Paperbacks, like Ann Beattie's short-story collection, *Where You'll Find Me*, are plentiful and cheap; it was seen here recently for just $4. And Isak Dinesen's *Out of Africa*, paired with *Shadows On the Grass*, was another beaut of a bargain at $3.

Aspidistra (gesundheit!) is open late six days a week; from 11-9:30 daily, and Sundays from noon to 7:30 p.m. Also, be sure to check out the **Aspidistra Annex** at 3250 N. Lincoln Ave., telephone (312) 549-7867 for further bargains on clearance books. This shop is only open Monday, Thursdays, and Fridays from 2-8 p.m.; Saturdays and Sundays from noon to 5:00.

B. Dalton Bookseller
- 129 N. Wabash St., Chicago; (312) 236-7615
- 645 N. Michigan Ave., Chicago; (312) 944-3702
- 175 W. Jackson Blvd., Chicago; (312) 922-5219
- 222 Merchandise Mart Plaza, Chicago; (312) 329-1881

And many other suburban locations
Yet another biggie in the bookselling wars, B. Dalton wins the race in its computer section, which encompasses more subjects than many competitors do—and in remainders, yet, at greatly reduced prices! Dalton's also discounts *New York Times* best sellers, as so many stores now do.

In the remainders section, Nikos Kazantzakis' *The Last Temptation of Christ*, basis for the controversial film, was seen here for only $2.98 in paperback. At that price, you can rent the movie too without being guilty of gluttony! Another great remainder spotted in the Wabash store was *Unseen Beatles, Photographs by Bob Whitaker*, a great coffee-table book

in hardcover for only $9.98.

Here's another Mr. C moneysaving tip: If you join B. Dalton's Booksavers Club, you get an automatic ten percent off every book every day, even if they're already discounted, along with other special offers. The club costs $10 to join, but for true bookworms, it soon pays for itself.

Barnes & Noble Booksellers
- 659 W. Diversey Pkwy., Chicago; (312) 871-9004

The bookstore wars in Chicago can be fierce, and Barnes & Noble is right up there with the other biggies offering everyday discount prices, including major reductions on *New York Times* bestsellers. This spiffy, refined shop is part of B & N's new wave of "superstores." It's big, but comfortable. Classical music wafts softly in the background. There's even a coffeeshop selling espresso, muffins, and biscotti.

Everything here, except for magazines and newspapers, sells for at least 10% below retail. Books on the NYT paperback list are sold at 30% off the cover price, as are the books on the staff-recommendation table; hardcover NYT bestsellers are sold at 20% off.

Special-ordering is a breeze here, and B & N's own publishing house offers classic hardcovers in easily-readable print at super savings. Their edition of Thoreau's *Walden* is only $4.98.

Overstocks are also super-deals, and there's a wider selection here than in most downtown stores. A recently spotted example was the oversized paperback *Bloom County 1986-1989* by Berkeley Breathed, selling for just $3.98.

Booksellers Row
- 408 S. Michigan Ave., Chicago; (312) 427-4242
- 2445 N. Lincoln Ave., Chicago; (312) 348-1170
- 1520 N. Milwaukee Ave., Chicago; (312) 489-6200

The three locations of this bookstore vary widely in selection and size, but all have great bargain shelves and

MR. CHEAP'S PICKS
Books

✔ **Bookseller's Row**—Three used bookstores of varying size, all crammed with bargains.

✔ **Bookworks**—A used bookstore with a high degree of organization and cleanliness.

✔ **O'Gara & Wilson Booksellers**—Near the University of Chicago, this is another large shop with used books right up to the high ceilings.

✔ **Powell's Bookstores**—New and used books arranged and divided into the most esoteric of categories.

✔ **The Stars Our Destination**—Great bargains on used science fiction books.

✔ **Super Crown**—Drastically reduced prices on remainder books, as well as *New York Times* best sellers.

highly knowledgeable staff, as well as extensive sci-fi, drama, poetry, and children's collections. The Lincoln Park store even has sections devoted to "Radical Activism" and "Poverty and Deprivation." Talk about *detail*. The South Loop branch, meanwhile, has great 99 cent shelves on the lower floor, and a section of books marked at 50% off retail, as well as a further remainders area. All three stores discount everything they sell by at least 10 percent.

Among the used books, Mr. C spied a paperback copy of Aeschylus' *The Oresteia* for $3.25, and a mint-condition hardcover of William H. Pritchard's *Randall Jarrell: A Literary Life* for $15, ten bucks off the original price. Thomas Pynchon's

Gravity's Rainbow, a heavy 750 pages worth, was buoyed by a price of only $6.45.

In children's books, a new copy of Maureen Galvani's *Me And My Dog* was seen marked down to $3.98.

The remainders section may yield up a brand-new copy of Merrill Schleier's *The Skyscraper in American Art 1890-1931*, reduced from $12.95 to just $4.98. David E. Greenberg's *The Construction of Homosexuality*, listed at $35 for the hardcover, was $6.98.

The Milwaukee store also has shelves with Spanish translations of American works, including those of Steven King and Alice Walker. In their 99 cent section, they had a used copy of *The Chicago Daily News Cookbook*, dating from about 1935, in excellent condition. The store also carries tons of greeting cards and postcards featuring artwork by the likes of Frieda Kahlo and Bruce Weber. Open from 11 a.m. to 10:30 p.m. for evening browsing, seven days a week.

Bookworks
- 3444 N. Clark St., Chicago; (312) 871-5318

Another of Chicago's great used bookstores, Bookworks is for the bookworm in us all. If cluttered and chaotic used bookstores just frustrate the heck out of you, this is the one to use. Its shelves are impeccably arranged and—could it be true?—totally dust-free.

The majority of the stock is used books, but there are some new volumes at discount thrown in for good measure. For example, a new copy of Jack Kerouac's *Pomes* (yup, this is how he spells it) *All Sizes*, listed at $8.95, was seen for $8.05.

The store's cookbook section is huge, with lots of titles on vegetarian and ethnic cooking. These included *The Complete Cookbook of American Fish and Shellfish* by Jean F. Nichols, in hardcover, selling for $8—and originally listed at $19.50. The fiction and literature section is almost overwhelming. Cheap buys abound.

These included a practically new-looking copy of *Damage*, Josephine Hart's paperback, listed at $5.99 but selling for just $3; in biography, Penelope Niven's account of Carl Sandburg's life was going for $17.50, half its original price.

The extensive animal book collection yielded more great buys, like *Peterson's Field Guide to Western Birds* for $8; it would sell for twice that if new. Used children's books like the "Disney Golden Book" favorites are also half off retail.

Even collector's editions of classics aren't priced ridiculously, like a leather-bound volume of John Milton's works, printed by the Easton Press of Connecticut. It was seen here for $22.50. The Franklin Library's leather-bound copy of Moby Dick was on sale for $12.50.

Open daily at noon, Bookworks closes at 10 p.m. weekdays, 11 p.m. on Fridays and Saturdays, and at 6 p.m. on Sundays.

Crown Outlet
- 26 N. Wabash St., Chicago; (312) 357-1150

Another part of the "superstore" wave, Crown's high-volume national operation allows it to sell tons of books, mostly recent leftovers, dirt cheap. If you're kicking yourself for missing one of last year's hot books and prefer reading hardcover to paperback, this outlet may be your saving grace. Although all Crown stores sell books at discount, this particular branch is their real clearance store.

Paul Theroux's mystery *Chicago Loop*, for example, originally retailing for $20, sold for only $3.99 here; and *New York Times* columnist Anna Quindlen's novel, *Object Lessons*, was reduced from $15 to $5. In paperbacks, Anne Stevenson's *Bitter Fame: A Life of Sylvia Plath*, retailing for $10.95, was here for only $4.48.

The store carries a surprising selection of videos and books on tape. Since this is manufacturers' overstock, you never know what you may find; Mr. C noticed one of his all-time faves, *The Graduate*, on video for $15.

Crown Outlet is open seven days a week. One other note: The atmosphere control sometimes runs off kilter, so be prepared to sweat or freeze—the price of a bargain.

Dan Behnke Bookseller
- 2463 N. Lincoln Ave., Chicago; (312) 404-0403

This used bookstore specializes in wonderful (but expensive) out-of-print and rare hardcovers and paperbacks. But wait—there are lots of similarly wonderful and less pricey popular books to be had. The stiff-neck factor in this place is intense; even if you're Lurch-height, you'll need a stepladder to see it all.

The sports section is gigantic, and if you're into woodworking or celebrity biographies, don't miss those sections, either. The *1983 Rolling Stone Rock Almanac*, while a decade old, is a hoot, especially the photos; and at only $9, the price has gotten better with time also. In literary biography, *The Loves of George Bernard Shaw*, a first edition in very good condition, is $8. You'll find plenty of other, better-selling-the-first-time-around first edition books by anyone from E.L. Doctorow to G. Gordon Liddy.

The Fiery Clock Face
- 5311 N. Clark St., Chicago; (312) 728-4227

You can't miss this Andersonville shop, with its spring green facade and homey screen door. Don't be intimidated by the decor—the place looks like a mansion's library with plaid-upholstered Hepplewhite chairs and classy knick-knacks. Head straight for the room in back, where used books—most of them classics—can be had for spare change.

There are lots of children's books here, like Dennis Kendrick's *The Three Billy Goats Gruff*, selling for merely $1.00. For the grownups, a 1962 Dell Laurel edition of Thomas Hardy's *Tess of the D'Urbervilles* was seen for $1.50. The back room also holds many foreign language books, in Russian, French, Spanish, and many others.

Flashback Collectibles

- 3450 N. Clark St., Chicago; (312) 929-5060

For a good belly laugh—not to mention the chance to buy an old Charlie's Angels lunchbox—find your way to Flashback. The merchandise and the salesmen are rather trippy (there's a "DRUGS OK" bumper sticker over the front window), but there's a good chance you'll find a funky gift for that friend who never got over his huge crush on Suzanne Somers during her "Three's Company" phase.

Lots of great finds lurk among the magazine racks, where a 1980's issue of *Rolling Stone* with James Taylor gracing the cover goes for a mere $2. *Life* magazines from the 1960's are priced between $3 and $5, and back issues of *Spy, Time, Newsweek, Musician, Circus*, and *Playboy* are all well-kept in plastic bags and are in miraculously superb condition.

For your book collection, how about a copy of *Kristy and Jimmy, TV's Talented MacNichols*, for $2? That's one dollar a Mac. So what if the original cover price on this paperback was $1.50—it's a collectors' item now! Also gracing the shelves during Mr. C's visit was the entire *Room 222* series for $3 or so a copy. When did these get turned into books? More importantly, why??

Miscellaneous buttons, pins, patches, pencils, and stickers are also here for those wishing to have a Flashback of their own. The store is open daily from noon until 10 p.m., and on Sundays until 6.

Kroch's and Brentano's

- 29 S. Wabash St., Chicago; (312) 332-7500
- 230 S. Clark St., Chicago; (312) 553-0171
- 516 N. Michigan St., Chicago; (312) 321-0989
- 30 N. LaSalle St., Chicago; (312) 704-0287
- 2070 N. Clybourn Ave., Chicago; (312) 525-2800
- Water Tower Place, 835 N. Michigan Ave., Chicago; (312) 943-2452
- 1530 E. 53rd St., Chicago; (312) 288-0145

And many suburban locations

This store, a Chicago mainstay since 1907, recently upped its discount on *New York Times* bestsellers to 40% and still promises to meet or beat any competitor's advertised title price. Along with some remainder tables, this is the primary moneysaver at K & B.

There is one other interesting option here: Kroch's "Good Sense" card gives you a $15 gift certificate for each $100 you spend in the store. The card costs $10, but book addicts soon recoup their Hamilton.

Free readings by authors like Isabel Allende, Barbara Kingsolver, Scott Turow, and Calvin Trillin add to the glamor at this venerable bookseller.

Louis Kiernan, Bookseller

- 1342 E. 55th St., Chicago; (312) 752-2555

One of several used bookshops in the Hyde Park/University of Chicago area, Louis Kiernan is a bit removed from the campus center—but the academic influence is no less keen. Tall bookshelves are lined with tomes dealing in all aspects of literature, the sciences, philosophy, and the like. Yes, if it's a weighty volume on the mechanics of cytochrome systems you're after—just the thing for reading on the beach—you can find it here, not at its $60 cover price, but selling instead for $15. It must mean something to some of you out there.

Perhaps of more usefulness to the general public are Kiernan's shelves of used computer guidebooks, all selling at half the cover price. Titles like "Symphony Made Easy" are easier to grab indeed when reduced from $25 to $12.50. And, lest you think that dry technical manuals are all you'll find here, the fiction section is lined with the works of James Michener, Gore Vidal, William Styron, and more. Michener's *Poland*, originally $17.95 and still looking like new, is marked at $4.95. In the paperback section, Mr. C found everything from those Penguin editions of Shakespeare's plays (you remember those from school days) to Sue Miller's best seller *Family Pictures* and tons of science fiction novels, all priced between $1.50 and $3.

Many of the hardcovers are clearly marked with any imperfections; being a college store, a proviso like "Notes in the margins" is especially helpful. You'd hate to get home only to discover that Keats wasn't the only one who'd waxed poetical between the covers. The shop is open from noon into the early evening, seven days a week.

O'Gara & Wilson Booksellers, Ltd.

- 1311 E. 57th St., Chicago; (312) 363-0993

The U of C's literary companion to Louis Kiernan, O'Gara & Wilson claims to be nothing less than the oldest bookstore in all of Chicago. It was founded in 1882, and indeed, the store has a Dickensian air—right up to the genuine hand-cranked cash register and the fluffy old cat sleeping beside it.

Literature, history and the arts are big here, in more ways than one. There is a large selection, for instance, of large-sized art books; Mr. C enjoyed leafing through *100 Masterpieces of the Art Institute of Chicago*, with lots of color plates, selling for half its original price at $30. The literary collection *Steinbeck: A Life in Letters*, edited by his wife, was available in both hardcover ($12.50) and paperback ($7.50). And, like any good used bookstore, there are plenty of paperback mystery and crime novels for $1.50-$3.00. Open until 10 p.m. every day.

Powell's Bookstores

- 2850 N. Lincoln Ave., Chicago; (312) 248-1444
- 828 S. Wabash Ave., Chicago; (312) 341-0748

- 1501 E. 57th St., Chicago; (312) 955-7780

This trio of bookstores is related to the gigantic Powell's Bookstore in Portland, Oregon, one of the biggest and busiest bookstores in the nation. They all carry fine used, out-of-print and rare books, though the Chicago shops unfortunately are not equipped to perform out-of-print searches.

The stores carry everything from classic literature and poetry to more esoteric categories. They don't just stock an American history section— they have a "Western American History" section. But that's hardly the end of it. Within this area, you'll find an entire shelf dedicated to "Outlaws." Now, *that's* specialization!

Powell's extensive science fiction and children's areas in the Wrightwood location included a used paperback copy of Ursula K. LeGuin's *The Left Hand of Darkness*, in very good condition, for $1.95, a wide choice of "Dr. Who" paperbacks for $1.50 each, many new hardcover copies of the "Curious George" series for $5, and multiple copies of Shel Silverstein's children's poetry collection *A Giraffe and a Half* in hardcover for $5. The latter was a British version, originally priced at about $9.

Literary criticism yielded a likenew copy of Camille Paglia's controversial *Sexual Personae* for $15, a savings of $20 off the publisher's list. The back room holds Powell's bargain collection, with books priced from 95 cents to $1.95.

The Hyde Park store is open from 9 a.m. to 11 p.m. daily; the Lincoln Ave./Wrightwood location, from noon to 9 p.m. daily, except Saturday, when it's open 10 to 10; and the smaller Burnham Park branch is open from 10:30 a.m. to 6 p.m. during the week, 10-6 on Saturday and 12-5 on Sunday.

Rosenblum's World of Judaica, Inc.

- 2906 W. Devon Ave., Chicago; (312) 262-1700

Rosenblum's, on that bargain avenue

of Devon, sells a surprising variety of good overstock books—from the paperback edition of Alan Dershowitz's *Chutzpah* for $7, instead of the cover price of $13, to photographer Richard Nagler's *My Love Affair With Miami Beach*, in hardcover, reduced from $30 to $14.98.

Anne Frank Remembered: The Story of the Woman Who Helped to Hide the Frank Family by Miep Gies, selling for $7 at the publisher's list price, was marked down to $5 here.

Rosenblum's also has a "baker's dozen" deal. When you buy twelve books from either their book club or their music club, you get the next one free, based on the average prices of the previous purchases. The store is open from 9-6 weekdays and 10-4 on Sundays, and is closed Saturdays for the Jewish sabbath.

Shake, Rattle and Read
● 4812 N. Clark St., Chicago; (312) 334-5311

Here's a funky combination store selling used books, old magazines, and used tapes, CDs and records. If you're a collector looking for that hard-to-find old issue of Life or if you're in search of an old Dylan record, shake, rattle and roll yourself over to this Uptown shop.

The store has racks of old magazines including *Vanity Fair, National Geographic, Scientific American*, and *Playboy* from as far back as the 1960's, most in mint condition, selling for as little as $2. They're wrapped in plastic and carefully displayed, ensuring that they don't get damaged. SR&R also features many entertainment industry magazines, such as *Premiere* and *Show Business*.

Paperbacks stocked here range from classics to comics; from Tennessee Williams' 1956 *Baby Doll* for $6 to a whole collection of *Mad Magazine* cartoon books from the 1970's for about $4 each. An untouched-looking Vintage International edition of Faulkner's *As I Lay Dying* was seen for $6, and a more worn copy of Glenn Savan's *White Palace* was $2.

Shake, Rattle and Read is open every day from 11-6, except Sundays from 12-6.

The Stars Our Destination
● 1021 W. Belmont Ave., Chicago; (312) 871-2722

As you may gather from the name, this bookstore is solely devoted to the science fiction and fantasy genre—for which "devoted" is the perfect word. Alice Bentley, a die-hard fanatic herself, created this large, bright shop and runs it with a meticulous hand; although she sells new and used books, Mr. C was primarily interested in the used section, which may be the largest in town for sci-fi.

There are three separate sections of used hardcovers and paperbacks lining the walls; the first is a section of books in only "fair" condition, as well as book club editions, all of which are priced at one dollar apiece Next comes the "average" section, priced in the $1-$5 range, offering better quality and more well-known authors, such as Asimov, Heinlein, Clarke and Bova. Then there is the section of very recent used titles; here, Mr. C found Asimov's *Prelude to Foundation*, like new, reduced from a cover price of $18.95 to just $9.00. The anthology *Legacy of Heorot*, written by Larry Niven, Jerry Pournelle, and Steven Barnes, was not its original $17.95, but just $6.00. And Stephen King's *Four Past Midnight* was reduced from $22.95 to a spine-tingling $8.00.

Owner Bentley knows that there may be some collector's editions mixed in on these shelves, but she doesn't try to price them at market rates. Not only would this require a lot of extra effort, but she also prefers to keep the stock moving. Used paperbacks, for instance, are uniformly sold at half the cover price (or a $1 minimum). "I want to unite books with people," she says of her philosophy, "not keep the books around for ten years." For those who do want to follow the collector's market, she does provide a reference section of the latest price guides. The store is open seven days a week, including weeknights and Saturdays until 9:00. It all makes for quite a successful, er, enterprise.

Super Crown

- 105 S. Wabash St., Chicago; (312) 782-7667

Larger than the regular Crown stores, this store carries few remainders, but slashes the *New York Times* bestseller prices to bits. Paperback bestsellers are 25% off and hardcovers are 40% off cover prices! All other hardcovers are permanently 20% off, too, while all other paperbacks are reduced by 10 percent.

So, if you were to buy Robert Parker's "Spenser" mystery *Paper Doll* here, new and in hardcover, the book would cost you only $11.97— off the publisher's list of $19.95! Robert James Waller's *The Bridges of Madison County* was only $8.97, cut from a list price of $14.95.

If you're looking for something other than a bestseller, though, prepare for disappointment. Literature and general fiction aren't found here in plentiful supply. Whatever you end up getting, by the way, you'll more than likely have to queue up like cattle in order to check out.

Tower Records/Video/Books

- 2301 N. Clark St., Chicago; (312) 477-5994

Most people associate Tower with records, tapes, and CDs; rightly so. Fewer folks are aware that this na-

tional monolith also sells books at discount, applying its high-volume approach (no pun intended there) to the print medium. As with many of the downtown bookstores, this Lincoln Park store discounts bestsellers by 30% off the cover price; in addition, they have a large selection of overstocks and remainders, all at big reductions. It makes surprisingly good browsing. Best of all, you can do just that from 9:00 in the morning until midnight, every day of the year.

Waterstone's Booksellers

- 840 N. Michigan Ave., Chicago; (312) 587-8080

The British are coming! Located at Michigan and Chestnut, this three-level store is the second landing of this classy chain in The States. They too discount *New York Times* bestsellers, by 30 percent; in addition, staff recommendations sell for 20 percent off the cover. Apart from these bargains, everything else sells at full price.

The sales staff is very knowledgeable, and stand ready to place special orders, especially for British editions. The reference, literature and classics sections are especially deep here. And many prominent authors visit Waterstone's for free readings; in recent months, these have included Barbara Kingsolver, Cynthia Heimel, Madison Smartt Bell and Robert Parker. Open daily 10-10, Sundays 11-7.

CDS, RECORDS, TAPES, AND VIDEOS

You can save extra money on music by shopping for *used* items. Like used book shops, many of the stores below will allow you to trade in music you no longer want. Alas, they won't take just anything; used LPs, in particular, have become less marketable. Most stores will give you a choice of cash or in-store credit; you'll usually get a higher figure by choosing the credit. It's a good, cheap way to check out artists you might not take a chance on at full price.

Disc Is The Place

- 50 E. Chicago Ave., Chicago; (312) 337-5401

For cheap CDs in the Near North area, this may be the place indeed. While the prices on their used discs may not be the best around, they still beat the cost of new ones. Rock, soul, rap, and dance are the main rhythms you'll find here, along with smaller selections in jazz, country, and classical. The rather odd pricing scheme puts most CDs at $9.29 to $10.79; also, some new releases can be found on sale at $10.99.

Among the bins, Mr. C noticed Mariah Carey's *Emotions* for just $8; *Frank Sinatra In Concert* for $9.79; and the same price for discs by Genesis, Bob Dylan, Kenny G, and others. There is also a "Budget Bin" of discs for $3-$5, though most of these seemed to be from obscure rock bands.

Discover Cafe

- 2436 N. Lincoln Ave., Chicago; (312) 868-3472

There's more to discover here than coffee. Note the first four letters; this is not just a cafe, it's also a music store, and the combination is a winner. At one counter, you can order up a cuppa their basic joe for a dollar (refills just 50 cents each). At the other, you can snap up a Miles Davis CD for just $9. Most of their 6,000 discs here are used, and almost all of them go for that same price—from Miles to Gershwin to Jimmy Buffett to Peter Gabriel to the Replacements. Mr. C also noted a "Lollapalooza" bin, for you alternative rockheads.

There is a more limited selection of cassettes, all priced between $3 and $5; discs are the main currency here. In fact, the music counter has a pair of portable CD players with headphones, so that you can try out the tunes before you buy—the sign of a true connoisseur's shop. They're also eager to buy up your used CDs, offering cash on the barrelhead. You can even trade CDs for food—though this creates all kinds of ethical dilemmas. Is Coltrane worth a chicken

sandwich? Perhaps two? And, if you brought in a Barry Manilow disc, would you still starve?

Food for thought. But wait, there's more! The cafe presents a live jazz trio during Sunday brunch, free of charge (the music, that is), from 10:30 a.m. until 2:00 p.m. Jazz also rings forth on Thursday evenings, while on Monday evenings there is a more eclectic grabbag of live performance. In any case, it's always offered as a free accompaniment to the food, which is of the sandwiches/salads/eggs/pastries variety. Or, just have a cappuccino and enjoy the bohemian atmosphere. You can sit at a table, or on one of the comfy couches, and while away an hour or two. Of course, you can hang out here any day of the week, with or without the jazz. Plenty of good music is always playing and works by local artists adorn the walls.

Hmm....With CDs, live music and food, this may be one of the only places in this entire book which fits into all three sections—shopping, restaurants and entertainment. And it's all cheap. Quite the discovery.

Dr. Wax Records

- 2529 N. Clark St., Chicago; (312) 549-3377
- 5210 S. Harper Ave., Chicago; (312) 493-8696

The Lincoln Park branch of this store carries over 6,000 used CDs and caters to the alternative music crowd, while the smaller Hyde Park shop leans more toward blues, jazz, and hip-hop. When you walk into these shops, it may be a good idea to have a bit of wax in your own ears in order to prevent hearing loss; you may also trip over holes in the weary-looking gray carpet. Still, most other stores can't hold a candle to Dr. Wax's selection.

Recordings aren't quite alphabetically arranged, so if you're looking for a particular artist, it may take a lot of searching. Most used CDs sell in the range of $6.99 to $8.99; you'll also find used cassettes for $3.99, and even good ol' hot wax for as little as 99 cents a disc, including lots of dance singles.

Dr. Wax also sells new releases at discount; Lyle Lovett's eponymous CD was seen here for $11.99. The North side shop also has a huge movie soundtrack section, among it the music to *The Firm* on CD for $9.99.

Open daily 11:30 a.m. to 9:00 p.m.; Sundays, 12-6.

Earwax Cafe
- 1564 N. Milwaukee Ave., Chicago; (312) 772-4019

It is certain that nowhere, throughout the annals of time, has anyone ever considered putting these two words together before. Yet here we have them, improbably describing this grunge-rock-meets-nouvelle-cuisine spot in Wicker Park. It is truly a place of odd pairings, being both a restaurant and a record store all in one.

The main room is a large and airy cafe, with a lengthy bar running along one side, and big storefront windows. Walk through the restaurant to the rear, you'll come to the record shop, which stocks lots of used cassettes and CDs. Tapes go from $1.99 to $10, while most CDs are in the $6-$10 range; most are $9. Every style of music is mixed into one alphabetical hodgepodge, where Tom Petty, Ray Charles, Shawn Colvin, and David Sanborn are all thrown together. Perhaps they prefer it that way—though it does make searching for a particular title more difficult. Think of it as a serendipitous experience, a good way to approach this entire wacky place.

Evil Clown CDs
- 3418 N. Halsted St., Chicago; (312) 472-4761

You may not find the latest Paula Abdul or Michael Bolton album here. And that's the way they want it. Evil Clown CDs, as befits the name, specializes in punk and alternative music. They carry new CDs starting at $10.99, going up to about $15.99. But, it's used CDs where the bargains are to be found, of course. These

discs start at $5.99 and go up to $9.99. What's more, they let you listen to any CD *before* you buy it; no more "Oh, no, why did I buy *this*?" Your neighbors, however, will end up thinking the same thing, which may be your intention.

Evil Clown also has used cassettes and LP's at even lower prices; and they carry books, posters, and a whole range of CD accessories. This is also not a store for the early riser: Hours are from noon to 10 p.m. Mondays through Fridays, 11 a.m. to 10 p.m. on Saturdays, and noon to 7 p.m. on Sundays.

The Inside Track
- 825 W. Armitage Ave., Chicago; (312) 348-1045

Here's a small Sheffield-area shop specializing in new and used CDs only. Nearly all of the used CDs— mainly rock, soul and jazz—are priced at $7.99. The selection, while not vast, offered up such artists as Pete Townshend, James Brown, and Luther Vandross on a recent visit; used jazz discs, in the separate jazz section, included titles by Pat Metheny, Frank Sinatra, and "soft jazz" fave Richard Elliott. There is a small classical section, too.

Prices on new compact discs are competitive with those of major stores, starting around $10.99 and going up from there. Mr. C has a particularly budget-conscious friend, though, who has found the store owners willing to deal on higher prices. For such items as boxed sets and videos (which they also carry in limited supply), find the best price you can elsewhere; then stop in, and see if they'll beat it. Can't hurt to try!

Jazz Record Mart
- 11 W. Grand Ave., Chicago; (312) 222-1467.

Looking to jazz up your LP collection with a decades-old Fats Waller 78? Come on in. Jazz Record Mart carries a huge number of 78s and 33s, out-of-prints, cassettes, and used CDs, as well as new stuff; and a lot of it is surprisingly cheap. In fact, this is the world's largest blues and

MR. CHEAP'S PICKS
CDs, Records, Tapes

✔ **Discover Cafe**—A great selection of used CDs, plus food, coffee, and live music—all under one Lincoln Park roof.

✔ **Dr. Wax Records**—Over 6,000 used CDs at great prices.

✔ **Jazz Record Mart**—Bargains on jazz and blues, for the vinyl fans among us.

✔ **Rose Records Classical Outlet**—The North Broadway branch of this regional chain is a clearance center for classical discs, reduced by 15% to 25% from the marked prices.

✔ **Video Beat**—Despite the name, you can find bargains here not only on used music videos, but on CDs, records, and tapes as well.

---

jazz shop (3,000 square feet, but who's counting?).

It may not appear that large when you walk in the front, but wait until you see the warehouse-sized back room. Among the recent finds, on LP: Chuck Berry's *St. Louis to Liverpool* for $4.99, *Mack the Knife: Ella Fitzgerald in Berlin* for $1.99, and Weather Report's *Heavy Weather*, just 99 cents.

The old meets the new in the used CDs bin; these are priced at 99 cents and up. *Tommy Dorsey's Greatest Hits* was seen for $5.99. Good rhythm and blues and gospel sections, too. Located near the courthouse district, you'll find lawyers and musicians shopping side-by-side here. The store is open weekdays 10-8, and Sundays 12-5; they are closed on Saturdays.

Reckless Records

- 3157 N. Broadway, Chicago; (312) 404-5080

Here's a sort of full-service rock music store, with good prices on new recordings (including lots of imports and EPs) and a big selection of lower-priced secondhand discs. They also sell videos, posters, books, T-shirts, and other rock memorabilia. It's one of the only stores Mr. C has found in his travels with a section entitled "Thrash"; this should give you some idea of the atmosphere.

Used compact discs start as low as $1.00 each, with the majority of desirable titles in the $3.49-$8.99 range. These include things like Steely Dan's *Pretzel Logic* and U2's *The Unforgettable Fire*. Used cassettes are mostly $3.99 and $4.99; among these, Mr. C found music from Midnight Oil, Cher, and *Eric Clapton Unplugged*.

Record albums make up a good portion of the store (hey, let's hear it for vinyl). These are mostly $5.99, such as Elvis Costello's *Spike*, though many go as low as $2.99. A friend of Mr. C's found a German import of Depeche Mode's *Meaning of Love*, made on yellow vinyl, for $7.99. A sticker on each LP rates its condition: Mint, very good, good, and so on. And then there's a separate bin of older records in poor shape, priced from 29¢ to 99¢. Among these were albums by Phil Collins, the Eagles, and Crosby, Stills and Nash.

RR also sells used videos; among the titles recently seen there were *A Room with a View, Out of Africa, 48 Hrs.*, and *Honey, I Shrunk the Kids*, as well as some concert videos. Just about all of these are priced at $8.99.

Rose Records

- 300 W. Washington St., Chicago; (312) 629-1802
- 820 W. North Ave., Chicago; (312) 482-8228
- 3155 N. Broadway, Chicago; (312) 472-2114
- 3259 N. Ashland Ave., Chicago; (312) 880-0820

- 214 S. Wabash St., Chicago; (312) 987-9044
- 1634 E. 53rd St., Chicago; (312) 752-3700

And many other suburban locations.
Rose Records does not discount across the board as much as competitors like Tower; big-deal sales run about 15% off retail here. But Rose's $10.99 CD sales are good, and its overstocks are fun to rummage through. On a recent visit, Mr. C spotted the two-CD soundtrack to the Broadway show *Tommy* for $24.99, and Sting's *Ten Summoner's Tales* was $10.99 in the hit bin.

There are a surprising number of good ol' LPs, not used, like *The Best of Arlo Guthrie* for $2.99. Overstock cassettes run around $1-$3; Suzanne Vega's *Days of Open Hand* was $3.99.

Classical music fans will want to check out the North Broadway store, which is Rose's classical clearance outlet. It's a full range store like any other, but classical CDs in here are sold at 15% off the sticker price— and some at 25% off. Mr. C found a Vox Box (two CDs) of Beethoven piano sonatas, played by Alfred Brendel, reduced from $9.99 to $8.49; and a disc of Jessye Norman arias in the Philips "Classics" series for $9.35. Budget label CDs and cassettes go even lower.

Rose Records also sells movie and concert videos. While most of these ain't exactly Academy Award-winners, they're only a little more expensive than rentals. *Hell Night*, with a post-Exorcist Linda Blair can be had for $3.99; while music videos like *The Jesus and Mary Chain: The Videos 1985-1989* average $5.99.

2nd Hand Tunes

- 2604 N. Clark St., Chicago; (312) 929-6325
- 2550 N.Clark St., Chicago; (312) 281-8813
- 1375 E. 53rd St., Chicago; (312) 684-3375

And other suburban locations.
This store got so busy, it had to split itself in two. The 2604 Clark location

carries LPs; 2550 Clark has CDs and tapes. Both stores display stock almost to the ceiling, as does the Hyde Park branch, which continues as yet undivided.

In compact discs, 2HT recently had New Order's *Substance 1987* for only $5.99—it goes for about $25 retail now. U2's *Boy* was seen for $9.99. The limited folk and new age sections almost aren't worth bothering with; the Broadway show tunes, soul, and disco sections are more impressive.

On the record side of things, in addition to rock 'n roll, there's a comedy and an international section; and there are lots of LPs and 45s selling for a whopping 99 cents. The store also has lots of boxed sets and even 8-track tapes (aaarrgghhhh!).

Security helps keep costs, and thus prices, down. Only the liner notes are within the customers' reach; the CDs themselves are up behind the front counter.

Shake, Rattle and Read

- 4812 N. Clark St., Chicago; (312) 334-5311

Here's a funky combination store selling used books, old magazines and used tapes, CDs, and records. If you're a collector looking for that hard-to-find old issue of *Life*, or if you're in search of an old Dylan record, shake, rattle and roll yourself over to this Uptown shop.

Vintage vinyls yielded up all sorts of interesting nostalgia—including the soundtrack from *Flashdance* for $2.99, and Gilda Radner's *Live from New York* for $3.99. And a July, 1975 issue of *Rona Barrett's Hollywood* magazine, with Cher and Gregg Allman on the cover, was $5. What ever happened to her, anyway? Rona, that is.

Shake, Rattle and Read is open every day from 11-6, except Sundays from 12-6.

Topper's Records, Tapes, and CD's

- 4619 N. Broadway, Chicago; (312) 878-2032.

Not too far from the Wilson "el,"

you'll find this small shop which primarily sells teenybopper music, but also some classic blues and soul CDs. The alternative selection is not that expansive, and the classical is non-existent; but if you're looking for rap, pop, or hip-hop, you can't top Topper's.

Steve Winwood's *Back in the High Life* CD was selling for $6.99 during a recent visit, while Echo and the Bunnymen's eponymous disc was only $7.99. Whitney Houston's debut was a not-so-cheap $14.99, since it's become a collector's item, but used discs by hubby Bobby Brown were selling in the $8 range.

Other cheap picks were the recent release *Lyle Lovett and His Large Band*, selling used for $7.99; and a used cassette, Van Morrison's *Moondance*, yours for a mere $2.99.

Tower Records/Video/Books
- 2301 N. Clark St., Chicago; (312) 477-5994

Nocturnal music lovers can't beat Tower, located at Clark and Belden in Lincoln Park. After all, this national mega-chain stays open until midnight every single night of the year.

The nation's top bestselling records, tapes, and CDs are always discounted 30% off list price; newer releases, rising up the charts, also tend to be marked down—usually to about $11.99 for CDs, $7.99 for cassettes. And be sure to check the cutout bins, where overstock music is always drastically reduced. You can usually find all formats, and all varieties of music, represented.

Oh, by the way, Tower opens at 9:00 a.m. for you early risers.

Video Beat
- 2616 N. Clark St., Chicago; (312) 871-6667

In spite of the name, there's more to meet the eye than just videos in this packed Lincoln Park shop. The videos are of the musical variety, rock in particular; they are used, and sell for $8-$10 each. You'll find titles like *The Doors Live in Europe, James Brown and Friends,* and Prince's movie *Purple Rain.* Oh, and if you'd like a copy of *Mike Ditka and the Grabowski Shuffle,* just ask—they're giving 'em away. Ah, how fleeting is fame.

Having set the beat with videos, the store is mainly given over to music—in the form of used records, CDs, and tapes. It's a truly vast selection, one that collectors of every stripe will want to check out. CDs and cassettes favor rock again; on disc, Mr. C found Hammer's *Too Legit to Quit* for $7.99, and *The Who Live at Leeds* for $8.99. Tapes, mostly $2.99 and $3.99, included Joni Mitchell's *Court and Spark,* Laurie Anderson's *Home of the Brave,* and titles by everyone from Sinead O'Connor to Paula Abdul.

The record section, meanwhile, is a jazz lover's dream. Priced from $1.99 and up, the bins are packed with Sinatra, Coltrane, the Crusaders, and more, going all the way up to Kitaro. Mr. C found Bobby McFerrin's debut LP, *The Voice,* along with the Oscar Peterson Trio's *Night Train,* each for $4.49.

Records are labeled with notes like "Not Perfect" and "Very Rough Shape," to alert you to their condition—and the friendly guys behind the counter will be happy to play any disc to further evaluate the sound quality. You will also find plenty of rock here, including collectibles like Monkees LPs, as well as a good selection of rock 'n roll books. Open seven days a week.

CAMERAS

There are lots of places to save money on appliances and electronics in Chicago. Some, unfortunately, are as far below repute as they are below retail. With merchandise that is imported from foreign countries, there is a greater possibility of shady deals, or inferior quality. Mr. C says this not out of any kind of prejudice, but because he wants you to be careful.

One of the best ways to protect yourself, if you have doubts as to *any* store's reliability, is to ask about their guarantee policy; make sure the item you want carries an American warranty. Since some stores deal directly with manufacturers in the Far East, their merchandise may carry a foreign warranty instead. Even for identical products, a foreign warranty can make repairs a hassle—unless you don't mind paying the postage to Japan. Remember, you are perfectly within your rights to inquire about this in the store.

Central Camera Company
- 230 S. Wabash St., Chicago; (312) 427-5580 or (800) 421-1899

You know that a company that has been around since before the turn of the century must know what it's doing. Central Camera, open since 1899(!!) in the heart of the Loop, definitely does. Selling both new and used cameras, along with scads of lenses and other equipment, it's heaven for both amateur and professional photographers.

The selection of used equipment offers the best bargains, with stock changing constantly. A 35mm Olympus OM-10 camera with a 50mm lens was recently available, priced at $150; and a Canon FTb was seen for $180, including a six-month warranty. Central Camera also maintains an impressive selection of used Leicas. Even secondhand, these are still pricey; but they last a lifetime, and Leica fans find them worth every penny for those silent shutters.

Used Canon zoom lenses are priced in the $100-$200 range, depending on age and condition. Pentax and Konica lenses are also well-represented, as is Oriental paper (25 sheets of the 8 X 10 portrait paper runs about $11) as well as printing papers by Kodak, Agfa, Ilford, and Forte.

Darkroom Aids Company
- 3449 N. Lincoln Ave., Chicago; (312) 248-4301

In the 1940's and 1950's, this place used to manufacture stainless steel nitrogen agitation equipment, whatever that is. Today, they buy and sell used photography equipment. Used equipment has been completely refurbished in their repair shop on the premises, and all used items carry a full 90-day warranty.

Prices will vary depending on how old a piece is, and its condition; but, as a general rule, you'll probably pay about half of what the camera was worth when it was new. And there's a special bonus for area college students: Show your valid student ID, and get an additional five percent off. Cool, huh?

Most of DA's stock is used, but they do carry some new stuff, enlargers, for instance, and other stuff that they can't find on the used market. The store is open daily from 9 a.m. to 6 p.m., except Thursdays when they stay open until 8 in the evening. They're closed on Sundays.

Helix Camera and Video

- 310 S. Racine Ave., Chicago; (312) 421-6000
- 141 W. Van Buren St., Chicago; (312) 663-3650
- 2 Illinois Center (Concourse), Chicago; (312) 565-5901
- 3 First National Plaza, Chicago; (312) 444-9373

And other suburban locations
The West Loop branch is the main store for this full-service photography chain. Helix offers competitive prices on a wide range of instamatic, 35mm, and video cameras, along with film, tape, accessories, and film processing. Save on the latest models from all the big names—Nikon, Canon, Kodak, Fuji, Sony, and more. The Canon EOS Rebel II, for instance, is a serious 35mm compact SLR camera with many automatic features, including motorized film advance. It was recently priced at $199 (for the body alone). It normally sells here for $229, and can be even higher at other stores. Canon lenses to go with it start around $100.

At the extreme opposite end of the spectrum, you can find the Fuji Quicksnap—disposable camera and 24-exposure film all in one—for just $4.95. In between are the fully automatic mini-35s so popular these days, like the Minolta Freedom Tele, with wide angle and close-up lens settings, selling here for $109.

Helix also carries other optical products, such as binoculars. The Nikon "Windjammer" model, offering 7 x 50 magnification, waterproof and fogproof with a 25-year warranty, was spied here at $149, about $70 below retail. And, in the world of video, you can find a Yashica Hi-8 camcorder, model KXV1, selling at $899. A package of two TDK 8mm videocassettes for it is $7.99. Good prices also on Kodak film (Kodacolor 35mm Ultra 400, 36 exposures, $5.80), batteries, blank videotapes for your home VCR, and just about anything else you might need.

John's Electronics

- 5322 N. Broadway, Chicago; (312) 878-3716.

Specializing in stereo and electronics, John's is an authorized dealer for many of the big name brands it carries. In the camera department, Mr. C found a Minolta Freedom 202 35mm camera, with automatic features, for just $109; and a Canon Sure Shot Telemax 35mm camera, with a zoom lens, for $149.

John's is also a good place for budget-priced cameras, like the Minolta "Memory Maker," a fully automatic 35mm model. It comes in a kit which includes batteries and film, for $39.95. Good prices on film and accessories, too. The store is open Mondays through Saturdays from 10 a.m. to 7:30 p.m.

Triangle Camera

- 3445 N. Broadway, Chicago; (312) 472-1015

Here's a photo shop that takes "full service" to the max. This Wrigleyville store does a lot more than sell film. For starters, they sell a complete line of new equipment and accessories at very competitive prices; many items are sold at or near cost. Some even go below cost, like a 35-mm Nikon N-90 camera which was seen here recently selling for $836. Due to market fluctuations, its wholesale cost had actually gone up to $862, but owner Linda Ogata doesn't see fit to keep needling with her prices—she'd rather have the business, and sell out the current stock at a low price. So, you never know what hidden bargains may be, er, exposed here.

But there are other ways to save here, too. One option is the used camera department, where you may find all kinds of goodies at up to half their original prices. Mr. C noticed the ever-popular Canon AE-1, with a 150mm lens, selling for $175, and a Minolta Freedom Zoom 70c for $105. There are usually several used flash units and lenses available too, like a Vivitar 5200 flash for $50. Used equipment carries no store war-

MR. CHEAP'S PICKS
Cameras

✔ **Central Camera**—An extensive selection of used cameras, including high-end Leicas.

✔ **Triangle Camera**—New cameras of every kind, near wholesale (sometimes below!). Used models, too.

✔ **Wolf Camera and Video**—Good to excellent prices on new 35mm and video cameras and supplies.

ranty, but what you can do is rent these cameras and apply the rental fee to the cost of buying.

Some of the cameras in this section may even be unused, discontinued models; these are sold at dealer cost, and still carry the full manufacturer's warranty. On display during Mr. C's visit was a Fuji Discovery 3000, with a built-in zoom lens, reduced from $320 to $250. It included a flash attachment—and a five-year warranty.

If you're serious about your snaps, another option to consider is the Triangle Camera Club. This entitles you to 10% discounts on film processing, studio darkroom rates, plus bulk prices on new film. At biweekly gatherings, you can exchange tips and ideas with fellow photographers. You also get half-price admission to special seminars and workshops with camera professionals, and a chance to display your work in the Triangle Gallery. And, every summer, Triangle hosts outdoor "Photo Fairs," even more prominent

exhibitions where you can show and sell your work. A six-month membership is $30.00. See? This store gets *involved*! Open seven days a week.

Wolf Camera and Video
- 1919 N. Clybourn Ave., Chicago; (312) 528-5535
- 42 S. Clark St., Chicago; (312) 759-8030
- 66 E. Madison St., Chicago; (312) 346-2288
- 750 N. Rush St., Chicago; (312) 943-5531

And other suburban locations.
Don't let anybody take your Kodachrome away, and don't buy a new camera anywhere without first checking out the goods at Wolf. A Nikon "Light Touch" 35mm camera, well priced at $140, is just one of the many good deals you can find here. It's one of the current, compact, point-and-shoot varieties, with automatic focus and exposure, and red-eye-reducing built-in flash.

Wolf is a full service store, offering equipment and photographic supplies as well. A 24-exposure roll of Kodak Gold 100 film sells for $2.89, and 24-exposure Fuji ISO 100 color print film is $2.99. Kodak fixer mix (enough to make a gallon) for $3.99 is a good price, as is $17.25 for 25 sheets of 8" X 10" Kodak FD glossy polyfiber paper.

Video recorders are also pretty cheap here. Mr. C saw a Sanyo 8mm camcorder selling for under $500, and a Sony 8mm camcorder with automatic features was $50 off retail, putting it under $700. Binoculars are also sold well below retail prices, like a Nikon 7x20 compact with a 25-year warranty for $80.

The chain's super store at 8361 Golf Road in Niles, (708) 967-0580, caters to commercial and industrial photography needs as well as retail. With any purchase, Wolf offers free introductory photography classes, held once a month at this location.

CARPETING AND RUGS

Carpet Market
- 1532 N. Milwaukee Ave., Chicago; (312) 384-4700

At this store, prices are labeled by the square foot, not yard, so you think you're hardly spending any money. The truth is, you can save money here, but you'll have to multiply all the prices by nine to figure out exactly how much!

The remnant selection is not spectacular, but worth at least a glance. A 10' x 12' remnant is usually priced at $159; a 12' x 16' plush carpet remnant is $229, and a 5' x 12' Berber leftover is $119.

Oriental rug runners sell for $5.95 per linear foot; and 9' x 12' area rugs, made in China and Belgium are $149. Berber rugs by Salem Carpets are regularly $4.99 a square foot but may go on sale for as low as $2.29. Wool/acrylic blend berber-style carpets, much softer than the really cheap all-nylon kind, are $2.69 per square foot. There is an extra charge of about 45 cents a square foot for installation, too.

The store is open Mondays through Thursdays from 9 a.m. to 6 p.m.; Fridays from 9 a.m. to 7:30 p.m.; Saturdays 9-6, and Sundays 11-5.

Carpet Warehouse Center
- 1640-52 N. Milwaukee Ave., Chicago; (312) 384-2600

The extensive address of this carpet company should give you a clue as to how big they are. Located in a rather dismal stretch of Wicker Park, this young company is a great place for remnants. Unfortunately, the buyers seem to be bent on stocking too many purple and green shades, but you can find gray, beige, and blue rugs too.

CWC discounts previously used remnants here, but most of the carpeting looks brand new. A lot of it gets used just for a day or two, in displays at McCormick Place and other convention centers, and is then returned to the store. Some carpets need to have coffee stains removed; others have small cut-outs that can be camouflaged by a sofa or bookcase. Because the carpets were used for special displays, some are odd-sized, like a used 2' X 11' hall runner or stairway carpet for a modest $13. A 12' x 17' remnant, originally $255, was seen on sale for $135.

Of course, Carpet Warehouse does sell new carpeting as well. Check the tags carefully; some of the brand-new carpeting includes padding and installation, but a lot doesn't, such as the remnants. New carpets by Columbus, at $20 per square yard, include installation, while Berber texturized carpets, at $12.99 a square yard, do not.

D & R Carpet Wholesaler's, Inc.
- 3028 N. Lincoln Ave., Chicago; (312) 880-5440

And other suburban locations

Would you buy carpet from a place with a grammatical mistake in its name? Or one with chain-smoking sales help? This store has both, but if you're willing to forgive them their faults, you can get a rug here with padding and installation included in the ultra-low price. The remnant and area rug selections are nothing to holler about, and neither is their miniscule vinyl flooring section, but for wall-to-wall carpeting, this wholesaler has good deals indeed.

D & R brags about its four million yards of carpet in stock, but the Lincoln Park showroom sure doesn't seem like it could hold that much. No doubt they mean chainwide. At any rate, carpeting by Queen was only $15.99 per square yard, on sale from its already low $19.99. With Stainmaster treatment, the sale price was still only $18.99 a square yard, down from $22.99. The color variety isn't gigantic, however, but the basic roses, blues and beige shades are represented.

Carpeting by Canterbury, which had a slightly tighter-woven feel than the Queen carpet, is normally $26.99 a square yard, but was on sale for $21.99 a square yard. All of these prices include padding and installation.

Remnants don't come with the same installation deal, but, on the other hand, didn't have as many imperfections as remnants in some other carpeting places. A 12' x 15' beige remnant was selling for $129; a 12' x 9' for $100; and a 12' x 18' patterned carpet was seen for $146. A woven candy-striped remnant—the kind good for a child's room or a playroom, where it's bound to get beat up immediately—was only $162 for a big 12' x 20' size.

In tapestries, an 11' by 7' Persian-style rug (it's actually made in the state of Georgia), was recently on sale for $309. It regularly sells for $359, and is valued at about $400, retail.

Because D & R is a wholesaler, most of the carpets don't have brand names on the backings of samples; but the carpeting is straight from the mill and in very good shape. The store is open from 9-9 weekdays, 9-6 Saturdays and 11-5 Sundays.

Exposition Carpet Company
- 5718 N. Broadway, Chicago; (312) 784-5600

Way up on Broadway, in that part of town known as Epic, is one of Mr. C's favorite places in all of Chicago to buy a carpet, remnant, or area rug. Direct purchasing from mills in Philadelphia, along with Exposition's super-high sales volume, helps keep prices ultra-low; and yet, the salespeople still manage to steal the show with their friendliness.

Stores buy their carpets at Exposition, since commercial carpeting is only $6.95 a yard and up. Sculptured

nylon carpeting starts at a mere $8.79 per square yard. Household broadloom, like designs by J.C. Stevens at $19 per square yard installed, are also super deals. Coronet carpeting, available in a whopping 150 colors, is only $20 a square yard. And soft, fuzzy bathroom carpeting, with a list price of $8.95 per linear foot, sells here for $6.50.

Area rugs are another scene-stealer here, with a pure wool hand-woven Turkish rug—valued at about $2100—selling for $699. Nine by twelve-foot Oriental rugs are $800, about half of their listed retail prices, and Oriental runners, 27" wide, are only $4 per linear foot. Regular nylon spot rugs are also half off retail (a 2' x 4' was only $13).

There are thousands (yup, thousands!) of remnants in stock, which sometimes go on sale for 10%-70% off their already-cheap-as-heck prices. A 12' x 20' remnant, listed at $615, recently sold for $389; and another, a 12' x 16' remainder, was only $105 since a couple of hardly-noticeable spots were made during installation of the original roll. If perfect, it would sell for $210. Mr. C also saw some berber remnants, like a 12' x 24' piece for $300, half of its original $599 list price.

Exposition, which has been around for twenty years, offers to "meet or beat" any competitor's price. They will make delivery for a mere $15. All marked prices, meanwhile, include padding and installation—such a deal! Open weekdays from 10 a.m. to 9 p.m., Saturdays from 10-5, and Sundays from noon to 5.

New York Carpet World
- 3425 W. Devon Ave., Chicago; (312) 267-7486

And many other suburban locations
You know how the song goes: If you can make it there, you'll make it anywhere. Well, this place can really paint the town red—or rather, carpet it in red, and dozens of other colors, for that matter. There is indeed a "world" of carpeting to be explored

MR. CHEAP'S PICKS
Carpeting and Rugs

✔ **D & R Carpet Wholesaler's**—Go for the carpet bargains, not their punctuation. Padding and installation are included in the low prices.

✔ **Exposition Carpet Company**—These guys buy direct from the mills, and many businesses buy from these guys. You should, too.

✔ **New York Carpet World**—Another mega-store, with thousands of colors and styles at rock-bottom prices.

✔ **Show Carpet**—This South Sider has an extensive selection of carpeting and remnants, many of which come with padding and installation included.

---

here, with thousands of rolls in just about every name brand. Many are treated with stain protection, and come with multi-year warranties.

Prices here drop through the floor. You can find synthetic plush broadloom for as little as $3.97 per square yard, with tweeds as low as $2.99. DuPont Stainmaster carpets begin at just $5.77 per square yard, including berber styles from $9.88, with dozens of colors to choose from.

There are tons of options in the budget price range of around $5 a yard. Again, these include commercial, cut-pile, plush, and berber weaves. Many of these prices are as much as 50% below comparable department store merchandise.

New York Carpet World also has a good selection of area rugs, as well as vinyl and wood floor coverings. They even offer a shop-at-home serv-

ice, and free credit for up to 180 days if approved. The store is open seven days a week; daily from 9:30 a.m. to 9:00 p.m., and Sundays from 11-5.

Olympic Carpet Center
- 2719 N. California Ave., Chicago; (312) 276-1212

Just off of the Kennedy Expressway, Olympic offers good prices on a variety of rugs and carpets, especially international styles of handmade rugs. Here, you can find a 5' x 8' hand-knotted wool tapestry from India for as low as $399, or even an 8' x 11' model from the Philippines for the same price. If you can't quite spring for these discount prices, and don't mind a machine-made copy, you may want to go for a 9' x 15' Oriental for only $249.

Of course, Olympic has discount prices on broadloom too, well below retail prices. But, perhaps the biggest deal here is their remnant selection—so large, they can't even fit it all in this store! The rolls spill over into not one, but two **Olympic Warehouse** locations. One is a block away at 2614 N. California Ave., telephone (312) 276-0384; the other is located at 3017 N. Central Ave., telephone (312) 763-3390. At any of these three spots, you may find 9' x 12' remnants for as little as $39, or 12' x 12' squares starting from $49. These prices are as much as 80% below original retail rates. They claim to stock some 40,000 square feet of rems, which Mr. C calculates to be roughly the amount required to carpet Lake Michigan shore-to-shore, and still have enough left over to do most of Daley Plaza.

Olympic is open seven days: Weekdays from 9 a.m. to 9 p.m., Saturdays from 9-7, and Sundays from 10-6. Free parking is available.

Show Carpet
- 4319 S. Archer Ave., Chicago; (312) 927-1177

They sure put on a "really big show" here. Show Carpet has two huge showrooms filled with broadloom and rugs, all selling at 40% to 70% below retail prices. These are closeouts and overstocks from mills all around the country, in a great selection of colors, patterns, and textures. Among the brands you'll find here are Anso, DuPont, Trevira, and others. Many of them are treated with "Scotchgard" stain protection.

Prices here are by the square foot, not the square yard, making comparisons tricky; but be assured that these prices are good indeed. Mr. C noticed a medium-pile sculptured synthetic, for example, in a handsome burgundy color. Its retail price was $3.39 per square foot, and it sells here for $2.39; it was on special sale that week, however, further reduced to $1.89 per foot. This carpeting was Scotchgarded, and carried a ten-year warranty. Good deal—one of many.

Attractive Oriental runners were also on sale during that visit. They had a list price of $8.95 per linear foot, and the normal selling price was $4.69 a foot; buy thirty feet or more, and the price came down another buck, to $3.69. Speaking of Orientals, a machine-made 6' x 8' rug was seen with a retail price of $249, marked down to just $79. Some 9' x 12' styles, with list prices of up to $350, sell for a mere $99.

By the way, Show does sell current broadloom styles, also at discount—anywhere from 35% to 60% below list prices, or about $1-$2 off per square foot. Plenty of durable tight-weave commercial carpeting, too, in broadloom and runners—some as little as 99 cents per foot!

And we haven't even gotten to the other room yet. That's where you'll find Show's incredible selection of remnants—over 4,000 of them, in a vast range of sizes and materials. Whether you want a little 2' x 5' bound rug for $8.50, all the way up to a 12' x 36' piece for $119 (enough to cut and fit into two or three rooms), chances are good you'll find lots of choices here. Rems in 4' x 6' and 6' x 9' sizes are priced from just $19 and up; 9' x 12' sizes start at $49. Any remnant in this size or larger will include foam padding free with your purchase. As a matter of fact, any purchase of wall-to-wall carpeting includes free padding and installation into the bargain. A DuPont remnant, 12' x 18' in sculptured, stain-resistant nylon, was reduced twice—from $399 to $260 to a final price of $188. You may even find some natural fiber rems, like a bound 6' x 9' wool berber marked down from $199 to just $57. Get the picture? This place is one of the best in town. There's even a waiting area with a TV set, for reluctant tagalongs.

Show Carpet offers a delivery service, as well as financing and layaway. It's open seven days a week, from 10 a.m. to 8:30 p.m. on weekdays, 10-5 on Saturdays and 12-5 on Sundays. Free parking lot, too.

CLOTHING—NEW

Know what you're buying! Clothes, like anything else, are sold at discount for many reasons. Let's quickly go over some basic terms.

With new merchandise, "First-quality" means perfect clothing—it has no flaws of any kind, as you would find in any full-price store. Such items may be reduced in price as a sales promotion, because it's left over from a past season, or because too many were made. Some stores are able to discount first-quality clothing simply through high-volume selling, and good connections with wholesalers. "Discontinued" styles are self-explanatory; again, these are usually new and still perfectly good.

"Second-quality," sometimes called "irregulars," "seconds," or "IRs," are new clothes which have some slight mistakes in their manufacture, or which have been damaged in shipping. Often, these blemishes are hard to find. Still, a reputable store will call your attention to the spot, either with a sign near the items, or a piece of masking tape directly on the problem area.

If you're not sure whether you're looking at a first or a second, ask!

MEN'S AND WOMEN'S WEAR—GENERAL

A & M Furs
● 613 W. Roosevelt Rd., Chicago; (312) 332-4064

West of the Loop, this block of Roosevelt is sort of a discount district, with a little bit of everything—even furs. A & M imports and makes some of its own merchandise, selling primarily to department stores; but you can save a bundle by shopping here directly.

There are high-quality furs of every color and style for men and women, along with some leather fashions as well. A full-length men's mink coat imported from Finland, for example, in a rich mahogany color, was seen here for $2,500; in other stores, it may sell for as much as $7,000. In leather, Mr. C saw a black bomber jacket from Argentina, reduced from $1,250 to $495. There's also a half-price rack, for even better bargains.

More importantly, the friendly folks in here are willing to negotiate a bit on their prices; you may be able to create a hot deal on a warm coat. Layaway plans are available, too, and A & M does storage, cleaning, and repair work on the premises.

The Answer
● 180 N. Wabash Ave., Chicago; (312) 419-1801
● 6560 W. Fullerton Ave., Chicago; (312) 237-3388
● 9601 S. Western Ave., Chicago; (312) 238-9390

For larger-size women, this discount chain offers fashions for work and weekends, and even dresses for the mother of the bride. Name brands like Maggie McNaughton are mixed with moderate labels, and it's all priced at 20% to 40% off retail everyday.

During a recent sale, all Jones New York career wear was 25% off—including dresses and two-piece suits. A beautiful dress of rayon viscose/linen blend, originally priced at a serious $120, was reduced to a svelte $74.99. Another super deal was a rayon Karin Stevens dress, in a tasteful floral print; originally $123, it was reduced by 35% to a more moderate $74. At that price, you can still afford to buy some accessories to go with it!

Arbetman and Goldberg
● 350 N. Orleans St. (Arcade Level), Chicago; (312) 467-0377

Next to the Merchandise Mart and its new arcade of hoity-toity shops, the more modern Apparel Center houses still more wholesalers of the clothing trade. One important difference is that there are a handful of shops downstairs, one level below the street, where the public can shop at bargain prices. King of the bunch is Arbetman and Goldberg, a large, full-service men's store with prices of 30% to 70% below retail.

With over 35 years of experience "upstairs," not to mention contacts all over the country, A & G has access to some spectacular deals in fine men's suits, sportcoats, raincoats, dress shirts, ties, and sweaters. Most of the styles are European classics, with some American traditionals among the racks. Everything is first quality—no irregulars—from some of the big names in the clothing biz.

Mr. C saw an all-wool suit by Yves Saint-Laurent, certain to sell for $600 on the Magnificent Mile, priced here at $349. Another suit, a double-breasted Courreges-Homme with a retail price of $500, was selling for $299. And a cashmere-wool blend sportcoat by Konen of Munich was reduced from $590 to a much slimmer $249.

A & G has a large selection of cashmere blend overcoats, made to sell for $300-$400, here just $199. Cotton dress shirts can go as low as two for $35. And a wall full of $45-$65 silk ties from Italy are on sale for $25 each—unless you want to look at another section of sale ties which are $15 each. In fact, about the only things you won't find here are socks and shoes.

Also, perhaps by the time you read this, the store will have expanded to include leather fashions with the same high quality and low prices. These will include styles for men, women, and kids, including jackets, skirts, etc.

As with many stores of this type, these great prices come from a low-rent (i.e., out-of-the-way) location and no advertising. How, then, do people find out about their special weekend-only sales? Why, by mailing list, of course. Ten times a year, A & G opens up on weekends for extra bargain binges—normal hours, like the rest of the building, are Monday-Friday, 9-5 only—and they send out postcards advertising the next weekend dates. Stop in, chat with the friendly folks, get on the list, and shop where the insiders shop.

Back Room Designer Outlet
- 11 E. Chestnut St., Chicago; (312) 664-3295

You can expect to find chi-chi fashions by Escada, Versace, and Donna Karan here in the ritzy Gold Coast area, but you'd *never* expect to find them at less than half-price. How is it possible? Because owner Marina Dolgonos snaps up closeouts, overstocks, and shipments that have been refused by major stores because they arrived

MR. CHEAP'S PICKS
Men's and Women's General Wear

✔ **Arbetman and Goldberg**—Worth finding, below the Apparel Center, for fantastic buys on fine men's suits. Across the hall, the **I.B. Diffusion Clearance Center** is an outlet for this popular maker of casual women's fashions.

✔ **Back Room Designer Outlet**—Drastically reduced prices on new designer clothing for men and women. In the Gold Coast area, yet!

✔ **Buy-A-Tux Superstore**—Discounts on designer formalwear for guys; budget brands too.

✔ **Filene's Basement**—The Boston legend has arrived in Chicago. Great clothing and accessories for the whole family—practically for beans.

✔ **Knitpickers Knitwear Outlet**—This Lincoln Park shop sells first-quality overruns with fancy names at 20% to 70% off.

✔ **Lands End Outlet Stores**—On Elston Ave., two shops a block apart—one for men, one for women—clear out the shelves for this popular mail-order company.

✔ **Meystel's Warehouse**—In the South Loop area, surplus stock from famous designers for men and women at rock-bottom prices.

✔ **Morris & Sons**—West of downtown is another out-of-the-way spot for incredible bargains on the latest high-end fashions imported from Europe.

MR. CHEAP'S PICKS
Men's and Women's
General Wear

✔ **Mark Shale Outlet**—Great deals on past season clothing, some slightly damaged, and all vastly discounted.

✔ **Spencer**—The shop looks a bit worn, but the men's suits and shoes inside are first-rate.

✔ **Spiegel Outlet Store**—Another catalog clearance center, and a gigantic one, at that.

too late in the season. These are all new, first-quality clothes and accessories for men and women, and it's quite a selection.

Ladies, here's your chance to get fashions like a two-piece Escada suit—originally priced at $1,475—for a mere $525. Or a snazzy red Donna Karan blazer, not for $1,600, but just $480. On the racy side, a lace bustier and jacket by Krizia, meant to sell for $2,150, was seen for $660.

There is a somewhat smaller, but no less impressive, selection for guys. Look sharp in a Paolo Uomo double breasted suit, reduced from $815 to $365, adding a Hugo Boss silk print tie for $40; or, ditch the suit for a casual Versace sportshirt, marked down from $265 to a more comfortable $80.

Sure, these prices are still not "cheap," but then, neither is the clothing. For many folks, a store like this can mean the difference between owning such fashions at all, or just wishing. There is a sale rack too, where items are knocked down another 50 percent; here, you may see a Karl Lagerfeld sundress ensemble for $230, or a dress by Michael Kors reduced from $370, to $170, to $49.

The store has much in the way of accessories, too, including shoes (Escada flats marked down from $395 to $89), belts, and jewelry.

The Back Room, literally at the rear of a little courtyard plaza, is open Mondays through Saturdays from 11 a.m. to 6 p.m.

Bagatelle
- 70 E. Randolph St., Chicago; (312) 332-5544

Right in the heart of the Loop, Bagatelle is a large shop specializing in fine, first-quality leather clothing for men and women. The merchandise is sold on consignment direct from several international factories, and the prices show it—like suede bomber jackets from a Canadian manufacturer, made to retail at $299-$700, priced here as low as $99-$199. A women's full-length black leather coat from England, with a retail price of $1150, may sell here for $695. Men's three-quarter length jackets, all the rage this year, sell for about half of retail at $250. Mr. C even saw a rack of parka-style leather jackets for children (!) priced at $150.

But you can bag more than just leather at Bagatelle. They also carry things like sandwashed silk blouses for $12, women's wool gabardine suits for $66 in a variety of colors, and other accessories. And don't miss the clearance room at the back, where everything is $20—including denim skirts, Italian cashmere/wool sweaters, and some designer separates. The stock is ever-changing, making this a regular lunch-hour stop for the downtown professional crowd.

Belmont Army/Navy Surplus
- 945 W. Belmont Ave. (2nd Floor), Chicago; (312) 975-0626

Inside and upstairs from an otherwise ordinary-looking clothing store (just head for the central stairway), you'll find this rugged and more offbeat army/navy. Up here, you can find all things military, from combat boots to gas masks (!) and everything that goes in between. That includes more practical gear, like heavy wool cable-knit sweaters for $17.99; lined nylon raincoats for $24; sailor shirts for $12.99; and more. Get a camouflage T-shirt for $7.99, or the real thing—an army-issue full camouflage shirt for $17.99.

Those combat boots are as low as $25-$30 a pair, and unlike some of the clothing, they are not previously used. The merchandise here runs about half new and half used. Then, there are all kinds of accessories, like sleeping bags for $45, and duffel bags (in all sizes from manageable to enormous), as low as $19.99, and all kinds of camping gear.

Sharing this space with the army/navy is **J. Park Company**, which overlaps a bit by selling new bags and backpacks, as well as new and vintage clothing. Among the new items are lots of ethnic fashions, like Mexican flour-sack pullover shirts ($15.99), and cotton skirts from India ($18.99). Also, women's stretch jeans for $13.99, and other separates, sterling silver rings from $2.99 to $10.00, handbags, and other accessories. Both stores are open seven days, including every night but Sunday until 8:00 p.m.

Buy-A-Tux Superstore
- 615 W. Roosevelt Rd., Chicago; (312) 243-5465

A member of the retail trade told Mr. C he considers this shop to be perhaps the only one of its kind in town, if not the entire midwest. Certainly, for anyone who uses formalwear frequently—musicians, say, or people who attend movie premieres—buying a tux makes more sense than renting all the time. Especially when you can save as much as $100 off the prices found at fancier specialty stores.

These are snazzy duds indeed, designer formalwear and all the accessories. A Bill Blass outfit, for example, was seen here recently for $300, reduced from $400. Perry Ellis, Joseph Abboud, and others are well represented in this good-sized store, which—unlike most others on the block—is *not* a no-frills bargain joint.

If those designers are fast company for you, even at reduced prices,

don't despair. Basic poly-blend tuxes start as low as $169.95, complete with cummerbund and bowtie. While on that subject, Buy-A-Tux is a complete outfitter, with lots of shoes, cufflinks and studs, ties, and other accessories to choose from, all at discount prices. They also have fashions for slightly less formal situations, like glittery looks for a night on the town, and Nicole Miller silk print neckties reduced from $50 to $39. The store is open seven days a week.

Cary and Company, The Leather Outlet
- 350 N. Orleans St. (Arcade Level), Chicago; (312) 329-9583

Another of the few shops open to the public at the Apparel Center, the Leather Outlet is a tiny new store which makes and sells its own line of leather fashions for men, women, and children. They sell direct to you at good prices, in a wide variety of styles and colors. Suede jackets start at $85, with kids' sizes starting at $55. Men's leather bomber jackets, in lambskin, are $99 and up. And they've got more than just basic black—Mr. C looked at an eye-catching purple and gold model, among others.

Also noteworthy is the fact that, because Cary and Co. make their own clothing, you can custom order larger sizes at no extra cost. "Big and tall" people know how important that can be; especially with leather fashions.

But leather isn't all you'll find here. Cary frequently gets deals on consignment, which can mean just about any kind of clothing from suits and dresses to ties and T-shirts, all at big discounts. On Mr. C's visit, there was a large display of first-quality women's separates woven of Italian linen by a local designer. Overruns from last season, these earth-tone tops and skirts originally sold for $90 apiece; here, they were down to just $25. Men's tops by Polo and Henry Grethel were on sale for half-price—again, top-quality overstocks. Folks who work in the Loop area may want to drop in occasionally—you never know what may be available. Open Monday to Friday from 9:00 to 5:00 only.

Joseph Cinofsky, Inc.
- 560 W. Harrison St., Chicago; (312) 922-5560

For no-nonsense discount clothing, head to Cinofsky's, as well-dressed gentlemen have been doing since 1940. It's around the corner from the Greyhound Bus station west of the Loop, and just south of the Eisenhower Expressway. Oh, and don't be scared by the nine-foot-long hammerhead shark mounted on the back wall, caught by Mr. Cinofsky himself; everyone here is quite friendly, really.

You can save big bucks by shopping Cinofsky's factory seconds and irregulars. Basics like Wrangler jeans at $14.95, Haggar "almost perfect" slacks for $14 (cotton) and $17 (corduroy), and worsted wool dress pants for $25 (solid or pinstripe) are all stacked up on plain tables. Some clothing is displayed in cardboard boxes, and the $4 silk ties, valued at $40, are hung on a rack that just may be as old as the store itself.

Stock up on accessories, like nylon dress socks at three pairs for $2.95, irregular briefs by BVD, three pairs for $5, or a five-pack of cotton handkerchiefs for $2.50. Better yet, for just $3, you can get one of those silk mini-hankies that tuck into the pocket of your blazer for that dashing touch. Canvas belts are as low as $3 each; suede gloves are $4 a pair.

Summer fashions: A box of cutoff denim shorts, including names like Calvin Klein, Rustler, and Wrangler, was seen at $1 a pair. Dressier cotton plaid shorts, obviously made by a well-known designer since the tags were cut out (the Gap would be a likely suspect), were only $3. Same price for blue plaid swim trunks, also by a mystery designer. Sport shirts by Seafarer were a mere $6 (these are genuine Navy issue!). For colder weather, cotton/poly blend turtlenecks are just $7, and a lined poplin

jacket by Alpine Ski was seen for only $40.

Also at Cinofsky's, you can choose from clothing in hard-to-find sizes, such as large-waisted pants and ties for tall men, all in good supply. One gripe: Whatever your size, he-man or average Joe, there are no complete suits to be found here, at least during Mr. C's visit.

The shop is open from 9-5 weekdays, 9-4:30 Saturdays and 9-2:30 Sundays. Along with the super deals you'll find inside the store, you'll also get an hour of free parking with a $10 purchase.

Mort Cooper
- 161 N. State St., Chicago; (312) 332-8410

Look spiffy for cents. Well, almost! By not advertising, Mort Cooper's shop in the Loop can afford to sell high-quality clothing for men, both career wear and casual, at inexpensive prices. The store has survived this way since 1921, operating mostly on word-of-mouth to draw in new customers. Free alterations, in addition to the personal attention given to shoppers, keeps them coming back.

Not all of the brands here are well-known designers, but all of the looks are sharp. Recently, the store was offering a tremendous selection of Givenchy silk ties for a wee $10. Pure wool dress pants by Greg Peters were only $55, valued at $95. A navy blue Yves St. Laurent wool suit, which would retail at $595, sells for only $300; and a wool blend suit under Mort Cooper's private label was only $165, although valued at $315.

While average-sized men will find a bonanza at Cooper's, big and tall sizes are hard to find in this shop. None of the shirts had sleeves longer than 35 inches. Open Mondays through Saturdays, from 9:00 a.m. to 5:15 p.m.

Designers Mart
- 170 W. Washington St., Chicago; (312)368-1980

This store's name is a bit misleading, since there aren't a heck of a lot of big-names represented, and the atmosphere is cavernous and no-frills. The store does have four amazing floors of reduced-price clothing for the entire family, for practically any occasion. Careful on the stairs here, though—this Loop building is a bit old, to say the least. The steps leading up to each warehouse-sized floor seem to, er, lean to one side.

The quality of clothing varies, including perfect and imperfect merchandise. This is definitely a good place to stock up on basics like undies and t-shirts. Men's generic-brand cotton briefs sell for 50 cents apiece. Dressy leather belts were an amazing $3.99, and past-season Christian Dior silk ties were recently seen for $15. Also, keep an eye out for occasional sidewalk-type sales here. One recent sale cut the prices on men's suits from a everyday low $120 to $29, blazers from $50 to $7 and socks to $1 a pair. A Christian Dior trench coat was reduced from $400 to a dapper $100.

Upstairs, ladies' fake fur coats can be found for $39. The store recently had a shipment of tank tops from the Gap going for $3.90, mostly in petite sizes. Clothes from Avon Fashions can also be found here, and J.C. Penney closeouts up to size 24. The $3 and $5 racks do have some treasures hidden among them, but you'll have to dig deep; and the store even has a huge selection of bargain wedding gowns. Tons of stuff for kids here, too.

Speaking of sizes, this issue can be a boon or a bane to you at Designer's Mart. For average folks, selection can be quite limited, since much of the stock here consists of closeouts and leftovers. If, however, your dimensions run to the small or large, you'll probably love this place; in fact, for big and tall men, clothing often goes all the way up to size 54.

Designers Mart is open from 9 a.m. to 6 p.m. on weekdays, and Saturdays from 10:30-5.

Discovery
- 3348 W. Belmont Ave., Chicago; (312) 463-3700

At the corner of Belmont and Kimball, right across the street from the subway station, is this store full of inexpensive urban-style women's clothing, where "everything is on sale every day." New merchandise does arrive daily, keeping the store full of contemporary styles.

Latino music blaring in the background, a bit loud, sets the tone here. There are no dressing rooms; but if you know your exact size, you can save big on flashy fashions for the nightclub scene, as well as pants and everyday clothes. A cotton chambray shirt was seen for $12.99, and bodysuits by Instant Action were just $8. Cotton twill pants in eight bold colors were just $15, as were denim skirts by True Blue. Discovery also offered a polyester/rayon blazer that looked like linen, on sale for just $15. More casual styles included hooded Georgetown University sweatshirts for only $7; and many other items on "one price $5" racks.

Filene's Basement
- One N. State St. (Lower level), Chicago; (312) 553-1061.

Boston's original Filene's Basement is the king of all bargain treasure troves. Normally-sane women pounce upon tables strewn with piles of clothing closeouts, flinging wrong sizes into the air, in search of The Find. If and when they come up with this, they clutch it tightly and head immediately for the nearest register—or, to another table. The place can be a real madhouse...which is part of its charm.

The atmosphere of Chicago's outpost is more refined, but it matches Boston's huge selection of jewelry, cosmetics, first-quality clothing and houseware closeouts, and irregulars. Mr. C noticed well-coiffed women with Gucci bags and men with diamond cufflinks—perhaps they can afford these fancy trinkets by saving on their wardrobe at the Basement. The selection changes constantly; many customers make a regular pass through here on a lunch hour or after work.

Ladies may find an Evan Picone suit, which would cost almost $300 retail, knocked down to $140. Girls' Keds sneakers were just $20, and juniors' Esprit cotton pants were only $15. A juniors' all-wool Laura Ashley dress was only $20, down from a retail price of well over $100. The ladies' expansive (not expensive!) petite section yielded Battenburg lace-inset cotton blouses by Carry Back Petite for $20, and Willi Wear Sport denim shirts for just $19.

On the men's side, Levi's Dockers pants were seen for $20, half their retail price; Perry Ellis silk ties, at the same price, were more than half off. Yves Saint Laurent dress shirts were just $20, and all-cotton Ralph Lauren dress shirts were $38, down from $60. Boys' twill Timberland shirts were cut from $65 to $35.

Filene's is also a good place to buy better-name cosmetics, which run at least 10% or more below retail. A 1.7-ounce spray bottle of Shalimar eau de toilette was 25% off retail, selling for $32. Lots of great jewelry buys, too.

So what if the Basement can get messy during sales? For the money you can save, it's well worth fighting the crowds, and rummaging around for your size. And it's good practice in case you ever go to Boston.

Frank's Second Stop Resale Shop

- 547 W. Roosevelt Rd., Chicago; (312) 733-7766, (312) 733-7733

In spite of the name, this store actually combines secondhand clothing with unused closeouts, a mix of items that ranges from ratty to gorgeous. It's surprisingly big, with a variety of clothes for men and women; the stock was good, though not spectacular, when Mr. Cheap visited. They're getting new stuff in all the time, though, and have some great finds in previously-owned clothing, much of which has never been worn and still bears the original tags.

Women's clothing ranges from casual to careerwear. An Outlander acrylic/wool dress, for example, looked almost brand new and was selling for only $15. Women's shoes are well-stocked but include some bloopers—be sure to check out the condition of the heels and the leather or uppers before you make that impulse purchase! A used pair of navy Ann Taylor heels, for example, were only $5, but badly needed some polishing. Ditto for a pair of red leather pumps by Nickels, selling here for $8. But either pair can be restored, and will save you at least $50 off the specialty and department store prices; Ann Taylor heels go for around $100 or more, brand new.

For men: A past-season pair of Armani trousers, never worn, were $50 here—they can cost $200 in retail stores. One hundred percent silk men's boxer shorts by Kikit were seen here for $45, bought from a store that was going out of business. The new and used tie selection is substantial, with names like Brioni (only $12 for a silk tie, new) and Yves St. Laurent (a used one for $6) popping up in the racks.

Gap Outlet

- 2778 N. Milwaukee Ave., Chicago; (312) 252-0594

This store sells both the current Gap line as well as irregular, discontinued, and store-damaged items.

If you're looking in the blooper sections, the staff will help you stay on the lookout for sun-faded spots, makeup, tiny holes, stains, pantlegs that are slightly different lengths, missing buttons, uneven stitching, broken zippers, and other boo-boos running from mild to very noticeable. Then, you can make an informed decision as to whether the price makes the blemish worth living with. Irregular or damaged items are automatically 20% to 40% off retail, and sometimes more.

Some of the clothes are so slightly damaged or defective that even the sales staff can't tell you what's wrong with it. Fortunately, almost everything is clearly labeled with its problem. If there's no tape marking the imperfect spot on an irregular item, there may be a size irregularity; sometimes, only by trying it on will you know what the problem is.

A unisex denim jacket, marred only by a slightly frayed cuff that can be rolled up anyhow, was seen reduced from $52 to $29.99. Irregular jeans (always try these on, for sure) sell for $9.99; they may have been as much as $44 at full price. The quintessential Gap T-shirt, the perfect thing to wear with those jeans, is $9.99 when imperfect—and you can still find it in half a dozen colors.

Men's green and white striped swim trunks, in their prime season $24, were only $3.99 after the season—another way clothes end up here. Seersucker shorts for men, $32 in the spring, can be found for $14.99 in the fall. You may also find young adults' leftovers too, like girls' floral bathing suits for $3.99 ($22 if first quality), and bright red sneakers for $9.99.

Gentry Men's Clothier

- 1445 W. Webster Ave., (Webster Place Shopping Center), Chicago; (312) 528-6400
- 29 S. LaSalle St., Chicago; (312) 553-9000

And other suburban locations
Gentry specializes in overstocks from well-known manufacturers, as well as copies by lesser-known counterparts. Either way can save you lots of money; you just have to successfully dodge the overzealous salespersons. Ignore their incessant inquiries and take a look at the store's stock of casual fashions and businesswear. While the special sale displays can get messed up, the fancier suits and separates are well-organized.

A rugby shirt by Perry Ellis America, which retails for $54, was marked all the way down to $10. Gant rugby shirts, retailing for $55, are $19. A summer weight all-wool suit by Gerald Austin of Bond St. was seen here for only $145, and

dress shirts by Cromwell and Worth were marked down from $45 to $29. Givenchy shorts, retailing for $18.50, sell at Gentry for $13, but were marked down to $10 during a recent summer sale.

One bummer: You have to pay for parking in the lot in the Webster Place store. Open 10-9:30 Mon.-Sat., Sundays 11-6.

I.B. Diffusion Clearance Center

- 350 N. Orleans St. (Arcade Level), Chicago; (312) 836-8275

Ladies who love shopping for this bright, contemporary sportswear at the I.B. Diffusion store on Michigan Avenue will be delighted to discover the company's outlet store, where a lot of the same clothing is always on sale at 30%-50% below retail prices. With its three labels—Santoria, Marie Diamond, and I.B. Diffusion—the company manufactures complete collections of knitwear, two-piece ensembles, and outerwear.

The outlet store, located next to the corporate offices, helps to clear out the stock and keep the main branches up-to-date. Thus, you can find sweaters, made to sell at $60 and $75, on sale for just $19.99. There's quite a variety of sizes, designs, and bold colors. One-of-a-kind designer samples, used only to show off the latest styles, can sometimes be found here as well.

Toward the rear are racks of past-season clothing, at even better discounts. An oversized, heavy wool sweater-coat—just as perfect for next fall as it was for last—was reduced from $168 to a mere $84.99. And IBD makes its own line of accessories to match its outfits; at the clearance store, you can add color-coordinated belts, earrings and hosiery at 50% and more off retail prices.

Three times a year, the outlet store runs its warehouse clearance sale, when prices zoom to 70% off; these usually take place in March, June, and October. Watch the newspapers for advertisements.

Knitpickers Knitwear Outlet
- 2659 N. Clark St.; (312) 472-6239

This Park West store boasts that they sell "the nicest knits for next to nothing," and Mr. C isn't going to get nitpicky with that notion.

They carry women's fashions by great names, like Oscar de la Renta and Bill Blass—not what you might expect from a rather tiny shop in a bustling stretch of Clark Street. Knitpickers buys first-quality overruns directly from the mills that supply such stores as Lord & Taylor, Victoria's Secret, and Casual Corner. New shipments arrive every week or so.

Bill Blass sweaters, skirts, and pants are 20% to 70% below retail prices. T-shirts are only $10. Oscar de la Renta cotton pants are only $20, and skirts normally going for at least $40 retail may also be only $20. Oleg Cassini jeans were seen here for just $25.

Clifford and Wills, Jordache and Chadwick's of Boston are just a few of the many other brands you may find among the neatly-organized racks. Open weekdays 11-7, Saturday 10-6, and Sundays 12-5.

Land's End Outlet Stores
- *Women:* 2317 N. Elston Ave., Chicago; (312) 384-4170
- *Men:* 2241 N. Elston Ave., Chicago; (312) 276-2232

And many other suburban locations. Only first-quality catalog overstocks are shipped to the Elston Avenue stores, which neighbor the *Sun-Times'* production plant in an industrial section of the Clybourn Corridor.

In the women's store, you can find cotton twill dresses, priced at $72 in the catalog, for only $35; and $40 swimsuits are $9.50. Nothing imperfect about them, remember. Long sleeve T-shirts are $12, knit pants are $15 (originally $29), and chinos are $20, ten dollars below the catalog price. A seersucker suit that would have cost over $150 through the mail may be only $55 here.

Espadrille sandals were recently seen for half price, just $9; and nubuck suede shoes were also half-off at $25. Cotton knit skirts, once $27, were only $5.

Some little girls' items are also on sale, although the children's selection can't compare with the womens' clothing. Sleeveless mock turtlenecks are $5, canvas belts are $4 off, and polos, rugby shirts, and sweatpants (some of the sweats are unisex) are usually better than half off the mail-order price.

Land's End sells home furnishings, too, and you may find such items as a twin-size waffle-weave cotton blanket for $16. A king-size quilted comforter, originally $209, was seen for $149. Hand towels, $5 in the catalog, are just $3 here.

In the men's store a few doors (actually, one warehouse) down the street, golf shirts are often reduced from $25 to $15, heavy-weight cotton sweatshirts are also $15 (half-off), and print bathing suits once priced at $16.50 are $9.50—even during the summer, which stores consider post-season. Purple nylon windbreakers (sometimes, you only get one or two colors to choose from), were reduced from $60 to $47.50. Most of the clothing in the store is casual, but dressier items are also included, like classic wool suits—once $165, now $132; and button-down collar shirts for $22, originally $31.50. Silk print ties, originally as much as $30, are plentiful here at $12. And brightly colored cable-knit wool sweaters, retailing for $45, were marked down to just $15.

Outdoor accessories are here too. Duffel bags get reduced from $50 to $38; rubber sandals, usually $36, are $18.50. Two-tone hiking shoes made of nylon and leather go for $38, usually $47.50, and leather moccasins are 1/3 off at $19.

Among the many Land's End stores in the suburbs, the Evanston location is their "Not Quite Perfect" store, stocking irregulars only, at further discounts.

Leather Warehouse

- 2428 N. Ashland Ave., Chicago; (312) 296-6300

Located in a non-descript building on a rather quiet stretch of Ashland, you could easily pass by this place without knowing it. But would you want to? Not if you like leather and shearling coats at big discounts, you wouldn't. LW makes its own clothing, and sells it from their workshop directly to you at about one-third of the retail prices. These are high-quality items, just as easily found in fancy boutiques and department stores.

A full-length shearling coat, for example, would sell at over $1,000 in a store; perhaps, noted the owner, it might be found on sale for $800-$900. But here, you can buy the same coat for $300 to $400, depending on the style. Bomber jackets, which retail for up to $700, sell here for only $250. And leather skirts go for anywhere from $70 to $90.

Leather Warehouse is open seven days a week; daily from 11 a.m. to 7 p.m., and Sundays from 11-5.

Mad Max's Cheap Stuff

- 852 W. Belmont Ave. (2nd Floor), Chicago; (312) 883-1800

With a name like this, how could Mr. Cheap pass it by? This quirky shop is sort of a clearance center for several other unusual businesses under the same roof, known collectively as "The Alley." These include Taboo Tabou, which sells racy lingerie, and The Architectural Revolution, which sells plaster-cast decorations for buildings. So at Max's, for instance, you could buy a nice gargoyle for your house—and some purple glitter to put in its hair—all at 50% to 80% below their original prices.

Perhaps that's not quite up *your* alley. Max's has lots of clothing in new wave styles, like black rock 'n roll T-shirts marked down to three for $10, flowery linen skirts reduced from $25 to $10, and other items featuring leopard-print, fishnet, and spandex. In addition, about one-third of the clothing here is good ol' vintage.

Beyond that, Mad Max's is a haven for novelty items, from wild sunglasses to wind-up toys, badges, and tattoos (non-permanent). Come up here anytime to stock up for Halloween; there are shelves of old packaged costumes for $5 each, along with such staples as vampire fangs and rubber rats. Y'know, wandering around in here is just plain fun. The store is only open weekends: noon to 7:00 p.m. on Fridays and Sundays, 10:30 a.m. to 8:00 p.m. on Saturdays.

Mark Shale Outlet

- 2593 N. Elston Ave., Chicago; (312) 772-9600
- Route 59 and Aurora Ave., Naperville; (708) 355-8200

Next to Cub Foods (a good place to save dough on food) in the Clybourn Corridor, is the outlet store for this popular men's and women's clothier. It is as bright and fashionable, with as much selection, as any full-price store; the only difference is in the prices, for clothing that's past season or a bit damaged.

In addition to its own lines, the Mark Shale Outlet mixes in bargains from other well-known brands. The styles here are mostly casual, for folks who are young and active, or who at least want to look that way. Men's wool sweaters in bold color prints, imported from Italy, may be found here reduced from $95 to $40; a recent sale knocked a further 20% off. Denim shirts were reduced from $45 to $22. And spring dresses, just a few months past their prime selling season, were $99 and under—from original prices of $198 to $350.

There are some dressy and professional looks here as well: Linen blazers for women, in a palette of bright solid colors like fuchsia and scarlet, were seen here for $60, a hundred bucks off the original price. A full rack of men's traditional suits were priced at $199 each, in all-wool and blends. Nearby, an "Everything $9" table was laden with shirts, belts, socks, and silk ties.

Toward the rear of the store is Shale's "Bumped, Bruised, Dented" area, with final sale merchandise at 50% off and more. A pair of men's leather loafers by Cole-Haan, once $275, was selling for $79; a suede skirt, slightly scuffed, was reduced from $165 to just $34. All "IR" (irregular) merchandise, anywhere in the store, is clearly tagged with a diagram indicating the flaw, a marvelous idea.

Also helpful is the large erasable sign over the cash register, highlighting the store's newest arrivals. Hours: Weekdays from 10 a.m. to 8 p.m., Saturdays from 10 a.m. to 6 p.m., and Sundays 12-5. Plenty of free parking, too.

McCoy Men's & Women's Apparel
- 1124 W. Bryn Mawr Ave., Chicago; (312) 334-4911

Selling both retail and wholesale clothing, McCoy's is a truly good place for young folk's "urban" clothing and casualwear.

Men's dress pants by brands like A.A. Fogley Co., Cotler, and Primavera were recently selling at two pairs for $24.99, from a regular retail price of $24.99-$39.99 each. Multicolor rayon dress shirts, suitable for the nightclub scene were two for $19.99, regularly $24.99 each.

For young women, an acetate rayon velvet semi-formal strapless dress was $34.99, reduced from $90. The store stocked racks and racks of lycra/acrylic bodysuits by Elite for $12.99 and $9.99, depending on the style—some were short-sleeved, others long, and some had cut-out shoulders and other looks-of-the-moment. Stonewashed jeans by Used were also reduced, selling for $19.99 a pair.

Meystel's Warehouse
- 1222 S. Wabash Ave., Chicago; (312) 347-3500

Meystel's has been in business since 1923, when the original Mr. Meystel came here from Russia and began selling textiles on the South Side. Today, the business has grown to sell quality men's, women's, and children's apparel—at prices as close to wholesale as possible. Their merchandise, from basic casual looks to the best in designer fashions, comes from leading mills and importers.

The current Meystels consider this facility to be quite spartan, keeping prices low with minimal overhead and efficient service. That doesn't mean there are no amenities: Dressing rooms, layaway, credit cards are all available. The staff is courteous, and the environment is comfortable and neatly laid out.

The store buys up surpluses and overstocks from leading makers. Part of their deal is that they don't advertise the brand names they carry, which Mr. C will respect; trust him, once you get there, you'll know you're getting a bargain. One nationally-advertised jacket, retailing for $95, was recently selling here for just $20. Designer suits with retail price tags around $300 to $500, sell here for more like $125 to $150. How about a designer shirt to go with it for just $6.50? And that's not all: Men's and women's nationally-known jeans for just $13.50, a huge discount off retail prices of up to $50. There are even jeans and pants for $4, fleece jogging suits for $20, two-piece skirt outfits for $10, and ladies tops as low as $3. At these prices, can you afford not to shop here?

Meystel's Warehouse is open every day except Saturday. Call the number above for information on specials, store hours, and more.

Morris & Sons
- 555 W. Roosevelt Rd. (2nd Floor), Chicago; (312) 243-5635

Located upstairs in a nondescript building next to a bank, this shop is one of Chicago's true shopping discoveries. It's a goldmine of current-season *couture*—designer sportswear, suits, dresses, and accessories. Prepare to be astonished by the discounts and selection, and pleased by the knowledgeable, friendly service.

This family-run business has been around for over forty years, sending its buyers to annual designer shows in New York and Europe, with a special emphasis on Italian merchandise (hint, hint; they asked Mr. C to not mention any names in the book). For many prominent Italian designers, in fact, this is the *only* current-season discounter in the United States. Morris & Sons sells clothing from 30% to as much as 70% below current, regular prices. How? Because they buy direct, because of their low-rent location, and because they offer no tailoring services.

Morris stocks over four thousand men's suits alone—in everything from wool blends to cashmere. This is the kind of place where you can *save* $1,000 on a suit. Don't worry, there are plenty of suits in more reasonable price ranges. Dress shirts by a very famous designer (who also happens to sell a lot of luggage) are over half-off, and athletic shirts by another Italian maker are at least 30 percent discounted.

Men and women's leather coats and wool longcoats are similarly priced. Some of these are salesmen's samples, barely used, at even greater discounts. A women's two-piece rayon/nylon/lycra suit from a very famous American designer was marked several hundred dollars from its retail price. And save 50% on dressy shoes, in traditional styles, for men and women. Morris & Sons are complete outfitters, from top to toe.

In the store's large clearance section, skirts regularly selling for $100 in department stores were slashed to just $25. A shirred polyester dress, looking like something out of *Dynasty*, was reduced from $250 to $100.

If you've never heard of this place, don't feel slighted; Morris saves more on its costs by not advertising. They do enough business strictly through word-of-mouth, and from regular customers who come in every year from as far away as London and Japan. Once you spend $350 or more in the store, you'll be added to the mailing list—and, you'll be allowed into their annual private clearance sale. That's when, for ten days only, everything in the store is sold at wholesale cost.

Nine Months New

- 2633 N. Halsted St., Chicago; (312) 296-MAMA (6262)

Nine Months New caters completely to mothers and mothers-to-be. It is the only shop Mr. C has found in Chicago which mixes new and used maternity consignments, creating a surprisingly diverse (and very classy) selection for such a small store.

Among the new clothing was a rack of very pretty blouses designed for nursing mothers, with a convenient flap (Mr. C is blushing a bit at this moment, talking about such things—but, a mission is a mission). These are sold in retail stores for about $50, but here they are $38.50. Also, a Pomponi skirt suit was seen, valued at well over $100; it sells here for $88, and was further reduced to $66 at the time of this visit.

Owner Holly Lane has several local designers who create something unique: Maternity formalwear. Talk about meeting a specific need—in style! Many of these are one-of-a-kind fashions, and they are expensive. But you *can* rent them, another of the many ways in which Nine Months New serves its particular clientele. Gowns rent for as little as $40 per night, going up to about $140, depending on the design.

The store is closed on Mondays and Tuesdays. Hours on Wednesday through Friday are from noon to 6:00 p.m. (Thursdays until 8:00); weekend hours are Saturdays from 11-5, Sundays from 12-5.

One Price Clothing Store

- 232 S. State St., Chicago; (312) 939-8007
- 6560 W. Fullerton Ave., Chicago; (312) 804-1899
- 2901 W. Addison St., Chicago; (312) 583-6844
- 800 N. Kedzie Ave., Chicago; (312) 826-2450
- 3900 W. Madison St., Chicago; (312) 722-2027
- 5160 S. Pulaski Rd., Chicago; (312) 284-0475
- 3465 S. Dr. Martin Luther King Jr. Dr., Chicago; (312) 791-0371

- 112 W. 87th St., Chicago; (312) 874-2377
- 1300 N. Ashland Ave., Chicago; (312) 772-6947
- 3546 E. 118th St., Chicago; (312) 646-4665

This is one "dollar" store that stays true to its name. Misses, juniors, plus-size, and children's clothing are in good supply here, all at the same price of $7. Accessories are also included in the $7 one-price promise, but are sold in multiples (two satin ponytail bows for $7, or three pairs of socks, for example). The quality of the clothing is not by any means superb, but it's good for everyday casual usage.

Some of the things $7 will get you here include all-cotton broomstick skirts, Justin Allen plaid cotton shorts, and silk tank tops and shorts by names like Manisha, Whistles, and Louise Paris.

All the items here are first quality; there are never irregulars or seconds. One Price Clothing Stores are open weekdays from 8-6, Fridays until 7, and Saturdays 10-6.

Something Old, Something New
- 1056 W. Belmont Ave., Chicago; (312) 271-1300

True to its name, this large storefront near the Belmont "el" station carries both old and new clothing, split evenly down the center as you come in. To your left, half of the place is a huge thrift shop, with racks and racks of ultra-low price clothing.

But wait. The other half of the store is filled with almost as much in the way of unused clothes. More interesting still, nothing on this side is priced above $5. This is liquidation stock, most of it second quality, from stores all over the country. Some of it is marked or damaged, but there is still plenty of good digging to be done. Men may find Oxford-style dress shirts from Christian Dior, Perry Ellis, and others—Mr. C found some from Lord & Taylor with the original $40 price tag still on them—all for $5 each. Women can get linen and cotton sundresses, or even a Liz

Claiborne blazer, for the same price; plus stretch denims, lingerie, and more.

Whichever side of the store you choose to browse, you can definitely fill your closets with entire wardrobes for very little cash.

Spencer
- 3031 N. Central Ave., Chicago; (312) 777-5556

A liquidator of men's clothing closeouts from around the country, Spencer has a very large assortment of everything to furnish the well-dressed guy from head to toe. Most of the stock is first-quality, and much of it is by top designer names—though you'd never expect it by looking at the faded storefront in this low-rent neighborhood. 'Twas not always thus. Inside, the warehouse atmosphere is strictly no-frills; clothing hangs from every rack and rafter, boxes of shoes are piled on top of each other, and cartons of jeans sit open in the center of the floor. The place goes on and on, though, and there's quite a lot to see.

Spencer does have some items for women, particularly in leather fashions. First-quality short jackets for men and women sell around $150; full-length coats go for $300 to $400, and leather skirts start at just $29. Mostly, though, this is a man's emporium. Would you believe perfectly good sportcoats from Hickey Freeman for $150, or a 100% wool double-breasted suit from the same esteemed maker, reduced from $550 to just $200? Wow. There are lots of suits, in classic and European styles, with poly-blends going for as little as $69 on sale. Many others are $150 each. Another rack is lined with trousers, originally listing for $80-$100 a pair, selling for $35 each; Mr. C found a snazzy pair by Louis Raphael among them.

There are lots of dressy shoes to go along with these dressy looks—overstocks by Pierre Cardin, Ferragamo, Giorgio Brutini, Stacy Adams, Nunn Bush, Timberland, and more, are all priced at $59 a pair. Sizes, unfortunately, are limited, but with so many to look through, you may just find something great.

Because Spencer snaps up left-over garments from so many clothiers, this becomes a very good place indeed for big and tall men. Suits range all the way up to size 62; one style, for instance, an all-wool crepe suit in size 52, was marked down from $375 to $200. Dress shirts to go with them, underwear, bathing suits, and more are also well-stocked. At the other end of the spectrum, there are plenty of young men's outfits, such as woolen suits suitable for graduations and the like (Mr. C found one by Pierre Cardin!) priced at $49 each.

Guys will also find some casual fashions here, like Boss jeans (these were irregulars) in bright solid colors, reduced from $60 retail to just $20. Plus silk shirts, jogging suits, and some athletic shoes. It seems that something great is always on sale here. Spencer is open all seven days, from 10:00 in the morning; they close at 7 p.m. Monday, Thursday, and Friday, at 6 p.m. Tuesday, Wednesday, and Saturday, and at 5 p.m. on Sunday.

Spiegel Outlet Store
- 1105 W. 35th St., Chicago; (312) 254-1099

And many suburban locations.
Just down the road apiece from Comiskey Park, the Spiegel Outlet is just what you'd expect—a clearance center for catalog items that haven't sold as well as expected. Does that mean they're trying to unload five thousand cases of polyester leisure suits? Not at all. The city branch has two floors of great clothes for men, women, and children—as well as housewares, furniture, electronics, and other goodies—at up to half off their original prices.

After all, there's nothing too shabby about men's Christian Dior dress shirts for $9.99, suede bomber jackets by Alan Michaels reduced from $289 to $120, or Reebok "Pump" sneakers for $70. On the gals' side, try a royal blue blazer by Leslie Fay, reduced from $78 to $50, a Daniel Niveau wool skirt suit, al-most half-price at $70, bathing suits from just $4.99 (at the end of the sea-son, always the best time to look), or anything from three long rooms' worth of professional outfits, fancy eveningwear, lingerie, and outerwear.

Even in this clear-the-decks set-ting, you can return purchases for cash or credit within thirty days (al-ways save your receipts!)—better than many full-price stores. Also worth noting, Tuesdays are discount days for senior citizens: 10% off the total purchase. Spiegel outlets are open daily from 10:00 a.m. to 7:30 p.m.; weekends, until 5:00.

The Urban American Club
- 1925 N. Clybourn Ave., Chicago; (312) 642-1500
- 1003 N. Rush St., Chicago; (312) 587-1500

Billing themselves as "The men's store women love," the Urban Ameri-can Club actually makes shopping for guys a pleasure. And, despite the im-maculately dressed sales help and the fancy flagstone flooring, it won't burn a hole in your wallet, either.

Shirts and ties are the main com-modity here. A wall of silk ties, for example, were all recently selling for $19 each. The store stocks the latest trendy styles and prints, as well as classics. Free alterations on shirts are offered, except on sale items.

The flagship location on North Clybourn Avenue is open Monday through Thursday, 11 a.m. to 8 p.m., Friday, 11 a.m. to 7 p.m., Saturday, 10 a.m. to 6 p.m., and Sunday noon to 5 p.m.

CHILDREN'S WEAR

The Family Shopper
- 5555 N. Broadway, Chicago; (312) 784-8082

No fancy brand names here, but a good selection of basic new clothing, for young girls, primarily. You'll find good prices on anything from casual separates and ensembles to party outfits and communion-style dresses. A girls' size 6 sundress by Kohana, for example, is $6.99. There is clothing for the little guys, too; a lined nylon winter jacket, size 7, sells for $29.99. The store is open daily from 11:00 a.m. to 7:00 p.m.

Let's Go Buy-Buy
- 2921 W. Devon Ave., Chciago; (312)764-3861

This resale store doesn't just sell babywear; moms-to-be can find clothing here as well. For the latter, Mr. C found a corduroy maternity jumper by Laura Ashley—hardly worn-looking at all—for a mere $11. Some of the clothes here may not have been worn since the days of the Brady Bunch, but you never know what you may find hidden among the racks. There are many great buys on toddlers' clothes, like an Izod virgin wool sweater, size 8/10, for only $8; or a little girls' size 14 leotard for just $3.80. Footed sleepers for babies and toddlers run around $6.

LGBB also has a moderate selection of used books and toys. Among these, Mr. C found a copy of *Opposites*, featuring Sesame Street's Big Bird, for $2.25; the stuffed animals, meanwhile, seem a bit overpriced. And if you're lucky, you may also find such necessities as a sturdy Maxi-mite baby carrier, seen for just $13.50; or car seats, strollers, and the like. These can be so expensive when purchased new—and how long would you use them?

The store can be as chaotic as a daycare center. Children roam freely while their parents shop for their forthcoming siblings, or for themselves. The shop is open 7 days a week, but closes three hours before sunset on Fridays for religious reasons.

The Second Child
- 954 W. Armitage Ave., Chicago; (312) 883-0880.

The Second Child advertises itself as "an upscale children's resale boutique." The phrase "resale boutique" may sound like an oxymoron, but it does describe this store perfectly. The racks are crowded with adorable outfits, all name brands, all previously worn—but not worn out, by any means. This stuff has been taken care of. To give you an idea of what the clientele brings in, many of the consigners drop off their used items in bags from Burberry's and such.

The Second Child accepts only current fashions. For expecting moms, a pair of Guess? maternity overalls were only $20, and would probably sell for at least $80 if new. A plaid jumper by ReCreations was only $15, and a knit sweater/skirt set by Lanz was $32. A gingham dress, perfect for the office, was only $38.

For the baby, Gerber onesies (one-piece sleeper outfits) may cost as little as $1. Snowsuits for tiny tots are priced in the $15-20 range. For little girls, a striped cotton top by Esprit was $6, and a velvet "Rare Editions" party dress was $18. A boys' size 6 Osh Kosh oxford was seen for $12.

The store is overflowing with shoes, and among those recently noted were girls' size 13 leather slip-ons by Capezio ($5.50), and other styles by names like Nike and Sam & Libby. Boys' black suede lace-ups by Playskool, size 5, were only $8; and Sporto winter boots for kids were about $10. A pair of little girls' roller-skates was also found, for $10.

The store also sells accessories like strollers and car seats here, as well as maternity clothes. Strollers by Graco, regularly selling for $100 and up, are priced in the $60-75 range.

Spiegel Outlet Store
- 1105 W. 35th St., Chicago; (312) 254-1099

MR. CHEAP'S PICKS
Children's Wear

✔ **The Second Child**—Used children's fashions—some quite fancy—at a fraction of their original prices.

✔ **Spiegel Outlet Store**—A huge room full of recent overstocks for kids from toddlers to teens.

And many other suburban locations
Just down the road apiece from Comiskey Park, the Spiegel Outlet is just what you'd expect—a clearance center for catalog items that haven't sold as well as expected. Does that mean they're trying to unload five thousand cases of polyester leisure suits? Not at all. The city branch has two floors of great clothes for men, women, and children—as well as housewares, furniture, electronics, and other goodies—at up to half off their original prices.

The South Side store's street level has racks and racks of clothing for kids, from toddlers to teenagers. A girl's jumpsuit from Gilda Marx was marked down from $26 to $15; two-piece snowsuits from Tidykins, once $95, were seen here for $40. Plus brightly colored sweatshirts by Crayola and Hush Puppies, reduced from $26 to just $5.99.

Even in this clear-the-decks setting, you can return purchases for cash or credit within thirty days (always save your receipts!)—better than many full-price stores. Also worth noting, Tuesdays are discount days for senior citizens: 10% off the total purchase. Spiegel outlets are open daily from 10:00 a.m. to 7:30 p.m.; weekends, until 5:00.

ACCESSORIES

Berry-Cutler Hosiery
- 546 W. Harrison St., Chicago; (312) 939-5777

For stocking up on stockings, not to mention crew socks and other undies, check out this inexpensive, no frills wholesale/retail store. It's part of a loose district of cut-rate shops just across the river from the South Loop area.

Basics for everyone in the family can be bought in one stop here. For ladies, slightly imperfect ultrasheer nylons are just 89 cents a pair, or $11 a dozen; they're available in neutral shades, as well as bright colors like hunter green, peach, fuchsia, and teal. Queen-size hose are just 30 cents more per pair. Slouch socks are $1.50 a pair, and come in so many different shades that their display completely covers a corner wall. Bikini briefs by Fruit of the Loom are only $3.89 for three pairs, and short-sleeved Lee sweatshirts are only $4.93 apiece.

Little girls' socks by Hanes, made of an 80/20 cotton-poly blend, are just $1.93 for three pairs. Lacy anklet socks for toddlers are $2.50 for three pairs.

For little boys, Bloopers! irregular T-shirts are two for $2.69. Fans of "Barney the Dinosaur" will love Fruit of the Loom with his picture on them; a three-pack is $4.99. Six pairs of cotton crew socks were just $4.50. Shorts for boys with various sports teams motifs are just $5.00.

Men can find irregulars in Lee sweatpants and sweatshirts for $8 each. There are also some unexpected goodies, like lined leather work gloves for $7, packed among the displays. And be sure to watch for Berry-Cutler's super sidewalk sales.

I. Blaustein & Company
- 2852 W. Devon Ave., Chicago; (312) 761-5355

One of the many bargain stores on this stretch of Devon, Blaustein's no-nonsense shop caters primarily to men's clothing; but there are a few items for females in its stock, notably flannel pajamas.

Ultra-cramped is the most concise way of describing the sales floor. It's teeming with cardboard boxes of merchandise that the store just wants to get the heck outta there. Blaustein doesn't bother to put prices on the clothes; you have to ask, at which point you can probably haggle him down a notch.

At these prices, of course, that's hardly necessary—it's already been done for you! Basics, like underwear and socks, are real bargains here. Irregular Hanes t-shirts for men run $5 for a three-pack, while colored t-shirts run from as low as $3 apiece. For women, two-piece pajama sets by Omni II were just $7 a pair.

There is a mix of first and second quality merchandise among the boxes. The store is open six days a week; it's closed on Saturdays to recognize the Sabbath.

Sun King
- 44 E. Chicago Ave., Chicago; (312) 649-9110

Must be a Beatles fan. Actually, this little step-down shop packs big bargains on all kinds of sunglasses and designer eyewear. The owner, who prefers to go by his annointed title, is an enterprising young man who began just over three years ago selling from a pushcart. Having moved up to a proper store, he still maintains a low overhead by running the shop himself. Thus, he can offer discounts of 20% to 50% below retail prices on Ray-Bans, Vuarnet, Revo, Serengeti, Armani (yes, he makes eyeglass frames too), and lots more.

Ray-Ban's classic Wayfarers sell here for $45 a pair; Sun King stocks the largest selection of Ray-Bans in the midwest—"Basically, we sell everything they make," pronounced the king. R-B's "Club Master 1" model, seen at Marshall Field's and similar stores for $125 to $180, sells here for $99.50. Serengeti aviator sunglasses, made by Corning, have a retail price of $140; most competitors

sell them for $120; here, they are a cool $77.

The service here is personal and laid-back. There are two certified opticians on the staff, and discounts on fancy prescription eyeglasses are clearly as good as the sunglasses. Those Armani frames, for instance, are about $40 below retail.

You may have an audience with the Sun King seven days a week; daily from 11 a.m. to 6:30 p.m., and Sundays from noon to 5:00.

That's Our Bag
- 50 E. Randolph St., Chicago; (312) 984-2626
- 200 N. Michigan Ave., Chicago; (312) 984-3510
- 734 N. Michigan Ave., Chicago; (312) 984-3517
- 230 N. Michigan Ave., Chicago; (312) 984-2628

It's this store's bag that you get reduced prices on super name brand purses, backpacks, luggage, briefcases, and wallets from names like Coach, Samsonite, and Kenneth Cole's Unlisted. You'll really regret it if you miss their end-of-season inventory clearance sales.

During Mr. C's visit, he found a leather Anne Klein II shoulder bag, in that trendy basket-weave design. Originally retailing for $102, it was marked down 20% to a price of $79. A Silhouette soft suitcase by Samsonite was a mere $119, almost half its retail price of $215; and an Irina Maxim camera-case shaped purse, in buttery-soft leather, sold for $25 off at $100.

Not everything in the store is leather, however. Black bags by Unlisted (Kenneth Cole's alter ego, of sorts) were only $50, but looked like they should cost four times that much. Surprise—they're not leather! For many people, that's an important philosophical option. If you simply can't afford the real thing, at least you can fake everyone out with these.

Uhlemann Optical
- 1135 W. Berwyn Ave., Chicago; (312) 878-5197

MR. CHEAP'S PICKS
Accessories

✔ **Berry-Cutler Hosiery**—This no-frills shop is a great place to stock up on stockings.

✔ **Sun King**—As in sunglasses. Save 20% to 50% on Ray-Ban, Vuarnet, and even designer eyeglass frames as well.

✔ **V.I.P. Handbag and Accessory Outlet**—Save big on bags, next to the Mark Shale Outlet.

- 3 First National Plaza, Chicago; (312) 346-8478
- 141 W. Jackson Blvd., Chicago; (312) 427-9555

The Berwyn shop is billed as an eyewear factory outlet, and while the focus is on prescription frames, you can also get bargains on sunglasses here.

Ray Ban sunglasses, in the Wayfarer II or Large Metal II (aviator) styles, were only $49 during a recent stop, and regular Wayfarers/Large Metals were selling for only $39.95. Vuarnet "Skylynx" sunglasses were only $81, and Laura Biagiotti shades, regularly going for $90-$150, sell here for only $45-75.

Open Mondays and Wednesdays 11-8, Tuesdays, Thursdays, and Fridays from 11-7, and Saturdays 10-5. Closed Sundays.

V.I.P. Handbag and Accessory Outlet
- 2603 N. Elston Ave., Chicago; (312) 489-7690

Located on a street lined with outlets (sandwiched between Cub Foods and the Mark Shale Outlet), V.I.P. is the place to find department store surpluses at significant savings. The selection is not gigantic, and you may have to fight someone for the last available bag in the style you want.

V.I.P. carries many very-important designers, as well as lesser-known brands. Either way, you'll save money.

For example, an Anne Klein II handbag with a goldtone twist chain—which might sell for $130 in a hoity-toity boutique—sells for $90 here. A backpack by Kenneth Cole's Unlisted label is $28, ten dollars below its department store price. Other name brands sold here include Unisa, Capezio, and Etienne Aigner, although not all brands are available everyday. The store receives shipments frequently, though, so it's the kind of place to check regularly.

Laura bags, knock-offs of Coach products made with the same leather and hardware, can also be found: A Laura briefcase with buckle closure, worth about $275 in Coach's version, sells for only $155. The colors—red, black and brown—are a bit off the Coach shades, but close enough to pass for the real thing.

V.I.P. has extra-discount tables, where bags sell for $10.99, and discounted wallets, too. An eelskin wallet, normally $30, is only $16 here. Mundi wallets are sold at about half off retail.

The store also sells Givenchy, Trifani, and Karl Lagerfeld jewelry at reductions of at least 15% off retail prices. Special sale items offer further markdowns, of as much as 50 percent off.

I. Weinberg Hosiery
- 632 W. Roosevelt Rd., Chicago; (312) 922-3710

Some first quality socks and pantyhose are mixed in with lots of irregulars in this University-area store—a long, narrow warehouse piled high with hosiery for both adults and children. If you don't mind rummaging through cardboard boxes of plastic-wrapped socks, stop in here sometime and stock up on bargains.

Get six pairs of men's argyle socks for $4.50, while cotton crew socks by Champion, slightly irregular, are $3.50. First-quality silk socks are only $1 a pair, and a four-pack of men's handkerchiefs here is only $1. For gals, items like light support nylons go for $1 a pair.

Plenty of stuff here for the kids, as well. A three-pack of multicolored tube socks costs just $1.00; or, $2.50 for six pairs of plain white ones. Toddlers' cotton blend socks by Nursery Rhymes are $2.50 for three pairs.

The store is open daily from 8 a.m. to 4:30 p.m. (sharp!), and weekends 10-2. The salespeople speak both Spanish and Polish, in addition to English.

CLOTHING—USED

Used clothing is another great way to save lots of money—and don't turn up your nose at the idea. Recycling doesn't just mean bottles and cans, y'know. In these recessionary times, people take this approach to nearly everything, and it makes a lot of sense. There is a wide range of options, from trashy stuff to designer labels. Again, a few terms:

"Consignment" and "resale" shops are all the rage these days. Most sell what they call "gently used" clothing—the original owner wore the article only a few times, then decided to resell it. Often, these are fancy outfits in which such people don't want to be seen more than that. Fine! This is how you can get these high-fashion clothes at super-low prices. Since they still look like new, your friends will never know the secret (unless, of course, you want to brag about your bargain-hunting prowess).

You can also sell things from your own closets at these shops, if they are recent and in good shape; the store owners will split the cash with you.

"Vintage" clothing is usually older and more worn-looking, often still around from other decades. Sometimes, it can cost more than you'd expect for used clothing, depending on which "retro" period is back in style at the moment.

Finally, "thrift shops" sell used clothing that has definitely seen better days. Generally, these items have been donated to the stores, most of which are run by charity organizations; in such places, you can often find great bargains, and help out a worthy cause at the same time.

CONSIGNMENT AND RESALE SHOPS

Buy Popular Demand
● 2631 N. Halsted St., Chicago; (312) 868-0404

In this store's packed showroom, better designer suits, shoes, and jackets for women and men are sold on consignment. BPD only accepts clothing that is less than two years old. Items sell here for about one-third of their average original price; and anything that hasn't sold after four weeks in the shop is further reduced until it does.

Rita LaFollette, one of the owners, showed Mr. C a number of great bargains. There's lots of stuff for the office, like a two-piece Liz Claiborne rayon suit with peplum waist, in barely-worn condition, going for a remarkable $40. A set of Ann Taylor silk-print shorts and top, in a sarong style, was on sale for $15. And formal evening gowns by Victor Costa tend to sell in the $60-$120 range. Rita also pointed out a two-piece Armani suit for women, and showed Mr. C a catalog in which this outfit was selling for $1200; this used model, with a barely-noticeable fabric distortion, was only $100.

The shoe selection includes dressier styles by Via Spaga, Calvin Klein, and Ferragamo, starting as low as $15. A pair of Naturalizer pumps were on sale for $20, in excellent condition. Some of the belts and costume jewelry border on outlandish, but more conservative styles can always be found among the selections. Designer handbags range from $10-$60.

Buy Popular Demand is one of the few consignment stores to sell men's clothing too; there isn't nearly as much, but Mr. C did see an Yves St. Laurent suit for $150, and a Missoni Uomo sport jacket—something you can expect to find in Neiman Marcus—selling for $100.

Don't miss their end-of-summer and end-of-winter sales, by the way. That's when everything in the store suddenly goes to half-price. Call or stop in to find out when the next sale is on. BPD is open daily 11-7, Sundays 11-5.

Cactus Trade
● 1103 W. Webster Ave., Chicago; (312) 472-7222

Open only since the beginning of '93, Cactus Trade is a small, handsome shop selling new and used designer clothing for women. Like many such stores, it's run by a former model who is using her wardrobe, experience, and contacts to good advantage. Resale makes up the majority of the racks, but you'll find new items mixed right in. Although some of the clothing is fancy, the emphasis here is on the casual side—like a Joan Vass knit top seen for $18, or a zip-up cardigan sweater from Ann Taylor for just $26.

A Leslie Fay floral print top and skirt was found here for $64; and a bright red wrap top and skirt by Armani, originally $220, was seen for just $95. There is also a good selection of shoes (Paloma suede heels, like new, $24) and handbags, many of which are new and at discount. And Cactus Trade has a lovely selection of handcrafted jewelry which is definitely new, made by local designers. Here's hoping the shop catches on.

The Chicago Fur Outlet
● 777 W. Diversey Pkwy., Chicago; (312) 348-FURS (3877)

This shop specializes in "previously owned" (or what they like to call "pre-furred") fur and leather jackets for men and women. Some of the merchandise is bought from shops that have gone out of business, some is consigned by individual owners and stores, and other coats are closeouts or bought outright from other fur stores.

To give you an idea of the savings, a dyed, sheared mink coat from Denmark sells here for $600. "Swing" coats, so popular in recent seasons, are fully stocked; so are those with detachable liners and fur collars. The store also packs in suede coats, fur hats, slippers, and boas.

The Chicago Fur Outlet is open Tuesday, Wednesday, and Friday from 11 a.m. to 6 p.m.; Monday and Thursday from 11-7; and Saturday, 11-5. During the peak season from October to March, it's also open Sundays 12-4. Their "de-furred" payment plan and 0% financing are very helpful options for those on a budget.

Cynthia's Consignments Ltd.
● 2218 N. Clybourn Ave., Chicago; (312) 248-7714

Cynthia is a former model (and one-time Miss Illinois) who has gone into the consignment business. So, you *know* she's got fashion sense—and connections. From her own closet, and those of other models, she fills this bright, spare shop with great used designer clothing. None of it is over two years old, and much of it is quite stunning.

Mr. C was shown a blue suede

skirt and top set by Peggy Martin, selling for $98; also, a two-piece plaid suit by Ann Taylor for $52. A pair of Liz Claiborne houndstooth slacks was selling for $32. Shoes, in fine condition, included a pair of Escada grey linen-finish pumps for $32; he also saw a pair of suede flats from Bloomingdale's private label, never worn—the original sticker was still there. It said $59; Cynthia's said $18.

Some of the merchandise here is brand new, coming directly from manufacturers and designers. These tend to be overstocks from current lines, like an Anne Klein navy blue suit for $72; or a Biba skirt suit, originally $600, selling for (are you sitting down?) $62. Cynthia likes to keep prices at the low end, preferring to get clothes out of her store and onto her customers. There's also a bargain table, where you may see a yellow Polo sweater for $10, or Esprit print shorts for $8.

There are lots of fancy dresses and formal gowns, many of which can be rented as an inexpensive alternative to buying. The store also offers resale designer bridal gowns and accessories. Gowns that sell for $3,000 to $5,000 at the Ultimate Bride on Oak Street can be found here for as little as $550.

Consignments run only 60 days, so the selection is always changing. Hours are Tuesday-Saturday from 11:00 a.m. to 6:00 p.m., and Sundays from noon to 5:00. The store is closed on Mondays.

Designer Resale of Chicago

- 6522 N. Lincoln Ave., Lincolnwood; (708) 674-7989 or (312) 973-1987

Mr. C has strayed a bit outside of Chicago City Limits (well, just barely) to tell you about another wonderful shop which sells used designer clothing for women at terrific savings. Among the names you'll find here are Versace, Armani, Escada, Ungaro, Liz Claiborne, the Kleins (Anne and Calvin), and many others.

Everything here is carefully appraised to high standards, but it sells at low prices; there is also a wide range of sizes, from petite to large. The store is open Monday, Tuesday, and Friday from 11:00 a.m. to 6:00 p.m.; Thursday, from noon to 8:00 p.m.; Saturday 10-5, and Sunday 12-5. Closed Wednesdays.

Entre Nous Designer Resale Shop

- 21 E. Delaware St., Chicago; (312) 337-2919

Just between us (ha-ha), nobody will know the difference if you shop here or if you go to Saks. This is a classy all-consignment shop with some of the best women's designer fashions you can find anywhere. It's mostly career-oriented and casual wear—not too many ultra-fancy dresses here, but the shoes and accessories selection in this closet-sized Gold Coast store are also exceptional.

The sales help is certainly spunky, and keep the store super-organized despite the lack of space. Among the treasures recently found here were a pair of Neiman Marcus patent leather shoes for $45, and a powder-blue silk shirt by Moda for $18. In accessories, Entre Nous had a Chanel handbag in almost-new condition for $65. They also have lots of hats and costume jewelry to jazz up any outfit.

Entre Nous is open weekdays from 11:00 a.m. to 6:00 p.m., and Saturdays until only 5:00.

Frank's Second Stop Resale Shop

- 547 W. Roosevelt Rd., Chicago; (312) 733-7766 or (312) 733-7733.

In spite of the name, this store actually combines secondhand clothing with unused closeouts, a mix of items that ranges from ratty to gorgeous. It's surprisingly big, with a variety of clothes for men and women; the stock was good, though not spectacular, when Mr. Cheap visited. They're getting new stuff in all the time, though, and have some great finds in previously-owned clothing, some of which has never been worn and still bears the original tags.

Women's clothing ranges from

MR. CHEAP'S PICKS
Consignment Shops

✔ **Clybourn Avenue shops**—There are several terrific resale stores near each other along Clybourn. **Cynthia's Consignments** and **Selections** feature designer women's clothing; **A Rubens Woman** specializes in new and used fashions for larger women.

✔ **The Chicago Fur Outlet**—Used furs? Why not. The prices will certainly warm you right up.

✔ **Halsted Street shops**—Here's another cluster of resale shops, including **Buy Popular Demand** for women's professional outfits, and **Nine Months New** for maternity wear.

✔ **McShane's Exchange**—Two branches packed with gently-used designer clothing for women.

✔ **Suitsmart**—A resale shop for men's suits, quite the rarity. The suits are in great shape; only the prices are threadbare.

casual to careerwear. An Outlander acrylic/wool dress, for example, looked almost brand new and was selling for only $15. Women's shoes are well-stocked but include some bloopers—be sure to check out the condition of the heels and the leather uppers before you make that impulse purchase! A used pair of navy Ann Taylor heels, for example, were only $5, but badly needed some polishing. Ditto for a pair of red leather pumps by Nickels, selling here for $8. But either pair can be restored, and will save you at least $50 off the specialty and department store prices; Ann Tay-

lor heels go for around $100 or more, brand new.

For men: A past-season pair of Armani trousers, never worn, were $50 here—they can cost $200 in retail stores. One hundred percent silk men's boxer shorts by Kikit were seen here for $45, bought from a store that was going out of business. The new and used tie selection is substantial, with names like Brioni (only $12 for a silk tie, new) and Yves St. Laurent (a used one for $6) popping up in the racks.

McShane's Exchange
- 815 W. Armitage Ave., Chicago; (312) 525-0282
- 1141 W. Webster Ave., Chicago; (312) 525-0211

This pair of resale shops has a fabulous selection of designer clothing for women at very good prices. How about a print dress by Escada for just $88? Not bad! Nor is an Albert Nipon blazer for the same price. You may find a black wool pleated skirt by Adrienne Vittadini for $34; and a linen blazer from Anne Klein II was seen reduced from an already-great $58 to an even better $30.

Chicago models consign their barely-worn clothing here, and shop for more of the same. The place was certainly hopping when Mr. C visited. Of particular note was the extensive selection of shoes, many of which were like new or in very good used shape; such as gold lame strap heels by Charles Jourdan for just $12, or a pair of Kenneth Cole flats with crepe bows for $30. Other names seen included Bandolino, Nine West, and Via Spiga.

Nine Months New
- 2633 N. Halsted St., Chicago; (312) 296-MAMA (6262)

Nine Months New caters completely to mothers and mothers-to-be. It is the only shop Mr. C has found in Chicago which mixes new and used maternity consignments, creating a surprisingly diverse (and very classy) selection for such a small store.

Many of the used items, furthermore, are designer samples, so they just barely fall into the used category. A handsome two-piece pantsuit by Japanese Weekend, for example, gives new style to the maternity look—for only $68. Other used fashions seen during Mr. C's visit were a Kik Kin knit jacket and skirt set for $50, and a three-piece ensemble by Pomponi for $70.

Owner Holly Lane has several local designers who create something unique: Maternity formalwear. Talk about meeting a specific need—in style! Many of these are one-of-a-kind fashions, and they are expensive. But you *can* rent them, another of the many ways in which Nine Months New serves its particular clientele. Gowns rent for as little as $40 per night, going up to about $140, depending on the design.

The store is closed on Mondays and Tuesdays. Hours on Wednesday through Friday are from noon to 6:00 p.m. (Thursdays until 8:00); weekend hours are Saturdays from 11-5, Sundays from 12-5.

A Rubens Woman
- 2216 N. Clybourn Ave., Chicago; (312) 477-0011

The artist Rubens is perhaps best known for the graceful, large-figured women in his paintings—precisely the opposite of the rail-thin models so idolized today. This consignment shop takes the Flemish master as its inspiration, selling new and used designer clothing in sizes from 14 up to, yes, size 60—well beyond what most stores consider "large sizes." Owner Lynette Wood has created a true specialty store.

There is no reason, after all, why clothing in these sizes cannot be as stylish as any other. ARW sells creations by women designers from all over the country—from formal wear to professional looks to casual stuff. You can even have something custom-designed here, at a very low cost for such personal service.

But it is the used clothing, of course, which saves you the most cash. You may find an $800 sequined evening gown by New York designer Jovani selling here for $395; or a $500 business suit for only $75. Clearance racks, where everything is $9.95 or less, may yield a pair of Gloria Vanderbilt jeans for $4, or a Villager all-wool skirt suit for $25. There are lots of accessories, new and used; hats for $5 and $10, jewelry, handbags, and more.

Special sales offer such deals as half-price on all business suits. And twice a year, the invite-only "Customer Appreciation Night" is like an in-store party, with free wine and all merchandise priced at $29.95 and under.

Open Tuesday through Friday from 11:00 a.m. to 7:00 p.m.; Saturday from 11-6 and Sunday from 12-5. Closed Mondays.

Selections
- 2512 N. Clybourn Ave., Chicago; (312) 296-4014

An upscale resale shop featuring both consignments and designer samples, Selections is a fantastic place to buy anything from an office outfit to an evening gown at greatly reduced prices. It's also one of the few such shops which carry a good range of used men's designer clothes. The stuff is fancy; even fur coats are sold here, in season. As a matter of fact, this store has so much stock, they put out only the appropriate clothing for each season.

Men's fashions may include such items as a double-breasted Armani wool suit for $320; or brand-new silk ties, valued at $65-$95, selling for $16-$20. Mr. C saw a sharp-looking dress shirt from Saks Fifth Avenue for just $14.

Women, of course, have a much larger Selection to choose from (c'mon, guys, let's get into this consignment thing!). Mr. C was shown a Kasper linen skirt suit for $48, an Anne Klein II blazer in mustard and rust plaid for $60, and a white merino wool sweater by Henri Bendel for *un petit* $28.

Ladies will no doubt enjoy the good variety of shoes and accessories too. A pair of Via Spiga flats or Evan

Picone dress pumps for $28 ain't bad; nor is a Louis Vuitton bag, originally $300, reduced to $55. And there's a long display case of costume jewelry, like a pair of Austrian crystal earrings for $12.

As you can see, things are priced to move. If they don't move after one month, prices are cut further—and twice in their second month. A pair of Basile women's wool slacks, $250 when new, was priced at $60 here; they were marked down to $18 before they sold.

Selections has a limited amount of children's clothes too, from time to time. All sales are final, and the store firmly maintains that prices are not negotiable.

The store is open Tuesday through Friday from 11:00 a.m. to 6:00 p.m., Saturday from 10-6 and Sunday from 12-5. Closed Mondays.

Suitsmart

- 115 N. Wabash St. (2nd Floor), Chicago; (312) 553-0200

Dan Hooson had this idea for a shop that would cater to businessmen, in the business district, saving them big money on their business attire. But would it work? After all, men aren't as keyed in to the world of resale clothing. They tend to prefer buying new, and keeping their clothing forever, to cleaning out the closet. Well, open for just a few months when Mr. C dropped in, Dan already had far more stock than he could display in the store.

Dan is truly a man for the 90's. This store combines all of the current trends, from recycling to computerized marketing analysis and a return to good old fashioned personal serv-

ice. It seems to work. Suits and sportcoats by Bill Blass, Brooks Brothers, Givenchy, Ralph Lauren, Giorgio Armani, and many others sell here for as little as $70 to $150. New, of course, they'd each go for hundreds of dollars more; the amazing thing about Suitsmart, though, is that everything in here has been so well-kept that it all *looks* new.

"People come up to me with a particular suit and ask me if I have it in another color," grinned Hooson. "Some don't even realize that these are used clothes. They think I can bring out three more sizes from the back." There are some new items, closeouts on smaller things like silk ties (just $10 apiece). Dress shirts, hosiery, and other accessories are here too. Suitsmart even offers bargain rates on alterations, having worked out a deal with a semi-retired tailor from Italy who prefers a relaxed workload.

Hooson has one more point to make, to anyone who intends to donate fine clothing to charity: Don't. "They'll only mishandle them, the pants will get separated from the jackets, and I hate to see that happen to a good suit. Charities aren't prepared to deal with the merchandise; they'd rather just have the money. Bring your old suits to me instead—I'll pay you for them, and then you can donate the money and save them a step."

So, is it Suits-mart or Suitsmart? It's both. All this, upstairs from a McDonalds, yet! Find out for yourself, Mondays through Wednesdays from 9 a.m. to 6 p.m., Thursdays and Fridays until 7, and Sundays from 11-4. Closed Saturdays.

VINTAGE SHOPS

Belmont Army/Navy Surplus

- 945 W. Belmont Ave. (2nd Floor), Chicago; (312) 975-0626

Inside and upstairs from an otherwise ordinary-looking clothing store (just head for the central stairway), you'll find this rugged and more offbeat army/navy. Up here, you can find all

things military, from combat boots to gas masks (!) and everything that goes in between. That includes more practical gear, like heavy wool cable-knit sweaters for $17.99; lined nylon raincoats for $24; sailor shirts for $12.99; and more. Get a camouflage T-shirt for $7.99, or the real thing—

an army-issue full camouflage shirt for $17.99.

Those combat boots are as low as $25-$30 a pair, and unlike some of the clothing, they are not previously used. The merchandise here runs about half new and half used. It's not all from "our guys," either; you may find French army parkas ($39.99) or German khaki pants ($13.99). Plus all the accessories, like sleeping bags for $45, and duffel bags (in all sizes from manageable to enormous), as low as $19.99, and all kinds of camping gear.

Sharing this space with the army/navy is **J. Park Company**, which overlaps a bit by selling new bags and backpacks, as well as new and vintage clothing. Among the vintage clothes items are everything from wool overcoats for $30 and tuxedo jackets for $35 to denim skirts for $12 and blue jeans for $2.99. Not to mention sterling silver rings from $2.99 to $10.00, handbags, and other accessories. Both stores are open seven days, including every night but Sunday until 8:00 p.m.

Chicago's Recycle Shop
• 5308 N. Clark St., Chicago; (312) 878-8525

Or, as it's known to its devotees, George's. Mr. C isn't sure whether to file this one under "Vintage" or "Thrift"; the stock is vintage, but the store looks more like a thrift shop. Possibly like a mega-garage sale gone haywire. Whatever you call it, this Andersonville store has an unbelievably large collection of clothing, furniture, and bric-a-brac at prices that are dirt cheap. Tightly packed aisles are jam-packed with tons of clothing, almost all of which is less than $5 apiece—like Hawaiian shirts for $3.50, or a full-length velvet evening gown for $1.95. That's not a typo, folks.

You can find pointy horn-rimmed eyeglass frames from the 1960's for just $6, and lots of antique jewelry for as little as a buck. Most is in the $1-$10 range. The rear half of the shop does the same for furniture,

although Mr. C felt that the prices don't quite match the condition of some of these pieces. But, you may find a china cabinet you like for $125, or a pair of armchairs straight out of some old black-and-white movie for $85. Oh, and the walls are lined with lots of truly tacky paintings.

As big as the store itself is, George barely has the room to hold it all. In fact, the merchandise spills over into the basement, where you can find the genuine vintage articles—prom dresses, military and marching band uniforms, shoes and boots, and the like. Most of these are not priced; presumably, there is some room for negotiation. Costume buyers from professional theaters, film, and TV crews frequently prowl around down here. Accordingly, the area is closed to the general public— that is, unless you ask to go down. Mr. C learned this simple trick from a friend with lots of experience in local theater. It's a flimsy but effective way to keep the riff-raff away from the "good stuff," and it works; even on a busy Saturday when the main floor was humming with activity, the basement was cool and quiet. Go ahead, ask.

Mad Max's Cheap Stuff
• 852 W. Belmont Ave. (2nd Floor), Chicago; (312) 883-1800

With a name like this, how could Mr. Cheap pass it by? This quirky shop is sort of a clearance center for several other unusual businesses under the same roof, known collectively as "The Alley." These include Taboo Tabou, which sells racy lingerie, and The Architectural Revolution, which sells plaster-cast decorations for buildings. So at Max's, for instance, you could buy a nice gargoyle for your house—and some purple glitter to put in its hair—all at 50% to 80% below their original prices.

Perhaps that's not quite up *your* alley. Max's has lots of clothing in new wave styles, like black rock 'n roll T-shirts marked down to three for $10, flowery linen skirts reduced

MR. CHEAP'S PICKS
Vintage Shops

✔ **Chicago's Recycle Shop**—Like a vintage warehouse, huge and dirt-cheap.

✔ **Strange Cargo**—A funky shop filled with fancy stuff for men and women.

✔ **Urban X**—Racks and racks of clothing, surrealistically suspended from the ceiling of this cavernous basement.

from $25 to $10, and other items featuring leopard-print, fishnet, and spandex. In addition, about one-third of the clothing here is good ol' vintage; jeans for $10, wool overcoats for $30, well-worn leather jackets from $10-$25, shoes for $1, and print shirts for 25¢. That's cheap stuff. Most of these are in slightly-above-thrift-shop shape.

Beyond that, Mad Max's is a haven for novelty items, from wild sunglasses to wind-up toys, badges, and tattoos (non-permanent). Come up here anytime to stock up for Halloween; there are shelves of old packaged costumes for $5 each, along with such staples as vampire fangs and rubber rats. Y'know, wandering around in here is just plain fun. The store is only open weekends: noon to 7:00 p.m. on Fridays and Sundays, 10:30 a.m. to 8:00 p.m. on Saturdays.

Strange Cargo
- 3448 N. Clark St., Chicago; (312) 327-8090

If you were on the Titanic as it was sinking, Mr. C bets that you'd risk your life to run back and save your clothes if you had bought them at Strange Cargo. One of the few vintage stores in town that includes as much clothing for guys as it does for gals, this is a ten-year old goldmine

of casual clothes, suits, shoes, hats, and jewelry. Lots of the pants and some of the sweaters and dresses still have their tags on, testimony to the fact that some of this garb has never been worn at all.

For men, a brown leather Gucci jacket—worn, but still sharp-looking—is almost a steal at $45. If you can't afford a vacation this year, Hawaiian shirts for just $11 will make you look like you've been there. Add a pair of seersucker shorts, also $11. Leather belts are a slimming $10, bow ties run $4-$8, and tuxedo cummerbunds average $12. A pair of genuine German work boots (already broken in for you) was seen for $30. If you can imagine an outfit which could incorporate all of these, you're starting to get the feel of the place.

Ladies will be impressed by the eccentric collection of dresses, from baby doll to wedding to leopard-print lycra. A wedding gown, with cap sleeves and an outer layer of tulle, was priced at $50. Strange Cargo is a good bet if you need a black evening gown and you only have ten dollars and one hour to find one. A fancier spaghetti-strap satin dress was seen for $35, which will leave you money to even get a pair of shoes to match it. A more casual cotton shift dress, circa 1970, in a crazy rainbow-colored kaleidoscopic pattern, was on sale for $12.

Accessories for body and home are plentiful, too. Women's cowboy boots were priced at $20. Cats-eye sunglasses are $10, and tons of crinolines, slips, camisoles, and teddies are priced about $10 and up. Now, *there's* an ensemble for you. And no home is complete without totally tacky drapes—the type with those little fuzzy balls hanging off the bottom, you know. Get a set for only $5.

Toad Head Reincarnated Stuff
- 2009 W. Fremont St., Chicago; (312) 404-5633

Mr. C isn't sure what the first half of this store's name means, although there is indeed a large, papier-mache amphibian acting as a sort of mascot behind the counter. The second half of the name is easier to decipher; everything in this delightful shop is vintage, or made from vintage materials. So, you could go basic and get a nicely broken-in pair of jeans for $17, or be a bit more creative and go for a brightly colored cotton dress for $38. A selection of these managed to look retro and new at the same time—that's the idea here.

There is also plenty of jewelry, again fashioned from materials which may or may not have been jewelry in past lives; Mr. C saw lots of drop-style earrings for $10 and $12 a pair. Likewise, sterling silver rings were $15 and up. Adding to the interesting variety of this cozy shop are framed vintage photographs, and hand-painted furniture. It's definitely a unique blend of stuff, an offbeat stop on the resale trail. It's off the beaten path, too, a block in from Armitage (look for their sign at the corner of Fremont). And they're only open Wednesdays through Sundays, from 11:00 a.m. to 6 or 7 in the evening.

Urban X
● 1529 W. Armitage Ave., Chicago; (312) 252-8009

Just west of the river, an old industrial building has been turned into a mini-mall of antique and vintage stores. While unique and fun, these are not all necessarily cheap; but downstairs in the basement, Urban X is the exception. They have 5,000 square feet of clothing for men and women, all on long racks suspended from the high ceilings. They look like they're hanging in mid-air.

Anyway, the clothing is fun, with an emphasis on the 1950's and 1960's (yes, including leopard-skin coats). The store is divided in half, one side for women and the other for men. Women's stuff consists of lots of dresses, from fancy- to house-, priced in the $5 to $25 range. Name your color and style; it's probably here. A shimmery, strapless cocktail dress in powder blue was among the finds, for $25. There are sweaters for $8-$12, like an Icelandic wool pull-

over for $8. And well-worn leather jackets (gives 'em more character, that's the ticket) are $10-$25. Lots of antique and handcrafted jewelry, too, as well as shoes and handbags to complete the outfit.

The guys' side sports tons of sportcoats for $10-$20 each; enough to outfit dozens of lounge rock bands. If they want fancier threads, there are also lots of tuxedo jackets for $30. Find a matching pair of trousers for $8, and you're in business. Vintage suits are all in the same $30-$40 range.

The whole place is tidy and neat as a pin (stripe); and there are several fitting rooms at the rear of the store. This could be one of the largest vintage clothing stores you'll ever see. But you can only see it on weekends; store hours are 11-6 on Fridays, Saturdays, and Sundays. There is also a bit of furniture here, classic rec-room couches and such; but you'll find more of these at Urban X's sister store, **Swank**, newly relocated at 1450 W. Webster Ave.; telephone, (312) 348-4283.

Wacky Cats
● 3109 N. Lincoln Ave., Chicago; (312) 929-6701

Selling funky vintage dresses, suits, undergarments, and shoes from the 1940's through the 1970's, this Lake View shop sells boutique-y vintage clothing at non-boutique prices. The store caters mainly to women, but there are some great men's suits and overcoats here, too.

A men's lined leather bomber jacket, for example, was recently seen for only $55. A snazzy sharkskin suit at $75 won't take a big bite out of your wallet, either. For the ladies, a metallic silver and black tank dress was $19, and a lacy wedding dress with fitted bodice and flared skirt was $49. A 1940's slip, perfect to wear underneath, was $19.

Nobody can call you wacky when paying only $9 for a pair of Levi cut-offs, or $18 for a wool houndstooth jacket by h.i.s. Wool stirrup pants, with the Carson Pirie Scott label, were seen for a trifling $19. To go with them, an Italian mohair and wool blend sweater will keep you

warm for only $21.

The shop opens daily at noon.

THRIFT SHOPS

The Ark Thrift Shops
- 3345 N. Lincoln Ave., Chicago; (312) 248-1117
- 1302 N. Milwaukee Ave., Chicago; (312) 862-5011
- 4833 N. Broadway, Chicago; (312) 275-0062

Perhaps the ultimate in Chicago thrift stores when it comes to selection, the Ark sells donated clothing and furniture at some of the lowest prices you may see anywhere. Lots of designer goodies are hidden among the dozens of racks and shelves in these warehouse-sized stores. And you'll feel good knowing that all the proceeds go to charities providing medical care to the needy.

In addition to clothing, these thrift shops have a good selection of household items and furniture. Many of the recliners and sofas should be categorized as dorm room, frat house, or first apartment variety—like a $28 velour recliner, or an easy chair (in a lovely shade of chartreuse) for $18. Other household goodies seen were a five-setting china set, including plates, saucers, tea cups, and bowls, along with a sugar bowl and creamer. These were in impressively good shape, all for just $22. Lots of cheap vases, like a green glass rosebud vase for 50 cents. The Ark also carries wide selections of other useful items, such as suitcases—there were about three dozen to choose from when Mr. C visited the Lincoln Avenue store.

In the overwhelmingly vast clothing department, Mr. C spotted an incredible buy: A pair of Salvatore Ferragamo shoes for ladies, with nary a scuff, for $2. Much of the selection is rather worn out, but you never know when you may come across such a find.

The Ark adheres to a one-price minimum policy on its clothing. All suits start at $5, and ladies' dresses

start at just $2.50, to name two examples. Some of the better-quality items Mr. C noticed were a plaid cotton Avon Fashions dress, a man's grey Botany 500 suit, a woman's London Fog trench coat, and a man's Scottish Tussah silk jacket by Arthur Dickson.

Lots of toys, like a $25 wide-handlebar Schwinn bicycle, are crammed into the stores, too. Be wary of the appliances, though, since most look like they may be able to qualify as antiques instead.

The Ark stores are open daily at ten, and stay open Mondays and Thursdays until 7, Tuesdays and Wednesdays until 5:30, Fridays until 3, and Sundays until 4:30. They're closed on Saturdays.

Brown Elephant Resale Shop
- 3641 N. Halsted St., Chicago; (312)549-3549

The Brown Elephant sure is huge, all right—8,200 square feet of clothes, housewares, and whatever various and sundry items get donated. As with all resale shops, prices vary with the value of the merchandise. But much of the clothing items have set prices: Most pants are $6, men's button-down dress shirts are $3.50, belts and ties go for $3, sweatshirts are $4, and sweaters are $4.50. Shoes are just $4 a pair, though boots go for $5. There may be exceptions to these rules, of course; a pair of lizardskin dress shoes, for example, would not sell for $4.

Brown Elephant also carries a good deal of housewares, which generally are a good deal indeed. A set of dishes, service for four, sells for about $8. Lots of books and jewelry, too. And then there are the occasional, shall we say, extraordinary items. Someone recently donated a Norton, which is an English motorcycle, worth $3,000; it sold here for $900. Someone else even donated a

Rolls Royce, which was auctioned off. Mr. C can't promise that you'll see *these* items everyday, but you never know...

Why, you may ask, are people so generous? Well, all of the proceeds from the Brown Elephant benefit the Howard-Brown Memorial Health Center, an AIDS clinic in town. The Center helps people living with AIDS pay for rent and utilities, and provides medical support. Many of the items in the store, like those fancy wheels, have come here instead of being sold off in estate sales. There's nothing like bargain-hunting for a good cause.

Changing Closets Resale Shop
- 1931 N. Halsted St., Chicago; (312) 751-2800

Get ready for a search. This store is located behind the offices of the Infant Welfare Society (whose sign is obscured by trees), then down a flight of stairs, way back on the right. Once you find the place, not only can you benefit this worthy cause, but you may find some real treasures.

All of the clothing is donated and naturally some is in rough shape, but Mr. C did spot a real mink cape, never worn, with the tags still attached, for $18. And no, it wasn't a misprint, the volunteer saleswoman verified the whole thing; needless to say, this is hundreds less than what you'd pay in a fur shop.

The racks here are dominated by children's clothing. A royal blue Gap children's sweater, with only a few pills on the sleeves that need picking off, was seen for $2. A child's unisex argyle sweater by the very preppy Boston Traders was only $1.50. Changing Closets also stocks plenty of jumpers and baby clothes.

Depending upon recent contributions, you may also be able to find an ultra-cheap child's suitcase here for as little as $2. Shoes included real Mary Janes, but tend to be in rather rough shape and may not even be worth the couple of bucks they cost. Toys and electronics are also tricky. During Mr. C's visit, a customer returned with a broken transistor radio; you may just want to skip these kinds of items. The 25 cent paperback section, however, is great! Nora Ephron's *Heartburn*, basis for the Meryl Streep movie, was found among this selection.

The back room is locked, but it can be opened upon request. This is where you'll find more valuable (yet inexpensive) items like that mink cape, as well as wool overcoats for $5 or so.

The store is open from 10 a.m. to 4 p.m. on Mondays and Tuesdays, 9-4 Wednesdays and Fridays, 9-6 on Thursdays, and 10-2 on Saturdays. Also on weekdays, it's closed from 1-2 for lunch.

Finders Keepers
- 2467 N. Lincoln Ave., Chicago; (312) 525-1510

A fairly large thrift with much of its merchandise in good condition, Finders Keepers divides itself almost evenly into a clothing section and a furniture/housewares section. The well-filled clothes racks may yield up such "finds" as a denim dress by Allan Toussaint for $18, Bandolino sandals for just $3, in good shape for used shoes, or a classic navy blue men's suit by Brittany for $30. There's plenty of stuff for outfitting your kids from head to toe, whether it's a boy's satin-style baseball jacket for $5, or infantwear separates for just a couple of bucks apiece.

On the home furnishing side, there are desks, table, and chair sets, shelf units, and more. A tweed couch, big enough for three potatoes, was seen for $130; put a table lamp beside it for $40. Lots of books, too, all 50¢ for hardcovers and 25¢ for paperbacks, as well as encyclopedia sets. Housewares include curling irons, coffee makers, and the like, all in working order; Mr. C found a Toastmaster portable griddle for $10.

You can find yourself in Finders Keepers daily from 10 a.m. to 4 p.m. Proceeds benefit the Latin School of Chicago.

MR. CHEAP'S PICKS
Thrift Shops

✔ **The Ark**—An incredible selection of cheap used clothing—enough for forty days and nights of shopping.

✔ **Brown Elephant Resale Shop**—Tons of clothes, most of which are uniformly priced (pants $6, shoes $4, etc.). Plus the occasional Rolls Royce—honestly.

✔ **Something Old, Something New**—Something unique: A store divided in half, with cheap closeouts on one side and thrift stuff on the other. Big selections and small prices on either side.

✔ **Village Discount Outlets**—The slightly modernized Salvation Army outposts.

The Right Place
• 5219 N. Clark St., Chicago; (312) 561-7757.

One of Andersonville's many resale shops, The Right Place has a decent assortment of clothing, furniture, and thrift shop bric-a-brac. Some of the items seen on Mr. C's visit included a 10 X 12-foot Oriental rug for $125, and a handsome cream-colored dresser in fine condition for just $50.

Among the clothing finds was a woman's three-piece linen suit—skirt, top, and blazer—for $65; plenty of children's clothing, too, not to mention a good selection of popular toys and games, many in their original boxes. Though much smaller than the king-sized Chicago Recycle Shop across the street, the merchandise here is more recent, and frequently in better shape. As such, the two stores complement each other nicely.

"A Second Chance" REMAR Shops
• 921 S. Western Ave., Chicago; (312) 243-3304 or (312) 243-3406
• 1539 N. Milwaukee Ave., Chicago; (312) 384-0819
• 3102 W. 25th St., Chicago; (312) 521-1551

REMAR, which is the abbreviation for the Spanish phrase translating to "Rehabilitation of people on the margin of society," is an international organization which helps drug addicts and homeless people recover from their problems and find employment. The Chicago shops sell donated items from suits to phonographs, and the money directly benefits those in need.

The Milwaukee Avenue store is the newer of the two, and wasn't as fully stocked during Mr. C's visit—though that should have improved by the time you read this. The stuff you will find in these shops can be fantastic, making the "Second Chance" stores worth a second look.

In clothing, a Gilligan and O'Malley cotton/poly dress was seen for just $3, as was a rayon jumpsuit by Liz Claiborne. The store also featured a selection of bridesmaid's dresses, like a red satin one for just $6. Pappagallo shoes, a bit scuffed but always stylish-looking, were a mere $2 for the pair. Boys' SpotBilt soccer shoes were only $4, and the men's racks yielded a $2 John Henry oxford shirt and a dapper Ungaro silk suit, custom made for Morry's, at a negotiable price (most of the non-designer suits were priced at $5 or so, many even less).

The home furnishings selection is full of surprises, like an old Singer sewing machine table for $75, a $40 recliner, an $8 movie projection screen, and a $35 ceiling fan. Just $7 gets you a framed print of Grant Wood's famous "American Gothic." Start your own Art Institute.

Books found here included a 50 cent paperback copy of Douglas Adams' *Life, the Universe, and Everything*, from the *Hitchhiker's Guide to the Galaxy* series (a 1 intergalactic forerunner to the *Mr. Cheap's* series) and a $1 hardcover edition of Garrison Keillor's *Lake Woebegone Days*. Record albums, just $1 each, ranged from Beethoven's Symphony No. 3, "Eroica," to Bob Dylan's *Nashville Skyline*. Pick up a Fisher turntable for $12, and you can get a whole stereo system for less than you might spend on one new CD!

Something Old, Something New
- 1056 W. Belmont Ave., Chicago; (312) 271-1300

True to its name, this large storefront near the Belmont "el" station carries both old and new clothing, split evenly down the center as you come in. To your left, half of the place is a huge thrift store, with racks and racks of ultra-low price clothing. Suits and dresses for $2, jeans for $5 ($8 if they're Levi's), shirts and blouses for $2, and tons of kids' stuff. The quality is of Salvation Army grade and better; you may find some name brands mixed in among the racks.

But wait. The other half of the store is filled with almost as much in the way of unused clothes. More interesting still, nothing on this side is priced above $5. This is liquidation stock, most of it second quality, from stores all over the country. Some of it is marked or damaged, but there is still plenty of good digging to be done. Men may find Oxford-style dress shirts from Christian Dior, Perry Ellis, and others—Mr. C found some from Lord & Taylor with the original $40 price tag still on them— all for $5 each. Women can get linen and cotton sundresses, or even a Liz Claiborne blazer, for the same price; plus stretch denims, lingerie, and more.

Whichever side of the store you choose to browse, you can definitely fill your closets with entire wardrobes for very little cash.

Village Discount Outlet
- 2032 N. Milwaukee Ave., Chicago
- 2855 N. Halsted St., Chicago
- 3301 W. Lawrence Ave., Chicago
- 4635 N. Elston Ave., Chicago
- 2043 W. Roscoe St., Chicago
- 4898 N. Clark St., Chicago
- 6419 S. Kedzie Ave., Chicago
- 4020 W. 26th St., Chicago
- 2515 Chicago Rd., Chicago
- 2514 W. 47th St., Chicago
- 7443 S. Racine Ave., Chicago

No phones in stores; central office, (708) 388-4772

This isn't an outlet at all, really, but a chain of thrift stores run by the Salvation Army in a slightly more upscale style. Some of these stores are in converted warehouses, and are not climate controlled (read: hot as heck inside). Still, they're worth venturing into for aisle after aisle of men's, women's, and children's clothing at rock-bottom prices.

Do a careful lookover of your choices before leaving. Some booboos that Mr. C discovered were ink spots (not the singing group), torn seams, and tiny holes; other shirts and pants just looked like they had been worn every day for a year.

Some of the goodies found here included men's silk ties for just 90 cents, Izod boys' rugby shirts for 75 cents, and girls' suede Minnetonka moccasins for just $2.20. Evan-Picone shoes for women were $1.50 for the pair, and only needed a coat of polish to look just fine.

While clothes shopping, you may come upon some cute toys for the kids, like a stuffed rabbit for a quarter. Otherwise, skip the beaten-up appliances and fragile-looking furniture, and stick to the clothing.

Most branches are open weekdays from 9 a.m to 9 p.m., Saturdays from 9-6, and Sundays from 11-5.

The White Elephant Shop
- 2380 N. Lincoln Ave., Chicago; (312) 281-3747, (312) 281-0063

Purchases at this popular thrift store in Lincoln Park benefit the nearby Children's Memorial Medical Center. It's big, but it can get crowded in here—especially in the clothing racks. The selection of furniture is not that expansive, but the home furnishings like lamps and dishware keep shoppers happily occupied here.

Full sets of dishes tend to be incomplete, but at only $1 per three pieces, nobody's complaining. Lamps with paper shades, circa 1950 but still in working order, start at around $7 and up.

A blue corduroy sofa, still in good shape, was seen for $140. Old comforters, $10 and up, still have plenty of warmth left in them. Stereos, typewriters, and portable radios are unlikely prospects due to their advanced age (many were dust-covered), so you should check these out carefully—ask if you can try them in the store. But the White Elephant is a definitely a good spot if you need a quick wool overcoat for $15, or a kid's bike, cheap.

COSMETICS AND PERFUMES

Beauty Warehouse
- 2065 N. Clybourn Ave., Chicago; (312) 880-5700

This store primarily sells salon-brand shampoos and conditioners—even the ones you can "only" get in salons—at savings of several dollars off the retail prices.

Paul Mitchell's "The Conditioner" is $10.95 for a pint, and his Awapuhi shampoo is $6.95 for the same size. Ten ounces of Sebastian Cello Shampoo is $4.97. Climatress deep conditioner, by Redken Classic, is $7.20 for five ounces; and Nexxus Dandarest shampoo is $6.50 for an 8.4-ounce bottle.

A liter of Apple Pectin shampoo sells for $6.87, while Zotos conditioning kelp masque by Bain de Terre is about $6 for five ounces. Sample-size designer perfumes are also sold here, many priced around $2.00.

Beauty Warehouse is open seven days a week; hours are from 9 a.m. to 8 p.m. on weekdays, 9-6 Saturdays, and 12-6 Sundays.

The Cosmetic Center
- 2817 N. Broadway, Chicago; (312) 935-2600
- 4747 N. Harlem Ave., Harwood Heights; (312) 775-0080

The Cosmetic Center has everything from generic cotton balls to eye shadow from Charles of the Ritz. There's nothing ritzy about the prices, however, making this a good place to stop in every once in a while with a forklift truck and stock up.

Also worth noting: The lighting here isn't the kind of harsh glare often found in drugstores. No more "lipstick that looks pink in the store yet somehow changes to orange by the time you get home" disasters.

The aisles are quite cluttered with cosmetics—an impressive variety of products at substantial savings. Basic items like Vidal Sassoon shampoo, normally retailing for $5.49, sell here at $3.99 for a 17-ounce bottle. Nice 'n Easy hair color was seen for $5.19—it can cost up to eight bucks elsewhere. And you can also find brands normally sold in hair salons, including Aveda, Nexxus and Paul Mitchell, at discount. They also have a selection of curling irons and hair dryers, like a Sassoon model (sorry about the pun) marked down from $38 to just $25.99.

The store's main attraction, though, is its superior designer cosmetics aisle. Clinique, Estee Lauder, Lancome, Christian Dior and Ultima II are among the fancy names sold at about 30% below department store "sticker shock" prices. Depending on the item, you can save as much as $10 on a single product, such as Elizabeth Arden's ceramide complex capsules.

Skin care products cover several aisles; at these reduced prices, you can really afford to take better care of yourself. Neutrogena Sesame Body Oil is $7.49 a bottle—nearly $3 off the retail price. Save about $1.50 on an eight-ounce bottle of Lubriderm skin lotion.

The discounts go on and on! Save $1.20 on Old Spice cologne for men, or as much as $10 on Samsara eau de parfum spray. Stock up on stockings from Burlington and No Nonsense, about 20% off retail. You get the idea.

One thing you'll notice here, by the way, is some rather tight security; this cuts down on shoplifting, which helps keep the prices down. Meanwhile, the store will be happy to replace any defective items (Mr. C says: Always keep your receipts!) or issue a refund, if you prefer.

Devon Discount
- 2454 W. Devon Ave., Chicago; (312) 743-1058

Wow. Devon Discount looks like a large, corner drugstore, but in fact it's a wholesale/retail distributor offering great savings on the basic stuff you use everyday, from soap and tooth-paste to Spic-n-Span and even some small appliances. The prices on these household items are good; where this place really stands out, though, is in its perfumes and personal care products.

Vitabath gel, for example, usually costs up to $20 in fancy-schmancy department stores; it's only $9 here for 10 1/2 ounces—and all three Vitabath scents are available, not just the green version. Vaseline Intensive Care Moisturizing Bath Beads sell for only $1.50 for a 15 ounce box, which is at least 50 cents below Osco or Walgreens.

Designer fragrances for both men and women are stocked in mass quantities. Two long walls are lined with names like Gucci, Armani, Paco Rabanne, Chaps, Paloma Picasso and just about any other brand you can think of. All are sold at 25% to 50% below retail prices; and there are test-ers for each one, so you can try them in the store.

Mr. C was asked not to mention prices, but you can save big on Chloe body powder, Ellen Tracy eau de toi-lette, and Liz Claiborne eau de par-fum spray. You will definitely like the discounts. Devon offers you other ways to save even more, such as ge-neric copies of famous fragrances, all under $10 for large bottles; also, if only the genuine article will do, they may have your brand in a bottle that's missing its cardboard box or protective cap. These may sell at less than half-price.

Filene's Basement
- One N. State St. (Lower level), Chicago; (312) 553-1061

Boston's original Filene's Basement is the king of all bargain treasure troves. Normally-sane women pounce upon tables strewn with piles of clothing closeouts, flinging wrong sizes into the air, in search of The Find. If and when they come up with this, they clutch it tightly and head immediately for the nearest register—or, to another table. The place can be a real madhouse...which is part of its charm.

The atmosphere of Chicago's outpost is more refined, but it matches Boston's huge selection of jewelry, cosmetics, first-quality cloth-ing and houseware closeouts, and ir-regulars. Mr. C noticed well-coiffed women with Gucci bags and men with diamond cufflinks—perhaps they can afford these fancy trinkets by saving on their wardrobe at the Basement. The selection changes con-stantly; many customers make a regu-lar pass through here on a lunch hour or after work.

Filene's is also a good place to buy better-name cosmetics, which run at least 10% or more below retail. A 1.7-ounce spray bottle of Shalimar eau de toilette, for example, sells for $32, a savings of 25% below retail. Plenty of good prices can be found on facial care products, makeup, and much more.

So what if the Basement can get messy during sales? For the money you can save, it's well worth fighting the crowds, and rummaging around for your size. And it's good practice in case you ever go to Boston.

Modern Overseas Appliances
- 2334 W. Devon Ave., Chicago; (312) 761-7665

MR. CHEAP'S PICKS
Cosmetics and Perfumes

✔ **Beauty Warehouse—**
Exclusive salon brands of hair care products, all below salon rates.

✔ **The Cosmetic Center—**
Anything and everything you might want, from designer names, all at good discounts.

✔ **Devon Discount—**Fabulous savings on name brand perfumes and colognes for men and women.

No, this is not a mistake; don't worry about the name. One of the many international-flavored electronics stores along Devon, Modern Overseas stocks a typical assortment of appliances, electronics, and—fitting right in—cosmetics. Find a 3.9-ounce bottle of Halston Z-14 eau de cologne, for example, nicely priced at $32.99; or a box of 60 Wilkinson razor blades for just $4.99.

The store also sells items like a Norelco rechargeable triple-head rotary shaver for $33.99, as well as Seiko watches and Cross pens at discounts of up to 50% off retail prices. It's open seven days a week, from 11:00 a.m. to 8:00 p.m.

Sav-A-Lot
- 1953 N. Clybourn Ave., Chicago; (312) 472-4177
- 2204 N. Clark St., Chicago; (312) 929-1770

Almost hidden in a little Clybourn Corridor strip mall, this store routinely discounts great names like Neutrogena, Bonne Bell, and L'Oreal by as much as 30 percent.

Bonne Bell's classic 10-O-6 Lo-

tion in the pint bottle, selling in most drugstores for almost $10, was seen here for just $6. The big 24-ounce bottle of Vaseline Intensive Care lotion was similarly reduced, to only $4.99.

Feeling stuffy and sneezy? Nyquil is only $5.49 for the six-ounce size at Sav-a-Lot. Contact lenses wearers will see big savings by getting their saline solution here—Bausch & Lomb's Sensitive Eyes solution is only $2.49 for twelve ounces!

Other recent deals here included a 6.4 ounce tube of Colgate for $2.39, a 15-ounce bottle of Halsa shampoo or conditioner for $2.59, and L'Oreal lipstick, retailing for over $6.50, here only $5.29. A 1.5-ounce Shalimar eau de toilette, priced at $22 and up in department stores, was seen for $18 at Sav-a-Lot.

In addition to cosmetics and perfume, you'll also save on some household necessities, like Wisk laundry detergent in the quart bottle for $3.49.

Valentine & Son Beauty and Barber Supply Center
- 34 W. Van Buren St., Chicago; (312) 939-3221

You can really fall in love with the bargains at Valentine's, which offers everyday discounted prices on hair products at a convenient Loop location.

Revlon hair relaxer kits, including Fabu-laxer and Realistic, regularly retailing for $9.95, sell for $7.95 here. Miss Clairol tints and toners, in hard-to-find shades, are stocked in good supply. Valentine's also carries specialized items like Egyptian Henna powder, with the 2.75-ounce size selling for $3.25. Jheri Redding Extra Awapuhi Moisturizing Shampoo, in the 15-ounce bottle, was seen here for the discount price of $3.75.

The store is open from 9:30 a.m. to 6:00 p.m. weekdays (stop in on your way home from the office), and from 10-3 on Saturdays.

DISCOUNT DEPARTMENT STORES

Goldblatt's

- 4772 N. Broadway, Chicago; (312) 989-3270
- 5630 W. Belmont Ave., Chicago; (312) 685-4700
- 1615 W. Chicago Ave., Chicago; (312) 421-5300
- 2600 N. Western Ave., Chicago; (312) 227-6600
- 3311 W. 26th St., Chicago; (312) 522-4900
- 4700 S. Ashland Ave., Chicago; (312) 247-0773
- 9100 S. Commercial Ave., Chicago; (312) 768-2000
- 125 W. 87th St., Chicago; (312) 224-4040
- 7538 S. Stony Island Ave., Chicago; (312) 288-6300
- 7975 S.Cicero Ave., Chicago; (312) 838-0010

Goldblatt's blasts away the competition. A Chicago institution for decades, they sell everything from 99 cent ceramic coffee mugs to super-cheap clothing to laundry detergent—all in a crazed, bargain-hunter, "get-out-of-my-way-that's-mine!" atmosphere.

It's a good place to buy children's clothing, if you're adept at fighting crowds and rummaging through racks and display tables. A little boys' lined nylon baseball jacket by DG Sportswear was seen for $3.99, and girls' size 7-8 black leggings were an ultra-cheap $2.99. That's not per leg, either. For adults, men's cotton pants by Westend were seen for only $3.99. Irregular Liz Claiborne nylons, retailing for $6.50 if perfect, go for only 99 cents here.

Elsewhere around the store: Goldblatt's is a find for party supplies, like crepe paper and table-cloths. Eight "Barney" party favors sell for only $2.39. In the luggage department, a weekender bag by Bonjour was only $25, far below its $65 list price.

Upstairs in the health and beauty aids department, Robitussin DM cough syrup sells for $3.29 for the four-ounce bottle. A bottle of Snuggle super-concentrated fabric softener is only $1.39.

Skip the bookcases and desks and other pressed woodchip furnishings upstairs; they're simply not sturdy enough and not as durable as they ought to be for their prices. Other kinds of home furnishings, though, are better buys—like a white ceramic table lamp, listed at $39, selling for $25 instead.

Shopper's Corner

- 150 N. State St., Chicago; (312) 346-0825

Billed as "The Loop's only discount store," Shopper's Corner sells everything from shot glasses and key chains to watches, costume jewelry, and electronics. Most of the stuff is clearly aimed at tourists. If you're looking for something basic, though, you'll probably be able to find it cheaper here than you could at major department stores.

Among the more practical items found here are a Panasonic Easa-Phone with automatic dialing, priced at $59.98, and a Westclox electric alarm clock with battery backup for just $7.98. Be warned, however: If anything breaks, you're out of luck—all sales are final here.

Spiegel Outlet Store

- 1105 W. 35th St., Chicago; (312) 254-1099

And many other suburban locations
Just down the road apiece from Comiskey Park, the Spiegel Outlet is just what you'd expect—a clearance center for catalog items that haven't sold as well as expected. Does that mean they're trying to unload five thousand cases of polyester leisure suits? Not at all. The city branch has

two floors of great clothes for men, women, and children—as well as housewares, furniture, electronics, and other goodies—at up to half off their original prices.

After all, there's nothing too shabby about men's Christian Dior dress shirts for $9.99, suede bomber jackets by Alan Michaels reduced from $289 to $120, or Reebok "Pump" sneakers for $70. On the gals' side, try a royal blue blazer by Leslie Fay, reduced from $78 to $50, a Daniel Niveau wool skirt suit, almost half-price at $70, bathing suits from just $4.99 (at the end of the season, always the best time to look), or anything from three long rooms' worth of professional outfits, fancy eveningwear, lingerie and outerwear.

Downstairs, there are racks and racks of clothing for kids, from toddlers to teenagers. A girl's jumpsuit from Gilda Marx was marked down from $26 to $15; two-piece snowsuits from Tidykins, once $95, were seen here for $40. Plus brightly colored sweatshirts by Crayola and Hush Puppies, reduced from $26 to just $5.99.

In the home department, check out Dundee bath towels, reduced from $10 to $3.99 each; a comforter ensemble from Dan River, marked down twice from $195 to $99 to $59; European-style table lamps from $29; woven country-style rugs at 50% off their original prices; wicker armchairs reduced from $299 to $199, and sometimes even exercise equipment. Mr. C saw "Alpine Tracker" ski machines, originally $299, selling here for much slimmer $129. You'll see some electronics, too, like a Sharp camcorder (brand new, a discontinued model) for just $599, a savings of $300 off the list price.

Even in this clear-the-decks setting, you can return purchases for cash or credit within thirty days (always save your receipts!)—better than many full-price stores. Also worth noting, Tuesdays are discount days for senior citizens: 10% off the total purchase. Spiegel outlets are open daily from 10:00 a.m. to 7:30 p.m.; weekends, until 5:00.

Value-Mart
- 628 W. Roosevelt Rd., Chicago;(312) 461-0722

While it's a stretch to call this shop a department store, it's not quite a dollar store and it sells more than clothes, so here it is. In the midst of a strip of great wholesale and discount clothing stores, Value-Mart sells clothes, toys, household goods—a little bit of everything, really—at ridiculously cheap prices.

Men's Sasson jeans are $17.99, as are little boys' nylon sports jackets with various sports team logos. Toddlers' shorts by Sun Hot Sea are $4.99.

Meanwhile, you can also pick up VO5 shampoo, Rave hair gel, or Condition hairspray for $1; or, generic brands of ketchup, mustard, and other packaged foods for $1 each. Even ant and roach spray. This place resembles the common "all for a dollar" stores, but there's a much better range of goods here than those tend to offer.

Open seven days a week; Mondays through Saturdays from 8:30-5:30, and Sundays 9:30-3:30.

Woolworth Value Store
- 1134 W. Bryn Mawr Ave., Chicago; (312) 784-0467

Everyone is familiar with the inexpensive merchandise available daily at good ol' Woolworth, but this far north mega-store really takes the cake. It's a one-stop shopping haven for bargains on clothing (especially for children), candy, home furnishings, and cleaning products, and even pet supplies.

Not all the clothing is of fantastic quality, as we know, but some better-maker brand names can be found among the aisles. Cotler men's tank tops at $5 are a good buy; and with acrylic/nylon socks at $1 a pair, you can afford to stock up. Children's rompers for just $3 are also welcome bargains indeed for families on a budget.

For the home, a five-piece "bath ensemble," including toilet cover, mat, and rug, was priced at $11.99. Keeping the bathroom Spic-n-Span will only cost $2.39 for the 17-ounce package.

MR. CHEAP'S PICKS
Discount Department Stores

✔ **Goldblatt's**—The decades-old Chicago institution is still a good place to shop for family clothing, home needs, and the like.

✔ **Spiegel Outlet Store**—Can't say enough about the bargains found here in clothing, housewares, and linens.

✔ **World Distributors**—Not really a department store, but a wholesaler with nearly as much to choose from in cameras, jewelry, small appliances, cosmetics, toys, and more.

"Baker's Secret" 12-muffin tins by Ecko are $3.99 each, and pot holders are usually no more than $1 each.

The pet and pet supplies department in this store is surprisingly large, with angora hamsters just $8.99 and Sun Seed finch mix bird seed at only $2.19 for a 2 1/2-pound bag.

Discount toys for the kiddies can always be found here. A Woolworth "super soaker" water gun was just $12, while its fancier equivalents cost as much as $20 in many other stores. For the kiddies' party, $3.99 will buy a Sesame Street character kit with cups and plates for eight and a matching tablecloth.

World Distributors

• 3420 N. Milwaukee Ave., Chicago; (312) 777-2345

Okay, this isn't exactly a proper department store. In fact, it's a wholesale distributor of everything from socks to stereo; and, amazingly enough, it's open to the general pub-

lic. You can shop here and get the same prices that dealers get—in other words, "at cost." Selection may be limited in many areas, but there are lots of major brand names at incredible savings. These are all first-quality, in current models and styles.

For instance, a Sharp 8mm "Twincam" camcorder, meant to sell for as much as $1,999, sells here for exactly half of that price. Seiko watches are similarly reduced, like a ladies' Movado-style model with a jet-black face and one jewel in the "12" spot, listing for $175 but available here for $102.90. Lots of other jewelry, too, including 14K gold and sterling silver.

You'll find a good variety of small appliances, such as a Remington Micro-Screen rechargeable shaver, not $120, but just $45.90. A Welbilt 1-cubic foot microwave oven, retail price $319.95, sells for $159; a seven-piece set of Regal aluminum non-stick cookware is marked down from $110 to $46; and a Eureka 5-amp upright vacuum cleaner sells for $84, as opposed to $220.

You want more? Well, there is baby furniture, toys, sporting goods, leather wallets and purses, luggage, tools, car accessories, Christmas decorations, and tons more, all stocked right there on the showroom shelves. It's all at wholesale prices, meant for other stores to purchase in quantity, but also available to you without any membership deals or special rules. Pick up a catalog ($2, or free with any purchase), with its separate "insider" price list stapled into the middle. Stop in seven days a week, daily from 9 a.m. to 6 p.m., and Sundays from 11-5.

About a block away, **Star Distributors** at 3500 N. Milwaukee Ave., telephone (312) 725-7770, is a competitor with World. This shop is a bit smaller and much more cluttered; it offers much of the same merchandise, and most of its prices are comparable, though some appeared to be higher.

ELECTRONICS—AUDIO, VIDEO, COMPUTERS

There are lots of places to save money on appliances and electronics in Chicago. Some, unfortunately, are as far below repute as they are below retail. With merchandise that is imported from foreign countries, there is a greater possibility of shady deals, or inferior quality. Mr. C says this not out of any kind of prejudice, but because he wants you to be careful.

One of the best ways to protect yourself, if you have doubts as to *any* store's reliability, is to ask about their guarantee policy; make sure the item you want carries an American warranty. Since some stores deal directly with manufacturers in the Far East, their merchandise may carry a foreign warranty instead. Even for identical products, a foreign warranty can make repairs a hassle—unless you don't mind paying the postage to Japan. Remember, you are perfectly within your rights to inquire about this in the store.

AUDIO AND VIDEO

Aronson Furniture and Appliances

- 3939 N. Ashland Ave., Chicago; (312) 871-6900
- 5657 W. Belmont Ave., Chicago; (312) 889-0312
- 1379 N. Milwaukee Ave., Chicago; (312) 235-9000
- 4630 S. Ashland Ave., Chicago; (312) 376-3401
- 3401 W. 47th St., Chicago; (312) 376-3400
- 2301 W. 95th St., Chicago; (312) 445-1888
- River Oaks West Shopping Center, Calumet City; (708) 891-1700

Since 1940, Aronson has been offering mid-range brands in all kinds of major goods for the home. Over the years, it has grown into one of Chicago's high-volume retailers, yet it hasn't lost sight of its own humble beginnings. As you can see above, it maintains branches in all parts of the city, north and south; this is the kind of place for regular folks who need to stretch the budget, but want good value for their money. Prices here can range from 30% to 60% off retail

for furniture, appliances, and even jewelry.

Wandering into the appliances and electronics department, Mr. C found an RCA Home Theater television—the kind with a projector screen and stereo speakers—selling for $999, about $500 off the list price. You may sometimes see floor samples on sale, like a Samsung stereo VCR and TV all-in-one unit selling for $499. There's a fairly good selection of audio equipment, especially in portables, boom-boxes and compact rack systems. Among components, a Kenwood CD player was seen for about $50 below retail, at $299.

Aronson's stores are open seven days a week, including weekday evenings. They also offer very flexible credit plans—as one person here put it, "If people see something they like, we'll give them every chance to buy it."

But wait—there's more! Aronson also has two clearance centers, the **Aronson Bargain Warehouses**, located at 2440 N. Milwaukee Ave., telephone (312) 276-2066, and 8530 S. Cottage Grove Ave., telephone (312) 873-8999. At these cavernous, no-frills places, you can find incredible savings on leftovers, closeouts, and slightly-damaged floor models. You never know what will turn up here, but there is sure to be a vast selection of furniture, televisions, lamps, and lots more. Everything is sold "as is," of course, with all sales final.

Discount Stereo and Photo

● 243 S. State St.; (312) 786-0442

This Loop shop is crowded and not always that super-cheap, but some items, especially floor samples, are great deals when you can find them. The store is an authorized Sony dealer—always a reassuring sign—so you can trust that what you're getting is of "genuiune" quality (not always the case with electronics stores, especially in the Loop!).

A Sony Sports Walkman with an auto-reverse tape player (model SXF30) sells for up to $100 in other places, but was seen for $80 here. A floor sample JVC 5-disc front loading compact disc player, with remote, was only $180. Another bargain was a pair of gigantic, powerful Fisher ST-410 speakers for $70 each, well below their list price of $150 apiece.

A word of warning: The store cranks up the volume on its own stereo system. If you have a hearing aid or are shopping with someone who does, it's a good idea to turn it down a mile or so before reaching the shop. If you don't, you may need one after spending any length of time here.

Douglas the TV Giant

● 4027 N. Lincoln Ave., Chicago; (312) 281-7600

● 7243 W. Touhy Ave., Chicago; (312) 763-4300

And other suburban locations

Sometimes, big savings require a big store. As in, "How do we do it? VOLUME!!" Such is the case with Douglas, the TV Giant (sounds like he should be a TV show instead of a TV dealer). These stores have a huge selection, not just in televisions of every kind, but also in high quality stereo.

You can get a Magnavox 13" color television for as little as $147, and a Sharp four-head VCR, with on-screen programming, for $188; great prices, both. Meanwhile, when it comes to giant-sized televisions, Douglas has a giant inventory—like a 30" Toshiba (picture tube) model with stereo sound for $998, or a Pioneer 45" wide-screen projection TV for $2,298.

Monthly payment plans, or 90 days with no interest, are both available, as is free delivery and installation on 27" sets and larger.

On the audio side of things, Douglas recently had an Onkyo CD player with remote control for $169; and a JVC dual cassette deck for just $99. Plus similarly competitive prices on speakers, amplifiers, and laser disc players. Open seven days a week, except for the Touhy store, which is closed Tuesdays (that should be easy enough to remember).

John's Electronics

● 5322 N. Broadway, Chicago; (312) 878-3716.

Panasonic, Fisher, Technics, VHS, Sony, and Minolta are among the big names available at reduced prices at this shop. You can rest assured that the merchandise is A-OK, despite the great deals, since the store is an authorized Sony dealer.

You'll find anything from small to large here—from a Sony SPP-57 cordless phone for $69.95, to a big screen projection television, also by Sony, selling for $1,159.

A Pioneer GR-555 model graphic equalizer was seen here for $199. One boom box, with a double tape deck by Panasonic, was $219; another, by JVC, combined a CD player with a double tape deck for $249. Put some Maxell XLII 90 Gold blank tapes in; they're $2.59 each. John's is open Mondays through Saturdays from 10 a.m. to 7:30 p.m.

JP'S Super Store

● 2425 W. Devon Ave., Chicago; (312) 761-4422

JP's is a mish-mash of merchandise in a gigantic, no-frills (read: cardboard boxes all over the floor) set-up. You'll find some great brand names here as well as some mystery manufacturers. Like so many of the importers along this stretch of Devon, they offer a little bit of everything from small appliances to stereo and video.

In JP's audio/video department, you can find good deals on blank tape, like a six-pack of Sony 60-minute HF cassettes at $5.59. Looking for a karaoke boom box? Who isn't? Mr. C found a Berecha (never heard of it either), with double cassette tape players, recently offered for just $109—almost half its list price.

A word of warning: Do watch your step as you wander around the warehouse. With lots of stray boxes lying around on the floor, to say you can really trip over a bargain here is true in more ways than one. JP's is open from 10:30 a.m to 7:30 p.m., seven days a week.

Modern Overseas Appliances
● 2334 W. Devon Ave., Chicago; (312) 761-7665

One of the many international-flavored electronics stores along Devon, Modern Overseas stocks a typical assortment of appliances, electronics, and—fitting right in—cosmetics. Among the bargains you may find here are such items as a portable stereo unit from Sony, with a cassette deck and four-band radio built in, for $32.99; Panasonic cordless telephones from $60; plus VCRs, camcorders, televisions, stereo components, and much more. As with all of these shops, do be careful to get units that are intended for use at American voltage levels (110 or 120 volts); many items are built to foreign standards, which will not work in this country. The store is open seven days a week, from 11:00 a.m. to 8:00 p.m.

Across the street is another, slightly larger shop selling much the same stuff: **International Video and Electronics**, at 2355 W. Devon Avenue, telephone (312) 338-9033. At both shops, by the way, you may want to try your hand at negotiating the prices down a bit. The language barrier can make it tough, but all of these places are competing with each other. You can always find another store to try.

Saturday Audio Exchange
● 2919 N. Clark St., Chicago; (312) 935-USED (8733)

High-fidelity buffs, listen up. Beginning a dozen years ago as a resale shop for used stereo equipment, Saturday Audio Exchange now sells a large variety of new, used, and second-quality new audio components, all at low-fi prices. And they carry many of the finest names in the business.

Used pieces may range from a Denon turntable (hard to find these anymore, new or used!), repaired by the manufacturer to be like new, for just $229—and several other brands under $100. A Harmon Kardon cassette deck, which sold for $265 new, was seen here for $129. These are reconditioned in the store, and they guarantee their work for a period of 90 days—as good a policy as you'll find in used stereo.

New and "B" stock equipment is also well-priced. "B" stock is the merchandise that gets a bit scuffed in shipping, but is still brand-new and perfectly good on the inside. Mr. C saw a Harmon Kardon power amplifier, with a wall-blasting 200 watts per channel, reduced from a list price of $1149 to just $499, simply because of a "blemish" on the casing. Mount it in your audio rack, and you'll never see the scratch.

Sometimes, you can even get a choice; Saturday recently had several pairs of JBL bookshelf speakers, list priced at $600, selling for $479 in "A" stock and $439 in "B" stock. And a compact disc player by NAD, unblemished but a discontinued model, was reduced from $429 to $259. "B" stock items, by the way, still carry the manufacturer's full warranty.

The salesmen here are friendly

MR. CHEAP'S PICKS
Electronics—Audio and Video

✔ **Saturday Audio Exchange**—New and used stereo components at hundreds of dollars off. So good, they now open *twice* a week.

✔ **20th Century TV and Stereo Center**—Don't buy cheaply made audio and video equipment; not when you can get top-of-the-line used components for less—the kind that can be kept going forever. This is the place to buy them and have them maintained.

guys who genuinely seem to enjoy what they're doing. The fact that they don't work on commission keeps them honest, too, notes owner Andy Zimmerman. And the atmosphere is always bustling in this tiny shop, since it's only open two days a week: Thursday evenings from 5:30 to 9:00, and of course, Saturdays from 10:30 a.m. to 5:30 p.m. These hours help keep the business brisk, and the overhead low—hence, the great deals.

20th Century TV and Stereo Center
- 1611-15 W. Montrose Ave., Chicago; (312) 528-1728

You'd never guess by looking at this humble Uptown storefront, but what lies inside for stereo enthusiasts is nothing less than salvation. Husband and wife tech wizards Mitch and Ursi Lewczuk run the sort of sales and repair shop that is quickly dying out in this age of shopping malls and chain stores. They buy and sell high-quality new and used components, from the ordinary to the exotic; from good ol' record players to laser disc video to speakers the size of phone booths.

Mitch believes passionately that many of the audio and video items being made today—even by well-known names—is of such shoddy quality as to be almost worthless. Yes, you can walk into Circuit City and walk out moments later with a VCR for $200, but it's likely to break down a year later; and when people bring these into his store, he finds they were so cheaply made in the first place that he cannot repair them. Better, he says, to buy something that's built to last, even if it's an older, used piece; and why not, when these folks can keep it going forever.

After all, they have a staff of certified electronic engineers. They have the manuals for everything ever made, which they've acquired as other stores have gone out of business. The files fill an entire room. And they have 15,000 replacement needles for phonograph cartridges.

They've got it all.

So, what can you get here? On the lowest price level, you can find used cassette decks, receivers, and other components—carefully repaired and guaranteed for 90 days, parts and labor—for around $100 or less. And it's not just old-timer stuff, though many items date back to the 1960's; Mr. C saw a Sony CD/laser disc player for $315, a Fisher CD player for $95, and an RCA Super VHS video deck with stereo sound—originally a $1,000 item—for $375.

Mitch's tastes run to the unusual, too. He'll happily show you a Sony DAT recorder in mint condition, list priced at $900, selling here for $450; the ten-cassette audio changer, a failed marketing concept from the 1970's; or a Nagra tape recorder, used to record sound for professional film cameras. Closer to home (stereo), but at the high end, are Macintosh power amplifiers, a Nakamichi dual-cassette deck with brand-new heads at half its original price, and an Akai four-track reel to reel stereo recorder—never used—for just $400, also half-price. Oh, and don't forget those six-foot tall speakers, from

Acoustat; they're actually quite thin for their height, and so is the price—$875 for the pair, marked down from $1,700.

20th Century also sells a few other kinds of appliances. During Mr. C's summertime visit, they had 5,000-BTU air conditioners by Gibson, new and with a ten-year warranty, for $349. Anything you don't see can be ordered from manufacturers' catalogs, at good rates. And the folks are very flexible about your purchases, with layaway plans and the occasional willingness to bargain. Open seven days a week until 9:00 p.m.

COMPUTERS

Chicago Computer Exchange
- 5225 S. Harper Ave., Chicago; (312) 667-5221

It's a little tricky to find this place, located in the "planned community" of Harper Court just below Hyde Park Boulevard. And once you make your way inside their solid blue front door, it's even more fun wandering around the cluttered shop, in which every square inch seems to be piled high with various bits of old computers.

Yes, "CCEX" is one of the few stores in all of Chicago selling new and *used* computers, a relatively new retail arena—and an important one for those who think they'd have to refinance their car in order to get into computing. Well, just like a used car lot, this store sells older machines that have been reconditioned (with warranty!) and still have plenty of life left in them. Meanwhile, if you don't need a computer with all the latest bells and whistles, you can save a lot of money this way.

For example, if all you want is something basic for word processing, spreadsheets, and the like, you can get an older IBM system—complete with keyboard, monitor, and dual floppy disk drive—for $500. It ain't fancy; the monitor is not in color, and it's as fast as a turtle compared to today's quick-like-a-bunny versions. But as we all know, turtles do win races. And if you only intend to write a college thesis, or want an inexpensive starter system for your children, this will do quite nicely.

Something more recent you might find could be a Macintosh LC II system, with a 40-megabyte hard drive and 4MB of RAM (apologies to non-techies), complete for $850. You may even come across used laptops, which are all the rage these days, and therefore continue to be the priciest units on the market; most brand-new ones sell for anywhere from $1,500 to $2,500. Mr. C saw a Toshiba 3200SX laptop here for just $750. Used printers start around $75; a used HP Laserjet printer may go for only $300. All used items carry a 90-day store warranty.

If you already have a computer, you may want to check out CCEX for its stock of used "innards" as well—their service department can upgrade your old model to the very latest specifications for a lot less than buying new components. Service really is the name of the game here; even if you want to buy a new computer, they will discuss your needs, check around with national distributors, and piece together a complete system at the lowest possible price. Open Monday through Thursday from 10 a.m. to 7 p.m., Fridays and Saturdays until 5:00 p.m.

CompUSA
- 7011 N. Central Ave., Skokie; (708) 677-3644
- Butterfield and Finley Drive, Downers Grove; (708) 241-1144
- 1057 E. Golf Rd., Schaumburg; (708) 619-7638

Mr. C is cheating a bit by taking you out of the city (not too far), but only because he loves this giant store so much. The superstore approach of this fast-growing national chain gives them tremendous buying power, which means good selection and bargain prices on the very latest in this try-and-keep-up technology.

Perhaps the best feature of the store is the fact that almost everything is out on display, so you can try things out and get a true feel for them. That includes the teensiest mouse and the most powerful PC (they carry Apple products now, too), as well as laptops and printers. The service is good, too, with salespersons who actually seem to know what they're talking about—a rarity in the chain-retail world.

Among the recent bargains here were the Compudyne 486 "SubNote" laptop, weighing in at under four pounds and under $2000—both excellent specs. Some laptops even approach the $1000 threshold, while the basic Apple Macintosh PowerBook was recently on sale for $2129. Desktop 486s start around $1200, the price on a Compaq "ProLinea" model.

Among peripherals, the Hewlett Packard DeskJet 500 printer was recently on sale for $349. Scanners start as low as $99. And CompUSA has tons of software (including bargain bins), supplies, magazines, and everything else you could possibly need. They even have training centers, where you can learn how the heck to work these dang things once you open the boxes.

Computer Discount Warehouse

- 315 W. Grand Ave., Chicago; (312) 527-2700
- 2840 Maria Ave., Northbrook; (708) 564-4900

CDW is one of the nation's only retail/direct marketing catalog discounters. It offers great prices on computers and peripherals, disk drives and memory expansion, software, floppy disks, and pretty much everything else you could need. They are authorized resellers for major brands like Toshiba, NEC, Texas Instruments, Hewlett Packard, Panasonic, and more, although they do not sell Macintosh products.

Desktop 486 personal computers start under $1,000 (without monitor); get a complete package, or design your own system. Loads of laptops, too, like a Toshiba Satellite T1850

model, recently seen for $1,399. And the Texas Instruments TravelMate 4000 WinSX/25 color laptop, a 486 with a 120MB hard drive (apologies to you non-technical folks), was recently selling for $2588, a savings of $600 from its regular CDW price.

In printers, Okidata's new OL400E laser printer had just arrived in the store when Mr. C dropped in. It was selling for $499. Dot matrix printers, meanwhile, started as low as $115, for the Epson AP-2250.

All of these prices are well below retail, though determined shoppers may find better deals on particular items with a lot of research into those tiny-type mail order ads in trade magazines. CDW, however, combines that approach with a retail store, in which you can talk to bright, knowledgeable salespeople and see everything before you buy. There is a very good selection in all areas, with over 15,000 products in stock. Most items are stocked right in the store—no waiting.

All of the latest software titles are here at discount; Borland's Quattro Pro for Windows was seen for $10 below its retail price at $89.99. Microsoft's MS-DOS 6.0 upgrade, newly released, was priced at $47.75.

CDW has a full support staff, including a free technical helpline for its customers. You can order by phone, too, with their toll free line (1-800-829-4CDW). Most orders are shipped the same day. This place has been doing right by folks for over ten years, and has been favorably written up in publications from PC Magazine to the *New York Times*. Open from 9 a.m. to 7 p.m. on weekdays, and from 10-5 on Saturdays.

Hyde Park Computers

- 1466 E. 53rd St., Chicago; (312) 288-5971
- 2850 N. Clark St., Chicago; (312) 248-6200

And suburban location
This is the type of computer store which "makes" its own units by purchasing components directly from manufacturers and assembling them

MR. CHEAP'S PICKS
Electronics—Computers

✔ **Chicago Computer Exchange**—Did you know you could get *used* computers? Wouldya believe, a whole system for $500, complete? With a warranty, even.

✔ **Computer Discount Warehouse**—If only new will do, get big discounts from the showroom of this national mail-order distributor.

cerned. From there, they take a sort of "a la carte" approach; when you buy the basic system, you can also add various options for a little more money—but only the ones you actually need.

Thus, you can get a basic 486 computer, currently the top level of sophistication, for as little as $899. This does not include a monitor, which you select separately (from $150); but it does include everything else to get you up and running at a fine price. These are also designed to make expansion easy, saving you cash when you decide to add more memory or upgrade to the "586" system that will inevitably make "486" obsolete (that's the way it goes, folks).

HPC also sells printers, CD-ROM devices, and other accessories, again getting the best prices they can from the industry. And they do occasionally sell used computers in the older "286" and "386" varieties, though these are only sold "as is" with a 7-day warranty.

into their own models. This can mean substantial savings on brand-new computers, compared with many other retailers. Three locations, on the South Side, North Side, and North Shore, make Hyde Park big enough to offer good deals, while staying small enough to offer good service too. And they've been doing this for ten years—a lifetime in the computer business.

HPC deals only in PCs (IBM clones), and only at the "486" level. That's the top current industry standard, as far as the insides are con-

Hyde Park's prices on new systems may not always be "unbeatably" low; you may find better deals here and there, often on cheaper-grade machines. But if the prices are close enough, the additional attention to quality, flexibility, and service can more than make up the difference.

FLEA MARKETS AND EMPORIA

Clark Mall
* 7212 N. Clark St., Chicago; (312) 764-8794

Unlike the weekend flea markets which make up most of this chapter, the Clark Mall is a permanent, commercial emporium open every day. Its interconnected booths, with merchandise of all kinds strung along the tops and lining every pole, give Clark the feeling of some foreign bazaar. These also lend much color and vis-

ual interest to the place, which is otherwise a bit dingy and rather quiet.

There are dozens of booths, neatly arranged on a grid system; walk up and down the rows, and you'll see jeans and leather jackets, jewelry and cosmetics, housewares and furniture, stereos and televisions, and almost anything else you can think of. All of this is new merchandise, from major brand names and lesser-known imitations. Are these all bargains? No, not necessarily—but don't be afraid to try a bit of haggling. Certainly, renting a booth means a lower overhead than owning a store, so many things are going to be less expensive than they might be elsewhere.

At the rear of the mall, there is also a grocery section billing itself as having "wholesale club" prices. The shelves are mostly filled with knock-off and generic brands of foods and beverages, many of which are truly cheap—like a 30-oz. jar of "Red Label" spaghetti sauce for 35 cents. Worth a try? Your call. Mr. Cheap is merely here to report cheap prices, wherever he finds them.

Clark Mall is open seven days a week, until 8:00 in the evening.

Halsted Street Art Fair
• 2853 N. Halsted St., Chicago; (312) 404-2889

Back in 1990, artist Claudia Webb had an idea for a cooperative store in which artists could sell their creations together under one roof. The result actually feels more like something from back in the 1960's. Vendors each rent a bit of space, coexisting cheek-by-jowl with one another, and dealing directly with shoppers in this modern-day bazaar. The atmosphere is extremely mellow. You may find tie-dyed cotton sundresses for $15, right next to crocheted floppy hats for $35, and hand-crafted silver earrings for $4 (or wooden bead necklaces for 75 cents). Guatemalan handbags and knapsacks in those bright red, blue, and gold colors range from $15-$20, and there's even a bin of old movie stills for $3 each. Mr. C also marveled at sets of chess pieces carved into elaborate African, Oriental, and classical Greek figurines. Some of these are priced as low as $25 per set.

So successful was Ms. Webb's idea that a second, much larger version was spawned in Lincoln Park. **Urban Underground** is literally underneath a now-vacated Woolworth's at 2418 N. Lincoln Avenue; telephone 528-1213. This location boasts 8,000 square feet of similar merchandise, along with books, toys, furniture, gift baskets, and "metaphysical goods." Hmm...perhaps that's some kind of new age way to shop-at-home.

Maxwell Street Market
• Maxwell and S. Halsted Sts., Chicago; no phone

Every Sunday morning, seemingly since the dawn of time, the desolate little streets of this South Side neighborhood have awakened to become a sprawling, chaotic, outdoor bazaar. Over the decades, as any city's neighborhoods will evolve, the faces of the merchants have changed—at this point, they are mostly Hispanic and African-American—but they've all been trying to do the same thing. Make a few bucks.

With that in mind, most of the stuff for sale here consists of things people need: Clothing, but primarily basics like shoes, socks (six pairs, three bucks!), and belts, used kitchenware and bric-a-brac, retreaded tires and salvaged auto parts (need an engine? Maybe a headlight?), secondhand portable TVs, and fresh produce (whole watermelons, two for $5).

The mix of new and used merchandise is about half and half, but it's all cheap. Like the brand-new luggage, whose largest size costs only $30. Or flowery Mexican blouses for $4.50. If you do find yourself interested in something a bit higher in price, make 'em an offer—bargaining is definitely part of the adventure. Couldn't hurt.

The market is as much a spectacle in itself as a place to actually do any shopping. The Chicago Bluesmobile, a blue-painted schoolbus loaded up with blues cassettes, is parked at one corner. Tapes by all the legendary howlers are $5 each, or three for $12. Oh, and they've got 8-track tapes, too. And chances are, somebody's got an old 8-track player sitting on a table nearby.

Do be careful as you wend your way through the crowds, or back to your car. Everyone seems to be genuinely there for the market, but this

MR. CHEAP'S PICKS
Flea Markets and Emporia

✔ **Maxwell Street Market**—Still the biggest and craziest in all Chicago. Perhaps this should be filed under "Entertainment."

✔ **South Loop Marketplace**—More recent and just as sprawling, this weekend flea market is cleaner than Maxwell Street—and it's indoors.

neighborhood is definitely on the down side.

Morgan Market
• 375 N. Morgan St., Chicago; (312) 455-8900

Only a year old, the Morgan Market has taken up residence inside an old railroad station that's been completely emptied and cleaned out, down to a plain, cement floor. Still, the building lends character to this West Town flea market, which makes a neater, more yuppified complement to the gritty environs of Maxwell Street.

Each Saturday and Sunday from 8:00 a.m. to 5:00 p.m., vendors of all stripes take up their assigned spaces and sell their wares. In true flea market fashion, these may consist of just about anything, from new merchandise to old junk. Among the nicer stuff, you may find plants, sunglasses and watches, flags and bandannas, handmade earrings (Bijouterie, a store described in the jewelry chapter of this book, has a table here), antique furniture, historic newspapers, and more—much of which is inexpensively priced.

The ambiance here is definitely quiet and laid-back, weekend style. Part of that has to do with the fact that only half of the spaces are filled; at least, that was the case when Mr. C

visited. The creator of the market, who was looping lazily around the premises on an old bicycle, noted that it was taking time for his enterprise to catch on—but people are beginning to discover it. He hopes to build up the attraction by adding a restaurant and bar on the premises, a fine idea which may even be a reality by the time you read this. Discover it for yourself.

South Loop Marketplace
• 509 W. Roosevelt Rd., Chicago; (312) 226-5800

Operating every weekend out of a huge old freight warehouse, South Loop Marketplace is another heir to the Maxwell Street tradition. It seems to be just about as large; room after room (so many that they are color-coded) is filled with vendors selling everything from antique junk to brand-new VCRs. Some are as organized and well-stocked as a mini-store, such as Sonia's Bath Shop, where you can get a ten-piece Cannon bath towel set for $25; others are just open tables piled with goods.

Like any good flea market, it's impossible to detail what you may find on any given visit; at the various booths selling new items, Mr. C found such things as a table full of women's casual shoes by Buffalino, in their original boxes, for $20....6 X 9 bound rugs for $45....gold and silver jewelry from $5 and up....and cast-iron cookware, including nice big skillets for $12.

Among the used tables, bric-a-brac browsers will be in heaven. There is seemingly no end to the parade of vintage clothes, furniture, salvaged auto parts, bits of nostalgic Americana, housewares and more. Mr. Cheap found a coffee machine by his counterpart, Mr. Coffee, for a mere 25 cents. Does it work? he asked the vendor. "Hey, for a quarter, do you care if it doesn't?" Good point.

More so than at Maxwell Street, you could probably spend an entire day prowling around here (the atmosphere is more low-key, and there's a snack bar, for refueling). That day would be Saturday or Sunday from 8:00 a.m. to 4:00 p.m., South Loop's only days of operation. And, just to keep a healthy flow of merchandise,

they hold public auctions on the first and third Sundays of every month. Antiques and other furniture make up most of the action. These start at 10:00 a.m., with viewing from 8:30.

FLOWERS AND PLANTS

Blanca's Flowers
- 5603 N. Clark St., Chicago; (312) 878-3017

The salesperson at Blanca's told Mr. C, "We are cheaper than you are," and this may just be so! One dozen long-stem roses cost just $11.99, a rosy price indeed. You can also purchase roses singly, for 99 cents each. Carnations are $3.60 a dozen. It's all cash and carry only, no delivery, but hey—when the price is right, you shouldn't be too critical about the lack of other amenities.

Devon Angie's Flower Shop
- 2959 W. Devon Ave., Chicago; (312) 761-2900.

Almost as cheap as the Flower Bucket chain, Devon Angie also happens to be a whole lot friendlier (see listing below). Long-stemmed red roses sell for $20 per dozen, boxed and delivered; better yet, they're only $14.95 if you go "cash and carry." Other blooms are well-priced here, too. Carnations, for instance, run $7.99 per dozen; but they can be gotten for as little as $5 a dozen during Angie's frequent sales.

Flower Bucket
- 158 W. Washington St., Chicago; (312) 346-9773
- 1201 Belmont Ave., Chicago; (312) 935-9773
- 1164 N. LaSalle St., Chicago; (312) 943-9773
- 1377 E. 53rd St., Chicago; (312) 955-5700

You've probably heard by now that Flower Bucket sells long-stemmed roses for an amazingly cheap $8.00 a dozen, cash & carry. Their "extra fancy" bouquets are nothing to

sneeze at, either, starting at just $3.99, with the larger bunches usually selling for about $7.

Fancier stems, like irises, were recently selling for $7 a bunch; and super-healthy spider plants, with plenty of offshoots were just $10.

The counter help's attitude, unfortunately, varies from store to store. The folks in the LaSalle shop seemed genuinely happy to help during Mr. C's visit, while their counterparts in the Loop can throw you for one with their frowns. Well, when their prices are just a drop in the bucket, you can't complain.

Henry Hampton Inc.
- 720 S. Michigan Ave., Chicago; (312) 461-1460
- 828 S. Wabash Ave., Chicago; (312) 461-0066
- 17 E. Monroe St., Chicago; (312) 917-1775

This Loop area chain is *the* place to go for beautiful carnations, priced at only $6.00 a dozen. Alas, their prices on other flowers, such as roses and arranged bouquets, aren't as inexpensive. Still, that's better than nothing; and Hampton's is convenient, of course, with its three downtown locations.

Silkcorp Factory Outlet
- 363 W. Ontario St., Chicago; (312) 335-1034

Okay, here's the ringer for this chapter. Walk into Silkcorp, and you'll swear you are suddenly lost deep in some Amazon jungle, surrounded by huge trees with shady green leaves of every shape and size. Lush flowers in every color grow at your feet. Only....they aren't actually growing.

MR. CHEAP'S PICKS
Flowers and Plants

✔ **Flower Bucket**—A dozen roses for $8. Need Mr. C say more?

✔ **Silkcorp Factory Outlet**—A flower factory? Yes, for these flowers, trees, and shrubs are handmade from silk—and perhaps the most realistic you'll ever see. At 50% to 70% off retail prices, even these can start to grow on ya.

Everything here is made of silk, and so craftily done that from a slight distance, you'd hardly know the difference. Silkcorp imports the leaves and flowers from China, and assembles them in their own local, er, plants. They make them very realistically, us-ing natural materials too. Giant banana trees, for instance, are made with silk leaves inserted into actual wood tree trunks. These are sold to department stores (including Marshall Field), restaurants, film companies—and, at this store, you can buy the same items at 50%-70% off retail prices.

That twelve-foot tall banana tree is made to sell for $600; here, it's priced at $200. Smaller ficus trees, list priced at $75, are just $25. Get a hanging basket of azaleas for $20, reduced from $50, a stalk of gladiolas for $8.75, or a pot of African violets for $4.20. And don't forget—you'll never have to water them and they'll always look healthy!

There is room after room of plants, each of which is clearly marked with the retail and sale prices. Custom arrangements can be made to order; the staff is friendly and as knowledgeable as any horticulturalist. Open seven days, including evenings.

FOOD SHOPS

Quoting prices on fresh foods, like meat and produce, is about as smart as quoting politicians on *their* promises. Neither one seems to keep very long. The prices mentioned herein, like everything else in this book, are simply examples which should give you some idea of each store's general pricing.

However, it's important to note that the shops below were all visited at the same time of year, summer; that's more or less the height of the season for many of these categories, when prices are at their lowest. Because Mr. C checked them all around the same time, you can certainly use these descriptions for comparison with each other.

BAKERIES

The Baker's Daughter
- 1563 N. LaSalle St., Chicago; (312)
- 2218 N. Lincoln Ave., Chicago; (312)

These two shops are part of a baking tradition that goes back to 1886, when Kathi Wendell's great-grandfather began a bakery in Germany. The story takes a number of twists and turns, but it basically leads to Kathi growing up over her father's bakery, joining in as she got older, and eventually spinning off into her own separate business (hence, the name).

She took over Danegger's in Arlington Heights, a longtime neighborhood bakery; and, more recently, added the Baker's Daughter shops downtown in that same tradition. All three are what Kathy calls "full service bakeries"; in this age of specialization, her shops make breads, cakes, doughnuts, croissants, and more—all delicious.

Another downside to the modern era of product-pushing is that many bakeries sell to middlemen, driving the price up before you buy these goodies. There are no hidden forces at the Baker's Daughter, which is why Kathi's prices are so good; her scones, pecan rolls and other delectable pastries are made and sold here for under a dollar each. Try matching that at Starbucks. She also makes a variety of coffee cakes, which you can't even find in most bakeries; and wacky, unique cakes for special events, custom decorated with just about any image you ask for.

Now, Kathi hopes her kids will join *her* in the family business, making a fifth generation. It's all part of "Schmidt Family Baking Since 1886." The Baker's Daughter is open seven days a week.

The Bread Shop
- 3400 N. Halsted St., Chicago; (312) 528-8108

A true vegetarian heaven in the heart of Lake View since 1971, the famous Bread Shop can stock you up with goodies without breaking the bank. An attached deli, grocery, and juice bar-cafe make for healthy one-stop shopping. The Bread Shop caters, too, and it's open every day of the year.

Some of the pluses of the Bread Shop are that they recycle practically everything, and use eggs obtained from free-range, antibiotic-free chickens. They don't use refined sweeteners or white flour (both of which are processed using ground bones, be-

lieve it or not). Their chocolate is sweetened with barley malt instead of sugar, and is just as tasty as any. Most of the grains in the recipes are organic, and the folks who do the cooking will be happy to adapt their recipes to specifically fit any diet, for those allergic or sensitive to different foods.

Of course, the main attraction here is the bread. Caraway rye, country rye, onion dill, sprouted wheat, molasses wheat, garlic, and even Pritikin loaves are just $2.29 each—a good price for such high-quality stuff. Challah, Swiss muesli, baked potato, orange bran, and pesto breads are just $3.29 a loaf, as are the sourdough choices: Rye, raisin walnut, brown rice, jalapeno rye, cornmeal rye, onion herb, and multi-grain. Again, your local supermarket is cheaper, but do they *sell* orange bran bread?

Dozens of different cookies sell for $7.40 a pound, such as spritz, coffee chip, sesame banana, gingersnaps, and carrot butter. Non-dairy choices feature banana chip chews, coconut macaroons, carob walnut kisses, tahini oat, and almond thins. And your sweet tooth will be further satiated by truffles, $1.25 each, in almond, cherry, mint, mocha, raspberry, and rum flavors.

The shop is open Monday through Saturday from 8 a.m. until 10 p.m.; and on Sundays from 9 a.m. until 9 p.m.

Butternut Thrift Store
- 40 E. Garfield Blvd., Chicago; (312) 536-7700
- 1837 W. 35th St., Chicago; (312) 927-5849
- 6655 S. Pulaski Rd., Chicago; (312) 582-5461
- 3236 N. Damen Ave., Chicago; (312) 528-4004
- 2925 W. Montrose Ave., Chicago; (312) 478-8875

And many other suburban locations
Butternut is a thrift store selling bread and Dolly Madison snack products at substantial discounts. Like such other bakery thrift outlets run by

Sara Lee, Wonder Bread, and Entenmann's, Butternut gets food that has come back from supermarkets and convenience stores, but has not yet reached its expiration dates. Thus, you can save anywhere from 20% to 50% off the prices marked on the packages.

You can buy three loaves of Butternut bread for $1.29, three boxes of Dolly Madison snack cakes for $1.09 and all sorts of other bargains. Butternut is open Monday through Friday from 9 a.m. to 7 p.m., Saturday from 9 a.m. to 5 p.m., and Sunday from 10 a.m. to 3 p.m.

Byblos 1
- 5212-14 N. Clark St., Chicago; (312) 271-1005

One of several great bakeries in Andersonville, Byblos 1 is a combination bakery-grocery-deli selling many grains, spices, and nuts in bulk, which can save you bundles.

Some of the great buys seen here were Aris olive oil, just $7.99 a gallon, and basmati rice for $1.29 a pound. Legumes and beans are also available in bulk—lentils are just 69 cents a pound. Go nuts with the roasted pistachios, just $3.99 a pound, and almonds for only $2.99 a pound. Byblos also has a wall of fresh spices for sale, blowing away regular grocery store prices. For example, curry is only $2.99 a pound—about the same you'd pay for a tiny canister of the stuff at Jewel.

The bakery is open daily from 9 a.m. until 9 p.m., and on Sundays from 9 a.m. until 2:30 p.m.

The Corner Bakery
- Union Station, 210 S. Canal St., Chicago; (312) 441-0821
- 516 N. Clark St., Chicago, (312) 644-8100

A bakery with more than just sweets, the Corner Bakery's Union Station branch is a favorite among harried Loop office workers who gobble down their lunches in five minutes or less (not required, of course). At either location, the portions are good-sized, and the help is extremely friendly without being overbearing—

even during lunch and dinner rushes. And all the baked goods are really made on the premises. While the regular bakery items can thin your wallet (a loaf of chocolate cherry bread is $6.50), this is a good spot for lunch or breakfast with a number of different salads and sandwiches offered daily. Wheat berry salad, made with two kinds of peppers, is $3.50 for a small, $5.95 for a large. Curry chicken salad, with grapes and parsley is $3.85 and $6.95; and a hefty tuna salad sandwich with sprouts, on olive bread, is $4.50. For snacks, desserts or whatever, the Corner's popular pretzel rolls are just 75 cents each, and giant fudge brownies sprinkled with confectioner's sugar are $1.50.

The Union Station location is open Monday through Friday, from 6 a.m. to 10 p.m., on Saturday 8 a.m. to 8 p.m., on Sunday 8 a.m. to 7 p.m. Hours on Clark Street are Monday through Friday, 7 a.m. to 10 p.m., Saturday 7:30 a.m. to 11 p.m., and Sunday 8 a.m. to 9 p.m.

Eli's Bakery Outlet
- 6510 W. Dakin St., Chicago; (312) 736-3417

This outlet is a bit different from the other name-brand bakery thrifts in this section, which offer savings on foods that are a bit past their prime. Here at Eli's home base, you can find their great cakes, just as fresh as the ones in stores, for less than half price. Why? Because they are "seconds," or slightly imperfect. They may have gotten jostled around, perhaps a little smushed or crumbled; but other than these visual defects, the cakes are perfectly good.

The end result is that you can get a nine-inch cheesecake, which is meant to sell for up to $17 in stores, for as little as $4-$8. These come in varieties from plain to caramel-apple. Chocolate cakes and carrot cakes, with retail prices of $20, sell here for $8 also. And muffins—in such flavors as chocolate chunk, blueberry, and sugar-free apple bran—are just $3 for a dozen. In stores, you only get two muffins for $1.98!

MR. CHEAP'S PICKS
Bakeries

✔ **The Baker's Daughter**—
There really is a baker's
daughter running these
old-fashioned shops. She's
grown up, but the prices have
hardly budged.

✔ **Eli's Bakery Outlet**—Famous
cheesecakes, slightly bruised,
but fresh and wonderful. Also,
less than half-price.

✔ **Swedish Bakery**—A loaf rises
in Andersonville. Inexpensive
Scandinavian breads and
pastries, plus free coffee while
you wait.

Eli's, a block south of Irving
Park Road, is open weekdays from 9
a.m. to 4:30 p.m., and Saturdays
from 9-1.

El Nopal Mexican Bakery
• 1844 S. Blue Island Ave., Chicago;
(312) 226-9861
• 3648 W. 26th St., Chicago; (312)
762-9204

In the Pilsen section of town, Chicago's "Little Mexico," Mr. C found
this absolutely wonderful bakery specializing in fresh, hot breads and pastries. The place is clean and bright,
with all sorts of wonderful smells as
soon as you walk in the door. If you
don't speak Spanish, you may have a
tough time; but you can always just
point to the various items in the glass
counters. Loaves of bread cost as little as a dollar or so; crusty rolls are a
quarter, and most pastries go for 60
to 90 cents each. Best time to get the
freshest, hottest bread is from 5:00
a.m., when the store opens daily, until about noon. Otherwise, the bakery
is open until 10:00 every night.

Entenmann's Bakery Thrift Store
• 3031 N. Pulaski Rd., Chicago;
(312) 283-5105
• 4400 S. Pulaski Rd., Chicago;
(312) 376-1609

And many other suburban locations
Many well-known baking companies,
national brand names like this one,
run direct-to-you bargain outlets.
That's because they crank out so
much food, constantly turning their
stock over in the supermarkets, that
they invariably have lots of leftovers.
These items have come back from
stores as fresher boxes replace them
on the shelves; they may not be hot
out of the oven, but they're far from
stale. And you can buy them at
greatly reduced prices.

A danish twist cake, for instance,
with apricot or raspberry filling, is
marked to sell at $2.49 in stores;
here, you'll find the same item selling for $1.09. Or, you may find a
chocolate loaf cake for the same
price. Banana crunch loaves are
about half-price at $1.69. Enten-
mann's offers other kinds of bargains,
like a special table piled high with
cakes priced at just 25 cents with any
$5.00 purchase. And Wednesdays are
"Super Saver" days, with more special deals.

The store also sells lots of food
items by other manufacturers, including frozen goods like Boboli pizzas.
Snack foods abound, like pretzels
and popcorn, too.

Most Entenmann's branches are
open seven days a week; Monday
through Saturday from 8:00 a.m. to
6:00 p.m., and Sunday from 10-3.

Holsum Bakery Thrift Store
• 3230 N. Milwaukee Ave., Chicago;
(312) 725-3399
• 1814 W. 87th St., Chicago; (312)
779-4991

And other suburban locations
Another big-name bakery outlet, buying your Holsum bread here can save
you a "hol" lot of money over the supermarket. Loaves of their "Jumbo"
sliced wheat bread, for instance, sell
here for just 67 cents each, as op-

posed to $1.89 in stores. Get a bag of twelve hoagie rolls for 80 cents; and eight-packs of hot dog buns or sesame-seeded hamburger buns go for just 50 cents each, even though they're marked at $1.79 on the bag.

You can save bread on more than just bread; it's like snack-food heaven in here. Some of Mr. C's finds: A two-liter bottle of Coke for 99 cents, a box of Health Valley fat-free cookies for $2.19, nine-ounce packages of Finley Gourmet whole bean coffee at $3.79 for French roast or Italian espresso, a Jubilee whole Dutch apple pie for $1.99, plus candy, popcorn, and pretzels, and lots more. The store is open seven days a week.

Home Bakery
• 2931 N. Milwaukee Ave., Chicago; (312) 252-3708

One of the treasures of Polish Village, Home Bakery is as high on value as it is low on aesthetics—but nobody's complaining. This is among the best of the Milwaukee Avenue bunch.

Heavy accents sometimes make the counter staff difficult to understand, but they're very friendly and make you feel right at home. For your own home, pick up some of the very sweet pastries called *bezy moregi*, made entirely with sugar and eggs, for 40 cents a pop. Or, maybe some apricot cookies, sweet rolls, or tortes. Tasty butter cookies, one of very few items not baked in-house, are $3.99 a pound (available for some reason in pumpkin and Santa Claus shapes, even in the middle of summer—hmm, maybe that's why they're cheap).

An entire cheesecake is $2.99, as is a good-sized lemon roll cake. Super-fresh baguettes and loaves of bread cost about a dollar each, while dinner rolls are $2.99 a pound.

Both the bakery, and the adjoining restaurant (see listing under "Restaurants: West of Town") are open from 8:00 a.m. to 9:00 p.m. daily, and on Sundays from 9-9.

Middle East Bakery and Grocery
• 1512 W. Foster Ave., Chicago; (312) 561-2224

This tidy little shop, along with such other food businesses as Reza's Restaurant around the corner on Clark Street, creates a bit of a Mediterranean district in the heart of traditionally Swedish Andersonville. But then, it's that kind of diversity which makes cities fun. At the Middle East Bakery, they have glass cases filled with every variety of baklava imaginable—filled with walnuts, filled with pistachios, in round shapes, in triangle shapes....Grab a piece of this sweetness to go for just 75¢, or $5.00 a pound. Other delicacies here include falafel for $1.50 a dozen, and bags of pistachio nuts at $3.99 a pound. Lots of spices and cooking ingredients, too, such as olive oil at $9.99 for a one-liter container.

Panaderia Roman
• 5705 N. Clark St., Chicago; (312) 769-2548.

A wee bit north of Andersonville, this bakery creates all the Mediterranean specialties you can imagine. Baklava, various kinds of salt and sugar breads, plus other, more Americanized desserts. A big roll of salt bread will cost you about a quarter, as will a corona, which is a sugar-topped sweetbread-like dessert. Kind of resembles a spider with too many legs.

Panaderia Roman's chocolate chip cookies are loaded with chips, and muffins are only 30 cents. The bakery is open daily from 6:30 in the morning to 9:30 at night, and weekends from 7 a.m. to 6:30 p.m.

Pan Hellenic Pastry Shop
• 322 S. Halsted St., Chicago; (312) 454-1886

Located in the heart of Greek Town, this faded but busy shop makes—guess what?—all kinds of Greek specialties, from baklava to cookies and cakes. And they are delicious, as testified by one of Mr. C's friends of Greek extraction. Pastries, like baklava and galactobourikos, are just 95 cents each; try getting them for such a price in any of the area's many restaurants.

Sara Lee Outlet Store

- 3247 N. Harlem Ave., Chicago; (312) 202-0093
- 6210 N. Western Ave., Chicago; (312) 973-6210
- 7650 W. Touhy Ave., Chicago; (312) 763-4785
- 4028 W. 59th St., Chicago; (312) 581-9408
- 742 E. 87th St., Chicago; (312) 783-6585

And many other suburban locations
"Nobody doesn't like Sara Lee," as their commercials used to tell us (are they still running?). Well, nobody doesn't like saving money on these pastries even less...wait a minute, we're getting too many negatives in these sentences. The point is, you can save as much as 50% off the supermarket prices on the full range of Sara Lee baked goods—pound cakes, those ever-popular refrigerated chocolate cakes, pies, danish, cheesecakes, and even bagels and croissants. Again, these are goods which have been replaced in supermarkets and convenience stores by fresher packages, even though they haven't yet reached their expiration dates. In recent years, Sara Lee has branched out into other kinds of packaged foods, too, including deli meats and frozen dinners—some of which you may also find here at discount. You can save even more by purchasing in bulk quantities.

Most Sara Lee branches are open seven days a week, including some evening hours on weeknights.

Schmeissing's Bakery

- 2679 N. Lincoln Ave., Chicago; (312) 525-3753

This Lincoln Park bakery isn't half as busy as it should be, probably because the variety of cookies and other desserts isn't as wild as it is other places. But their butter cookies are heavenly, whether plain or chocolate-dipped. The dipped cookies are actually two cookies separated by a filling—the whole shabang decorated with colored, shredded coconut.

These go for $7.25 a pound, which translates to about 30-40 cookies if they're dipped, or double that if they're plain. Their white butter-top bread is $1.50 a loaf, tortes start at $12.95, and layer cakes are priced at a reasonable $7.95 and up.

Sholly Bakery

- 137 W. Leland Ave., Chicago; (312) 334-4415

The jolly people at Sholly bake only one thing—tart-shaped pies. But they sure do them well, and sell them for next to nothing. Why, if they had their way, you could have a complete "pie" meal from start to finish.

A spinach pie could be your appetizer; move on to a chicken pie for your main entree, and finish with a fruit pie for dessert. Apple and cherry are their specialty. Each of these, meanwhile, sell for a trifling $1.25. As an added bonus here, you can watch the bakers at work; they use no preservatives in the process, by the way.

This Uptown store is located just off of Broadway, a block below Lawrence, and is open weekdays only from 8:00 a.m. to 7:00 p.m. Special party orders are welcome.

Swedish Bakery

- 5348 N. Clark St., Chicago; (312) 561-8919

Up in Andersonville, this bakery invariably has a line running straight out the door. These folks don't seem to mind the wait; they take advantage of the free coffee to the right of the counter.

The Swedish Bakery's egg twist bread is only $1.50, and *skradda kaka*, a sweet rye bread, is only 95 cents a loaf, while *limpa* is priced at $1.95. Truffles are, for some reason, 56 cents a pop; and croissants are only 45 cents each. Kringles are $4.15. You like, yah?

Even the fanciest items on the list aren't too pricey. Marzipan torte is $11.30, and a mocha log is $5, while an entire Boston creme pie is $4.20.

The counter help can get rather brusque during the daily rushes, but you'll probably agree it's all worth putting up with when you taste the results. Open weekdays 6:30-6:30, Fridays until 8, Saturdays 'til 5; closed Sundays.

Wonder/Hostess Thrift Store

- 1301 W. Diversey Pkwy., Chicago; (312) 281-6700
- 5702 W. 55th St., Chicago; (312) 585-7474

Alphabetically only, this is the last stop on our tour of Chicagoland's many bake-factory outlet stores. Wonder/Hostess sells its famous breads and pastries here at about 40% to 70% off marked prices. As Mr. C has noted before, these are returns from retail stores which are not superfresh, but not yet stale, and at greatly reduced prices. Depending on the nearness of the expiration dates, different color stripes dashed across each box tell you how much of a discount you'll get.

Of course, with some of the sweets, the expiration date hardly matters. Thanks to the miracles of modern science, the Twinkies you buy for your kids today will still be edible when they get out of college. Get a twin-pack of Hostess fruit pies, that brown-bag staple, for 49¢; or a box of ten HoHo's for the same price.

Loaves of good ol' Wonder Bread can go for as little as 49¢ for two; you can save a dollar or so on a loaf of Wonder's "Beefsteak Rye" bread—about two-thirds off its supermarket price. And, if you're planning a cookout, this is the place to get all the hamburger and hot dog buns you need. On the average, most of these bread items tend to be about three days away from their expiration dates (which are a bit on the early side, themselves). So, if you have a big family which goes through bread quickly, or if you have room in the freezer to stock up, freshness should not be a problem.

Nor, by the way, is parking in the store's ample lot, or finding a time to shop here; Wonder/Hostess is open seven days a week. Hours are from 9 a.m. to 8 p.m. on weekdays, 9-6 on Saturdays, and 10-4 on Sundays. They accept food stamps, too.

CANDY AND NUTS

Blommer's Chocolate Factory

- 600 W. Kinzie St., Chicago; (312) 226-7700

Cooks who work with chocolate do their shopping here. They rave about how Blommer's melts better than any of the stuff you can get in the grocery store. It costs a heck of a lot less, too. What more could anyone ask?

Well, how about *free* chocolate? Okay! Samples of hard candy and chocolate chips are yours for the munching in the store, while for a mere 94 cents you can pick up two pounds—yup, that's right, two *pounds*—of cocoa powder, great for baking and for making homemade hot chocolate. A bag of Blommer's darker cocoa, made with beans imported from Sudan, is only $1.20 for the same size. The store offers several kinds of chips: Regular semi-sweet chips are $2.02 for a two-pound bag, while the same size of butterscotch-flavored and white chocolate chips are only $1.88 each.

Ardent chocoholics can buy a ten pound block of chocolate—dark, milk or white—for $14.80 to $15.24. Go nuts! Speaking of which, a half pound of salted mixed nuts in a gift box sells for $2.50, and the store has also created unusual gift sets of nuts and candies. How about a miniature chocolate golf caddy, with dyed white-chocolate coated golf balls? Blommer's store is open weekdays only, from 9-4.

Byblos 1

- 5212-14 N. Clark St., Chicago; (312)271-1005

One of several great bakeries in Andersonville, Byblos 1 is a combination bakery-grocery-deli selling many grains, spices and nuts in bulk, which can save you bundles. Go nuts with the roasted pistachios, just $3.99 a pound, and almonds for only $2.99 a pound. Byblos also has a wall of fresh spices for sale, blowing away regular grocery store prices.

Byblos is open daily from 9 a.m. until 9 p.m., and on Sundays from 9 a.m. until 2:30 p.m.

Farley's Outlet Store

- 3025 N. Pulaski Rd., Chicago; (312) 725-1661
- 3057 W. 26th St., Chicago; (312) 376-8105

Want to feel like a kid in a candy shop? Between the jars and bins filled with colorful sweets, and the low prices, you're sure to go wild in Farley's. Grab a bag and scoop up a pound of Tootsie Rolls for $1.65, or a pound of big, fat gumdrops for 59 cents. Or carob-covered raisins for a buck a pound. A two-pound container of nonpareils costs just $3.25, while a one-pound bag of chocolate-covered almonds is $1.39.

Which brings us to nuts. There are several different kinds of peanuts alone, starting at $1.95 per pound (not to mention those big, goofy marshmallow peanuts, three 12-ounce bags for a dollar); pistachios are $3.95 a pound, as are cashew "butts" (pieces). At these prices, you may go a bit nuts yourself.

Oops! Almost left out Farley's own brand of Teenage Mutant Ninja Turtle Fruit Snacks; the 30-ounce box sells for $2.50. Cowabunga, dude.

Gregory and Son Nuts Factory Outlet

- 2850 W. Devon Ave.; (312) 465-6787

Another great store for the nut in all of us. In addition to such staples as cashews and macadamia nuts, Gregory and Son also sells dozens of different hard candies, many of them sugarless and thus safe for diabetics. In fact, this store is a distributor for a company called Regal Health Foods (in spite of all the candy), and here, they bring their snacks directly to the public at reduced costs.

The lollipops aren't quite lollipop-shaped—they're more like mini-

blobs—but taste fine just the same and come in exotic flavors like watermelon and tangerine, along with the old favorites like orange and lime. Licorice twists, Jolly Rancher hard candies, and sugar water taffy are all priced under $2 a pound. Carob, cherry or chocolate chips are priced from $1.29 to $1.99 a pound—about half of what you'd pay for the same in grocery stores.

Pesto lovers rejoice—pine nuts are only $7.49 a pound here. Spanish peanuts are $1.70 a pound if roasted, and regular peanuts are $1.39 per pound, in the shell. Almonds, about $4 a pound, are available with or without salt. Pistachio meats are a steal at just $3.99 a pound, and sunflower seeds at $1.19 a pound make a great high-fiber snack. Various types of raisins and trail mixes are also for sale.

Those hard candies for diabetics (and anyone else interested in avoiding sugar) come in citrus and other neat flavors like pina colada, licorice, and coffee. The store is open from 9 a.m. to 8 p.m., Monday through Saturday; and on Sunday from 9-6.

Middle East Bakery and Grocery

- 1512 W. Foster Ave., Chicago; (312) 561-2224

See listing under "Bakeries," above.

Nuts on Clark

- 3830 N. Clark St.; (312) 549-6622
- Union Station Concourse, Chicago; (312) 876-NUTS (6887)

And other suburban locations

The selection here may drive you crazy, but you'd be nuts to not get your pistachios, almonds, or even chocolate here. The stores frequently offer tantalizing samples to shoppers, including caramels and salted peanuts.

"Nuts" has been in business for about fifteen years; during that time, it's established a substantial mail-order business. Buying in bulk allows them to pass savings on to customers. So do their no-frills shops, where fold-out tables covered with simple cloths serve as displays.

Some of the goodies you can af-

MR. CHEAP'S PICKS
Candy and Nuts

✔ **Blommer's Chocolate Factory**—Where the pastry chefs shop. Free samples too!

✔ **Superior Nut and Candy Bulk Stores**—Discount prices by the pound on name brand candies and fresh roasted nuts.

---

ford to squirrel away are Turkish pistachios for $7.99 a pound (unshelled are a buck more), squash seeds for $3.99 a pound, and sweetened banana chips for $3.19. Macadamias are under $11 a pound—still expensive, but probably as cheap as you'll find. Peanuts in the shell are priced at $2 a pound, and a half-pound bag of semi-sweet chocolate chips is $1.64.

Not all of the candies are made on the premises, such as the wide selection of "Jelly Belly" flavors; but the store's volume purchasing allows them to sell these for only $5.89 a pound.

Cholesterol-free candies, sugarless items, and carob-covered nuts and sweets are a focal point of the backroom, where you'll also find a miniature shrine to the Cubs and autographed photos of Nutty fans from coach Mike Ditka to Roger Daltrey of The Who.

NOC also sells fresh coffee beans, although these prices are not so remarkable—some varieties start at under $8.00 a pound. Meanwhile, gift baskets for every occasion are a specialty here, so if you're stuck wondering what to get your boss or cousin Quentin, stop in or call to check out their wide selection and prices.

Superior Nut and Candy Bulk Stores

- 3102 N. Central Ave., Chicago; (312) 237-4340
- 3243 N. Harlem Ave., Chicago; (312) 282-3930
- 4038 N. Nashville Ave., Chicago; (312) 282-3930
- 4408 S. Pulaski Rd., Chicago; (312) 247-1940
- 3046 W. 77th St., Chicago; (312) 434-5500

And other suburban locations

Everything in this store's name is true. You can save lots of money by purchasing these fine nuts and candies out of bulk dispensers, with a wide variety to choose from. Fresh roasted in-the-shell peanuts, for example, are just 99 cents a pound; raw Brazil nuts go for $2.59. And an assortment of roasted mixed nuts (the good ones, without any peanuts) sells for $3.69 a pound. Jumbo cashews get a bit pricier, but then, they always do; at $5.19 a pound, they're still better here than at other places. Sometimes, they may go on sale for as low as $3.99 a pound.

You can also find related items, like trail mix for $1.99 per pound, and "Hawaiian Delight" for the same price—a mix of dried fruits, peanuts, and macadamia nuts. Freshly ground natural peanut butter sells for $1.49 a pound. All of these nuts are roasted in cholesterol-free oil, in Superior's own factory.

Lest your sweet tooth be ignored, there is a treasure trove of candies here, too. These are *not* roasted in their own factory. Instead, they bear such familiar names as Tootsie Rolls and Mary Janes, just $1.79 a pound; a five-pound bag of Gummi Bears for $7.50; and jelly beans, 99 cents a pound. Superior also carries a selection of sugar-free and salt-free candies, including Eda "gourmet" candies at $4.99 per pound. Absolutely nobody need be left out of these bargains!

All Superior stores are open seven days a week.

COFFEE AND TEA

Coffee Chicago
- 801 N. Wabash Ave., Chicago; (312) 664-6415
- 1561 N. Wells St., Chicago; (312) 787-1211
- 2922 N. Clark St., Chicago; (312) 327-3228
- 3323 N. Clark St., Chicago; (312) 447-3323
- 6744 N. Sheridan Ave., Chicago; (312) 274-1880
- 828 N. State St., Chicago; (312) 335-0625

What an anomaly: A coffee shop that's bright and airy, roomy, but not exorbitantly priced! For gourmet java, Coffee Chicago's prices hover in the $7-$8 a pound range. Their Chicago Blend, Costa Rica, Kenya AA coffees, and Moka Java are $7.95 a pound, as are the espresso and French roast. Decaf versions are available for many of these flavors, mostly about $8.45 a pound. The most expensive of the lot is Hawaiian Kona, rocketing out of Mr. C's range at $12.50.

Coffee & Tea Exchange
- 3300 N. Broadway, Chicago; (312) 528-2241
- 833 W. Armitage Ave., Chicago; (312) 929-6730

With all the coffee craze going on in Chicago, it's a wonder there aren't more places like this where you can buy your own fresh gourmet beans to take home—at reasonable prices. After all, even if you have a Starbucks on your corner (at this point, who doesn't), you still need something to get you up and out of the house, right?

At the Broadway location, C & T roasts its own coffee beans in dozens of flavors. At both stores, these are sitting out in huge bins, ready to be scooped up for you by the busy clerks. Their pace is understandable, considering that most varieties are in the price range of $4-$5 per pound—several dollars less than at the trendy cafes, which are really geared to business by the cup.

Coffee & Tea Exchange always features weekly specials at incredible prices. One "Coffee of the Week" is always available at just $3.44 a pound, easily half the price you'd find anywhere else; it may be a basic French roast, or a unique house blend of two or three types of bean. Then there's the "Flavor of the Week" for $4.95, which on Mr. C's visit was "Tiramisu"; you'll also find a "Decaf of the Week," like Viennese Roast, for $5.49 a pound.

Of course, you can getta cuppa fresh-brewed here if you wish, and sit at the natural wood counter (not that much room for sitting, though; great for carry-out). Again, these prices are an improvement over the high-powered cafes. A single cup of the house blend is 74 cents; a double espresso is just a dollar. And you can get a whole mocha steamer for $1.80. Similar prices for cappuccino, flavored coffees, and iced coffees as well.

C & T also sells a myriad selection of loose teas, too; these start at just 69 cents per ounce, with exotic flavors such as "Passion Fruit" and all kinds of English and Oriental brews. Needless to say, they also sell all the apparatus you could ever need to get you the most out of the above-mentioned delights.

Cool Beans
- 2562 N. Clark St., Chicago; (312) 665-2700

Cool Beans is a gourmet coffee shop that's every bit as good as Starbucks—only cheaper, less crowded, and less yuppified. Having just opened in 1993, they have already expanded to include a larger retail space and a full cafe serving basic vegetarian meals. Cool!

In the bulk coffee section, prices start at $5.99 per pound, ranging up to $7.99. Columbian Supremo is $6.50 a pound. Kenya AA (use it to make a mean *tiramisu*) is $7.50 a pound, as is decaf espresso and the "Roaster's Choice" blend. Other un-

MR. CHEAP'S PICKS
Coffee and Tea

✔ **Coffee & Tea Exchange—**
Gourmet coffee beans as low as
$3.44 a pound. Won't lose any
sleep over *that*.

---

usual flavors at the high end include
hazelnut truffle and chocolate raspberry.

Cool Beans is open early and
late seven days a week, from 6 a.m.
to 11 p.m.

Gold Standard/Chalet Wine Shops
- 40 E. Delaware St., Chicago; (312) 787-8555
- 405 W. Armitage Ave., Chicago; (312) 266-7155
- 3000 N. Clark St., Chicago; (312) 935-9400
- 1525 E. 53rd St., Chicago; (312) 324-5000

And many other suburban locations
Located all over town, these large
shops proffer a vast selection of
wines, spirits, beers, champagnes,
and even some of the fine foods to go
with them—all at good prices. Wander through the winding aisles, pick
up a catalog of the latest deals, sample a bite of cheese. Everything is
very clearly marked with prices and
full-bodied descriptions, and the low-
pressure salespeople are quite helpful
if you need them.

Along with its wines, Gold

GENERAL MARKETS

Asia Provision Company
- 5426 N. Broadway, Chicago; (312) 769-1553

Mr. C often advises that you stick to
small ethnic food markets, like this
Chinese one in Edgewater, if you
want to buy fresh food at ridiculously

Standard/Chalet also sells gourmet
coffee by the pound at amazing
prices. Columbian supremo and espresso roast were recently seen selling for just $3.99 a pound, while
gourmet flavors like hazelnut and mocha java start slightly higher at $4.99
a pound. These stores are open seven
days a week.

Bourgeois Pig! Coffee, Tea and Spice Co.
- 748 W. Fullerton Ave., Chicago; (312) 883-JAVA (3282)

The tongue-in-cheek name of this
cafe lets you know that it's not a
hoity-toity place. It is located in Lincoln Park, just east of Halsted, but
for a gourmet cup o'joe, its prices are
reasonable.

This newly-opened store was
still experimenting with its house
roast when Mr. C stopped in, and
hadn't yet settled upon the formula at
the time of this writing. They do have
a good selection of beans from
around the world, at reasonable
prices: French roast sells for $7 a
pound, mocha java is $8, dark Suma-
tra is $7.75, and dark Columbian cof-
fee is $6.75.

For teatime, a quarter pound of
loose chamomile is $3.75, rose hip
tea (chock-full of vitamin C!) is
$1.75, and exotic lemon grass tea
sells at $1.63 for a quarter pound.

The shop, which is primarily a
sit-down cafe, opens at 6:30 a.m.
weekdays and stays open til 11 p.m.
Monday through Thursday and until
midnight on Friday. On weekends
they open at 9 a.m., closing at midnight Saturday and 10 p.m. Sunday.
All the requisite board games, Trivial
Pursuit et. al., are on hand.

low prices. Once you start this, you
may never go back to Jewel again!

Asia Provision Company, like
many of these tiny stores, sells in
bulk to restaurants—but is also open
to the general public, all at wholesale
or near-wholesale prices. Some of the

MR. CHEAP'S PICKS
General Markets

✔ **Chicago Meat House**—This South Side butcher and grocery is like a discount supermarket.

✔ **Cub Foods**—This one, to the north, *is* a discount supermarket.

---

bounty found here recently included cashews at $2.85 a pound (great to toss in stir-fry), bean thread noodles at $1.12 a package, and Chinese almond cookies—just $3.70 for a box of about 100.

Veggie prices, of course, vary with the season; but fresh broccoli was seen here in summer for only 85 cents a pound(!) when Mr. C went shopping. Peppers, carrots, cabbage, and other vegetables that are staples of Chinese cooking, as well as fruits and other produce, are super-fresh here, just out of the boxes.

Chicago Meat House
● 4750 S. California Ave., Chicago; (312) 927-3200

Don't be misled by the name—there's more here than "meats" the eye. This is a complete discount supermarket, where bulk fresh and frozen meat is just the beginning of the savings. Yes, you can get their freshly made Polish sausage for $1.98 per pound, lean ground beef for $1.89 a pound, or a 2 1/2 pound package of thick center cut pork chops for $5.20. And there is a full service deli counter, slicing up things like pastrami or roast beef for $3.29 a pound. And yes, you can also buy massive quantities of frozen meats, such as a 20-pound box of spare ribs for $25, or similar deals on frozen hamburger patties and chicken breasts.

But there's so much more here! Also in the freezer aisle, for instance, Mr. C found a two-pound box of

Alaskan sea scallops for $13.95, and further along, all kinds of Stouffer's frozen prepared foods. Not the kind you usually see in the little boxes, but bulk "food service" packages, like a six-pound lasagna for $14.95. Enough to feed the whole family, and then some. Or, how about six portions of chicken Kiev for $5.99, ready to heat and serve?

Elsewhere in this clean and bright store, you may find eggs from 85 cents a dozen; as well as milk, packaged foods, and just about anything else you'd expect in any grocery store. There is also a soda and liquor section, with similarly discounted prices. A 1.75 liter bottle of Smirnoff vodka sells for $14.99, and one liter of Bailey's Irish Cream is $23.95; lesser-known brands offer even better deals, like a 1.75 liter bottle of Hannah and Hogg whiskey for $10.99. Sodas, such as Royal Crown cola and A & W root beer, are priced at $6.25 for a case of 24 cans. Plus bags of ice and styrofoam coolers.

The Chicago Meat House (see what we mean about the name?) is open from 8 a.m. to 5:30 p.m. on weekdays, and from 8-5 on Saturdays. They have a spacious parking lot, and they accept cash, checks, credit cards, and food stamps.

Cub Foods
● 2627 N. Elston Ave., Chicago; (312) 252-6400
And many other suburban locations

This popular supermarket chain has one branch in town, smack dab in the middle of a "miracle mile" of outlets in the Clybourn Corridor. It's a full-service, discount store, claiming to offer lower prices than its competitors in every department—including meats, produce, deli, and all the rest. It would be rather pointless to relate any specific examples, grocery prices fluctuating as they constantly do; suffice it to say, lots of folks swear by this place, and will drive a bit out of their way to shop here. Cub Foods also has an in-store pharmacy, with equally competitive prices on items like aspirin, cold remedies, beauty products, and vitamins; this is a particularly useful thing to remember, especially since Cub is open 24 hours a day. So, whether you're up at 4:00 in the morning with a cold, or a hankering for Pop-Tarts, you'll find 'em here and save some money in the process.

Old World Market
- 5129 N. Broadway, Chicago; (312) 989-4440

Caribbean, African, and Latin American foods are sold pre-packaged, as well as in bulk, at this cosmopolitan market just above Argyle Street.

A twenty-five pound sack of Uncle Ben's rice was priced at $14.99. Goya coconut milk is $1.09 a can. Knorr's Tamarind Soup Base is just 65 cents, and banana chips are $4 a pound. The store also independently distributes a variety of staples under the Little Africa label, such as a hefty five-pound bag of rice flour for just $2.49.

At the deli, catfish, and tripe are just 79 cents a pound each. Dried goods like alligator peppers, African beans, bitter leaves, and dried crayfish are also for sale. Produce items like yucca at 89 cents a pound, and tomatillos at $1.49 a pound, will let you tally up a lot of food without a lot of cash. Exotic delicacies like fresh lotus roots are $2.25 a pound, and canned quail eggs are only $1.09 for a 425-gram jar. Free parking is provided in the adjacent lot.

HEALTH FOOD AND VITAMINS

Broadway Vitamins
- 3321 N. Broadway, Chicago; (312) 404-9000

This small Wrigleyville shop manages to pack a punch with vitamins and related health care products at very good prices. In fact, their everyday discounts range from 10% to 30% below retail prices. And there are always several selected items that are further reduced as in-store specials. Among the bargains Mr. C found on his visit were a 100-capsule bottle of Nature's Way echinacea, a sort of organic cold-stopper, reduced from a regular price of $9.95 to $6.95; and a 100-tablet size of Source Naturals time-release vitamin C, with 1000 mg, marked down from $10.98 to $7.98. Broadway also carries body-building products, like Champion's "Heavyweight Gainer 900" powdered mix. A 3.3-pound tub was recently on sale for $19.95, reduced (pardon the pun) from $23.95. The store is open seven days a week.

The Organic Tomato
- 22 W. Maple St., (312) 935-7783

This is an all-purpose market, featuring a wide selection of well-priced, non-irradiated herbs and spices and freshly prepared vegetarian items. Veggie burritos, for example, are huge. A chili burrito, made with soy cheese and cilantro, is $3.95—and quite possibly enough for two meals. Japanese nori rolls are similarly gargantuan, and only $2.95 each. Falafel burgers are also $2.95.

Other items, such as cosmetics, are not necessarily bargains here. But some good buys can be spotted in the main grocery area of the store, such as Rainforest Crisp cereal, $2.95 for the 13.5 ounce box, about 70 cents off retail.

Sherwyn's Health Food Shop
- 645 W. Diversey Pkwy., Chicago; (312) 477-1934

For the serious vegetarian, homeopathy enthusiast, food allergy sufferer or the just plain health-minded, this enormous store (it carries over 17,000 products) is a haven that's been in business for over twenty years. The crowded bicycle racks out front make it easy to spot the store from Clark Street. With so much to see—granola, grains, and spices in bulk, walls of vitamins and even over a dozen kinds of honey, you can spend hours and hours here.

The staff is as cruelty-free as the cosmetics; they're always happy to explain products and answer questions, especially in the homeopathy

MR. CHEAP'S PICKS
Health Food and Vitamins

✔ **Sherwyn's Health Food Shop**—Here's a health food supermarket, with prices to keep your wallet in good shape.

department (where Longevity brand hayfever pills sell for $3.95 for the 100 count package). In the cosmetics section, a pint of Kiss My Face SPF 15 lotion for $7.99 was just one of the many bargains seen recently.

Vegetarian staples like Edensoy soy milk are always price-reduced. Ice Bran frozen desserts are sixty cents off at $2.19 a pint—with many flavors, such as Carob Super Crunch, Strawberry and Almond Espresso, in stock.

Fantastic Foods' Nature Burger mix is just $1.59, fifty cents off re-

tail; and Yoshi's Tofu is priced at a mere 89 cents a pound. After the Fall raspberry lemonade is only $1.49 a quart; a 16.9-ounce bottle of Evian water (that's Naive spelled backwards, y'know) is just 85 cents; and loose chamomile flower tea is about $2.50 per quarter pound. Sherwyn's busy juice bar serves up carrot juice ($4.49 a quart), beet-carrot juice, and drinks made from mixed vegetables including spinach.

Bulk foods are available prebagged or do-it-yourself. Raw almonds are a good deal at $3.19 a pound, and organic, sulfur-free raisins are only $1.69 a pound. Blue corn meal and quinoa flour spaghetti both sell for $3 a pound. Buy as much as you like—stocking up here can keep you and your budget healthy.

Sherwyn's is open daily. Monday to Friday hours are from 10 a.m. to 8 p.m; Saturdays from 10-7, and Sundays 10-6. Delivery is available and parking is free with a $25 purchase—another good argument for bulk shopping!

MEAT AND FISH

Chicago Meat House
• 4750 S. California Ave., Chicago; (312) 927-3200
See listing under "General Markets," above.

Columbus Meat Market
• 906 W. Randolph St., Chicago; (312) 829-2480
Just west of the loop, the Fulton Market area is where restaurants buy much of their meat, fish, and other provisions. Most of the businesses here are wholesale only, but Mr. C has found a few in which you can get the same great deals. Columbus is one of several; a small but friendly shop offering choice cuts of beef, lamb, pork, and chicken. On any given visit, you may find such specials as T-bone steaks at $3.69 a pound, or New York strip steaks at a dollar more. Pork loin goes for $1.79 a pound, lamb chops for $1.99, and

so on. You can also get a ten-pound box of breaded veal patties for a mere $19. The selection here is not extensive, "but what's there is cherse," to quote an old Tracy-Hepburn movie.

Gabriel & Gabriel
• 5621 N. Clark St., Chicago; (312) 275-5635
Specializing in fresh seafood, this neighborhood family market caters to Philippine and Oriental customers. Lobster meat sells for as low as $3.99 a pound, or it can go up to $9.50, depending on the season and other market conditions. There are other supermarket-type provisions, such as Chef's Choice coconut milk, only 75 cents for a 13.5-ounce can.

Open daily from 8:00 in the morning to 8:30 in the evening; Saturdays 7:30 a.m. to 8:30 p.m., Sundays 7-7.

MR. CHEAP'S PICKS
Meat and Fish

✔ **Pepe's Meat Packing**—You can buy where the restaurants buy, in the Fulton Market area, and save big bucks.

✔ **L. Isaacson & Stein Fish Company**—Same idea, same area, different kettle of fish.

Good Morgan Kosher Fish Market
• 2948 W. Devon Ave., Chicago; (312) 764-8115

Straight from the dock to you, Good Morgan sells the freshest fish at great prices on the corner of Devon and Sacramento.

Mr. C would like to remind you that these prices fluctuate widely due to market conditions; but, during a recent visit, lake perch was $2.98 a pound, smoked whitefish was $3.95, Boston cod was under $6, and yellow fin tuna was under $10 a pound.

Good Morgan is open Monday through Wednesday from 7:00 a.m. to 5:00 p.m., Thursday from 7 a.m. to 6 p.m., and Friday from 7-3 only. It's closed on Saturdays for Sabbath, but reopens Sunday from 7 a.m. to 12.

L. Isaacson & Stein Fish Co.
• 800 W. Fulton St., Chicago; (312) 421-2444

At the eastern edge of the Fulton Market itself, Isaacson & Stein is a large operation selling freshly-caught and frozen fish to the restaurant business and to the public. Walk in and browse around, and you'll see open bins of whatever happens to be in season. Mr. C found such delicacies as fresh shrimp for $6 a pound, red snapper for $4.50 a pound, mussels for $1.40 a pound—and oysters in the shell, just 35 cents each (ever tried prying one of these suckers open?).

In the freezer cases, you may see even better deals, like a five-pound box of shrimp for just $15, or hefty swordfish steaks for $7.00 a pound. Oh, and if you're buying whole fresh fish, the nice folks at I & S will clean and fillet them for you at no charge. And, unlike many wholesale operations which close up by midday, this store is open all day, regular business hours.

Nearby, another great place to go fishing for bargain seafood is **Pick Fisheries**, at 702 W. Fulton St., telephone (312) 226-4700. Open Monday through Friday, 7 a.m. to 4:30 p.m., and Saturday 6 a.m. to 2 p.m.

Olympic Meat Packers
• 810 W. Randolph St., Chicago; (312) 666-2222

Also along the two-block "meat district" stretch of Randolph, Olympic Meat Packers is another small shop which has good deals on interesting items along with cuts of meat. T-bones here may go as low as $2.99 a pound, and center cuts of roast beef for $1.79; but, in addition, this place has things like "Mississippi sausage," a spicy blend stuffed into a bright red casing, at $2.29 a pound. Your basic Polish sausage goes for $1.79 a pound. Or, try some frozen pork shishkebabs, ready for grilling; a case of twenty costs $13.

Pepe's Meat Packing
• 853 W. Randolph St., Chicago; (312) 421-2488

Across the street from Olympic, Pepe's is a much larger operation offering a more extensive variety of similar deals. Here, T-bones were seen at $8.99 for three pounds; pork loin, whole or split, for $1.69 a pound; and a five-pound box of ground chuck was on sale for $8.45. Mr. C also saw some meaty-looking baby back ribs for $1.69 a pound. Obviously, the prices at each of these stores will rise and fall over time; but with the closeness and competition between them, you can easily shop around to get the best prices and selection.

Robert's Fish Market
- 2916 W. Devon Ave., Chicago;
  (312) 761-3424

A few doors down from Good Morgan, Robert's is another market selling fresh-from-the-dock stuff, and all pure Kosher. But psst! Hey Bob! The fake hammerhead shark on the wall by the phone really ought to go...

Tacky plastic wall hangings notwithstanding, the prices here are fantastic. Per pound, Robert's sells fresh lox for $12.98, sea bass for just $5.89, perch for $3.89, whitefish for $3.29, red snapper for $6.89, and rainbow trout for only $4.09. Free delivery, too.

Robert's is open six days a week, and closed on Saturdays for the Jewish sabbath.

Vienna Beef Outlet Store
- 2501 N. Damen Ave., Chicago;
  (312) 235-6652

You'd think that, in almost any kind of shopping, there's a bargain to be found by going directly to the source. Alas, Mr. C has found, this is not always the case. There is no shortage of places to buy Vienna Beef products, whether cooked up or frozen, around Chicagoland; coming here to their factory and corporate offices,

you can get 'em both ways—but, surprisingly, you may not necessarily save much money by doing so.

There is both a deli and a store on these premises. The deli offers hot and cold sandwiches, plus cold cuts by the pound, like any sandwich shop; it's also priced like any sandwich shop, so Mr. C will conserve his ink. It's not overpriced, certainly, but nothing to write home—or a book—about.

For packaged goods, again, the prices are not spectacular. A 16-ounce package of Jumbo Beef Franks, for instance, costs $3.49—about what you'd expect to pay at your local supermarket. A 12-ounce package of knockwurst goes for $2.49; same price for a 12-ouncer of Deli-Lite Beef Franks, 91% fat free. They ought to be similarly reduced in price, but sorry, they just aren't.

They also have a freezer section, which includes lots of non-Vienna and non-meat items, such as a two-pound frozen cheesecake for $4.25, or a 15-ounce package of blintzes for $2.00. Some of these products appear to have been in the freezer cases for quite a while. The store is open weekdays from 9:00 a.m. to 4:45 in the afternoon, and from 9-2 on Saturdays.

PRODUCE

Fruit Wagon Produce and Deli
- 2958 W. Devon Ave., Chicago;
  (312) 338-2296

One of the dozens of bargain shops on Devon, Fruit Wagon is a neighborhood store that sells just gorgeous fruit at great prices.

When Mr. C went for a visit, blueberries were a mere 89 cents for 3/4 of a pound, and seedless green grapes were just 29 cents a pound. Fresh okra was 49 cents a pound and plump tomatoes were flying off the shelves at just 39 cents for a pound.

Jump on the wagon and buy one of their bowling-ball size cantaloupes for $1.69 apiece, or red delicious apples for only 69 cents a pound. These prices are, of course, subject to change—but they're sure to be as

good as the produce.

Monroe Finer Foods
- 1619 N. Damen Ave., (312)
  862-0700

James Monroe, the owner of this tiny but busy Bucktown produce market, is at O'Hare every morning at 4:30 waiting for the freshest shipments of fruit and vegetables from all over the country. The produce is oversized and in great shape, prompting many shoppers to leave with more than what was on their lists.

Prices here may not always beat your local supermarket, but they are competitive—and the quality is first-rate. Gargantuan grapefruits were seen here for 79 cents a pound. Mt. Ranier cherries are $2.89 a pound, giant eggplants are 69 cents a pound,

MR. CHEAP'S PICKS
Produce

✔ **N & G Produce**—Again, in the Fulton Market district, this fruit, vegetable, and grain wholesaler is open to the public.

and unbelieveably huge Kentucky tomatoes are $1.19 a pound. Zucchini are 98 cents a pound and a ten-ounce bag of fresh spinach is $1.49. Humungous cantaloupes are $1.49 each, avocadoes are 69 cents each, and almost-ripe green figs (these are supposed to be green) are 39 cents apiece. Red delicious apples are only 69 cents a pound.

N & G Produce
* 902 W. Randolph St., Chicago; (312) 226-7552

Along with all of the wholesale/retail butcher shops along Randolph Street, you'll find this produce market which sells to restaurants, hotels, and the public. It's more like a mini-farmer's market, with plenty of fruit, vegetables, grains and nuts all sitting in open bins. A large blackboard overhead lists most of the prices; anything else you see, just ask. Mr. C found iceberg lettuce at 75 cents a head, four-pound sacks of red potatoes for a dollar, green grapes at $1.25 a pound, and much more.

There is a large section with several varieties of rices—brown, long-grain, even jasmine—all at 75 cents a pound. Same price for bins of beans: Red, kidney, lima, lentil....and, in the same area, you'll go nuts over salted-in-the-shell peanuts for a dollar a pound, or pine nuts for $9.50 a pound.

In addition to produce, N & G sells all kinds of imported products; dried pastas, spices (a 16-oz. jar of ground nutmeg for $3.75), condiments, and more. Get a three-liter can of extra virgin olive oil for just $13.00. If buying in bulk is good for you, so is this store.

Stanley's Fresh Fruit and Vegetables
* 1558 N. Elston Ave., Chicago; (312) 276-8050

Located at the busy intersection of North and Elston, this free-standing building looks more like it should be a convenience store. In a way, perhaps it is; surrounded by a parking lot, it's a place where you can park the car and dash in to pick up some fresh veggies for dinner tonight. The selection, meanwhile is far greater than any such store, or even many supermarkets. And the prices can't be beat.

Pick a pint of blueberries for just 98 cents, or four pounds of bananas for a dollar. At the height of the summer season, cantaloupes were seen selling here for a mere $1.49—for *three* melons! And three pounds of plum tomatoes were $1.99, while red potatoes went for 49 cents per pound. These prices, of course, will change throughout the year; but they, like the quality of the food itself, should remain consistently good.

FURNITURE

NEW

Affordable Portables
- 2608-10 N. Clark St.; (312) 935-6160
- Plaza Del Grato, 1736 Algonquin Rd., Arlington Heights; (708) 398-3717

This spunky, family-run store has been around for fifteen years, specializing mainly in futons, sofas, and contemporary furniture. Some of the frames and tables are made from particleboard and veneer, but at least the finishes here are more realistic-looking than those in other inexpensive stores. Factory seconds, mixed in among the first-quality items, will save you even more bucks.

The store is crowded with more merchandise than there's room for, and more customers than the help can handle. When they do get to you, the salespeople can be on the pushy side, but not to the point of annoyance.

Futon frames start as low as $80 here. Aspen Frame futons sell for $200 (futon extra), which is $100 less than retail, and these are all made from solid hardwood. An all-hardwood frame sofa was seen for $329. Other bargains include such items as a four-drawer writing desk for $99, and a queen-size platform bed for $120 (down from $200). They also carry some European designs, like the ever-popular Wassily chair for $149.95.

The North Clark store opens daily at 10:30 a.m., and stays open Monday and Thursday until 8, Tuesday, Wednesday, and Friday until 7, and Saturday until 6. Sundays are the exception, with hours from 12-5. Hours are slightly different at the Arlington Heights location, which is also open seven days a week.

Aronson Furniture and Appliances
- 3939 N. Ashland Ave., Chicago; (312) 871-6900
- 5657 W. Belmont Ave., Chicago; (312) 889-0312
- 1379 N. Milwaukee Ave., Chicago; (312) 235-9000
- 4630 S. Ashland Ave., Chicago; (312) 376-3401
- 3401 W. 47th St., Chicago; (312) 376-3400
- 2301 W. 95th St., Chicago; (312) 445-1888
- River Oaks West Shopping Center, Calumet City; (708) 891-1700

Since 1940, Aronson has been offering mid-range brands in all kinds of major goods for the home. Over the years, it has grown into one of Chicago's high-volume retailers, yet it hasn't lost sight of its own humble beginnings. As you can see above, it maintains branches in all parts of the city, north and south; this is the kind of place for regular folks who need to stretch the budget, but want good value for their money. Prices here can range from 30% to 60% off retail for furniture, appliances, and even jewelry.

Starting from scratch? Aronson has complete room ensembles at discount, in traditional and contemporary styles. A ten-piece living room set, with a total list price of $4599 if everything was purchased separately, was recently offered as a package deal for $2500. It included a two-piece sectional sofa and chair, upholstered in a bold and splashy modern print; plus a cocktail table, two wood-and-glass end tables, and two lamps (the other "pieces" were fabric coating for the sofa and chair, and a warranty). You can, of course, purchase individual items. Mr. C saw a leather-upholstered Stratolounger chair, listed at $1050, selling for $650. Among the brand names sold here are Bassett, Singer, Broyhill, and many other well-known names.

Bedrooms work the same way, again with many different styles to choose from. One complete set featured the popular black-lacquered look; it consisted of a queen-size mattress and boxspring, black-and-mirrored headboard, matching dresser, mirror, chest, two nightstands, and two lamps. The retail value was $3699; Aronson's price was $1899. If you just want the bed alone, the extra-firm Ther-A-Pedic set was reduced from $879 list to $549.

Aronson's stores are open seven days a week, including weekday evenings. They also offer very flexible credit plans—as one person here put it, "If people see something they like, we'll give them every chance to buy it."

But wait—there's more! Aronson also has two clearance centers, **the Aronson Bargain Warehouses**, located at 2440 N. Milwaukee Ave., telephone (312) 276-2066, and 8530 S. Cottage Grove Ave., telephone (312) 873-8999. At these cavernous, no-frills places, you can find incredible savings on leftovers, closeouts, and slightly-damaged floor models. You never know what will turn up here, but there is sure to be a vast selection of sofas selling for as little as $120, bedroom sets as low as $200, refrigerators under $300, and color televisions from $166, plus lamps, chairs, and lots more. Everything is sold "as is," of course, with all sales final.

Brook Furniture Outlet
- 2525 N. Elston Ave., Chicago; (312) 593-5940

At Brook's regular stores throughout the region, you can rent (or rent-to-own) handsome contemporary furniture for every room in the house. At their clearance center, along this outlet-laden stretch of Elston, you can

get new and used furniture at savings of 30% to 70% below the manufacturers' suggested prices. Those makers include such estimable names as Bassett, Sealy, and La-Z-Boy. In the front room, there are sofas, loveseats, tables, and dining room sets; further into the back, they have bedding and desks, including office furniture.

Among the new pieces, you may find a sofa with a list price of $700 selling for $465; or an upholstered easy chair for $200, about $100 off list. These are available in tweeds, bold colors, and prints, as well as some traditional looks. Inexpensive veneer-covered coffee tables, like a round cherry-finished model about two feet in diameter, may sell for as little as $60—some $35 below the list price. You can rent these at a monthly rate (after twelve months, they're yours), but the finance charges in this arrangement seem to bring the cost back up to the original retail price. Better to buy.

Cash, checks, and credit cards are accepted; Brook offers a 90-day layaway plan, and delivery is available for a fee. Hours are Tuesdays through Fridays from 10 a.m. to 6 p.m., and Saturdays from 10-4. Closed Sunday and Monday. Brook also has a suburban outlet store, located in Elk Grove Village.

Buycorp
- 4301 S. Pulaski Rd., Chicago; (312) 523-1590

This may be a Mr. Cheap first—a furniture store located inside of a supermarket. Talk about "special on aisle seven"...crazy! This is really two businesses running side by side, but yes—walk in, through the produce section to the rear, and you'll find the entrance to a large warehouse room filled with new, contemporary furniture, most of which are closeout models which this enterprising place has bought up. They're in fine condition, a mix of solid wood furniture and some cheaper, pressed-wood-and-veneer models. Mr. C found a 68-inch tall armoire (of that cheaper variety) for $199; same price for a glider easy chair upholstered in a handsome blue pin-dot fabric. Other easy chairs, stationary ones, were reduced from a list price of $279 to just $149; and a two-piece sofa and loveseat ensemble, retailing for $1,090, was seen for a more comfortable $699. Put an attractive ceramic table lamp next to these for $45. There are also lots of dining room table and chair sets; and, in fact, chairs of every kind are stacked up to the high ceiling, and sofas are even loaded onto deep metal shelves. There's quite a lot to see.

European Furniture Warehouse
- 2145 W. Grand Ave., Chicago; (312) 243-1955

Sometimes, you have to go a bit out of your way to find something out of the ordinary. West of downtown, European Furniture Warehouse is a vast treasure trove—70,000 square feet, in fact—of modern, fancy furniture at fantastic savings. The prices on these living room and dining room pieces can be as much as 20% to 60% below retail prices. Why? Because this family operation makes and sells *copies* of trendsetting designs by Barcelona, Breuer, Mies van der Rohe, and others.

A chaise lounge, for instance, in the Le Corbusier style, made to sell elsewhere for $1,129, was recently seen here for $799—in leather or dappled ponyskin coverings. A Biedemier chest, with a marble top, was not $1,695 but just $995. And a stack of Bauhaus-style Wassily chairs was on sale for $139 each, in chrome and grey, tan, or black leather. The warehouse goes on and on, with coffee tables, sectional sofas, dining sets and more.

Upstairs in a loft space, EFW has its collection of traditional English and French designs. Mr. C's home furnishings expert also noticed a steel and brass "sleigh bed," which she had seen at Bloomie's for over $4,000, selling here for $2,399. And a French country-style writing desk, in burled walnut, was a handsome find at $1,200—well below its list price of $2,000.

In addition to stylish furniture, the owner evidently has a taste for sports cars as well. One side of the warehouse is stocked not with Le Corbusiers, but with Corvettes, lovingly (and noisily) being restored during Mr. C's visit. Somehow, these seem to complement each other perfectly. EFW is open seven days a week.

Furniture Connection
- 3128 N. Broadway (2nd Floor), Chicago; (312) 281-7411

Upstairs from one of Mr. C's literary haunts, Barbara's Bookstore, is this large and attractive shop selling contemporary furniture and bedding at good discounts. There are some traditional looks too, but you'll probably want to go for the trendy Euro and Far East styles. Prices can be as much as 40% below retail, especially during special promotions.

Mr. C relaxed luxuriously in an imported Italian leather sofa, sale priced at just $599 and available in three different colors. Upholstered couches and chairs come with your choice of fabrics, which can be custom-ordered at no extra charge. A full-length black futon and matching metal frame was seen recently for $250; put a Japanese tri-folding rice-paper screen beside it for $79, or a 500-watt halogen torch lamp for $27. The store even offers free decorating consultation, to create that special look for your living room, dining room, or bedroom.

Speaking of which, Furniture Connection also sells name-brand mattresses at discounts of 25% to 50% off retail. These start as low as $43 for a firm twin mattress or boxspring; in full size, each piece is $57. They go up through several grades, all the way to "Ultra pillow top super plush," in which queen sets are $569 and king sets are $769, top o' the line. These fancier models include a frame, and delivery, at no extra charge.

The store is open weekdays from 10 a.m. to 8 p.m., Saturdays from 10-5, and Sundays from 11-5.

Furniture Liquidation Center

- 5923 N. Clark St., Chicago; (312) 275-5888
- 2600 W. 79th St., Chicago; (312) 778-8727

This large, rambling showroom is absolutely jam-packed with closeouts taken directly from national manufacturers in furniture for the living room, dining room, and bedroom, along with mattress sets and decorative items. The materials range from chintzy to solid, and styles range from elegantly traditional to brightly modern; there's plenty to see in everything.

A European-style glass top dining table was seen by Mr. C, with four high-backed chairs in black wood and burgundy upholstery; its retail price was $849, but the set was selling for $549. If that's not your speed, choose instead from five-piece dining table and chair sets for $99 and $129; they're more of the assemble-it-yourself variety, but not bad looking.

For the living room, you may like a traditional, very American blue-checked sofa, loveseat, and chair combination, selling for nearly half-price at $799. And you can class up the bedroom with a cherry wood set by V.B. Williams, including a queen-size headboard, triple-dresser, hutch, mirror, and armoire. It should sell for over $3,000 at fancier stores, but here, it's only $2,100. Again, at the other end of the spectrum, FLC has things like bunk beds from $39 (Mr. C liked a handsome one with a dark pine frame, reduced from $399 to $249). They also have closeouts on Sealy mattress sets.

To add some spice to these rooms, there are table lamps, floor lamps, and framed prints of every size, shape, and color scheme. The salesmen are friendly, and financing is also available. Furniture Liquidation Center just opened its South Side location in the spring of '93. Formerly a lumberyard, this branch is even bigger than the Uptown store, and similarly crammed with bargains. Open seven days a week; daily from 10 a.m. to 8 p.m., and Sundays from 11-5.

The Furniture Store

- 222 W. Kinzie St., Chicago; (312) 661-0124

From a $9 brass magazine rack to $119 Italian beechwood chairs, you'll find a lot more than just sofas and loveseats here, all high-quality in classic to contemporary styles. The store is simple to find, located right across the street from the Merchandise Mart.

A cherrywood Shaker-style coffeetable is just $109, and a big, comfy sofa upholstered in a soft burlap-like material was seen for $500. For elsewhere around the house, an all-glass dining table was $299; a six-drawer oak armoire was $699; and six-foot tall halogen torch lamps were just $39. A recent special sale included Windsor chairs, perfect for the dining room or kitchenette, at $40 apiece—from a list price of $60. There's not enough room to display everything on the main floor, so check out the not-so-tidy lower level room for more bargains.

How do they manage the savings? The Furniture Store buys directly from manufacturers—and, in many cases, you have to do your own assembly. Since they buy direct, you can pick out your own fabric on upholstered items, too.

More bonuses: Free popcorn to munch on while shopping, and a sense of humor evident on the assembly ratings tags attached to each piece—ranging from "Easy" to "Don't make plans." Open seven days a week. Hours on weekdays are from 9:30 a.m. to 6:00 p.m., Saturdays 12-6, Sundays 12-5.

Gaines Furniture Outlet

- 4944 W. 73rd St., Chicago; (708) 496-0355

Newly relocated into a giant warehouse just below Midway Airport, this South Side store buys out factory overstocks and second-quality merchandise, and resells them at super-cheap prices. Wouldya believe a four-piece bedroom set, including headboard, bed frame, mirror, and dresser, for $145? Or a sofa, with matching loveseat and chair, for $138 (plus other styles at $268 and $399)? Well, believe it—though, before we go on, Mr. C should point out that this is one of those instances where "you gets what you pays for." Naturally, you're not going to find too many major brand names at these prices. Much of this stock is made from cheap wood, or that pressed-chips-and-veneer material. But hey, this may be all you need. It's hard to argue, after all, with a pine dinette table and four chairs for $99, or a glass and brass set for $89.

You can find good deals on inexpensive accessories for the home, such as halogen torch lamps for $19, or brass-plated coat trees for $10. Gaines also sells mattresses and bed frames; Mr. C found a white lacquered brass daybed frame (no mattress) for a mere $38. Mattresses themselves sell for as little as $12 per twin-size piece; even at this price, these are innerspring mattresses, not foam. You do have to buy them in sets, though. Better models range from $49 per piece in full size, for example, up to $89 per piece; even king size only goes up to $109 per piece. These carry limited warranties of up to twenty years.

Gaines is open until 8 p.m. on weekdays, and until 6 p.m. on Saturdays and Sundays.

The Great Ace Warehouse

- 2950 N. Oakley Ave., Chicago; (312) 880-7390

Everybody knows about the Great Ace stores; one at the Clark/Broadway split, the other at the Webster Place shopping center on Clybourn. These have plenty to offer in the way of reasonably priced furniture, shelving and storage units, lighting, accessories, and hardware. Spare, modern, and ultra-functional is the house style.

Less well-known is the Great Ace Warehouse, where they sell floor models, overstocks, and damaged goods at reduced prices. This may be due to the fact that the warehouse is in the middle of nowhere; more precisely, at the place where residential

Oakley Avenue dead-ends by the Chicago River, just below Clybourn. The building is virtually undistinguished, except for the big loading dock doorway, which only welcomes you on weekends.

Inside the cavernous warehouse, the available stock has been more or less lined up for your inspection. Mr. C found a free-standing bar finished in black formica, with two matching stools, for $75; black or white laminate kitchen tables for $30 each; several armoires, each $50; European-style black aluminum chairs for the living room, $30, and similarly techno-modern desk lamps for $15.

The selection is not vast. Many items are one-of-a-kind; at most, you may find three or four of an item. Yes, many of these pieces are scratched or scuffed in some way. It's up to you how noticeable these blemishes are, and how much this matters, given the drastically reduced prices. The warehouse also has some carpet remnants and mattresses to check out, as well as bathroom accessories, dishware, and assorted hardware items at half-price.

All sales are final, of course, and payment is accepted in cash or check only. The Great Ace Warehouse is open Saturdays and Sundays from 11:00 a.m. to 4:00 p.m.

Harris Lamps Factory Outlet

- 1200 W. 35th St., Chicago; (312) 247-7500

Not far from Comiskey Park, this factory has opened a showroom displaying a large inventory of lighting in classic and contemporary styles. These range from your basic ceramic-base table lamps, in a variety of solid colors with white linen shades ($17 apiece), to wild-looking floor lamps that swoop up and over in a giant arc toward a plastic scallop-shaped light ($40 and $50).

Harris also makes some furniture, mostly chairs, available here singly or in sets. Traditional-style upholstered armchairs go for $75 each; Mr. C also saw a cane chair with linen upholstery—which absolutely belonged on some outdoor patio in Jamaica—for $60. The showroom is only open on Fridays, from 11:00 a.m. to 6:00 p.m., and Saturdays from 8:00 a.m. to 4:00 p.m. No delivery, layaway, refunds, or exchanges are available.

House of Teak Scandinavian Furniture Centers

- 2112 N. Clybourn Ave., Chicago; (312) 248-4444

And many other suburban locations
The name should more accurately read teak-*finish* furniture, and a lot of it is actually from Belgium; still, you can find quality contemporary furniture here at discount prices. Of course, the bookcases and consoles have unfinished backs, but who will see? The drawers open and close very smoothly, too. You may also get a good buy on sofa and table samples, but check them thoroughly for such defects as ink stains, which Mr. C found on some pieces.

Here at House of Teak, a rosewood-finish console table with a glass top is $875, reduced from a list price of $1168. A natural-wood finish queen-size bed frame was $600, and a teak-finish dinette table was $199. A gray leather sofa, big enough for three people, was seen for $1099, about $700 off; and a beautiful mahogany-finish bookcase was $130, valued at about $200.

Hufford Furniture

- 310 W. Washington St., Chicago; (312) 236-4191

Wow! What a place. If big-name, traditional furniture for the home is your style, you can save yourself a lot of money by purchasing it here. Hufford has long been known only to the most inside of the insiders, but has more recently opened its doors to a wider audience—winning rave reviews in the process.

Fancy brands like Stiffel, La-Barge, and many others can be bought in this huge warehouse in the Loop, at discounts of up to 40% below list price. Make no mistake: These pieces were expensive to begin

with, and technically, they still ain't cheap. But you *can* save hundreds, even thousands of dollars by shopping here, and this furniture will be heirloom material for generations to come. Wander around through dining room table and chair sets, hutches and cabinets, bedroom wardrobe units, chests and desks, cocktail tables for the living room, and all the rest—in real mahogany, cherry, walnut and other rich woods. And yes, many of the larger items are more than a thousand dollars below their retail prices.

Hufford Furniture is open on weekdays from 8:30 a.m. to 5:30 p.m. (Monday and Thursday evenings, they stay open until 7:00). They're open from 8:30 to 3:30 on Saturdays, and closed Sundays.

Interiors by Renee

- 3036 N. Lincoln Ave., Chicago; (312) 404-8660

Talk about a success story. Renee and Scott Lynn, a mother and son team, began selling furniture out of their garage just a few years ago; now, they own a three-story building in Lincoln Park, with a vast showroom filled with handsome modern furniture at catalogue prices. In fact, that's really the hook here—as a family operation in a building they own, the overhead stays low, and so do the prices. They can order directly from big-name factories, and keep the figures just above cost.

There is plenty to see, in a wide range of prices and grades. Complete bedroom sets range in price from as little as $149 up to $10,000. A Bassett cherry wood bedroom set was seen for $599. Queen-size mattress sets start as low as $95. For the living room, how about a Natuzzi sofa and loveseat in brown leather, imported from Italy; it might sell for up to $3,000 at Bloomingdales, but here it's $900. Put a halogen torchiere lamp beside it for just another $20.

This is the kind of place to check out after you've shopped around a bit, and found a good price on some-

MR. CHEAP'S PICKS
Furniture—New

✔ **European Furniture Warehouse**—High-quality replicas of trendy and classic designs, at 20% to 60% off.

✔ **Hufford Furniture**—More big names, all in traditional styles, at big discounts.

✔ **Interiors by Renee**—You name it, Renee can get it for you wholesale.

---

thing you like. Bring in the make and model number, and the chances are very good that these folks will beat it by a mile. Unlike other retail stores, they're really into bargaining. And they have catalogues from just about any major line of furniture and bedding; if you don't see it, they can order it.

Krause's Sofa Factory
● 2111 N. Clybourn Ave., Chicago; (312) 935-3900

Take a seat. You'll have to wait a bit to get a sofa or chair from Krause's, but that's because everything here is made to order. They offer a choice of about one thousand different upholstery styles, including Ralph Lauren and Laura Ashley-imitation prints. Unfortunately, there's even more of a wait on the more tasteful and popular fabrics.

The deals you can end up with, however, are often worth the wait (it can take about a month for orders to arrive from Krause's manufacturer in California). The frames have a lifetime guarantee, and you can even save a bit more when the store holds frequent "no sales tax" sales. Mr. C found a handsome leather sofa for $999, reduced from an original $1349; fabric-upholstered sofas run about $600, and chairs, about $349. They're very comfortable, too.

Many other kinds of items are available here to finish outfitting any room, such as coffee tables and lamps. These are not factory-direct, though, and the prices show it.

La-Z-Boy Gallery
● 5353 N. Broadway, Chicago; (312) 784-0113
● 3232 N Harlem Ave., Chicago; (312) 237-6116

If you're looking for a recliner and only a recliner, you can afford to be lazy about it by making this your only stop. There is a fine selection of these popular chairs, available here direct from the factory.

The sales help can be a bit pushy, but the best part about shopping here is getting to try out the chairs. Upholstery coverings are available in the full range, from corduroy on up to leather. The chairs also come with a full La-Z-Boy factory guarantee.

A swivel rocker recliner, retailing for $429, sells here for $269. A top grain leather version, regularly $1149, was reduced to $900. And an 83-inch sofa, with a retail price of $1100, was here for $900. These are still high prices, yes, but Mr. C is interested in savings at both ends of the spectrum. If this trusted, quality brand is your fancy, you'll find it for less here.

Marjen Furniture
● 2707 N. Halsted St., Chicago; (312) 929-0008
● 8121 N. Milwaukee Ave., Niles; (708) 966-1088

First of all, a point of order. Within Chicago City Limits, there are two stores called Marjen. Both sell inexpensive furniture and bedding. And, although they were once related to each other, both are now separate businesses.

Specializing in living room furniture, particularly sofas, the Lincoln Park/Niles Marjen doesn't offer the greatest everyday discounts (many sofas, for instance, hover in the $1000 range). Their frequent advertised specials, however, can save you a bundle. One sofa and love seat pair was recently on sale for $599, marked down from $1499.

Another deal was being offered on a genuine leather L-shaped sectional, with a reclining chair and fold-out sleeper built in. Retailing for $2499, it was on sale at Marjen for $1659, available in a dozen different shades.

Open weekdays from 10:30 a.m. to 8 p.m., Saturdays 10:30-5:00, Sundays 11:00-5:00.

Mar-Jen Furniture

• 1536 W. Devon Ave., Chicago; (312) 338-6636

Okay, here's the other Mar-jen (note the spelling difference, too). This uptown competitor focuses more on low- to mid-range price and quality, in a wider variety of furniture for all rooms in the house.

European-style sofa and loveseat sets start as low as $399, and offer you a choice of fabric coverings. A dinette table and two chairs can be as low as $129; Mr. C also saw a solid butcher-block table and four chairs for $199.

Modern-looking leather sofas start under $600; put a halogen torch lamp beside one for just $25, the lowest price Mr. C has seen anywhere. While much of the furniture here is modern in style, including glass-top varieties, there are some traditional looks available here as well.

Upstairs in a low-ceilinged loft space, Mar-jen has its clearance area of leftovers and floor samples. Many of these are scuffed or even broken, but you may find a buried treasure up here, like a mirror-top end table, reduced from $200 to $139. Just remember to watch your head.

Mar-jen offers free delivery to any part of the city, north or south. Free layaway plans are available, too. They're open from 10:30 a.m. until 7 or 8 p.m. on weeknights, 10-6 on Saturdays, 11-5 on Sundays.

Naked Furniture

• 5725 N. Broadway, Chicago; (312) 784-1616

The prices at Naked Furniture will make you (almost) jump out of your clothes with glee. Naked Furniture is a true bargain, selling high-quality, but affordably priced pinewood tables, chairs, and bookcases, and other handy handcrafts like compact disc holders and magazine racks, and wine racks. Why naked, and why the savings? Same answer—this is unfinished furniture. Take it home, throw on a coat of lacquer, and you've got a handsome, natural wood bargain.

Some furniture is ever-so-slightly chipped in spots, but nothing too major. Other items were marred by being constructed with heartwood, meaning lots of knots; you decide whether these features are charming or marring. Knots may also make furniture (especially bookcases and beds) weaker, depending where they appear, so do be careful.

Otherwise, everything in this store will save you lots o' cash. Prices listed are for the items in their unfinished states only; you can choose to keep the furniture unfinished, have the store finish it for you, or do-it-yourself with their kits for creative types and novices alike. In addition to classic finishes, the store offers novelty patterns like sponge painting and marble-look finishes. If you bring in a photo or sample of a look that you prefer, the store will duplicate it for you.

A bookcase/desk combination was $270, for example, and will be $370 if the store finishes it for you. Elsewhere around this huge showroom, Mr. C saw a ten-compartment entertainment center selling for $380; a queen-size, mission-style bedframe for $400; and a walnut dining table set with six chairs for $1300 complete. Lots of sofas, too, like a sleep sofa with a funky southwestern print fabric for $689.

Floor samples make even better bargains. Case in point: a large, maple-finished armoire with two glass doors was seen recently for $800. Another sample seen was a blue and white-striped queen sleeper sofa, only $400. That's less than half of what you'd spend for a plain couch at many stores. Other advantages here include free parking, as well as layaway and financing plans. Naked Furniture is open weekdays 10-8:30, Saturdays 10-5:30, and Sundays 12-5.

Nelson Brothers

- 2750 W. Grand Ave., Chicago; (312) 235-3414
- 4840 N. Broadway, Chicago; (312) 561-3900
- 6250 S. Cottage Grove Ave., Chicago; (312) 324-6551
- 6535 S. Halsted St., Chicago; (312) 487-2123

And other suburban locations
The "sales counselors," as they're dubbed here at Nelson Brothers, could use a little help themselves; when asked, two of them began arguing over where their store's other branches were located. If you can put up with this, give the store a shot for mid-quality furniture in traditional American and Euro-modern styles, as well as brand-name appliances and home furnishing accessories.

Nelson specializes in complete-room package deals. A sofa, loveseat and chair set was selling for $1500 on a recent visit. Some groupings combine their dual furniture/electronics approach, throwing a color TV in with a living room set, for example. Such a TV wouldn't be a top-of-the-line model, natch; but you can get a sofa, loveseat, easy chair, coffee table, two end tables, two lamps, a 9' X 12' rug, a framed print for the wall—oh, and the TV—all on sale for $1099.

You can, of course, get many of these items individually, like a mint green and black chintz floral print sofa for $659, or a table lamp with a mauve-colored glass shade for $59. Open seven days a week.

Sheldon Cord Products

- 2201 W. Devon Ave., Chicago; (312) 973-7070

If you absolutely need a sofa or a mattress ASAP, and don't give a hoot about luxurious comfort, try Sheldon. Prices always run about 70% below retail, which is great; but the quality can be sub-par as well.

Don't get confused when you

first walk in and spot the toys and tools they sell super-cheap here—this store caters to flea market people, selling items from "super-soakers" and dolls to screwdrivers and electrical cords. These are sold only by the dozen, and just to flea market vendors.

The furniture, however, is fair game to all. Prices are almost too good to be true, but check these pieces out carefully. On his visit, Mr. C found some of the mattresses to have rather noticeable springs, while others were okay. A queen-size mattress and box spring set by Regal Splendor brand was seen for just $240. If you've never heard of this brand, well, neither has your humble scribe; the set does come with a twenty-year warranty, though.

Couches run in the $200-$400 range, and some of the lower-quality ones are even cheaper. For example, the store was heavily advertising a three-piece set—sofa, love seat and chair—for an absolutely ridiculous $149.95! Again, check them thoroughly. Some of the sofas make odd noises when you sit on them; not the whoopie-cushion variety, but the overstuffed, "Ouch, you're hurting me!" smush kind. Other low-grade sofas, meanwhile, were understuffed.

Bedroom sets include the often-seen Italian black lacquer look, five pieces for $290. Dressers, chests, and the like are primarily of the particle-board-and-veneer sort, and many of the drawers opened very clumsily. But, if you're just starting out and want some furniture that hasn't already been through the wringer—say, for a dorm or a frat house—Sheldon Cord is a wholesaler to check out. Open seven days a week.

Southwest Furniture and Appliance

- 2934 N. Milwaukee Ave., Chicago; (312) 227-4224
- 3239 S. Halsted St., Chicago; (312) 567-9752

In addition to saving folks money on appliances by repairing and reselling used models (see listing under "Shopping: Appliances"), Southwest offers good deals on furniture as well.

No, the styles here are not exactly southwestern (the name is more likely due to the two store locations), but it is cheap—due to high volume and low overhead. Southwest is so packed with sofas that it's difficult getting from one area of the store to another. A sofa, love seat, and chair set by Lagniappe is $799. The identical set was spotted in other stores for a couple hundred dollars more. A wood veneer bookcase with three shelves is $59, and may be found for as much as $119 in other stores.

Southwest Furniture and Appliance is open Mondays through Saturdays from 10-7, and 11-5 on Sundays.

Spiegel Outlet Store
* 1105 W. 35th St., Chicago; (312) 254-1099

And many other suburban locations
Just down the road apiece from Comiskey Park, the Spiegel Outlet is just what you'd expect—a clearance center for catalog items that haven't sold as well as expected. Does that mean they're trying to unload five thousand cases of polyester leisure

suits? Not at all. The city branch has two floors of great clothes for men, women, and children—as well as housewares, furniture, electronics and other goodies—at up to half off their original prices.

In the home department, check out Dundee bath towels, reduced from $10 to $3.99 each; a comforter ensemble from Dan River, marked down twice from $195 to $99 to $59; European-style table lamps from $29; woven country-style rugs at 50% off their original prices; wicker armchairs reduced from $299 to $199, and sometimes even exercise equipment. Mr. C saw "Alpine Tracker" ski machines, originally $299, selling here for a much slimmer $129.

Even in this clear-the-decks setting, you can return purchases for cash or credit within thirty days (always save your receipts!)—better than many full-price stores. Also worth noting, Tuesdays are discount days for senior citizens: 10% off the total purchase. Spiegel outlets are open daily from 10:00 a.m. to 7:30 p.m.; weekends, until 5:00.

USED

Brook Furniture Outlet
* 2525 N. Elston Ave., Chicago; (312) 593-5940

At Brook's regular stores throughout the region, you can rent (or rent-to-own) handsome contemporary furniture for every room in the house. At their clearance center, along this outlet-laden stretch of Elston, you can get new and used furniture at savings of 30% to 70% below the manufacturers' suggested prices. Those makers include such estimable names as Bassett, Sealy, and La-Z-Boy. In the front room, there are sofas, loveseats, tables, and dining room sets; further into the back, they have bedding and desks, including office furniture.

Brook's used furniture department consists of much the same merchandise as its new lines; these are items which have been rented and re-

turned. Y'know, it's funny how people don't take such good care of stuff they don't own. A lot of this stock is rather worn, and some of it is downright beaten-up; still, new stuff is always coming in, and you never know what you may find. Sofas generally begin as low as $149 each; kitchen and dining room table-and-chair sets start around $119. You may even find mattress and boxspring sets for $80, or executive desks for $249. For someone starting an office, or moving into a first apartment, the condition may not be so critical. These furnishings, especially at these prices, will do just fine.

Cash, checks and credit cards are accepted; Brook offers a 90-day layaway plan, and delivery is available for a fee. Hours are Tuesdays through Fridays from 10 a.m. to 6 p.m., and

---

MR. CHEAP'S PICKS
Furniture—Used

✔ **Interiors on Consignment**—Exquisite estate furniture, in top condition, far below original prices.

Saturdays from 10-4. Closed Sunday and Monday. Brook also has a suburban outlet store, located in Elk Grove Village.

Interiors on Consignment
- 2150 N. Clybourn Ave., Chicago; (312) 868-0797

The amazing thing about this store is the consistently high quality of its merchandise. Owner Ellen Kohn says that people often stroll in and scarcely notice that everything here is used, and it really does look like a designer showroom. That's because she and her husband Kenneth are very selective about which items they'll take in; they personally visit the homes of the people who want to sell their furniture through this store. Items must be in excellent condition, and not everything makes the cut.

Each piece is priced at one-third to one-half below the value of a comparable new version; and, in order to keep things moving, the price is further reduced by 15% after one month.

OFFICE—NEW AND USED

Direct Office Furniture Warehouse
- 5041 N. Western Ave., Chicago; (312) 271-3000
- 7232 N. Western Ave., Chicago; (312) 465-3300

This duo of warehouses has an incredible amount of office furniture, stacked into row after row, in several rooms, upstairs and down. The Ra-

After two months, the best offer takes it, provided the original owner agrees to the price. The Kohns clearly know their stuff, because even as fussy as they are, this large store is packed with antique and modern furniture, paintings, jewelry, and other estate items.

Among the items Mr. C found during his visit were a Barcelona chair and ottoman set by Knoll, valued at $9,000 new; here, it was selling for $4,000. Speaking of design pieces, you may also find furniture which literally doubles as an art object, like a colorful hand-painted coffee table for $649, that is undeniably one of a kind.

A European-style formal dining table in black marble, with eight matching leather chairs, was seen here for $3,000—and could easily cost almost twice as much. And don't worry, not everything here sells in the thousands. A handsome antique washbasin stand, in solid oak, was seen for $298; a bow-front mahogany chest, with two sets of double doors, was $260; and a butcher-block rolling cart, never used, was $159. There are also things like halogen torch lamps, table lamps from $40, ceiling fixtures, mirrors, antique headboards, and much, much more.

It's a beautiful shop just to browse. New items are added frequently; a bulletin board displays photos of incoming pieces that have been scouted and are soon to arrive. Sort of a "coming attractions" for furniture, and another smart touch by this well-run business.

venswood location sells a mix of new and used stock, either one of which can save you lots of cash; the far north branch deals primarily in used merchandise only.

Among the bargains in new items, a recent sale featured a variety of products by Hon, one of the leading manufacturers in the business furniture business. Several types of

MR. CHEAP'S PICKS
Furniture—Office

✔ **Direct Office Furniture Warehouse**—Actually, two gigantic barns full of new and used bargains, some dirt cheap.

---

filing cabinets were as much as 50% off their retail prices, like a four-drawer letter-size model with a list price of $222 selling for $109. The legal-size version was reduced from $260 to $159. Ergonomic chairs in a variety of styles were on sale too, such as one with padded armrests and a pneumatic lift, marked down from $230 to $135. Basic models were as low as just $69.

New executive desks start from $149 everyday, with many choices in the $599-$799 range; these are still several hundred dollars below retail. Direct Office also sells lines like Sauder assemble-it-yourself furniture; some of these desks can be had for a mere $195. Computer tables begin at just $75 each, for a rolling metal stand model.

In used furniture, at either location, you can find basic office chairs from $20, and upholstered models in the $50-$75 range; standard metal folding chairs, the kind you see in any auditorium or meeting room, are just $8 apiece. Mr. C saw a handsome oak-laminate executive's credenza for $250, very slightly scuffed; other desks can be as cheap as $50—perfect for the startup office. And dozens of file cabinets start around $50. The selection in this stacked room is huge in just about anything you may need.

And we haven't even gotten to the basement yet. Down in this rather musty area, you'll find older, more banged-up pieces—some of which you can probably get for a song.

Poke around through more desks, chairs, filing cabinets, and bookshelves, and you may uncover a hidden treasure; Mr. C saw a four-foot wide drafting table, still in quite good shape, for $350 (but probably negotiable). There was even a big old schoolteacher's desk (used, of course, by big old schoolteachers) and a rusty set of gym lockers.

DOFW also has a limited selection of office accessories, such as bookends, letter trays, and the like. The 7232 Western location hosts public auctions on Tuesday evenings, where you can get real dirt-cheap deals. Oh, and at the 5041 branch, if you want a good laugh, ask to see the elephants.

Both stores are open Mondays through Saturdays from 9:30 a.m. to 5:30 p.m.

Gently Used Office Furniture
- 1300 W. North Ave., Chicago; (312) 276-6200

Just moved into brand-new digs a few blocks from its previous location, GUOF has been a hit for over five years. They sell both new and used office furniture, accessories, and supplies, all at discount. "We cater to the entrepreneur," manager Steven Schwartz is proud of saying, "the kind of person who wants to set up an office quickly and cheaply." Indeed, whether that may be a corner of your apartment or a downtown suite, there's plenty here to check out.

Mr. C saw an L-shaped executive's desk by Alma, for instance, which might have sold for $2,000 originally, on sale for just $500. It was still in very good shape, and most impressive-looking. Other, smaller desks, with retail prices over $1,000, often sell here for around $200. And chairs are priced from $5 and up. There are file cabinets in all sizes and shapes, from such top manufacturers as Steelcase; originally $500 to $1,500, they are in the $150-$400 range here.

The old location featured a huge, dusty basement stacked with older items at even cheaper prices; not just furniture, but all kinds of rare and un-usual office equipment. Schwartz says, "we loved to set people loose down there—some came in once a week, just to wander around for fun on their lunch hour." Whatever floats your boat. The new location doesn't have a basement, but there is still an area piled high with this corporate flotsam and jetsam.

GUOF also sells new furniture, in stock exclusively from the Global catalogue; everything from ergo-nomic chairs to conference tables and modular systems—all readily avail-able at discount prices. They stand prepared to beat the prices of any competitors. Plenty of free and easy parking at the new location, too.

HOME FURNISHINGS

1730 Outlet Company
- 1730 W. Wrightwood Ave., Chicago; (312) 871-4331

1730 Outlet Company is the clear-ance center for the Trade Associate Group, an importer/exporter of fancy home furnishings—they sell to many of the stores you probably pass by all the time. Why gaze wistfully in the expensive shops, when the leftovers and discontinued items come back here? The same housewares are sold off at near-wholesale prices. You may find gorgeous candleholders for 50 cents apiece, as well as a great selec-tion of candles to put into them; or, a colorful linen tablecloth for $5. All of their textiles are 100 percent cotton, including dishtowels seen for 95 cents, placemats for $1.50, and cloth napkins for a tidy 75 cents each. They also carry picture frames, plas-tic containers, rugs, and more. The 1730 Outlet is open Mondays through Saturdays from 10:00 a.m. to 4:00 p.m.

Artists' Frame Service Inc.
- 1915 N. Clybourn Ave., Chicago; (312) 248-7713 or (312) FRAMING

And other suburban locations
While AFS touts itself as the world's largest framing service, artists flock here for the plain frames themselves. Everyone who works here has at least some training, if not a degree or ad-vanced degree, in art or a related field; you can check out their (beauti-

fully) framed diplomas in the center of the store. They're busy, but knowl-edgeable and willing to help with any questions you may have.

Whether you're looking for a regular silver or goldtone frame for a gift, an antiqued metal one for some-thing historic, or a painted ceramic multiple display frame for children's pictures, you'll find good buys here. The high volume of sales allows them to offer such discounts. Pine frames by Burnes of State Street, in a 3½" x 5" size, are only $5.50. An-other wooden frame, handmade in Thailand, is $10 for the 2½" x 3½" size.

A 5" x 7" marquetry frame, with wood-on-wood inlay by Beacon Hill (which Mr. C noticed in another store for $30), was priced here at just $16; and a pastel-painted ceramic 2" x 3" frame, suitable for a baby or child's photo, was only $3.50.

Brass Works
- 2142 N. Halsted St., Chicago; (312) 935-1800

You don't necessarily have to be big brass to shop here. Some of the bed-frames, lamps, and antique items are wildly expensive, but you can jazz up your apartment for practically nickels (well, ok, not quite) if you check out the smaller fixtures.

The stuff in this store is mostly salvaged from older buildings or at estate sales, so the selection varies widely and is always different. For little touches, check out the doorknobs and brass door hinges in the front display cases; these go for about $30 and up. Perhaps you'll find a brass number for your front door, or a wall sconce that is selling for far below its original value. Always worth a look! Store hours are from 10-6 weekdays, and 11-5 Saturdays.

Crate & Barrel Outlet Store
- 800 W. North Ave., Chicago; (312) 787-4775

The very popular Crate & Barrel is more fun than a barrel of monkeys if you're searching for anything from glassware and dishtowels to briefcases and storage racks. This outlet is C & B's clearance center, selling off factory seconds, special purchases, leftovers, and closeouts. Selection can be limited, and some items are defective; the prices make it worthwhile. If you don't mind tiny bubbles in your glassware, stock up here.

Some examples of the cheapies found here recently were Marimekko fabric for $6.95 a yard, marked down from $26; a large rectangular glass vase, worth $27 if perfect, selling for $19; and a beechwood finish, three-shelf bookcase for half its original price at just $30.

Decorative items here make interesting gifts; unfortunately, there are no gift boxes or wrapping available at the outlet. The store is open seven days a week, from 10 a.m. to 8 p.m. on weekdays, Saturdays 10-6, and Sundays 11-5.

Edward Don & Company Outlet
- 2525 N. Elston Ave.; (312) 489-7739

One of several super outlets on this stretch of Elston, Edward Don is not to be missed. It's a restaurant supply house that's open to the public, with lots to see for your kitchen and dining rooms. The back room here is full of discontinued and close-out kitchen supplies and appliances, while the front area offers a wide range of regularly-priced kitchen accessories.

It's kind of fun to wander through the behind-the-scenes side of the restaurant biz; past big bottles of cleansers and stacks of plastic ashtrays, paper plates, napkins, punch bowls, and much more. Lots of this stuff would be appropriate for wedding receptions or big parties—another angle to consider here.

In the front room, a Mirro 22-quart stockpot sells for $22; plastic fajita dishes are $4 apiece, and colandars, stainless steel wisks and cookie sheets are well-priced. So are party decorations and accessories (24 birthday candles for 69 cents— cheaper than the Hallmark store).

That back room, however, is the true bargain bonanza. Votive candles are $9.99 for six dozen; stainless steel cutlery is $4.50-$5 a dozen, depending on the type of utensil and design; and a closeout on a 30-cup Regal coffeemaker was seen for $44.

The store is open Mondays through Fridays from 10:00 a.m. to 6:00 p.m., Saturdays from 9-5, and Sundays from 11-4.

Erickson Jewelers
- 5304 N. Clark St., Chicago; (312) 275-2010

This Andersonville store draws as many of its customers from the far-away suburbs as from in town, since it sells great watches, jewelry and china at everyday discounts of at least twenty percent—it's like going to the outlet malls, without the drive. Erickson would make a great place for a wedding registry; they sell Omega and Citizen watches, Waterford crystal, Lenox china, and Lalique glass accessories—always well below retail prices.

In the home furnishings half of the store, Waterford Crystal candle stick holders are $159 each and a Waterford ring holder is $49, again much less than what you'd pay for at a store like Marshall Field's. Towle silver plated picture frames were $46 for a set of three—a fine bargain. Dansk dinnerware is always 20% off list; and, when it goes on sale, can be almost half off retail.

The Great Ace Warehouse
- 2950 N. Oakley Ave., Chicago; (312) 880-7390

Everybody knows about the Great Ace stores; one at the Clark/Broadway split, the other at the Webster Place shopping center on Clybourn. These have plenty to offer in the way of reasonably priced furniture, shelving and storage units, lighting, accessories, and hardware. Spare, modern, and ultra-functional is the house style.

Less well-known is the Great Ace Warehouse, where they sell floor models, overstocks, and damaged goods at reduced prices. This may be due to the fact that the warehouse is in the middle of nowhere; more precisely, at the place where residential Oakley Avenue dead-ends by the Chicago River, just below Clybourn. The building is virtually undistinguished, except for the big loading dock doorway, which only welcomes you on weekends.

Inside the cavernous warehouse, the available stock has been more or less lined up for your inspection. Mr. C found a free-standing bar finished in black formica, with two matching stools, for $75; black or white laminate kitchen tables for $30 each; several armoires, each $50; European-style black aluminum chairs for the living room, $30, and similarly techno-modern desk lamps for $15.

The selection is not vast. Many items are one-of-a-kind; at most, you may find three or four of an item. Yes, many of these pieces are scratched or scuffed in some way. It's up to you how noticeable these blemishes are, and how much this matters, given the drastically reduced prices. The warehouse also has some carpet remnants and mattresses to check out, as well as bathroom accessories, dishware, and assorted hardware items at half-price.

All sales are final, of course, and payment is accepted in cash or check only. The Great Ace Warehouse is open Saturdays and Sundays from 11:00 a.m. to 4:00 p.m.

Harris Lamps Factory Outlet

- 1200 W. 35th St., Chicago; (312) 247-7500

Not far from Comiskey Park, this factory has opened a showroom displaying a large inventory of lighting in classic and contemporary styles. These range from your basic ceramic-base table lamps, in a variety of solid colors with white linen shades ($17 apiece), to wild-looking floor lamps that swoop up and over in a giant arc toward a plastic scallop-shaped light ($40 and $50).

Other, more traditional floor lamps include the sort that are set into a glass table base, priced at $35 and $40; and there are also several styles of genuine brass table lamps for just $30 each. A selection of replacement lampshades is spread out on a long table, most of which are $6-$8 each.

The Harris showroom is only open on Fridays, from 11:00 a.m. to 6:00 p.m., and Saturdays from 8:00 a.m. to 4:00 p.m. No delivery, layaway, refunds, or exchanges are available.

Orient Midwest Gallery

- 740 N. Franklin St., Chicago; (312) 664-6309

Primarily an art gallery, Orient Midwest presents an interesting selection of contemporary art from Central and East Asia. You'll see examples of *sumi'e*, traditional paintings in black and white; Asian influenced paintings in oils and watercolors; Chinese papercuts, carvings, and more. OMG has furniture and decorative arts like lamps, Korean *tansu* chests, tapestries, kimonos, and jewelry. The gallery also has a longstanding reputation for its collection of handwoven Tibetan carpets.

Particularly interesting for collectors, and anyone looking to artistically furnish their home on the cheap: OMG uses many pieces of furniture and accessories to "enhance" its art displays. As the exhibits here change (usually every month or so), these items are often sold at a significant discount; as much as 40% to 50% off their original values. In addition to these sales, OMG holds an annual clearance sale on accessories, furniture and porcelain at the beginning of each August. The gallery is open from 10 a.m. to 5 p.m., Monday through Saturday.

Picture Us Galleries
- 2828 N. Clark St., Chicago; (312) 281-5558
- Two N. LaSalle St., Chicago; (312) 726-6334

And many other suburban locations
Picture yourself saving big bucks at this store, which specializes in framing but also has walls and walls of framed prints for sale. Matted and framed Ansel Adams prints were seen selling at two for $39 in 8" x 10" sizes; and a print of Georgia O'Keeffe's *Sky Above Clouds IV*, as seen in the Art Institute, was only $15.

Larger prints will also save you large amounts, as compared to other framing stores. Gustav Klimt's *The Kiss* was spied at $220 for the 32" x 54" print, complete with a goldtone frame; and Joan Miró's *Abstrait* was only $190 for the enormous, framed 39" x 55" size.

Plain ol' photograph frames are also a deal here. An 8" X 10" goldtone frame was selling for only $13.99; and a silver-plated, hinged double frame imported from China was only $20. The framing services offered by Picture Us are reasonably priced as well.

Poster Plus
- 210 S. Michigan Ave., Chicago; (312) 461-9277
- 3366 N. Clark St., Chicago; (312) 929-2850

Some of the foreign and vintage out-of-print posters in these shops can get pricey; but many others, including copies of paintings in the Art Institute, as well as more unusual posters and photographs, are surprisingly inexpensive. Everything here, though, is of museum quality.

An unframed copy of Jackson Pollock's *Number 31* is $54, while a Philippe Halsman photographic portrait of Georgia O'Keeffe is only $15; and Salvador Dali's famous *The Persistence of Memory*, which will persist in college dorm rooms for eternity, is $19 unframed. Cozily enough, the store's Michigan Avenue location is right across the street from the Art Institute itself.

Private Lives Bed and Bath Linens
- 39 E. Oak St., Chicago; (312) 337-5474
- 662 W. Diversey Pkwy., Chicago; (312) 525-6464
- 3011 N. Clark St., Chicago; (312) 348-4646

And other suburban locations
The Diversey branch of this chain is probably your best bet for discounts; while the other stores do have markdowns, this one is the company's warehouse location. Everything from sheets and comforters to shower hooks and stuffed animals are for sale at price-slashed savings.

If you search hard enough, you can find sheet sets even in those hard-to-find sizes. Some may have been discontinued, and you may not be able to find the pillowcases to match a particular set of sheets. Clever shoppers work around this problem by mixing and matching; you can find coordinated prints that work well together, or prints with matching solids.

Mr. C spotted a Ralph Lauren cotton blanket discounted by almost $40, depending upon the size. The twin size, retailing for about $90, was only $69.99, while the king size was marked down from $170 to $135. Kitchen accessories like fashionable dish towels for only $1.99 also make for big savings off department store prices. Open seven days a week.

Reiter's Warehouse Outlet
- 2460 W. George St., Chicago; (312) 267-4669
- 4635 S. Ashland Ave., Chicago; (312) 376-2666
- 8643 S. Cottage Grove Ave., Chicago; (312) 783-0700

Reiters stores are already inexpensive, but their warehouse outlets are even better. They sell overstocks, discontinued merchandise and irregulars, mixing famous names in with mid-grade brands. All sales are final

MR. CHEAP'S PICKS
Home Furnishings

✔ **1730 Outlet
Company**—Tucked away in
Wrightwood is this clearance
center for fancy decorative
objects and gifts.

✔ **Crate & Barrel Outlet
Store**—Another clearance
outlet, full of trendy and useful
items for all around the house.

✔ **Edward Don & Company
Outlet**—This clearance center
focuses on restaurant supplies,
with lots of great stuff for any
kitchen.

✔ **Reiter's Warehouse
Outlet**—Super-cheap deals on
bedroom and bathroom
accessories.

at these outlet stores, but if you're
willing to take a chance, you can
change over your kitchen and bathroom for small change indeed. Low
overhead is more than a pricing philosophy here; in fact, the ceiling was
leaking during Mr. C's visit, and the
floors are uneven, so watch your step!

Watch the savings, too. For the
bedroom, a four-piece Criterion by
Dan River queen-size sheet set was
on sale for only $22.99; drapes for
just $9 and mini-blinds for $8 were
also on special sales. Quilts for twin
beds were selling briskly at $14.99,
as were the $12.99 comforter covers.
And standard-size pillows at just $7
will let you rest easy, knowing that
you saved over 50% over regular retail prices.

Need stuff for the bathroom?
Full-size bath towels were going for
only $3.79 apiece, and soft toilet
seats by Classique were just $9. Area
rugs were seen at $8 for a 3' X 5'
size. Facecloths in pastels and

brights, irregular closeouts, were selling at two for $1; and vinyl shower
curtains were reduced to $3.99, in-
cluding a set of matching hooks.

Spiegel Outlet Store
- 1105 W. 35th St., Chicago; (312)
254-1099

And many other suburban locations
Just down the road apiece from
Comiskey Park, the Spiegel Outlet is
just what you'd expect—a clearance
center for catalog items that haven't
sold as well as expected. Does that
mean they're trying to unload five
thousand cases of polyester leisure
suits? Not at all. The city branch has
two floors of great clothes for men,
women, and children—as well as
housewares, furniture, electronics and
other goodies—at up to half off their
original prices.

In the home department, check
out Dundee bath towels, reduced
from $10 to $3.99 each; a comforter
ensemble from Dan River, marked
down twice from $195 to $99 to $59;
European-style table lamps from $29;
woven country-style rugs at 50% off
their original prices; wicker armchairs reduced from $299 to $199,
and sometimes even exercise equipment. Mr. C saw "Alpine Tracker"
ski machines, originally $299, selling
here for a much slimmer $129. You'll
see some electronics, too, like a
Sharp camcorder (brand new, a discontinued model) for just $599, a sav-
ings of $300 off the list price.

Even in this clear-the-decks setting, you can return purchases for
cash or credit within thirty days (always save your receipts!)—better
than many full-price stores. Also
worth noting, Tuesdays are discount
days for senior citizens: 10% off the
total purchase. Spiegel outlets are
open daily from 10:00 a.m. to 7:30
p.m.; weekends, until 5:00.

That Porcelain Place
- 2239 S. Wentworth Ave., Chicago;
(312) 225-3888

Along the main stretch in Chinatown,
this shop is lined with traditional
Eastern earthenware (try saying *that*
three times fast). Buy a wide ceramic

soup spoon for your own hot and sour creations, just 39¢; and a matching saucer to rest it upon for 85¢. Chinese tea cups and saucers are $2.00 per set. They've got all of these by the ton; enough for you to do your whole service in cheap chic.

For other rooms in the house, there are decorative glazed porcelain planters for as low as $7.00 apiece, in several varieties; one-foot tall porcelain flower vases range from $10-$19, and porcelain figurines of traditional Oriental characters are $10 each. They'll look great in your living room or in your garden. You can also find basic clay planters here in many sizes, some of which are big enough for a tree. The shop stays open into the evening, nice for an after-dinner browse.

JEWELRY AND CRAFTS

Aronson Furniture and Appliances

- 3939 N. Ashland Ave., Chicago; (312) 871-6900
- 5657 W. Belmont Ave., Chicago; (312) 889-0312
- 1379 N. Milwaukee Ave., Chicago; (312) 235-9000
- 4630 S. Ashland Ave., Chicago; (312) 376-3401
- 3401 W. 47th St., Chicago; (312) 376-3400
- 2301 W. 95th St., Chicago; (312) 445-1888
- River Oaks West Shopping Center, Calumet City; (708) 891-1700

Since 1940, Aronson has been offering mid-range brands in all kinds of major goods for the home. Over the years, it has grown into one of Chicago's high-volume retailers, yet it hasn't lost sight of its own humble beginnings. As you can see above, it maintains branches in all parts of the city, north and south; this is the kind of place for regular folks who need to stretch the budget, but want good value for their money. Prices here can range from 30% to 60% off retail for furniture, appliances, and even jewelry.

Not all Aronson branches have a jewelry department; for some reason, the Belmont, North Ashland, and Calumet stores do not. At the other locations, though, a small but serviceable counter features rings and bands, watches, necklaces, and more, all at discounts of 10% to 15% below retail. Often, you'll find some even better deals on discontinued styles. Recently, a selection of diamond bands with regular prices from $179 to $450 were selling at 50% off; one model, for instance, was a 14-karat gold band, set with seven diamond chips, reduced to $90.

Aronson's stores are open seven days a week, including weekday evenings. They also offer very flexible credit plans—as one person here put it, "If people see something they like, we'll give them every chance to buy it."

Bijouterie Jewelry Outlet

- 645 W. Grand Ave., Chicago; (312) 733-5600

If the name of this store sounds French, perhaps it's because founder Fred Mandolini was born and raised in Louisiana Cajun country. Appropriately, then, the baubles he makes and sells have less to do with European fashion than with the rugged style of the American southwest. Jewelry made not with precious gems, but with stones like agate and turquoise. With mule teeth and camel bone. Trader stuff.

Fred gets the raw materials, and with his son Chris, he manufactures unique necklaces, rings, and other pieces. He's been doing it for decades. Bijouterie sells to retail stores mainly, but at this hideaway west of

MR. CHEAP'S PICKS
Jewelry and Crafts

✔ **Erickson Jewelers**—Discount prices on fancy watches for men and women.

✔ **Great Lakes Jewelry**—An inexpensive jewelry shop in the Gold Coast area? Believe it.

✔ **I. Harris and Son**—A gold and diamond wholesaler which has opened its doors to the public. Family-run, great service, fine deals.

✔ **Wabash Jewelers Mall**—Similar approach from dozens of dealers under one roof. "Shop around" with just one stop.

downtown, you can buy at below retail prices. That mule teeth and camel bone necklace, f'rinstance, would fetch $99 in a boutique; here, it's $49. Another version, made from buffalo horn, retails for $90, sells here for $45. And a simpler goatskin necklace strung with agates would sell for $12-$16 in town, but you can get it here for $6-$10.

Bijouterie sells more conventional jewelry, though more as a distributor than a manufacturer. Basic 14-karat gold chains range here from $15-$30; sterling silver goes for $8-$15. You can go super-cheap, too: Men's and women's gold-plated rings, flashing stones of cubic zirconia (that Home Shoppers Club favorite), are half off their retail price at $22. There are necklaces of fake pearls. And you can put a copy of a $75,000 bejeweled ring worn by Princess Diana into your hands for a mere $15. They've got knockoffs of famous designer watches here too, from $11-$22; at least the leather bands are real. In all, it's quite an in-teresting mix of stuff. Closed Sundays.

Busch Jewelry Company
- 214 S. State St., Chicago; (312) 782-4700
- 6343 S. Halsted Pkwy., Chicago; (312) 487-1120
- 6465 W. Diversey Ave., Chicago; (312) 237-7300

The selection isn't tremendous at this Loop jewelry store, but you can find some good prices here. A man's gold water-resistant Seiko watch was spotted here recently selling for $236, almost $60 off the original retail price.

A gold ring featuring a tiny emerald, surrounded by two even-tinier diamonds, was only $99. The gold was only 10 karat, however, and the diamonds were not of the most outstanding quality. Much of the women's jewelry is of similar quality; well above costume-variety, but not anything that will appreciate much with age, either.

Erickson Jewelers
- 5304 N. Clark St., Chicago; (312) 275-2010

This Andersonville store draws as many of its customers from the faraway suburbs as from in town, since it sells great watches, jewelry, and china at everyday discounts of at least twenty percent—it's like going to the outlet malls, without the drive. Erickson would make a great place for a wedding registry; they sell Omega and Citizen watches, Waterford Crystal, Lenox china, and Lalique glass accessories—always well below retail prices.

Tissot rock-face watches from Switzerland, while by no means inexpensive, are still better than they could be at $225. No retail prices were listed, but these go for much more in Carson Pirie Scott and other department stores. Diamonds sell for as much as 40% off suggested retail prices, and emerald rings and other gold and sterling silver jewelry are usually found at 30% off suggested retail.

Filene's Basement
- One N. State St. (Lower level), Chicago; (312) 553-1061

Boston's original Filene's Basement is the king of all bargain treasure troves. Normally-sane women pounce upon tables strewn with piles of clothing closeouts, flinging wrong sizes into the air, in search of The Find. If and when they come up with this, they clutch it tightly and head immediately for the nearest register—or, to another table. The place can be a real madhouse...which is part of its charm.

The atmosphere of Chicago's outpost is more refined, but it matches Boston's huge selection of jewelry, cosmetics, first-quality clothing and houseware closeouts, and irregulars. Mr. C noticed well-coiffed women with Gucci bags and men with diamond cufflinks—perhaps they can afford these fancy trinkets by saving on their wardrobe at the Basement. The selection changes constantly; many customers make a regular pass through here on a lunch hour or after work.

Filene's jewelry department offers lots of great buys, like 14-karat gold hoop earrings for $50, as well as necklaces, chains, and fine costume jewelry.

So what if the Basement can get messy during sales? For the money you can save, it's well worth fighting the crowds, and rummaging around for your size. And it's good practice in case you ever go to Boston.

Great Lakes Jewelry
- 104 E. Oak St., Chicago; (312) 266-2211

It's the Gold Coast, Chicago's ritziest neighborhood. It's a jewelry shop. And it's in *this* book? Yup! For almost twenty years, owner Maria Alexander has been designing and manufacturing her own jewelry—changing with the times as necessary to keep prices affordable. "I used to sell a lot of gold stuff in the 1980's," she says of the boom years. "These days, it's mostly silver."

In this dazzling little jewel of a shop, half a flight down from the street, every square inch seems to be brimming with bright objects in all kinds of styles and materials. Many of the current looks are in the fashion of Native American crafts, like a pair of sterling silver and malachite drop earrings reasonably priced at $20. Silver bracelets start around $25; and pins and necklaces set with all kinds of colorful, genuine gemstones, like amethyst, garnet and topaz, begin at $29.

There is also a lovely selection of men's and women's watches, starting as low as $35 each. Many of these are copies of famous designer styles, which would cost hundreds of dollars. Unlike the super-cheapo copies so often hawked on street corners, however, these quality reproductions will last longer than one sweep of the hour hand. What's more, if they *should* break, they can be repaired instead of tossed out.

The shop offers repair services on all of its jewelry and watches, and is open Mondays through Saturdays from 10:30 a.m. to 5:30 p.m.

Healing Earth Resources
- 2570 N. Lincoln Ave., Chicago; (312) EARTH-59 (327-8459)

From candles to jewelry to incense to $4 change pouches woven in Guatemala, Healing Earth Resources is bound to carry something gift-worthy, and boasts a vegetarian cafe next door, too.

Much of the jewelry is made of semi-precious stones like turquoise, making for very attractive and elegant-looking gifts which are still quite inexpensive. Rose quartz and blue lapis necklaces hung on leather strings sell for about $16. The store is open seven days a week.

Heritage Jewelry
- 114 W. Grand Ave., Chicago; (312) 664-4664

Heritage sells kitschy vintage jewelry and cheaper costume jewelry, by such lesser-known names as Napier. They carry everything from the safely sedate to the truly tacky, including overdone necklaces and earrings that you wouldn't be caught dead in—unless, of course, you're going for that certain look.

Do beware: Some of the older rhinestone pieces have cleverly had missing stones replaced. You'll have to look closely to find some of these boo-boos; but then, with costume jewelry, perhaps you don't mind such easily-missed flaws. Among the many pieces Mr. C saw here, a silver-plated blue and white rhinestone brooch was priced at about $30.

Hubba-Hubba
- 3338 N. Clark St., Chicago; (312) 477-1414

This Wrigleyville boutique sells rather pricey vintage and new clothing, but its costume jewelry isn't as expensive. The stock consists mostly of rhinestone and faux-pearl necklaces and earrings, meant to jazz up an outfit for a night on the town.

Mr. C saw a double-take fake topaz ring, only $15. A rhinestone brooch was only $8.50, and huge, bordering-on-gaudy rhinestone cluster rings were $12.50. Classy faux pearl drop clip-on earrings were $28.50, a bit much—but perhaps affordable if you get your dress to go with it at one of the vintage clothing stores in this book. A jet black and clear glass "crystal" bracelet was seen for $24.50. Oh, and they even have mood rings for $7.50. Hubba-hubba!

I. Harris and Son
- 2 N. Wabash St., Chicago; (312) 263-5552

This is the classic downtown, family-run, fancy jewelry store. The big difference between this and many other similar-looking businesses: The prices. Three years ago, after nearly sixty years in the wholesale diamond trade, current owner Brian Harris moved to his present location and began selling directly to the public at wholesale rates. With stores in New York and Europe, and connections worldwide, he imports his own diamonds—keeping costs down.

Wedding rings are the specialty here. Gold bands start around $40.

Engagement rings and wedding bands start as low as $100 for the semi-set; once you've chosen the band, you'll sit privately with a salesperson to look at various stones which can be mounted in it. Thus, you get extremely personal service, and each ring is custom made—factors which should *add* to the price, and yet it actually saves you money! And, if you have something unique in mind, they even have designers who will work from your ideas at no extra charge.

Harris also sells earrings, necklaces, and watches. He even has a stock of used Rolex watches in top condition; a watch originally valued at $4,000 may sell here for $1,500. Sure, that's still out of Mr. C's price range, but it *is* a bargain. Open Mondays through Saturdays from 10 a.m. to 5:30 p.m.

Kongoni Traditional American Handicrafts
- 2480 ½ N. Lincoln Ave., Chicago; (312) 929-9749

Authentic imported African and Asian jewelry, charms, clothing, accessories, and home decorations are attractively displayed in this Lincoln Park store. Zambian "Moon babies" made from clay, which are used as worry stones, are $2.25 each. Sterling silver jewelry from Yemen runs in the $30-$40 range, depending on the style.

There are symbolic scarab bracelets for $42, as well as a variety of *ankhs*, the Middle Eastern religious charm. A malachite bracelet from Zaire was recently spotted for $15. Small statues, drums, carvings and masks are also sold, as are the popular Kente hats and scarves from Ghana.

Kongoni is open weekdays from 11:30 a.m. to 6:30 p.m., Saturdays from 11-6:30 and Sundays from 12-5.

Studio V
- 5246 N. Clark St., Chicago; (312) 275-4848
- 672 N. Dearborn St., Chicago; (312) 440-1937

Studio V offers a fun assortment of

both new and vintage items, from fine articles to the truly kitschy. Owner Jack Garber also specializes in doing business with those people looking for "something old, something new" for wedding gifts.

Vintage silver lockets start at around $20, and marcasite jewelry—pins, earrings, and necklaces—range from $18-40. Garber makes a point of stocking lots of sterling silver and handcrafted jewelry from local artists in his huge display cases. Lapis and wooden items are modestly priced for their looks.

Vintage compacts, including those made with mother-of-pearl, are big sellers, as are new and used perfume bottles. For men, there are dozens of southwestern bolo ties in stock, as well as lots of money clips and cuff links.

The Dearborn store is open Mondays through Saturdays from noon to six p.m., while the Andersonville location is open Wednesdays through Fridays from 11-7, Saturdays from 10-5, and Sundays from 11-4 only.

V.I.P. Handbag and Accessory Outlet

- 2603 N. Elston Ave., Chicago; (312) 489-7690

Located on a street lined with outlets (sandwiched between Cub Foods and the Mark Shale Outlet), V.I.P. is the place to find department store surpluses at significant savings. The store primarily deals in leather bags and purses (see listing under "Shopping: New Clothing/Accessories"), but they also have a limited selection of jewelry sold at discount.

Merchandise changes frequently, but on any given visit you may find designs by Givenchy, Trifani, and Karl Lagerfeld at reductions of at least 15% off retail prices. Special sale items offer further markdowns of up to 50 percent off.

Wabash Jewelers Mall

- 21 N. Wabash St., Chicago; (312) 263-1757

Here's a new concept for an old business (actually, it's been here for ten years). The Wabash Jewelers Mall consists of 23 separate vendors, all at one address. As you walk in the door, you see row upon row of glass counters, each with a different merchant selling his or her own stock. The advantage for them is lower overhead costs; the advantage for you is bargain prices. Competition amongst the dealers, as you may guess, can be sharp, though they claim it's all friendly enough—but, depending on what you're looking for, you may be able to do some very convenient comparison shopping and come away with a sweet deal.

Prices can be as much as 50% below retail value; many are near wholesale, plus sales tax. And with so many mini-shops, just about every kind of item is represented: Diamonds, colored gemstones, pearl, watches and watch repair, estate jewelry, and more. Here's an example of a recent bargain from one of the dealers (it gets rather technical, but Mr. C was implored to get all the facts exactly right so that there could be no disputing the truth): A customer had seen a particular diamond in a retail shop, a 3/4-karat stone of SI-2 quality and F-color, priced at $4,250. He then came to this particular dealer in the mall, who was able to sell him a higher-quality diamond—VS-2, F-color—for $2,800. Now, there's an example that speaks for itself...even if you can't understand what it's saying.

The Wabash Jewelers Mall is open Mondays-Fridays from 10 a.m. to 5:30 p.m. (Thursdays until 6:30), and Saturdays from 10-5. For yet another goldmine of jewelers under one roof, you may also want to walk through the **Jewelers Center at the Mallers Building**, just down the street at 5 S. Wabash. This building houses no less than 135 separate businesses, many of which are wholesale only; you'll have to wander around and find the ones which sell to the public, but it may be worth your while.

LIQUOR AND BEVERAGES

Adelphi Liquors
- 2351 W. Devon Ave., Chicago; (312) 973-4466

Here's a small neighborhood liquor store which nevertheless carries its own weight with good prices, especially on wines. Burati Asti Spumante light sparkling wine was recently selling at $7 for the 750ml bottle, and Blue Nun white wine from Germany was $6 for the same size.

Corona "Extra" beer was priced at $5.99 for a six-pack. More serious stuff, like a 750ml bottle of Smirnoff vodka for $7.99 won't break the bank, either. And not-to-be-overlooked tonic water from Schweppes was just 90 cents for a one-liter bottle.

The store provides free delivery for orders of twenty dollars or more.

Armanetti Beverage Mart
- 3066 N. Lincoln Ave., Chicago; (312) 935-0505
- 515 N. Western Ave., Chicago; (312) 226-4600
- 4430 S. Kedzie Ave., Chicago; (312) 847-1166
- 10000 S. Western Ave., Chicago; (312) 239-2800

And many other suburban locations
Buying from any of the Armanetti chain stores is a good idea since their large-volume buying translates to big savings for you. The Lincoln Park store, open since 1938, is a case in point (no pun intended).

The store vehemently claims that it will meet or beat any price at Walgreens or Osco. In many instances, these prices are still not the absolute lowest you can find, but they're good—and the staff is genuinely helpful.

At the low end of the scale, a six-pack of Busch beer (in cans) is just $1.99, while Carlsberg bottles are $4.89 for a six-pack. Leinenkugel

cans in a twelve-pack were recently on sale selling for $4.49.

Prices on fancier liquors include J & B scotch at just $12.99 and Remy Martin Cognac VSOP for $28.95, both in the 750ml size. Freixenet Cordon Negro champagne was a very reasonable (one might almost say bubbly) $6 a bottle.

If you're having a party, it's reassuring to know that local delivery is free; and an eight-pound bag of ice will put you back only another $1.19.

Buy-Low Liquors
- 5201 N. Clark St., Chicago; (312) 338-5560

While this Andersonville shop doesn't carry the widest selection of beers, Mr. C will forgive it for the low prices on the stuff it does stock. In fact, this place has a rather eclectic selection of obvious choices and more unusual brands. The store is well-arranged, and the sales help is more than willing to give you a hand.

Buy-Low was recently selling a six-pack of Beck's beer for $5.99, a good deal indeed. Meanwhile, a tall, 750ml bottle of a Japanese beer called Sho Chiku Bai was only $5.39. And, for you champagne lovers, Cordon Negro was only $7.99 for the 750ml bottle.

Cardinal Liquors
- 3501 N. Central Ave., Chicago; (312) 725-0900
- 4905 N. Lincoln Ave., Chicago; (312) 561-0270
- 4132 W. Peterson Ave., Chicago; (312) 545-6661

And many other suburban locations
This local chain gives good discounts on a full range of liquors and wines. Whether you want a 30-pack case of Old Style in cans for $8.99, or a 1.75 liter bottle of Gordon's vodka for the same price (both as offered in recent sales), you can do very well with

your cash at one of these stores. Other good prices seen here in recent months included a 750ml bottle of Kahlua for just $7.99, a 1.75 liter bottle of Myers rum for an incredibly low $9.99 (with a mail-in rebate), and your choice of blended liquor "coolers" from Jack Daniel's, Southern Comfort, Jose Cuervo, or Bacardi, each $3.99.

Wines here tend toward the inexpensive brands, such as Almaden and Gallo. A 750ml bottle of Sutter Home white Zinfandel may go for just $3.99 here, or you can lay in a good supply of Inglenook's version at $6.99 for the three-liter jug. Cardinal stores are open daily from 9:00 a.m. to midnight, and Sundays from 11 a.m. to 8 p.m.

Casey's Liquors

- 1444 W. Chicago Ave., Chicago; (312) 243-2850

While this west-of-town store has good deals on all kinds of liquor, Casey's is particularly renowned for good deals on all kinds of beer. Whether your taste runs to great domestic microbrews like Sierra Nevada Pale Ale (at just $4.99 for a six-pack of bottles), or good ol' Budweiser (24 cans, $9.99), you'll find excellent prices here. Kegs start as low as $39.95, for Bud, Miller, and Old Style.

Chicago Meat House

- 4750 S. California Ave., Chicago; (312) 927-3200

Don't be misled by the name—there's more here than "meats" the eye. This is a complete discount supermarket, where bulk fresh and frozen meat is just the beginning of the savings. Along with just about all the foods you'd expect at any grocery store (only better priced), there is also a soda and liquor section with similarly discounted prices. A 1.75 liter bottle of Smirnoff vodka sells for $14.99, and one liter of Bailey's Irish Cream is $23.95; lesser-known brands offer even better deals, like a 1.75 liter bottle of Hannah and Hogg whiskey for $10.99. Sodas, such as Royal Crown cola and A & W root

beer, are priced at $6.25 for a case of 24 cans. Plus bags of ice and styrofoam coolers.

The Chicago Meat House (see what we mean about the name?) is open from 8 a.m. to 5:30 p.m. on weekdays, and from 8-5 on Saturdays. They have a spacious parking lot, and they accept cash, checks, credit cards, and food stamps.

Crown Cut-Rate Liquors

- 2821 N. Milwaukee Ave., Chicago; (312) 772-9227

This Polish Village shop specializes in imported beers. Expect a crowd to be streaming through here evenings, and especially on weekends.

Watney's Red Barrel or Stout English beer is just $5.99 a 6-pack. Domestic beers are also low-priced, such as Miller Lite in cans at $3.29 for a six-pack.

Jack Daniel's, at $10.99 for a 750ml bottle, and Johnnie Walker Red, at $19.98 for the 1.75 liter bottle, are among the good buys seen here. The folks who inhabit this neighborhood, however, probably prefer Luksusowa Polish Vodka—just $8.99 for the 750ml bottle.

You can afford to throw an elegant party with Martell VSOP Cognac for $23.99, Courvoisier for $13.99, and Bacardi black rum for around $9 a bottle (all in the 750ml size). Soda prices, including Dr. Pepper, Coke, and harder-to-find Orange Crush and Strawberry Sunkist, are only $1.99 for a six-pack.

Electra Liquors

- 5556 N. Broadway, Chicago; (312) 784-0601

This Edgewater shop is a good spot for deals on liquor, with free delivery to boot. Freixenet Cordon Negro champagne is $6.99 for the 750ml bottle; Malibu rum is $10.99 for the 750ml bottle. Absolut is also well-priced here, at $15.49; and the store carries lesser-known brands for extra savings, like DeBouchett black brandy, $2.79 for a one-pint bottle.

A six-pack of Busch beer was on sale for a mere $2.09, less than what you'd pay for Diet Coke in many

MR. CHEAP'S PICKS
Liquor and Beverages

✔ **Gold Standard/Chalet Wine Shops**—Chain-store prices, with boutique-style service.

✔ **Sam's Liquors**—These guys put the fun back in liquor shopping.

✔ **Wine Discount Center**—A small shop with an amazing selection of top-quality wines (only!) at up to 25% less than most other stores.

✔ **Zimmerman's Discount Liquor Store**—Another mega-discounter, with everything under the sun at great savings.

places; Miller Genuine Draft was only $6.49 for the suitcase of twelve 12-ounce bottles.

Electra will also give you special discounts if you're buying in large quantities for a party or other occasion.

Gold Standard/Chalet Wine Shops
• 40 E. Delaware St., Chicago; (312) 787-8555
• 405 W. Armitage Ave., Chicago; (312) 266-7155
• 3000 N. Clark St., Chicago; (312) 935-9400
• 1525 E. 53rd St., Chicago; (312) 324-5000

And many other suburban locations
Located all over town, these large shops proffer a vast selection of wines, spirits, beers, champagnes, and even some of the fine foods to go with them—all at good prices. Wander through the winding aisles, pick up a catalog of the latest deals, sample a bite of cheese. Everything is very clearly marked with prices and full-bodied descriptions, and the low-pressure salespeople are quite helpful if you need them.

Quality American wines may start as low as $4.49, for a sauvignon blanc seen here recently from Caymus Vineyards of California. The case price was just $50. Wines from New York state and Washington state offer more good deals. Other wine bargains hail from Italy and France, as well as Spain, Australia, Chile, and Israel; Aussie wines start at $4.99 a bottle, and Mr. C saw several Chilean wines from the Santa Carolina winery priced at just $3.99.

A bottle of Dry Sack sherry from Spain was seen on sale, reduced from its already-good regular price of $13.99 to a very dry $9.99. Among harder liquors, several 12-year-old single malt scotches were recently on sale at $19.99 for a 750ml bottle, including Glenlivet (normally $26.95). The 1.75 liter size of Dewar's White Label scotch was seen for $23.99; and the same size of Smirnoff vodka was seen for $13.99. Good prices on beer too, like a six-pack of Pete's Wicked Ale for $4.99, and many other large and small brands. And one-liter bottles of Canada Dry ginger ale were recently on sale for 59 cents apiece.

Gold Standard/Chalet also sells gourmet coffee by the pound at amazing prices; Columbian supremo and espresso roast were seen for just $3.99 a pound, and flavors like hazelnut go for $4.99 a pound. To go with your wine, French Emmental cheese sells for a low $2.99 per pound; Claudel brie is $4.99 a pound, and Valbreso sheep's milk feta cheese (also from France!) is $3.99 per pound. You'll also find imported crackers, mustards and vinegars, extra virgin olive oil, and other packaged gourmet foods at good prices. Open seven days a week.

Sam's Liquors
• 1000 W. North Ave., Chicago; (312) 664-4394
This large, well-stocked, full-service liquor store rambles on and on; every section is bulging with cases of wine, beer, liquor, champagne, cordials, or sodas. Each week brings special sales

on many items, to which you are alerted by electronic message boards overhead. The sales clerks are kept very busy, squeezing through the aisles crowded with displays and customers (at least, this was the case on a weekend visit by Mr. C). Still, they are super-friendly, and will stop the moment you ask for help, and give you any information you may need.

Mr. C uncorked several good deals on champagnes, including Bollinger's Special Cuvee, marked down from $38 a bottle to just $22; and a 1985 vintage Dom Perignon, reduced from $89 to $69. There are rows upon rows of wines to choose from; you can find good prices in all varieties, but for dependable and inexpensive options, try some of the lesser-known wine producers, like Chile. A bottle of Caliterra Sauvignon Blanc sells for just $3.99, marked down from $5.50.

It seems that Sam's carries every beer made in the world, especially those from American microbreweries. A recent sale featured a six-pack of Snakebite beer (from Australia, mate) for a low $2.99, or $10.99 per case. *That's* a deal. In the liquor section, Mr. C noted Bushmills Irish Whiskey at $19.99 for a 1.75 liter bottle; and a one-liter bottle of Tanqueray English gin for $15.75.

Another fun (and definitely cheap!) feature at Sam's Liquors is the free wine tastings, which take place every Saturday right in the store. In fact, Sam's hosts several tasting events every month, like "Champagne Night" and lecture visits by renowned wine experts. Not all of these are free, though. For more information, call or stop in to get on their mailing list. The store is open daily from 8 a.m. to 9 p.m., and Sundays from 11-6. As you can see, there's quite a lot going on here!

Treasure Island

- 3460 N. Broadway, Chicago (312) 327-3880
- 1639 N. Wells St., Chicago (312) 642-1105

- 75 W. Elm St., Chicago (312) 440-1144
- 680 N. Lake Shore Dr., Chicago (312) 664-0400
- 2121 N. Clybourn Ave., Chicago (312) 880-8880

And other suburban locations.
Treasure Island is a paradise for yuppies buying brie and marzipan and imported food at far-out prices; but its liquor department offers surprising bargains. You can afford to celebrate when Moet & Chandon champagne is only $32.99 for the 750ml bottle. Absolut vodka is only $15.79 for the same size. And—great Scotch!—a liter of J & B is just $21.99.

Beer drinkers will appreciate the prices on quality brands like Samuel Adams—only $5.99 for a six-pack. At the other end of the spectrum, Milwaukee's Best is just $1.99.

More news from the grapevine: Wines, like Beringer White Zinfandel at $6.49 a bottle, and Sutter Home Chenin Blanc for just $4.99, are some of the buried treasure you may find here.

United Liquor Marts

- Various Chicago locations; see below

Not a store in and of itself, United Liquor Mart is a loose confederation of independent stores which feature many of the same prices all over town. At any one of the merchants listed below, you may find such deals as a 750ml bottle of Seagram's 7 Crown whiskey for $6.99; the same size of Absolut vodka for $13.99; a 1.75 liter bottle of Cuervo Gold tequila for $20.99; or the same size of Hiram Walker's Ten High bourbon for $9.99.

In wines and champagnes, 1.5 liter bottles of Sebastiani Zinfandel or Beaujolais were recently selling for $5.99, while Tott's Champagne was $4.99 for the 750ml bottle. And a special 20-can case of Old Style beer was on sale for $6.99, in regular, light, and "Classic Draft" varieties.

So, where are these deals to be found? Here is the list of stores in the United Liquor Mart chain:

American Liquors, 1515 W. Roosevelt Rd., Chicago; (312) 243-5056

Archer Liquors, 5996 S. Archer Ave., Chicago; (312) 582-2176

Armanetti Wine & Liquor, 5130 W. Fullerton Ave., Chicago; (312) 237-0298

Banner Discount, 10558 S. Ewing Ave., Chicago; (312) 721-9393

Eddie's Liquor, 4321 S. Ashland Ave., Chicago; (312) 247-5881

Edison Park Liquors, 6694 Northwest Hwy., Chicago; (312) 631-4630

Gee Jay Liquors, 8550 S. Pulaski Rd., Chicago; (312) 582-8550

Gonzalez Liquors, 4027 W. 26th St., Chicago; (312) 521-7425

Hani's Liquor Station, 2601 W. 51st St., Chicago; (312) 436-8822

Kimbark Liquors, 1214 E. 53rd St., Chicago; (312) 493-3355

Manhattan Liquors, 4200 N. Broadway, Chicago; (312) 404-8600

North Shore Beverages, 1677 W. Howard St., Chicago; (312) 764-2423

Oasis Liquors, 3184 N. Clark St., Chicago; (312) 525-1000

Park Food and Liquor, 2610 W. 71st St., Chicago; (312) 776-1821

Park West Liquors, 2581 N. Lincoln Ave., Chicago; (312) 935-8197

Saginaw Liquors, 2615 E. 83rd St., Chicago; (312) 721-1060

Talman Liquors, 2627 W. 63rd St., Chicago; (312) 737-2813

Wine Discount Center

● 1826 ½ N. Elston Ave., Chicago; (312) 489-3454

For over six years, people have been flocking to this Clybourn Corridor shop for unbeatable values on fine wines. Owner Bud Schwarzbach gets about fifty to seventy new labels in each month, with an eye toward high quality in every price range. His prices are nearly always a few dollars below other stores—about 25% less than full service stores, and even 10% to 20% below Osco and Walgreens, which cannot offer nearly the same selection, or certainly the service.

Being a small store, every wine is carefully selected for quality; the people on the sales staff have tasted each wine, and can also suggest foods to go with every one. A few examples of recent bargains: Korbel champagne, which may sell for $7.99 to $9.99 in discount stores, and even higher elsewhere, is priced at $6.99 here. A Kendall-Jackson chardonnay, often found for $10.99, sells here for $7.99. And you may find highly-rated 1990 vintage Bordeaux for as little as $5.99 to $8.99 a bottle.

As Bud says, everyday prices at his store are like the "special sale" prices at other shops. He even stocks good wines for just $1.99 a bottle— the well-respected Duna wines from Hungary, available in chardonnay, cabernet and merlot. "They're not as good as $5 or $10 wines," he notes, "but they are definitely comparable to the $3 and $4 American wines." The Wine Discount Center is open daily; from 10 a.m. to 7 p.m. on weekdays, 9-5 on Saturdays and 12-5 Sundays. It offers a free monthly mailing to customers, announcing the latest arrivals; call or drop in to get on the mailing list.

Zimmerman's Discount Liquor Store

● 213 W. Grand Ave., Chicago; (312) 332-0012

Zimmerman's touts itself as the world's largest discount liquor store, and they're not kidding. Once you find the entrance from the street (down a couple steps and around the corner), this River North store can save you plenty, from diet soda to champagne. They also hold occasional (but large-scale) wine-tasting sessions.

A bottle of Chateau Malmaison Bordeaux, which the store tells us is highly recommended by the wine critic of the *New York Times*, sells here for $14. In the champagne department, Moet & Chandon goes for an incredible $15.99 for the 750ml bottle. And good ol' Gallo Chablis Blanc goes for just $2.79 in the same size.

Not only does Zimmerman's import wines from France and Italy, but it also stocks many wines from less snooty (therefore, less expensive) countries, such as Spain and Australia. These places produce wines which are considered comparable to many of the fancier vineyards, at several dollars less per bottle—a great way to save.

Hard liquor is also reduced dramatically; Jack Daniel's is $11.99 for a 750ml bottle, and the 1.75 liter size of Stolichnaya Russian vodka is $18.99.

In the extensive beer section, a six-pack of Samuel Adams is $5.65; and Bud Light cans are $10.99 for a suitcase of 24. A six-pack of Diet Coke, meanwhile, is only $2.40, saving you about 50 cents off most other places. Evian water is $1.59 for the 1.5 liter bottle.

Zimmerman's is open Mondays through Saturdays from 7:30 a.m. to 8:00 p.m., and Sundays from 11-5. They have free parking, too—if you can maneuver into a spot while their shipping trucks are unloading.

LUGGAGE

Emporium Luggage
- 128 N. LaSalle Ave., Chicago; (312) 372-2110

This Loop store has been selling fine luggage, briefcases, and other business accoutrements since 1945. They sell a good variety of well-known name brands at very competitive prices; and you can always expect to find a selection of sale items, where the discounts are even better. Mr. C found a Hartmann garment bag, the sort that folds over into a soft suitcase, reduced from a list price of $460 to just $190. A selection of genuine leather briefcases was on hand, with prices starting as low as $49. Emporium also carries things like Liz Claiborne handbags, and Filofax leatherbound organizers—a group of which were recently on sale for $30, a terrific price. The service is friendly and helpful, in a relaxed atmosphere.

Kaehler Luggage
- 2734 N. Clark St., Chicago; (312) 525-5705

And other suburban locations
Kaehler, which sells both luggage and leather goods, is an oldie (around since 1920) and carries quite classy, high quality merchandise. Their special purchases and closeouts, along with occasional sales, make them one

to check out early in your search for a new suitcase or briefcase, or carry-on.

A leather briefcase by Atlas, for example, originally selling for almost $400, was seen for only $180. A ladies' handbag by Kenneth Cole, in either black or red leather, was only $110, while a binocular-case shaped Coach bag (the real thing!) was selling for $94. These usually retail around $150.

Luggage by great names like Lark, Delsey, and Boyt are here, but you'd be wise to wait for a sale on these. A large Samsonite weekender duffel bag, usually $150, was cut to $90 on such a sale; and the popular Tumi wheel-away carry on suitcase,

---

MR. CHEAP'S PICKS
Luggage

✔ **Kaehler Luggage**—Check out their closeout bargains, especially at their suburban outlet branches.

---

retailing for $375, was only $329 here. A Hartmann garment bag was $20 off at $140. Kaehler also makes its own bags, sold under the rather original name, Outta Here. One Outta Here nylon duffel bag, retailing for up to $80 elsewhere, was seen for $55.

Kaehler recently closed down its Gold Coast shop on Oak Street, reducing their overhead and helping to keep prices down. For even bigger savings, you should definitely pack yourself off to visit their outlet stores in the Deerbrook and Town & Country Malls.

That's Our Bag
- 50 E. Randolph St., Chicago; (312) 984-2626
- 200 N. Michigan Ave., Chicago; (312) 984-3510
- 734 N. Michigan Ave., Chicago; (312) 984-3517
- 230 N. Michigan Ave., Chicago; (312) 984-2628

It's this store's bag that you get reduced prices on super name brand purses, backpacks, luggage, briefcases, and wallets from names like Coach, Samsonite, and Kenneth Cole's Unlisted. You'll really regret it if you miss their end-of-season inventory clearance sales.

During Mr. C's visit, he found a leather Anne Klein II shoulder bag in that trendy basket-weave design. Originally retailing for $102, it was marked down 20% to a price of $79. A Silhouette soft suitcase by Samsonite was a mere $119, almost half its retail price of $215; and an Irina Maxim camera-case shaped purse, in buttery-soft leather, sold for $25 off at $100.

Not everything in the store is leather, however. Black bags by Unlisted (Kenneth Cole's alter ego, of sorts) were only $50, but looked like they should cost four times that much. Surprise—they're not leather! For many people, that's an important philosophical option. If you simply can't afford the real thing, at least you can fake everyone out with these.

MUSICAL INSTRUMENTS

Here's another category in which you can save money by "going used"—though many instruments actually increase in value as they age. Often, a better-quality instrument which can be repaired is a better investment than a cheaper, newer version.

Biasco Pianos
- 5535 W. Belmont Ave., Chicago; (312) 286-5900

And other suburban locations
Biasco sells major American and international brands of traditional and electronic pianos. Their prices on new models are competitive, but the way to score really big savings is with their used, reconditioned units. New spinet pianos start from around $1,400; baby grands are priced from $3,990 and up, and digital models can be found for as little as $495.

Among used pianos, though, you can select from dozens of choices which begin for as little as $485. Most, in fact, are priced under $1,000; grands start over a grand, at around $1,400. All of these carry a five-year store warranty, and monthly payment schedules are available. Biasco's Chicago branch is open seven days a week, while its suburban warehouses in Elk Grove and Lisle are open from Thursdays through Sundays only.

Field's Piano Company, Inc.
- 4735 W. 120th St., Alsip; (708) 389-6400

At Field's Piano, just a bit outside of

town, you'll find new and used pianos and organs, as well as brand-new digital pianos and keyboards—over 400 pieces in all—at 40% to 60% off retail. These prices are sure to make your heart sing.

For example, at Field's you may find a Yamaha Grand Piano for $5,975. Sounds like a lot? The same piano, if new, would retail for $8,400. If you'd prefer something that *is* new, how about a grand piano by Hyundai (and you thought they only made cars!). Ignore the retail tag reading $10,950—Field's was selling them recently for just $4,995. For something a little smaller, a Sangler and Sohne console piano, with a retail price of $3,495, was seen on sale at Field's for just $1,695. In fact, pianos start here for as little as $395.

Field's also sells organs. A used Hammond B3 or C3, each retailing at about $7,100, can be had here for around $3,400. By way of new organs, a Viscount RBX 950 was seen for just $1,425, a substantial savings from the $2,490 retail price.

Field's doesn't carry used electronic keyboards, but there is still a bundle to be saved on their new models. A Casio CPS 300, retail price $695, was on sale here for just $395; and a Casio CPS 350 with a list price of $1,695 could be bought here for $795.

This may be a warehouse, with prices to prove it, but it is definitely not a "no-frills" joint. Field's offers free delivery, a free bench with your purchase, and a free tuning. They have warranties from 90 days to five years, depending on the merchandise, and they do their own repairs.

Kagan and Gaines Music Company
- 216 S. Wabash St. (4th Floor), Chicago; (312) 939-4083

In what is sort of Chicago's closest thing to a music district, you could easily miss Kagan and Gaines—since the only thing seen at the street level is a door leading to an elevator. Make your way upstairs, though, and you'll enter a no-frills, professional store

that is just packed with musical instruments of every kind. Guitars, keyboards, woodwinds and brass, violins, they're all here. The salesmen will walk you down a hallway lined with little side rooms and closets, each one of which is filled to capacity (in fact, their crunch for space has led to the opening of a second store, in Forest Park).

The instruments here are both new and used, all mixed together by type. In this business, used isn't necessarily cheaper; a top-quality brand name may actually increase in value as it gets older and rarer. But there are some bargains to be found, like an all-wood clarinet which could be worth $800 new, but sells here for $350. Or a Gibson acoustic guitar, half of its original price at $500. It takes a bit of searching.

If the brand name isn't crucial to you—say you're just noodling around, or you want a cheap instrument for your ten-year-old prodigy who may chuck it all for baseball instead—there are plenty of good, used instruments at bargain rates. Trumpets from $250, electric guitars from $150, acoustics for $75. You can find amplifiers and empty cases here, too, not to mention strings, sticks, reeds, and just about any other accessory you need.

Meanwhile, K & G also discounts its new instruments—by as much as 30% to 40% below list price. And they're sometimes willing to deal; you'll get a bigger discount, for instance, if you pay in cash. That's music to anyone's ears.

Music House, Inc.
- 2925 W. Devon Ave., Chicago; (312) 761-3770, (312) 262-2051.

It's hard to find a street better for bargain shopping than Devon, and this tiny store has great prices on guitars. They're marked way down from original prices, because they are used; but they're in good condition. The selection varies, depending on what owner Richard Trumbo can find. Recently a used full-size Goya classical acoustic was $139, and a

MR. CHEAP'S PICKS
Musical Instruments

✔ **Biasco Pianos**—Quality used pianos, reconditioned in the store, starting under $500.

✔ **Pinter's Violin Shop**—Top-notch used violins, lovingly restored, sell here at low-octave prices.

---

black bass guitar by Stinger was $150, knocked down from $325. Trumbo also offers lessons.

Musician's Network
- 5505 N. Clark St., Chicago; (312) 728-2929

Located in Andersonville, this music shop sells new and used instruments that can save you plenty. You'll probably want to shy away from the vintage instruments, many of which have been carefully refurbished and run $1,000 and up.

The store did have a used George Washburn acoustic guitar for $350, though, and a used drum set by Pearl on consignment for the same price. A four-piece Pearl drum set (missing the snare drum, though) was only $300.

The store has a high rate of turnover, mostly on its more inexpensive trade-ins, so the selection varies widely from week to week. Definitely worth a look.

Pinter's Violin Shop
- 3804 N. Clark St., Chicago; (312) 248-6536

Pinter's is a charming Wrigleyville repair shop selling discounted used violas, violins, cellos, and basses. You can watch the technicians stringing horsehair, polishing a violin body, or fixing bridges. In-house repairs cut down on overhead, which means

lower prices—that's always music to Mr. C's ears...and yours! And the prices are often negotiable, a nice feature of small shops like this one; you can deal with Mr. Pinter himself, who has run the place for 26 years.

For children just beginning to take lessons, or adults looking to start up again, this is an excellent place to buy a violin. What would cost up to $2,000 if new, may be only $425-$450 here. A twenty-year old full-size German violin by William Lewis & Co. was selling for $350, but valued well over $400 for its fine quality spruce and maple body.

Some of the instruments are investment-quality, though, and not quite in Mr. C's price range. On a recent visit, Pinter's had seven bass violins in stock, from a gorgeous 1825 American spruce priced at a cardiac-arrest inducing $13,000, to a Czechoslovakian model made in the 1920's priced at $4,000. Pinter's handmade violins are of beautiful quality, but are also pricey.

Mr. Pinter keeps his shop open six days a week in the summer, but stays open only until 3:00 in the afternoon on Saturdays. Call ahead to double-check if the store is open.

Kurt Saphir Pianos
- 310-322 W. Chicago Ave., Chicago; (312) 440-1164

And other suburban locations

A store that has stayed in the same family for six generations, Kurt Saphir restores old pianos, many of which come to the store through estate sales and the like. Roger Ebert bought his piano here; Mr. C adds his own thumbs-up. Saphir also sells brand-new models, in the middle- to upper-end price range.

Mason & Hamlin and Kawai are the two predominant brands carried here, and these are discounted due to the volume of sales and low overhead in this River North warehouse. If you're pricing around, be sure to check them out.

PARTY SUPPLIES

Card and Party Warehouse

- 1265 N. Milwaukee Ave., Chicago; (312) 227-9900
- 4216 W. Belmont Ave., Chicago; (312) 736-4900

And other suburban locations

It doesn't look like a warehouse. It looks like a festival in here, with balloons and streamers and bright colors everywhere. Yet, these decorative items are being sold at prices of up to 70% below retail. Save 25%-50% on packs of invitations, and 50% off all greeting cards, all the time—except for the extra clearance section, where all cards are just a quarter apiece.

A complete set of plastic utensils for eight people is just 63 cents; a pack of fifty plastic 10-ounce drinking cups goes for $3. Mylar balloons, with prints for every conceivable occasion, are priced at three for $5, and those little exploding champagne bottle party favors are six for a dollar. And, if you want to decorate a complete theme party from floor to ceiling, whether for children or grownups, this is a great place to look—and save. Open seven days a week.

Edward Don & Company Outlet

- 2525 N. Elston Ave., Chicago; (312) 489-7739

One of several super outlets on this stretch of Elston, Edward Don is not to be missed. It's a restaurant supply house that's open to the public, with lots to see for your kitchen and dining rooms. The back room here is full of discontinued and close-out kitchen supplies and appliances, while the front area offers a range of regularly-priced kitchen accessories and party supplies.

It's kind of fun to wander through the behind-the-scenes side of the restaurant biz; past big bottles of cleansers and stacks of plastic ash-

trays, paper plates, napkins, punch bowls, and much more. Lots of this stuff would be appropriate for wedding receptions or really big parties—another angle to consider here.

In the front room, Mr. C found all kinds of party decorations and accessories, such as a package of 24 birthday candles for 69 cents—cheaper than the Hallmark store. That back room, however, is the true bargain bonanza. Party planners can find votive candles at $9.99 for six dozen; ten-ounce glass wine goblets for just $1 each, a pack of 250 paper doilies for $1.25, and Dixie paper bowls at $6 for a 125-pack.

A set of eight linen napkins, regularly $20, sell here at half-price. Paper napkins, in many bright and pastel colors, sell at 50 for $3.50, and 250 drinking straws are just $1.29. Check 'em out!

The store is open Mondays through Fridays from 10:00 a.m. to 6:00 p.m., Saturdays from 9-5, and Sundays from 11-4.

Factory Card Outlet

- 6560 W. Fullerton Ave., Chicago; (312) 622-3338
- 4604 S. Damen Ave., Chicago; (312) 927-8927
- 8059 S. Cicero Ave., Chicago; (312) 582-7787

This chain takes the "superstore" approach to the greeting cards and party supplies market. Sooner or later, y'know, there's gonna be at least one superstore for absolutely *everything*. Anyway, for starters at FCO, all holiday and greeting cards are priced at 39¢ each. Period. And they don't just have a few, yellowing leftovers from last Arbor Day—it's a huge, current selection. Obviously, high-volume business allows them to make up the difference elsewhere.

What else do they sell here?

MR. CHEAP'S PICKS
Party Supplies

✔ **Factory Card Outlet**—A party supply "superstore."

✔ **Pyramid Cards and Gifts Outlet**—A new clearance center for these trendy card and knick-knacks shops.

Everything you need to invite people to a party, decorate it, and serve them food and drink. And it's all sold at 30% to 70% below retail prices. Whether you want to go simple, with color-coordinated plates and napkins, or go all out—with ten-inch tapered candles in a palette of colors (four for $1), 80-foot rolls of streamers (68¢ each), paper or plastic tablecloths, "Batman" napkins, and helium balloons (59¢ each, inflated for you in the store), chances are you'll find what you need here at discount.

Seasonal supplies, of course, are a specialty, well in advance of major holidays. Do people make fun of you for doing your Christmas shopping in July? Come in here—you'll be among friends, not to mention bargains on cards, wrapping paper and so on. This is also a good place to stock up on school supplies in August, and picture postcards anytime, at five for a dollar.

Pyramid Cards and Gifts Outlet
• 2574 N. Lincoln Ave., Chicago; (312) 665-9550

Opened in the summer of '93, this Lincoln Park shop is a clearance center for its two larger siblings at 3021 N. Clark and 1461 W. Webster, at Clybourn. At first glance, it looks just like any fully-stocked card shop; ah, but there are big differences here. All of the greeting cards in the shop are sold at half-price. And these include plenty of major lines, not some yellowing rejects that have been sitting in warehouse basements for years. The same half-off deal goes for novelty post-its, gift wrap, posters, and novelty items.

Wrapping paper, for example, that had been sold in the other stores at $4 a roll, sells here for $2, in plenty of varieties of colors and prints. Novelty jewelry, cheap stuff to begin with, is even cheaper here, like a pair of Chicago Cubs earrings—just the thing for the avid fan. Originally $5.95, they sell now for $2.99. A selection of humorous T-shirts are reduced from $14.95 to $9.95. And Mr. C loved a table clock in the shape of an orchestra conductor, originally $40, now $19.95. Since this is a clearance outlet, you never know quite what will show up here; but again, they have all the basics and then some. So why shop at full-price?

Sills Paper Company
• 841 W. Randolph St., Chicago; (312) 666-6387

This isn't really a party goods store; located in the wholesale food district near Fulton Market, it's mainly geared to serving restaurants. But, if you need large quantities of basic supplies, such as disposable plates, utensils, and cups, you're as welcome to shop at this no-frills place and get the same prices as the food business.

Plastic knives and forks, for instance, come in boxes of 25 (not an outrageous amount) for $1.50. Sixteen-ounce clear plastic cups by Solo cost $3.75 for a pack of fifty. A 125-pack of three-section dinner plates, of extra heavy cardboard by Chinet, goes for $10.95. And you can get fancy two-ply dinner napkins, in a variety of colors, at $5.95 for a package of 125. If you're planning a really big party, you may make out very well here—and they're certainly not likely to run out of stock.

PET SUPPLIES

Animal Kingdom

- 2820 N. Milwaukee Ave., Chicago; (312)227-4444

Animal Kingdom sells both supplies and pets, from puppies to kittens to more exotic beasts, like the occasional capuchin monkey. The back area, where the animals are kept, can get doggone rowdy, especially if there's a myna bird present; it certainly adds to the liveliness of the shop.

Among its selection of pet supplies, a forty-pound bag of Iams puppy food is well-priced at $30.88; and a Ro-pa bone for those in-between meal snacks is $5.29. Fuzee Muzzles are $9.99.

As mentioned above, the store has a good range of birds, and supplies. Ultra Blend Parakeet Condition Food, by 8 in 1, costs $1.99 for an eight-ounce bag.

For the aquarium, snails are 99 cents each, small angel fish are $3.99, and Marble Mollies are $1.99. A nine-inch air grass plastic aquarium plant by Plantastics is $2.39.

Animal Kingdom opens its gates to you from 10:00 a.m. to 9:00 p.m. on weekdays, Saturdays from 9-6, and Sundays from 10-6.

Famous Fido's Doggie Deli

- 1533 W. Devon Ave., Chicago; (312) 761-6029

Would you feed your dog brownies? Or, for that matter, cookies, doughnuts, pretzels, pizza, and bagels? Gloria Lissner does. And she's foisting them upon more and more innocent pooches all the time. Now, before some animal rights activist tries to collar Mr. C or Ms. Lissner, an explanation is necessary.

Of course they're not real. And yet they are, in a way, since Famous Fido's motto is "Real Food for Dogs." What all this actually means is real *ingredients*, healthy stuff only, with no preservatives, fats, sugar, salt, meat, or by-products. For the last dozen years, Ms. Lissner has been developing wholesome foods for dogs, shaped and colored to look like human foods just for fun—and to drive home the message that we should take as much care with our pets' diets as with our own.

The idea began in her own kitchen, on her own dog, Fido; careful experimenting with the help of vets and food analysts, along with—er—dogged marketing have led to a million-dollar business. Famous Fido products are sold around the country, from upscale pet shops right on up to Bloomingdale's. "I started with things that I would want to eat, and that were healthy," says Lissner, who uses grains, oatmeal, honey. "I've found that even the most finicky dogs love this food."

And now she's renovated her shop to look like, well, a fancy deli. Tiled floors, a glass counter brimming with colorful cookies (boy, do these things look *good*), and booths with red-checked tablecloths create a festive atmosphere—which is just the idea. Y'see, what people do is bring their pup pals in for birthday parties. Yes, that's right. It's a full meal, including cake and ice cream; owners bring something for themselves, and everyone eats together. Talk about your party animals.

Sure, it's fun, but is all this cheap? Well, not as cheap as bringing home a can from the supermarket—but don't forget how much healthier Famous Fido's food is. It's gotta be cheaper to come in and buy direct from the source than to get it in Bloomics, that's for sure. And in small quantities, you can certainly give your dog a special treat without a major spending splurge. The parties

MR. CHEAP'S PICKS
Pet Supplies

✔ **Famous Fido's Doggie Deli**—Buy your pooch a slice of pizza (made of ingredients he can really eat) for 75 cents.

✔ **PetCare and PetCare+ Superstores**—Great prices on foods of all kinds.

---

cost $12 per pooch, but that includes four courses. You can also shop for take-out; a tray of assorted "cookies and pastries" is only $4, and the above-mentioned "pizza" is 75¢ a slice. And check out the new walk-in "meat freezer," where you and your pet can pick out something fresh for dinner together.

One Pet Plaza
● 1533 W. Devon Ave., Chicago; (312) 973-3436

Located at the rear of Famous Fido's Doggie Deli (see listing above), One Pet Plaza is a more traditional pet shop offering every kind of product and accessory imaginable. They have good prices on high-quality pet foods like Iams, Science Diet, and other popular health brands. An eight-pound bag of Eukanuba dry dog food for adults is $9.50; a twenty-pound sack of Nutro Max "Natural Choice" for dogs is $17.50.

On the feline side of things, the Nutro Max is $23.50 for a twenty-pounder (the food, not your cat). Natural Life Feline Adult is $6.29 for four pounds, and $11.39 for eight pounds; Eukanuba dry cat food is priced at four pounds for $7.10 and eight pounds for $13.00.

Yet another business, the third under one roof, offers all kinds of pet grooming services. One Pet Plaza is one busy place.

PetCare and PetCare+ Superstores
● 2053 N. Clybourn Ave., Chicago; (312) 348-0550
● 8117 S. Cicero Ave., Chicago; (312) 735-3250
● 4072 N. Milwaukee Ave., Chicago; (312) 777-7387

And many other suburban locations
With four locations in Chicago proper and twenty more throughout Chicagoland, PetCare and PetCare+ stores probably have the area's best deals on pet food and accessories. IAMS canned dog food sells for just 89 cents a can, and Friskies Buffet cat food is only 28 cents a can. These are just a couple of examples of their prices, which are good all the way up to the forty-pound bags of dog food. There are plenty of supplies for other kinds of pets, including fish, birds, and guinea pigs. Pet's Pal pine shavings, used for lining the bottoms of cages, are only $2.49 for the 2,000 cubic-inch size.

Petland
● 6560 W. Fullerton Ave., Chicago; (312) 237-0202

As the name suggests, Petland takes a sort of theme-park approach to pet shops. They call it a safari, and you do almost have to cut a swath through the aisles. The place is just packed with fish tanks, bird cages, the requisite puppies, kitties, and bunnies...and kids. On a weekend, anyway, which is when Mr. C happened to venture in. It's lively, to say the least.

With Petland's good prices, it's no wonder the store is so popular. Here are just a few representative prices: A five-pound bag of Nutro Max puppy food sells for $5.99; Iams kitten food is $12.99 for the eight-pound bag, while Science Diet Maintenance dog food comes in a twenty-pound sack for $17.99. Cans of Science Diet Feline Maintenance food are 69¢ and $1.29 for the small and large sizes, respectively. And they also carry similar selections of food for birds, fish, and other small domestic animals.

Along with these everyday prices, Petland runs monthlong sales, when you can get specials like a Doskocil "Kennel Kab" for $19.99 or dog shampoo for $5.99 a bottle. And if you join their "Club Pet" (for an an-nual fee of $7.99), you'll be entitled to all sorts of further discounts, such as 10% off all non-sale pet foods, 15% off cat furniture, free bird grooming, and all sorts of one-time-only deals. Woof!

SEWING AND CRAFT SUPPLIES

Creative World Superstore
● 418 S. Wabash Ave., Chicago; (312) 922-6767

This three-level South Loop store is staffed by friendly, well-informed art-ists. The dizzying selection, from paints to easels to Plaster of Paris, is chock-full of discounts. Looking up at the clouds painted fresco-like on the ceiling will make you dizzy, too.

The store's own brand of acrylic paints are $1.79 for the 1.25-ounces size. Black display easels by Chart-Pak are $135 here, priced well below the suggested retail of $180. And similar savings can be found on leather portfolios, page protectors, lamps, pens, and markers, among other supplies. The store also offers a framing service.

Loomcraft Home Decorating Fabrics
● 3330 N. Clark St., Chicago; (312) 404-1100
● 640 LaSalle St., Chicago; (312) 587-0055

And many other suburban locations
Buying mill-ins in big lots allows this chain to cut prices. Their selection is geared towards material for uphol-stery and drapes. The stores are neatly organized by color and pat-tern, which saves time, though it can be a bit dizzying. The majority of fab-rics here are cottons, with some syn-thetic blends in the upholstery section. Their remnant table is super-cheap, but good luck finding a roll with enough for whatever project you're working on.

Pinstripe fabric, in pastel colors, is $9.99 a yard; they note that it sells for $18-$25 in other stores. First qual-ity floral prints, similar to Laura Ashley designs, were seen for $12.99 a yard, with a retail value of up to $32 elsewhere. Heavyweight cotton, suitable for sofas and chaircovers, is reduced from a comparable $25 to just $9.99 per yard; same price for a *moire* print, offered in ten colors. A very sturdy cotton weave was priced at $19.99, as compared to $35-60 elsewhere.

Two caveats: If you see some-thing you like, buy it right away—since Loomcraft can't guarantee what stock they will ever get again. Also, their upholstery service prices can hardly be considered a bargain. But, for the do-it-yourselfer, this is the place!

Minnesota Fabrics
● 3326 W. Belmont Ave., Chicago; (312) 463-0180
● 3016 N. Ashland Ave., Chicago; (312) 549-6300
● 3000 S. Ashland Ave., Chicago; (312) 808-0491
● 7601 S. Cicero Ave., Chicago; (312) 767-2254

And many other suburban locations
For sheer selection at great prices, Minnesota Fabrics has got the city covered. They are a full service chain, with fabrics, patterns, tools and supplies, fillings, and even sew-ing classes.

They've got vinyl and burlap for upholstery. Cotton cloth for draper-ies. Lace for bridal gowns. Lycra for swimwear. Supplies for making and stuffing quilts and pillows. You name it. Furthermore, there are always

MR. CHEAP'S PICKS
Sewing and Craft Supplies

✔ **Minnesota Fabrics**—A chain
of sewing and fabric
"supermarkets."

plenty of these items on sale—below
MF's already-low prices.

One recent sale offered stretch
terry cloth at half of its usual discount price, bringing it down to just
$1.75 a yard. The above-mentioned
bridal lace was on sale for $2.88 a
yard; some 50/50 blends are just
$1.00. Cotton knit solids were half-
price at $1.50, and cotton prints start
as low as $2.00 per yard, from 60-
inch-wide bolts.

There are lots of remnants, generally selling at half of the original bolt
price, and other clearance tables
where fabrics are 20% to 50% off.
Most branches also have a monthly
senior citizen's discount day, when
they'll take a further 10% off the total purchase.

You get the idea. This place is
like a fabric supermarket; they even
have shopping carts for the truly industrious. The staff is extremely courteous and helpful, guiding you about
the store or cutting lengths of fabric
for you; they can also custom order
anything you may need. They offer
sewing machine repair and scissor
sharpening services (try saying *that*
three times fast) at fair rates. And, as
noted above, you can register for
classes in sewing, craft-making, creating your own Christmas presents, and
the like. Many of these vary from
store to store, so you'll want to check
in with the branch nearest you.

SHOES AND SNEAKERS

Adams Factory Shoe Outlet
• 3655-3659 W. Irving Park Rd.,
Chicago; (312) 539-4120
Here at the Adams Factory Shoe Outlet, you can save from 10% to 60%
off retail on all kinds of shoes for
men, women, and children. Adams
sells factory overstocks, samples,
slight irregulars, and closeouts—in
styles from casual to dress shoes,
work shoes to athletics. They also
sell accessories, like hosiery and
handbags. The store aims to carry
only American made products.

They actually have a unique pricing system here. If a price ends in
"8," say, $49.98, then the shoe is first-
quality. If the price ends in "9" (such
as $49.99), the shoe is slightly irregu-
lar. And, if the price ends in "0"
($49.90), the shoe is a closeout, over-
run, or sample. Shoes are cleaned and
repaired, if necessary, before they are

put on display; and irregular shoes
are clearly labeled as such.

There is also a good selection of
specialty shoes. Women's therapeutic
shoes, which normally cost $117 to
$170, sell here for $44.99 to $89.99.
Men's therapeutic shoes, which can
cost $200 and more, sell here for
$59.99 to $99.99.

Or, just come in for coffee.
Adams serves free coffee and tea in
the store, plus lollipops for the kids.
And here's something you seldom
see anymore: Full service, including
sizing. All at a store that charges less
money than at downtown shops!
Open seven days a week, from 9 a.m.
to 6 p.m. daily, and 10 a.m. to 4:30
p.m. on Sundays.

Alamo Shoes
• 5319-25 N. Clark St., Chicago;
(312) 784-8936
When a store takes up more than one

street number, you know that the selection has got to be pretty impressive. Alamo more than meets this expectation, with boxes and boxes of shoes for children, men, and women. All of the big names like Tretorn, Timberland, and Reebok are here, with displays of discounted shoes making for great buys. Mr. C did feel, though, that the overly attentive clerks who kept hovering about could use some Valium.

Some shoes on the discount rack are ever-so-slightly to rather-obviously scuffed; these are probably returns, so do check them over carefully.

Seen recently in this Andersonville store were Candies sandals for just $15, or three pairs for $40. For men, Frye boots were a ridiculously low $150 for two (yup, pardner, that's *two*) pairs, or one pair for $80. These can retail for $180 or more! Men's Rockport wingtips, regularly retailing for $100, were reduced to $80.

The prices aren't so fantastic on Birkenstocks, Hush Puppies, or Nine West shoes; it may be prudent to wait for sales on these if you're shopping here.

Two other Chicago stores are affiliated with Alamo: **Izen Shoes** at 4023 W. North Ave., telephone (312) 235-9375; and **Kay Shoes** at 2839 N. Milwaukee Ave., telephone (312) 489-4350.

At Kay Shoes in the Polish Village, Reebok Fitness Walkers for women were selling briskly at $50, about $20 off the retail price. Child Stride leather-upper dress shoes or sandals were $15 a pair; not-as-durable-looking children's sandals by Li'l Prints were just $5. Also, nursing shoes by Nurse Mates were almost $15 off the manufacturer's list price, selling for $50.

Chernin's Shoes
- 606 W. Roosevelt Rd., Chicago; (312) 922-4545
- 2665 N. Halsted St., Chicago; (312) 404-0005

- 1001 S. Clinton St., Chicago; (312) 922-5900

And other suburban locations.
Chernin's has a pretty solid foothold in Chicago's discount shoe biz, having been at it since 1907. Their service matches their prices; this is one store where you don't have to wait for a sales assistant—ever.

The selection in women's, men's, and children's shoes is all-encompassing. Designer names like Via Spaga, Esprit, Nickels, Mia, and Charles David are at least $10 off retail. Etienne Aigner heels were only $65 at Chernin's recently, and go for over $80 in many department stores.

For men, Florsheim dress shoes were recently selling at two pairs for $110. Sperry's classic "Top Siders," originally $75 retail, were seen for $60 at Chernin's. Bostonian, Easy Spirit, Dexter, Rockport, Zodiac, Hush Puppies, New Balance, and more are all discounted daily, too.

For children: Converse All-Stars, practically a part of the school uniform for guys, usually sell for $32; here, they are only $26. The sneaker selection also includes models by Ryka, KSwiss, Avia, Keds, Nike, and L.A. Gear...all price-reduced as well.

Chernin's ShoeMart Express
- 3035 N. Pulaski Rd., Chicago; (312) 282-2626
- 5139 S. Pulaski Rd., Chicago; (312) 284-7272
- 6560 W. Fullerton Ave., Chicago; (312) 804-0494

And other suburban locations
"ShoeMart Express" is the clearance side of the Chernin empire. These smaller shops are popping up all around town, selling off overstocks and discontinued shoes and sneakers, for men, women, and kids. Honestly, there is just about as much selection—usually at better discounts—than you'll find at many regular shoe stores.

Women's leather loafers by Dexter, for instance, were seen here recently at half of their original price, just $30. A pair of shiny silver leather shoes from Nine West was reduced from $45 to just $19. And gals who wear small sizes will love rummaging through the samples table, where size 5 and 6 shoes with list prices of up to $80 all sell for a mere $12.99. Dexter, Selby, and Timberland were all seen here on a recent visit.

For men, slip into a pair of tassel loafers from Stanley Blacker, once $80, here $58. A pair of smart-looking patent leather shoes by Steeple Gate was reduced from $100 to $60, and Mr. C lassoed a pair of Zodiac western boots for just $78—originally, they were $145. Sturdy looking Bay Colony suede work boots, meanwhile, were 30% off at $50.

Athletic shoes are here too, like Reebok basketball hi-tops, slam-dunked from $60 to $48 in a good range of sizes. ShoeMart Express is a no-frills set up, with all shoes sitting out on racks for you to search through and try on in the aisles. These stores also have some accessories, such as socks and hosiery, at discount. Open seven days a week.

Chicago Shoe Market

● 1541 W. Chicago Ave., Chicago; (312) 733-3822

This busy store in a Hispanic section west of town specializes in top brand-name sneakers for the entire family, at good discounts. A recent sale featured a variety of children's Reeboks, with list prices of $45-$75, selling for just $27.90. L.A. Gear shoes for infants were $23 off at $12.99. Men's leather hi-tops by Converse were marked down from $43 to $19.99, while similar styles by Pony were reduced from $70 to $24.95.

For women, Reebok's pink-and-white "Princess" sneakers were cut from $55 to just $34.90; and casual sneaker/shoes by L.A. Gear's "Pier Avenue," once $45, sold for $19.90. Plus canvas shoes for $5.99. Other brands found here include Nike, Fila, Puma, and more.

Now, many of the shoes found here are not current models; these tend to be leftovers and discontinued styles, and some are only available in certain sizes. But it's definitely worth

a look, especially for families on a tight budget. Open seven days a week.

Chicago Shoe Outlet

● 3212 N. Lincoln Ave., Chicago; (312) 528-4433

This store specializes in athletic shoes and men's casual footwear, at discounts of anywhere from 10 percent to 50 percent below retail prices. They carry such brand names as Reebok, L.A. Gear, and Fila. Among the bargains recently found were a pair of Nike running shoes with a list price of $60, selling instead for $45. Timberland boots were another good deal at $85, a substantial savings from their $110 retail price.

The Chicago Shoe Outlet opens weekdays at 10 a.m., closing at 7 p.m. on Mondays and Thursdays, 6 p.m. on Tuesdays and Wednesdays, and 8 p.m. on Fridays. Saturday hours are 9:30 a.m. to 7 p.m.; Sundays, 11:30 a.m. to 5:30 p.m.

Famous Footwear

● 2731 Clark St., Chicago; (312) 477-0400
● 6560 W. Fullerton Ave., Chicago; (312) 804-1100
● 9645 S. Western Ave., Chicago; (312) 238-2876
● 6199 N. Lincoln Ave., Chicago; (312) 478-9275
● 1730 W. Fullerton Ave., Chicago; (312) 528-0077

And other suburban locations

Always selling shoes and sneakers at 10% to 50% off manufacturer's suggested retail prices, Famous Footwear can make you look like a celebrity for less. With the money you save, perhaps you can afford that chauffeur you've been meaning to hire....

All shoes are first-quality, with savings provided to customers by cost-cutting within the company on shipping, billing, and such. Recent bargains found at Famous Footwear include women's Esprit sandals for an unheard-of $5, L.A. Gear sneakers for $39 (listed at $46), Naturalizer high heels reduced from $57 to $32, and Mootsies Tootsies shoes for $10.

Doc Marten boots, listed at $120

MR. CHEAP'S PICKS
Shoes and Sneakers

✔ **Adams Factory Shoe Outlet**—Up to 60% off on shoes for the entire family, in a good ol' family-style shop.

✔ **Chernin's Shoes**—For discounts on current styles, shop Chernin's; for better deals on closeouts and overstocks, check out Chernin's ShoeMart Express.

✔ **Famous Footwear**—This chain sells many "famous" brands at up to 50% off.

✔ **Lori's Shoes**—Good discounts on the most current fashions in women's footwear.

✔ **Nine West & Company Outlet**—Clearance prices on this popular brand, as well as a few others.

a pair, were marked down to $100 here. Nike cross-trainers and Reebok high-tops for girls sell for about $10 off retail, and girls' Tretorn tennis shoes scored an ace at twenty percent off retail, only $30.

Men can jog out of the store having saved big on Saucony Jazz running shoes, ten bucks off at $50, and Fila high-tops, regularly $85, selling for $75. Boys' Air Sonic basketball sneakers by Nike, with a suggested retail of $70, were only $60.

There's plenty of stuff for your famous child here, as well. Playskool sneakers for toddlers, for example, sell for $20, which is almost $10 off the list price.

Almost as impressive as the savings was the fact that the sales floor was extremely neat and organized—despite the massive sales event which happened to be taking place during Mr. C's visit.

Giorgio Brutini
- 132 S. Wabash St., Chicago; (312) 263-2551

This shop, not much bigger than Mr. C's closet, is the only store in the city specifically selling Brutini shoes. They do carry some other brands, but these are overshadowed by the presence of GBs.

Despite the tiny selection (and lack of larger sizes), this shop is worth checking out. If you get lucky and find something you like, you're bound to save up to 50% off retail here. Some examples were a pair of Botany 500 leather dress shoes with tassels, recently seen for only $49.95; and casual, sandal-style Brutini shoes on the specials rack selling for only $29.95.

A word of note: Even the selection of Brutini shoes is not huge, making Mr. C wonder how long this shop will stay in business; perhaps it was just a case of the in-between-season blahs.

Hanig's Shoe Rack
- 2754 N. Clark St., Chicago; (312) 248-1977

Unless you're a millionaire, pass up Hanig's Footwear on the corner of Diversey and head right for the adjacent Rack. It's tiny, messy and crowded, but full of bargains brought in from the ritzy Michigan Avenue and LaSalle Street branches. The main store carries everything from Doc Martens to Birkenstocks to Clarks to Rockports—but only the Rack will offer any real savings.

Be aware, though: Some shoes, particularly the dressier styles, are scuffed and were probably exchanged. But for men, if you're in between sizes 7-11 only, and women with feet size 7-10, you may be in luck. The shoes are well-organized by size, although they tend to get piled up on top of each other. Rummage and ye shall find good stuff.

A pair of men's Florsheim leather wing-tips were seen here for $40; Johnston and Murphy loafers were $80; and Cole-Haan sneakers were a remarkable $20. For women, recent selections included Bandolino high heels for $20, pumps from the Nine West "Spa Collection" for $29.90, and Easy Spirit shoes for just $30 (that's over $25 off retail). Nothing for the kiddies here, alas.

Lebo's Shoe Outlets

- 2037 N. Clybourn Ave., Chicago; (312) 871-0004
- 7939 S. Cicero Ave., Chicago; (312) 585-9004

And many other suburban locations. This 'Bo knows good sneaker and shoe prices. Almost everything you see in these shops is a well-recognized national name-brand, and the help won't hover over you, helicopter-style. The selection is constantly changing. They deal in overstocks in dress shoes, casual sandals, sneakers, and even hiking boots and roller-blades.

For women, Gloria Vanderbilt leather pumps were selling for $19.95, marked down from $36. Only two colors were available, but they were neutrals, not the hard-to-build-on purple or orange leftovers sometimes found in such outlets. Easy Spirit leather pumps, sold for up to $75 in department stores, were seen for only $45 at Lebo's; but once again, only two colors were stocked.

Keds canvas sneakers for girls and women, regularly retailing for $26 or so in other stores, were found at Lebo's for $19.95. The leather versions, usually $44, were $10 off here.

For men, Eastland penny loafers were $10 off, selling for $36.95. Avia tennis sneakers were on special sale; normally retailing for $50, the regular price of $43 was further reduced to just $35.

Lebo's also stocks a variety of children's shoes and sneakers at similar discounts. The variety, as you can see, is not fantastic—but checking in every once in a while may turn out to be worth your while.

Loop Footwear

- 142 S. Wabash St., Chicago; (312) 368-5010

This store sells urban casual and dress shoes at very competitive prices, with terrific special sales. In one recent promotion, shoes by Giorgio Brutini and Botany 500 were offered at two pairs for the price of one. Expect this store to have just as good prices as the Giorgio Brutini store, which is practically next door at 132 South Wabash.

Lori's Shoes

- 808 W. Armitage Ave., Chicago; (312) 281-5655
- 311 Hap Rd., Northfield; (708) 446-3818

Many of the stores listed in this chapter offer deals on "past season" leftovers. Lori's Shoes, however, discounts overstocks of current styles. They carry a wide range of women's brand names, from Keds to evening shoes to western boots, and everything in between. The discounts are not as deep as at other places, naturally; but, at 5 to 30 percent below retail prices, you can do quite well. There is also a good range of sizes. The atmosphere, despite its trendy look, is rather like a chic bargain basement; it's strictly self-serve, resulting in a room full of women all standing around on one foot at a time.

Lori's also has accessories like socks, hosiery, purses, and some jewelry. Among the names you'll find here are Hue, Calvin Klein, Giorgio Armani, Joan & David, Anne Klein, and Paloma. The Lincoln Park store is open seven days a week; their Northfield location is closed on Sundays.

Morris & Sons

- 555 W. Roosevelt Rd. (2nd Floor), Chicago; (312) 243-5635

Located upstairs in a nondescript building next to a bank, this shop is one of Chicago's true shopping discoveries. It's a goldmine of current-season *couture*—designer sportswear, suits, dresses, and accessories. Prepare to be astonished by the discounts and selection, and pleased by the knowledgeable, friendly service.

This family-run business has been around for over forty years, sending its buyers to annual designer shows in New York and Europe, with a special emphasis on Italian merchandise (hint, hint; they asked Mr. C to not mention any names in the book). For many prominent Italian designers, in fact, this is the *only* current-season discounter in the United States. Morris & Sons sells clothing from 30% to as much as 70% below current, regular prices. How? Because they buy direct, because of their low-rent location, and because they offer no tailoring services.

In addition to its (literally) thousands of suits, dresses and separates, Morris can save you 50% on dressy shoes, in traditional styles, for men and women. Morris & Sons are complete outfitters, from top to toe.

If you've never heard of this place, don't feel slighted; Morris saves more on its costs by not advertising. They do enough business strictly through word-of-mouth, and from regular customers who come in every year from as far away as London and Japan. Once you spend $350 or more in the store, you'll be added to the mailing list—and, you'll be allowed into their annual private clearance sale. That's when, for ten days only, everything in the store is sold at wholesale cost.

Nine West & Co. Outlet
- 2739 N. Clark St., Chicago; (312) 281-9132

Selling high-quality leather shoes is Nine West's specialty, and this is the place to get past-season styles for a fraction of their original prices. As is the norm (at *any* shoe store), it helps to be a size 7 when it comes to selection availability—but have no fear, the smaller and larger sizes are here, too.

Enzo Angiolini heels were $29.97, a remarkable price considering these Italian-made shoes sell in the $100 range at fancier boutiques. Nine West's own leather flats, selling

for $64 in their specialty stores, are $45 at the outlet; they come in nubuck, patent leather, and regular leather styles. The shoe colors are generally tasteful here, and styles from platforms to pumps to cowboy boots are stocked.

Spencer
- 3031 N. Central Ave., Chicago; (312) 777-5556

A liquidator of men's clothing closeouts from around the country, Spencer has a very large assortment of everything to furnish the well-dressed guy from head to toe. Most of the stock is first-quality, and much of it is by top designer names—though you'd never expect it by looking at the faded storefront in this low-rent neighborhood. 'Twas not always thus. Inside, the warehouse atmosphere is strictly no-frills; clothing hangs from every rack and rafter, boxes of shoes are piled on top of each other, and cartons of jeans sit open in the center of the floor. The place goes on and on, though, and there's quite a lot to see.

The main attraction here is the huge selection of fancy men's suits. To go along with these dressy looks, there are lots of dressy shoes, too—overstocks by Pierre Cardin, Ferragamo, Giorgio Brutini, Stacy Adams, Nunn Bush, Timberland, and more, are all priced at $59 a pair. Sizes, unfortunately, are limited, but with so many to look through, you may just find something great. There are also some athletic shoes, sometimes on sale for as little as $10 a pair, as well as jogging suits and separates.

Spencer is open all seven days, from 10:00 in the morning; they close at 7 p.m. Monday, Thursday, and Friday, at 6 p.m. Tuesday, Wednesday, and Saturday, and at 5 p.m. on Sunday.

141

SPORTING GOODS

Calcoastal Volleywear and Activewear Outlet
- 2420 N. Clark St., Chicago; (312) 327-6067

For the Sinjin Smith in the family, volleyball clothing and accessories can be found here on the cheap. The store also keeps its shoppers informed of activities on the local volleyball circuit. The store isn't huge, but they manage to pack in warm-up suits, shorts, and tank tops. The sales help is friendly, yet unobtrusive.

While many of the shirts can really be considered unisex, men's clothing dominates the store. A men's nylon windbreaker by Sideout, with a retail price of $68.50, sells here for $44.95. Matching pants, for $36.50, were $12 off retail. A $32 heavy cotton sweatshirt by Leggoons, stocked in bright colors, also sells at similar savings. And women's racing swimsuits, by Arena, sell for $40.

The store's focus, though, is on volleyball shorts. A nylon/polyester pair by Red Sand were $30, about $6 off retail. The ever-important sun visors, again mostly by Sideout, are about $3 off retail prices, selling for about $14 a pair.

Chicago Sports Exchange
- 4159 N. Western Ave., Chicago; (312) 583-7283

Mr. C thinks used sporting goods stores are one of the best aspects of the recycling 90's. After all, you *want* a baseball mitt to be broken in, right? And these things can be sooooo expensive. Yet, for some reason, it's a concept that seems to be striking out in the business world.

Well, Chicago Sports Exchange carries a wide range of new *and* used sporting goods, all at discount prices. Whether your passion is baseball, football, scuba diving, hockey, or ice skating, you can probably find the equipment you need here, for up to 50% less than retail. Among the second-hand equipment, Mr. C found some Spaulding baseball gloves, which retail for about $69, for $35. Soccer and football spikes, usually about $39, can be had here for as little as $15. Prices are low even on new merchandise, which tends to be discontinued stuff and last year's overstocks.

The Chicago Sports Exchange also has a selection of bicycles; mountain bikes, f'rinstance, start from just $75. A repair service, for all items, is offered as well. CSE's hours are from 10 a.m. to 7 p.m. Tuesday through Friday, and 10-3 on Saturday and Sunday. Closed Mondays.

Chicago Tennis Company
- 1000 W. North Ave., Chicago; (312) 951-2941

Tucked into a shopping center between Sam's Liquors (which you will find elsewhere in this book) and the Whole Foods Market (which you will not), Chicago Tennis Company sells equipment and clothing for all racquet sports—tennis, racquetball, squash and, badminton—at good discounts. They offer a combination of new and used equipment on consignment, which can be a great way to add to your arsenal of weaponry and still have enough left over to hit the juice bar at the club.

A Prince Lite I Classic tennis racquet, with a list price of $150, normally sells here for $130; recently, it was further reduced on sale for $110. Same thing for a Dunlop Pro Pulsar; list $129, regular price $99, sale $75. There is a wall full of new racquets to choose from, and all new racquets include basic (synthetic) strings.

Among the other new items seen here were a Dunlop Airfoil squash racquet, reduced from a list price of

MR. CHEAP'S PICKS
Sporting Goods

✔ **Chicago Sports Exchange—** Why pay full price for a stiff new baseball mitt, when you're only going to break it in anyway? Good new and used equipment here.

✔ **Chicago Tennis Company—**Everything you need for all racquet sports, all at discount, plus a "testing" alley.

✔ **Recycle—**Bicycles, that is. Cheap deals on new and used wheels.

$110 to $70; and an Ektelon racquet-ball model marked down from $120 to $80. You'll find balls and accessories here as well, all at good discount prices.

But, as Mr. C often suggests, do consider going with used stuff! This is an especially good idea for folks who want to try the game, but aren't sure if they'll stick with it—parents of little ones, take note too. There are two such options here. The "Demo Sale" rack has plenty of brands, sizes, and styles to choose from, most priced around $80 (all used just a few feet away in CTC's "Indoor Demo Lane," another nice feature of the store). Another, smaller rack has consignment racquets in good shape, all clearly tagged with the price, model and owner's name. Mr. C saw a fine looking Dunlop "Max Classic" for just $50. You can, of course, sell your own used equipment here as well.

Kozy's Cyclery and Fitness
- 601 S. LaSalle St., Chicago; (312) 360-0020
- 3712 N. Halsted St., Chicago; (312) 281-2263
- 1610 W. 35th St., Chicago; (312) 523-8576
- 1451 W. Webster Ave., Chicago; (312) 528-2700

Mr. Kozy is an adamant believer in customer service. Shopping at any of his locations is truly a pleasant experience, with knowledgeable, athletic sales associates who can tell you all about the products. They're not nosy at Kozy's, though. If you want to just poke around, they'll let you.

Bicycles at Kozy's consist mainly of the middle-grade brand names, well-known ones like Schwinn. Recent buys included a GT Tequestra, with a list price of $520, selling for $470. A Schwinn Crisscross bike, listed at $350 retail, sells here for $300, and a Giant Option mountain bike was just $240.

Kozy's downtown branch is in big competition with the nearby Village Cycle Center, which has the high-end Trek business sewn up. Kozy's does have an excellent selection of accessories, though, with prices that are quite competitive themselves. A Kryptonite Kryptolock, for example, is about $30 at Kozy's. The Kryptonite Evolution 2000 Vetta LiteGel series saddles, available in racing, men's, women's, and wide styles, are each about $25.

MC Mages Sports
- 620 N. LaSalle Dr., Chicago; (312) 337-6151

And many other suburban locations
This River North store is an eight-level heaven for sports fiends, from golfers and hunters to scuba divers and campers. You can find the cap for almost any sports team in the country here, for instance; they line an entire wall.

MC Sporting Goods doesn't list comparable retail prices, but their high volume of sales allows them to sell their merchandise at reduced rates. For example, a Mitre soccer ball was selling for $20, about $10 below its retail price. A Wilson Fore 250 Racquetball racquet goes for $19.99.

For the weekend sports enthusiast, MC sells the Rubbermaid Sidekick Ice Chest for $9.99, and padded seats for bleachers are $14.99. Adidas logo T-shirts are $9.99. And racks and racks of sneakers for women, men, and kids—including Converse, Tretorn, Puma, and Reebok—are on sale, some priced as low as $10.

Minky's Bicycle Sales & Repairs

- 2834 W. Devon Ave., Chicago; (312) 743-9292

If you're looking for a used bicycle for a quickly-growing child, try Minky's—where they fix up old bikes and resell them super-cheap. It's also a good spot for adults who just want a reliable bike for errands or whatever, but don't want to have to worry about the thing being stolen. Some of these bikes look as if they've been around the block a few times, and some look as if they've been ridden around the world; but they'll still get you to where you need to go. Children's bikes tend to be in better shape than the often rusty-framed adult models.

Among the bargains, a Columbia Tourist V bike, suitable for a five- or six-year-old, was recently spotted for $65 at the Devon shop. A Sears Free Spirit 3-speed was only $60, and a Ross Countdown mountain bike, in super shape, came and went quickly at $90.

Which brings up a significant point. If you see something you really like in one of these stores, grab it! Minky's will warn you that these bikes practically fly out the door, especially ten-speeds.

Nevada Bob's Discount Golf and Tennis

- 60 E. Lake St., Chicago; (312) 726-4653

And many other suburban locations
A national chain, Nevada Bob's carries a huge selection of golf club sets, gloves, and shoes, tennis and squash racquets, and apparel—lots of equipment for men, women, and children, too. Tommy Aaron and Lady Aaron golf sets are as low as $240 for eight irons and $150 for three metal woods. Or, get a complete set of irons, woods, bag, and head covers, by Cyclone, for $300. Spikeless golf shoes start at $20. Stylo waterproof

shoes are $60, about a third of their pro shop price.

Prince tennis racquets are as low as $80, even lower during special closeout sales. And they have tennis socks for 99 cents to $1.99 a pair, along with clothing for both sports. Bob's also offers racquet restringing, as low as $10 for synthetic gut. Open seven days a week.

Recycle

- 1234 S. Wabash Ave., Chicago; (312) 987-1080

Mr. C loves a good pun, and the name of this place is certainly that. But Mr. C loves a good bargain even more, and they have plenty of those here, too. Recycle sells both new and used bicycles, with used bikes starting as low as $50. They carry a good range of brand names, including Raleigh, Peugot, and Schwinn. "Cheap rent means low prices," say the folks here, and they ain't kidding. Well, even if this place may be a bit out of your way, it's bound to be worth the trip.

All used bikes are fully reconditioned; they do their own repairs in the shop. The store is open Mondays through Fridays from 10 a.m. to 6 p.m., and Saturdays and Sundays from noon to 4 p.m.

Sportmart

- 440 N. Orleans St., Chicago; (312) 222-0900
- 6560 W. Fullerton Ave., Chicago; (312) 804-0044
- 3100 N. Clark St., Chicago; (312) 871-8501

And many other suburban locations
Sportmart is your basic, all-American, all-around sports center, with competitive prices every day (pun intended) on equipment and clothing for just about any athletic endeavor. From baseball, football, and basketball to jogging and hiking, there are plenty of choices to meet your every need.

Clothing and gear are a big part of the store, with things like NFL and NBA replica jerseys by Champion for adults and kids, not to mention caps for seemingly every single professional and college team ever to play. Save big on shoes from Reebok, Nike, Asics, Converse, and more; Reebok aerobic shoes for women were recently seen for just $29.96. Lots of shoes for kids, too, as low as $20.

Wilson "Hammer System" tennis racquets start at $29, while Ektelon racquetball weapons begin as low as $23. For hikers, there are full lines of backpacks from Eastpak, Jansport, and High Sierra, like the popular Jansport styles with leather bottoms for $29.94. And Nike small duffel bags were recently reduced from $19.96 to $9.93.

Sportmart stores are open seven days a week.

Universal Bowling and Golf Corporation

- 619 S. Wabash Ave., Chicago; (312) 922-5255
- 1926 S. Mannheim Rd., Westchester; (708) 562-3431

It's Al Bundy's dream come true. Not too big and not too fancy, Universal primarily sells bowling balls and shoes at discount, with some golf clubs added in—almost as an afterthought. The women's selection is miniscule, but what they do have is cut-price.

Bowling balls by Columbia and Brunswick, some of them discontinued, are almost always available at greatly discounted prices. Men's Brunswick X-Cell shoes were $58.95 on a recent visit, available in sizes 7-12 and 13. Women's shoes by Dexter, in the Raquel style, were $37.95.

Close-outs on men's and women's golf clubs, mostly by Universal's own brand, are $9.95 for iron and $16.95 for wood. Universal Classic clubs in the Open Stock models are $16.90 each for wood and $11.90 for iron. Woods are $22.95 each.

The store is open from 8:30 a.m. to 5:30 p.m. Monday through Saturday, but they close at 2:00 on Saturdays in the summer.

Village Cycle Center

- 1337 N. Wells St., Chicago; (312) 751-2448

For a store that sells ten thousand bikes a year, the front sales area of Village Cycle Center is not huge by any means. But don't be misled—they have four floors worth of stock that simply can't fit on the display floor. Only about 250 bicycles are shown in the front sales area, but about twenty times that number are stored in this Old Town shop.

Village Cycle lays claim to being the largest Trek store in the world. Their high volume equals low prices, but that's not all—each bike comes with a lifetime warranty, and two free fall tune-ups. Furthermore, any adjustments you may need during the first year of ownership are also done free of charge.

The shop is largely devoted to mountain bikes, although a few racing bikes can be found among the racks. A Trek 700, retailing for $335, was recently seen for $280; and a Trek Composite 8300, retailing for $970, was selling for $100 off. A Specialized Crossroads bike is a whopping $200 off, yours for $395. In fact, every bike in the store is discounted by at least $30, but most tend toward more dramatic reductions. Schwinn racers are all around $50 below retail, more or less, depending on the model.

Village Cycle is open weekdays from 10:00 a.m. to 9:00 p.m., and weekends from 9-6.

TOYS AND GAMES

The world of retail toys is a very competitive one; fun 'n games are serious business to such stores. They all tend to keep pace with each other, and so there aren't many places to save money beyond the well-known retail giants.

FuncoLand

- 1730 W. Fullerton Ave., Chicago; (312) 549-0885
- 6560 W. Fullerton Ave., Chicago; (312) 637-2727
- 7947 S. Cicero Ave., Chicago; (312) 284-5599

And many other suburban locations
Can't keep the kids in computer games? It's an expensive little habit, these Nintendos et. al., but there is a way to beat the system at its own game. The trick is to go with *used* software. Hey, why not? After all, how long would your child let a new game sit in the box anyway? They all look the same on the screen, and that's where it counts.

This national chain, based in Minneapolis, buys and sells games for Nintendo, Sega Genesis, Gameboy, and other formats, as well as the actual systems and accessories. Given their popularity, the stock of titles is enormous—it fills four pages of tiny type in a sort of catalog/flyer, which lists the names and prices that may be available at any branch. Of course, availability changes all the time, so not every title you see listed will be in any one store. The prices themselves, while below retail, are rather like those of old coins or baseball cards; the savings vary according to each game's popularity, supply, and demand.

Mr. C conducted a direct study, comparing the prices of games at random with those at a well-known national toy discounter. In most cases, the savings were good to excellent. "Zelda," for instance, selling for $30 new in the standard Nintendo format, can be gotten for $8 at FuncoLand. Meanwhile, the Gameboy version of "Home Alone," based on the movie, which was also $30 new at the big store, was only reduced to $22 at Funco. It's still a hot one, evidently.

A Sega Genesis version of "WWF Super Wrestlemania," featuring a character based on Hulk Hogan, was seen for $39, a savings of $10 below the department store; and "Roger Clemens Baseball" throws a strike at $44, a savings of $16.

The store also sells used, reconditioned, equipment and accessories. You can also save money on carrying cases, joysticks, power supplies, and other accessories, depending on stock; or, upgrade your older system instead of tossing it out and starting all over. Everything comes with a 90-day warranty, and you can always try out any games or equipment before purchasing. You'll love these stores because of the prices; your kids will love it because it's the modern version of a candy store, complete with several screens available for play. And you can sell them your old games too, for payment by check or store credit. Again governed by supply and demand, the amount paid out for certain games may be a small fraction of its original price; you'll get more, by the way, if you opt for store credit.

FuncoLand is open seven days a week, including weeknights until 9:00. Considering how quickly the novelty wears off on some of these games, the concept of paying less up front—and selling them off at the other end—may be the best way to score a win.

Mad Max's Cheap Stuff

- 852 W. Belmont Ave. (2nd Floor), Chicago; (312) 883-1800

With a name like this, how could Mr. Cheap pass it by? This quirky shop is sort of a clearance center for several other unusual businesses under the same roof, known collectively as "The Alley." These include Taboo Tabou, which sells racy lingerie, and The Architectural Revolution, which sells plaster-cast decorations for buildings. So at Max's, for instance, you could buy a nice gargoyle for your house—and some purple glitter to put in its hair—all at 50% to 80% below their original prices.

Beyond that, Mad Max's is a haven for novelty items, from wild sunglasses to wind-up toys, badges and tattoos (non-permanent). Come up here anytime to stock up for Halloween; there are shelves of old packaged costumes for $5 each, along

MR. CHEAP'S PICKS
Toys and Games

✔ **FuncoLand**—If your kids (or you) are hooked on Nintendo and Sega games, you can support your habit for less with used software here.

✔ **World Distributors**—A world of toys, among other things, at wholesale prices.

with such staples as vampire fangs and rubber rats. Y'know, wandering around in here is just plain fun. The store is only open weekends: noon to 7:00 p.m. on Fridays and Sundays, 10:30 a.m. to 8:00 p.m. on Saturdays.

Woolworth Value Store
● 1134 W. Bryn Mawr Ave., Chicago; (312) 784-0467

Everyone is familiar with the inexpensive merchandise available daily at good ol' Woolworth, but this far north mega-store really takes the cake. Along with bargains on clothing for the entire family, household needs and pet supplies, discount toys for the kiddies can always be found here. A Woolworth "super soaker" water gun was just $12, while its fancier equivalents cost as much as $20 in many other stores. For kids' parties, $3.99 will buy a Sesame Street character kit with cups and plates for eight and a matching tablecloth.

World Distributors
● 3420 N. Milwaukee Ave., Chicago; (312) 777-2345

Okay, this isn't exactly a proper department store. In fact, it's a wholesale distributor of everything from socks to stereo; and, amazingly enough, it's open to the general public. You can shop here and get the same prices that dealers get—in other words, "at cost."

Among the toys well-known and less-so, you can find all sorts of Fisher-Price and Sesame Street products at less than half-price; the "Musical Peek-a-Boo Big Bird," which retails for $22, sells here for just $6.50. Can you say "bargain," kids? As you might expect from an importer, there are lots of electronic toys, such as a rather sophisticated toy guitar (with strings and buttons). It includes a headset microphone for singing along, through a miniature speaker. The ensemble has a retail price of $75, but here it's just $24.90.

Not to mention walkie-talkies, race cars, educational games, dolls, and plastic tricycles. Everything is stocked right there on the showroom shelves. It's all at wholesale prices, meant for other stores to purchase in quantity, but also available to you without any membership deals or special rules. Pick up a catalog ($2, or free with any purchase), with its separate "insider" price list stapled into the middle. Stop in seven days a week, daily from 9 a.m. to 6 p.m., and Sundays from 11-5.

About a block away, **Star Distributors** at 3500 N. Milwaukee Ave., telephone (312) 725-7770, is a competitor with World. This shop is a bit smaller and much more cluttered; it offers much of the same merchandise, and most of its prices are comparable, though some appeared to be higher.

UNUSUAL GIFTS

This is Mr. C's "catch-all" chapter, in which he's put some of the stores which just don't fit anywhere else in the book. Many of the stores below are places to find truly nice gifts, while others fall more into the realm of the fun and decidedly offbeat.

Cross Cultures
- 2055 W. North Ave., Chicago; (312) 486-8689

All of the artwork, jewelry, and apparel in this shop on the Wicker Park-Bucktown border is handmade in Guatemala. For $12-$15, you can buy a ceremonial mask; terra cotta masks of different animals, such as pigs and monkeys, are also about $12. The store owners hang them from a string as door ornaments.

Cactus-shaped candles, selling for $3 apiece; a bracelet made from old silver coins, for $25; and colorful hand-woven Native American place-mats, just $5, are some of the many other interesting decorative and functional gifts which can be found in this lovely shop.

Flashback Collectibles
- 3450 N. Clark St., Chicago; (312) 929-5060

For a good belly laugh—not to mention the chance to buy an old Charlie's Angels lunchbox—find your way to Flashback. The merchandise and the salesmen are rather trippy (there's a "DRUGS OK" bumper sticker over the front window), but there's a good chance you'll find a funky gift for that friend who never got over his huge crush on Suzanne Somers during her "Three's Company" phase.

A poster for the above-mentioned friend is only $4, as is one of Andy Gibb or the Bee Gees. Rambo, Peanuts and *Close Encounters of the Third Kind* lunchboxes are about $5, with matching Thermoses a mere $1 more. And would your life be complete without *Battlestar Galactica* trading cards, selling at Flashback for just pennies apiece? Sorry, Lorne.

Have no fear if you scratched your old Pat Benatar LPs; you can replace them here for about $2 a pop. For your book collection, how about a copy of *Kristy and Jimmy, TV's Talented MacNichols*, for $2? That's one dollar a Mac. So what if the original

cover price on this paperback was $1.50—it's a collectors' item now! Also gracing the shelves during Mr. C's visit was the entire *Room 222* series for $3 or so a copy. When did these get turned into books? More importantly, why??

David Cassidy figures prominently around the store—you can get a gigantic sticker-backed photo of him for only $5. Somewhat classier memorabilia items, like movie posters (*Shoot the Moon*, starring Albert Finney, or Neil Simon's *Last of the Red Hot Lovers*) start as low as $4 each. And 8" x 10" advertising cards from the 1960's, for such products as Tang and Kellogg's Corn Flakes, are only $1.

Miscellaneous buttons, pins, patches, pencils, and stickers are also here for those wishing to have a Flashback of their own. The store is open daily from noon until 10 p.m., and on Sundays until 6.

Healing Earth Resources
- 2570 N. Lincoln Ave., Chicago; (312) EARTH-59 (327-8459)

From candles to jewelry to incense to $4 change pouches woven in Guatemala, Healing Earth Resources is bound to carry something gift-worthy, and boasts a vegetarian cafe next door, too.

Need a kilogram of incense? It'll be $80 here. If you're not that much into buying in bulk, you can buy an individual stick for about 25 cents. Large herbal candles are $6.25 each; while fat rainbow-striped votives, made entirely from beeswax, are $1.50 each.

Much of the jewelry is made of semi-precious stones, making for very attractive and elegant-looking gifts which are still quite inexpensive. Rose quartz and blue lapis necklaces hung on leather strings sell for about $16. The store is open seven days a week.

MR. CHEAP'S PICKS
Unusual Gifts

✔ **Illinois Artisans Shop**—
Ceramics, jewelry, ornaments
and more, all handmade by
local craftspeople.

✔ **Okee-Chee's Wild Horse
Gallery**—Native American
crafts, very inexpensive.

✔ **Uncle Fun**—An old-fashioned
"joke shop" with nostalgic
merchandise culled from
novelty warehouses around the
country. It's fun just to browse.

Illinois Artisans Shop
• 100 W. Randolph St., Chicago;
  (312) 814-5321

In the State of Illinois Center, home
also to the Illinois Art Gallery (see
listing under "Entertainment: Art Galleries"), this shop is dedicated to the
art of American crafts. From ceramics and jewelry to more unusual tradi-
tions like quilling and lace-making,
the shop has a fascinating selection
of both whimsical and practical art.
Specific crafts shown here have included Mexican printmaking, Native
American deerhide ornaments, wood
carving, Chinese clay figures, and
Jewish paper crafts and calligraphy.

It's all part of the Illinois Artisans Program, sponsored by the Illinois State Museum, which is
dedicated to promoting the work of Illinois craft artists. In addition to
showing work by local artists, members of the program also participate
in educational outreach. To this end,
the Illinois Artisans Shop features a
number of free workshops and demonstrations to introduce the public to
the tradition of crafts. Call them for a
schedule of upcoming events.

Kongoni Traditional American Handicrafts
• 2480½ N. Lincoln Ave., Chicago;
  (312) 929-9749

Authentic imported African and
Asian jewelry, charms, clothing, accessories, and home decorations are
attractively displayed in this Lincoln
Park store. Zambian "moon babies"
made from clay, which are used as
worry stones, are $2.25 each. Sterling
silver jewelry from Yemen runs in
the $30-$40 range, depending on the
style.

There are symbolic scarab bracelets for $42, as well as a variety of
ankhs, the Middle Eastern religious
charm. A malachite bracelet from
Zaire was recently spotted for $15.
Small statues, drums, carvings, and
masks are also sold, as are the popular Kente hats and scarves from
Ghana.

Kongoni is open weekdays from
11:30 a.m. to 6:30 p.m., Saturdays
from 11-6:30, and Sundays from 12-5.

Nuts on Clark
• 3830 N. Clark St., Chicago; (312)
  549-6622
• Union Station Concourse, Chicago;
  (312) 876-NUTS (6887)

And other suburban locations

The selection here may drive you
crazy, but you'd be nuts to not get
your pistachios, almonds or even
chocolate here. The stores frequently
offer tantalizing samples to shoppers,
including caramels and salted peanuts.

"Nuts" has been in business for
about fifteen years; during that time,
it's established a substantial mail-order business. Buying in bulk allows
them to pass savings on to customers.
So do their no-frills shops, where
fold-out tables covered with simple
cloths serve as displays.

Gift baskets for every occasion
are a specialty here, so if you're
stuck wondering what to get your
boss or cousin Quentin, stop in or
call to check out their wide selection
and prices.

Okee-Chee's Wild Horse Gallery
• 5337 N. Clark St., Chicago; (312)
  271-5883

Don't be led astray by the name—you won't find mares and stallions running amok in this Andersonville shop. You will find inexpensive jewelry, baskets, candles, and handcrafted Native American art here, though.

Beaded necklaces sell for only $3 apiece; and while it may sound odd, necklaces made with dyed corn ($6) are actually quite funky-looking. Wooden knick-knacks like a handpainted cactus ($5) or wolf ($7) line the shelves. Peach-colored pottery jars with handpainted southwestern designs, perfect for holding plants or votive candles, are also only $5, and other inexpensive works of art like God's eyes can be found in the gallery.

The large, framed Native American Indian-themed paintings on the walls can get into a more expensive price range, many going for a couple hundred dollars each; but they are authentic, and Okee-Chee herself can tell you all about the artists.

Omiyage, Ltd.

- 2482 N. Lincoln Ave., Chicago; (312) 477-1428

From gags like a whoopie cushion for $2 or a $1.50 pack of glow-in-the-dark sticky worms, to gorgeous $40 fancy cotton robes hand-made in India, Omiyage carries such a wide range of interesting imported goods that it's hard to categorize. Mr. C has placed it in this chapter, since it's a great place to check in with when you're stuck for a "different" gift idea.

Stationery, pill boxes and greeting cards are reasonably priced; and, mercifully, they're quite different from the same old stuff you can get at Walgreens. Metallic wrapping paper is sold here, too.

Cloisonne picture frames aren't super-cheap, but are reasonably priced for their fanciness. Clothing gets quite ornate indeed, but at $78 for a 100% silk dress, these are a real deal.

More of those gag items include door knob signs—like the kind you see in hotels—for $2.25. With these, however, you can warn people of a PMS attack or scare them away with language that isn't appropriate to print in a fine, family publication such as this. You'll just have to go and see them for yourself!

Pachamama's Hovel

- 1583 N. Milwaukee Ave., Chicago; (312) 235-MAMA (6262)

In the heart of funky, artsy Wicker Park, this relatively new shop sells an eclectic variety of Native American crafts (as well as some from Africa and the Far East) at affordable prices. The name, by the way, does not refer to something you do to your mother's head. Pachamama is an Earth goddess of the Andes, and it's this Peruvian culture which inspires so much of the merchandise in the store. Sterling silver drop earrings, delicately hand-crafted, are priced at $8.50, $10, and $12 a pair. A woven handbag from India was recently seen on sale, reduced from $48 to just $18. Good prices also on rings, scarves, and batik-dyed cotton dresses; as well as fascinating folk art pieces, like dolls and rain sticks.

Paper Source

- 232 W. Chicago Ave., Chicago; (312) 337-0798

If you're looking for some different gifts for creative children, or the artsier of your friends, try this River North store, located right next to the Ravenswood "el" stop.

The name is no joke; this store runs classes on paper-making, and so it truly is a paper source. All of the papers sold here are handsome indeed, and can make an elegant, yet inexpensive gift idea.

But it was the rubber stamps in the cramped back room which attracted Mr. C's eye for the offbeat. For about $5 and up, you can buy rubber stamps of everything from elaborate initials to pictures of celebrities to constellations and more. Paper Source can also supply you with the ink pads to go with these, in a variety of colors. Some pads even come rainbow-striped.

This can be a good place to look for inexpensive party, shower or wedding invitations; save some cash, and impress your friends, by making your own. The "It's A Shower!" stamp is only $2, and the sheets of paper start about 45 cents. What could be easier? Glitter-ized and other kinds of novelty print paper can be a bit more expensive, but will still save you money in the long run. The store is open weekdays from 10 a.m. to 6 p.m., Saturdays from 10-5, and Sundays 12-4.

Studio V

- 5246 N. Clark St., Chicago; (312) 275-4848
- 672 N. Dearborn St., Chicago; (312) 440-1937

Looking for kitschy costume jewelry or funky frames, as a simple gift for either a guy or a girl? Studio V offers a fun assortment of both new and vintage items, and owner Jack Garber specializes in doing business with those people looking for "something old, something new" for wedding gifts.

Vintage silver lockets start at around $20, and marcasite jewelry—pins, earrings and necklaces—range from $18-40. Garber makes a point of stocking lots of sterling silver and handcrafted jewelry from local artists in his huge display cases. Lapis and wooden items are modestly priced for their looks.

Vintage compacts, including those made with mother-of-pearl, are big sellers, as are new and used perfume bottles. For men, there are dozens of southwestern bolo ties in stock, as well as lots of money clips and cuff links. Picture frames start at about $12.

The Dearborn store is open Mondays through Saturdays from noon to six p.m., while the Andersonville location is open Wednesdays through Fridays from 11-7, Saturdays from 10-5, and Sundays from 11-4 only.

Uncle Fun

- 1338 W. Belmont Ave., Chicago; (312) 477-8223

It sure is. Kind of a variation on the good ol' joke shop, Uncle Fun is crammed with every novelty item you ever got caught with as a kid, from joy buzzers to fake you-know-what. It's somehow reassuring to know that someone is still making this stuff—and that today's jaded MTV-generation kids are still coming in to see it and spend their lunch money on it.

But owner Ted Frankel has gone beyond whoopee cushions. He has unearthed buried treasure from warehouses around the country—cases of "vintage" novelties you may have easily forgotten about. Remember things like "Magic Rocks" and "Sea Monkeys?" Ted's got 'em. Did you grow up with a 1960's character called "Ratfink?" He's here, too—in plastic rings for just 50 cents. Speaking of jewelry, let us not forget the height of fashion statements, the mood ring. Find a trove of them here for $2 apiece.

The store has a vast stock of items that verge on the world of collectibles. Wind-up cars from the 1950's; "bride and groom" decorations for wedding cakes made of plaster, not plastic, from the 1940's; and thousands upon thousands of old postcards, at six for a dollar. Plus movie and rock 'n roll memorabilia, like products from early Beatles and Monkees merchandising campaigns. Oh, and black velvet Elvis portraits—can't leave those out. Mr. C found a selection of them, framed and ready for enshrinement at $14.

Because Frankel isn't interested in these period pieces for the sake of collecting, his prices are often below market value. He'd rather keep his inventory moving at low prices, clearing a bit of space for whatever blasts-from-the-past that the next basement may yield. And he loves the fact that, with zillions of items under a dollar or two, those kids keep streaming in daily. They know they can always walk out with something fun.

Open at noon; closed Mondays and Tuesdays.

ENTERTAINMENT

Chicago is truly an amazing city for all kinds of entertainment that is inexpensive and often free. Movies, concerts, theater, museums, nightclubs . . . you name it, there's a way to experience it on the cheap.

Nearly everything in this section of the book is free, or only a few bucks; in some cases, Mr. C has found activities that are a bit more expensive, but discounted from their full prices.

There is no reason why a limited budget should keep anyone from enjoying the arts!

ART GALLERIES

Most city dwellers know that browsing through art galleries is one of the truly enlightening and (best of all) *free* cultural activities around. For no more than the price of an espresso at a nearby cafe—you *have* to do that, right?—you can while away a fine afternoon or early evening.

River North has Chicago's highest concentration of art galleries; it's become one of the city's trendiest districts, though not in an over-blown manner. In summer especially, there are gallery openings just about every Friday evening. Wander in, have some wine and cheese, dahling, and enjoy.

The Bucktown/Wicker Park area has become Chicago's second art center, with more of a gritty, experimental focus. Other galleries are scattered all around the town.

Some galleries may require you to buzz in, only for security purposes. Don't fear that you're being kept out because of an annual income below that of, say, Ross Perot; go on in! After all, the richer people are, the less they have to care about their appearances—for all the gallery owners know, someone in torn jeans could be an eccentric millionaire. Be sure to sneer at one or two paintings, as though you *could* buy one if it were any good.

American West Gallery
- 2110 N. Halsted St., Chicago; (312) 871-0400

This Lincoln Park gallery shows contemporary Southwestern and Western art, including seriographs, lithographs, paintings in oil, acrylic, and watercolor, and a number of mixed media pieces. Shows have presented such national artists as Hal and Fran Larson, husband and wife painters who work in watercolors and acrylics, respectively.

The American West Gallery represents some fifty artists and sculptors, including about twenty Native American artists. With so much recent interest in the culture of the southwest, this is a great place to get an overview of contemporary Native American art, including monoprints and sculptures in wood, bronze, and other metals. American West is open Tuesday through Friday noon to 6 p.m., Saturday 11 a.m. to 6 p.m., and Sunday noon to 5 p.m.

Atlas Galleries
- 549 N. Michigan Ave., Chicago; (312) 329-9330
- 900 N. Michigan Ave., Chicago; (312) 649-0999
- 41 E. Oak St., Chicago; (312) 266-0772

This trio of Gold Coast art galleries, which first opened in 1967, displays everything from Rembrandt to up-and-coming (read: unknown) artists in a variety of media. They feature original oils, etchings, watercolors, sculpture, graphic art, and museum-quality prints. With the likes of Renoir, Whistler, and Maimon, this is no lightweight collection. Very nice folks, too. All three locations are open seven days a week.

Douglas Dawson Gallery
- 814 N. Franklin St., Chicago; (312) 751-1961

The Dawson Gallery specializes in native handcrafted art from Africa, Asia, and the Americas—including textiles, ceramics, furniture, and sculpture. A recent exhibit,"Temples," featured vintage photographs of archeological sites. The Dawson is open from 10 a.m. to 5:30 p.m., Tuesday through Friday and on Saturdays from 10 a.m. until 5 p.m.

Michael Fitzsimmons Decorative Arts
- 311 W. Superior St., Chicago; (312) 787-0496

This River North gallery is filled with antiques. More specifically, the decorative arts, including furniture, lighting, metalware, paintings, and textiles, particularly from the early 20th century Arts and Crafts Movement. Mr. Fitzsimmons describes this "vigorous and all-encompassing" movement as a reaction against the decorative and social excesses of the late 19th century, also known as the "Gilded Age." Artists like Charles Limbert and Frank Lloyd Wright were thus inspired to create simpler, freer designs. Talk about rebels with a cause.

In addition to antiques by Limbert and Wright, Fitzsimmons also shows the work of Fay Barnes, Gordon Thompson Pritchard, and Oscar B. Erickson. Works are shown in period room settings so you can get a real feel for the era and its art. The gallery is open Tuesday through Friday from 11 a.m. to 6 p.m. and on Saturdays from 11 a.m. to 5 p.m.

Gallery 37
- N. State St., between Washington St. and Randolph St., Chicago; (312) 744-6630.

For six weeks every summer, this program provides Chicago's teens with the perfect blend of art, education, and temporary employment. Eleven large, open tents occupy an entire city block next to the Daley Center, transforming it into a giant, festive open-air art workshop.

Stroll through and watch these serious folks at work, Mondays through Fridays from 10 a.m. to 4 p.m.; they'll be creating anything from beaded jewelry to colorfully handpainted park benches. Social observers may even find this a fascinating glimpse into what's influencing young people at the moment.

Admission is free. So are the classes you can take yourself, taught by faculty members from the School of the Art Institute of Chicago, offered from 10-4 on Saturdays. And, at the big tent near the State Street entrance, you'll find all kinds of this artwork for sale. Proceeds help fund the program, which employs some 400 kids a year from the Chicago area. There are satellite locations in several neighborhoods as well. For more information call them at the number above, or the Chicago Cultural Center at (312) 346-3278.

Grayson Gallery
- 207 W. Superior St., Chicago; (312) 266-7766

The Grayson Gallery specializes in ancient and primitive art, and since there is a finite supply of this category of art the exhibits only change about twice a year. But the pieces they show are unlike anything else you may see as you ramble around the River North galleries. Recent exhibits have included art from the ancient Americas, African ritual objects, Native American beadwork, and Pre-Colombian effigy vessels. Grayson Gallery is open Tuesday, Wednesday, Friday, and Saturday from 10 a.m. to 5 p.m.

Mur Mur Box
- 1255 S. Wabash St., Chicago; (312) 871-8732

This hip little South Loop gallery shows art in all media, focusing primarily on photography and sculpture. But, as an alternative space for emerging artists of all types, they don't limit themselves and have had shows ranging from paintings to more unusual installation works. As a relative newcomer to the gallery scene, they have already racked up several well-received shows, including photography by Tor Dettwiler and steel sculpture by Eric David Hamilton.

Mur Mur Box is part of the South Loop Arts Building at 1255 S. Wabash Street. This building also houses the **Matrix Gallery, Ltd., World Tattoo, MWMWM Gallery**, and recently became the new home of the well-known, not-for-profit **N.A.M.E. Gallery**. Openings at these galleries often coincide; and at this buzzing facility, you can see lots of up-to-the-moment art in one place.

Orca Aart Gallery
* 300 W. Grand Ave., Chicago; (312) 245-5245

The Orca Aart Gallery, located in the gallery-dense River North District, shows native art from Canada and the Pacific Northwest—including Artic Quebec, Greenland, and Alaska. The pieces, mainly by Inuit and other peoples of the Pacific Northwest, include sculpture in stone and wood, jewelry, and tapestries.

Orca Aart installs about eight to ten shows a year, so there's often something new and exciting to see. Recent shows have highlighted women artists of the North, along with works by woodcarvers Beau

---

MR. CHEAP'S PICKS
Art Galleries

✔ **Atlas Galleries**—Three Gold Coast galleries offer a wide variety from masters to modern.

✔ **Gallery 37**—Every summer, this *plein-air* happening is a marvelous opportunity for city teens and viewers alike.

✔ **Riverfront Gallery**—The hip art scene lies to the west. Bucktown, to be specific. Here's a huge place with a lot going on under one roof.

Dick, Tony Hunt, Jr., and Terry Starr, featuring masks, totem poles, and more. Call it "River Northern Exposure." Orca Aart is open Tuesday through Saturday from 11 a.m. to 5 p.m., on Fridays until 7 p.m.

Orient Midwest Gallery
* 740 N. Franklin St., Chicago; (312) 664-6309

The Orient Midwest Gallery carries an interesting selection of contemporary art from Central and East Asia. You'll see examples of *sumi'e*, traditional paintings in black and white; Asian influenced paintings in oils and watercolors; Chinese papercuts, carvings, and more. OMG has furniture and decorative arts like lamps, Korean *tansu* chests, tapestries, kimonos, and jewelry. The Orient Midwest also has a longstanding reputation for its collection of hand-woven Tibetan carpets.

An interesting feature for collectors on the cheap: OMG uses many pieces of furniture and accessories to "enhance" its art displays. As the exhibits here change (usually every month or so), these items are often sold at a significant discount; as much as 40% to 50% off their original values. In addition to these sales, OMG holds an annual clearance sale on accessories, furniture and porcelain at the beginning of each August. The gallery is open from 10 a.m. to 5 p.m., Monday through Saturday.

Perimeter Gallery, Inc.
* 750 N. Orleans St., Chicago; (312) 266-9473

Exhibiting contemporary art by established artists, as well as those the gallery calls "mid-career" artists, the Perimeter's offerings range from abstract to representational. The Perimeter features paintings, drawings, prints, and sculpture. Recent showings have included paintings by John Colt, sculpture by Ben Pranger and photographs by Roxana Keland. Gallery hours are 11 a.m. to 5:30 p.m., Tuesday through Saturday.

Posters Plus
* 210 S. Michigan Ave., Chicago; (312) 461-9277

- 3366 N. Clark St., Chicago; (312) 929-2850.

For those who know that posters are truly high art, this is the place to be. Posters Plus features a large selection of fine art reproductions, contemporary works, and Chicago-related posters. They also have a large selection of vintage posters from France, Britain, and other countries.

If it's vintage posters you go for, try the **Colletti Gallery** at 67 E. Oak St., Chicago; (312) 664-6767. The Colletti features lithograph posters dating as far back as the 1890's including American turn-of-the-century posters such as advertisements for Buffalo Bill's Wild West shows and the Ringling Brothers and Barnum and Bailey Circus.

The Riverfront Gallery

- 2929 N. Western Ave., Chicago; (312) 252-2500

Just above the happening Bucktown area, the Riverfront touches on a little bit of everything in the world of art. They have oil paintings, antique prints, mirrors, and more, including work by local artists. Everything here is for sale, though you are perfectly welcome to wander through and admire it all. A team of muralists and decorative artists have a workshop on the premises; they also offer framing, restoration, and portraiture. All this in one place! It's part of the sprawling Chicago Riverfront Antique Mart which features, among other things, The Rocking Chair Cafe. Survey works of art, shop for antiques, sip espresso—it can all make for a fine day of inexpensive pleasures.

State of Illinois Art Gallery

- 100 W. Randolph St., Chicago; (312) 814-5322

Located on the second floor of the State of Illinois Center, this small but serious gallery shows work by Illinois artists, both historic and contemporary. Operated by the Illinois State Museum and Arts Council, their offerings span all media including paintings, sculpture, photography, and even film and video. Richard Hunt, Gertrude Abercrombie, Roger

Brown, Margaret Warton, and Carl Weirsom are just a few of the famous Illinois artists who have had work shown there. Several times a year, the gallery also hosts panel discussions with artists; specific lectures for school groups can even be arranged in advance.

The atrium of this massive building, a work of art in itself, functions as a second gallery space. In fact, the center has its own permanent collection, comprised of winners from statewide competitions in painting, photography, ceramics, and glass, printmaking, drawing, and sculpture. On display throughout the atrium, these pieces are part of the largest single collection of contemporary Illinois artwork. The Illinois Art Gallery is open Monday through Friday from 9 a.m. to 6 p.m.

613 Tree Studio Gallery

- 613 N. State St., Chicago; (312) 337-7541

If you didn't get your fill of Chicago's Roaring Twenties at "Capone's Chicago," then pay a visit to the Tree Studio Gallery, which specializes in city art from the 1920's, 30's, and 40's. The gallery carries a good deal of Art Deco antiques and collectibles, as well as furniture inspired by the designs of Frank Lloyd Wright.

613 Tree also displays work in other media, such as oil paintings, watercolors, and sculpture. They've shown work by Louis Grell, who created the murals seen in the Chicago Theater, and Allen St. John, who illustrated books for Edgar Rice Burroughs, author of *Tarzan*. These treasures can be seen on Mondays and Tuesdays, from noon to 6 p.m. and Wednesdays through Saturdays, from 11 a.m. to 6 p.m.

Uncomfortable Spaces

Not a gallery in itself, Uncomfortable Spaces is an affiliation of four galleries, whose owners share a like-minded approach to contemporary art, particularly conceptual art. Two West Town galleries, one South Loop gallery, and one Bucktown gallery, address what they perceive as a lack of spaces showing the newest generation of Chicago artists. So, they've banded together and committed themselves to showing cutting-edge contemporary art.

The above-mentioned **MWMWM Gallery**, at 1255 S. Wabash St., (312) 786-0782, and **Tough Gallery**, at 415 N. Sangamon St., (312) 829-7100, focus primarily on sculpture and installation pieces. **Ten in One Gallery**, at 1510 W. Ohio St., (312) 850-4610, and **Beret International**, at 2211 N. Elston Ave., (312) 489-0282, add paintings and works in other media to their installation displays.

Each gallery exhibits about eight to ten shows a year, so there's always something new and different coming down the pike. Like most galleries, their hours vary and are often limited, so it's best to call ahead and find out when they'll be open.

The group's occasional newsletter, also called "Uncomfortable Spaces," contains a list of upcoming shows; articles and maps tell you about other off-the-beaten-path places to explore. Copies can usually be found in galleries and cafes around the city, especially in the artsy Wicker Park area.

Wood Street Gallery
- 1239 N. Wood St., Chicago; (312) 227-3306

Wood Street Gallery is dedicated to showing work by contemporary Chicago artists, reflecting social, political, and cultural themes. A recent show on protest art, for instance, included woodcuts of famous labor leaders made by a former member of the International Workers of the World. Not everything here is ardently radical, though; another recent exhibit featured fantasy-based Celtic kites by Frank Crowley.

The Wood Street Gallery also has a backyard, which is being developed into a sculpture garden. It currently contains several large-scale pieces, including a sculpture in aluminum and neon by Tom Scarf. Wood Street often hosts lectures by its artists, which are free and open to the public. Find out the story behind the work! They're open from 1 p.m. to 5 p.m. Wednesday through Saturday.

CHILDREN'S ACTIVITIES

See also the "Museums" and "Outdoors" chapters for listings on zoos and other activities suitable for children.

Adler Planetarium
- 1300 S. Lake Shore Dr., Chicago; (312) 322-0300

Here, the stars shine even in the daytime, whatever the weather, but they sparkle even more brightly on Tuesdays, when you can see them for free. Get up-close and personal with galaxies, telescopes, and inventions used by people hundreds of years ago in their attempts to chart the world and beyond. The Adler has a comprehensive collection of early scientific instruments, including telescopes used by Galileo and William Herschel, discoverer of the planet Uranus.

The planetarium's three floors of exhibits look not only into the past, but also the future—with "Space Transporters" which take you to the Sun, Mars, and other heavenly bodies. The Hall of Space Exploration features 3-D scale models of the planets and their moons. Included in the price of admission is the Sky Show, where dazzling special effects allow you to watch as a star is born (no, not Judy Garland or Barbara Streisand).

Adler Planetarium also offers courses in astronomy. Classes start at just $5 for a two-hour class of "Star Stories," which explores the mythical tales behind the constellations. Call 322-0323 for an up-to-date schedule of courses. Another fun feature of the Adler Planetarium is the Nightwatch Hotline: Call 322-0334 to hear a free recorded message about which planets and constellations are "up" at the moment.

Regular admission is $4 for adults, $2 for children under 17 and senior citizens—great deals, even at full price. Open daily from 9:00-5:00, plus Fridays until 9:00 in the evening.

Barbara's Bookstore
- 1350 N. Wells St., Chicago; (312) 642-5044
- 1800 N. Clyburn Ave., Chicago; (312) 664-1113
- 3130 N. Broadway, Chicago; (312) 477-0411
- 1100 Lake St., Oak Park; (708) 848-9140
- Also Barbara's Bestsellers, 2 North Riverside Plaza, Chicago; (312) 258-8007

Barbara's Bookstore does its all-out best to encourage reading for people of all ages, and one way it accomplishes this is through children's storytelling. The Broadway store has a children's story hour at 10:30 a.m. every Saturday morning. And for those of you out in the 'burbs, the Oak Park location features volunteers reading stories of their young audience's choosing, held at 11:00 a.m. every Saturday. Both of these series are free and open to all. Now, isn't that better than cartoons?

Barnes and Noble Booksellers
- 659 W. Diversey Pkwy., Chicago; (312) 871-9004

This spacious Lincoln Park shop, brand-new and extremely comfortable, sponsors "Kids' Story Times" every Thursday afternoon at 4:00 p.m. and every Saturday morning at 11:00 a.m. They have a regular roster of storytellers, with the occasional guest author added in to read from his or her latest release. It's a fun fam-ily activity for the young and the young-at-heart.

Capone's Chicago
- 605 N. Clark St., Chicago; (312) 654-1919

If you thrill to the romance of gangsters and the images that are conjured up when one thinks of Prohibition-era Chicago, this recently opened attraction is the place for you. Using "Audio-Animation" and other high-tech gadgetry, Capone's Chicago takes you to this bygone era and lets you experience the people, places, and events that have become the stuff of legend.

While the people who actually lived in Chicago during the 1920's may not have appreciated the "excitement, adventure and mystery" that surrounded them, Capone's Chicago is a much safer—and fairly inexpensive—way to spend the day.

Admission is $4.75, $3.75 for senior citizens and children. Located in River North near the Hard Rock Cafe, it's open daily from 10 a.m. until 10 p.m.

Chicago Children's Museum
- North Pier Festival Market (2nd Floor), 435 E. Illinois St., Chicago; (312) 527-1000

Make your own West African jewelry. Star in your own TV news broadcast. Visit the Three Bears' Cabin. Learn how to recycle. But most importantly: Touch Everything!

The Chicago Children's Museum is dedicated to helping kids learn and have fun at the same time. That's why you will not see "Do Not Touch" signs anywhere. They want everyone to touch and to explore and to DO! with a variety of programs, exhibits and workshops.

The museum is open daily from 10 a.m. to 4:30 p.m. With admission prices of $3.50 for adults and $2.50 for children, this is one of the few things you'll find at the North Pier Festival Market that is not overpriced. But wait, it gets better! Every Thursday from 5 p.m. to 8 p.m., admission is free (the word Mr. C loves to hear). And that's for all ages, folks!

Chicago Historical Society

- 1601 N. Clark St., Chicago; (312) 642-4600

From the drama of the early frontier days to the tragedy of the Great Chicago Fire, and the rebuilding that followed, the story of Chicago is an exciting and unique one indeed. And the CHS sure knows how to tell it, combining artifacts, photos, and paintings, with hands-on displays. Suddenly, you realize "history" wasn't all that long ago—and it's still unfolding.

This is another great place where you can have fun, learn a lot, and not empty your wallet to do it. Admission is a suggested donation of $3, $2 for students and seniors, and $1 for children. Better still, admission is free to all every Monday. Open Mondays-Saturdays, 9:30 a.m. to 4:30 p.m.; Sundays, noon to 5:00 p.m.

David Adler Cultural Center

- 1700 N. Milwaukee Ave., Libertyville, (708) 367-0707

On the fourth Sunday of the month at 2 p.m., the David Adler Cultural Center sponsors a children's concert at Libertyville High School Studio Theatre. Tickets are just $6 for adults and $4 for children and seniors. It's quite a ways out, but if you live north of the city, this may be convenient for you. Your kids will certainly think so!

The music is geared toward children from ages three to ten; some concerts include elements of dance and theatre. Past performances have featured troupes like the Chicago Moving Company and Metamorphosis Theatre. How will kids be able to resist a show with a name like "Ooooogy Green and Other Fables"?

Field Museum of Natural History

- S. Lake Shore Dr. at Roosevelt Dr., Chicago; (312) 922- 9410

Q: What's four stories high, 75-feet long and *really* bony? A: The Brachiosaurus, the largest mounted dinosaur in the world, on permanent display at the Field Museum. And you can visit this Jurassic creature any Thursday for free.

Of course, that's not all there is to see here. With over nine acres of exhibits and over nineteen million artifacts and specimens from around the world, there is bound to be something for any interest. Whether you want to explore ancient Egypt, travel the Pacific, or experience life in a Pawnee earth lodge, you can do it here. Got a big school project? Get a jump on it at the Webber Resource Center, where you can browse through maps, books, artifacts, and videotapes. The Resource Center staff is available to answer any questions.

Regular admission is $5.00; $3.00 for children under 17, students, and senior citizens. The museum also has a special one-price family rate, which gets absolutely everybody in for $16. Decent savings for small families, and really great for Brady Bunch-sized broods. Meanwhile, the Field is free to all on Thursdays. Open daily, 9-5.

57th Street Books

- 1301 E. 57th St., Chicago; (312) 684-1300

This cozy, quiet bookstore near the University of Chicago in Hyde Park offers free storytelling hours for children. Readings take place every other Saturday morning, from 10:30 to 11:30; and, for an extra family activity tip from Mr. C, there's an Ann Sather's restaurant just down the block, convenient for brunch before or after.

Kiddieland

- 8400 W. North Ave., Melrose Park; (708) 343-8003

Can't make it down to Disney World on your budget? Spend the day at Kiddieland instead. Admission is $2.95, with an additional charge of 50 cents per ride. Now, with over 30 rides, that can really add up; however, for only $10.95 you can get a "Super Saver All Day Ride Pass" good for unlimited rides. Mr. C has done the math for you—if you plan on going on more than sixteen rides, then the pass is worth it; if not, skip it and pay as you go.

The bottom line is that even if you pay the general admission price and pay 50 cents to ride 30 rides, it would still be cheaper than Six Flags Great America, where the admission price is $22-$26.

And hey, with a name like Kiddieland, could this place be anything but fun? All the basics are here—a ferris wheel, water slides, an arcade and other games. It's open seven days a week during the summer; weekends and evenings during the spring and fall. Hours vary through the season.

Kohl Children's Museum

- 165 Green Bay Rd., Wilmette; (708) 256-6056

Another museum with an aim to teach through touch, the Kohl Children's Museum offers a variety of exhibits designed to both educate and entertain. Features include a human bubble machine, a reproduction of an Egyptian tomb, a King Solomon exhibit, and an exhibit called "Be a Star!" in which kids can get dressed up and see themselves on video. Another exhibit, "Recollections," features a giant video screen on which kids can see their own movements reflected in multiples and in colors.

Kohl also offers story hours, hands-on workshops, experiments, parties and more. These activities usually revolve around themes such as "Wacky Water Fun," "Comedy Days," and "Henry Ford's Birthday Celebration."

Admission is $3; $2.50 for senior citizens. To get information on current exhibits, programs, and special events, call the Kohl Activities Hotline at (708) 251-7781.

Mont Clare Coffeehouse

- 6935 W. Medill Ave., Chicago; (312) 714-0328

This coffeehouse offers something unique—entertainment for the whole family. Just $4 gains you admission to an evening of folk music and story-telling, presented on the second Saturday of each month from September through June. Admission for children ages twelve and under is only $1. The coffeehouse begins around 8

p.m., and features regional and national folk artists.

Other occasional events include participatory dances with live music, usually for the same admission; and singarounds with an admission charge of just $2, free for children 12 and under. And don't miss the one-day Mont Clare Folk Festival, held each August; admission is free to all.

It all takes place at the same hopping location. These industrious folks also put out a quarterly newsletter, *Common Times*, which you can pick up at area coffeehouses; or, subscribe to it for just $5 per year.

Museum of Broadcast Communications

- Chicago Cultural Center, 78 E. Washington St., Chicago; (312) 629-6000

Lights! Camera! Action! Learn about the history of radio, television, and its famous broadcasters. Get a feel for television of today by sitting behind the anchor desk of your own newscast. And do it all for free. Now, that's news!

Newly housed in the Chicago Cultural Center (see listing under "Entertainment: Multicultural Centers), this museum takes you behind the scenes of broadcasting from its inception to the present day. An exhibit of Edgar Bergen's famous trio, Charlie McCarthy, Effie Klinker, and Mortimer Snerd, plus showings of award-winning commercials, only scratch the surface of the fun to be had. Exhibits on subjects like the Nixon/Kennedy debate illustrate the impact television has had on our lives.

Along with their permanent collections, the museum creates special exhibits like the recent "My Little Margie to Murphy Brown: Images of Women in TV." Along with the exhibit, panel discussions explored the portrayal of women as housewives and superheroines in the workplace. It all comes alive when, in the words of Walter Cronkite, "You are there."

Museum of Holography

- 1134 W. Washington Blvd., Chicago; (312) 226-1007

MR. CHEAP'S PICKS
Children's Activities

✔ **Adler Planetarium**—Every kid wants to learn about the stars. Like so many of Chicago's museums, the Adler offers one free day (Tuesday) per week.

✔ **Chicago Children's Museum**—Tucked into the North Pier Festival Market is this wonderful place where kids can play and learn at the same time—if you can wrest them away from the glitzy stores downstairs.

✔ **Field Museum of Natural History**—Is there a kid alive today who doesn't go gaga over dinosaurs? This is the place.

✔ **Mont Clare Coffeehouse**—Something unique in the entertainment biz: Live music, family-style.

✔ **Players Workshop Children's Theatre**—Top-notch short plays, with lots of audience participation.

Like most museums, you can look around in here—but you can't touch anything. In this case, it's because the exhibits aren't really there. Holograms are three-dimensional images made with lasers into tantalizingly real-looking displays with no physical substance at all.

For the nearly non-existent price of $2.50 (under age six, free admission), you can experience the wacky world of holograms, along with special exhibits. One recent exhibit demonstrated how computers are used to generate these very holograms. Open 12:30 p.m. to 5:00 p.m., Wednesdays through Sundays.

Museum of Science and Industry
- 57th St. at S. Lake Shore Dr., Chicago; (312) 684-1414

This massive building opened as part of the great Columbian Exposition of 1893, and it's the only remaining structure from that historic event. Offering literally thousands of exhibits on science and technology and their industrial applications, the museum is big on visitor participation. Visit the "Communications" gallery, which takes you from the invention of the telephone right all the way to fiber optics and other up-to-the-moment technologies. See how things like computers and television will be different in the near future. Explore the workings of the circulatory system by walking through a 16-foot pulsating model heart. Or, experience a miniature fairyland in "Colleen Moore's Fairy Castle," which contains over 1,000 tiny treasures.

One of the MSI's biggest attractions is the Omnimax Theater, part of the Henry Crown Space Center, which adjoins the main building. The Omni is a five-story, 350-seat theater which boasts the largest sound system in the world. It shows everything from scientific subjects like "Ring of Fire," which takes you inside a burning volcano, to fun films like "Rolling Stones At the Max." The Space Center, of course, is where you can see what it's like to be on the Space Shuttle, or even on another planet!

The MSI is open every day from 9:30 a.m. to 5:30 p.m. (until 4:00 from Labor Day to Memorial Day), with Omnimax shows added on Friday and Saturday evenings. Admission to the museum alone is $5.00 for adults, $4.00 for senior citizens, and $2.00 for children under twelve; admission is free to everyone on Thursdays. Children under 5 are free at all times, and are admitted to the Omnimax free if seating is available. The Omni, of course, has a separate admission fee; combination Museum/Omni tickets are sold at the box office.

Oriental Institute Museum

- 155 E. 58th St., Chicago; (312) 702-9521

On the campus of the University of Chicago, this museum has one of the world's foremost collections of artifacts from the ancient lands of Nubia, Persia, Mesopotamia, Assyria, and other places in what we now call the Middle East. Measure yourself next to a twenty-foot-tall statue of King Tut, carved in red quartzite stone, from Thebes in the year 1330 B.C. See how modern-day language experts decipher ancient hieroglyphic writing, step by step. Gaze upon gigantic ceremonial objects and delicate handcrafted jewelry. Room after room is filled with incredible sights—and all of it is free and open to the public.

The museum also offers a number of special programs to shed more light on these artifacts. Special interest tours, given Friday mornings at 11:30, highlight a particular gallery. On Sundays at 2:00, short films are shown on specific subjects, again followed by a gallery tour. And on Thursdays in the summer, there are special activities geared especially toward children.

Admission to the museum is free at all times, though groups of ten or more must phone ahead to arrange a tour. Hours: Tuesdays through Saturdays, 10:00-4:00 (plus Wednesday evenings until 8:30); Sundays, noon to 4:00. The museum is closed on Mondays and holidays.

The Power House

- 100 Shiloh Blvd., Zion; (708) 746-7080

Here's a way to learn about energy and have fun at the same time, all for free. Run by Commonwealth Electric, the Power House is like a small museum, but hey—7th grade science class should have been like this! Interactive exhibits and hands-on programs use French fries and snowballs to teach thermodynamics. You can experiment with magnetic attraction. Learn what lit up Chicago when your great-grandparents were young. And

in the process, you and your kids will become experts on energy consumption, alternative energy sources, and conservation.

The Power House also has an Energy Resource Center with computerized information, videotapes, books and magazines, and a resource specialist to help you find and use the materials. So, whether you have a big school project on the history of nuclear power, or you're just curious about the world of energy, go on in and browse.

Admission to the Power House is free; reservations are required for groups of 15 or more. Hours are 10:00 a.m. to 5:00 p.m., Tuesday through Saturday. Closed Sundays and Mondays.

Players Workshop Children's Theatre

- 2636 N. Lincoln Ave., Chicago; (312) 929-6288

The Players Workshop presents regular shows for children, most of which are presented on Sunday afternoons in this Lincoln Park studio. Their recent "Not Ready for Bedtime Stories" was a musical version of three Washington Irving tales, including *The Legend of Sleepy Hollow*. Admission to these shows is just $5, for all ages.

Sometimes Players Workshop takes its act on the road, as with their recent presentation of "Monkey Kings and Other Things," a collection of musical tales from old England and ancient India. The show was presented at the Body Politic Theater, 2261 N. Lincoln Ave., on Saturday and Sunday afternoons.

Shows are generally about an hour long (more precisely, the length of time a kid can keep from fidgeting), and often include audience participation. Another great feature: you can have your birthday party with the Players for free! You and your guests pay the admission price, and bring whatever food you want; they'll supply the entertainment, and everyone gets to join in at the end. Call them for details.

The Puppet Parlor

- 1922 W. Montrose Ave., Chicago; (312) 774-2919

The Puppet Parlor features European-style puppeteers in a jewelbox theatre with admission prices that are as small as their stars.

Children's shows on Saturdays and Sundays at 2 p.m. are only $5 per person. Weekend matinee performances have included *Babes in Toyland* and *Hansel and Gretel*.

But the fun doesn't end there. The Puppet Parlor also features adult shows on Saturday evenings at 8 p.m. for just $8. These shows are generally follies or operas, such as *The Merry Widow*, Mozart's *Impresario*, and *La Petit Follies: An Opera in Miniature*.

The European-style puppet show means the puppeteers are seven feet above the stage. They use a number of special effects, making scenes magically transform before your eyes—it really is a highly stylized, almost unknown art form in this country. Give them a call for information on upcoming shows.

John G. Shedd Aquarium

- 1200 S. Lake Shore Drive, Chicago; (312) 939-2438

While Mr. C doesn't like to look a gift horse, or shark, in the mouth, it is important to point out that free admission on Thursdays isn't exactly free. The Oceanarium, a re-creation of a Pacific Northwest coastline complete with beluga whales, white-sided dolphins, sea otters, and harbor seals doing their thing in a natural environment, is always an additional $4.00 ($3.00 for children under twelve and senior citizens). But the usual aquarium admission is waived (or is that "waved"?) on Thursdays.

Of course, you could save the four bucks, skip the Oceanarium and still have a whale of a time. The Aquarium itself is home to some six thousand aquatic animals from every one of the seven seas. You can observe such exotic creatures as electric eels, sea anemones, and piranhas. The Aquarium also houses the Tropical

Coral Reef exhibit, a 90,000-gallon tank filled with sea turtles, sharks, moray eels, and more. If you're there at the right time, you may even get to see a diver hand-feed these animals while talking with visitors through a dive mask microphone.

Regular admission to the Aquarium is $3.00 for adults, $2.00 for children and seniors—already a bargain price. Regular admission to the Aquarium and the Oceanarium is $7.00 ($5.00 children and seniors) and you should purchase these tickets in advance. Children under three are free at all times for all exhibits. The Aquarium also runs a number of special programs throughout the year including scientific courses and hands-on workshops. Call the education department for information.

The David and Alfred Smart Museum of Art

- University of Chicago, 5550 S. Greenwood Ave., Chicago; (312) 702-0200

Really, no price would seem too high for the chance to view over 7,000 works of art spanning over 5,000 years. But admission to this museum is free, making its collection truly priceless.

The museum, named for the founders of *Esquire* magazine, was designed by renowned architect Edward Larrabee Barnes. It contains precious works in a number of media, from ancient Greek vases, with a rare example by Euphronios, to furniture by Frank Lloyd Wright. Not to mention sculpture by Degas, Matisse, Moore, and Rodin; photographs by Walker Evans; watercolors by Grosz, Heckel, and Nolde; and collections of ancient Chinese bronzes and modern Japanese ceramics. Whew!

Free lunchtime tours of the special exhibits are offered, as well as regular tours of the permanent collection. And there are children's programs like "Valentine's Day Fun and Games," in which children were supplied with ribbons, papers, and markers to create their own artistic valentines. While the kids were busy being creative, adults were invited on a special tour of the collection. The theme? Love, of course. All this fun for free! Stop in for a listing of upcoming events.

Spertus Museum of Judaica
- 618 S. Michigan Ave., Chicago; (312) 922-9012

Do any of your kids want to become an archaeologist? The Rosenbaum Artifact Center at Spertus Museum has a hands-on exhibit designed to allow children to explore the ancient Near East using the same techniques as real archaeologists.

The Spertus Museum covers 3,500 years of Jewish history with over 3,000 works in its main galleries. In addition, it houses the Zell Holocaust Memorial and sponsors special exhibits on Judaic themes. Recent exhibits have included "Yiddish Theatre in Chicago" and "Stars of David: Jews in the World of Sports."

Admission is $3.50 and $2 for children, students, and senior citizens. Spertus has a maximum family admission of $8—an idea of which Mr. C highly approves. Better yet, on Fridays the museum has free admission for everyone, all day.

Harold Washington Library Center
- 400 S. State St., Chicago; (312) 747-4800

Mr. Cheap always says that the library is a great place to look for fun and inexpensive activities. Working in tandem with the Chicago Cultural Center, the Washington Library Center presents a full slate of movies, music, dance, art exhibits, and children's activities—all free.

In their spacious auditorium, you can enjoy events from the classical, with concerts performed on their Steinway grand, to the extraterrestrial—yes, E.T. himself, part of the Midweek Matinee movie series.

The auditorium also offers dance performances, children's theatre, even opera. In their other venues around the building, there are art exhibits, career workshops, and a permanent exhibit on the tenure of the library's namesake, Mayor Harold Washington. You can take a free public tour of this large, beautiful building; group tours can be arranged by calling (312) 747-4136. All programs here are free of charge, though some programs may require advance reservations. The library is open Tuesdays and Thursdays from 11 a.m. to 7 p.m.; Wednesdays, Fridays and Saturdays from 9-5; closed Sundays and Mondays.

Women and Children First Bookstore
- 5233 N. Clark St., Chicago; (312) 769-9299

In addition to their literary programs for adults, Women and Children First sponsors a program called "Kiddielit for City Kids" every Wednesday at 10:30 a.m. Geared towards ages two to four, the series features lively stories, finger-puppet plays, and humorous poetry. W & C also hosts a monthly "Young Feminists Round Table" on Sundays at 6:15 p.m. This gives high school and college-age women a chance to get together and discuss the important issues of the day. Stop in for a schedule of events.

COLLEGE PERFORMING ARTS

The Chicago area's many college campuses offer a wealth of music, dance, theater, and films which don't require much personal wealth to attend (unlike the colleges themselves). Many events are free to students, of course (don't forget your ID!), but they are also open to the general public. If you want to put culture into your life on a regular basis, this is a great way to do it.

DePaul University

- School of Music, 804 W. Belden Ave., Chicago; (312) 362-NOTE (6683)
- The Theatre School, 60 E. Balbo Dr., Chicago; (312) 362-8455

Perhaps the best feature of college and university performances (besides low admission prices) is the diversity of their presentations. Professional venues which like to refer to themselves as "eclectic" don't hold a candle to a place where you can hear a symphony orchestra one night and a jazz ensemble the next. **The DePaul University School of Music** has a performance schedule that includes wind ensembles, opera, wind symphonies, jazz combos, and more.

And what about those low admission prices? Most of the concerts are free and open to the public. There are a few concerts each season, perhaps a half-dozen out of thirty, which charge an admission fee. Tickets to those shows can be very pricey, over $20, although DePaul students can get them for half-price. But the rest of the shows, ensembles, opera, symphonies, festivals, are absolutely free for everyone.

Concerts take place in the late afternoon or evening, and there are performances every day of the week, throughout the semester. Write or call them and they will put you on their mailing list to receive a calendar of events.

The Theatre School at DePaul University also provides a great opportunity for adults and children to enjoy the arts. The "Showcase Series" includes about five productions each season, with tickets priced at $5-$10. Each of these includes a night, usually the second Wednesday of the run, when DePaul students can get two-for-one tickets. Discounts are also available for seniors, alumni, and DePaul employees; subscription rates are available, too. Many of these shows have received critical ac-

claim, including a recent presentation of the Tony Award-winning *Into the Woods*.

The Theatre School also offers "Chicago Playworks," a series of shows geared towards families and young children. Playworks was founded in 1925 as the Goodman Children's Theatre, and recent performances have included *Snow White and Rose Red* and an adaptation of *The Miracle Worker*. Ticket prices are only $5 and group rates are available.

They also have a "New Directors" series, which features free productions directed by M.F.A graduate students. The number of these shows varies with the number of M.F.A. candidates each year. All DePaul University Theatre School productions are held in the Merle Reskin Theatre (formerly the Blackstone for you theater buffs), at the address shown above.

Loyola University

- 6525 N. Sheridan Rd., Chicago; (312) 274-3000

Each semester, **Loyola University Theatre** sponsors some nine performances, four large Mainstage productions, and five smaller Studio works. Mainstage shows cost about $5 admission, with tickets for Studio shows a mere $2 apiece. Series tickets can also be purchased, such as a series of all four Mainstage performances for only $15. Call the theater department at (312) 508-3830 for a schedule of upcoming performances.

The **Loyola University Music Department** also sponsors performances by its student and faculty ensembles, and all of these are free. The different groups include a gospel choir, a symphony orchestra, jazz bands, and more. Give the music department a jingle at (312) 508-8300 for more info.

While you're here, take a stroll through the Fine Arts Gallery, which brings the work of professional artists to the campus. If you don't find the canvas landscapes exciting, you can gaze at the real thing, too—a wall made entirely of glass overlooks Lake Michigan.

Northwestern University

- School of Music, Pick-Staiger Concert Hall, 1977 S. Campus Dr., Evanston; (708) 491-5441

For music lovers, Northwestern University makes a trek (just barely) into the suburbs well worth the trip. Pick-Staiger Concert Hall is the scene of some forty concerts each semester, and most ticket prices fall within the $3 to $7 range. These performances include everything from the University Symphony Orchestra to a "Jazz Night" featuring the Jazz Lab Band, the Jazz Ensemble, and the Jazz Chamber Ensemble.

NU also presents some half-dozen concerts through the year featuring international guest artists; tickets for these performances are a still-reasonable $13-$20 apiece. Recent guests have included the Suk Chamber Orchestra, a 14-member ensemble from the Czech Republic, conducted by violinist Josef Suk. To hear a recording of the current week's offerings call (708) 467-PICK (7425).

And there's more! "Kids' Fare" is a series of Saturday morning programs giving children a chance to experience the arts by getting involved. Whether singing and dancing to popular Cole Porter songs, or stepping in formation with the NU Wildcat Marching Band, little ones won't have a chance to get fidgety in these shows. Admission is just $3—low enough to keep room in your budget for ice cream afterwards.

As if all that were not enough, NU's **Theatre and Interpretation Center** offers drama, dance, and stuff that defies simple description, at reasonable prices. Some shows can be expensive with tickets around $20, especially their Mainstage productions. But there are definite bargains, especially on dance concerts. Recent performances included such troupes as the Ballet Gran Folklorico de Mexico. Tix to several of these events range from $12 to $15.

MR. CHEAP'S PICKS COLLEGE ARTS

✔ **Northwestern University**— Dozens of low-priced concerts each semester, plus theater, dance, and children's shows.

✔ **Sherwood Conservatory of Music**—Free student and faculty recitals every week during the school year.

✔ **University of Chicago**—In Hyde Park, a packed slate of theater, comedy, and music; including a low-priced concert series featuring internationally renowned classical artists.

Then, there is the "N.U.D.E. Showcase." No, wait—it's not what you're thinking. This stands for Northwestern University Dance Ensemble, and admission to their live, onstage acts is only $5. And finally, they have "Performance Hours," an eclectic blend of drama and experimentation, which are free and open to the public. For more info. call (708) 491-7282.

Roosevelt University

- 430 S. Michigan Ave., Chicago; (312) 341-3720

For fun and inexpensive theater, give Roosevelt University a try. They present about a half-dozen shows a year, to which general admission is a very reasonable $10. Tickets for students and seniors are only $6, and for children they're just $5. You can also get group rates, bringing the cost of each ticket down to $3-$5.

Recent performances have included such drama classics as *The Madwoman of Chaillot* and *To Kill a Mockingbird*. Shows specifically geared to children are also offered, including *The Wind in The Willows* and *The Velveteen Rabbit*.

Sherwood Conservatory of Music

- 1014 S. Michigan Ave., Chicago; (312) 427-6267

Since student musicians look for any opportunity to play in front of an audience, you can often see their first-quality performances without paying first-quality prices. At the Sherwood Conservatory, in fact, you can enjoy such performances for free.

Sherwood presents student recitals on the first and third Saturday of every month during the school year, which usually begins in October. Most concerts begin at 1:30 p.m.— though they'll sometimes split the performers into two concerts, one at 12:30 p.m. and the other at 1:30 p.m.

The faculty, prominent musicians all, give performances of their own every Friday night at 7:30 p.m. In addition, the conservatory has two open houses every quarter; one for adults on Thursdays at 6:30 p.m., and one for children Saturdays at 10 a.m. These events feature all kinds of ensembles performing live, and they'e free and open to the public. Call to get on the mailing list.

University of Chicago

- Department of Music, 1010 E. 59th St., Chicago; (312) 702-8484
- University Theater, 5706 S. University Ave., Chicago; (312) 702-3414

U of C's **University Theater** provides top-notch dramatic performances at bottom-notch prices. Admission to these fine productions is only $3 to $6. And that isn't the student rate—that's the ticket price for Joe and Jane Public.

University Theater has two kinds of performances: UT Mainstage and UT Studio. Mainstage productions are the group's BIG shows. They get the most amount of time and resources and therefore charge the most admission, usually $6. Mainstage performances run the gamut from Shakespeare to Sam Shepard, dramas to musicals, and include the improvisational comedy revue "Off-Off-Campus."

Studio productions are smaller,

simpler shows, focusing on the acting challenges at hand; tickets usually go for about $3. This is where you'll have a chance to see student-written work, experimental shows, and one-act plays. Recent offerings have included "A Night of One Acts" and "An Evening of Performance Art." Call to receive their quarterly publication, "Spotlight," which includes a calendar of events and articles about University Theater.

On a similar note (pun intended), the **University Department of Music** offers a number of musical delights for little or no money. Each season, they present their professional concert series which they bill as "the world's greatest musicians at Chicago's lowest prices." Individual tickets are $18 for the general public, and just $8 for students. If that still seems a bit steep, it isn't—not for musicians and ensembles on the national and international circuit, such as the Chamber Music Society of Lincoln Center and soprano Julianne Baird. Subscription tickets are also available, six tickets for $89; the same deal is only $45 for students. The savings aren't that big over the regular cost, but other benefits, like priority seating and pre-concert programs, make the subscriptions more enticing. It is important to mention that students at institutions other than U of C can also take advantage of these student rates. Call (312) 702-8068 for more info.

If you are like Mr. C, you may know that music doesn't necessarily have to be professional to be enjoyable. The University of Chicago presents a number of other concerts fitting a range of musical tastes at super-low prices. The University Symphony Orchestra, for one, performs major works each season at prices around $5 per ticket, and $2 for students. There are several concerts each season by a number of groups in this price range.

Many other assorted concerts are free, such as those given every Thursday during the school year at 12:15 p.m. in Goodspeed Recital Hall. But the fun doesn't end there. There are dozens of concerts, ranging from cabaret songs from 1920's Berlin to the University Chamber Orchestra playing selections from Mozart and Bach, which don't even cost one thin dime. Call (312) 702-8484 for a schedule of upcoming events.

University of Illinois at Chicago

- Department of Performing Arts, 1040 W. Harrison St., Chicago; (312) 996-2939

Music, drama, and dance are combined by the UIC Theatre in productions that will make your heart soar, with admission prices that are never a tragedy. The majority of UIC theater productions can be seen for a mere $10. Tickets for major presentations by the UIC Dancers are just $9 each, and their smaller studio performances are free of charge.

There are, of course, some exceptions. When UIC hosts guest troupes like the Theatre of Moscow-Southwest, performing *Hamlet* and *Romeo and Juliet*, you can expect to pay as much as $18 a ticket. Still pretty low, for artists on the international touring circuit; and UIC students are admitted for just $6 to these performances.

COMEDY

In Chicago, it's getting harder and harder to find the dividing line between comedy and theater. This town is pretty much considered the birthplace of improvisation, and these ensembles dot the landscape like one-liners in a Vegas lounge. New ones crop up all the time; older ones may switch locations, or disappear and regroup. Listed below are many of the current standouts. Meanwhile, comedy fans should also check the other side of the line—theater companies which have incorporated the improv sketch style into their plays. Find out about them—where else?—under "Theater."

As for regular standup, the best cost-cutter in the biz remains the open mike night, when you can get in for a very low cover charge and see up-and-coming "stars of tomorrow." Guaranteed, there'll be plenty of klunkers (does the name Rupert Pupkin ring a bell?); but the shows are hosted by headliners, so you're sure to get plenty of good laughs no matter what. Most clubs, some of which are listed here, have open mike shows; they tend to be early in the week. Call your favorite venue to see what they offer.

Blue Velveeta

- The Improvisation, 504 N. Wells St., Chicago; (312) 527-2500

A spinoff of the ImprovOlympia troupe (see listing below), Blue Velveeta relies on audience suggestions for its entire performance—and the wackier your ideas, the better. Check 'em out on Saturday nights at 8:00 and 10:30 p.m.; admission is $7, quite good for a weekend show downtown, plus a two-drink minimum.

ComedySportz

- Congress Hotel, 520 S. Michigan Ave., Chicago; (312) 549-8080

Just below the Loop, you'll find this ensemble cutting up with the very latest trend in improvisational comedy: The sports format. Two teams of comedians square off, scoring points along with the laughs—as well as penalties for violations of the improv

MR. CHEAP'S PICKS COMEDY

✔ **ComedySportz**—The latest hybrid for our times: Competitive improv. It works!

✔ **Second City**—Who else? The folks who started the whole Chicago comedy thing. They make so much comedy, they're even *giving* it away; check out the free late-night shows.

rules. These may include anything from misusing imaginary doors to just plain "bad acting." Who wins at the end of the night? Different every time. Face-offs are Fridays and Saturdays at 8:30 p.m. Tickets are $8, plus a $5 drink minimum; but here's an extra tip—this is one of the few comedy shows which turn up at the Hot Tix booth on State Street, where you can get tickets for half-price on the day of the performance, if available.

Comedy Womb
- 8030 W. Ogden St., Lyons; (708) 442-0030

Sometimes, going a bit outside the heart of Chicago's bustling comedy scene is the way to save money. Just to the west of town, the Comedy Womb (Mr. C, who loves puns, has decided to leave this one alone) has a top ticket price of only $6 per person. There's also a two-drink minimum, but for a Friday or Saturday night out, this deal is nothing to laugh at.

Even better, check out "New Talent" night on Thursdays. There's still a two-drink minimum, but the cover charge is only $1. All right, so you're not going to see nationally-known acts, but funny is funny, and the price works out to just pennies per comic. And who knows, you may spot a diamond in the rough.

The Funny Firm
- 318 W. Grand Ave. (2nd Floor), Chicago; (312) 321-9500.

This spacious and comfortable River North club presents comedians from the local and national circuits seven nights a week. Cover charges vary, but can go as high as a rather serious $10-$15. How to beat this? Two ways. First, call to buy your tix in advance; that knocks $3 off each admission, even on weekends.

Better still, visit The Firm on Sunday or Monday nights. On Sundays, "The Wunce a Week Pickle Show" is a kind of no-holds-barred variety extravaganza; Mondays are showcase nights, when new young comics get to strut their stuff in the company of seasoned vets. For these shows, the cover is only $5; in fact, if you arrive before 7:30 on Mondays, you'll get in free. Showtimes are 8:00 both nights.

Improv Institute
- 2319 W. Belmont Ave., Chicago; (312) 929-2323

Are you able to think fast on your feet? Can you make it really funny? Or would you rather leave this to talented professionals who can spin hilarious sketches at the word "go"? The Improv Institute features fully-improvised comedy shows where every performance is different, led by suggestions from the audience. Play as much a part as you want.

Now this kind of fun doesn't come cheaply (hey—isn't that the point of this book? Yeah, yeah hold on. . .). Regular shows on Fridays at 8 p.m. and Saturdays at 8 and 10 are $10 each. But, on Wednesdays they have "Fun Night" for professional "guest" improvisors—it seems Chicago is full of 'em—for only $5. Also, the show "Mooky Soup" is currently enjoying an open run on Thursday nights with tickets priced at $7. This endeavor claims to create nothing less than an entire play on the spot, based on your suggestions. So go on down, bring some ideas (after all, everyone's a comedian) and have some truly cheap laughs.

ImprovOlympia

* 3527 N. Clark St., Chicago; (312) 880-0199

At the Wrigleyside Bar every Thursday and Friday evening, this comedy ensemble brews up a unique blend of comedy and theater. It's really closer to theater, in fact, than standup comedy and even some other improv shows—very sharp, avant-garde improv. Showtimes are 8 p.m., and admission is just $7, plus a two-drink minimum.

Sarantos Studios

* 2857 N. Halsted St., Chicago; (312) 528-7114

Always trying to be the life of the party? You can be a part of the evening's entertainment when you "Improv the Night Away" at Sarantos Studios. Every Friday night at 7:30 p.m., this show rollicks in audience-driven sketch comedy—though, of course, no one is going to force you to take part. Much.

Don't worry, there are plenty of highly-trained comedy professionals on hand to take on the dangerous stuff. With so much of the material generated on the spot, this is the kind of show you can see again and again; it will be a very different experience every time. It's a good thing, then, that admission is an affordable $8.

Sarantos Studios runs a teaching studio for improvisation as well, and so they host occasional live showcases featuring student performers. These performances are often free; some have a small admission price. Call to see if any showcases are coming up.

Shay's

* 1615 N. Clyboum Ave., Chicago; (312) 664-1427

Many comedy troupes base their sketches upon suggestions from audience members. Many audience members would prefer to just kick back and watch the show, free of this responsibility. If you fall into the latter category, walk into Shay's on Sunday nights to see "A Mean Watusi." This wacky evening features the groups Level 6 and Free Pickles, both graduates of Second City. "Level 6," by the way, is a bit of a wink at the venerable Second City training school, which has five levels of study—presumably, these performers go them one better.

"A Mean Watusi" is performed every Sunday at 7:30 p.m., and admission is only $5.00—a true bargain among improv comedy clubs. Other nights at Shay's feature local rock and alternative bands; the cover charge is usually just $3, and never more than $5. They also have a jukebox and CD player loaded up with alternative music, while paintings by local artists adorn the walls.

Second City

* 1616 N. Wells St., Chicago; (312) 337-3992

Second City E.T.C.

* 1608 N. Wells St., Chicago; (312) 642-8189

In the ever-more expensive world of comedy clubs, it's nice to know that even premier venues like Second City may yield the occasional bargain. In fact, they have a couple. On Monday nights at 8:30 p.m., Second City features its local touring company, "The Best of Second City" for only $5. This is a considerable savings over their usual ticket prices of $10-$15. And for you night owls there is an even bigger bargain to be had. Every night, except Friday, Second City presents a free (yes, free—no joke!) improv show after the last regular show of the evening. That's 10:30 p.m. Mondays through Thursdays, 1:30 a.m. on Saturdays, and 10:00 on Sundays. These shows last from 45 minutes to an hour. Lots of folks stay on after the main show, so seating can be limited, even on a weeknight; get there a bit early, and stick close to the theater entrance for the moment when the doors open.

While hanging out in the lobby, it's fun just to look at the hundreds of photos lining the walls, reminding us why Second City is such a comedy powerhouse. It seems that every big name of the last three decades has worked here. Alumni include Robert

Klein, Joan Rivers, Bill Murray, Gilda Radner, John Candy—actually, just about everyone who ever appeared with SCTV and Saturday Night Live. Second City revues are known for their clever titles, like the recent "Take Me Out to the Balkans" and "Disgruntled Employee Picnic, or The Postman Always Shoots Twice."

As you may have noticed above, there are two Second City stages next door to each other; both offer the same wild brand of sketch comedy, as well as the free apres-show improv (although Second City E.T.C., the one at 1608 N. Wells, only does so Wednesday-Thursday and Saturday-Sunday). Furthermore, for you suburban yukmeisters, there is **Second City Northwest** at 1701 Golf Road in Rolling Meadows; telephone (708) 806-1555.

DANCE

Alas, the dance scene in Chicago is not nearly as expansive as the jazz or theater scenes, and so there are fewer opportunities to experience dance inexpensively. There are several top-quality professional dance companies in Chicago; but these better troupes tend to play the fancier venues, which charge a hefty price for tickets. Summer festivals like the Grant Park Music Festival often offer opportunites to see these better companies for less money. And don't forget the dance programs at various colleges and universities in the area—check the listings under "Entertainment: College Performing Arts."

Meanwhile, there are a number of troupes and venues seeking to nurture young dancers, which also present affordable dance concerts to create a larger audience overall. Here are a few companies offering dance concerts for reasonable prices.

Academy of Movement and Music
- 605 Lake St., Oak Park; (708) 848-2329

Many of the Academy's concerts will take you into the 'burbs but the money you save will make the trip worthwhile if you're coming from the city. These concerts are performed by AMM's company-in-residence, MOMENTA. They focus on reconstructing historical American modern dance, particularly the work of choreographer Doris Humphrey.

Tickets start at only $10 for adults, and about $8 for students and seniors. And, even when their performances are held in downtown locations, tickets still only run about $12. Many concerts include matinee performances that start at just $5.

Boulevard Arts Center
- 6011 S. Justine St., Chicago; (312) 476-4900

Home to the Body Language Dance Company, this South Side arts center presents dance concerts for about $10 a ticket. Body Language works in the tradition of modern dancer Katherine Dunham, and they do so with authority: Artistic Director Tommy Gomez danced in her company. The troupe also performs in other venues, and even then tickets still usually run in the $10 range.

The Boulevard Arts Center also presents a number of independent theater productions, with ticket prices usually between $7 and $10. Call them for a full schedule of upcoming events.

Chicago Dance

- Chicago Cultural Center, 78 E. Washington St., Chicago; (312) 744-6630

Each spring, the Chicago Cultural Center—that wonderful home of free arts performances—hosts this festival of modern, classical, and ethnic dance. See such troupes as Gus Giordano Jazz Dance Chicago, the Boitsov Classical Ballet Company, the Royale Polynesian Review, and many other local and international companies. All concerts are free of charge; call or write the CCC to get on the mailing list for "City Arts," their regular newsletter and calendar of events.

DéjAvant Performance Series

- Performing Arts Chicago, 410 S. Michigan Ave., Chicago; (312) 663-1628

For top-name dance performers and companies, with a unique discount program, the DéjAvant Series is the way to go. Here's how it works: Buy a "DéjAvant Pass" for $50. This then entitles you to buy any tickets in the series at a substantial discount. This most recent season, passholders were frequently able to purchase tickets to some of the best seats in the house for $10—tickets which normally go for $25 to $35.

You'll need to attend about three or four events before you see substantial savings, of course; but, if you plan on seeing more than a few of the shows in the series, this is a deal that cannot be beat.

And just who can you see from these wonderfully cheap seats? Recent offerings through the DejAvant series have included performances by Ann Carlson, winner of the New York Dance and Performance Award; the nationally-renowned Bill T. Jones/Arnie Zane & Company; and the Grammy Award-winning gospel choir, Sounds of Blackness. Call for more info.

Grant Park Music Festival

- Petrillo Band Shell, 235 S. Columbus Dr., Chicago; (312) 819-0614.

The Petrillo Music Shell, at the cor-

MR. CHEAP'S PICKS DANCE

✔ **Boulevard Arts Center**—Inexpensive, high-quality modern dance on the South Side.

✔ **Chicago Dance**—A spring festival bringing troupes from all over the city to the Chicago Cultural Center.

✔ **Hedwig Dances**—Performances, school tours, informal hip hop lessons in Grant Park—it's almost impossible *not* to run into these ambitious folks.

ner of Columbus and Jackson Drives, is a delightful setting for a wide variety of free concerts and performances every summer. Green trees laced with delicate lights, the skyline looming above them, are your backdrop for classical music featuring the Grant Park Symphony Orchestra.

The festival, in existence for sixty years, also presents the "Dance at Dusk" series on Monday evenings at 7 p.m., featuring such troupes as Ballet Chicago and the Joseph Holmes Chicago Dance Theatre. In addition, there are performances of ethnic dance in Hispanic and African styles. The schedule begins in mid-June and continues through the end of August. There are plenty of folding chairs, set up like any auditorium, or you can bring a blanket and relax on the lawn. Stretch out and have a picnic. Shows take place on afternoons and evenings, weekdays and weekends—call (312) 819-0614 for a current schedule.

Hedwig Dances

- 4753 N. Broadway, Suite 918, Chicago; (312) 907-2192

The dance company-in-residence of the Chicago Department of Cultural

Affairs, Hedwig Dances doesn't waste much time hanging out at the local barre. They conduct classes for teens and adults in their studios, take their educational outreach program to area schools, perform in summer festivals, lead aerobics sessions, and more. Many of their performances are inexpensive; lots of them are free, taking place in their studios at the Chicago Cultural Center at 78 E. Washington Street (see listing under "Entertainment: Multicultural Centers").

Similarly, while Hedwig charges nominal fees for many of its dance classes, they also conduct free workshops that can introduce you to the world of movement and dance—and they really mean *the world*. A recent summer program, held just outside the center in Grant Park, gave people an opportunity to take classes in African Dance, Tai Chi, Aikido, hip hop, modern, and improvisational styles.

You can get on their mailing list by writing or calling the office above, or by stopping in to the Chicago Cultural Center.

Links Hall
- 3435 N. Sheffield Ave. (2nd Floor), Chicago; (312) 281-0824

What you see here is not strictly dance, but it *is* strictly cheap: Every show is $7. What you'll see at Links is a mixture of modern dance, dance improvisation, performance art, and whatever else gets thrown into the mix. Recent performers have included Jan Erkert and Dancers and The Next Generation Project.

You may not believe this, but they have shows that go even cheaper. Tickets to their "Shopworks" series, which presents the work of students in the Shopworks Performance Workshop, are just $2. And "Chance Dance," featuring choreographer Bob Eisen is always surprising and just $5.

The Ravinia Festival
- Lake Cook and Green Bay Rds., Highland Park; (312) 728-4642 (R-A-V-I-N-I-A)

For nearly sixty summers, the Rav-

inia Festival has presented the finest names in classical and popular music in its bucolic indoor/outdoor setting. While it's not located in Chicago proper, it makes a fine change-of-scenery getaway—which couldn't be easier, by car or by buses and Metra trains which go directly to the main gate.

Ravinia's season runs from June through September, with a few off-season programs tossed in. The Chicago Symphony Orchestra takes up residence here for eight weeks every summer, frequently joined by internationally known guest stars. In addition, Hubbard Street Dance Chicago does a shorter residency in September, running a repertory of programs during a week of performances.

Ticket prices for dance shows are slightly different than for music concerts, since lawn seats (while still available) aren't a desirable option. There is a range of prices, all within the pavillion; top prices are as high as $25, but you can get "limited view" seats off to the side for just $10 apiece. Call them starting in mid-May for more detailed schedule information.

"Under The Picasso"
- Daley Civic Center, 50 W. Washington St., Chicago; (312) FINE-ART (346-3278)

Every weekday, promptly at noon, the Chicago Department of Cultural Affairs brightens up the downtown lunch hour with free arts performances on the plaza in front of Picasso's famous sculpture. These events may consist of anything from a celebration of Jamaican Independence Day, full of music and colorful dance, to standup comedy or ballet. In the summer, there are even open-air farmers markets. Inside the building lobby itself, a small but serviceable art gallery offers more free culture, such as works from the Chicago Print and Drawing Fair. To find out what's on tap this week, call the hotline number above for a recorded message.

MOVIES

Unfortunately, there's not much to be done about the ever-rising prices of first-run Hollywood movies. Some theaters do cut the price a bit on their first shows of the day (see "Reduced-price Matinees" below). But don't despair! There are lots of alternative options for the budget moviegoer.

Chicago Cultural Center
- 78 E. Washington St., Chicago; (312) 744-6630

What a wonderful, civilized offering this is—the kind of facility which makes a city great. Looking to see a movie or hear a concert on a limited budget? Need a quiet place to cool your jets after a day of downtown shopping? New to town, and in need of helpful info to get around? Stop into the Chicago Cultural Center, where you can find all this and more, all for free.

Run by the city's Department of Cultural Affairs, the Cultural Center is committed to making lively and enriching entertainment accessible to the public. Along with the concerts and art galleries, they show movies geared to both grownups and children. These may include golden oldies like *Casablanca*, recent hits such as *The French Lieutenant's Woman* and *Blazing Saddles*, and ethnic films, as in their recent "Viva Latina!" series showing Spanish language films. For children, there are films like *Bon Voyage, Charlie Brown, Black Beauty*, and *The Little Prince*.

Before or after these events, relax in the Randolph Gallery and Cafe on the main level. You can sit over a cup of gourmet coffee and some pastry, and read or chat; best of all, it's air-conditioned in the summer. The building is open seven days a week, except holidays: Mondays through Thursdays from 10 a.m. to 7 p.m., Fridays from 10-6, Saturdays 10-5, Sundays 12-5. For more info about arts events here, call (312) FINE-ART (346-3278).

Chicago Filmmakers
- 1543 W. Division St., Chicago; (312) 384-5533

Chicago Filmmakers screens the kind of films, shorts, documentaries, and experimental works that may not even be seen in most art houses. The films seen here are among the newest and gutsiest being made in the city. Many are short works gathered under titles like "With No Apologies" and "Bodies in Crisis" and "Cultivated Fear: Encountering Violence in the U.S." CF has also presented evenings of locally made music videos. Screenings are usually held once or twice a week, unless there's a festival, and admission is just $5.

Better still is the deal for members, who get admission to all screenings for $2.50. A regular membership costs $25, so if you see ten or more films you'll have made up for the membership fee. What's more, you get four free tickets to regular CF events, as well as free sneak preview screenings. Membership does have its privileges. Give them a call and they'll send you a calendar of events and membership info.

Doc Films
- Max Palevsky Cinema, 1212 E. 59th St., Chicago; (312) 702-8575

Well, it's officially known as the Documentary Film Group at the University of Chicago. But Doc Films screens a lot more than documentaries: Vintage films, cult classics, and recent hits all turn up. Admission is just $3 at all times; films are generally shown Wednesday through Saturday nights.

Can you really see good movies

MR. CHEAP'S PICKS
MOVIES

✔ **Doc Films**—All kinds of classic movies for $3, open to the public at the University of Chicago.

✔ **Facets Multimedia**—The *avant-garde* is well-represented here, from historical groundbreakers to the latest from Chicago and the world.

✔ **Talman Home Savings**—Classic movies for $2, in a bank auditorium. Go figure.

✔ **The Vic**—"Brew and View" is a double feature of recent hits for $2.50 at this grand old movie palace, refitted with tables and chairs, so you can eat and drink while you watch.

for only $3? How about the Marx Brothers comedies, *Cocoanuts* and *Duck Soup*? Or, for that matter, *Some Like It Hot*, *The Manchurian Candidate*, and *Gaslight*. Among the art favorites that have been recently screened: Almodovar's *Tie Me Up, Tie Me Down*, the bio-pic *Henry and June*, and *My Beautiful Laundrette*, an early Daniel Day Lewis role. For those of you who want to see movies that are a little more mainstream, they've shown *My Cousin Vinny*, *Prelude to a Kiss*, and *Dead Again*.

Doc Films also has some other unique screenings like *THX—1138*, the movie George Lucas made as his senior project at USC. Give them a call and they'll send you a schedule of their upcoming shows.

Facets Multimedia
● 1517 W. Fullerton Ave., Chicago; (312) 281-9075

Near Clybourn and the river, Facets is the textbook definition of an "art house." On its film and video screens, it programs an ever-chang-

ing lineup of foreign films, silents, and the kind of on-the-edge flicks that win awards at Cannes but don't show up at the local megaplex. Recent offerings have included such "rediscovered" silents as *Diary of a Lost Girl*, from 1929, starring Louise Brooks; early works by Spanish director Pedro Almodovar, who gave us the classic *Women on the Edge of a Nervous Breakdown*; and the annual Blacklight Film Festival, featuring works by local and national black filmmakers.

And what price, for such priceless films? Why, only $5, all seats, all shows. If you're a real film buff, consider becoming a Facets member. Memberships start as low as $20; and these bring individual ticket prices down to $3. And they also rent videos; two-day rentals are $5, $3.50 for members. Call to get on their mailing list, and you will receive a monthly schedule.

Fermilab Film Society
● Fermilab Auditorium, Kirk Rd. and Pine St., Batavia; (708) 840-3000

Movies at a science lab? It's proven here on the second and fourth Friday of each month. A program of the Fermi National Accelerator Laboratory, the Fermilab Film Society features exotic films without charging exotic prices. These may include foreign films, independent productions, and other films that don't get a wide distribution. Recent offerings ranged from Peter Greenaway's British black comedy *Drowning by Numbers* to Laura Dern's provocative performance in *Rambling Rose* and the Canadian family pic *Black Robe*. Tickets for all this celluloid culture are only $3.00 each; kids are admitted for just 50 cents.

Film Center at the School of the Art Institute
● Columbus Dr. and Jackson Blvd., Chicago; (312) 443-3737

You are not likely to see multi-gazillion-dollar movies like *Jurassic Park* at the Film Center, but you will see all sorts of interesting cinema from around the world for just $5. Each month brings a group of films selected around a few themes, like "Films from the Middle East," or "Women's Vision in Film." Other individual movies are selected for their cultural or artistic qualities. The Film Center also sponsors lectures and special study screenings, which are free.

Admission is $5 at all times, which is already better than the mall; but, become a member and tickets are just $3. Memberships start for as little as $35. Besides discount admission, they include other great benefits like free classes, free tickets and discount merchandise. For more information, or to get on their mailing list, call (312) 443-3733.

Music Box
● 3733 N. Southport Ave., Chicago;
  (312) 871-6604

The story behind the Music Box is as dramatic as any of the films they show—an old-time theater, fallen into disrepair, then rescued by die-hard movie buffs who renovate it into a beautiful and popular showplace once more. What's more, they show an amazingly diverse schedule of current art films, old favorites, animation festivals, and other special-interest series.

See classics like *Roman Holiday*, the 1955 pic that made Audrey Hepburn an instant star; Walt Disney's *Snow White*; or Greta Garbo in the rediscovered *Flesh and the Devil*, a silent film with live organ accompaniment. *Far Away So Close*, German director Wim Wenders' sequel to *Wings of Desire*, had its Chicago premiere here. And recent festivals have focused on movies from China, gay and lesbian films, and the 29th Annual Chicago Film Festival.

Regular admission is $6.50, not that much of a bargain; however, there are other options. Weekend matinees, showing films from the entire broad Music Box spectrum, are only $5 a ticket, every Saturday and Sunday at 11:30 a.m.; you can also purchase a discount card, giving you six admissions for $28, or about $4.50 each.

Talman Home Savings
● 4901 W. Irving Park Rd., Chicago;
  (312) 443-2704

What better place to save money than at a bank? Seriously folks, this may not be the first place you think of to go for entertainment, but wait. Talman happens to have a 300-seat theater attached to it, where they show great, low-priced, old movies. The movies shown here are classics like *The Jazz Singer* (the real one, from 1927), *Oliver!*, *The Petrified Forest*, and *The Snake Pit*.

Admission is only $2. Movies are generally shown once a week, usually on Saturday nights. Showtime is 8:00 p.m., but you should arrive about a half-hour early to get a ticket. Call them to get a schedule of upcoming screenings. And you thought the most fun you could get here was a toaster oven.

The Vic
● 3145 N. Sheffield Ave., Chicago;
  (312) 618-8439 (VIEW)

"Brew and View" is a whole new experience in the world of second-run cinema. Another old movie palace that's been given a modern twist, the Vic combines the best aspects of renting videos at home with the experience of going out to the movies. Here, you see hit films that have just left the mainstream houses, on the big screen—but you sit at tables, eat and drink as you watch. They've taken out the seats; they've also added draft beer, Bacino's pizza and other "real" food (well, more real than Jujyfruits) to the popcorn stand. The pizza is $2 a slice; beers are $1.75 each. And on Thursdays, they only cost a quarter.

Admission, meanwhile, is a mere $2.50. And that's for a double feature, folks—anybody remember those? Recent offerings included *Cliffhanger*, *Dave*, and *Indecent Proposal*. But wait, there's more. On Saturdays, they add a midnight movie to the regular 8:00 and 10:00 starts. Three movies, one price. Add it all up—did you ever think you could go out to dinner and a couple of movies

177

for under $10? Such a deal!
    The Vic changes its lineup almost every week. They also frequently interrupt the movie schedule for live rock concerts (not as cheap), so call or check the newspapers for info.

Second-run Movies

There are many other theaters besides the Vic which exclusively show second-run features after their initial runs. If the picture was a flop, it may turn up in these places just weeks after its debut. But sometimes, a movie you'd never pay $7 to see is worth a try at $1.50 or so. Second-run houses can come and go, or their prices may change; but here is a listing of theaters to check out in the Chicagoland area. Most of them tend to be in the suburbs.

400 Theater
- 6746 N. Sheridan Rd., Chicago; (312) 764-9100
    $5, $3 before 6 p.m. on Saturdays and Sundays.

Bensenville Theatre
- 9 S. Center St., Bensenville; (708) 860-7774
    may be an exception on one first-run feature

Bremen Theatre
- 6813 159th St., Tinley Park; (708) 429-1010
    only $1.00 before 6:00 p.m.

Centre Cinema
- 116 Centre St., Park Forest; (708) 503-0707
    All movies $1.50.

Davis Theatre
- 4614 N. Lincoln Ave., Chicago; (312) 784-0894
    $1, $2 after 6 p.m. weeknights and all day Saturday and Sunday.

Des Plaines Cinema
- 1476 Miner St., Des Plaines; (708) 298-6715
    All movies $1.50, plus 50¢ admission on Tuesdays.

Elk Grove Cinema
- 1050 S. Arlington Heights Rd., Elk Grove; (708) 228-6707

Glenwood Theatre
- 18233 S. Halsted, Glenwood; (708) 754-7469
    $2.00, matinees on Saturday, Sunday, and Wednesday for $1.00

Highland Park Theatre
- 445 Central Ave., Highland Park; (708) 432-3300
    All movies $1.50

Lake Theatre
- 1020 Lake St., Oak Park; (708) 848-9088
    $2.00

Logan Theatre
- 2646 N. Milwaukee Ave., Chicago; (312) 252-0627
    $2 all seats, all times and that added bonus: Double features!

Morton Grove Cinema
- 7300 W. Dempster, West Harlem; (708) 967-6010
    All movies $1.50.

Olympic Theatre
- 6134 W. Cermak Rd., Cicero, (708) 652-5919
    $2.00

Patio Theatre
- 6008 W. Irving Park Rd., Chicago; (312) 545-2006
    $2.00.

Pickwick Theaters
- 5 S. Prospect Ave., Park Ridge; (708) 825-5800
    All movies $1.50.

Portage Theatre
- 4050 N. Milwaukee Ave., Chicago; (312) 202-8000
    $2.00, $1.50 on Mondays

Three Penny
- 2424 N. Lincoln Ave., Chicago; (312) 935-5744
    General admission $4.50, seniors $3.00.

Tivoli Theatres
- 5021 Highland Ave., Downers Grove; (708) 968-0219

Tivoli South
- 2119 63rd St., Downers Grove; (708) 968-0219

Tradewinds Cinema
- 1452 Erving Park Rd., Hanover Park; (708) 289-6707
  This one shows films for just 99¢, all seats, all times.

The Village Theater
- 1548 N. Clark St., Chicago, (312) 642-2403
  $2.75

Reduced-price Matinees

There are savings to be had on first-run movies if you like matinees. These may change from time to time, especially as the price of primetime films goes up. Call your local cinema to see if they're currently offering any bargain matinees. The following theaters have recently advertised earlybird deals:

Wilmette Theatre
- 1122 Central St., Wilmette; (708) 251-7411
  $2.00 until 4:00 p.m., $4.00 until 6:00 p.m.

Lake Zurich Theaters
- 755 S. Rand Rd., Lake Zurich; (708) 550-0000
  $3.00 until 5:00 p.m.

Lake Art Theatre
- 1020 Lake St., Oak Park; (708) 848-9088

$3.00 before 4:00 p.m., $5.00 after 6:00 p.m.

Yorktown Cinemas
- 97 Yorktown Shopping Center, Lombard; (708) 495-0010
  $4.00 before 6:00 p.m.

Lincoln Mall Cinema
- 4647 Lincoln Mall Dr., Matteson; (708) 481-4770
  $3.75 before 6:00 p.m.

And for something both cheap and romantic, there is the drive-in. **The Cascade Drive-In Theatre,** North Ave., W. Chicago; (708) 231-3150, may not seem all that cheap at $6.00 per person. But for that price you get to see two first-run flicks, these movies are still hot in the box office, and children under twelve get in free. **Cicero Twin Drive-In,** (708) 534-6050, also offers first-run double features at only $5.00, children under nine free.

MULTICULTURAL CENTERS

Chicago is blessed with several arts centers, public and private, which offer a full range of cultural activities at low prices—or even free! Here are some of the best.

Beacon Street Gallery and Performance Company

- Uptown Hull House, 4520 N. Beacon St., Chicago; (312) 528-4526

This Uptown multicultural arts center, just above Graceland Cemetery, is dedicated to bringing a variety of performances to a variety of people. To that end, their exhibition and performance schedule combines equal parts of traditional and ethnic offerings with more experimental and avant-garde works.

Beacon Street has a number of traditional ethnic dance companies in residence, including troupes dedicated to Guatemalan folk dance and Laotian classical dance. Their gallery exhibits have included work by Vietnamese, Native American, and West Indian artists. The theme of a particular exhibit is often matched with live performances. Tickets to these presentations are usually about $5—and sometimes they're free, as was a recent Native American concert of dance and poetry.

On the experimental and avant-garde side, Beacon Street has hosted such nationally known performance artists as Tim Miller, Karen Finley, and Holly Hughes. Along with its resident theatre ensemble, the Beacon Street Performance Company, these guest artists add further depth to the offerings. Their work really breaks boundaries, as with a recent show which combined music, video, and theatre.

Tickets to most events are about $8 to $10, with the national acts, like Tim Miller, going up to about $15. Admission to the art exhibits is always free. It all takes place under one roof, at the Uptown Hull House. Give them a call to get a full schedule of upcoming events.

Chicago Cultural Center

- 78 E. Washington St., Chicago; (312) 744-6630

What a wonderful, civilized offering this is—the kind of facility which makes a city great. Looking to see a movie or hear a concert on a limited budget? Need a quiet place to cool

your jets after a day of downtown shopping? New to town, and in need of helpful info to get around? Stop into the Chicago Cultural Center, where you can find all this and more, all for free.

Run by the city's Department of Cultural Affairs, the Cultural Center is committed to making lively and enriching entertainment accessible to the public. They present all kinds of events in the building's many galleries, concert halls, and studios. During one recent month alone, you might have taken in a harp and oboe recital; an exhibit of Japanese ceremonial kites, made by senior citizens; a slide lecture on the Hebrides islands of Scotland; a tap dance class; and movies for children, like *Bon Voyage, Charlie Brown*, or for grownups, like *Blazing Saddles*.

They also sponsor things like participatory dance in modern styles from around the world, and children's storytelling hours, taking place just outside the center in Grant Park; art exhibits at other galleries in the downtown area; a visitor information center, with all the brochures and free advice you could want; and guided tours of their own historic landmark building—the original location of the Chicago Public Library. The Museum of Broadcast Communications is in here, too (see listing under "Entertainment: Museums").

Before or after these events, relax in the Randolph Gallery and Cafe on the main level. You can sit over a cup of gourmet coffee and some pastry, and read or chat; best of all, it's air-conditioned in the summer. The building is open seven days a week, except holidays: Mondays through Thursdays from 10 a.m. to 7 p.m., Fridays from 10-6, Saturdays 10-5, Sundays 12-5. For more info about arts events here, call (312) FINE-ART (346-3278).

Why, you don't even have to leave the house to take advantage of CCC programs; call their "Dial-A-Poem" line at 744-3478, and you can enjoy a bit of culture in the comfort of your own home.

Fermilab Art Series

- Wilson Hall, Kirk Rd. and Pine St., Batavia; (708) 840-ARTS

The Fermi National Accelerator Laboratory, site of the highest energy particle accelerator in the world, may seem like an unlikely place to go for the performing arts. Nevertheless, this laboratory presents a series of nationally renowned artists at very affordable prices. Recent performers have included the Saturday Brass Quintet, bluegrass group Alison Krauss and Union Station, mandolin folkie Peter Ostroushko. The series also presents choreographer's showcases and Celtic music festivals, as well as jazz, theater, and opera.

Individual ticket prices go as high as $15, but most are in the $8 to $10 range. Series subscriptions offer additional savings. A reception follows every performance so you'll get a chance to socialize and maybe even meet the evening's artists. You can call to order tickets or to get a calendar of upcoming events and ticket information.

Harold Washington Library Center

- 400 S. State St., Chicago; (312) 747-4300

Mr. Cheap always says that the library is a great place to look for fun and inexpensive activities. Working in tandem with the Chicago Cultural Center (see listing above), the Washington Library Center presents a full slate of movies, music, dance, art exhibits, and children's activities—all free.

Find everything from the practical, like a lecture on how to repair bad credit, to the whimsical, such as poetry readings by local authors. And in their spacious auditorium, you can enjoy events from the classical, with concerts performed on their Steinway grand, to the extraterrestrial—yes, E.T. himself, part of the Midweek Matinee movie series.

The auditorium also offers dance performances, children's theatre, even opera. In their other venues around the building, there are art ex-

MR. CHEAP'S PICKS
Multicultural Centers

✔ **Beacon Street Gallery**—An arts center whose resident companies reflect the Uptown melting pot, while also bringing in nationally-known guest artists.

✔ **Chicago Cultural Center**—Mr. C's favorite. The reason why cities are great places. Free concerts, dance, movies, or just a quiet place to sip coffee and read.

✔ **Fermilab Art Series**—Concerts at a research lab? Believe it. Out in Batavia, this auditorium offers music, dance, opera, and theater by nationally renowned artists.

✔ **The Ravinia Festival**—International stars of classical music, dance, rock, and jazz all shine here. Avoid the expensive tickets by sitting on the open lawn.

✔ **Under the Picasso**—This city-run program brings free performances to downtown lunch crowds all summer.

hibits, career workshops, and a permanent exhibit on the tenure of the library's namesake, Mayor Harold Washington. You can take a free public tour of this large, beautiful building; group tours can be arranged by calling (312) 747-4136. All programs here are free of charge, though some programs may require advance reservations. The library is open Tuesdays and Thursdays from 11 a.m. to 7 p.m.; Wednesdays, Fridays and Saturdays from 9-5; closed Sundays and Mondays.

North Lakeside Cultural Center

- 6219 N. Sheridan Ave., Chicago; (312) 743-4477

Housed in an old mansion near the Loyola University campus, North Lakeside Cultural Center presents a wide variety of inexpensive music and theater performances. Their regular "Sunday Afternoon at the Mansion" series can offer anything from classical piano one week to Gershwin the next. The "Theater at the Mansion" series features productions by the much-respected Equity Library Theatre company; and there is also a regular "Jazz Night at the Mansion" series as well.

Tickets to any and all of these events are just $5 at the door; tickets are $3 if purchased in advance, senior citizens pay just $2.50. The Center also has an art gallery, with exhibits that change monthly. Call them for a schedule of upcoming events.

The Ravinia Festival

- Lake Cook and Green Bay Rds., Highland Park; (312) 728-4642 (R-A-V-I-N-I-A)

For nearly sixty summers, the Ravinia Festival has presented the finest names in classical and popular music in its bucolic indoor/outdoor setting. While it's not located in Chicago proper, it makes a fine change-of-scenery getaway—which couldn't be easier, by car or by buses and Metra trains which go directly to the main gate.

Ravinia's season runs from June through September, with a few off-season programs tossed in. The Chicago Symphony Orchestra takes up residence here for eight weeks every summer, frequently joined by such guest stars as Yo-Yo Ma and Itzhak Perlman. They also offer a June jazz series, as well as pop music, country, gospel, ballet, and more. Pop stars

seen here have included Ray Charles, the Neville Brothers, Natalie Cole, Peter, Paul and Mary, Spyro Gyra, the Mighty Clouds of Joy, and many others.

Ticket prices can be expensive, anywhere from $18-$35. What, then, is Ravinia doing in Mr. C's book? Well, there's another option: Lawn seats. Or rather, lawn folding chairs, lawn blankets, lawn-whatever-you-bring-to-sit-on....A $7.00 general ticket admits you to the lawn area, behind the concert-hall seating. Kids under ten are only $5. You can even bring a picnic, spread out and relax. Of course, you won't see as much, though you can wander up to the semi-enclosed auditorium to have a look at the stage; but you will hear every note perfectly, and if the weather cooperates, you'll hear them under the stars. It's a delightfully different way to experience a concert.

"Under The Picasso"

- Daley Civic Center, 50 W. Washington St., Chicago; (312) 346-3278 (FINE-ART)

Every weekday, promptly at noon, the Chicago Department of Cultural Affairs brightens up the downtown lunch hour with free arts performances on the plaza in front of Picasso's famous sculpture. These events may consist of anything from a celebration of Jamaican Independence Day, full of music and colorful dance, to standup comedy or ballet. In the summer, there are even open-air farmers markets. Inside the building lobby itself, a small but serviceable art gallery offers more free culture, such as works from the Chicago Print and Drawing Fair. To find out what's on tap this week, call the hotline number above for a recorded message.

MUSEUMS

Mr. C firmly believes that *all* museums are bargains. Consider how many treasures you can see, for less than the price of a movie! Still, everything is relative; with many museums raising admission fees, it's great to know two important things. One is that Chicago has lots of free and inexpensive museums, somewhat less famous but just as worthy of your attention. The other is that most of the biggies offer free admission one day a week. These are highlighted at the end of this chapter.

If you really enjoy a particular museum, by the way, consider becoming a member. This usually gets you free admission anytime, including perhaps your family, for the price of a couple of visits. It's a money-saver, and it helps out your beloved institution as well.

Adler Planetarium
- 1300 S. Lake Shore Dr., Chicago; (312) 322-0300

Here, the stars shine even in the daytime, whatever the weather, but they sparkle even more brightly on Tuesdays, when you can see them for free. Get up-close and personal with galaxies, telescopes, and inventions used by people hundreds of years ago in their attempts to chart the world and beyond. The Adler has a comprehensive collection of early scientific instruments, including telescopes used by Galileo and William Herschel, discoverer of the planet Uranus.

The planetarium's three floors of exhibits look not only into the past, but also the future—with "Space Transporters" which take you to the Sun, Mars, and other heavenly bodies. The Hall of Space Exploration features 3-D scale models of the planets and their moons. Included in the price of admission is the Sky Show, where dazzling special effects allow you to watch as a star is born (no, not Judy Garland or Barbara Streisand).

Adler Planetarium also offers courses in astronomy. Classes start at just $5 for a two-hour class of "Star Stories," which explores the mythical tales behind the constellations. Call 322-0323 for an up-to-date schedule of courses. Another fun feature of the Adler Planetarium is the Nightwatch Hotline: Call 322-0334 to hear a free recorded message about which planets and constellations are "up" at the moment.

Regular admission is $4 for adults, $2 for children under 17 and senior citizens—great deals, even at full price. Open daily from 9:00-5:00, plus Fridays until 9:00 in the evening.

American Police Center and Museum
- 1717 S. State St., Chicago; (312) 431-0005

The American Police Center and Museum is dedicated to educating the public about the work police officers do, and explaining the role of average citizens in helping to prevent crime.

Examine badges and shields from across the country and 'round the world, or trace the progress of police communications from the early days of whistles to the current use of two-way radio. They also have educational exhibits that explain such serious topics as the effects of legal and illegal drugs.

The museum caters to tour groups, from schoolchildren to senior citizens, particularly on Saturdays; call for more information. They often conduct special workshops to teach people what they can do to reduce crime, and to avoid becoming victims themselves. The museum is open from 9 a.m. to 4:30 p.m. daily; admission is a suggested donation of $2 for adults, and $1 for children. Admission is free to all on Mondays.

The Art Institute of Chicago
- 111 S. Michigan Ave., Chicago; (312) 443-3600

For a suggested donation of $6.50 ($3.25 for students and seniors), you can view one of the world's finest collections of paintings, sculpture, photography, decorative arts, architecture, and more from all over the world. The museum's permanent collection boasts such masterpieces as Georges Seurat's famous "A Sunday on La Grande Jatte" among its quarter-of-a-million art objects from the classical to the contemporary.

Considering how much you can see, that price is a bargain. But if that's still too steep for you, the museum is free to all on Tuesdays—and they even stay open extra late, from 10:30 a.m. until 8 p.m. As another part of the bargain, the museum holds lectures by renowned artists, art historians, and curators every Tuesday evening at six. Free gallery tours are given every day at 2:00 p.m., with a tour in Spanish on the first Saturday of every month; and half-hour walks through selected galleries take place every day at 12:15 p.m.

In addition to looking at art, talking about art, and hearing about art, you can also read about art in the Ryerson and Burnham libraries, the second-largest museum libraries in the world. The museum also sponsors frequent demonstrations, workshops, storytelling, and other special activities. Stop into the lobby for a calendar of events.

Mary and Leigh Block Gallery
- Northwestern University, 1967 S. Campus Dr., Evanston; (708) 491-4000

The fine arts museum of Northwestern University, the Block Gallery is free and open to everyone. The Block's seemingly endless array of tours, lectures, concerts, and other activities make it a popular stop for visitors, students, and local residents alike.

The gallery's sculpture garden (which, amazingly enough, never closes) offers visitors a chance to sit and relax among 20th-century sculptures by such renowned artists as Henry Moore, Joan Miro, Jacques Lipchitz, Jean Arp, and more. Admission, again, is free to all.

Chicago Academy of Sciences
- 2001 N. Clark St., Chicago; (312) 871-2668

The Chicago Academy of Sciences is the city's oldest museum, founded in 1857. Since then, it's been offering exhibits and programs to teach Chicagoans the rich natural history that is all around them. From the Great Lakes to the Great Plains, the Midwest has a rich store of natural history that goes back as far as when dinosaurs ruled the earth.

Here, the scientists seem to have brought all of the great outdoors inside for study. Trees and animals "live" in these fascinating rooms, one of which is a tropical rainforest entirely recreated to show you what Chicago looked like 300 million years ago. And the Atwood Celestial Sphere gives you a much better look at the stars seen from the city than you could ever really get in the city, where too many lights spoil the view.

Enjoy it all for a mere $2 per adult; senior citizens and children ages 3-17 are admitted for only $1, and kids under three get in free. Reservations are required for groups of ten or more. Call the number above for recorded info about upcoming events.

The Chicago Athenaeum: The Museum of Architecture and Design
- The Daniel H. Burnham Center, 1165 N. Clark St., Chicago; (312) 280-0131

The only independent museum of architecture and design in the country, the stated mission of this museum is to educate the public on the importance of "Good Design." The Athenaem sponsors a variety of programs including gallery walks, walking tours around town, special performances and events, and competitions. Recent exhibits have highlighted the contributions of women and African Americans to the field of architecture and design.

Admission is a suggested donation of just $2 for all ages. Group visits are available at reduced rates and require advanced registration.

The Athenaeum has several smaller branches around town. The main number, above, will give you info. about all of them. Branches are located at the John Hancock Center, 875 N. Michigan Avenue; Gallery I, 515 N. State Street; and the 333 W. Wacker Drive Gallery, 333 W. Wacker Drive.

Chicago Historical Society
- 1601 N. Clark St., Chicago; (312) 642-4600

From the drama of the early frontier days to the tragedy of the Great Chicago Fire, and the rebuilding that followed, the story of Chicago is an exciting and unique one indeed. And the CHS sure knows how to tell it, combining artifacts, photos, and paintings, with hands-on displays. Suddenly, you realize "history" wasn't all that long ago—and it's still unfolding.

This is another great place where you can have fun, learn a lot, and not empty your wallet to do it. Admission is a suggested donation of $3, $2 for students and seniors, and $1 for children. Better still, admission is free to all every Monday. Open Mondays-Saturdays, 9:30 a.m. to 4:30 p.m.; Sundays, noon to 5:00 p.m.

DuSable Museum
- 740 E. 56th Pl., Chicago; (3123) 947-0600

Named after Chicago's first permanent citizen, a black Haitian named Jean Baptiste Pointe DuSable, this museum is dedicated to preserving African-American culture and heritage. Frequent special exhibits highlight current themes. Recently the museum presented "African-American Architects in the Design of the Urban Community" and "African-Americans in Cinema," a collection of film posters. Their new Harold Washington Wing houses a permanent exhibit, "Washington On the Air," showcasing the career of the late Mayor Harold Washington.

DuSable also hosts the "Black Light Film Festival," featuring films by and about black people from around the world. Held each summer, this annual festival includes workshops and seminars with screenwriters, directors, and producers.

Admission for adults is only $3.00. Senior citizens and students pay $2.00; children under age thirteen get in for $1.00. Thursday is this museum's free day, when all ages are admitted at no charge.

Field Museum of Natural History
- S. Lake Shore Dr. at Roosevelt Dr., Chicago; (312) 922 9410

Q: What's four stories high, 75-feet long and *really* bony? A: The Brachiosaurus, the largest mounted dinosaur in the world, on permanent display at the Field Museum. And you can visit this Jurassic creature any Thursday for free.

Of course, that's not all there is to see here. With over nine acres of exhibits and over nineteen million artifacts and specimens from around the world, there is bound to be something for any interest. Whether you want to explore ancient Egypt, travel the Pacific, or experience life in a Pawnee earth lodge, you can do it here. Got a big school project? Get a jump on it at the Webber Resource Center, where you can browse through maps, books, artifacts, and videotapes. The Resource Center staff is available to answer any questions.

Regular admission is $5.00; $3.00 for children under 17, students, and senior citizens. The museum also has a special one-price family rate, which gets absolutely everybody in for $16. Decent savings for small families, and really great for Brady Bunch-sized broods. Meanwhile, the Field is free to all on Thursdays. Open daily, 9-5.

Lizzadro Museum of Lapidary Art

- 220 Cottage Hill Rd., Elmhurst; (708) 833-1616

If you like your art to sparkle, then this is a must-see. The Lizzadro features a world-famous collection of Oriental jade and hardstone carvings along with gemstones, animal dioramas, fossils, and a variety of earth science exhibits.

The Lizzadro also sponsors special interest films on the first and third Saturday of the month at 2:00 p.m. and "American Gemstones" every Sunday at 3:00 p.m. Recent exhibits have focused on the handiwork of German bowls and the work of Olive Colhour. Admission is $2.50 for adults, $1.50 senior citizens, $1.00 students, and free to children under 13.

May Weber Museum of Cultural Arts

- 299 E. Ontario St., Chicago; (312) 787-4477

This is the kind of place that makes Chicago a great city. Hidden away in an otherwise nondescript office building, the Weber Museum is a small gallery begun by Ms. Weber, a local physician who also happens to travel to far-off, exotic lands most of us will never see. In addition to displaying artifacts from her own vast personal collection, she has been able to borrow other rare objects from friends and fellow collectors.

The result is an oasis of quiet beauty amidst the hubbub of busy downtown life; but for the sign out front, you could walk past it every day and never know of its existence. Restaurants and shops crowd the unadorned entrance to a hallway, which takes you back to the rear of the building. There, what could have been a boring old office suite has instead been transformed into rooms filled with exhibits like the recent "A

Single Blade of Grass: The Japanese Vision." Graceful paintings, vases, kimonos, and other items from several centuries were on display; the exhibits change every few months.

Admission is only $1.00, and the hours are 12-5 p.m., Wednesdays through Sundays. Unfortunately, at the time of this writing, the museum is facing a financial crisis that may close its doors for good; and, according to articles in the newspaper, Ms. Weber is working hard to find some funding to keep alive what is clearly a labor of love. Call ahead to find the museum's current status.

Mexican Fine Arts Center Museum

- 1852 W. 19th St., Chicago; (312) 738-1503

Located in the South Side neighborhood of Pilsen, the heart of Chicago's Mexican population, the Mexican Fine Arts Center Museum represents nothing less than the entire spectrum of Mexican art and culture. It's the largest such institution in the United States, with exhibits ranging from the traditional to the avant garde. And admission is free to all ages, all the time.

Four major exhibits take place each year in the main gallery. One showcases contemporary art, another folk art; a third, art from some of the 56 indigenous peoples of Mexico. The fourth exhibit is the annual "Day of the Dead" show. Based on beliefs of people in pre-Colombian Mexico, this November holiday combats our own mortality with humorous displays of skeletons and other gruesome figures. In the modern world, the themes have advanced to include such topics as AIDS, hunger, and gang violence.

The Mexican Fine Arts Center Museum's west wing gallery shows work from its permanent collection. In their courtyard gallery, you can see work by today's emerging artists, as well as by students in the museum's children's art education programs. Hours are from 10 a.m. to 5 p.m., Tuesday through Sunday.

Mitchell Indian Museum

• Kendall College, 2408 Orrington Ave., Evanston; (708) 866-1395

Located on the campus of Kendall College, the Mitchell Indian Museum collects and exhibits art and artifacts of the native peoples of the United States and Canada. The museum was founded in 1977 to display the collection of John and Betty Mitchell, who collected art and ethnographic material from many North American tribes for over sixty years. It's grown significantly since then, and you can see it all for a one-dollar donation.

Compare the pottery, basketry, clothing, beadwork, quillwork, jewelry, musical instruments, toys, carvings, paintings, and more from various regions. There are also several "touching tables," where you're actually encouraged to pick things up and handle them—stone tools, rawhide, deerskin, and dance rattles. How many museums let you do that?

In addition to their permanent displays, special exhibits offer a deeper exploration of a single theme. Pueblo pottery, Native American dolls, and contemporary Native American art have all been the subject of special exhibits.

The museum also sponsors lectures and other educational programs. Call them for more info. They are open Monday through Friday from 9 a.m. to 4 p.m., and Sunday from 1 p.m. to 4 p.m. The museum closes during the month of August.

Museum of Broadcast Communications

• Chicago Cultural Center, 78 E. Washington St., Chicago; (312) 629-6000

Lights! Camera! Action! Learn about the history of radio, television, and its famous broadcasters. Get a feel for television of today by sitting behind the anchor desk of your own newscast. And do it all for free. Now, that's news!

Newly housed in the Chicago Cultural Center (see listing under "Entertainment: Multicultural Centers), this museum takes you behind

---

MR. CHEAP'S PICKS
Museums

✔ **The Art Institute of Chicago**—One of the world's greatest art museums, and it's free on Tuesdays.

✔ **Chicago Academy of Sciences**—The natural history of the Midwest region, marvelously brought to life.

✔ **DuSable Museum**—African-American history and popular culture is explored in this fine Hyde Park museum. Free on Thursdays.

✔ **Museum of Contemporary Art**—Another world-class art museum, focusing on modern works, again free on Tuesdays.

✔ **Museum of Science and Industry**—A gigantic place, all whirring, flashing, and generally bopping. Free on Thursdays.

✔ **The David and Alfred Smart Museum of Art**—Also in Hyde Park, a broad collection of over 7,000 works spanning 5,000 years. Admission is free every day.

---

the scenes of broadcasting from its inception to the present day. An exhibit of Edgar Bergen's famous trio, Charlie McCarthy, Effie Klinker, and Mortimer Snerd, plus showings of award-winning commercials, only scratch the surface of the fun to be had. Exhibits on subjects like the Nixon/Kennedy debate illustrate the impact television has had on our lives.

Along with their permanent collections, the museum creates special exhibits like the recent "My Little Margie to Murphy Brown: Images of Women in TV." Along with the exhibit, panel discussions explored the portrayal of women as housewives and superheroines in the workplace. It all comes alive when, in the words of Walter Cronkite, "You are there."

Museum of Contemporary Art

- 237 E. Ontario St., Chicago; (312) 280-2660

Known for its challenging and controversial exhibits—including photography by Robert Mapplethorpe—the MCA prides itself on provocative contemporary art. At the MCA you'll have a chance to see work by established artists as well as experimental work by those who are up-and-coming. Recent exhibitions have included photographs by Emmet Gowin, paintings by Libby Wadsworth, and early handpainted pop art by Roy Lichtenstein, Andy Warhol, and others.

The admission price of $4.00 ($2.00 for students, seniors, and children under sixteen, free for children under ten) is a bargain, especially since exhibitions are accompanied by lectures, panel discussions, and artists' talks. It's an even better bargain on Tuesdays, when the MCA is free for everyone. Guided tours of current exhibits are offered Tuesday through Friday at 12:15 p.m., and Saturday and Sunday at 1:00 and 3:00 p.m.

Museum of Contemporary Photography

- 600 S. Michigan Ave., Chicago; (312) 663-5554

Shutterbugs and admirers alike would be crazy not to go to Columbia College to snap a peek at the treasures hidden there. First of all, it's free. So, really what have you got to lose?

More importantly, beautiful, contemporary photographs in a variety of styles have gained this museum an international reputation. Artists often lecture on their work and you can take classes through Columbia College that will help bring these pictures (and your own) into sharper focus. Group tours can be arranged. The museum is open Monday, Tuesday, Wednesday, and Friday from 10 a.m. to 5 p.m., Thursday from 10 a.m. to 8 p.m., and Saturday from noon to 5 p.m.

Museum of Holography

- 1134 W. Washington Blvd., Chicago; (312) 226-1007

Like most museums, you can look around in here—but you can't touch anything. In this case, it's because the exhibits aren't really there. Holograms are three-dimensional images made with lasers into tantalizingly real-looking displays with no physical substance at all.

For the nearly non-existent price of $2.50 (under age six, free admission), you can experience the wacky world of holograms, along with special exhibits. One recent exhibit demonstrated how computers are used to generate these very holograms. Open 12:30 p.m. to 5:00 p.m., Wednesdays through Sundays.

Museum of Science and Industry

- 57th St. at S. Lake Shore Dr., Chicago; (312) 684-1414

This massive building opened as part of the great Columbian Exposition of 1893, and it's the only remaining structure from that historic event. Offering literally thousands of exhibits on science and technology and their industrial applications, the museum is big on visitor participation. Visit the "Communications" gallery, which takes you from the invention of the telephone all the way to fiber optics and other up-to-the-moment technologies. See how things like computers and television will be different in the near future. Explore the workings of the circulatory system by walking through a 16-foot pulsating model heart. Or, experience a miniature fairyland in "Colleen Moore's Fairy Castle," which contains over 1,000 tiny treasures.

One of the MSI's biggest attractions is the Omnimax Theater, part of the Henry Crown Space Center, which adjoins the main building. The Omni is a five-story, 350-seat theater which boasts the largest sound system in the world. It shows everything from scientific subjects like "Ring of Fire," which takes you inside a burning volcano, to fun films like "Rolling Stones At the Max." The Space Center, of course, is where you can see what it's like to be on the Space Shuttle, or even on another planet!

The MSI is open every day from 9:30 a.m. to 5:30 p.m. (until 4:00 from Labor Day to Memorial Day), with Omnimax shows added on Friday and Saturday evenings. Admission to the museum alone is $5.00 for adults, $4.00 for senior citizens, and $2.00 for children under twelve; admission is free to everyone on Thursdays. Children under 5 are free at all times, and are admitted to the Omnimax free if seating is available. The Omni, of course, has a separate admission fee; combination Museum/Omni tickets are sold at the box office.

Oriental Institute Museum
● 155 E. 58th St., Chicago; (312) 702-9521

On the campus of the University of Chicago, this museum has one of the world's foremost collections of artifacts from the ancient lands of Nubia, Persia, Mesopotamia, Assyria, and other places in what we now call the Middle East. Measure yourself next to a twenty-foot-tall statue of King Tut, carved in red quartzite stone, from Thebes in the year 1330 B.C. See how modern-day language experts decipher ancient hieroglyphic writing, step by step. Gaze upon gigantic ceremonial objects and delicate handcrafted jewelry. Room after room is filled with incredible sights—and all of it is free and open to the public.

The museum also offers a number of special programs to shed more light on these artifacts. Special interest tours, given Friday mornings at 11:30, highlight a particular gallery. On Sundays at 2:00, short films are shown on specific subjects, again followed by a gallery tour. And on Thursdays in the summer, there are special activities geared especially toward children.

Admission to the museum is free at all times, though groups of ten or more must phone ahead to arrange a tour. Hours: Tuesdays through Saturdays, 10:00-4:00 (plus Wednesday evenings until 8:30); Sundays, noon to 4:00. The museum is closed on Mondays and holidays.

Peace Museum Archive
● 350 W. Ontario St., Chicago; (312) 440-1860

The Peace Museum preserves the art and artifacts of peace movements and other political struggles, much of which is done by local grassroots organizations. A video, for example, documents a program instituted by the museum which brought local artists into the inner-city to teach art to young people. After you watch the video, you can look at the actual artwork these kids created.

The museum also presents special exhibits like the recent "Artifacts of Vigilance: Selections From the Permanent Collection." On display were political buttons, fliers, posters, letters, photos, quilts, and more. Not all of the subjects portrayed here deal with war; they also deal with things like the women's movement, and their campaigns against violence.

Admission is a suggested donation of $3.50 for adults and $2.00 for seniors and children. The Peace Museum is open from 11 a.m. to 5 p.m., Tuesday through Thursday, and from 11 a.m. to 6 p.m., Friday and Saturday.

The Polish Museum of America
● 984 N. Milwaukee Ave., Chicago; (312) 384-3352

The Polish Museum is among the oldest and largest ethnic museums in the United States. Its location, south of what is now called Polish Village, is in the heart of the first Polish neighborhood in Chicago. Admission to this treasure trove of Polish art and history is free, but they do request a $2 donation.

The museum mostly exhibits works by Polish and Polish-American artists; paintings, sculpture, drawings, lithographs, and more. The accomplishments of noted Polish men and women are seen in documents and personal effects. Military leaders Pulaski and Kosciuszko, scientists Copernicus and Sklodowska-Curie, and musicians Paderewski and Chopin all have their place in the Polish Museum.

The museum is open daily from noon to 4 p.m. The museum library, with 60,000 volumes, 250 periodicals, and a number of records, discs, and videocassettes, is open Monday through Saturday from 10 a.m. to 4 p.m.

John G. Shedd Aquarium

- 1200 S. Lake Shore Dr., Chicago; (312) 939-2438

While Mr. C doesn't like to look a gift horse, or shark, in the mouth, it is important to point out that free admission on Thursdays isn't exactly free. The Oceanarium, a re-creation of a Pacific Northwest coastline complete with beluga whales, white-sided dolphins, sea otters, and harbor seals doing their thing in a natural environment, is always an additional $4.00 ($3.00 for children under twelve and senior citizens). But the usual aquarium admission is waived (or is that "waved"?) on Thursdays.

Of course, you could save the four bucks, skip the Oceanarium and still have a whale of a time. The Aquarium itself is home to some six thousand aquatic animals from every one of the seven seas. You can observe such exotic creatures as electric eels, sea anemones, and piranhas. The Aquarium also houses the Tropical Coral Reef exhibit, a 90,000-gallon tank filled with sea turtles, sharks, moray eels, and more. If you're there at the right time, you may even get to see a diver hand-feed these animals while talking with visitors through a dive mask microphone.

Regular admission to the Aquarium is $3.00 for adults, $2.00 for children and seniors—already a bargain price. Regular admission to the Aquarium and the Oceanarium is $7.00 ($5.00 children and seniors) and you should purchase these tickets in advance. Children under three are free at all times for all exhibits. The Aquarium also runs a number of special programs throughout the year including scientific courses and hands-on workshops. Call the education department for information.

The David and Alfred Smart Museum of Art

- University of Chicago, 5550 S. Greenwood Ave., Chicago; (312) 702-0200

Really, no price would seem too high for the chance to view over 7,000 works of art spanning over 5,000 years. But admission to this museum is free, making its collection truly priceless.

The museum, named for the founders of *Esquire* magazine, was designed by renowned architect Edward Larrabee Barnes. It contains precious works in a number of media, from ancient Greek vases, with a rare example by Euphronios, to furniture by Frank Lloyd Wright. Not to mention sculpture by Degas, Matisse, Moore, and Rodin; photographs by Walker Evans; watercolors by Grosz, Heckel, and Nolde; and collections of ancient Chinese bronzes and modern Japanese ceramics. Whew!

The museum presents special exhibits, like the recent "German Print Portfolio 1890-1930: Serials for a Private Sphere" and "Art of the Persian Courts." Free lunchtime tours of the special exhibits are offered, as well as regular tours of the permanent collection. They also host free symposia, such as "Russia: The Land, the People" and "Sigmund Freud and Art." And there are children's programs like "Valentine's Day Fun and Games," in which children were supplied with ribbons, papers, and markers to create their own artistic valentines. While the kids were busy being creative, adults were invited on a special tour of the collection. The theme? Love, of course. All this fun for free! Stop in for a listing of upcoming events.

Spertus Museum of Judaica

- 618 S. Michigan Ave., Chicago; (312) 922-9012

The Spertus Museum covers 3,500 years of Jewish history with over

3,000 works in its main galleries. In addition, it houses the Zell Holocaust Memorial and sponsors special exhibits on Judaic themes. Recent exhibits have included "Yiddish Theatre in Chicago" and "Stars of David: Jews in the World of Sports."

The Spertus also offers many activities for children. Do your kids, or did you, ever want to be an archaeologist? The Rosenbaum Artifact Center at Spertus Museum has a hands-on exhibit designed to allow children to explore the ancient Near East using the same techniques as real archaeologists.

Admission is $3.50 and $2 for children, students, and senior citizens. Spertus has a maximum family admission of $8—an idea of which Mr. C highly approves. Better yet, on Fridays the museum has free admission for everyone, all day.

Swedish American Museum of Art
- 5211 N. Clark St., Chicago; (312) 728-8111

If you come to visit this museum you'll be in good company; King Gustaf stopped by in 1988 for an official dedication. All right, so Mr. C can't promise you'll see royalty when you go, but he can promise that for just $2 you'll see a variety of Scandanavian art from paintings to sculpture to lithographs. And, kids get in for just $1! The museum also sponsors a number of related cultural events including theater, jazz, folk music, and dancing. Call for info on their current schedule. Hours are Tuesday through Friday, 11 a.m. to 4 p.m., and Saturday and Sunday, 11 a.m. to 3 p.m.

Terra Museum of American Art
- 666 N. Michigan Ave., Chicago; (312) 664-3939

The focus of the Terra Museum is American art from the early 19th century, and their admission price will certainly make you feel like you're back in those good ol' days. Suggested donations are only $3.00 for adults; $2.00 for senior citizens and children under 14. Students with a valid I.D. get in free at all times, and all ages are admitted free on Tuesdays.

And what do you get to see for so few greenbacks? Terra's permanent collection includes works by Homer, Wyeth, and Cassatt. They also have frequent special exhibits, like their recent show commemorating Chicago's 1893 Columbian Exposition. Another recent exhibit, "American Abstraction at the Addison," featured the work of Arthur Dove, Georgia O'Keefe, Kenneth Noland, Man Ray, and many more.

Tours are offered Tuesdays through Sundays, at noon and 2:00 p.m. The museum also has a full-service education department, being affiliated with Northwestern University. You can even take courses that count toward credit at NU. Museum hours are noon to 8 p.m. on Tuesday, 10 a.m. to 5 p.m., Wednesday through Saturday, and noon to 5 p.m. on Sunday.

Ukrainian Institute of Modern Art
- 2320 W. Chicago Ave., Chicago; (312) 227-5522

Another of Chicago's many small but proud ethnic museums, the Ukrainian Institute of Modern Art existed here even before there was such a museum in Ukraine. Now that more attention has been focused upon former Soviet republics, it's a great time to have a look at this little cultural gem.

The permanent collection contains over 100 pieces by artists who share a Ukrainian heritage, from paintings and crafts to wood sculpture. The main exhibit hall has some six curated shows a year, while concerts, lectures, and other special programs round out the institute's offerings. Open from noon to 4 p.m., Tuesday through Sunday, admission is simply on a "donations appreciated" basis.

Ukrainian National Museum
- 453 W. Chicago Ave., Chicago; (312) 276-6565

Ukrainians have been calling Chicago their home for decades, and the

Ukrainian National Museum is dedicated to educating Chicagoans about the culture and history of this newly-independent land. Admission is free; donations, though, are gladly accepted.

The museum's historical collection includes portraits of prominent Ukrainians, as well as Ukrainian banknotes and other artifacts. They also have a large art collection, including paintings and sculpture by Ukrainian artists. Their folk art collection includes embroidery, wood and metal carvings, ceramics, beadwork, and *pysanky*, the Ukrainian art of painting Easter eggs.

The museum is open Thursday through Sunday from 11 a.m. to 4:30 p.m., though other hours can be arranged by appointment. Tours are available, but must be requested in advance.

FREE ADMISSION DAYS AT CHICAGO-AREA MUSEUMS

Not only is Chicago packed with world-class museums of every kind, but many of them offer free admission at least one day each week. Here is a listing of those free days.

Free every day:

Mary and Leigh Block Gallery
- Northwestern University, 1967 S. Campus Dr., Evanston; (708) 491-4000

Mexican Fine Arts Center Museum
- 1852 W. 19th St., Chicago; (312) 738-1503

Museum of Broadcast Communications
- Chicago Cultural Center, 78 E. Washington St., Chicago; (312) 629-6000

Museum of Contemporary Photography
- 600 S. Michigan Ave., Chicago; (312) 663-5554

Oriental Institute Museum
- 155 E. 58th St., Chicago; (312) 702-9521

The David and Alfred Smart Museum of Art
- University of Chicago, 5550 S. Greenwood Ave., Chicago; (312) 702-0200

Free on Mondays:

American Police Center and Museum
- 1717 S. State St., Chicago; (312) 431-0005

Chicago Historical Society
- 1601 N. Clark St., Chicago; (312) 642-4600

Free on Tuesdays:

Adler Planetarium
- 1300 S. Lake Shore Dr., Chicago; (312) 322-0300

The Art Institute of Chicago
- 111 S. Michigan Ave., Chicago; (312) 443-3600

Museum of Contemporary Art
- 237 E. Ontario St., Chicago; (312) 280-2660

Terra Museum of American Art
- 666 N. Michigan Ave., Chicago; (312) 664-3939

Free on Thursdays:

DuSable Museum
- 740 E. 56th Pl., Chicago; (312) 947-0600

Field Museum of Natural History
- S. Lake Shore Dr. at Roosevelt Dr., Chicago; (312) 922 9410

Museum of Science and Industry
- 57th St. at S. Lake Shore Dr., Chicago; (312) 684-1414

John G. Shedd Aquarium
- 1200 S. Lake Shore Dr., Chicago; (312) 939-2438

Free on Fridays:

Spertus Museum of Judaica
- 618 S. Michigan Ave., Chicago; (312) 922-9012

MUSIC

CLASSICAL

Chicago String Ensemble
- 3524 W. Belmont Ave., Chicago; (312) 332-0567

The Chicago String Ensemble is a 22-member group that has been together for almost twenty seasons, enjoying great critical acclaim during that time. The ensemble's repertoire includes selections from 18th, 19th, and 20th century composers. Concerts frequently add guest soloists of one sort or another, including singers. And one of the half-dozen concerts they do each season is a showcase of work by Chicago-based composers.

The most expensive ticket to these performances is $20; Mr. C doesn't find this to be overpriced, especially since the CSE is the only professional string orchestra in the Midwest. What's even better is that you can get lesser-priced tickets for just $15; seniors and students get the best deal of all, tickets for $12.

Performances take place regularly at three venues. St. Paul's Church, 655 W. Fullerton Ave., Chicago; St. Luke's Church, 939 Hinman Ave., Evanston; and Emmanuel Episcopal Church, 203 S. Kensington St., LaGrange. Call them for information about their schedule and about money-saving subscriptions.

Chicago Symphony Orchestra
- Orchestra Hall, 220 S. Michigan Ave., Chicago; (312) 435-6666

If you think you'd have to mortgage your home to pay for an evening at Orchestra Hall, hang on a moment. While the best box seats in the house can go up to $130 per ticket (yikes!), there *are* alternatives. First, it is worth noting that not every seat in the hall is so outrageously priced; while many tickets are $50 and higher, there are several sections in the $20 to $30 range and even some for $15 and under, depending on the concert.

Option number two: Students and senior citizens can take advantage of rush tickets. These tickets are available after 5 p.m. on the day of a performance (after noon on matinee days) and are priced at just $12.50. Remember, you must have valid identification to obtain discounted tickets.

Also, the CSO has a number of

MR. CHEAP'S PICKS
Music—Classical

✔ **Chicago Symphony Orchestra**—Don't pawn Aunt Myrtle's glass unicorn collection—there are several inexpensive ways into the hallowed halls of the CSO.

✔ **Dame Myra Hess Memorial Concerts**—Free chamber music at the Chicago Cultural Center.

special programs with ticket prices that won't break your budget. "Sundays at Orchestra Hall in the Ballroom" are early evening performances priced at only $10 per ticket. In addition, the audience is invited to enjoy light refreshments and conversation with the musicians after the performance. In a similar vein, "Fridays at Loyola University in the Madonna della Strada Chapel" are also $10 concerts. No, you won't see the Material Girl, but you will hear chamber music played by members of the Chicago Symphony and enjoy the beauty of the Lake Shore campus.

For a pleasurable mixture of music and art, try "Sundays at The Art Institute in Fullerton Hall." This series consists of five concerts, each of which includes members of the CSO, exploring connections between music and the fine arts. The $15 ticket price includes admission to the Art Institute of Chicago, a slide presentation and lecture, full-length concert in the museum, and a self-guided tour of selected galleries.

Back at Orchestra Hall, the CSO also presents a "Family Concerts" series providing a great opportunity to introduce children to the joys of classical music. Ticket prices range from $5.50 to $13; box seats can be had for just $22 apiece. These concerts

take place on Saturdays at 2 p.m.

We're not finished yet! If all that isn't enough, how about free open rehearsals and performances by the Civic Orchestra of Chicago, the training orchestra of the Chicago Symphony? There are generally six programs per season, and they include a pre-concert lecture. Other special events include the Chicago Youth Symphony Orchestra, the Apollo Chorus of Chicago, and Performing Arts Chicago. One phone call can get you a program schedule listing all of these events, times, and ticket prices. And you thought you had to be rich? Save Mr. Cheap the aisle seat!

Dame Myra Hess Memorial Concerts

• The Chicago Cultural Center, 78 E. Washington St., Chicago; (312) 346-3278.

Every Wednesday at 12:15 p.m., the Chicago Cultural Center presents free classical music recitals. The delightful repertoire leans particularly toward chamber ensembles.

The Dame Myra Hess series is not the only time you can hear free classical music here. The Chicago Cultural Center has a number of free concerts each month, including regular performances on Sunday afternoons. Notable concerts have included the Chicago Chamber Musicians and the Chicago Chamber Orchestra. Call the above number (it's easy to remember; it spells FINE-ART) to get on their mailing list. They'll send you a monthly calendar listing all of their free events, including concerts, literary events, lectures, and more.

Evanston Symphony Orchestra

• Evanston Township High School, 1600 Dodge Ave., Evanston; (708) 864-8804

Sometimes, a short drive into the 'burbs can reap unimagined benefits. Away from the (expensive) hustle and bustle of the city, you can find the Evanston Symphony Orchestra, a fine community orchestra with ticket prices that will make you smile.

The ESO presents four concerts

per season and the entire series can be purchased for $25. That's only $6.25 per concert! At most performances, professional guest soloists join the orchestra as they play compositions by the likes of Rachmaninoff, Dvorak, Wagner, Tchaikovsky, Gershwin, and Puccini.

If you've always wanted to be a patron of the arts, the ESO offers a great opportunity to do so without selling off the family cubic zirconia heirlooms. For only $60, you can become a Patron of the Evanston Symphony. You'll receive a pair of tickets to each concert in the series (only $10 more than the total cost anyway), and your name will be listed in the program as a supporter. Why, that's cheap enough to rent a Rolls for the evening and really play the part!

All concerts begin at 8 p.m., and they are held in the Evanston Township High School. Call the number above for more information.

Geja's Cafe
- 340 W. Armitage Ave., Chicago; (312) 281-9101

Okay, so it's not opening night at Orchestra Hall, but this Lincoln Park restaurant is a great place to go for live classical and flamenco guitar, presented every night of the week.

The specialty of the house is fondue; cheese, seafood, and chocolate, as a snack, meal, or dessert. Two people can share to keep the tab reasonable; Geja also has a good wine list. Yet, there's never a cover charge or a drink minimum; so feel free to stroll on in and enjoy the music—tap your feet all night long.

Hyde Park Chamber Music Festival
- 1100 E. 55th St., Chicago; (312) 493-2409

Every summer, this series based in the University of Chicago area, presents a half-dozen concerts by a resident ensemble. They play chamber music by such composers as Bach, Haydn, Debussy, and other traditional names, as well as modern composers. Some programs are grouped around a central theme, such as "Music for Soprano, Flute, and Guitar" or simply "French Music."

Concerts take place in various church halls around the campus area, usually on Monday or Thursday evenings at 8 p.m.; ticket prices are a very reasonable $8 each, and $5 for students and senior citizens. Better yet, consider a "Series Ticket"—just $26 gets you a ticket to any four performances ($18 for students/seniors). The festival runs during July and August; call or write to the address above for schedules and order forms.

The Ravinia Festival
- Lake Cook and Green Bay Rds., Highland Park; (312) 728-4642 (R-A-V-I-N-I-A)

For nearly sixty summers, the Ravinia Festival has presented the finest names in classical and popular music in its bucolic indoor/outdoor setting. While it's not located in Chicago proper, it makes a fine change-of-scenery getaway—which couldn't be easier, by car or by buses and Metra trains which go directly to the main gate.

Ravinia's season runs from June through September, with a few off-season programs tossed in. The Chicago Symphony Orchestra takes up residence here for eight weeks every summer, frequently joined by such guest stars as Yo-Yo Ma and Itzhak Perlman.

Ticket prices can be expensive, anywhere from $18-$35. What, then, is Ravinia doing in Mr. C's book? Well, there's another option: Lawn seats. Or rather, lawn folding chairs, lawn blankets, lawn-whatever-you-bring-to-sit-on....A $7.00 general ticket admits you to the lawn area, behind the concert-hall seating. Kids under ten are only $5. You can even bring a picnic, spread out, and relax. Of course, you won't see as much, though you can wander up to the semi-enclosed auditorium to have a look at the stage; but you will hear every note perfectly, and if the weather cooperates, you'll hear them under the stars. It's a delightfully different way to experience a concert.

Summer Carillon Festival

- Rockefeller Memorial Chapel, 5850 Woodlawn Ave., Chicago; (312) 702-2100

Also on the U of C campus, this magnificent chapel is the setting for a summer music series of a different sort. Every Sunday evening in July and August, its tall, Italianate bell tower rings forth with the joyous sound of the carillon. With a total of 72 bells, this is the second largest carillon in the world! They don't mention where the largest one is, but you can bet it's gotta be in France. Anyway...

The concerts are free; the public is invited to sit on the chapel's broad lawn, spread out a blanket, bring a picnic and bask in the sun (or whatever). If you so desire, you can even climb up the bell tower with the "carilloneur" and experience the whole scene from the inside! If you do, though, it may be a good idea to bring along a bit of cotton for the ears. The music begins at 6:00 p.m.; be at the main door by 5:30 if you want to go up to the top.

By the way, if you've never been in this interdenominational chapel (they won't call themselves a church), be sure to step inside during your visit—it's a beautiful one.

FOLK

Abbey Pub

- 3420 W. Grace St., Chicago; (312) 478-4408

In addition to being a fine broth of a restaurant, the Abbey serves up healthy portions of Irish music, along with good ol' rock and blues. There's music every night except Monday; best of all, there is no cover Sunday through Thursday nights.

Music starts at 8 or 9 p.m. On Sundays and Wednesdays at 8, bring your fiddle and join in on the traditional Irish jam sessions (yes, you can just listen). Other nights feature local bands, with the occasional headliner, like the Clancy Brothers, mixed in. Cover charges on Friday and Saturday range from $2 to $15, but usually stay in the $4 to $5 range.

Beat Kitchen

- 2100 W. Belmont Ave., Chicago; (312) 281-4444

It's a bit out of the way, but Beat Kitchen is a fun place to see all kinds of live rock and folk music for very little money. BK sponsors a free songwriters showcase, usually happening on Monday or Tuesday. Other weeknights are especially good times to go; most offer two local bands at little or no cover charge, and no drink minimum.

Weekends, of course, are a different story, but still fairly reasonable.

Friday nights may feature four bands for $6. Admission can go as high as $10.00 on Fridays and Saturdays, depending on the act, but most weekends stay closer to $6 or $7. Music starts around 9:30, later on weekends.

Bub City

- 901 W. Weed St., Chicago; (312) 266-1200

Where can you hear live country and western music absolutely free? Why, here at Bub City, of course. This restaurant and bar turns into a venue for all kinds of C & W bands every Friday and Saturday night from 9 p.m. until 1 a.m. There is often music on Thursdays, too, from 7 p.m.

There's never a cover or drink minimum, and the eats—mainly barbecue and seafood—are reasonably priced. So mosey on in and listen to bands with names like Rick Pickeron and the Outriders, or Burning House of Love. You won't have to spend a plug nickel—except maybe to whet your whistle with a cold sarsparilla.

Chicago Brauhaus

- 4732 N. Lincoln Ave., Chicago; (312) 784-4444

Can't afford a trip to Bavaria? You can hear lively German-American music here Wednesday through Monday with no cover charge and no drink minimum. Of course, you'd be missing out on an essential part of the scene if you come here and don't try their old-world brew.

On Saturdays and Sundays, the fun starts at 1 p.m. with lively accordion music. Then at 6 p.m., the five-piece house band takes over for the evening. Oom-pah all you like; lederhosen optional.

The Brauhaus, of course, serves up traditional German and American dinners, including wiener schnitzel, bratwurst and the rest. Prices are fairly moderate, and reservations are recommended.

Clearwater Saloon

- 3937 N. Lincoln Ave., Chicago; (312) 549-5599

Every Sunday through Thursday at the Clearwater, you can hear great blues and rockabilly bands at no cover charge. Well, all right, there's one exception: Thursdays feature the "Chicago Songwriters Showcase," presenting members of the Musicians Network, and they ask for a $1 donation. C'mon, what's a buck? It's a good deal and it helps support the music.

Tuesdays feature open blues jam sessions. On Fridays and Saturdays there is a $5.00 cover, still not bad; and you can see acts like the Elvis Brothers and Blue Dixie. Yeeee haw!

David Adler Cultural Center

- 1700 N. Milwaukee Ave., Libertyville; (708) 367-0707

Well, this one's quite a ways out of town; but there's so much going on here, Mr. C just had to throw it in. Three Fridays a month, the David Adler Cultural Center presents an open stage and jam session. Admission is free, but donations are suggested (and greatly appreciated). Musicians from around the area come to sing and play folk music. You can just relax and listen, or, during the open mike part, enjoy your twenty minutes of fame by joining in with your own tunes.

But why only three Fridays, Mr. C? Well, on the *first* Friday of every month, the DACC presents a proper folk music concert. These feature local talent, with the occasional na-

---

MR. CHEAP'S PICKS
Music—Folk

- ✔ **Abbey Pub**—Irish jam sessions, on traditional instruments, Wednesday and Sunday evenings—with no cover charge.
- ✔ **Bub City**—Country and western music every weekend, with no cover or minimum ever.
- ✔ **Old Town School of Folk Music**—Every Friday night, folk players gather for a free, informal song circle at 6:30; a more proper coffeehouse follows at 8:30.

---

tional artist mixed in. Tickets are just $8, and the music begins at 8:00 p.m. They also have children's concerts (see listing under "Entertainment: Children's Activities").

Oh, and on the first *Saturday* of every month, the Cultural Center presents a barn dance at the American Legion Hall in North Milwaukee. Admission to the dance is also $8, and it too starts at 8:00 p.m. Then, there are the Center's music classes, art classes, children's classes....Call them for more information.

Java Jive

- 909 W. School St., Chicago; (312) 549-3500

Besides having a cool name, Java Jive has a number of opportunities for you to hear live music with no cover charge. They do ask that you spend something on sandwiches, pastry, or coffee, all of which are first-rate (see listing under "Restaurants: Lincoln Park"). And there is, of course, a tip jar for the musicians themselves, should you feel so inclined. They are generally quite deserving of a buck or two.

The music starts up around 8:00

p.m., playing on and off until 11:00 or so. Different nights bring different sounds; Tuesdays, for instance, are folksinger nights, while Fridays add a folk/rock edge. On Thursdays, there is usually a duo of flute and guitar, playing classical music and/or Irish folk melodies. And Sundays feature live jazz, in the evening and also at brunch. Another bonus, during nice weather, is the handful of patio tables outside the front door.

Kopi, A Traveler's Café
- 5317 N. Clark St., Chicago; (312) 989-KOPI (5674)

Here's another cafe, in Andersonville, with varied live music offerings to entertain you while dining (again, see a separate listing under "Restaurants: Uptown"). "Kopi" in case you're wondering, is in fact the Indonesian word for cafe.

Music at Kopi, which is known for this international flavor, takes place twice a week. Monday evenings feature various types of music from all around the world; on Thursday evenings, the bill usually consists of singer/songwriters. There is no cover charge, though of course you ought to eat something, and you should tip the musicians as well. Remember, Mr. C is no cheapskate.

Mont Clare Coffeehouse
- 6935 W. Medill Ave., Chicago; (312) 714-0328

This coffeehouse offers something unique—entertainment for the whole family. Just $4 gains you admission to an evening of folk music and storytelling, presented on the second Saturday of each month from September through June. Admission for children ages twelve and under is only $1. The coffeehouse begins around 8 p.m., and features regional and national folk artists.

Other occasional events include participatory dances with live music, usually for the same admission; and singarounds with an admission charge of just $2, free for children 12 and under. And don't miss the one-day Mont Clare Folk Festival, held each August; admission is free to all.

It all takes place at the same hopping location. These industrious folks also put out a quarterly newsletter, *Common Times*, which you can pick up at area coffeehouses; or, subscribe to it for just $5 per year.

Old Town School of Folk Music
- 909 W. Armitage Ave., Chicago; (312) 525-7793

There is another Mr. C in Chicago: Mr. Coffeehouse. Every Friday night (except holidays and during the summer), the Old Town School of Folk Music hosts an informal gathering of students, teachers, local musicians, and folk enthusiasts.

The evening begins at 6:30 p.m. with a song circle; admission is free, and everyone is welcome to join in the singing. Then, at 8:30 p.m. the more formal part of the evening gets underway with featured guests. These are usually established regional groups, preceded by a warm-up act of local musicians or students. There's a $3-$5 cover charge for the second half. What a bargain!

But that is not all the OTS has to offer. Sunday afternoons feature their "Showcase Series" of new talent, as well as a "Children's Concert Series"; tickets for these shows are usually priced at $8. Call for a brochure that details all of these, plus other concerts and class offerings.

Schuba's Tavern
- 3159 N. Southport Ave., Chicago; (312) 525-2508

Right around the turn of the century, this was a tap house for Schlitz beer. Today, it's a restaurant and bar located minutes from Wrigley Field, which features regular doses of live rock, country, and jazz—something different every night of the week, except Sunday. Cover charges average between $4 and $6, depending on the night and the band. Enjoy the latest sounds in a setting that's old enough to be hip all over again.

Whiskey River
- 1997 N. Clybourn Ave., Chicago; (312) 528-3400

Well, it's really closer to the Chicago River...but this club is one of the city's premier spots for country music, and it certainly looks the part. They'll even teach you the two-step; yessiree, free dance lessons are offered every night at 7 p.m. on their 1,200-square foot dance floor. Then, when you come to hear groups with names like West Confederate Rail-road and Born to Boogie, you'll know how. The cover charge varies; most live bands, which play on Friday and Saturday nights, get about $4-$5 at the door. There's never a cover charge during the week, when the whiskerandos spin records.

JAZZ AND BLUES

Andy's Jazz Club
- 11 E. Hubbard St., Chicago; (312) 642-0565

Looking for a different way to spend your lunch hour? Head over to Andy's, just across the river above the Loop, and hear great jazz with no cover charge any weekday at noon. The music generally progresses from solo piano at the beginning of the week, adding a piece each day, up to a lively quintet on Fridays. You can sit at the large central bar, or in the dining area for lunch (see listing under "Restaurants: Near North"). The players are a wide-ranging assortment of local musicians.

Nighttime prices aren't free, but they're not bad either. The cover charge is only $3 from 5 p.m. to 8:30 p.m., Monday through Friday; after that, it goes up to $4, for music until about 1:00 a.m. Sunday music starts up around 6:00 in the evening, going until midnight. Weekend cover charges are $5-$7. Music on these evenings may range from straight-ahead jazz to boogie-woogie blues.

Bistro 1800
- 1800 Sherman Ave., Evanston; (708) 492-3450

Tucked behind an office building, the Bistro 1800, and its adjoining My Bar, may be difficult to find—but they're worth the effort. They offer nightly entertainment, mostly jazz and blues, as well as a weekend jazz brunch.

There is no cover charge; there is a $4 minimum, but this may include both food and drink. Entertainment begins at 9:00 p.m., running until 11:00 p.m. on weekdays and 'til midnight on weekends. Another good feature here, especially for a cafe: A no-smoking section.

B.L.U.E.S.
- 2519 N. Halsted St., Chicago; (312) 528-1012

B.L.U.E.S. Etcetera
- 1124 W. Belmont Ave., Chicago; (312) 525-8989

This pair of nothing-fancy-just-hard-hitting-music clubs, one in Lincoln Park and the other in Lake View, have been around for about fifteen years. They rock well into the night, seven nights a week, shuttling great howlers from the national circuit back and forth between them. Son Seals, Luther "Guitar Jr." Johnson, Otis Rush, Billy Branch, and Chubby Carrier and the Bayou Swamp Band are just some of the many stars who play both clubs regularly, with cover charges usually in the moderate $5-$7 range.

B.L.U.E.S. Etcetera also hosts a free Wednesday night blues jam session, usually with reduced-price beer promotions as well. Music at both clubs starts up around 9:00 p.m. every night.

The Bop Shop
- 1807 W. Division St., Chicago; (312) 235-3232

This little bar/nightclub has so many different things to see and do that it's difficult to know where to begin. They have open-mike poetry nights. They have open jam sessions for professional musicians of all stripes, on Sundays and Tuesdays. And they have a regular lineup of jazz and rock bands. Cover charges vary from about $3 to as high as $7. Some nights, like those open jams, have no cover charge at all.

But that's not all. There is also an art gallery where you can view works by local artists, and even buy if you're so inclined. Pick up some art supplies for your next masterpiece, too. Nice way to blend art and music—there is a delightfully bohemian air to the Bop Shop.

Bossa Nova
- 1960 N. Clybourn Ave., Chicago; (312) 248-4800

Bossa Nova is a restaurant that also features jazz, salsa, and blues Wednesday through Saturday. Music begins about 8 p.m. on Wednesday and Thursday and at 10 or 11 p.m. on Friday and Saturday. On any given night, you can get anything from cool jazz to hot salsa.

The only time they charge a cover is on Saturday nights, but even then it's only about $5. They're open until 2 a.m. and they keep the kitchen open pretty late, so this is ideal for late-night munchies or after-hour snacks.

Brother Jimmy's BBQ
- 2909 N. Sheffield Ave., Chicago; (312) 528-0888

What a hopping place this is! When they're not raising the roof with live music, they're lowering the price on their great barbecued chow. Outside, all you see is a simple doorway. Inside, this is a huge, high-ceilinged version of a North Carolina roadhouse, right down to the "Duke" paraphernalia on the walls. There's a long bar area, lots of dining tables and booths, and a stage which features free, live music every Thursday, Friday, and Saturday night.

Music starts up around 9:00 each evening, with a strong bias toward hard rockin' blues. Mr. C stopped in on a Thursday evening and found the place packed with a lively, young crowd which was not only eating up the food, but also the fiery rockabilly music. The variations range from urban blues to country, to zydeco, to straight-ahead rock 'n roll. And, as mentioned above, there is *never* a cover charge. The friendly guy at the door just says, "C'mon in!"

The kitchen serves food until 11:00 p.m. on weekdays, and until 1:00 a.m. on weekends, while the club stays open for an hour or two more.

Buddy Guy's Legends
- 754 S. Wabash St., Chicago; (312) 427-0333

In this town, Buddy Guy *is* a legend—and the rest of the country is finally discovering this, too. Equally worthy is his music club, where you can enjoy live blues and a buffet every Friday from 5 p.m. until 8 p.m. for free. It's their "After Work" special, serving up chicken wings, fries, and other nibbles along with the music. It's not the most generous buffet ever seen, but you can make one good pass and have a nice snack—and hey, it's all free!

While that is one fine deal, the weeknight cost won't leave you cryin' the blues either. Cover charges for Sunday through Wednesday are only $4, and Thursdays are $5. Not bad for national stars like Ronnie Earl, Duke Robillard, Maria Muldaur, and Otis Rush. Weekends get more expensive; around $8-$10 depending on the musicians. If you're inclined to stick around, there are pool tables and a full menu of burgers and sandwiches.

The Bulls Jazz Club
- 1916 N. Lincoln Park West, Chicago; (312) 337-3000

"The Bulls" offers a good blend of jazz, Latin music, and reggae. Best of all, their $4 cover charge on weekdays is as good as a Jordan slam-dunk. Weekends, of course, get a bit more pricey. The atmosphere is intimate and the acoustics are fine—a great setting for many of Chicago's up-and-coming jazz artists. Sets start around 9:30 p.m., and the club jams until 4:00 in the morning—well past the coach's curfew.

Deja Vú
- 2624 N. Lincoln Ave., Chicago; (312) 871-0205

This may well be the only place in Chicago—perhaps anywhere—in which you can see live turtle races for $1.00. Not your thing? Don't worry. They also have live bands, for your listening and dancing pleasure. The music changes from night to night, ranging from country rock to progressive jazz. Sundays feature a jazz jam session, with no cover charge; on Tuesdays, the Deja Vú Big Band holds forth, with admission just a buck. Friday and Saturday nights, when the sound turns to country rock, cover charges average $2-$4.

Discover Cafe

- 2436 N. Lincoln Ave., Chicago; (312) 868-3472

There's more to discover here than coffee. Note the first four letters; this is not just a cafe, it's also a music store, and the combination is a winner. At one counter, you can order up a cuppa their basic joe for a dollar (with refills just 50 cents each). At the other, you can snap up a (used) Miles Davis CD for just $9.

But wait, there's more! The cafe presents a live jazz trio during Sunday brunch, free of charge (the music, that is), from 10:30 a.m. until 2:00 p.m. Jazz also rings forth on Thursday evenings, while on Monday evenings there is a more eclectic grabbag of live performance. In any case, it's always offered as a free accompaniment to the food.

Nibble on a hefty turkey sandwich ($5.25), or a plate of "Eggs Espresso" ($2.75). No, these are not coffee-flavored sunnysides; these eggs are steamed in an espresso machine, and thus made without butter. The place is also big on "comfort foods," like a pair of good ol' Pop Tarts for $1.50. Or, just have a cappuccino and enjoy the bohemian atmosphere. You can sit at a table, or on one of the comfy couches, and while away an hour or two. Of course, you can hang out here any day of the week, with or without the jazz. Plenty of good music is always playing, and works by local artists adorn the walls.

Hmm....With CDs, live music, and food, this may be one of the only places in this entire book which fits

---

MR. CHEAP'S PICKS
Music—Jazz

✔ **Andy's Jazz Club**—Free lunchtime jazz every weekday, plus other inexpensive shows each night.

✔ **Deja Vú**—Catch the Deja Vú Big Band every Tuesday night for only one dollar.

✔ **Discover Cafe**—Sunday jazz brunches with no cover charge.

✔ **Green Mill Lounge**— Straight-ahead jazz for little or no cover, from midnight into the wee small hours.

✔ **Tania's**—Salsa and other streams of Latin music at this Bucktown restaurant; no cover, and you don't even have to eat.

---

into all three sections—shopping, restaurants, and entertainment. And it's all cheap. Quite the discovery.

Elbo Room

- 2871 N. Lincoln Ave., Chicago; (312) 549-7700

Known primarily as a rock club, this cozy little downstairs bar also offers a rare and wonderful show once a week for jazz aficionados. Every Tuesday, drummer Barrett Deems— who once pounded the skins with the Duke Ellington Orchestra—now leads his own big band for two sets starting around 9:00 p.m. How they manage to fit eighteen musicians onto Elbo's small stage is but one of the miracles of these performances; the presence of Deems himself, several decades along in his career, is another.

Meanwhile, it's a great opportunity to hear good old big band jazz in a close-up, unmiked setting. The band plays a mix of standards and more recent arrangements. So, whether you remember the 1940's, or regret missing them altogether, you're sure to enjoy a couple of hours here. The cover charge for all this fun is only $4, and there's plenty of elbow room at the Elbo Room—including a dark nook lined with comfy couches off to the side.

Fitzgerald's
- 6614 W. Roosevelt Rd., Berwyn; (708) 788-2118

This club is best known for live blues, but that's not all there is to see here. Fitzgerald's Tuesday night "Open Stage" presents poetry, music, dance, and anything else that people may be willing to do in front of an audience. Admission is a super-cheap $2.00.

On Wednesdays, you can enjoy the sounds of big band jazz for an $8 cover. Wednesdays and Thursdays often feature local and national bands playing everything from bluegrass and rock to acoustic and folk acts. Fridays and Saturdays, of course, are reserved for the bigger national acts. Cover charges can get as high as $15, but often they're between $5 and $8.

And this is a club steeped in history. Los Lobos, Robert Cray, and Stevie Ray Vaughn have all played here. Lonnie Mack and Koko Taylor both made live recordings here. And Fitzgerald's has been the scene, quite literally, for a few big movies, including *The Color of Money*. Remember when Elisabeth Shue sang the blues in *Adventures in Babysitting*? She did it at Fitzgerald's. Or, in *A League of Their Own* when Madonna and her cohorts tore up the rug at a local roadhouse? That was here, too. So, stop in—you may end up seeing the next great act, or be in the next big movie.

Gold Star Sardine Bar
- 666 N. Lake Shore Dr., Chicago, (312) 664-4215

Cabaret is the house music at Gold Star. Sometimes, they toss in a bit of swing, too. They ask no cover charge, but there is a two-drink minimum per person, per set. If you were planning to go out for a few drinks anyway, then it's not a bad deal.

It's an especially good deal when you consider some of the acts that have played this club. How about Bobby Short (you know, the guy who sings in those "Charlie" perfume commercials)? Or maybe the Count Basie Orchestra? Liza Minnelli? There are also local regulars who play in between the big gigs.

Shows start at 8:30 p.m. and go until 12:30 a.m. on Monday and Tuesday; from 8 p.m. until 1 a.m. on Wednesday, Thursday, and Friday; and from 9 p.m. until 2 a.m. on Saturday.

The Green Mill Lounge
- 4802 N. Broadway, Chicago; (312) 878-5552

Walking into this Uptown club, once owned by Al Capone, feels like a trip back to that earlier time. The Green Mill has been carefully restored to speakeasy glory: Ornate bas-relief pictures set into the walls...red "lounge" lighting...high-backed upholstered booths...and of course, as you make your way in, the sounds of a sultry saxophone or a brassy big band fill the room.

Amazingly enough, the prices for this entertainment seem to be from a bygone era, too. There's live jazz seven nights a week, and the cover charges range from $3-$6 for music starting around 9 p.m. (8 p.m. on Saturdays, 11 p.m. on Sundays). Ah, but any die-hard jazz fan is just waking up at that hour. Make your way to the club at midnight on Fridays and Saturdays, when the second group hits the stage, and admission is only $2. Better yet, by 1:30 or 2:00 a.m., the Green Mill All-Stars take over—and from then, until they knock off just before dawn, there is no cover charge at all.

For a totally cheap and wonderful evening out, start or end the night at one of the many Vietnamese restaurants along Argyle Street, a couple of blocks to the north. Some caution is advisable, though, as this general area is not the safest part of town at late hours. Cars and cabs are preferable to public transit.

The Jazz Oasis

- 343 W. Erie St., Chicago; (312) 787-7788

Some jazz clubs are least expensive "after hours," very late at night. At the Jazz Oasis, the best deal comes early—before 6 p.m. on Wednesdays and Thursdays. Make a date to stop in on your way home from work, and it'll cost you just $1 to hear some fine tunes. After 6 p.m., the price goes up to only $5.

Fridays and Saturdays get a little expensive at $10, but Sundays are a more reasonable $8. With live acts nightly you can enjoy everything from traditional mainstream to the latest in Brazilian jazz. All this in an elegant and cozy setting that is sure to make you feel like you've been transported to another time and place.

Moosehead Bar & Grill

- 240 E. Ontario St., Chicago; (312) 975-8100

As a restaurant, this Streeterville spot is rather expensive. They also have entertainment, though, which is not so expensive. A mere $5 cover gets you in to hear all sorts of local jazz acts, Thursday through Saturday evenings. Music starts around 7 or 8 p.m., and the atmosphere is comfortable and casual. In fact, the only stuffy thing about the place may be the stuffed animal heads on the walls.

The Pump Room

- 1301 N. State Pkwy., Chicago; (312) 266-0360

Here's a somewhat creative alternative for anyone looking for an inexpensive, yet elegant evening out. The Pump Room is, yes, a rather expensive and dressy dining establishment; but there is no charge, in fact not even a drink minimum, to sit in the lounge and enjoy piano music Mondays through Thursdays—and a full orchestra on Fridays and Saturdays. Do note that a jacket is required after 4:30 p.m., but that only adds to the

---

MR. CHEAP'S PICKS
Music—Blues

✔ **Brother Jimmy's BBQ**— Raise-the-roof blues every weekend, never a cover charge.

✔ **Buddy Guy's Legends**—Free blues *and* food on Fridays from 5-8 p.m.

---

feeling of getting real elegance—cheap!

Schuba's Tavern

- 3159 N. Southport Ave., Chicago; (312) 525-2508

Another rock venue which, like the Elbo Room, has a regular weekly jazz gig. Every Monday night, jazz player and FM disc jockey Barry Winograd leads a big band which he calls the Alternatives. Music starts up at 9:30, and runs until about 1:00 a.m.; all this, plus reduced-price beer promotions, for a cover charge of $4.

Tania's

- 2659 N. Milwaukee Ave., Chicago; (312) 235-7120

Here's another restaurant where you can also enjoy great live music with no cover charge, though they do ask that you at least have a drink or two. So, even if you're not hungry, you can sit at the bar and enjoy the sounds of groups with names like Ases De Los Merengue and Sensación del Caribe.

The flavor at Tania's, you see, is strictly Latin—both the food and the music. Have a little salsa with your salsa. The music heats up around 10:30 p.m., Thursdays through Saturdays; at 9:30 p.m. on Sundays.

Rock/Pop

America's Bar
- 219 W. Erie St., Chicago; (312) 915-5988

America's Bar knows it's important to fortify yourself before a big night of dancing and partying. In that spirit, they feature a $1.00 dinner buffet every Thursday and Friday evening.

That's right—for one thin dollar, you can enjoy a dinner buffet and a night of music from their DJs and dancing 'til you drop. They play music from the '60's right up to this week's top hits.

There is no cover charge (and alas, no buffet) on Tuesdays and Wednesdays; there is a $5.00 cover charge after 7:30 p.m. on Fridays, and on Saturdays (when the doors open at 8:00 p.m.).

Avalon
- 959 W. Belmont Ave., Chicago; (312) 472-3020

Here'a a good place to go when you want to blast your ears out, but not your wallet. Tuesday is "Guest DJ Night" at this dance club, and there is no cover charge or drink minimum. On Tuesdays you can also order $3 pitchers and $2 mixed drinks. And you can play pool there any night of the week.

But the savings don't end there. Wednesday features live heavy metal bands; it's also "Ladies Night," when women get in free (but call ahead for a pass). The cover charge for men (and women without passes) is usually $4. Prices go up, of course, as the weekend approaches; but they are still pretty good, considering that there are two stages with anywhere from six to eight bands a night. That comes to less than a dollar a band! Shows usually start around 9:30 p.m.

Baja Beach Club
- 401 E. Illinois St., Chicago; (312) 222-1993

When it comes to nightclubs Mr. Cheap's favorite words are: "No cover, no drink minimum." This Streeterville club takes things a step further, because here you can actually get something for your nothing. Starting at 4 p.m. on Fridays, the Baja features a 30-foot-long complimentary buffet. It's served until 9:00 p.m. and it's a great way to kick off the weekend.

The first of Baja's two rooms features a DJ playing a variety of music including top-40, country, oldies, rock, and techno. It also has pool tables, video games, and the like. The second room is a piano bar where Baja's pianists play a variety of music—including your requests. And if they don't know the lyrics to your favorite song, they'll simply make them up. Be forewarned: they expect, if not demand, audience participation.

Berlin
- 954 W. Belmont Ave., Chicago; (312) 348-4975

This club doesn't feature live bands, but they do have video screens to keep you amused and high-energy dance music to keep you moving.

What really gets Mr. C dancing is the fact that Berlin is open every night of the week, and it's always free. Okay, not always. On Fridays and Saturdays after 10 p.m., admission is a whole three dollars. Oh yeah, and the last Wednesday of every month is disco night and that costs a whopping two dollars. But honestly, at all other times there's no cover charge. And this place is open until 4 a.m.; so even if you do pay, you'll get a lot of headbanging for your buck.

Bootleggers
- 13 W. Division St., Chicago; (312) 266-0944

At Bootleggers, you can request your favorite songs at the DJ booth and dance your cares away until the wee hours. There is never a cover charge or a drink minimum here, and the fun doesn't stop until 4:00 a.m. on Sundays through Fridays, and 5:00 a.m. on Saturdays.

Cairo
- 720 N. Wells St., Chicago; (312) 266-6620

Many clubs promise to have "something for everyone"; this chic, two-level nightclub seems to live up to this promise. Enjoy live music in their cabaret, from salsa to jazz to rock 'n roll. Every Tuesday from 6-9 p.m., in fact, they even offer free tango and salsa dance lessons.

The second level is called the Catacombs, appropriately enough; it's underground. This room features DJs playing hypnotic dance music. They call it the "check-your-inhibitions-at-the-door dance floor." Just about says it all, don't you think?

There is a $5.00 cover charge Monday through Thursday, $7.00 on Friday and Saturday. That's a bit more than most other nightspots in this book, but it gets you into both levels and includes any live shows they have going on in the cabaret.

Elbo Room
- 2871 N. Lincoln Ave., Chicago; (312) 549-5549

Every Wednesday night at Elbo Room, you can enjoy alternative rock sounds from three local bands with no cover charge. Aimed at the college crowd, Wednesdays also offer reduced prices on beer. On Thursdays, they present three bands for three bucks. Quite the deal.

Fridays and Saturdays feature headlining bands, including such national acts as Poi Dog Pondering, and less-than-national acts like Goober and the Peas. The admission price of $5 to $8 gets you in to see two to three bands from around the country.

Another alternative to high cover charges is the upstairs bar, where there is never a cover, Wednesday through Saturday. No live acts up here, but a sound and video system allows you to enjoy what's going on downstairs. The upstairs area also features a pool table, jukebox, and a more relaxed atmosphere.

MR. CHEAP'S PICKS
Rock and Pop

✔ **Baja Beach Club**—No cover, no minimum, and on Fridays, a free dinner buffet. DJs spin Top-40 dance music.

✔ **Elbo Room**—Wednesday nights: Three bands, no cover. Thursday nights: Three bands, three bucks. Dark, funky, downstairs atmosphere.

Walter Payton's Thirty-Four's
- 1850 E. Golf Rd., Schaumburg; (708) 605-8994

Usually, places named after famous people come with exorbitant prices just to get in. Former Bears running back Payton scores a game-winner with this dance club, which offers an affordable evening's fun. No live music here, but the DJ's spin top-40 hits all night.

On Tuesdays, the cover is just $1 from 5:00-7:30 p.m.; on Fridays, it's $3 all night. And both nights include a free dinner buffet! Now, Mr. C is not going to promise you filet mignon and caviar for your three bucks, but this is a full-dinner buffet featuring steak and chicken on Fridays and "chef's choice" on Tuesdays.

Meanwhile, there's dancing every night 'til the wee hours (Tuesday through Thursday until 2 a.m., Friday and Saturday until 3 a.m.). Wednesdays and Thursdays require no cover charge at all (but, of course, there's no buffet). That's enough to get anyone doing the end-zone dance.

OUTDOORS

Brookfield Zoo
- First Ave. and 31st St., Brookfield; (708) 485-0263

Unlike its Lincoln Park counterpart, this zoo isn't free; but there are savings to be found. On Tuesdays and Thursdays, groups of ten or less can get admission to the zoo and parking for the low, low price of $7.00. Total. Groups of 11 or more get the same deal for only $10.00. Pack the kids into the minivan and head on over!

With over 2,300 animal species, you'll see more than just lions and tigers and bears (oh my!). You'll see dolphins in the "Seven Seas Panorama"; giraffes, zebras, antelope, and wild dogs in "Habitat Africa!"; and gorillas, monkeys, and tropical birds in "Tropic World." Brookfield also features a Children's Zoo and a Motor Safari.

One extra note: some of the exhibits, such as the dolphin shows and the motor safari, do have additional costs. The Zoo's regular admission price is $4.00, $1.50 for children under twelve and senior citizens, and children under three get in free. Open 365 days a year.

Chicago Botanic Garden
- 1000 Lake Cook Rd., Glencoe; (708) 835-5440

Butterflies are free—and so is your admission to stroll through twenty different gardens on 300 acres. From the Japanese Garden to the traditional English Walled Garden, enjoy the beauty of nature in spring, summer, fall, or winter. You can take a narrated tram ride and get fascinating information about the horticulture around you; or, use the self-guided tour maps to enjoy this exceptional beauty on your own.

You can also walk through the educational greenhouses, a living catalogue of plants from around the world, ranging from the most common to the truly exotic. Special exhibits and family activities also take place year-round.

Dine in the education center's restaurant or pack your own lunch and eat at designated picnic spots. Although admission is free, parking is $4.00. The garden is accessible by public transportation (call for directions). The Garden is open every day, except Christmas, from 8 a.m. until sunset.

Forest Trails Hiking Club
- (708) 475-4223

The Forest Trails Hiking Club provides free hikes around Chicago and beyond, year-round. For $3.00 they will send you a year's worth of their bulletin which gives you all the needed information on their upcoming hikes.

Most of their hikes begin at forest preserves and parks within 40 to 50 miles of downtown Chicago. The majority of the hikes are from eight to fourteen miles in length, and the bulletin indicates whether the hike is very strenuous or hilly; some hikes allow for easy bail-out on public transportation if you get tired! The bulletin provides the name and phone number of the hike leader so you can call for specific information about the hikes that interest you.

More distant hikes are offered as overnight or weekend packages, with fees for food and lodging. Some of these trips go to places like Michigan's Porcupine Mountains Wilderness State Park and North Kettlemoraine State Park in Wisconsin.

Hikes are led year-round, except for certain holidays; most take place on Sundays, starting at 9:30 a.m., with a few on Saturdays as well.

Friends of the Chicago River Canoe Trips

- 407 S. Dearborn St., Suite 1580, Chicago; (312) 939-0490

In addition to their great $5 walking tours (see listing in "Walks and Tours") the Friends of the Chicago River sponsor monthly canoe trips each summer at very reasonable prices.

The registration fee for each trip is $25 for nonmembers, plus an additional $25 for the rental of a canoe and supplies. Now, if this is something you think you'd like to do more often, consider becoming a member; this knocks both fees down to $15 each. As a matter of fact, when you sign up for any trip, you can become a member for a mere $5. Since an individual membership is normally $25, this amounts to quite a savings. Rates do tend to increase annually, but you should always be able to get a deal along these lines.

Trips are usually on Sundays and begin about 9 a.m. Pre-registration is required; the trips last until around 4:00. Bring a brown bag lunch! The season runs from May through October, with about six canoe trips a year.

Garfield Park Conservatory

- 300 N. Central Park Blvd., Chicago; (312) 533-1281

Here at the Garfield Conservatory you can see 5,000 species of plants valued at around two million dollars. The good news is that you don't have to spend anywhere near this much to see them; in fact, admission is free.

The conservatory's six houses contain almost every type of plant imaginable, from the most exotic Bird of Paradise to more common varieties. Guides will show you around and trained personnel will answer your questions on house plants and gardening. You can even call them and they will answer your horticultural questions over the phone. The conservatory is open from 9 a.m. to 5 p.m. daily.

Four annual shows highlight chrysanthemums in November, Christmas plants in December, azal-

MR. CHEAP'S PICKS
Outdoors

✔ **Forest Trails Hiking Club**—A steady variety of free hikes all around Chicagoland, year-round.

✔ **Garfield Park Conservatory/ Lincoln Park Conservatory and Zoo**—Two wonderful collections of flora and fauna, right in town, open free all year.

eas, camellias, and rhododendrons in late January, and Easter blooms in early April. All plants used in the shows are grown at the conservatory; call them for the exact dates of upcoming shows. During flower shows they are open Saturday through Thursday from 10 a.m. to 6 p.m., and from 9 a.m to 9 p.m. on Fridays.

Lincoln Park Conservatory

- 2400 N. Stockton Dr., Chicago; (312) 294-4770

If you have a love for all things green, then you simply must take a walk through the Lincoln Park Conservatory. It's completely free and located near the Lincoln Park Zoo, which is also free; you can spend an entire day communing with flora and fauna without spending a dime.

As you wind your way around inside the glassed-in conservatory, you'll pass through its palm house, fern house, cactus room, and special exhibit room—each one a distinctly different, balmy habitat. The conservatory has outside gardens as well.

They hold four major shows a year (call for specific dates). In November they show chrysanthemums, so many you won't want to keep mum about it (sorry, couldn't resist). From December into early January, their Christmas show features poinsettias and other plants of the season; azaleas and camellias take center stage in February, and the Easter Show in March and April features lilies and other blooms of spring.

Open daily from 9 a.m. to 5 p.m., you can spend a whole day here—or just an hour at lunchtime to de-stress yourself.

Lincoln Park Zoo

- 2200 N. Cannon Dr., Chicago; (312) 294-4660

The Lincoln Park Zoo is, as a life-long Chicagoan boasted to Mr. C, one of the best in-city zoos anywhere; and it's true. Better yet, as just about everyone knows, it's free. Nine to five, every day, 365 days a year. What a delightful bargain for a city to offer. The zoo houses more than 1,600 birds, animals, and reptiles from all over the world, all hanging out in carefully reproduced versions of their natural habitats. Highlights include one of the world's largest collections of apes, polar bears enjoying a dip in their very own 266,000-gallon pool, and a tropical rainforest house with an aviary. You'll have to duck your head as exotic and colorful birds zip past you!

Lincoln Park also houses the Pritzker Children's Zoo, where kids can study their animal counterparts in a nursery setting; and the Farm-In-The-Zoo, a real working farm where you can observe cow and goat milking, horse grooming, butter churning, and more.

The zoo also sponsors summer "ZooCamps" which give children a hands-on opportunity to be with animals, visit behind-the-scenes, go on field excursions, make crafts and more. Camp fees can get pretty steep, but considerable savings are available to zoo members. Call for more information.

Morton Arboretum

- 4100 Lincoln Ave., Lisle; (708) 968-0074

Spread over 1,500 acres, the Morton Arboretum is home to more than 3,000 trees, shrubs, vines, and other woody plants from around the world. Admission to this natural paradise is only $5 per car; and, on Wednesdays, this is reduced to just $3 per car.

Once inside, you may of course ditch the car and roam about on your own; or you can take any number of different tours—on foot, in trams, and in open-air buses. The cost of these guided excursions is an additional $1.50 to $2, and many of the walking tours are free of charge.

Are your plants plagued? Your shrubs sick? Your trees tainted? From April to October, the Plant Clinic at the arboretum's Visitor Center is there to help. Trained experts will give you advice on everything from plant problems to landscaping. Exhibits illustrate common seasonal problems; and the staff will even answer your questions over the phone. Give them a ring at (708) 719-2424, from 1-4 p.m., any Monday, Tuesday, Thursday, or Friday.

The Arboretum also sponsors classes in botany, horticulture, and more. While some of these classes can be pretty expensive, $50 and up, there are a bunch in the $8 to $11 range. How about a bike tour, "Pedaling Through the Colors" for only $7? Or "Beginning to Watch Birds" and "Continuing to Watch Birds" for $8 each? They have several classes geared towards young children, including some that involve catching bugs and other creatures. They even have workshops for teachers so they can gain necessary skills to teach their classes about nature.

Contact the Visitor's Center at the main number above, and they will send you a calendar of events and give you information about classes and other special events.

POETRY AND LITERARY READINGS

Keep an eye out for free newspapers, like *Letter ex*, near the entrance of your local restaurants and cafes. These will keep you well informed of the ever-changing world of literary events and venues.

Barbara's Bookstore

- 1350 N. Wells St., Chicago; (312) 642-5044
- 1800 N. Clybourn Ave., Chicago; (312) 664-1113
- 3130 N. Broadway, Chicago; (312) 477-0411
- 1100 Lake St., Oak Park; (708) 848-9140
- Also Barbara's Bestsellers, 2 North Riverside Plaza, Chicago; (312) 258-8007

These stores are truly a book lover's paradise. Despite the ebb and flow of the publishing industry, they always schedule at least one or two readings a month. And we're talking big names here. Recent readings have featured Studs Terkel reading from *Race: How Blacks and Whites Think and Feel about the American Obsession*, Susanna Kaysen with *Girl, Interrupted*, and Eric Bogosian, author of *Talk Radio*, reading and performing from his latest work, *Notes from Underground*.

Barbara's has also hosted Allan Kornblum, publisher at Coffee House Press, talking about the history of book-making and how the publishing process works today. And don't miss their annual "Biblioboogie," a benefit event with proceeds going to Literacy Chicago. All readings are free and open to the public; stop in for a calendar of upcoming events.

Barnes and Noble Booksellers

- 659 W. Diversey Pkwy., Chicago; (312) 871-9004

In addition to selling books at discount prices, Barnes and Noble "books" (sorry, couldn't resist) popular authors for frequent readings and discussions. Recently, B & N featured Jill Nelson reading from her controversial work *Volunteer Slavery* and mystery author Mark Zubro with his book *Political Poison*.

In addition to the usual "author-on-a-book-tour" appearances, Barnes and Noble sponsors several book discussion groups which meet on Wednesdays at 7:30 p.m. Whether your passion is fiction, non-fiction, or science fiction there is a group for you. Each one meets once every three weeks or so on a rotating schedule; but fluctuations are bound to occur, so it's a good idea to stop in and get a calendar of upcoming events.

The Bop Shop

- 1807 W. Division St., Chicago; (312) 235-3232

This little bar/nightclub has so many different things to see and do that it's difficult to know where to begin. They have open-mike poetry nights. They have open jam sessions for professional musicians of all stripes, on Sundays and Tuesdays. And they have a regular lineup of jazz and rock bands. Cover charges vary from about $3 to as high as $7. Some nights, like those open jams, have no cover charge at all.

But that's not all. There is also an art gallery where you can view works by local artists, and even buy if you're so inclined. Pick up some art supplies for your next masterpiece, too. Nice way to blend art, words, and music—there is a delightfully bohemian air to the Bop Shop.

Cafe Voltaire

- 3231 N. Clark St., Chicago; (312) 528-3136

Tristan Tzara was a Hungarian poet

who, during World War I, helped invent "dada"—a kind of surrealist art. He also ran a cabaret in Zurich, in which he and his cohorts gave the performances that defined their art (Tzara created poems by cutting up a Shakespeare sonnet, dropping the words into a hat, and pulling out one word at a time). It is from this heritage that the Cafe Voltaire takes its name and inspiration.

In the cozy and definitely downscale basement space at this beatnik-style coffeehouse, "Better Late than Dead" is a performance showcase held every Thursday evening at 9:30. Along with "the underrated five-minute play" and a different featured performer each week, the mike is open to poets, storytellers, comedians, and just about anyone else who wants to share "valuable insights." Admission is $5; or $2 if you plan to participate. You even get free chocolate, as an enticement!

Cafe Voltaire's ongoing lineup of theater and performance art, at least two different shows every night of the week, includes other poetry-oriented works as well. Most have a cover charge in the $4-$7 range; call for info, or stop in and pick up a calendar.

Centuries & Sleuths Bookstore
● 743 Garfield St., Oak Park; (708) 848-7243 (PAGE)

This bookstore is for those who profess their bibliophilia to history and mystery. C & S carries a wide selection of books to satisfy your love for these genres, but they do more than just stock the shelves with them! They sponsor both a "Mystery Discussion Group" and a "History Discussion Group," in which the respective buffs can get together to socialize and discuss their favorite topic. The groups meet on Saturdays; membership is free and open to anyone interested.

C&S also hosts readings on a fairly regular basis (what kind of readings? C'mon, you've already had enough clues). Recent authors have included Max Allan Collins and his most recent Elliot Ness mystery, *Murder By Numbers*; William Martin with his true crime book, *The Crime of the Century*; and Bill Brashler and Rinder Jantil with their baseball mystery, *Fear in Fenway*.

Do Your Own Thang
● Cafe Beignet, 1004 Church St., Evanston; (708) 328-2221

Every Tuesday night at 8 p.m., this little New Orleans-style cafe becomes a bohemian paradise when it sponsors "Do Your Own Thang." This open mike night, started by mother-daughter team Helen Katz and Heidi Hendron, is very open; the only restriction is that work must be original. They welcome fiction, dramatic readings, improv, comedy, and poetry; they even hope to have some non-fiction readings, though that hasn't happened yet. Hmm, maybe Mr. Cheap himself will show up one night and perform from his vast repertoire of shopping tips. Admission charge is just $2—and you can get that for half-price if you participate in the entertainment.

Most shows begin with a 20-minute "Spotlight" act by a featured performer; then, it's time for people to do their thang, with a maximum stage time of ten minutes. While you're enjoying the fun, partake of food and beverages that you thought you could only find in the French Quarter of New Orleans. Chicory coffee, beignets, and gumbo are just a few of the down-home offerings.

But the fun doesn't end there. Katz and Hendron have found a Chicago home for their "thang": **Cool Temptations**, 2808 N. Halsted St., Chicago; (312) 348-5865. This ice cream shop now does its *own* "Do Your Own Thang" every Saturday night from 8 to 10 p.m., with the same assortment of original writing and music. Sounds like a "cool" idea to Mr. C. For more info about either "thang," call (708) 491-1571.

Guild Complex Readings
● HotHouse, 1565 N. Milwaukee Ave., Chicago; (312) 278-2210

Wicker Park is one of Chicago's burgeoning areas for the young, hip arts scene. This bar and nightclub is at the center of it all, with a focus on avant-garde jazz and rock. And, on Wednesday nights at 7:30, the Guild Complex, a performance art organization, hosts a literary evening. You never know what you may hear: Poetry and fiction readings, songwriters, and many other types of original performance by local and national artists have made up the slate for almost five years.

Recent performances have featured a Latin evening, with flamenco guitar music and a poet from Puerto Rico; dramatized stagings of poetic works; rap music; and even a "Poetry Video Festival." Admission is $4-$5, depending on the bill. Preceding the featured performers, the microphone is open to anyone who wants to try out his or her own new material; these folks also get a reduced admission price of $2. The Guild also offers workshops on how to write, perform, and publish poetry. Call for schedules.

McCabe's "Pong Jam"
- 2770 N. Elston Ave., Chicago; (312) 252-4822

Near the six-corner intersection of Elston, Western, and Diversey, McCabe's is one of the newest entries into the world of live poetry—and quite an interesting one. Every Thursday night at 9 p.m., poet Marc Smith hosts what he calls a "Pong Jam." This has nothing to do with that prehistoric video tennis game.

A "pong," in Smith's view, is a combination of a poem and a song. There is a band on stage, small but frisky; poets come up to join the band, requesting a certain type of music (which may include well-known or newly-coined genres). The group plays its idea of the request, while the author recites his or her poetry. The two art forms are blended with varying degrees of success; it's a fascinating experiment which can be moving, humorous, or anywhere in between. The "jam" comes when, at one point in the evening, the band kicks in and

MR. CHEAP'S PICKS
Poetry and Literary Readings

- ✔ **Cafe Voltaire**—A full slate of poetry and performance art, every night, including a weekly open-mike showcase.
- ✔ **"Do Your Own Thang"**—Wide-open-mike nights every Tuesday at the N'awlins-style Cafe Beignet in Evanston.
- ✔ **Guild Complex Readings**—At the Hothouse in Wicker Park, this group hosts Wednesday night readings of fiction, poetry and performance monologues.
- ✔ **Uptown Poetry Slam**—The words fly every Sunday night at the Green Mill Lounge.
- ✔ **Women and Children First Bookstore**—Readings and discussions on a range of important topics concerning today's society.

audience members are invited to walk up with a few lines each. The music twists and turns to keep up with the words. Give it a try!

The Poetry Center
- School of the Art Institute of Chicago, Columbus Dr. and Jackson Blvd., Chicago; (312) 368-0905

Next door to the Goodman Theatre, the Poetry Center calls itself "the city's premier sponsor of poetry readings." Their hyperbole is not unfounded. John Ashbery, Margaret Atwood, Robert Creeley, Allen Ginsburg, and Maxine Kumin are just some of the celebrated bards who have read from their works here.

Since its founding in 1974, the Poetry Center's aim has been to provide an accessible forum to bring great poets before the public. They present seven readings per season for a general admission cost of $7 per event. Students and senior citizens are admitted for only $4, and student groups can get a discounted price of just $2 per person.

It all makes for a great contribution to the city's cultural life. Along with its slate of well-established authors, the center presents lesser-known and younger writers in need of exposure as well as writers from other countries. Call them for a complete listing of their programs.

School Street Cafe
- 1011 W. School St., Chicago; (312) 281-4989

Everyone is welcome to participate in the School Street Cafe's weekly open mike night. Or, just come in and enjoy budding artists entertaining you with poetry, performance art, music, or whatever. It happens every Sunday night at 9 p.m. and, most importantly, it's free!

But wait—there's more. Friday and Saturday nights at School Street feature live jazz and blues for a cover charge of just $1. They also have occasional theater performances, to which admission is usually $7 or $8. Diamondback Theater and Imagine Theater are among the troupes who have trodden the boards here.

Spices Jazz Bar
- 814 N. Franklin St., Chicago; (312) 664-6222

Somewhat above the gallery scene of River North, this nightclub devotes one night a week to an open-mike poetry evening. Every Monday at 8:00 p.m., you can sit and listen to the art of the spoken word, or join in with a few couplets of your own. There is no cover charge. Spices is located downstairs from the street level, and right next to the Chicago Avenue "el" station.

Uptown Poetry Slam
- Green Mill Lounge, 4802 N. Broadway, Chicago; (312) 878-5552

Every Sunday evening from 7 p.m. until 10 p.m., a mere $4 will afford you entry to the "Uptown Poetry Slam." Yes folks, the beatniks battle it out in the ring—or rather, on the stage of this popular jazz club. The offerings will be good, the offerings will be bad, the audience will cheer, the audience will boo. Poetry slams are the latest thing in the world of words and performance art; catch all the excitement, and don't forget the popcorn.

Weeds
- 1555 N. Dayton St., Chicago; (312) 943-7815

This Old Town nightclub presents live rock music on the weekends (with no cover!); but, on Monday nights at 10:00 p.m., the stage is bare and the mike is open for poetry. Bring that journal you've been doodling in for the last seven years, take to the stage, and liberate your words. Admission is free to all.

Women and Children First Bookstore
- 5233 N. Clark St., Chicago; (312) 769-9299

As the name would suggest this bookstore carries stock with a feminist perspective and children's books. Accordingly their readings and other programs have similar themes (see separate listing under "Entertainment: Children's Activities"). Adult readings generally feature female authors discussing a range of topics from sexuality to the men's movement. The occasional poetry reading and performance art event round out their offerings. Programs are free and they are open to the public (c'mon guys, a little consciousness-raising never hurt anyone).

You can receive W & C's newsletter by mail, to follow their busy lineup in advance; $3 gets you a one-year subscription. Better yet, save the three bucks by stopping in and checking out the store.

SPORTS AND PLAY

No, Mr. C can't get you into the Bulls game for free—though don't forget that many of the big sports arenas and stadiums do have ticket prices that start around $10. One cheaper alternative is college sports; there are highly competitive schools throughout Chicago, and many have very affordable prices for football, basketball, hockey, and many more. There are often many different sports locations on each campus; the ticket offices, at the phone numbers listed below, can give you all the details. A few teams to check out:

DePaul University

A big basketball school in the middle of this big basketball town, DePaul is ranked in Division I of the NCAA. Despite its cream of the crop status, tickets to these games are only about $18 when they play other big name schools like Kansas, Georgetown, and Massachusetts, and about $15 when they play smaller-name schools. For more info call the ticket office at (312) 362-8010.

Illinois Institute of Technology

NAIA Division I sports events here are free of charge, except for some tournament competitions, and open to all. Call (312) 567-3296 for season schedules.

Loyola University

Tickets to most events at this NCAA Division I school are free. The main exception is men's basketball, their big draw; tickets to these games are $8. For ticket information call (312) 274-2560.

Northwestern University

A NCAA Division I school, Northwestern University's Wildcats are well-known throughout the world of college sports, especially in football and basketball. Accordingly, tickets to football games go up to $18, while tix to basketball games are a little better at $10 to $12. But don't despair; there's lots of other fun on tap, in the form of volleyball, softball, field hockey, soccer, and more. Admission to most of these sporting events is free or nominal. Call (708) 491-7070 for ticket info.

University of Chicago

Big draws at this NCAA Division III school include football, basketball, and track. Admission to all athletic events is free, except for football. Tickets to football games cost $2.50 for adults and 50 cents for kids. Call (312) 702-7681 for more info.

University of Illinois

Here at the Chicago campus, tickets to hockey and men's basketball are $8 for reserved seats and $6 for general admission. These are the kinds of bargains that make Mr. C cheer even louder! Tickets to all other events, including volleyball, soccer, gymnastics, baseball, softball, tennis, and swimming, are free. Call (312) 996-2772 for more info.

Meanwhile, why not consider some other kinds of sports—the kind in which your participation means more than just raising a bottle of beer?

MR. CHEAP'S PICKS
Sports and Play

✔ **ArtGolf**—Painting and putting meet on the greens of this wacky miniature golf course.

✔ **Batter Up!**—The modern, high-tech approach to good ol' batting cages; video backgrounds put you right into the ballpark.

✔ **College sports**—Bulls games too expensive? Don't pass up the opportunity to see tough competition at the college level, at much lower prices.

ArtGolf
- 1800 N. Clybourn Ave., Chicago; (312) ART-GOLF (278-4653)

What do you do when you want to play mini-golf but your date wants to go to an art exhibit? Do both! Each hole of this indoor miniature golf course was designed and built by a different artist. The holes are changed periodically to add a little excitement to your mini-golf life.

Eighteen culturally-enlightening holes of golf cost $5.50 per person; $4.50 for senior citizens, $4.00 for kids twelve and under. Not a bad price for an evening of fun that is definitely different.

Need somewhere to stage Uncle Joe's birthday party or the scout troop's annual fundraiser? Have it at ArtGolf. The entire course can be rented for a private party and adjacent mall space is available for even larger gatherings. ArtGolf also has group rates.

Batter Up!
- 2100 N. Southport Ave., Chicago; (312) 404-2287 (BATS)

This brand-new sports complex brings practice baseball into the 21st century. Now that Wrigley's got

lights, it was probably inevitable that batting cages should get...VIDEO! Yep, now, when that machine spits those rubber baseballs relentlessly your way, they appear to be thrown by actual pitchers. It adds a new dimension of realism to what was already a fun pastime for any baseball fan.

Choose your type of game and speed of delivery, from major league to little league, or slow-pitch softball. One round of sixteen pitches costs just $2.00. Of course, if that just gets you warmed up, get the three rounds for $5.00 deal, or seven rounds for $10. Batter Up! even offers its cages by the hour, or at group rates so that your whole bench can get its at-bats. And there are free clinics for Little League teams throughout the spring season.

For a better deal still, swing by on Monday or Thursday nights, when you can get "Unlimited Hitting" from 6-9 p.m. for $7.00.

Batter Up! doesn't stop at baseball. Try your best hook at "Bankshot Basketball," which squeezes eighteen different hoops into a single room. Each backboard has an oddly curved or angled surface, making it a real challenge to work your way along the course. Hourly rates are inexpensive; the best deal is netted on Saturday mornings from 10:30 to noon, when you can get unlimited play for $3.50 per person.

They've also added the video angle to golf, with a pair of driving cages that even tell you how far your shot has gone; and, what would a place like this be without a roomful of video games. There's even a snack bar serving up hot dogs and other stadium fare, giving Batter Up! all the necessities for a family outing or a birthday party that circles the bases.

CityGolf Chicago
- 435 E. Illinois St., North Pier, Chicago; (312) 278-4653.

Although the holes at CityGolf may not be as hip as the artist-designed holes at ArtGolf, these depict Chicago landmarks and there is still plenty of fun to be had. With two indoor miniature golf courses, CityGolf is a great way to get off the couch, have a good time, and not spend a whole lot of dough.

Admission to play 18 holes is just $4.95 for adults, and $3.95 for children under 12. Group rates and party packages are available; City-Golf also boasts a full-service bar.

Muddler's Pool Room
- 1800 N. Clybourn Ave., Chicago; (312) 944-7665

So you saw "The Color of Money" and you thought "Hey, I could do that. . . ." Well, you can give it your best shot on Muddler's antique, tournament-sized A.E. Schmidt tables. Hand-blown glass lampshades add an elegant but casual atmosphere, to make billiards a respectable and fun outing.

At $15.00 an hour on weekend nights and $12.00 an hour on week nights, a few games of pool can get pricey. But wait—there are savings. An hour of pool is only $8.00 during the day, including weekends. And Wednesdays, all day and evening, are "Ladies Days" when women play for free, and the men at their tables pay half-price. Muddler's also has a full-service bar and is available for private parties.

Sluggers Upper Deck
- 3544 N. Clark St. (2nd Floor), Chicago; (312) 472-9696.

Just around the corner from Wrigley Field, you can practice your swing in these good old fashioned batting cages. Its upstairs location means you'll work up a sweat as you hack away at a variety of pitches, assuming you're playing during the season. But Slugger's is open seven days a week, all year.

A mere $1.00 gets you a token good for fifteen pitches in any cage—slow, medium, fast, or softball; you can also get six tokens for $5.00.

This is considerably less than the fancy modern cages at Batter Up! (see listing above), but then, it's like the difference between some old minor league park and the new Comiskey. There are no video backgrounds here, just a bunch of screened-in cages—with a few basketball hoops, skee-ball alleys and pinball games wedged into the layout. It's no-frills and noisy, but y'know, it's just plain fun.

On Monday and Thursday evenings from 6-11 p.m., as long as there's not a Cubs game on, you can pay just $5.00 for unlimited hitting. The place is open until 1:00 a.m. on weekends. Oh, and by coincidence, Sluggers Upper Deck happens to be upstairs from Sluggers Bar. There's no obligation, of course, but it's a good place to knock back a frosty one after the "game."

United Skates of America
- 4836 N. Clark St., Chicago; (312) 271-6200

Mr. C loves a good pun, so the name of this place alone caught his attention. But an even better pun, and better savings, is their Wednesday night family "Cheap Skate." Admission is a low $2.50 for adults and $1.50 for children from 4:00 p.m. to 6:00 p.m., making this a good "quality time" afterschool activity. And, of course, it also counts as exercise (especially helpful to those who wish they were fitness-minded). Skate rentals are available; they cost $2.00 at all times.

Other savings include a Thursday "Ladies Night," from 9:00 p.m. to 2:00 a.m., when women can skate for free. Admission is $5.00 for guys, and you must be 18 or older. Admission prices and times are subject to change; call for their current calendar of events. They are also available for private parties, including birthday parties.

SUMMER FESTIVALS

Chicago loves to party. All summer long, the city sponsors outdoor festivals along the lakefront, each with its own unique theme—usually having to do with music or food. Best of all, they're free! Most of these last a day or two, with the exception of "Taste of Chicago," a ten day culinary extravaganza. Some of these festivals come and go, but many of them have been taking place annually for a decade or more. You should certainly expect to find the following fests advertised on subway posters and in newspapers; or, for more info, call 1-800-487-2446.

Chicago Blues Festival

Chicago calls itself the "Blues Capital of the World." It's considered one of the true birthplaces of this uniquely American music. For three days each June, on as many stages, you can find out why this is no empty claim. Festival-goers in past years have heard the likes of Junior Wells, Lonnie Brooks, Elvin Bishop, and Staple Sisters.

Chicago Gospel Festival

Somewhere in between jazz and blues, the joyous sounds of gospel also fill the air every year for a two-day festival, usually held in July. A parade of national stars and local choruses take the stage in these free concerts. Recent performers have included Al Green, The Chicago Mass Choir, Otis Clay, and Andre Crouch.

Chicago Jazz Festival

Chicago has an international reputation for jazz; for over fifteen years, this festival has been a testament to that fact. Two days of jazz headliners in mid-September make the approach of winter a little more bearable. The artists who've been heard here recently include Charlie Haden & The Liberation Music Orchestra, the Count Basie Orchestra, Dr. John, and Sir Roland Hanna.

Grant Park Music Festival

The Petrillo Music Shell, at the corner of Columbus and Jackson Drives,

is a delightful setting for a wide variety of free concerts and performances every summer. Green trees laced with delicate lights, the skyline looming above them, are your backdrop for classical music featuring the Grant Park Symphony Orchestra. The festival, in existence for sixty years, has also presented fully staged operas and ballets. Perhaps you'll enjoy an evening of scenes performed by the Shakespeare Rep, or one of the Petrillo's many other events—even movies, with live orchestral accompaniment. And don't forget "Concerts for Kids, Too!" featuring the Chicago Youth Symphony Orchestra. The schedule begins in mid-June and continues through the end of August. There are plenty of folding chairs, set up like any auditorium, or you can bring a blanket and relax on the lawn. Stretch out and have a picnic. Shows take place on afternoons and evenings, weekdays and weekends—call (312) 819-0614 for a current schedule.

Printers Row Book Fair

Okay, so this isn't a music festival, nor does it take place on the lakefront. But if you love books—and Chicago is certainly a book town—you shouldn't miss the Printers Row Book Fair. In the middle of June, this historic neighborhood just south of the loop hosts the country's third largest book fair.

Festivities include writers and

poets reading from their work, author signings, musical performances, lively panel discussions, and storytelling for children. Artists demonstrate the crafts of papermaking, hand marbling, calligraphy, and binding. And of course, there are plenty of booksellers and publishers selling new, used, and antiquarian books.

For nearly a decade, this fair has attracted some of the most celebrated names in publishing, including Sara Paretsky, Susan Sontag, Studs Terkel, and Kurt Vonnegut. Last year's event included a book drive for Chicago area hospitals, schools, and shelters; fairgoers were asked to bring a book as a donation. Otherwise, admission is free. Call (312) 987-1980 for more information.

Taste of Chicago

More than seventy restaurants from all over the city bring samples of their cooking to Grant Park for ten days of food and frolic, wrapping itself like a flag around the Fourth of July holiday. Tickets can be purchased singly or in books, for use at

---

MR. CHEAP'S PICKS
Summer Festivals

✔ **Grant Park Music Festival**—The grandaddy of them all. World-class music and dance of all kinds, all summer, all free.

✔ **Taste of Chicago**—Same idea, only culinary, for ten days each July. The ultimate pig-out festival.

---

all of the food vendors. Use them wisely, for this event is a true culinary safari. Entertainment, on three stages, includes lots of special events for the kiddies; and the Chicago Country Music Festival jumps in for two days to add some western spice to all that food.

THEATER

There are several interesting ways to save money on big-time, professional theater in town. Perhaps the best-known is **Hot Tix**, which sells many tickets at half-price (see below). **Rush tickets** are also available at many of the larger (you know, expensive) theaters; if seats are still available before curtain time, you may be able to get discounted tickets an hour or two before the show begins.

Finally, consider a lesser-known option: **Volunteer ushering**. Major theaters, including the Goodman, the Royal George, and the Steppenwolf (but not the Broadway-type houses like the Shubert), use regular folks to help rip tickets, hand out programs, or guide people to their seats. In exchange for your services, you can watch the show for free. Responsibilities are light; you'll have to dress nicely, arrive a bit early to learn the layout of seats, and then go to it. As soon as the show begins, find a seat for yourself and enjoy the show—you're all done. Ushering can even make for a fun cheap date—it's a guaranteed conversation starter afterwards! Best of all, you'll save yourself some cash *and* help that theater out at the same time. Call ahead to find out if that show you've been eyeing uses volunteers, and when they have slots available. Advertisements for ushers also appear in the classifieds of the Reader, under "Wanted."

Hot Tix

- 108 N. State St., Chicago; "Hot Tix Line," (312) 977-1755.
- Also at Rose Records, 820 W. North Ave., Chicago, and 1634 E. 53rd St. (Hyde Park), Chicago; and in Arlington Heights, Downers Grove, Evanston, Naperville, Oak Park, Orland Park, and Vernon Hills.

If you enjoy going out to theater a lot, but can't afford ever-rising ticket prices, stop by any of the ten Hot Tix booths spread around Chicagoland. Shows which have blocks of unsold seats for that evening's performance often make them available through Hot Tix at half-price, or $10 off. A service charge of $2.00-$3.50, depending on the theater, is added to each ticket.

You take your chances, of course, on what may be offered on any given evening; but among the companies and venues frequently "on the board" are the Steppenwolf, Royal George, the Auditorium Theater (even for ballet and other events) Shear Madness, Theater Building, Second City, Live Bait, Drury Lane, Candlelight Dinner Playhouse, and many others.

You must buy your tickets in person at any of the booths, paying either by cash or credit card; before possibly wasting a trip, though, you can always call the Hot Tix Line at

the above number for a recorded message of shows on sale for that day.

Hours at the downtown Hot Tix booth are from noon to 6:00 p.m. on Mondays, 10-6 on Tuesdays-Fridays, and 10-5 on Saturdays; the booth is closed on Sundays, but you can buy tickets to Sunday matinees on Saturday. Suburban hours vary.

Except for the Loop, Arlington Heights, and Evanston booths, all other "Hot Tix" outposts are located in Rose Records stores. And every branch of "Hot Tix" is also a Ticketmaster outlet, selling full-price tickets (cash only) to other kinds of events.

But wait—that's not all! To make discount theater tickets even more convenient, join **Hot Tix By Mail**, which offers dozens of the same shows at half-price, plus a service charge. For an annual membership fee of $10, you will receive a packed brochure every other month offering you the chance to actually order these "day of performance" bargains in advance. For most shows, you even get several dates to choose from. Talk about dramatic savings! To join, or get more information, write:

Hot Tix By Mail

- 67 E. Madison St., Suite 2116 Chicago, IL 60603

Inexpensive theater, meanwhile, abounds in Chicago. It seems that a new company hits the boards every ten minutes or so, performing late at night in some converted loft or basement. Many of them are creating and presenting their own original shows. Not all of these are ready for Broadway, but at ticket prices usually between $5-$9, you shouldn't mind the occasional clunker too much. The energy that drives these young troupes, not to mention the people who go out regularly to see them, is remarkable—and proof that George Bernard Shaw's notion of theater as "the fabulous invalid" is, well, invalid.

Of course, as easily as these troupes appear, they can also disappear. The listing below describes some of the well-established troupes which are working most of the year. As always, your local newspapers can give you the most up-to-date info.

The Annoyance Theatre

- 3153 N. Broadway, Chicago; (312) 929-6200

The shows seen here are not necessarily annoying, although there is lots of interaction with the audience, which a friend of Mr. C's considers an intrusion (at the worst, you may get zapped with Silly String, which isn't so bad). It seems that the name may have more to do with the things that annoy us all, which this troupe has a lot of fun skewering. With titles like *The Stinky Onion Gang* (a spoof of cutesy, corporate-sponsored children's theater), *That Darned Antichrist* (it's a musical...really) and *Co-Ed Prison Sluts* (take a guess), the Annoyance likes to go way off the deep end. Their parodies of modern life are truly wacky and often hilarious. Sets, costumes and props are extremely minimal, but this actually adds to the fun.

Many of their hour-or-so plays are offered as double bills, allowing you to see one show for $6 or two for $9—but no ticket price ever tops $10. Shows tend to run in a repertory rotation Tuesdays through Saturdays, including late-night performances on weekends.

Black Ensemble Theatre

- Uptown Hull House, 4520 N. Beacon St., Chicago; (312) 769-4451

The Black Ensemble Theatre has two main goals: To produce black-oriented theater for the enjoyment of all audiences, and to provide training and employment for black theater artists. The ensemble has produced over fifty plays, with such titles as *Ain't That Lovin' You Baby*, *Great African Queens*, *Out Here On My Own*, and *The Otis Redding Story*.

Tickets to their performances cost $15; there is a discount rate of $12 for seniors, students, and children. Actually, anyone can get that price by purchasing a subscription; their most recent season offered five

plays for just $60. Give them a call for information on their upcoming season.

Body Politic Theatre

- 2261 N. Lincoln Ave., Chicago; (312) 871-3000

This company is well-respected for its productions of such classics as *King Lear, All My Sons*, and *The Dresser*. Upstairs in its Lincoln Park home, the professional, arena-style seating surrounds the stage with good sightlines all around. Ticket prices vary, but they're seldom much above $12.

Of special interest to Mr. C's fellow lovers of theater, though, is the "Unknown Playwright Series" which presents staged readings (script in hand) of brand-new works by local authors. A discussion follows, in which you can give your own instant Siskel-and-Ebert-like critique if you wish. And you never know, you may discover a diamond in the rough. The price? It's free. Readings take place at 8:00 p.m. on the first and third Tuesdays of each month through the year.

Cafe Voltaire

- 3231 N. Clark St., Chicago; (312) 276-9425

Tristan Tzara was a Hungarian poet who, during World War I, helped invent "dada"—a kind of surrealist art. He also ran a cabaret in Zurich, in which he and his cohorts gave the performances that defined their art (Tzara created poems by cutting up a Shakespeare sonnet, dropping the words into a hat, and pulling out one word at a time). It is from this heritage that the Cafe Voltaire takes its name and inspiration.

Mixed in with its own offerings of poetry and music, Cafe Voltaire's low-tech basement auditorium is also home to fledgling theatrical productions of all kinds. Seating is on musty, thrift shop sofas, and there tends to be very little in the way of sets or lighting—the emphasis here is

MR. CHEAP'S PICKS
Theater

✔ **Annoyance Theatre**—No, not a "Saturday Night Live" sketch, but something home-grown and very similar, five nights a week.

✔ **Body Politic Theatre**—The "Unknown Playwright Series" gives you the chance to discover a hit play. Free admission, every other Tuesday night.

✔ **Hot Tix**—Half-price tickets on the day of performance, with outlets all over town.

✔ **Neo-Futurarium Theatre**—"Too Much Light Makes the Baby Go Blind" presents thirty plays in sixty minutes—can you get *better* value for your theater dollar?

on the acting work and scripts themselves. Both can be a bit of a gamble, to be sure; young, experimental companies know that they can take risks here, developing their work. Some shows catch on, and get longer runs, and a recent production of Dylan Thomas's *Under Milk Wood* became so successful that it actually transferred to an open run at a larger theater.

Admission usually costs $5-$7 or so, for shows taking place in early or late evening slots on just about any night of the week. Call the friendly folks at Voltaire to find out what's in the wings.

Court Theatre
- 5535 S. Ellis Ave., Chicago; (312) 753-4472

In residence at the University of Chicago in Hyde Park, the Court is a fully professional repertory theater company. They perform in a modern, arena-style theater arranged into just seven rows, making for an up-close

and intimate evening. Accordingly, their tickets don't come as cheaply as, say, the nearby University Theater (see listing under "Entertainment: College Arts"). But that doesn't mean there aren't savings to be had.

Rather not spend $26 apiece for tickets on a Saturday night, even for performances of plays by the likes of Edward Albee, Caryl Churchill, Moliere, and Oscar Wilde? Mr. C understands. At the Court Theatre, savings go to those who can pop out on the spur of the moment. Half-price tickets are available after 5:00 p.m. before any evening performance (or two hours before any matinee). The best part is that you don't even have to go to the box office in person to get this deal—you can order them right over the phone. Last minute planning was never so easy!

There are also savings for students and senior citizens: $2 off any ticket, except on Saturday evenings. Students can also get $7 rush tickets the day of any performance; just don't forget your ID when you go to pick them up. If you're not on or near the campus, the theater is easy enough to reach; just twenty minutes' ride from the Loop, whether by Lake Shore Express bus or by car. Free parking, too!

For those who prefer to plan ahead, the Court Theatre offers several subscription packages which also save you money. The "Flex-Tix" package, for instance, allows you to pick and choose any five weeknights or weekend dates for a set price as low as $80 (higher for weekends). You'll save about $5 to $6 per ticket. There is also an "Under 21" subscription offering all five plays for $65, with proof of age—an economical way for families to have evenings at the theater together.

The Goodman Theatre
- 200 S. Columbus Drive, Chicago; (312) 443-3800

No, this certainly is *not* an inexpensive little stage group. Everybody knows the Goodman—located behind the Art Institute, it's one of the country's foremost theater companies, where recent productions of *The Grapes of Wrath, Marvin's Room,* and *The Piano Lesson* all played before going on to Broadway. Unfortunately, art on this level can be expensive—ticket prices start around $20 and go up into the thirtysomething range.

But wait—Mr. C is here! Did you know about the Goodman's "Tix at Six" program? Stop by the box office before 6:00 p.m., and ask if they have any seats remaining for that evening's performance. If they do, hang around—starting at six, they go on sale at half-price. It's first-come, first-served, but it can definitely be worth the chance. For matinees, half-price tix go on sale an hour before curtain.

Live Bait Theatre
- 3914 N. Clark St., Chicago; (312) 871-1212

Live Bait Theatre was so named because they want to "lure" people in and "hook" their audiences. They do present some of the best in strong, new, local theater work. Ticket prices, therefore, can get a bit pricey—in the $10-$15 range. Mr. C knew there had to be another way!

Well, there is, in the form of two series that offer lower-priced tickets. For you night owls, there's the "Late Night" series, shows usually offered on Friday and Saturday nights at 11:00 or 11:30 p.m. Tickets for these shows are a more reasonable $5 to $10.

Live Bait also offers an "Off-Night" series. These shows, featuring a variety of local troupes, generally have an 8:00 curtain on Mondays, Tuesdays, and Wednesdays. Ticket prices range from $5 to $10 for these as well. No matter when you go, you're sure to see adventurous, cutting-edge theater and performance art.

Neo-Futurarium Theatre
- 5153 N. Ashland Ave., Chicago; (312) 275-5255

During the last four years or so, this ambitious company has written and presented over 2,000 plays. Honestly. How do they do it? Well, most of the plays are only 2-3 minutes long. In fact, the claim of their hit show, *Too Much Light Makes the Baby Go Blind,* is that you will see "Thirty plays in sixty minutes!"—and they actually do manage to pull it off.

Every aspect of this company and their show is given some clever twist. For starters, their current home is upstairs from a funeral parlor. Admission is $2 plus one roll of a die (no pun intended)—in other words, $3-$8. You're asked your name on the way in, and given a name tag with something nonsensical on it instead.

Then, there are the mini-plays themselves. There are indeed thirty to choose from, with titles like "Dysfunctional House Cleaning," "Leslie the Lobster Speaks Out," and "Lusia and Diana Can Talk Openly About Sex, But It Is Heather Who Can Say the Big Words With Ease." These are all developed in advance by the cast, with new titles added each week—hence, the prolific volume.

The plays are all numbered; the audience shouts out which one it wants to see next, but the actors usually manage to fit them all in anyway. It's a wild, fast-paced, and decidedly different evening of theater, offered Fridays and Saturdays at 11:30 p.m., and Sunday evenings at 7:00.

Theatre on the Lake
- Lake Shore Drive at Fullerton Parkway, Chicago; (312) 348-7075

Every summer, this spacious auditorium puts together an eclectic and interesting season by hosting a variety of non-profit and community theater companies from all over town. True to its name, the pavillion is located right on the lakefront, at the very beginning of Fullerton; its patio makes for lovely dusk viewing before the show. The whole show is run by the Chicago Park District, as it has been for over forty years.

Each week, a different troupe takes up residence for performances on Tuesday through Saturday evenings at 8 p.m. The choices can be as diverse as Charles Fuller's *A Sol-*

dier's Play (basis for the movie, *A Soldier's Story*) to the musical revue *Jerry's Girls*, a collection of songs from the career of Jerry Herman (the tunesmith behind such Broadway hits as *La Cage aux Folles* and *Hello, Dolly!*).

Theatre on the Lake provides a valuable opportunity for these talented companies to strut their stuff in a professional setting, before large audiences (ample seating is arranged on all four sides of the stage). Yet, tickets to all shows are a mere $4.00

each. Occasionally, the theater also hosts touring children's plays as well, with low or free admission. Refreshments are available at all performances, too.

TOTL's lakefront location is only semi-enclosed; this can also make for a rather breezy experience as the evening progresses. Unless there's a heat wave on, it's a good idea to bring a jacket or sweater along. The theater's season typically runs from mid-June until the Labor Day weekend.

WALKS AND TOURS

CBS Studio Tour
* 630 McClurg Ct., Chicago; (312) 944-6000

There are several museums in Chicago which let you experience work in a TV studio, such as the Chicago Children's Museum. But if you want the real, honest-to-goodness thing, head over to CBS Studios—tucked quietly into the Streeterville area—and take their free tour.

Tours last about a half-hour to 45 minutes. You'll be able to see working studios, the newsroom, behind-the-scenes control rooms, and more. Along the way, tour guides will explain what everyone is doing and how it all comes together before reaching your television.

CBS conducts tours year-round; reservations are required for groups of 40 or more. Call for schedules and more info.

Chicago Architecture Foundation
* 224 S. Michigan Ave., Chicago; (312) 922-3432

Chicago is renowned worldwide for its architecture, and the Chicago Architecture Foundation is amply prepared to show you why—through free exhibitions at their home office and guided tours all around the city. CAF conducts about fifty different

tours throughout the year and some of them, especially the bus tours, can get rather expensive. But there are savings to be found, specifically on several of their walking tours.

The foundation offers two tours of architecture within the Loop. "Early Skyscrapers" will introduce you to the work of Louis Sullivan and teach you to recognize such famous details as "Chicago windows." "Modern and Beyond" features the work of Mies van der Rohe and explores post-WWII developments. Each of these tours cost $9.00 per person, but you can get a deal by purchasing a $15.00 ticket that is good for both walks.

The near suburb of Oak Park has the highest concentration of designs by Frank Lloyd Wright in the world; for $9.00, the Wright tour takes you through these quiet streets past the exteriors of these homes. It winds up with a stroll through Wright's actual home and studio.

By far, the best bargain available is the tour of the Prairie Avenue Historic District. Two houses are explored on this tour: Clarke House, Chicago's oldest building, and Glessner House, a 19th century structure by H.H. Richardson. Each house costs $5.00 to tour; or, see them both for $8.00. On Wednesdays you can tour both houses for only $1.00. At that price, can you afford to stay in your own home?

CAF also sponsors Wednesday lunchtime lectures at 12:15 p.m. in their lecture hall. These are brown bag affairs and the lecture goes for about 45 minutes. A suggested donation of $2.00 is asked of non-members. Recent topics have included "Palace Cars & Paradise: Story of Pullman" and "Frank Lloyd Wright's Arizona Biltmore: Jewel of the Desert." Call or stop in to their tour office to get more information on all of these programs.

Chicago Architecture Foundation River Cruises
• (312) 922-3432

The esteemed Chicago Architecture Foundation, pretty much the city's authority in guided tours, can show you the town not only on foot, but by water as well. They offer cruises on the elegant ship, *Chicago's First Lady*, designed in the spirit of the 1920's presidential yacht, *Sequoia*.

Now, you *could* spend $41.50 per person to sail down the Chicago River for three hours on this vessel, supping on prime rib and tarragon chicken. Or, for a more affordable $15.00, you can spend 90 minutes gliding down the same river, on the same boat. And only this less expensive choice will give you expert commentary from CAF guides. Learn about more than fifty of the city's historically and architecturally significant sites in complete elegance.

The boat offers open-air and indoor seating; snacks and beverages are available (on the non-dinner cruise, that is). A group rate of $13.00 per person is available for parties of 20 or more. Other tours on this graceful craft include a two-hour Sunday brunch buffet cruise for $27.00, and a 90-minute luncheon buffet cruise for $24.00. You'll find this Lady on the south side of the river, on the western side of the Michigan Avenue bridge. Private charters are also available.

The Chicago Athenaeum: The Museum of Architecture and Design
• The Daniel H. Burnham Center, 1165 N. Clark St., Chicago; (312) 280-0131

The only independent museum of architecture and design in the country, the stated mission of this museum is to educate the public on the importance of "Good Design." The Athenaem sponsors a variety of programs including gallery walks, walking tours around town, special performances and events, and competitions. Recent exhibits have highlighted the contributions of women and African Americans to the field of architecture and design.

Admission is a suggested donation of just $2 for all ages. Group visits are available at reduced rates and require advanced registration.

The Athenaeum has several smaller branches around town. The main number, above, will give you info. about all of them. Branches are located at the John Hancock Center, 875 N. Michigan Avenue; Gallery I, 515 N. State Street; and the 333 W. Wacker Drive Gallery, 333 W. Wacker Drive.

Chicago Board Options Exchange
• 400 S. LaSalle St., Chicago; (312) 786-5600

If you want to remind yourself why you didn't major in business and finance, stroll on over to the Options Exchange and gawk from the visitors gallery at the mayhem that takes place on the trading floor. The exchange is open to the public, at no charge, weekdays from 8:30 a.m. to 3:15 p.m. There is a 20-minute video that will explain how options work and what is going on down on the floor below you; after that, you're on your way to becoming a financial wheeler and dealer, you'll be a multizillionaire, and you won't need this book anymore. But write once in a while, okay?

Formal tours must be booked in advance and require a group of ten or more.

Chicago Board of Trade
- 141 W. Jackson Blvd., Chicago; (312) 435-3590

In a gallery one level above the trading floor, the Chicago Board of Trade will provide a free 30-minute tour which explains the history of the exchange. This above-the-scenes look, including a short film, will show you how the trading of financial futures and agricultural commodities works.

Tours run about every hour from 8 a.m. to 12:30 p.m., Monday through Friday. Call for specific times. Groups of ten or more are requested to make reservations in advance.

Chicago Mercantile Exchange
- 30 S. Wacker Dr., Fourth Floor, Chicago; (312) 930-8249

If your idea of a good time is watching other people working their buns off, this is a great place to do it. From the visitors gallery above the trading floor, you can watch as grown men and women scream, yell, and make funny hand gestures in an attempt to amass vast quantities of money. Fun, huh?

This is the world's largest financial futures exchange. Bigger than in New York? Well, they claim to be the largest in square footage. What these folks trade is "futures"; so, for instance, folks here will be selling coffee that hasn't even been grown yet. Now, that's salesmanship.

The tours are free, but you must have a group of fifteen or more to get one. If you have less than that, call up that day and try to get on someone else's tour. Tours are usually given between 9 a.m. and noon on weekdays only; they last about twenty minutes, though they can go as long as 45 minutes if there are questions.

Chicago Motor Coach Company
- (312) 922-8919

See Chicago from the top of a double-decker bus and get a narrated tour of Chicago's landmarks into the bargain. You can catch the bus at the Sears Tower, the Art Institute, the Field Museum, the Water Tower, Chicago Place, North Pier, and Mercury Boats, plus a few other locations by request. Buses arrive about every five to ten minutes between 9:30 a.m. and 5 p.m. Once you've bought a ticket, you can get on and off as often as you like until your tour is complete. Your tour is over when you arrive back at the place you started. A great way to get around the city and see the sights.

The top deck offers open-air seating (but they can cover up when it's bad weather). The fare is $9 for adults; $5 for children six to eleven, senior citizens over 65, and military personnel in uniform.

Chicago Stock Exchange
- 440 S. LaSalle St., Chicago; (312) 663-2742

Here's another opportunity to watch hundreds of people run around like crazy chasing after the almighty dollar. The fifth-floor gallery is free and open to the public; as you watch, instructional tapes explain what is happening on the trading floor below. Meanwhile, you can enjoy the lively entertainment of watching all that money changing hands—comfortable in the knowledge that none of your own money has changed hands to do so.

Group tours can be arranged, but due to staff constraints they can only give tours to college groups, investment groups, and the like. It may be worth a call to see if your group qualifies.

Chicago Sun-Times Newspaper Tours
- 401 N. Wabash Ave., Chicago; (312) 321-3251

Ever been curious about what it's like to work at a big-city newspaper? The *Chicago Sun-Times* gives you an excellent opportunity to find out. Their free 45-minute tours allow you to visit the big daily's newsroom, composing room, photo-engraving room and press room—and you'll learn all about the paper's storied (sorry, folks) past.

Tours are given at 10:30 a.m., Monday through Friday. Reservations are required; children must be at least eight years old to participate.

Chicago Tribune Newspaper Tours

- Freedom Center, 777 W. Chicago Ave., Chicago; (312) 222-2116

Unlike the tours given by its archrival, the *Sun-Times*, the Trib's tours don't let you peek into the newsroom, which is a pity. Still, for less than the price of a paper—in other words, absolutely free—you can tour the *Chicago Tribune's* "Freedom Center." This houses the newspaper's five-story production and circulation facility. You'll see the paper's ten off-set printing presses (one of the largest press rooms in the world), learn about the history of the *Tribune* and its production, and find out about the telecommunications technology that allows the *Tribune* to print simultaneously in Illinois, Wisconsin and Michigan. Bet you didn't even know they could do that.

You must make a reservation for the tour. The *Tribune* will conduct tours for up to fifty people, but there must be at least one chaperone for every fifteen children. Children under ten are not admitted on the tour.

Daytime Talk Shows

- The Jenny Jones Show, NBC Tower, 454 N. Columbus Dr., Chicago; (312) 836-9485
- The Jerry Springer Show, NBC Tower, 454 N. Columbus Dr., Chicago; (312) 321-5365
- The Oprah Winfrey Show, Harpo Studios, 1058 W. Washington St., Chicago; (312) 591-9222

These aren't exactly walks or tours, but Mr. C wasn't quite sure where to put them. Since this chapter does list some TV studio tours, here they are. Unlike the tours, these shows will give you a more in-depth look at how these shows get put together. Besides, they're free.

Now, don't you have to be a transsexual politician, or a closet goldfish abuser to get on one of these shows? Relax—you won't be sitting in *that* part of the studio. The shows do need regular folks to sit in the audience and give their reactions to the goings-on, though. All you have

---

MR. CHEAP'S PICKS
Walks and Tours

✔ **CBS Studio Tour**—A free look behind the scenes in TV-land.

✔ **Chicago Architecture Foundation**—Two-for-one deals on guided tours of historic architecture.

✔ **Chicago Mercantile Exchange/Chicago Stock Exchange**—Two of the world's largest exchanges each have one commodity that never goes up: Free tours.

✔ **Chicago Sun-Times/Chicago Tribune Tours**—Flash! More free guided tours inside the media biz.

✔ **Friends of the Chicago River**—Inexpensive walking tours along different parts of the river, all summer long.

---

to do is call the numbers listed above, and request your tickets.

It can take anywhere from two to six weeks to get into a show. Be warned though: Oprah is, by far, the most popular. You may have a harder time getting these tix. To twist an old phrase: Call early and call often. You'll get through eventually.

Friends of the Chicago River

- (312) 939-0490

Every summer, this non-profit group sponsors a regular Saturday walking tour along the river for only $5 per person. As you stroll along its briny banks, a trained docent will explain the river's fascinating development, discussing important contemporary issues as well. Eight different tours rotate weekly; each begins at 10 a.m. and last until about noon. Sturdy shoes are strongly recommended! Each tour meets in a different location; call for a schedule of upcoming tours.

Goose Island Brewing Co.
- 1800 N. Clybourn Ave., Chicago; (312) 915-0071

Part of the 1800 Clybourn Center, which also houses retail stores, restaurants, and ArtGolf (see listing under "Entertainment: Sports and Play"), Goose Island is one of Chicago's most popular breweries.

Here you can tour a working brewery and see the process that goes into making beer—from grains to foam-covered vats to the finished product. Tours take place every Sunday at 3:00 p.m., and they include a tasting at the end. Of course, the tasting is only for those legally able to partake, but the tour itself is open to all ages. Admission is free.

"Here's Chicago!"
- 163 E. Pearson St., Chicago; (312) 467-7114

Located inside the Water Tower Pumping Station, one of the few buildings to survive Chicago's Great Fire of 1871, "Here's Chicago!" lets you tour the city without leaving your seat. This one-hour sound and sight show will take you through Chicago and fly you over the city with aerial and special effects photography.

"Here's Chicago!" also features life-like exhibits on the gangster era, Abraham Lincoln, and of course, that nasty fire. You can also take a tour of the Pumping Station itself, a waterworks which was built in the 1860's. Not only did it survive the 1871 fire, but it pumps water into the city to this day.

Shows run continuously from 9:30 a.m. until 4:30 p.m., Monday through Thursday, and until 5 p.m. Friday, Saturday, and Sunday. Admission is $5.75; $4.75 for senior citizens and students. An extra bargain for big families is the special family rate of $15, period.

Island Princess
- (312) 468-0069

What this Jamaican-style cruiseboat is doing on the Chicago River is a bit of a mystery. It also happens to be the lowest-priced deal on the riverfront, which is less of a mystery once the boat departs. This is, um, a modest operation, folks. The decks are painted in neon colors, meant to create a "party" atmosphere but looking instead like the owner got a good deal on some leftover paint. Your friendly captain chimes in with a few tidbits of information about the sights floating by, but these are decidedly selective and somewhat whimsical. Music plays from a tinny car stereo system, and the music choices seem also to have come from the bottom of a glove compartment (James Bond themes—huh?).

Still, if you want to get onto one of the river cruises for the least amount of cash, this is your baby. And after all, you're not there for the boat itself. The city is still the city. The 90-minute tour takes you both inland, along the business district, and out through the locks to Lake Michigan. Board on the south side of the river, west of State Street. Tickets for a one-hour cruise are $6.50; the hour-and-a-half version is $8.50, and two hours go for $10.00. Senior citizens receive a $1.00 discount on every cruise, and tickets for children under age twelve are half-price.

John Hancock Center Observatory
- 875 N. Michigan Ave., Chicago; (312) 751-3681

For the bargain-basement price of only $3.65, this tower has a spectacular view that is worlds above the basement level. Your adventure will begin below ground, where the world's fastest elevator whisks you to the Observatory on the 94th floor in a mere 39 seconds. Once your ears finish popping, you can enjoy a spectacular view from all four sides of one of the world's tallest buildings. On a clear day you may not see forever, but you can see four states: Illinois, Indiana, Michigan, and Wisconsin.

Admission is only $2.35 for senior citizens and children under 17, and children under 4 are admitted free. Members of the armed forces in uniform are also admitted free. Once you've paid your fare, you can stay up there as long as you want; and, since it's open until midnight, you'll have plenty of time to enjoy the scenery.

Mercury, Chicago's Skyline Cruiseline

- (312) 332-1353

Departing from the southwest side of the Michigan Avenue bridge, Mercury offers perhaps the best variety of budget-priced tours on the Chicago River and around Lake Michigan. Their modern boat, the "Skyline Princess," is comfortable, though Mr. C disapproves of the see-through blue plastic roofing over most of the top deck. Get there early and grab one of the open seats on the bow (that's the front, to you landlubbers).

Rates start at $7.00 for a one-hour "Skyline Special" ($3.50 for children under 12), which takes you out through the lock for a turn around the lake. The "Mercury Landmark Classic" is a 90-minute cruise for $9.00 ($4.50 for children under 12), which adds a spin upriver along Wacker Drive; and the two-hour "Summer Sunset Cruise," at $11.00 ($5.50 for children under 12) combines these with an extended circuit on the lake during the sunset hour. Charters and group rates are also available, as are scheduled children's tours and special theme tours. Call 332-1368 for more information on these.

Oak Park Visitors Center

- 158 Forest Ave., Oak Park; (708) 848-1500

The Oak Park Vistors Center has a number of ways to enjoy this suburb, one-time home of the famous architect Frank Lloyd Wright. There are two main tours, one focusing on Wright's home and studio, and the other a tour of thirteen Wright-designed homes in the Forest Avenue area. Admission to each is $6.00, and $4.00 for senior citizens and children under 18. For a bargain deal, you can purchase a package and get both for $9.00; $7.00 for senior citizens and children under 18. Children under 10 are free at all times.

The Visitors Center also offers a "Tour of the Month," at 2:00 p.m. on the first Sunday of every month from April through November. The rotating lineup includes the River Forest Walking Tour, the Victorian Walking Tour, the Prairie Bicycle Tour, and the Oak Park Hike. At $5.00 per person, these jaunts are a pleasant and inexpensive way to spend a Sunday afternoon.

But wait—there's more! The Visitor's Center offers two other low-priced tours. The Unity Temple Tour takes you through this national historic landmark edifice, built in 1905, and dubbed by Wright his "little jewel." The cost is $4.00, $2.00 for students and seniors, Monday through Friday. On Saturday and Sunday it's $5.00, $3.00 for students and seniors.

Finally, the Pleasant Home tour takes you around the 1897 estate designed by architect George Maher. This includes Oak Park River Forest Historical Society collections on display on the second floor. The cost is $3.00, and $2.00 for children under eighteen.

Sears Tower Skydeck Observatory

- 233 S. Wacker Dr., Chicago; (312) 875-9696

Okay, so this view is a little more expensive than the one over at the John Hancock Center; but it is, after all, the world's tallest building. The higher view gets a higher price—$6.00 for adults, $3.25 for kids ages five to fifteen—but those extra floors make it worth every cent. The observatory is, in fact, on the 103rd floor of this 110-story giant, located in the financial district.

The observatory is open every day of the year and, as with the John Hancock Center, once you're up there they won't kick you out until it's time to close. That's at 10:00 p.m. from October through February, and at 11:00 p.m. March through September. In any case, you're sure to have plenty of time to enjoy the magnificent beauty of Chicagoland.

RESTAURANTS

For the dining chapters of the book, which many folks consider to be its main course, Mr. C decided not to dig in alphabetically—but rather by geographical area. After all, when you're hungry, you want to eat *now*—no matter how appetizing some place halfway across town may sound. The city has been divided into six very broad sections, so that you can just pick up the book and find the cheap choices in your area. Or the area where you're going to be...coordinate it with the "Entertainment" chapters, to plan out a whole day or night on the town!

All of the restaurants in this book are places where you can eat dinner for around $10 per person, or less. Far less, in many cases; and lunch prices, of course, can be even lower. Still, these eateries all serve filling meals of "real" food, not phony fast food junk.

That $10 limit does not include alcohol, which is going to be expensive just about anywhere. In fact, many of these places can afford to serve good, cheap food *because* they make their money on the booze. But, if you're tight on cash, you can always nurse one beer or an overpriced soda, eat well, and still come out ahead on the deal. And check out Mr. Cheap's special "Tip-Free" list for establishments where you can safely save an extra buck or two in that department.

MR. CHEAP'S PICKS
TIP-FREE RESTAURANTS

The following fine establishments won't give you a dirty look if you head out the door without leaving a gratuity. Here's to them!

DOWNTOWN
Billy Goat Tavern and Grill, 232
Gold Coast Dogs, 235
Gourmand Coffeehouse, 236
Jacob Bros. Bagels, 236
Krystyna's Cafe, 237
Morry's Old Fashioned Deli, 238
Shalom Deli, 239
Stage Door Express, 239

LINCOLN PARK AREA
Boston Chicken Rotisserie, 254
Chili Mac's 5-Way Chili, 259
Discover Cafe, 261
Fazzio's, 262
Gold Coast Dogs, 263
Metropolis Rotisseria, 268
Muskie's Hamburgers, 269
Rocky Mountain Bagel
   Company, 273

NEAR NORTH
Au Marché, 275
Billy Goat Tavern and Grill, 276
Foodlife, 281
Gino's East (take-out side), 282
Jacob Bros. Bagels, 283
Lo-Cal Zone, 284
Michigan Avenue Hot Dogs, 284

SOUTH SIDE
Valois Cafeteria, 295

WEST OF TOWN
Joe's Fisheries, 301
Manny's Coffee Shop and
   Deli, 304
Red Apple Restaurants, 306

DOWNTOWN
(including the Loop, South Loop)

Artists' Restaurant and Summertime Cafe
- 412 S. Michigan Ave., Chicago; (312) 939-7855

Located in the Fine Arts Building, diagonally across the street from the Art Institute, this mostly-Greek restaurant attracts tourists from the Hilton, actors and students from nearby Columbia College, and everyone in between. Locals recommend the restaurant as *the* place to perhaps catch sight of a famous actor or actress; casts from shows at the Auditorium and the area's many theaters sometimes come here for a bite after the show. One such visitor was Clara Peller, the fussy grandma of "Where's the beef?" fame, whose autographed photo hangs by the door.

Clara would be satisfied here. The theatrically-large Artist's Salad, with lots of fresh tomato, and cucumber, is served with roll and butter for $4.50. Another popular plate is the open-faced hot roast beef sandwich with mashed potato for $6.75. Among the more innovative menu items are the huge Burgundy burger, sautéed with wine and mushrooms, topped with bacon and served with French fries and a pickle for $6.75; and "Pierre's Tuna Volcano" (a croissant with tuna, mushrooms, tomato and melted cheddar cheese) for $7.25.

Prices may not be the cheapest you'll find anywhere, but remember, this is a touristy area. For the neighborhood, and the portions, this place is okay. Other low-priced options here include linguine or cheese ravioli for $6.50. For $5.95, go for a gyros plate or souvlaki—a skewer of herbed lamb with hot pita bread, olives, cucumber, tomato, pepper and ultra-thin French fries. Getting up there in price (but not bad, considering what you get) is grilled swordfish at $9.95, served with potatoes and rolls.

Finish off with a potent cup of Greek coffee ($1.90) and a slice of lemony cheesecake ($2.95). The Artist's Restaurant also carries a full liquor license. The restaurant's pretty rose-print wallpaper and faux marble counter combine for a casual and pleasant atmosphere. It's a good rendezvous for before or after a nearby musical, a concert in Grant Park, or a movie at the Fine Arts Theater next door.

Two words of warning, though: The restaurant enforces its minimums—$1 if you eat inside, and $2 if you eat out in the cafe. More important: Wherever tourists abound, so do pick-pockets. A sign in the restaurant warns customers to keep an eye on their wallets and purses, and it's good advice.

Blackie's
- 755 S. Clark St., Chicago; (312) 786-1161.

Tiny but fun, this Printer's Row-Burnham Park neighborhood bar is rich in history. It's is also open for lunch, Monday through Saturday from 11 a.m. until 3 p.m. only. They make a point of running the place, as they put it, "free of snobbery and excessive prices."

The restaurant has been run by the DeMilio family since 1939, who are still present in conjunction with the Thomas family. In its heydey, Blackie's attracted such celebrities as Tommy Dorsey, Glenn Miller and even the Three Stooges. After many of the printing companies moved out and Dearborn Station closed in the 1950's, business slowed, but Blackie's was rehabbed in the 70's and is now quite a hopping place once again.

You can get a great breakfast for about $5—well, okay, so it's at brunch time. Blackie's banana pancakes with bacon, sausage, or ham are $3.95; and eggs any style, with an English muffin, hash browns and your choice of bacon, sausage, or ham, are $3.75. The OJ ($1.50) is fresh-squeezed, and it goes great with the lox and bagel platter, served with cream cheese and garnishes for $5.25.

For lunch, an all-white meat chicken salad plate is $4.75 with a choice of Russian, creamy dill or vinaigrette dressings, and a Caesar salad with albacore tuna is $3.25. Chili is just $1.50 a cup—plus 50 cents extra if you want it topped with sour cream or cheddar cheese, a pile of onions or jalapeños. And a big six-ounce steak sandwich with grilled onions and mushrooms is served with fries for just $6.95. If you've never stopped in here early enough in the day to grab some of these eats, Mr. C recommends that you do so in the near future.

Billy Goat Tavern and Grill
- 430 N. Michigan Ave., Chicago; (312) 222-1525
- 309 W. Washington St., Chicago; (312) 899-1873

Well, no discussion of cheap dining in Chicago would be complete without a mention of these cut-rate charcuteries. Is there anyone who *doesn't* know by now that this is the birthplace of John Belushi's famous cry, "Chizbugger, chizbugger, chizbugger....No fries—*cheeps*!....." So the legend is told and retold—including here at the Billy Goat itself. Hey, they're proud of it.

Those cheeseburgers are $2.30 each, flat and greasy. If you're feeling particularly brave, go for the double at $3.55. And by the way, you can get fries, for another buck. The BG also has breakfast specials each morning, most around $2-$3. A ham and cheese omelette, for instance, goes for $2.95. Let's face it, sometimes cheap is cheap; the place is certainly not going to win any awards for health food. Especially when you con-

sider that a full bar is positioned directly across from the grill—somehow, an odd sight, at least during the day. But it all makes for a nice, divey hangout that's popular with the working crowd.

Chicago Style Pizza and Eatery
- 122 S. Michigan Ave., Chicago; (312) 427-0968

Another dependable and inexpensive tourist spot across the street from the Art Institute of Chicago. You can get a decent pizza here, or just a slice, and not even have to leave a tip; it's counter service only, but this isn't just fast-food.

"Chicago style" means stuffed, which these pizzas definitely are; you will be, too. In addition to several varieties of fillings, there is a "Daley Special" (get it?) as well. Wash it all down with a tall Leinenkugel, only $2.15.

The restaurant can get very packed (especially on Tuesdays, when the Art Institute offers free admission all day); but, if you can't grab one of the vinyl-covered barstools, head outside to the patio. The pop/alternative rock music inside can get a bit loud, anyway.

Desserts are listed as "Oprah's downfall," and you can get sundaes soused with liqueur. Chocolate sodas are $1.89.

The Corner Bakery
- 210 S. Canal St., Union Station, Chicago; (312) 441-0821
- 516 N. Clark St., Chicago, (312) 644-8100

A bakery with more than just sweets, the Corner Bakery's Union Station branch is a favorite among harried Loop office workers who gobble down their lunches in five minutes or less (not required, of course). At either location, the portions are good-sized, and the help is extremely friendly without being overbearing—even during lunch and dinner rushes. And all the baked goods are really made on the premises.

While the regular bakery items can thin your wallet (a loaf of chocolate cherry bread is $6.50), this is a good spot for lunch or breakfast with a number of different salads and sandwiches offered daily. Wheat berry salad, made with two kinds of peppers, is $3.50 for a small, $5.95 for a large. Curry chicken salad, with grapes and parsley is $3.85 and $6.95; and a hefty tuna salad sandwich with sprouts, on olive bread, is $4.50.

For snacks, desserts or whatever, the Corner's popular pretzel rolls are just 75 cents each, and giant fudge brownies sprinkled with confectioner's sugar are $1.50.

The Union Station location is open Monday through Friday, from 6 a.m. to 10 p.m., on Saturday 8 a.m. to 8 p.m., on Sunday 8 a.m. to 7 p.m. Hours on Clark Street are Monday through Friday, 7 a.m. to 10 p.m., Saturday 7:30 a.m. to 11 p.m., and Sunday 8 a.m. to 9 p.m.

Deli on Dearborn
- 723 S. Dearborn St., Chicago; (312) 427-3354.

Tired of running to Au Bon Pain or Burger King for a rushed lunch? A bit south of the Loop, this is the deli to go to for a quick and healthy takeout. If you do have a minute to sit down and eat, though, you won't find any tables here; but Burnham Park's benches are just a block away.

The menu changes constantly. They do offer a weekly listing of the Monday through Friday lunch specials, though, so you can keep up with the daily soup, salad, and sandwich offerings, and hit the place on your favorite day.

The deli does tend toward fancy, yuppie-ish pasta salad concoctions, as well as many vegetarian selections; but there are plenty of trusted standbys, too. A dish of pasta primavera made with shells, broccoli, cherry tomatoes and carrots in a pesto sauce runs around $2.50 a serving; for a full, substantial lunch, try fettucini carbonara with a Caesar salad and homemade bread, for $6.25.

Homemade soups are moderately priced in the $2-$2.50 range. Some of the many interesting soup

---

MR. CHEAP'S PICKS
Downtown

✔ **Edwardo's Natural Pizza Restaurant**—For its stupendous lunch and dinner buffet deals.

✔ **El Taco Loco**—"Real" Mexican food at Taco Bell prices.

✔ **Morry's Old Fashioned Deli**—Like a trip back to the days of big sandwiches and small prices.

✔ **Surf Restaurant**—Another coffee-shop throwback, famous for its mouth-watering meatloaf.

---

choices in a recent week included Santa Rosa soup (Italian vegetables with orzo), seafood creole, curry chicken, mushroom barley, and tomato bisque.

The fancy sandwiches range from about $5 to $7, but they are created almost like works of art. The smoked turkey, for instance, is not "just" smoked; it's smoked with applewood, which imparts to it an especially piquant flavor. Another variation is served on walnut raisin bread with cranberry mayonnaise. Not your average brown-bag varities.

You can, of course, request individualized sandwiches and call your order in ahead of time. Deli on Dearborn is open until 6:00 p.m. on weekdays, and until 4 p.m. on Saturdays.

Edwardo's Natural Pizza Restaurant
- 1212 N. Dearborn St., Chicago; (312) 337-4490
- 521 S. Dearborn St., Chicago; (312) 939-3366
- 1321 E. 57th St., Chicago, (312) 241-7960

Many other suburban locations
Despite its yuppie exterior and award-

winning pizza, Edwardo's is not all that expensive, especially if you take advantage of their terrific lunch buffet. But you can split a pizza, order an individual salad and a soda at any hour, and still only spend $6 or so.

Now, about that buffet. It costs just $4.95 per person. First, fill up at the salad bar with fresh greens and tomatoes, multicolored rotini in a nutty pesto sauce, thick cantaloupe wedges, and tangy poppyseed dressing. Then, choose from four different pizzas (two with a whole-wheat crust, including their wonderfully tasty spinach pie), baked ziti, and other entrees. Don't forget frozen glacee or chocolate cake for dessert. This incredible deal is offered weekdays from 11:30 a.m. until 3 p.m., with a $6.49 dinner version offered daily from 5-9 p.m. The main difference between the two buffets is that the dinner buffet offers stuffed pizza while the lunch buffet does not.

If you're not in the mood for the buffet, the appetizer menu has great garlic bread for $1.75 (slather it with mozzarella for 50 cents extra), or a Caesar salad for $2.95. Stuffed pizzas start at $9.35 for a regular size mozzarella, which itself can be enough to share. Prices go on to $14.75 for a basic large pie, higher with extra toppings; but it serves four or five people. Thin crust pizzas run up to $19 for the large Edwardo's special, and a whole wheat crust is 75 cents extra for either style pizza. Other types of pies include vegetarian, with mushrooms, peppers and onions; pesto pizza, and several more. Desserts are on the rich side, with a slice of blueberry cheesecake about $3.

Edwardo's also offers delivery (not free) to limited areas.

El Taco Loco
- 5258 N. Lincoln Ave., Chicago; (312) 275-9892
- 645 S. Wabash Ave., Chicago; (312) 922-4125
- 1726 W. Lawrence Ave., Chicago; (312) 784-1881

El Taco Loco is a good quality, full-menu Mexican restaurant with south-of-the-border prices. Two people can easily stuff themselves here for less than $10, total; think of it as real Mexican food at Taco Bell prices.

Open for breakfast, lunch and dinner, the day starts off with the traditional huevos rancheros (two fried eggs in a mild ranchero sauce) or chilaquiles (scrambled eggs). Each plate, which comes with rice and beans, is priced at $3.75.

Moving on to lunch, you *could* have American-style sandwiches filled with pork, steak, chicken or ground beef for $2.95, with beans, lettuce, tomatoes, sour cream, and guacamole on the side. The truly non-adventurous can also bail out with a hamburger for $1.95. But why come here and not go Mexican? Mr. C liked the burrito grande, made with a choice of chicken, beef, pork, or beans. It'll fill you up for a mere $2.45. Add a generous side of fried rice—not too spicy, not too wimpy—for another $1.25. Sauces here really aren't too hot, unless you request them to be so.

Three big enchiladas go for $5.00, and tacos (soft or crispy) are only $1.25 a pop, $2.45 for the "grande" size. The chicken fajita dinner, served with plenty of lettuce, rice, beans, and tortillas to roll it all up, is one of the most expensive items on the menu, ringing in at just $7.95. Various combination plates are also offered. Wash it all down with sweet rice water, a Mexican favorite, for $1.

El Taco Loco offers little in the way of atmosphere (the south Loop Loco seems a bit out of place, right across the street from the Hilton). There is a tiny counter and a couple of booths—no frills. The restaurant also keeps costs down by offering everything a la carte, and by charging extra for condiments like jalapeños, hot sauce, and extra tortillas. You're only going to pay for what you want.

Gotta love the hours: Lincoln Avenue is open Sunday-Thursday from 11 a.m. to 5 a.m., Fridays and Saturdays from 10 a.m. to 6 a.m. The South Loop location runs from 7 a.m. until 3 a.m. daily, while the

Lawrence spot is open daily 24 hours. Both the Lawrence and Lincoln Avenue spots offer free parking.

Ferris Wheel Restaurant

- 120 S. State St., Chicago; (312) 236-4842

This thirty-year-old eatery in the State Street Mall is the kind of place you may remember your grandparents taking you to when you were a kid. Candy and gum for sale at the cash register and Muzak in the air combine for the old-fashioned atmosphere of the place. Mr. C likes the fact that the Ferris Wheel is one of the few business-district restaurants to remain open seven days a week.

It seems that the owners have tried to make the place romantic, with low lighting and cozy two-seater booths; but have no doubt, this is a family kind of place. Orders are put through to the kitchen using a microphone, a la Burger King. The friendly waitresses like to clown around with each other, lightening up the atmosphere.

The standard breakfast menu is chock-full of bargains, like three-egg Swiss cheese omelettes for $3.25. The vegetarian omelette, with mushrooms, green peppers, onions, and tomatoes, is only $3.45. A stack of pancakes is a mere $2.55; add ham, bacon, or sausage for $1.20 more. They also make a point of stocking up on bakery items, like pecan rolls for $1 apiece.

The lunch and dinner menu is not much different from any other family-style restaurant. A fried fish dinner, for instance, is served with a huge baked potato and mixed vegetables for just $6.95. Beverages are reasonably priced; the restaurant also has a full liquor license. And, for the kiddies (well, whomever), Mr. C *highly* recommends the chocolate milk shakes.

The Ferris Wheel opens bright and early to catch the above-mentioned business crowd: Mondays through Saturdays from 6 a.m. until 10 p.m., and Sundays from 7 a.m. until 10 p.m.

Gold Coast Dogs

- 325 S. Franklin St., Chicago; (312) 939-2624
- 2100 N. Clark St., Chicago; (312) 327-8887
- 418 N. State St., Chicago; (312) 527-1222

The Trib gave Gold Coast Dogs three stars, but patrons would seemingly give it four. This is a fast-food joint, granted, but a classy one using the freshest ingredients possible. And remember, Mr. C always says that counter service will save you dough—no tipping required!

Don't be put off by the line, snaking out the door, filled with businesspeople and families alike—it moves quickly. While you wait, you're more than welcome to read the dozens of praiseworthy newspaper and magazine articles framed on the wall.

Those who have already gone to these Dogs know that the One Magnificent Dog is $1.80, the plain ol' Red Hot Dog is $1.90, and the Char Cheddar Red Hot Dog (topped with fresh Wisconsin cheese) is $2.20. Beer bratwursts and Polish sausages go for $2.50 each. All sandwiches come with free condiments including mustard, ketchup, relish, onions, tomatoes, hot peppers, pickles, celery salt, and grilled onions.

But Gold Coast serves up more than just dogs. Catch the char-broiled swordfish sandwich, f'rinstance, made with fresh fish picked up daily at the dock. It's a deal at just $5.95. Turkey sandwiches are only $3.95. Chili is $1.95 for a bowl, and their ever-popular jumbo 1/3 pound charburgers are $2.95.

And there's more! Don't forget that they also serve breakfast here. Omelettes are only $3.50; get some grits or hash browns for 85 cents more. Herbie's Special—two eggs, sausage or bacon, hash browns, toast or bagel, and coffee for $1.95—may possibly be the best breakfast deal in all of Chicago. Unless you count Izzy's Special, that is—two scrambled eggs, cheese, and Canadian bacon on a toasted bagel for $1.89.

Gold Coast Dogs is open weekdays from 7 a.m. to midnight, from 10:30 a.m. to 8 p.m. on Saturdays, and from 11 a.m. to 8 p.m. on Sundays.

Gourmand Coffeehouse

- 728 S. Dearborn St., Chicago; (312) 427-2610

The Gourmand doesn't sound like the name of a shop that Mr. C would frequent, but for baked items, clever sandwiches and coffee at not-too-crazy prices, this Printer's Row/Dearborn Park hangout is certainly worth checking out.

Their breakfasts are true bargains. "Eggs espresso," two eggs steamed in an espresso maker, are served with cheese and two slices of toast for $3.50. Add coffee and orange juice for $1.50 more. A bowl of granola, topped with lowfat yogurt, is only $2.95.

"Gourmand" evidently means "world-traveler" to these folks. For lunch, you can have a panini sandwich—turkey and pesto, or eggplant and tomato with feta cheese, on crusty Italian bread for $3.25; or a pita sandwich loaded with hummus for $3.50. Japanese noodles and pasta primavera are two other good picks at just $2.75 each.

Desserts are the real treats here, with some items baked by the popular Third Coast Coffee House (see listing under "Restaurants: Near North"). Muffins are $1.50 each but are absolutely gigantic, offered in carrot, bran, lemon poppyseed, and chocolate cream cheese varieties. Rugelaghs, eastern European treats similar to tarts, are just $1 each and come in raspberry, apricot, and walnut raisin.

For your caffeine fix, try the "chocoloccino," or a cafe mocha, latte or americano for $1.60 a cup; a single espresso is $1.35, and a double costs $2. Sip to the sounds of blues or jazz, whether in the cozy coolness of the art-decorated interior or out at the sidewalk tables. The Gourmand gets a thumbs up for serving their in-house beverages in glasses and mugs, with patrons returning their cups to the counter in this tip-free setting.

Since the Gourmand is just three blocks west of Michigan Avenue, a five-minute walk from the Art Institute, consider eating here instead of one of the tourist-crowded eateries on the main drag. Open weekdays from 7 a.m. until 11 p.m., and weekends from 8 a.m. until 11 p.m.

Jacob Bros. Bagels

- 58 E. Randolph St., Chicago; (312) 368-1180
- 53 W. Jackson Blvd., Chicago; (312) 922-BAGL (2245)
- 50 E. Chicago Ave., Chicago; (312) 664-0026

With two locations tucked inside the Loop and one to the north, you can stop in here for a snack on the run or a quick meal. The prices, meanwhile, are nice and cheap—hardly what you'd expect from the fancy gold lettering on the door or the yuppified mauve and ivory color scheme.

Choose from 17 different types of bagels, from the standard ingredients to flavors like cheese and honey-oat bran. Bagels are all 50 cents each; slathered with various blends of terrific cream cheese, shipped in from Vermont, they go for $1.40.

Lunch items include pasta salad for 95 cents. Real deli-style sandwiches are all around $3.25; among the good picks are chicken salad, tuna, turkey, ham, Danish havarti, and kosher salami. Add a side order of fresh couscous salad for 90 cents more. There are several Middle Eastern items on the menu, in fact; take home a half pound of hummus for $2.65. Half a pound of their cream cheese or lox spread is about $2.50. Mr. C found the fruit salad, though, to be laden with that bitter-tasting sulfate flavor preservative.

Many of the "dessert" choices, while good, are geared to the ascetic: Oatmeal raisin bars, carrot-raisin bread, or zucchini bread. But don't worry—you can eschew the healthy for the sinful route and grab a rich brownie for $1, and a good cup of coffee for just 70 cents.

An obvious commuter stop, Jacob Bros. Bagels is open from 6:30 a.m. to 6:00 p.m. weekdays, and 10-3 on Saturdays.

Kaz's Restaurant and Bar

- 1154 S. Michigan Ave., Chicago; (312) 663-9318

Attached to the super-cheap Avenue Motel on the corner of Michigan and Roosevelt, Kaz's is one of the few inexpensive places along Grant Park where you can get a good basic breakfast, lunch, or dinner at basic prices. They're open seven days a week, to boot. A gritty, urban sort of place, Kaz's may also offer a bit of entertainment in some of the offbeat regulars who dine here. Don't worry—if they get too loud, there are also plenty of Chicago cops who eat here; the station is right around the corner.

Remember Mel's Diner on the TV show "Alice"? That's kind of what this place feels like, right down to the frequently-pounded waitress bell. Actually, Kaz's does hang some artsy black-and-white photographs of city scenes on its walls, somehow mixing with African masks and classical background music, but who the heck cares here? For 75 cents, you can sit over a cup of coffee and a nice view of Grant Park.

Kaz's breakfast special—French toast or three pancakes with two eggs, two bacon strips, and two sausage links—is $4.25. Three-egg omelettes are made with some quite unusual additions like sour cream, spinach, and sauerkraut; and the soups, as well as ten different salad dressings, are all homemade. The food is filling, cheap, and good stuff. There is also a full liquor license.

Kaz's opens up at 7 a.m. daily, 8 a.m. on Sundays; it closes at 9 p.m. Monday through Wednesday and Saturday, at 10 p.m. Thursday and Friday, and 8 p.m. on Sunday. It really makes a good breakfast and lunch bet, though, or perhaps for a pre-concert dinner, since this neighborhood after dark is not one of Chicago's best.

Krystyna's Cafe

- 8 E. Jackson Blvd., Chicago; (312) 922-9225
- 203 N. Wabash St., Chicago; (312) 750-0553

Krystyna's may try just a little too hard to be French (the piped-in music is more reminiscent of an Express store than of Paris), but it's one of the better places in the Loop to grab a quick and inexpensive bite on the way to work.

Croissants are priced around $1.50, and come with apricot, blueberry, cinnamon, peach, almond, or chocolate fillings. Actually, the prices here, while reasonable, are extremely precise; isn't that more Swiss than French? The plain "Normandy" butter croissant, for example, costs 91 cents. Almost two dozen muffins are offered (though not all are available at all times) at $1.54 each. "Verry Berry," cranapple, cheesecake streusel, lemon crunch, and wild raspberries in custard are among the delightful and interesting muffin offerings.

For a more substantial start to the day, there are egg dishes and the like. A cheese and ham omelette (billed as "*au fromage jambon-ham*") goes for $3.27.

At lunch, there is (of course) a soup du jour, priced at $2.22; cream of mushroom was the choice on Mr. C's visit. Individual pizzas are just $3.50 (beef stroganoff, spinach florentine, and ginger chicken—these are pizzas? Mmmmm). Pasta in pesto sauce and seafood Marseille are both $4.04 for a generous serving, and sandwiches like avocado Francaise ($3.17) and ham and brie ($3.22) are further French faves.

Sip an amaretto cappuccino ($2) or espresso ($1.40) with your meal. Perrier and San Pellegrino waters are here too, as well as pear and apricot nectars. Delivery is available for orders exceeding $8.00.

Monday's Restaurants

- 19 E. Jackson Blvd., Chicago; (312) 408-1120

- 75 W. Harrison St., Chicago; (312) 663-3647
- 120 S. Riverside Plaza, Chicago; (312) 372-9866
- 203 N. LaSalle St., Chicago; (312) 629-0444

Monday's Restaurants are best categorized as neighborhood bar/eateries, but they stand out from the crowd with their super-friendly service and unusual menu items. Start your weekend off right with their Sunday brunch, or try breakfast, lunch, or dinner any day of the week.

Some items are basic, like the big Belgian waffles ($3.50); but real maple syrup and whipped butter make it special. Other offbeat offerings include "Ka-Ya-Na" ($4.95), which is scrambled eggs with tomato, onion and feta cheese mixed in, European style, plus a muffin or toast.

Several omelettes are on the menu, all under $5.00; go for the zucchini—made with Swiss cheese and onions—or the crabmeat. All of these dishes come with fried potatoes, muffin or toast and jelly. Or, try nova lox and three eggs for $5.95. That Sunday brunch is $9.95, but well worth it for those with hearty appetites. It's an elaborate, all-you-can eat buffet of eggs, salmon, fresh fruit, breads, and other fixings.

Lunches and dinners are just as reasonably priced. Even at dinnertime, nothing on the menu tops $6.95, including burgers, ribs, and "evvvvvvvvverything," as one of the waiters here put it. Mondays also has a full liquor license, and a separate bar area. Dinner is only available, however, until about 8:00—after that, the place is strictly a bar.

All the Monday's branches have similar, though not identical, menus and decor. The Harrison location has funky splatter-painted floors, glow-in-the-dark steps from the bar area to the raised dining floor, and big, comfy green vinyl booths. It must have been a converted warehouse, with its super-high ceiling; but neon stars, hanging lights, and the raised television sets combine for more of a wacky nightclub effect.

Morry's Old Fashioned Deli

- 245 S. Dearborn St., Chicago; (312) 922-2932, (312) 922-2933

You've gotta love a place like Morry's, where coffee is still just 55 cents, and the food is self-service, so you don't even have to leave a tip. Pickle buckets with tongs sit on each of the tables, which are placed almost on top of each other in the crowded dining area. It gets downright noisy at rush times, but then that's part of the gritty charm here.

Start your day lightly with a bagel or bran muffin, plus a fruit cup, for only $1.35. Other breakfast goodies include two eggs with hash browns ($2), or a bologna omelette with hash browns ($3.55).

Lunch is the busy time. Could it be because the iced tea is fresh, the soups are all homemade, and the sandwiches are huge? You betcha. Nova lox sandwiches are just $3.50, or $4.55 with cream cheese. Liverwurst and salami sandwiches are $3.50 each, while jumbo sandwiches like the corned beef "Sandwich and a half," complete with artery-clogging potato salad, is $6.50. Italian and barbecued beef sandwiches are $4.85 each.

Morry's soups are all homemade and available in three sizes, priced from $1.40 for a small to $3.65 for the large (and worth it!). They're offered in mushroom barley, chicken matzo, split pea, vegetable, chili, chicken noodle, and chicken rice. They got chili here, too.

"Diet" dishes include your basic fresh fruit plate with cottage cheese, potato salad, cole slaw, Bermuda onion, tomato, cucumber, and roll for $6.95. Side orders like cheddar fries ($1.95) and veggie salad ($1.65) are also big sellers.

Desserts are all homemade too, and such a deal! Brownies or slices of apple pie are $1.20 each, and a piece of banana cake is just $1

The deli has a liquor license, with Bud Lite and Miller beer on tap for just 99 cents at the almost-microscopic bar. Free local delivery—another holdover from bygone days—is another reason why Morry's is a per-

ennial favorite with the downtown office crowd. The deli is open from
6:30 a.m. until 8 p.m. weekdays,
from 8 a.m. to 5 p.m. Saturdays, and
closed on Sundays.

North Loop Deli
- 205 N. State St., Chicago; (312)
  782-5678

You can gaze at photos of Betty
Grable, Dustin Hoffman in his "Tootsie" garb, and a baby-faced Robert
DeNiro (think they've all eaten
here?) while you chow down at the
North Loop. Open for breakfast and
lunch only, its portions are hefty and
the price is right. There's plenty of
room for eating in, or you can call
ahead for take-out.

Pancakes or French toast with
sausage, bacon, or ham will cost you
just $3.25. Three eggs, any style,
with toast and yummy potatoes go
for $2.35, and you can add bacon,
sausage or ham for just 50 cents
more. A ham and egg sandwich is
just 99 cents—and a heck of a lot
more appetizing than that culinary
phony they serve at McDonalds.

For lunch, sandwiches come in
three sizes—the "Pleaser" with three
ounces of meat for $3.25, the five-
ounce "Belt Buster" for $4.50, and
the seven-ounce "Heavyweight" for
$5.75. And they ain't kidding.
Choices include corned beef, pastrami, salami, egg salad, reuben, and
vegetarian.

Add one of North Loop's genuine malteds for $1.60 more. Or, how
about some of their hearty homemade soups ($1.25 a cup, $2.00 a
bowl)? Flavors include beef vegetable, chicken noodle, and chicken
matzo ball.

A true businessman's (and
woman's) haven, the deli is open
weekdays from 7 a.m. to 3 p.m. only.

Shalom Deli
- 7 N. Wells St., Chicago; (312)
  606-0371, (312) 606-0372

The Shalom Deli is a welcome sight
in the North Loop area for its quick,
friendly service and low prices. The
inside is a bit odd—lots of vertical
strip mirrors, and a half-exposed

brick wall—making Mr. C curious to
know if it's perhaps transformed into
a night club at closing time. Curiosi-
ties aside, check out their menu, with
every sandwich served with potato
salad and nothing on the list over $6.

A bagel is just 40 cents at Shalom, with butter just a dime more and
70 cents extra for a slab of cream
cheese. Sandwiches are served on
either white, wheat, rye, dark rye, or
onion bread or on a kaiser roll. Hot
corned beef, salami, turkey, ham, egg
salad, or chicken salad sandwiches
range in price from $2.95 to $3.95.
Giant combination sandwiches, like
ham and cheese or corned beef and
pastrami, are just $4.00-$4.50. Clubs
go for $5 or more, but they're piled
high with meat and cheese.

On the lighter side, tossed salads
are just $1.50; a fresh fruit salad with
cottage cheese on the side is just
$3.95. And on the heavier side, des-
serts like the $1.95 chocolate chip
cheesecake or carrot cake may set
your diet back, but not your wallet.
Don't forget coffee at an old-fashioned 55 cents a cup.

Tips are optional, since it's just
counter service, and in good weather,
you can people-watch from the patio
chairs on the sidewalk.

Shalom is open from 6 a.m. until
6 p.m., Mondays through Saturdays.
They also deliver, but there's a three-
sandwich minimum; so, that means
you're either ordering for your office,
or to lay in enough food to hibernate
for the winter.

Stage Door Express
- 20 N. Wacker Drive (3rd Floor),
  Chicago; (312) 346-1466

How do you get to Carnegie Hall?
Practice. To get into the Civic Opera
Building, there's a much easier way:
Follow your nose. Up the main lobby
elevators to the third floor, you'll find
this bustling deli/restaurant, quite
handsome with its dark wooden tables and panelled walls, brass trim,
and gaslight-type sconces. For all
these elegant trappings (not to mention what goes on downstairs), the
cafeteria-style place is surprisingly

casual and the menu is very inexpensive. It's an offbeat location for a good, downtown business worker's breakfast or lunch.

Sandwiches are the main act here, big enough to fill up the beefiest baritone, with dozens of choices all priced under $5. The basic corned beef, for example, is just $3.49, on your choice of ten different types of bread. There are two *dozen* choices of dressings and toppings for your sandwich, from mayo or Dijon mustard to teriyaki sauce and even bean sprouts.

Other popular choices include pastrami with Havarti cheese, chopped liver and black olives, all for $4.72; Oriental chicken salad ($3.49); bologna with horseradish, tomato and cream cheese ($3.86); roast turkey with egg and onion ($4.13); indeed, about a dozen variations for every kind of meat. There is one sandwich that tops $5 (by only twelve cents)—the jumbo combination of corned beef, pastrami, salami, chopped liver, Swiss cheese, onion, and Thousand Island dressing. Bravo!

Meanwhile, there are also hot sandwiches, including meatloaf, gyros, veal brisket (each $3.49), and even such rather exotic varieties as a roast duck sandwich or chicken salsa sandwich (each $3.99), and Louisiana shredded pork ($3.49). Not to mention kosher hot dogs and Polish sausages, stir-fried vegetables, soups, and fresh salad and pasta bars. Sweet tooth fanatics will love the ice cream and soft-serve frozen yogurt with a candy toppings bar, as well as fresh baked pastries.

Another surprise is that, considering its upstairs location, the windows are so small. Well above the business district on one side and the Chicago River on the other, there is not much in the way of a view. Stage Door Express opens every weekday at 7:00 a.m. for breakfast, and closes by 4:00. It's also closed on weekends. Free delivery service to area offices is available, with a minimum of ten sandwiches.

Surf Restaurant

- 1016 S. Michigan Ave., Chicago; (312) 427-2646
- 205 W. Wacker Dr., Chicago; (312) 346-0985

The writeups in the window rave about the meatloaf at this business-crowd hangout: It's the best in town, the best, the best. Well, Mr. C has two confessions to make. First of all, he has just never much cared for meatloaf—it's those traumatic childhood memories of dry, tasteless attempts while trying to be a polite dinner guest at a friend's house, and so forth. Confession number two: All those dreaded memories were wiped out instantly by the juicy, seasoned slabs served up here, with scrumptious gravy and real mashed potatoes. Lucky break for our hero, eh?

The meatloaf, just $4.95 for a big platter, is just one of the zillions of choices on the Surf's huge breakfast and lunch menu. By the way, you also get cooked vegetables and warm, homemade rolls to complete the picture. On the same side of the tracks, there are hand-rolled six-ounce burgers, starting at just $2.95; the "Surf Burger," at $4.50, is topped with Swiss cheese and grilled onions, plus good fries on the side.

Salads, a bit pricier, are nonetheless gigantic. Most are around $6.50, including your garden-variety Caesar's, chef's, and spinach. Or, try the "California Fruit Plate" ($6.25), with fresh fruit in season, cottage cheese, and homemade cinnamon bread. There are plenty of hefty sandwiches; the basics start at $3.95, moving up to fancier sorts like brisket of beef ($5.25, on great rye bread with French fries). Always plenty of daily specials, too. These include homemade soup or juice, an entree, coffee, and fresh cake or fruit for dessert—for around six bucks. The Surf also has a modest list of cocktails, beer, and wine.

Going back to breakfasts, available through the day, there are lots of omelettes—all around $4.95, served with toast or bagel, and fries. Check out the homemade cheese blintzes, thick-sliced French toast (each $4.50), smooth, butter cream pancakes made with blueberries or pecans (each $3.50)...or go hog-wild with the farmer's breakfast—two eggs, pancakes, and bacon or sausage, all for $5.25.

How many times has the word "homemade" appeared in this entry? That should give you a clue about the Surf. The daily crowds are another. The restaurant, renovated in coral pink and green, is bright, clean, and comfortable—a genuine, modern luncheonette. Service is friendly, too, whether or not you are one of the obvious regulars here. Open early, the place shuts down after everyone heads back to the office, around 3:00. It's located inside the Engineering Building, at the corner of Wells and Wacker; enter from the Wells Street side.

Taste of Siam
- 731 S. Dearborn St., Chicago; (312) 939-1179

Taste of Siam had just moved from its old Plymouth Court locale into its new digs on Dearborn when Mr. C visited. Despite a few kinks in the system—probably due to adjusting to a new spot—the meal was definitely good, cheap eats with atmosphere to boot.

Just a couple of blocks south of the Congress Parkway, Siam is an easy-to-find and popular spot in Dearborn Park—in fact, it's a good idea to arrive ahead of the lunch or dinner rush, or to call ahead for reservations.

While Mr. C was put off by the fact that the tables had numbers stickered to the wall to aid the waiters' and waitresses' order delivery, that was practically forgotten after the tasty chicken satay (six skewers for $4.50). Thai cucumber salads are supposed to be tiny, and the ones at Taste of Siam are exceptionally so—but crisper than many in town, and just $1 extra if they don't already come with your entree. Beef noodle soup ($2.25) with rice noodles, sprouts, celery, and green onion was good-sized and tasty, worth every penny indeed.

Other inexpensive appetizers include fried tofu ($2.50), prawn rolls (five for $5.25), shrimp and vegetable tempura ($5.25), and the Siam Platter, a sampler of satay, spring rolls, vegetable tempura, chicken golden cups, egg rolls and prawn rolls, for $9.95. All of these are big enough to share.

Entrees are wonderful and low-priced. Roast duck, at $5.95, is among the most expensive dishes; plenty of other choices include pepper steak ($4.50), ginger chicken ($4.75), and a mixed vegetable stir fry ($4.50). Thai custard, at $2 a pop, will finish off your meal on a sweet note.

If you would like your order prepared any special way—spicier, perhaps, with extra noodles, or whatever—the kitchen will be happy to oblige you. Taste of Siam is open Monday through Thursday from 11 a.m. until 9:30 p.m., Fridays and Saturdays until 10:30 p.m., and on Sundays from noon until 9:30 p.m.

FAR NORTH
(including Andersonville, Edgewater, Ravenswood, Rogers Park, Uptown)

Ann Sather
- 929 W. Belmont Ave., Chicago; (312) 348-2378

- 5207 N. Clark St., Chicago; (312) 271-6677

- 1329 E. 57th St., Chicago; (312) 947-9323

For true-blue Swedish dining, a significant part of Chicago's heritage, this famous restaurant has it all. The original Ann Sather in Lake View was formerly a funeral home, but you can't tell now with the way that they have it decorated. Well, the chairs and tables *are* black, but the restaurant is warmed up by a crystal chandelier, stained glass windows and red and gold trim.

The food will warm you up, too, with goodies like three-egg omelettes for $4.75, whether filled with peaches, cheddar cheese, broccoli, ham, or several other choices. Or, try one with crab, spinach, and sour cream for $6.25. And if you're watching your cholesterol, you can have any omelette made with just egg whites. Other breakfast "musts" at Ann Sather are their heavenly homemade cinnamon rolls (two for $1.50), and Swedish limpa rye bread, made tangy with anise seeds ($1).

Breakfast is served all day, while both the lunch and dinner menus start at 11 a.m. (who could eat dinner at that hour?) On the lunch menu, three Swedish pancakes are $4.25 (ice cream and strawberries are extra), grilled cheese and tomato sandwiches are $3.95, the veggie burger is $4.95 (both sandwiches served with cole slaw), and the Caesar chicken tortellini salad is $6.95. Add a cup of homemade soup to any salad or sandwich order for just $1 extra.

For big appetites, Ann Sather offers a long list of dinners under $10, complete with appetizer, two side dishes, dessert and beverage. They're also available as "lite" meals, in smaller portions with just the side dishes and drink. The roast duck dinner is $9.50 ($7.50 in the lite version); chicken croquettes are $8.50 ($6.50 lite); and baked meat loaf is $8.95 ($6.95 lite).

Several beers are available; though, for a true Scandinavian experience, you may want to try the potent Swedish glogg ($3.50)—a mixture of spiced sherry, red wine and brandy, with almonds and raisins, served warm. For those not wishing to be knocked out, one dollar gets you a bottomless cup of coffee, or Darjeeling tea.

By the way, you can take home a dozen of those famous cinnamon rolls or muffins for $6, or a loaf of their limpa bread for $3.75.

The Lake View restaurant is open from 7 a.m. until 11 p.m. Thursday through Sunday, and until midnight on Friday and Saturday. The Andersonville branch is open daily from 7 a.m until 10 p.m.; while the Hyde Park location, near the University of Chicago campus, is open from 7 a.m. only until 3 p.m. daily.

Campeche Restaurant
- 3606 N. Clark St., Chicago; (312) 327-1448
- 7124 N. Clark St., Chicago; (312) 761-8378

While this Mexican chain doesn't necessarily pack folks in, it does do a steady business from Wrigleyville residents, Cubs fans, and Chicago Transit Authority employees. The decor could stand some improvement, especially with the hanging foil curliques around the taco bar and an annoying electronic message board advertising their Sunday brunch. But the food isn't half bad, and Campeche is open late to accommodate nocturnal folks.

Their popular all-you-can-eat taco bar costs $4.50, giving you a choice of chicken or beef fillings and a slew of toppings. A dinner buffet, also an all-you-can-eat deal, is $7.99. Those with smaller appetites can choose from among the many burrito choices (plenty big themselves), ranging in price from $2.25 for the chicken, pork and beef to $3.75 for the steak burrito. Enchiladas and tacos are also available a la carte, starting at just 99 cents.

Larger meals include fajitas ($7.50); combination plates are also good values. The vegetarian combo includes a bean tostada, guacamole taco and cheese quesadilla, all for $6.25. If none of these fill you up, you can stuff yourself on the tortilla chips and salsa which come with most dishes.

Wash down all this spicy food with a good selection of Mexican beers, including Corona, Bohemia, Dos Equis and Carta Blanca, each $2.50. Fruit juices, like pineapple, papaya, orange and grape, are served in ridiculously tall glasses for just $1.25.

Campeche makes its own desserts. Flan topped with Rompope liqueur is the standout at just $1.60, and "Campechitas" (flour tortillas stuffed with fruit and topped with caramel) are $1.50.

While both branches open at 10 a.m, the Wrigleyville location (right across the street from the ballpark) stays open until 5 a.m.

The Dellwood Pickle
• 1475 W. Balmoral Ave., Chicago; (312) 271-7728

Located just east of Clark Street, in a quiet corner of Andersonville, this closet-sized restaurant is full of fun touches. Oversized paintings of frogs, caricatured into such notables as Cher and Toulouse-Lautrec, cover (*really* cover) the walls; tea is served in little handmade ceramic tea pots; and the tablecloths are decorated with eye-grabbing moire patterns. Everything, right down to the lavender floor, is in some way artistically done.

The atmosphere is decidedly casual, with waitresses in jeans, and easygoing pop music on the radio. A cozy pair of tables in the window, one step up from the main floor, are a charming feature. If you've brought kids along, the folks here will offer little baskets of crayons to keep them amused (non-parenting patrons may appreciate that just as much). The homey feel extends even to the stack of magazines provided in the unisex, er, reading room.

The menu is an interesting mix of nouvelle and comfort food. Mr. C tried the bruschetta, which was a little heavy on the olive oil but nevertheless tasty. It comes topped with pesto sauce and full slices of ripe tomatoes—a nice twist on the usual

chopped tomato style. Fusilli tri-color pasta salad, made with red onion, parmesan cheese, basil, and lots of garlic, is meant to be an appetizer. But it's really almost big enough to be a meal, at just $2.95. The veggie sandwich is packed with lettuce, cucumbers, tomato, sprouts, peppers, mushrooms—with homemade mayo—all on French bread for $4.50.

There are also hot entrees, like wonderful pot roast ($7.00), cooked with wine, celery and carrots, plus potato and vegetables on the side. Desserts usually come from the nearby Swedish Bakery around the corner. Speaking of pastries, Dellwood is open for breakfast, too; choices include the "Bowl o' Granola" for $1.50. Now, *that's* comfort food.

Don's Coffee Club
• 1439 W. Jarvis Ave., Chicago; (312) 274-1228

Carmen Miranda sings "Chattanooga Choo Choo" as you stroll in. A huge painted backdrop of a Hawaiian sunset fills the rear wall. The high-ceilinged, wide-open storefront cafe consists of tables and chairs which have come from local thrift shops, and so each set is from a completely different era. Don's itself, which just opened last summer, seems to be from some bygone era too. You almost expect Bogey to saunter by and ask you for a light.

That's what Don's is for, really—sitting back over a cuppa coffee and cigarettes to while away a few hours. In fact, when you order your brew, Don asks, "Cream?...Ashtray?" It's all part of the mood. Sit back, read, discuss matters trivial or important. Get up and thumb through the stacks of old LPs and 78s lining the walls by Billie Holliday, Dinah Shore, Tony Martin, Danny Kaye, Edith Piaf, Woody Herman, and This Thundering Herd. Ask Don to throw it on the vintage 1950's hi-fi.

The food menu is as quirky as everything else; the chalkboard on the wall lists a number of desserts, which is basically all that's offered here. The choices are whatever Don's

MR. CHEAP'S PICKS
Far North—Uptown

✔ **Mekong**—One of the best of Argyle Street's many Vietnamese restaurants—with super-cheap lunch buffets.

✔ **Nhu Hoa Cafe**—For something delightfully different on Argyle, try this Vietnamese/Laotian restaurant.

---

gotten in from local bakeries: New York cheesecake, German chocolate cake, hot strawberry rhubarb. Now, be prepared to forget about your diet. These come on a full-size plate—a gigantic slab of dessert, topped with about a pint of ice cream. Whatever you get, it costs $3.00 ($2.25 without the ice cream). Good luck finishing.

At the bottom of the board, you may see things like: "Peanut butter and jelly sandwich, $1.00. Oreo cookies, 25¢ each." Somehow, it all works. The coffee, meanwhile, is a strong brew which Don calls "Casablanca Roast." It's served in an elegant china cup for $1.50. The board says nothing about refills, but Don keeps coming around with a thermos jug anyway.

As you can see, there aren't too many rules here. The place runs the way Don wants to run it. That includes his hours, officially 3:00 in the afternoon until 1:00 in the morning every day; "But I'll stay open later, if people want to stay," says Don. "We've been here until two or three on the weekends." No surprise. This place is tailor-made for hanging out.

The neighborhood, next to the Jarvis "el," looks questionable—but it's quiet. Don has a patio out front, during the warm months. He even hosted a 1940's swing dance recently, as part of a block party. Local artists are finding Don's, too, like the pair of actors who asked if they could perform A.R. Gurney's romantic comedy Love Letters at the cafe. Suddenly, "Late Night Dessert Theater" was born, all free of charge. If you don't live in the vicinity of Rogers Park, but you dig the cafe scene, it's worth the trip to join the soiree at Don's Coffee Club.

El Taco Loco
- 5258 N. Lincoln Ave., Chicago; (312) 275-9892
- 645 S. Wabash Ave., Chicago; (312) 922-4125
- 1726 W. Lawrence Ave., Chicago; (312) 784-1881

El Taco Loco is a good quality, full-menu Mexican restaurant with south-of-the-border prices. Two people can easily stuff themselves here for less than $10, total; think of it as real Mexican food at Taco Bell prices.

Open for breakfast, lunch, and dinner, the day starts off with the traditional huevos rancheros (two fried eggs in a mild ranchero sauce) or chilaquiles (scrambled eggs). Each plate, which comes with rice and beans, is priced at $3.75.

Moving on to lunch, you *could* have American-style sandwiches filled with pork, steak, chicken, or ground beef for $2.95, with beans, lettuce, tomatoes, sour cream, and guacamole on the side. The truly non-adventurous can also bail out with a hamburger for $1.95. But why come here and not go Mexican? Mr. C liked the burrito grande, made with a choice of chicken, beef, pork, or beans. It'll fill you up for a mere $2.45. Add a generous side of fried rice—not too spicy, not too wimpy—for another $1.25. Sauces here really aren't too hot, unless you request them to be so.

Three big enchiladas go for $5.00, and tacos (soft or crispy) are only $1.25 a pop, $2.45 for the "grande" size. The chicken fajita dinner, served with plenty of lettuce, rice, beans, and tortillas to roll it all up, is one of the most expensive items on the menu, ringing in at just $7.95. Various combination plates are also offered. Wash it all down with sweet rice water, a Mexican favorite, for $1.

El Taco Loco offers little in the way of atmosphere (the south Loop Loco seems a bit out of place, right across the street from the Hilton). There is a tiny counter and a couple of booths—no frills. The restaurant also keeps costs down by offering everything a la carte, and by charging extra for condiments like jalapeños, hot sauce, and extra tortillas. You're only going to pay for what you want.

Gotta love the hours: Lincoln Avenue is open Sunday-Thursday from 11 a.m. to 5 a.m., Fridays and Saturdays from 10 a.m. to 6 a.m. The South Loop location runs from 7 a.m. until 3 a.m. daily, while the Lawrence spot is open daily 24 hours. Both the Lawrence and Lincoln Avenue spots offer free parking.

El Tipico

- 1836 W. Foster Ave., Chicago; (312) 878-0839
- 3341 Dempster St., Skokie; (708) 676-4070

Rather a lackluster name for a very comfortable and delicious restaurant. Friends of Mr. C's brought him to this spot, well off the beaten track in a quiet, residential corner of Ravenswood. The neighborhood may look almost suburban, but inside El Tipico, the decor looks authentically Mexican—with several dark and cozy *taverna*-style rooms off a winding hallway. One of these is a bar and cafe area; the other dining rooms maintain an intimate feeling.

The food here is a bit more than your typical Mexican chow, offering a few interesting twists on the same old fare. The fun starts right in with the appetizers; sure, you could begin with some good guacamole and chips (a good-sized plate, $3.50); but Mr. C's pals insisted upon the "queso fondue" ($3.75), a cast-iron skillet which arrives bubbling with tangy cheese and slices of mildly spicy sausage. Scoop some of this mixture onto one of the tortillas provided, roll it up, and enjoy. It's a tummy-warming start to the meal.

The large menu presents about fifty entree choices, with similarly intriguing variations turning up among the standard dishes. Steak Milanesa, for example, is seasoned, breaded, and then pan-fried; at $9.95 it's one of the few more expensive entrees, but it comes with home fries, sliced onions and tomatoes, rice, and beans. Just about all of the dinners, in fact, are served with rice and beans; among the many other options are five different enchilada plates (each $6.95), filled with beef, chicken, or sausage, and topped with a cheese sauce, or a tomato sauce, or a mole (unsweet chocolate) sauce....

Or, go for arroz con pollo ($6.95), chicken and rice colorfully decorated with green peas and red peppers; "El Tipico burrito verde" ($5.95), a huge tortilla filled with beef or chicken with cheese, avocado, tomato, and lettuce; a three taco plate, for $5.95; or the unusual shrimp fajitas, which tops the menu at $10.95. Several of these dinners frequently turn up as daily specials, priced a dollar or so lower than on the regular menu. If you have room after these generous portions, the flan ($2.75) arrives flaming; the nifty, but only occasionally seen "fried ice cream" ($2.50) is another fun dessert.

There is a good beer list, including Tecate and Negra Modelo, decently priced at $2.25 (domestic beers are just $1.75); plus wines, sangria, and cocktails. El Tipico serves dinner until about 1:00 a.m.; they're open for lunch, too.

Golden Waffle Restaurant and Pancake House

- 5600 N. Broadway, Chicago; (312) 271-3445

You have got to like a restaurant where they practically pour your cup of coffee before you have a chance to sit down. That's the modus operandi at Golden Waffle, where your coffee cup (and your wallet) will never run empty. A great place for the kids, they make chocolate chip pancakes the size of Frisbees for $2.95 a stack; and for $3.30, you can get your flapjacks served with strawberries, blueberries, cherries, apples, or peaches.

The "Club Breakfast" is your basic—two eggs prepared any style, home fries, and toast with strawberry preserves, for $2.35. Add a side of raisin toast for 85 cents more.

Mr. C also liked the potato pancakes ($2.95), made with chives and served with sweet-tart applesauce, and the Monte Cristo sandwich ($3.50), grilled ham and swiss on French toast. The colossal half-pound burger is a remarkable $3.25, plus a quarter more for extra cheese. Add a side of potato (French fries, mashed, baked, hash-browns) or the veggie of the day—just a buck.

It's a never-ending menu, continuing on with grilled cheese sandwiches for $1.95, a hot turkey sandwich for $4.45, and a pork chop sandwich for $4.10.

The kiddie menu is great, featuring combinations only a child could love, such as spaghetti with jelly bread for just $1.95—and they're sure to want a milkshake to wash it down (same price). Okay, so some of us kids don't look that small anymore...

HaShalom
- 2905 W. Devon Ave., Chicago; (312)465-5675

For a quick break while bargain hunting on Devon, this may be the ultimate place for cheap Israeli and Moroccan eats. Some folks do forget that, in addition to this street's well-known Indian district, there is a Middle Eastern stretch as well.

The restaurant is decorated with baskets, tapestries, copper pots, pans, and colanders. The crowd consists mainly of families from a variety of ethnic groups, with the occasional businessperson or couple taking a break from checking out the Devon shops.

Mr. C isn't sure just how the lone waitress managed to calmly handle the giant lunchtime crowd, but she did, and super-quickly at that. His falafel arrived less than five minutes after the waitress took the or-

der—a mean feat for both her and the chef. The falafel was not overly spicy, and was full of crispy, toasted sesame seeds—yum. And, at just $1.00 for five pieces, with thina sauce, it's hard to beat. A side order of baba ganoush was spiked with a good dose of paprika and parsley, and came with plenty of pita bread for only $2.25. Other appetizers include "Moroccan Cigars," which are ground beef, pine nuts and hot peppers rolled into filo dough ($2); and matbukha, which is chopped tomatoes cooked with hot peppers and spices ($2).

Entrees are served with soup or salad, rice or potatoes, and pita bread, and they're all priced under $10. Beef or lamb shishkebab dinners are $7.50 each, fish a la tveria (whitefish with thina sauce) is $6.50, and lahme (lamb sauteed with pine nuts and spicy cumin sauce, served with hummus) is also $6.50.

For lighter appetites, HaShalom offers sandwich plates like the lox platter (with two bagels, cream cheese, tomato, onion, pepper, and olives for $5.95, or with one bagel for $3.25) and the falafel sandwich ($2). Sandwich versions of the chicken, lamb, or beef shish kababs are only $4, served with pita, Israeli salad, thina sauce and French fries. There's American-style deli food as well, like kosher salami or corned beef sandwiches (also $4), or a tuna salad sandwich for $3.75. These come with French fries, a side salad, and, of course, a pickle.

Coffee is a mere 55 cents; Mr. C prefers dark, strong Israeli coffee, which is 85 cents. Cafe au lait is the most expensive beverage at $1. With food and drinks so cheap, you can afford to indulge in one of their desserts, like poppy seed cake and baklava (each $1.25), or creme caramel ($1.50). HaShalom is not only a miracle of diplomacy, bringing Arabs and Jews together, but a miracle of economics too.

Heartland Cafe
- 7000 N. Glenwood Ave., Chicago; (312) 465-8005

"It's healthier, but not necessarily *health food*," said one of Mr. C's friends of the earthy-crunchy Heartland Cafe. This Rogers Park establishment, sitting beside the Morse "el" station, has nevertheless been a fixture on the wholesome food scene for over fifteen years. Indeed, it offers plenty of variety for both the true vegetarian and the more average diner who just wants high-quality regular food. All of which is inexpensive enough to make everyone happy.

Oh sure, you'll find your tempeh burgers and your tofu platters here. Have a grilled cheese, avocado, and tomato sandwich, on thick wholegrain bread, for $4.75; and if you prefer soy cheese to cheddar, they've got it for fifty cents more. Turkey burgers ($4.50), of course, are a nice middleground alternative (no pun intended there, really); but the Heartland is not above serving up a good old cheeseburger ($5.95, with grilled onions and French fries)—made with farmraised beef, of course.

For light, simple fare, have a bowl of soup and a garden salad for just $3.25. On Mr. C's visit, the choices included a hearty black bean, with a handful of scallions tossed in and a dollop of sour cream. Salads are made with crispy, fresh vegetables and a pile of alfalfa sprouts on top. For perhaps the ultimate salad experience, the Heartland Supreme assembles avocado, cheese, mushrooms, peppers, tomatoes, red onions, sprouts, sesame and sunflower seeds, and raisins on a bed of greens, all for $6.25.

Entrees change seasonally. Recent specials included such delicious options as chicken fajitas (substitute seitan, if you wish), pan-blackened catfish, both served with rice and beans; or red pepper linguine in garlic-tomato salsa. All of these were $7.95 each, including homemade cornbread. Add soup or salad for a dollar more. And you'll always find things like stir-fried vegetables and

---

MR. CHEAP'S PICKS
Far North—Andersonville

✔ **Ann Sather**—The original Swedish pancake house lives up to its reputation.

✔ **The Dellwood Pickle**—Nouvelle cuisine meets comfort food at this artsy, health-conscious Andersonville spot.

✔ **Kopi Cafe**—This "traveler's cafe" is a hip place for globe-hopping on the cheap.

✔ **Reza's Restaurant**—A Middle Eastern classic, serving elegant food in an elegant setting...all of which should cost far more than it does.

---

brown rice ($6.25, or $7.25 with tofu and curry), or a hefty grilled turkey sandwich ($5.95) made with real hand-carved turkey, sauteed onions and cheese. Plus nachos, vegetarian chili, barbecued chicken wings, and more.

The mix of food is as eclectic as the decor, which looks like a saloon on the inside (there is a full bar, with good bottled beers under $3) and "Toys-R-Us" on the brightly multicolored patio outside. The crowd is just as diverse, ranging from folkies to yuppies. The indoor area also features a shop selling health food products, and a small stage which hosts live music, poetry readings, and even plays in the evenings. Call for a schedule of upcoming events. The full menu is served until 10:00 p.m., with a late-night menu available until 1:00 a.m.

Kopi Cafe
- 5317 N. Clark St., Chicago; (312) 989-KOPI (5674)

Calling itself a "traveler's cafe," Kopi is definitely far-out, especially with its elevated front-window area where you can actually kick off your shoes and sit on pillows while you sip your coffee and try some of their all-vegetarian specialties. Started by a group of twentysomethings who met in Indonesia, Kopi also offers travel books for sale, an art gallery, and a tiny boutique with international styles in bags and jewelry (but be aware that neither section is particularly cheap).

The cafe is a good deal, though, both for its food and the eclectic atmosphere. Where else in Chicago can you find a wall of clocks showing the times in locations like Kyoto and Kathmandu? The tables are hand-painted with funky designs—Mr. C sat at one decorated with quotes from the likes of Georgia O'Keeffe and Ranier Maria Rilke.

For breakfast, Kopi offers dishes like oatmeal with dried fruit ($2.25). Ginseng and other herbal teas will get you going for $1.50. Fresh focaccia bread is $3.75, with a 50 cent additional charge for extra black or green olives, garlic or pepperoncinis. The tempeh burger is a good bet, topped with lettuce and tomato for $4.75. A platter of smooth, thick hummus, served with warmed pita and crudites of crispy fresh celery, cucumber and carrots, is under $5.

On Monday and Thursday evenings from 8-10 p.m., you can enjoy live music free of charge. Mondays may feature world beat (natch), jazz or folk; Thursdays are generally singer-songwriter showcases. The Kopi is open from 7:30 a.m. until 11 p.m. Monday to Thursday, until midnight on Friday and Saturday, and from 9 a.m. to 11 p.m. on Sunday.

Leona's

- 3215 N. Sheffield Ave., Chicago; (312) 327-8861
- 6935 N. Sheridan Ave., Chicago; (312) 764-5757
- 1936 W. Augusta Blvd., Chicago; (312) 292-4300
- 1419 W. Taylor St., Chicago; (312) 850-2222

- 848 W. Madison St., Oak Park; (708) 445-0101.

Family-run (and darn proud of it) since 1950, Leona's has grown into a Chicagoland chain serving almost 50,000 people a week. A Mr. C warning: Not all of the entrees are under $10, but the pizza and the weekday lunch buffet can't be beat for great values in food.

The above-mentioned buffet includes your choice of turkey (a whole bird is out on the table for carving), boneless chicken breast, fried eggplant, meatballs, four kinds of pizza, super-fresh broccoli and zucchini, onion rings, and a slew of pasta and regular salads. Desserts, like cheesecake, brownie-bottom chocolate cake, and a slew of cookies and truffle-like treats are included in the tab. The whole shabang, all you can eat, is a reasonable $8.95. It's served from 11:30 a.m. until 2:00 p.m., weekdays only.

If you're not feeling that Bacchanalian, opt for a sandwich—and this is no short-changing compromise. Mr. C can't put into words just how huge the chicken parmesan sandwich is; it's comparable to a football (in size only). At $4.45, it's a great deal, loaded with marinara and provolone. $1.50 more gets you "broccoli slaw," fresh fruit, or Leona's homemade Italian cookies, plus a side of pasta, fries, pesto veggies, or salad. Tummy-stuffing indeed!

Of course, what would an Italian restaurant (or, in Chicago, any restaurant) be without pizza? Here, they come with a mind-boggling choice of 26 toppings—everything from turkey breast and giardiniera peppers to zucchini and soy cheese. A small thin-crust pie is $6.75; pan is $7.25 and stuffed is $8.50. Homemade pesto shrimp pie is a specialty, starting at $10.95 for the individual size.

Don't forget dessert if you can hack it. *Tiramisu* is $3.25, homemade cannoli are $2.25 each, and a dozen of those famous Italian cookies goes for $2.75.

Leona's has a promotional deal: Visit all five locations (with a tab of

$20 or more), and they'll give you a free dinner for two. Ask for a "Road Rally Challenge" form, to which they will attach a sticker at each place.

Mekong

* 4953 N. Broadway, Chicago; (312) 271-0206

Right on the corner of Broadway and Argyle, this is a good spot for Vietnamese on the cheap. Service is friendly, though it gets progressively lethargic during the course of your meal—but the food is just fine. The Christmas lights strung along the walls have got to go; though the picture of the Eiffel Tower over the bar is a nice try for decor.

Anyway, start off with the Mekong egg rolls with lemon sauce ($3.50) or shrimp rolls in a soybean sauce ($3). The pho tai, a tasty beef-noodle soup, also makes a good starter at $3.50. There are ten other soups, all under $4.

As you might expect, Mekong has lots of options for vegetarians, from sauteed bean sprouts ($3.25) to stir-fried noodles and veggies ($4.50). Carnivorous treats include ginger chicken ($4.75), sizzling platters of chicken, beef, or pork, with vegetables ($7.50), and steamed rice in a wok, with shrimp, squid, chicken, pork, and vegetables for $6.25.

Otherwise, seafood is the specialty of the house. Try the pepper shrimp ($6.25), mixed with pork and cucumber, or catfish soup served in a flaming bowl for $8.95. It's prepared in a tangy, slightly spicy lemon broth—a unique taste, to be sure.

Weekdays from 11 a.m. to 2:30 p.m., there is a lunch buffet featuring things like egg rolls, soup, chicken curry, and pepper steak—all you can eat for $4.95. Not bad!

Mekong carries a full liquor license. But instead of a cocktail on a hot day, try their yummy lemonade, which seems to have a twinge of lime in there too, for 85 cents a glass. Sweet-milk coffee ($1.30) makes a great way to polish off your meal. Oh, and when you pay at the cash register, you'll get a "Fortune Bub-

---

MR. CHEAP'S PICKS
Far North—Rogers Park

✔ **Don's Coffee Club**—Recently opened in Rogers Park, this cafe is like walking into an old movie. Coffee and desserts only.

✔ **Heartland Cafe**—Not strictly lacto-ovo vegetarian, but health-conscious and pleasantly peasant.

✔ **On the Tao**—Get it? Get it? This hip cafe/bar is perfect for conversation, meditation, and live music appreciation.

---

ble." Hey, it's something different, folks. The restaurant is open 7 days a week from 10-10, and until 11 on weekends.

Moti Mahal

* 1031 W. Belmont Ave., Chicago; (312) 348-4393
* 2525 W. Devon Ave., Chicago; (312) 262-2080

Moti Mahal is perhaps the king (or should that be rajah?) of Devon's many Indian restaurants, having spawned a busy Lake View location as well. Both are extremely popular for their daily lunch buffets, in which you can heap your plate with food for only $5.95. The buffet is offered from 11:30 a.m. to 3:30 p.m. every day of the week.

The extremely humble decor, lack of signs identifying each buffet item, and the long, communal dining tables make Moti feel almost like a soup kitchen; unattentive service, marked by a paucity of English, doesn't improve the atmosphere any. Why then, do so many people eat here on an almost-daily basis? Because the food is wonderful, of course—and cheap.

The buffet is really rather small, but offers just enough variety to give you some interesting choices. Appetizers include wonderful nan bread, a slightly spicy vegetable soup, and pakoras, deep-fried patties filled with vegetables. Grab a pile of saffron rice, and top it with things like sag paneer—cooked spinach with cheese (who says all Indian food has to be spicy?), or aloo gobhi, a sort of potato and cauliflower stew. You'll probably find tandoori baked chicken, your basic; but try the chicken tikka masala—an absolutely yummy dish in a creamy tomato sauce that's out of this world.

Sodas, coffees, and teas are not included in the buffet price; and you're welcome to bring your own beer or wine, with no corkage fee. Remember, "BYO" places invariably charge less for their food! The regular menu, by the way, is also very inexpensive. Only the big combination platters, enough for two people to share, top $10—no single item approaches this. The "Moti Mahal Mix," for instance, gives you tandoori chicken, chicken tikka, lamb kebabs, lamb curry, lentil stew, mixed vegetables, nan bread, and rice—all for just $11.95. The menu is available during buffet hours, too. Forget about ambiance....go for the food.

Near the uptown Moti Mahal, Mr. C also recommends **Viceroy of India** at 2516 W. Devon Avenue, telephone (312) 743-4100; and the spiffy new **Eastern Garden Restaurant** at 2340 W. Devon Avenue, telephone (312) 338-8550, both of which are larger and more elegantly appointed than Moti Mahal. Viceroy separates itself into two sides—one a quick-service and carry-out operation, the other a more formal restaurant. And Eastern Garden is quite fancy-looking indeed, all done out in jade green decor and muted lighting. Yet, both of these places offer $5.95 lunch buffets similar to those of Moti Mahal.

Nhu Hoa Cafe

- 1020 W. Argyle St., Chicago; (312) 878-0618

Among the zillions of Vietnamese restaurants on Argyle Street, Nhu Hoa offers something a little bit different: Laotian cuisine. If you've never tried this variation of Asian cooking, you're in for a real treat. Laotian flavorings are subtly different from those of their close neighbors, Thai and Vietnamese cooking—and very tasty indeed.

This particular restaurant can get a bit expensive, compared to the other places on the block, especially of course for seafood dishes. But then, the surroundings are correspondingly more upscale—from the pair of lions which greet you outside the door to the giant Buddha statue who welcomes you once inside.

Meanwhile, much of the vast menu is well within Mr. C's price range. Most of the main dishes range from $6.95 to $8.95, and portions are certainly ample. Start off with a bowl of *keng som kay*, perhaps the tangiest and tastiest soup Mr. C has ever had. Who knows what they put in the broth, along with chicken, vegetables, and lemon grass; but the flavors, without being spicy, quite literally dance on your tongue. $5.95 gets you an individual bowl big enough to be a meal by itself, although there are three larger sizes (!) for couples and groups to share.

For other authentic Laotian fare, try an order of Laos noodles ($6.95)—rice noodles with shrimp, chicken, eggs, and bean sprouts mixed in, plus ground peanuts and chilies over the top. For those with stronger tastes, there are three varieties of curry: Panang, which is the true style sauce, made with straw mushrooms and chili paste, as well as the more recognizable red and green curries. Whichever you choose, you can apply it to beef, chicken, or barbecued pork for just $5.95; to shrimp, mussels, or squid for $8.95.

There are lots of other items to choose from, including salads and vegetarian dishes. And yet, this is only about one-third of the menu, which covers the full spectrum of Vietnamese cooking as well—over 150 different examples of it, in fact. These options are a bit less expensive than the Laotian items, as Viet meals consist largely of soups, stews, and rice dishes—but they're no less filling and tasty.

A popular starter is the *chim cut quay* appetizer ($6.95)—four tiny, whole quail roasted to a crispy brown, with enough for two people to share. *Gui cuon* ($2.75) are shrimp rolls also filled with diced pork and vegetables. There are over a dozen steamed rice main dishes, all $5.95, mixing in such ingredients as grilled beef, shrimp, and pork in oyster sauce, or sauteed lobster meat. And *nem nuong*, $6.95, is one of several traditional meals similar to Chinese *moo shi*, in that you roll up your food in a thin rice-paper pancake. This particular choice consists of grilled beef meatballs, along with the standard veggies, bean sprouts, rice noodles, and fish sauce.

The list goes on and on. Add a Singha or Tsing Tao beer to your meal for $2.25, or house wine at $2.50 a glass. When you're done, try the wonderfully sweet, thick coffees made with condensed milk; or a fruit milk shake, made with pineapple, avocado, guanabana, and the like.

Nhu Hoa also offers lunchtime specials, including such dishes as lemon grass chicken and Vietnamese beef stew, for just $3.95 each; these are available Tuesdays through Fridays from 11:30 to 3:00. The restaurant is closed on Mondays.

On the Tao
- 1218 W. Morse Ave., Chicago; (312) 743-5955

Besides being a great pun, something Mr. C can't resist, this cozy Rogers Park restaurant/bar/cafe is a great hangout. Without being fancy, it manages to have the feel of a sophisticated private club. The front room is dominated by a long, curving bar; but near it you'll also find tables meant as much for sitting and reading as anything else. While away an early or late hour, while sitting over one of the many domestic and imported beers available, most of which are just $2-$2.50; or an espresso ($1 single, $1.50 double).

MR. CHEAP'S PICKS
Far North—Devon Avenue

✔ **HaShalom**—Flash! Arabs and Israelis make cheap culinary peace on Devon.

✔ **Moti Mahal**—The original outpost of this popular Indian kitchen is famous for its cheap, hearty lunch buffet—and deservedly so.

The next room is the larger, main dining and entertainment room, lined with couches and floor lamps in addition to the usual tables. Art works adorn the walls, and there's a small stage in one corner. Here, informal live music takes place several nights a week. There's jazz on Wednesdays and Sundays, with no cover charge; a singer's showcase on Thursdays, with a $1 admission; and rock takes over on Fridays and Saturdays, usually with a $4 or $5 cover.

The menu is simple, health-oriented, and almost entirely vegetarian. It includes breakfast (from 7:30 a.m. Tuesdays through Saturdays, 8:30 on Sundays), like eggs espresso with cheese ($2.50), cold cereal with fresh fruit, or granola with yogurt (each $2).

Later into the day or evening, we're basically talking sandwiches here, made on freshly baked bread. Have a grilled eggplant and mozzarella cheese sandwich for $3.50, or grilled chicken breast (the one nonveg item) with honey-Dijon sauce for $4. Rounding out a very quick world tour are snack plates like baba ghanoush and black bean quesadillas (each $3).

In addition to the basic house coffee (just 75 cents a cup, with a refill; or go bottomless for $1.25), there is a full coffeehouse menu. Cafe au lait, caffe latte, hot and cold, they're all here. Plus all kinds of regular and herbal teas, and fresh-squeezed fruit (and vegetable) juices.

You can spend your night On the Tao until 2:00 a.m., Tuesdays through Saturdays; and until 10:00 p.m. on Sundays. Closed Mondays.

Reza's Restaurant

- 5255 N. Clark St., Chicago; (312) 561-1898
- 432 W. Ontario St., Chicago; (312) 664-4500

This longtime Middle Eastern favorite in Andersonville serves up incredibly large portions of Persian specialties at surprisingly low prices. Many folks call it one of the best deals in town—though some instead swear by Andy's Restaurant right next door (see listing above). Either way, says Mr. C, you can't go wrong.

Reza's is a handsome and spacious dining room, done up in natural wood with brass trim and potted plants everywhere. The front opens up onto Clark Street for refreshing summer breezes. Reza's new location in River North is even larger and flashier, with outdoor tables for al fresco dining on a quiet stretch of Ontario Street. The new spot doubles as a brewery, dominated by huge copper vats behind the bar.

Both locations feature the same menu. Start off with one of two dozen appetizers, many of which are vegetarian—and nearly all of which are around $3 each. Falafel, of course, is a must; but try the vegetable casserole ($3.50), a blend of zucchini, eggplant, carrots, green

peppers, and scallions baked in a tomato sauce and served over rice. Mmmmmm.

Entrees divide mainly into two types: Stews and skewers. Both, again, come in gigantic proportions. Mr. C opted for what is simply called "The Combo" ($7.95): One skewer of char-broiled filet mignon and one skewer of marinated grilled chicken, separated by a mountain of dill flavored rice. Each skewer was big enough to be an entree in itself—a footlong strip of meat, juicy and delicious. And none of your "beef, tomato, pepper, onion, beef..." skewer; each one was all meat, and the vegetables came in a third strip on the side. It was all too much to finish, and tasted just as good the next day.

Mr. C's dining companion chose a bowl of "khoresht ghormeh sabzi" ($5.95—and don't worry, you can order any item by number). This is a savory soup of ground beef, kidney beans, chopped onions, and greens, all spiked with tangy lemon juice and other spices. The vast bowl was accompanied by another mound of rice (white, this time); and if you think this can't be enough by itself, think again. Scrumptious and filling.

There are plenty of seafood and vegetarian dishes on the large menu; with the exception of some seafood orders, almost every entree is priced under $10. And if you have room for dessert, try a strong cup of coffee and a piece of the homemade baklava (only 95¢) or zoulbia (75¢), a deep-fried pastry made without sugar.

LINCOLN PARK AREA
(including Lake View, Park West, Wrightwood)

Ann Sather

- 929 W. Belmont Ave., Chicago; (312) 348-2378
- 5207 N. Clark St., Chicago; (312) 271-6677

- 1329 E. 57th St., Chicago; (312) 947-9323

For true-blue Swedish dining, a significant part of Chicago's heritage, this famous restaurant has it all. The original Ann Sather in Lake View was formerly a funeral home, but you can't tell now with the way that they have it decorated. Well, the chairs and tables *are* black, but the restaurant is warmed up by a crystal chandelier, stained glass windows and red and gold trim.

The food will warm you up, too, with goodies like three-egg omelettes for $4.75, whether filled with peaches, cheddar cheese, broccoli, ham, or several other choices. Or, try one with crab, spinach, and sour cream for $6.25. And if you're watching your cholesterol, you can have any omelette made with just egg whites. Other breakfast "musts" at Ann Sather are their heavenly homemade cinnamon rolls (two for $1.50), and Swedish limpa rye bread, made tangy with anise seeds ($1).

Breakfast is served all day, while both the lunch and dinner menus start at 11 a.m. (who could eat dinner at that hour?) On the lunch menu, three Swedish pancakes are $4.25 (ice cream and strawberries are extra), grilled cheese and tomato sandwiches are $3.95, the veggie burger is $4.95 (both sandwiches served with cole slaw), and the Caesar chicken tortellini salad is $6.95. Add a cup of homemade soup to any salad or sandwich order for just $1 extra.

For big appetites, Ann Sather offers a long list of dinners under $10, complete with appetizer, two side dishes, dessert and beverage. They're also available as "lite" meals, in smaller portions with just the side dishes and drink. The roast duck dinner is $9.50 ($7.50 in the lite version); chicken croquettes are $8.50 ($6.50 lite); and baked meat loaf is $8.95 ($6.95 lite).

Several beers are available; though, for a true Scandinavian experience, you may want to try the potent Swedish glogg ($3.50)—a mixture of spiced sherry, red wine and brandy, with almonds and raisins, served warm. For those not wishing to be knocked out, one dollar gets you a bottomless cup of coffee, or Darjeeling tea.

By the way, you can take home a dozen of those famous cinnamon rolls or muffins for $6, or a loaf of their limpa bread for $3.75.

The Lake View restaurant is open from 7 a.m. until 11 p.m. Thursday through Sunday, and until midnight on Friday and Saturday. The Andersonville branch is open daily from 7 a.m until 10 p.m.; while the Hyde Park location, near the University of Chicago campus, is open from 7 a.m. only until 3 p.m. daily.

Batteries Not Included

- 2201 N. Clybourn Ave., Chicago; (312) 472-9920

Tucked inside a small wooden storefront, like a tiny island hideaway, this restaurant becomes a tropical paradise the moment you step through the door. Turquoise walls splashed with contrasting bright colors, indoor trees, and a long, inviting bar in the front room all combine to create that island charm—the sort Jimmy Buffet is always writing songs about. Sip a margarita or some rum punch over elegantly prepared food that is surprisingly affordable, given its French and Caribbean flair.

In fact, the pricing couldn't be simpler. Lunch entrees are all $5.95 each, served with bread and a side dish of pasta or red beans and rice. Choices include rainbow trout, stuffed with spinach, scallops and shrimp; grilled skirt steak with cilantro; Lamby, or conch meat, sauteed with a jalapeño-pimento sauce; a plate of sauteed vegetables with a tomato-cilantro sauce; about a dozen in all. Add a salad for $1.50; or one of several appetizers, each $5, like steamed mussels or seafood gumbo.

Dinner offers an expanded version of the same menu, with even more seafood options, including shrimp and calamari provencal (sauteed in white wine and garlic); chicken and shrimp piqué, spiced with jalapeño and cayenne peppers; cornish hen stuffed with spinach in a red wine sauce; and many others. Again, all dinners are price-fixed at $9.95, which includes both bread and salad, plus the rice/pasta sides. Desserts, $3.00, change daily. During Mr. C's visit, the topper was fresh strawberries in a Grand Marnier sauce.

For the money, Batteries Not Included is a most unusual place indeed. It's hip and trendy, but with a careful attention to detail. They also have a private party room, as well as a catering service. The restaurant serves lunch from noon to 5:00, Wednesday through Sunday only; dinner is served from 5:00 to 11:00 p.m. Tuesday through Saturday, and from 5-9 on Sunday. They're closed all day Monday—perhaps to recharge their batteries.

Located across Clybourn from the Webster Place shopping center with its multiplex movie theaters, BNI offers another deal: A special dinner/movie "Passport" combination. Just $15 per person gets you dinner and a Loews movie ticket, with some restrictions. Call the restaurant for more info.

Beat Kitchen
- 2100 W. Belmont Ave., Chicago; (312) 281-4444

Perhaps best known for the variety of great live music presented on its stage (see listing under "Entertainment: Folk"), Beat Kitchen has an equally eclectic and delicious menu. The name tells you—this is a place for good music and good food. And that goes for light snacks or hearty appetites.

The menu starts off, as so many in Chicago do, with pizzas. Nice-sized individual pies are $5.95 each, in several busy combinations—mozzarella, mushroom, garlic, onion, black olive, and tomato, for just one example. Ask about the pizza of the day, too; just a dollar more, these may consist of such unique varieties as smoked bacon and spinach, "Spring veggie," or even "Thai Pizza," topped with pieces of sesame chicken in a peanut plum sauce. This is pizza? Yum!

Chomp on hefty sandwiches like grilled bratwurst, boiled in beer ($3.95), blackened chicken breast ($4.95), or a good ol' cheddar cheeseburger ($4.95). All come with grilled potatoes on the side. There's an interesting choice of homemade soups, from gazpacho ($3.50) to chicken gumbo ($3.95), and salads too, making a meal out of any sandwich.

The long, cozy bar features a good selection of domestic and imported beers, both bottled and on tap. Beat Kitchen is open every day but Sunday, with live music every night; they serve lunches and dinners, with food available until 1:00 a.m.

Boston Chicken Rotisserie
- 2201 N. Halsted St., Chicago; (312) 549-5100
- 2619 N. Clark St., Chicago; (312) 404-5505

Hey, are these guys lost, or what? Nah. Boston Chicken began as a small, local eatery in none other than Mr. C's own home of Beantown, quickly expanding into a national chain. In Boston, you practically see one on every corner nowadays—in many instances, right next to another Pizzeria Uno. See, anybody can do it.

Anyway, BC is definitely *not* your typical fast food joint, mass-producing meals laden with chemicals. You can see the whole rotisserie chickens turning golden brown in glass ovens. The side dishes are just as fresh and hot, including real mashed potatoes, butternut squash (Mr. C's favorite), long-grain rice, and, of course, good ol' Boston baked beans.

Get a half-chicken with any two side dishes, plus corn bread, all for $6.49—probably as close to a hearty, home-cooked meal as you ever will find at a chain restaurant. A quarter-chicken, with the two sides and bread, is $5.49 with light meat and $4.49 with dark. You can even get a whole bird for $7.49, or $9.99 with mashed potatoes and corn bread.

There are a few other options, such as an individual chicken pot pie, a hot sliced chicken breast sandwich, or even a "Side Item Sampler" with any three side dishes (each $4.29). For the most part, though, it's a simple menu; make your choices and dig in.

The Bread Shop
- 3400 N. Halsted St., Chicago; (312)528-8108

A true vegetarian heaven in the heart of Lake View since 1971, the famous Bread Shop can stock you up with goodies without breaking the bank. An attached deli, grocery, and juice bar-cafe make for one-stop shopping. They cater, too, and stay open every day of the year.

Some of the pluses of the Bread Shop are that they recycle practically everything, and use eggs obtained from free-range, antibiotic-free chickens. They don't use refined sweeteners or white flour, both of which are processed using ground bones, believe it or not. Their chocolate is sweetened with barley malt instead of sugar, and is just as tasty as any. Most of the grains in the recipes are organic, and the folks who do the cooking will be happy to adapt their recipes to specifically fit any diet, for those allergic or sensitive to different foods.

Mr. C enjoyed a hearty serving of Chinese noodle pasta salad, which cost just under $3. It included broccoli florets, julienned peppers and carrots and sesame seeds, all with a tamari-ginger-garlic-onion dressing. Quite delicious. Some of the other carry-out items include baba ghanoush for $5 a pound, deviled tofu for $6, falafel for 30 cents each, and truffles for $1.25 (available in almond, cherry, mint, mocha, raspberry, or rum flavors).

Of course, the main attraction here is the bread, in varieties from caraway rye and onion dill to such exotic creations as baked potato and pesto loaves. The deli and bakery is open Monday through Saturday from 8 a.m. until 10 p.m.; and on Sundays from 9 a.m. until 9 p.m.

Brother Jimmy's BBQ
- 2909 N. Sheffield Ave., Chicago; (312) 528-0888

What a hopping place this is! When they're not raising the roof with live music, they're lowering the price on their great barbecued chow. Outside,

---

MR. CHEAP'S PICKS
Lincoln Park

✔ **Cool Beans**—Great coffee, yes, but also a sort of "veggie bar" for sandwich-making. Home-baked breads, too.

✔ **Red Lion Pub**—A bit of old Blighty in Lincoln Park, with authentic beers and British food.

✔ **Siam Delight**—A tiny but proud standout among Thai restaurants.

---

all you see is a simple doorway. Inside, this is a huge, high-ceilinged version of a North Carolina roadhouse, right down to the "Duke" paraphernalia on the walls. There's a long bar area, lots of dining tables and booths, and a stage which features free, live music every Thursday, Friday, and Saturday night.

The food consists mainly of burgers, barbecued chicken, and ribs, and variations thereof, and you get tons of food for your dough. Three flavors of ribs (spicy, sweet, and dry-rub) come in platters with two side dishes and corn bread, all for $12.95. That's a bit above Mr. C's usual $10 limit, but you sure won't go away hungry. All styles of meat are smoked over hickory wood. And there are a dozen of those down-home sides, like mashed potatoes, candied yams, collard greens, and baked beans.

Get a plate of chicken and ribs for $11.95, a chopped pork dinner for $9.95, and chopped brisket for the same price. For smaller appetites and/or wallets, there are sandwich versions of the same in the $6-$7 range, including one side dish. Plus chili, soups, salads, and Tex-Mex appetizers.

Mr. C has got to tell you, though, about the special deals here for you pig-out fans. On Tuesdays,

$11.95 per person gets you all the BBQ chicken you can eat, *and* all the draft beer you can drink (as long as you're still eating, that is). On Sundays, it's the same deal for ribs at $15.95. Wow.

The kitchen serves food until 11:00 p.m. on weekdays, and until 1:00 a.m. on weekends, while the club stays open for an hour or two more.

bw-3

- 2464 N. Lincoln Ave., Chicago; (312) 868-WILD (9453)

That's not a printing error, folks—the name of this place is "bw-3." It's short for "Buffalo Wild Wings and Weck"—but what the heck is a weck? Either way, it's a wacky name for this casual, comfortable Lincoln Park saloon. In fact, it's the sole Chicago outpost of a growing midwestern franchise; still, it looks individualized enough, with its large bar room and larger dining room all done out in a rustic natural wood decor.

bw-3 has the feel of a college hangout, and it attracts a youngish crowd. They are no doubt attracted by the large quantities of low-priced bar food: Buffalo wings (of course), hamburgers, nachos and several other unique items. Though these are all real, cooked to order foods, they have prices like a fast-food joint. Wings, for example, come in multiples of six—a half-dozen is $2.19, a dozen is $3.99, and so on. They come glazed in one of eight different sauces, from "Wild" (and look out, ye of faint heart, it really is) to "Mild," as well as curry, sweet BBQ and teriyaki.

Charcoal-grilled "Weckburgers" come in quarter-pound and half-pound varieties. The menu says they are "possibly the best burger in America"; Mr. C says, well, anything is possible. They're not bad, though, and you can't beat the price for real beef: $2.24 and $3.24 for the basic versions, going up to only $2.99/$3.99 for fancier sorts like the pizza Weckburger and the Mex Weckburger. Sides are extra, but worth it;

the French fries are thick slices of deep-fried potatoes, from 99¢ for a regular order, and $1.19 for "Cajun style." Go for 'em.

Chicken breast sandwiches are a good bet, from $3.39-$4.14 depending on extras like cheese, bacon or mushrooms. bw-3 also offers complete grilled chicken dinners for $7.99, half a chicken served with fries, slaw, corn, and a roll. Then we get to the Mexican side, with homemade chili ($2.79), chicken fajitas ($4.99), and taco salads ($3.29). Can one restaurant excel in so many different areas? Not exactly. Most of the items Mr. C and his party sampled were good, but not superior. "Pizza pockets," in particular, were a bit of a mystery—deep-fried dough filled with cheese and pepperoni. They were rather greasy, heavy and not as interesting as they sounded.

For the most part, though, you can do just fine, especially if you're looking for a friendly place to pig out. There are plenty of good beers on tap and in bottles; the place is open nice and late, from lunchtime until 2:00 or 3:00 in the morning. And they present live rock bands on Thursday, Friday, and Saturday nights for a cover charge of just $1.00.

Campeche Restaurant

- 3606 N. Clark St., Chicago; (312) 327-1448
- 7124 N. Clark St., Chicago; (312) 761-8378

While this Mexican chain doesn't necessarily pack folks in, it does do a steady business from Wrigleyville residents, Cubs fans, and Chicago Transit Authority employees. The decor could stand some improvement, especially with the hanging foil curliques around the taco bar and an annoying electronic message board advertising their Sunday brunch. But the food isn't half bad, and Campeche is open late to accommodate nocturnal folks.

Their popular all-you-can-eat taco bar costs $4.50, giving you a choice of chicken or beef fillings and a slew of toppings. A dinner buffet, also an all-you-can-eat deal, is $7.99. Those with smaller appetites can choose from among the many burrito choices (plenty big themselves), ranging in price from $2.25 for the chicken, pork, and beef to $3.75 for the steak burrito. Enchiladas and tacos are also available a la carte, starting at just 99 cents.

Larger meals include fajitas ($7.50); combination plates are also good values. The vegetarian combo includes a bean tostada, guacamole taco, and cheese quesadilla, all for $6.25. If none of these fill you up, you can stuff yourself on the tortilla chips and salsa which come with most dishes.

Wash down all this spicy food with a good selection of Mexican beers, including Corona, Bohemia, Dos Equis, and Carta Blanca, each $2.50. Fruit juices, like pineapple, papaya, orange, and grape, are served in ridiculously tall glasses for just $1.25.

Campeche makes its own desserts. Flan topped with Rompope liqueur is the standout at just $1.60, and "Campechitas" (flour tortillas stuffed with fruit and topped with caramel) are $1.50.

While both branches open at 10 a.m., the Wrigleyville location (right across the street from the ballpark) stays open until 5 a.m.

Cafe Voltaire
● 3231 N. Clark St., Chicago; (312) 528-3136

Tristan Tzara was a Hungarian poet who, during World War I, helped invent "dada"—a kind of surrealist art. He also ran a cabaret in Zurich, in which he and his cohorts gave the performances that defined their art (Tzara created poems by cutting up a Shakespeare sonnet, dropping the words into a hat, and pulling out one word at a time). It is from this heritage that the Cafe Voltaire takes its name and inspiration.

Check the Voltaire entry in this book's entertainment section for more details on the performances which help to define Chicago's art; right now, let's talk about the restaurant. In a way, it's hard to separate the two—the walls are lined with giant murals and other works by local artists, and even the tables are painted with lively designs, each one unique. As you might guess, the menu here is vegetarian, and most of the items are homemade. Start off with a cup of carrot-lentil soup, $2.50, made with organic ingredients; or, vegetarian chili for $2.75, topped with mozzarella or soy cheese (for the real purists) for another fifty cents.

Move on to mega-salads for $5.95 each, like the Voltaire: Romaine lettuce, tomatoes, mushrooms, carrots, onions, peppers, sunflower seeds, raisins, and alfalfa sprouts. Whew! Sandwiches, mostly the same price, include vegetarian sloppy Joes, burgers, and clubs. Hot entrees range from sesame noodles topped with cashews ($5.95) to black bean burritos filled with beans, corn, guacamole, and salsa ($7.95). Spinach lasagna ($7.95) comes with homemade garlic bread, topped with tomato and pesto. That's something even a non-vegetarian can order!

Save room—or, come in only for—the desserts. They may be a bit pricey, but they're worth it. Your waitperson (just call me Mr. PC) will, upon request, bring out a tray loaded with half a dozen tempting treats, like cappuccino cheesecake, banana truffle cake and chocolate mud pie. They're all $3.75 each, and fantastic. Or, for the same price, you can opt for a fresh fruit frappe (say that three times fast), made with no sugar or milk—just your choice of fruits (but why, with all that chocolate stuff around? Ah, never mind).

The above-mentioned wait staff is comprised of bright, personable folks who aren't above having a bit of fun with the customers. Cafe Voltaire is just a fun place to be, and you can be there until 1:00 a.m. on weeknights and 3:00 a.m. on weekends. The kitchen closes up half an hour earlier.

MR. CHEAP'S PICKS
Lincoln Park—Clybourn
and vicinity

✔ **Batteries Not Included**—The classy, Caribbean food in this tropical setting won't leave you worrying about your traveler's checks.

✔ **Beat Kitchen**—The beat goes on here for creative bar food (Thai pizza? Yes!) and live music.

✔ **El Presidente**—True Mexican food, 24 hours a day—a place even our own presidente would love.

The Chicago Diner
● 3411 N. Halsted St., Chicago; (312) 935-6696

Don't look for your average greasy burger and fries at *this* diner. While trying to shrug off Chicago's reputation as "hog butcher to the world," this twenty-year-old vegetarian restaurant in Lake View has developed a fine reputation in its own right. Not only is it a hangout for the health-conscious, but a super cheap eats haven as well. The owners are world travelers, which is reflected in the cosmopolitan nature of the menu. This sensibility extends to the cozy wooden booths and tiny tables with romantic pastel floral tablecloths, which lend a romantic air to the place.

Try the "Future Burger," which is made from basmati rice, couscous, and vegetables, garnished with lettuce, tomato, sprouts, carrots, onion, and pickles all on a whole wheat bun for $4.95. Add a cup of miso soup for $1.50 more, or a side order of tempeh strips for $1.95.

Instead, perhaps you'll opt for the macrobiotic plate: Vegetable, bean and grain of the day, plus kale, rice, sea vegetable, pickle, and a choice of tofu or tempeh with miso sauce or gravy for $7.25. It's as much of a mouthful to eat as it is to describe!

Soup of the day or a tossed salad can be added to any entree for just $1 extra; and most dishes are served with a choice of bread—homemade cornbread, whole wheat pita, seven-grain toast, sprouted English muffin, or walnut-raisin bagel.

Lacto-ovo vegetarians and other hard-core "vegans" can eat here without concern—any dish with dairy cheese can be made with soy cheese as a substitute. Now, if you're *not* a vegetarian, all of this probably sounds like a foreign language to you (there's that adventurer notion again). This includes Mr. C himself, who, in his never-ending quest for bargains, is willing to try almost anything...once. Especially if it's cheap *and* healthy, two qualities which rarely go hand-in-hand. Anyway, don't worry about the unfamiliar items on the menu; a handy glossary is provided, and many of these things taste better than you may think.

Despite the restaurant's relatively late opening time, it does serve breakfast, including tofu scrambles, granola, and French toast. Saturday and Sunday breakfasts offer additional choices like "Ex-Benedict" ($5.95), grilled tempeh patties on an English muffin, topped with poached eggs and cheese sauce, and served with home fries.

Beverages include herbal teas, carrot, beet, celery, apple or orange juices, soy milk, organic wine, and ciders. The diner has a children's menu, too.

No smoking is allowed in the restaurant at any time. The Chicago Diner is open at 11 a.m. weekdays, closing at 9:30 p.m. Monday through Thursday, and 10 p.m. on Friday. On weekends, it's open from 10-10. Hmm...is there some hitherto unseen connection between vegetarians and late risers?

Chili Mac's 5-Way Chili
- 851 W. Armitage Ave., Chicago; (312) 525-3232
- 3152 N. Broadway, Chicago; (312) 404-2898

Here's another new national chain offering decent food in a clean, bright setting—food that will really fill you up for just a few bucks. Chili Mac's claims to make a "healthier" chili that will also go easier on your stomach than most, thanks to their use of fresh ingredients and the fact that they drain all the fat from their beef as it cooks. Certainly couldn't hurt.

These restaurants are spotless in their white tile decor and red trim, with a counter where you place your order and lots of small tables for casual dining or a quick bite on the go. Meanwhile, Mr. C loves any place serving real food with a menu that never tops $5.95.

This chili comes in three varieties: A mild "Cincinnati," sweetened with cinnamon; the hotter "Texas Jailhouse," which tosses in jalapeños; and "Spicy Vegetarian," perhaps the first chili to be made with tofu (was this crying out to be invented?). Any one of these starts as low as $2.25, for a simple "Solo" bowl of chili. That's "1-Way." Throw it on top of spaghetti for $3, and that's "2-Way." Top it with cheddar cheese ($3.50), for "3-Way"; add kidney beans or onions ($3.75) for #4, and have 'em all ($3.95) for #5. Any "Way" you go, you can get a larger portion for another dollar, and you can also add a la carte toppings to solo chili.

Quite a flexible approach—and we haven't even gone to the dogs. All beef hot dogs, that is, just 95 cents each—or get various chili and dog combinations for $4-$5. And that $5.95 topper brings you "Jailhouse Grub," 5-Way chili with a salad and corn bread. They've got chips and salsa here too, and a liquor license to boot—draft beer by the glass, mug, or pitcher, plus margaritas. This is a fast food place? No way. *Yes* way!

Clarke's Pancake House
- 2441 N. Lincoln Ave., Chicago; (312) 472-3505

One of the city's many all-night pancake houses, Clarke's is distinctive for its clean, bright white interior and diverse menu—a real all-purpose kinda place. Oh sure, you can get pancakes. German, Swedish, apple, blueberry, carrot/zucchini, raisin/wheat germ....prices range from $3.85 to $5.85 a plate, and they're delicious.

But there's more here than silver dollars. Clarke's serves a whole coop of grilled chicken breast sandwiches in such variations as cajun, teriyaki, or honey mustard. They're all $6.25, which includes French fries. Other sandwiches start at $3.35 for grilled cheese, $5.05 for stir-fried veggies in pita bread, and $5.35 for the "San Diego Club" (that's the Padres, isn't it?)—a BLT with ham and cheese added. Big salad plates here, too.

And it doesn't stop there! Clarke's goes Mexican with quesadillas and burritos ($4.95 to $5.60), filled with your choice of chicken, steak, spinach (?), or vegetables. And their "Tijuana Pizza" is an individual pie made with salsa, onions, Jack cheese, and chorizo sausage for $5.35.

Desserts are a specialty here, from the "J.K. Sweets" counter at the front of the restaurant. Plenty of malts, floats, sundaes, etc. But then, why have ice cream when you can have chocolate chip pancakes? Which brings us back to breakfast. Mr. C has a theory about this: If you stay up late enough, you end up having breakfast—before you go to sleep. At Clarke's, you can have breakfast 24 hours a day.

Cool Beans
- 2562 N. Clark St., Chicago; (312) 665-2700

Cool Beans is a gourmet coffee shop that's every bit as good as Starbucks—only cheaper, less crowded, and less yuppified. Having just opened in 1993, they have already expanded to include a larger retail space and a full cafe serving basic vegetarian meals.

Hot beverages come in the same large selection of choices as at other cafes. House coffee starts under a dollar; espresso is $1 for a regular, and $1.20 for a double shot. Cappuccino and caffe latte are $1.70 for an eight-ounce cup, $1.95 for twelve ounces, and $2.55 for the scrape-you-off-the-ceiling sixteen ounce size.

The cafe serves up hearty sandwiches, filled with your choice of any four fresh vegetables, like avocado, roasted peppers, sprouts, and the like. Choose your bread, too, from such healthy homemade varieties as honey wheat, vegetable, and oatmeal. The sandwich costs $5, with a side salad; add extra veggies, cheese, or even (gasp!) ham or smoked turkey for another 50-75 cents. Homemade soups, $3 a bowl, change daily. They may include black bean, vegetarian chili, corn chowder, and creole bean. Quiche is served with slices of orange for $3; or, for $5, you can have it with soup or a salad.

You can, in fact, make up all sorts of different combinations, like a half-sandwich with soup or salad for $4, or soup, salad, and bread for $5. Clearly, the idea here is "give 'em what they want," and that's great for everybody. The newest thing they're giving Chicago is all-natural "Out of a Flower" lowfat ice cream; based in Dallas, this is one of the country's hottest new brands. So far, this is the only place in town where you can get it.

Cool Beans is open early and late seven days a week, from 6 a.m. to 11 p.m. They also offer free delivery in the local area. Way cool.

Corridor Cafe
- 2142 N. Clybourn Ave., Chicago; (312) 975-8999

The handsome Corridor Cafe manages to be both a yuppie, Crain's-reader haven, as well as a trendy place to take a date or such. The marble bar upstairs gets crowded at lunch and after work. They offer casual fare, mainly pizza, pasta, and sandwiches, and the presentation is fancy.

The help has something of an attitude problem, but then, they look suspiciously like out-of-work lawyers. Try to ignore this and order an individual garden pizza for $4.95, or such snacks as toasted raviolis or "peel 'em and eat 'em" shrimp. There are a variety of sandwiches, many of which are served on croissants; Mr. C found the cold roast beef on black bread ($5.95) a winner. The cafe also has a Sunday brunch from 10:00-2:00, which includes a children's menu.

Desserts are a house specialty, with such taste-treats as banana chocolate chip cake, key lime pie, or Snickers and Reese's pies, all at $3.75 a slice. A bit pricey, but....

The cafe is open 7 days a week, 11:30 a.m. to 2:00 a.m., with food being served 'til midnight only.

D'Agostino's
- 1351 W. Addison St., Chicago; (312) 477-1821

A chummy, neighborhood bar with a vast dinner menu, D'Agostino's is particularly interesting for its nightly specials—which, unlike those at many bars, are dependably unchanging. The favorite of Mr. C's local expert is the Wednesday night pizza special: Large, thin-crust pies, cheese or sausage, at half-price. Thus, a $12 pizza, big enough for four people, becomes a $6 pizza—or $1.50 per person. *That's* a bargain!

Among the other specials: Tuesdays offer a fried chicken dinner for $5.95, or a ravioli dinner for $5.25. Sundays, get a half slab of barbecued ribs for $6.75. And Thursdays, get a veal parmigiana dinner for $5.75. All dinners come with soup, salad, and bread, too. As Mr. C so often says, bar food is cheap food—these places make their money from the booze. Plenty of good beers on tap, by the way.

The regular menu dinners move toward the upper limits of the cheap range, though you get a lot for your money. Pastas, from $6.25 to $8.50, include mostaccioli, baked tortellini, and linguine with clam sauce.

Chicken dinners—fried, barbecued, or baked, all around $8.75—come with soup or salad, plus pasta and a vegetable.

You may prefer to stick with D'Agostino's hot and cold sandwiches, $5-$7, like the barbecue beef sandwich or breast of chicken. And there are all kinds of appetizers to snack on, such as fried zucchini sticks ($2.95), cheddar fries ($2.50), and even a whole potato with cheddar cheese baked on top ($2.50).

Needless to say, those specials make this a popular place—but it's big enough to handle the crowds. Give it a try some night, and pig out.

Discover Cafe
- 2436 N. Lincoln Ave., Chicago; (312) 868-3472

There's more to discover here than coffee. Note the first four letters; this is not just a cafe, it's also a music store, and the combination is a winner. At one counter, you can order up a cuppa their basic joe for a dollar (with refills just 50 cents each). At the other, you can snap up a (used) Miles Davis CD for just $9.

But wait, there's more! The cafe presents a live jazz trio during Sunday brunch, free of charge (the music, that is), from 10:30 a.m. until 2:00 p.m. Jazz also rings forth on Thursday evenings, while on Monday evenings there is a more eclectic grabbag of live performance. In any case, it's always offered as a free accompaniment to the food.

Nibble on a hefty turkey sandwich ($5.25), or a plate of "Eggs Espresso" ($2.75). No, these are not coffee-flavored sunnysides; these eggs are steamed in an espresso machine, and thus made without butter. The place is also big on "comfort foods," like a pair of good ol' Pop Tarts for $1.50. Or, just have a cappuccino and enjoy the bohemian atmosphere. You can sit at a table, or on one of the comfy couches, and while away an hour or two. Of course, you can hang out here any day of the week, with or without the jazz. Plenty of good music is always

playing, and works by local artists adorn the walls.

Hmm....With CDs, live music, and food, this may be one of the only places in this entire book which fits into all three sections—shopping, restaurants, and entertainment. And it's all cheap. Quite the discovery.

Duke of Perth
- 2913 N. Clark St., Chicago; (312) 477-1741

Yes, the menu gets a bit too cute ("haggis wings" turn out to be good ol' chicken), but Duke of Perth certainly feels a lot like an authentic Scottish pub. Sit at the dark wooden bar over a single malt scotch or one of their many English beers, or grab a table and try some quite authentic pub food. It's done to a nice turn in the kitchen, and of course this food is noted for its heaviness—so you won't leave hungry.

Mr. C particularly enjoyed a huge slice of shepherd's pie, tasty meat topped with a layer of mashed potato and served on a bed of green peas. It's a lot of food for a very reasonable $6.25. Hebridean leek pie, also $6.25, is sort of a veggie version of the same, with melted cheese over the top. Alas, no steak and kidney pie here, though.

They do, of course, serve fish and chips, and it's quite good. D of P uses codfish, deep fried in a beer batter, served with thick fries and the ubiquitous peas. It costs (surprise!) $6.25, but here's something to keep in mind—every Wednesday and Friday, it's all-you-can-eat fish and chips for $6.95. Good deal.

Other offerings include nice-sized burgers, named after some well-known Scots, all around $6; several chicken sandwiches as well, from $6.25-$7.25; and a number of thinly-veiled American entrees, like "Luigi MacPherson's Tomato Pasta Salad" ($5.95) and the "Nessie Steak Sandwich" ($6.95). The latter, in reality, is no lake monster, but a tuna steak marinated in beer and broiled up on a bun. Well, you've got to give them credit for trying. No matter—this is a cozy place to sit back and down a pint or two.

El Presidente

- 2558 N. Ashland Ave., Chicago; (312) 525-7938

It's 4:33 in the morning. You've just gotten off the graveyard shift. And all night, you've had this hankering for a humongous plate of huevos rancheros. Where do you go? El Presidente. This popular Mexican restaurant is open 24 hours a day, seven days a week. Sure, that makes the Wrightwood spot convenient (except for the lack of a parking lot, though that shouldn't be a problem at late hours), but can such nocturnal nachos be any good? Yes, says one of Mr. C's experts in the area. He's in there all the time. So, he notes, are members of Chicago's Finest—making the place safe for more than just your budget.

The appetizers alone can serve as mini-meals, since several of these come with beans and rice—like the tostadas quesadilla, which gives you all this for $4.50; or the chile relleno enchilada, with those sides, for $5.70. Several soups are offered in small and large portions, including beef, chicken, or tripe stew with vegetables (each $3.45/$4.90), and fine homemade chili, served with corn chips ($2.40/$3.60).

Being an all-night kind of place, there are actually several "huevo" dishes on the menu. Have your eggs with chorizo, a fairly spicy Mexican sausage, for $4.90; scrambled with onions, tomatoes, and peppers ($4.50); with ground beef ($5.95), or other styles; all include rice and beans.

All the other traditional entrees are here. A plate of three tacos, filled with beef, pork, or chicken, with r & b, is $5.65. Carne asada, the basic Mex-broiled steak, is just $8.25; add peppers and a cheese enchilada on the side, and it's $9.40. Chicken in mole sauce ($6.40) is another Mexican specialty, topped in that unique, not-dessertish chocolate sauce. And there are all kinds of combinations available, like the "El Presidente Spe-

cial" ($8) which gives you a beef taco, a bean tostada, a chicken enchilada, a tamale, rice, beans, and guacamole. Hey, even Presidente Clinton would love this place.

For something more unusual, try the "Vista del Mar"; shrimp and chicken sauteed in butter, mixed with crabmeat, with melted cheese, tomato, and avocado over the top. It's a hearty and yummy meal, served with rice for $8.70.

El Presidente does not have a liquor license; go for the agua de horchata ($1), instead. That's almond-flavored soda—sounds like "orzata," popular in Italian restaurants. The folks in the kitchen, by the way, are very accommodating; they'll make your food as spicy, or mild, as you request—whatever the hour. And if you still have any room, finish off with flan for only a dollar.

Fazzio's

- 2801 N. Lincoln Ave., Chicago; (312) 472-0787

Specializing in Italian beef sandwiches, freshly-squeezed lemonade and Italian ices, Fazzio's has been a tried-and-true Lake View favorite for years. The restaurant is plunked right in the heart of the six-corner confluence of Diversey, Racine, and Lincoln.

The counter help is remarkably polite and patient, quick to offer (friendly) suggestions for the indecisive. The menu is loaded with many homemade items, from minestrone soup ($1.05 for a cup, $1.60 for a bowl), to thick chili ($1.50 and $2.25) to delicious milk shakes ($1.99, and worth every penny).

But the sandwiches are the real stars here. The basic submarine, selling for $2.99, is stuffed with Plumrose ham, salami, capicolla, provolone, lettuce, tomato and onion, oil and vinegar, and Fazzio's special Italian spices. Gramma Fazzio's tomato sauce may be added free of charge to any sandwich. Vienna Beef hot dogs are only $1.49 here, and a marinated boneless skinless chicken sandwich (with six ounces of meat) is only $3.99—and that's the most expensive item in the place! Extra cheese, fiery-hot giardiniera sauce or sweet peppers on any item are 25 cents extra.

Side orders include onion rings for $1.59, fried mushrooms for $1.79 and garlic bread for a whopping $1.20. Don't miss the lemonade, though, which has been voted among Chicago's favorites. A regular size is $1.19; a large, $1.99. Lemon Italian ice, offered only in summer, is just 99 cents (large size, $1.76). Other dessert items include cannoli for $1.75 and homemade brownies for 99 cents.

No tips are required here, since it's order and pick-up at Fazzio's only, with its green counter running the perimeter of the restaurant and four tiny marble-topped tables in the dining area. Those who feed quarters to the juke box can listen to an oddball mix of Mariah Carey, Bonnie Raitt, Bette Midler, the Doors, and the Cure. Large plants temper the effects of the many neon signs inside, an unnecessary one of them reading "Eat at Fazzio's". In good weather, customers skip the neon and spill out onto the front patio to eat at umbrella-covered tables.

Fazzio's is open 7 days a week, until midnight in summer, until 10 p.m. otherwise. Delivery is available and there's free parking in the small front lot.

Gold Coast Dogs

- 325 S. Franklin St., Chicago; (312) 939-2624
- 2100 N. Clark St., Chicago; (312) 327-8887
- 418 N. State St., Chicago; (312) 527-1222

The Trib gave Gold Coast Dogs three stars, but patrons would seemingly give it four. This is a fast-food joint, granted, but a classy one using the freshest ingredients possible. And remember, Mr. C always says that counter service will save you dough—no tipping required!

Don't be put off by the line, snaking out the door, filled with businesspeople and families alike—it moves quickly. While you wait, you're more than welcome to read the dozens of praiseworthy newspaper and magazine articles framed on the wall.

Those who have already gone to these Dogs know that the One Magnificent Dog is $1.80, the plain ol' Red Hot Dog is $1.90, and the Char Cheddar Red Hot Dog (topped with fresh Wisconsin cheese) is $2.20. Beer bratwursts and Polish sausages go for $2.50 each. All sandwiches come with free condiments including mustard, ketchup, relish, onions, tomatoes, hot peppers, pickles, celery salt, and grilled onions.

But Gold Coast serves up more than just dogs. Catch the char-broiled swordfish sandwich, f'rinstance, made with fresh fish picked up daily at the dock. It's a deal at just $5.95. Turkey sandwiches are only $3.95. Chili is $1.95 for a bowl, and their ever-popular jumbo 1/3 pound charburgers are $2.95.

And there's more! Don't forget that they also serve breakfast here. Omelettes are only $3.50; get some grits or hash browns for 85 cents more. Herbie's Special—two eggs, sausage or bacon, hash browns, toast or bagel, and coffee for $1.95—may possibly be the best breakfast deal in all of Chicago. Unless you count Izzy's Special, that is—two scrambled eggs, cheese, and Canadian bacon on a toasted bagel for $1.89.

Gold Coast Dogs is open weekdays from 7 a.m. to midnight, from 10:30 a.m. to 8 p.m. on Saturdays, and from 11 a.m. to 8 p.m. on Sundays.

Golden Apple Grille and Breakfast House

- 2971 N. Lincoln Ave., Chicago; (312) 528-1413

This is a good ol' neighborhood kind of place, catering to policemen, retirees, and teenagers who seem to have nothing else to do. Many of these folks appear to be regulars, and the wait staff handles their sometimes cantankerous personalities with panache.

MR. CHEAP'S PICKS
Lincoln Park—Lake View

✔ **The Bread Shop**—Like, totally organic food that's as healthy for your wallet as for your body. And, just across the street, **The Chicago Diner** takes a similar approach, in spite of its greasy-spoon moniker.

✔ **Brother Jimmy's BBQ**—Check out their weekly "all-you-can-eat-*and*-drink" chicken and rib specials.

✔ **D'Agostino's**—Nightly specials, like half-price pizza every Wednesday, make this Lake View restaurant/bar a fine hangout.

✔ **Happi Sushi**—For Japanese dining, romantic yet inexpensive, this place will surely keep you happi.

✔ **Penny's Noodle Shop**—This Asian cafe near Wrigley Field hits a home run with its huge bowls of meat, soup and noodles—for less than five bucks.

Golden Apple is decorated with hanging ivy plants, and its back wall is lined with stained glass windows. Next to the cash register is the classic revolving-dessert display case that you expect from an older place like this; it's too bad that the sweets (including cheesecake and chocolate cream pie) aren't made on the premises.

The soup, however, *is* home-made; and the choices accompanying most entrees are designed so that you can't avoid getting a coupla veggies here too. Of course, the vitamin-phobic can have them in the form of French fries.

The wide-ranging cuisine runs from the familiar (pasta, barbecued chicken) to the improbable (enchiladas, served with tortillas and refried beans, are $4.50). Broiled scrod ($5.99) may not be fresh-caught, but it comes with garlic bread or dinner rolls, a mixture of broccoli, cauliflower, and big slices of carrot, and a choice of salad, juice, or soup.

Despite the dozens of entrees, though, the focus of the menu is actually breakfast food—as it should be. All the usuals are here, along with some surprises like banana pancakes ($3.99) and blintzes (cheese are $3.50, strawberry, blueberry, apple, or peach are $3.99). Mexican breakfasts, such as chilaquiles (scrambled eggs with tortilla chips, covered with Monterey jack cheese, $4.75) are also offered.

Nothing on the menu is priced over $7.95. There are almost twenty special items just for children, available to those age ten and under. Chocolate chip pancakes are $2.35, and for dinner, kids' portions of spaghetti or mostaccioli are just $2.75 each—same for hot turkey with gravy. Kiddies must be accompanied by an adult to take advantage of this menu, though.

The Golden Apple is a good bet if you're with a family or group of friends that can never decide on where to eat or what to eat. Or when, for that matter—since this place is open 24 hours a day. The diversified menu and quick service should keep everyone content; that, and the Dum-Dum lollipops handed out at the register.

No cigar smoking is allowed, although parts of the restaurant fill up with smoke from the regulars' regulars. There's also a semi-enforced minimum charge of $2.50 per person in the booths.

Goose Island Brewing Company
• 1800 N. Clybourn Ave., Chicago; (312) 915-0071

Named after that island formed by the branch of the Chicago River, bordered by Elston and Kingsbury, this microbrewery/pub/restaurant in the 1800 Clybourn Mall is worth the trip for its homemade potato chips alone. The huge, yet cozy, wooden bar in the center of one of the rooms—complete with green shaded lamps overhead—gives the place a classy but casual "Cheers"-like atmosphere. It all makes Goose Island a favorite among locals as well as businessmen negotiating power deals.

Can't decide which of their many homemade brews to choose? There are, after all, dozens of varieties, with selections varying by season. No problem—they'll let you try a free sample or two. Ales and lagers abound, but Mr. C swears by the "Chicago Weizen," a light wheat brew.

Along with its creative beer list, Goose Island gets kudos for its innovative appetizers and entrees, not to mention its incredibly friendly wait staff. Split an order of beer batter onion rings—you'll be stuffed—for $4.50, or try the mushroom, garlic, and brie quesadilla for $4.95, which is served with pico de gallo. The "goose" wings, available in buffalo-spicy, honey mustard, teriyaki, or barbecue sauces, are just $5.25 an order. Blue corn nachos taste just about the same as their yellow cousins, and are served with black beans, tomatillo salsa, and chihuahua cheese for $6, with guacamole an extra buck.

Sandwiches are plenty big, served with cole slaw and pickle on your choice of black, wheat, French, Italian, or onion bread. A Carolina pulled-pork sandwich, dripping with barbecue sauce, is just $7.95, as is the Cajun blackened catfish sandwich, served with cheddar cheese on Italian bread. Add French fries, pasta salad, baked beans, or fruit for just 50 cents more. And the grilled half-pound burger gives you a choice of seven cheeses, bacon, mushrooms, grilled onions, and any other toppings your little heart may desire, for $6.95.

And if you really feel like stuffing your face, or want to bring a doggie bag home, go for fish and chips ($7.95), or a half-slab of smoked baby back ribs ($8.95). All entrees are served with a salad or cup of soup, and rolls and butter. Of course, all this wonderful food is really just something to have between swigs of that great beer.

Happi Sushi Restaurant

- 3346 N. Clark St., Chicago; (312) 528-1225

Happi Sushi is a great spot for sushi on the cheap. It's as romantic as a sushi bar can get, with wicker chairs, blue and white china, and soft jazz music in the background. The sushi chef will greet you as soon as you step in, and the waitresses are ultra-polite. Happi's customers include families, couples, and movie-goers. You can sit at the 10-seat bar and watch the chef prepare your rolls, or glance over from your table.

The miso soup is excellent, with just enough green onion and tiny cubes of tofu. It comes with eight large rolls of California maki (crabsticks and avocado) and a bowl of white rice for only $7.50. Smaller appetites may opt for the finger-size rolls of tekka, or tuna maki (six rolls for $3.50). The spider maki appetizer rolls (soft-shell crabmeat) are $4.50 for four pieces.

A la carte sushi is also available at $1.00 apiece, with clam, mackerel, squid, and salmon roe among the choices. Family-style platters are also available. One platter gets you sixteen pieces (eight varieties) of sushi, plus California and tekka rolls, for $20.00; it's enough for two people, and bigger plates are also offered for parties of three, four, and five.

If you're here with a sushi fan, but not one yourself, try the combination plate of tempura shrimp and chicken teriyaki ($8.50); or, niku nabe (beef and vegetables) for $6.50. Fried chicken or pork is also $6.50. Like many of the small, ethnic eateries in the Wrigley area, Happi Sushi is open for dinner only.

Hog Head McDunna's

- 1505 W. Fullerton Ave., Chicago; (312) 929-0944

In the DePaul University area, there are any number of pubs which offer varying degrees of food along with the drink. Hog Head McDunna's has a fairly extensive menu at cheap prices, and they're geared to lots of lunch and dinner specials too.

It's a big, spread-out kind of place, with high ceilings and two large, open rooms. The first, as you walk in, is the bar room, though it has some tables; through the doorway is an even bigger dining room which includes a stage area for live bands. Both rooms, meanwhile, are dominated by numerous TV screens showing several different ballgames at once. They have an impressive array of beers on tap, including Fullers Ale, Harp Lager, Murphy's Stout, and Woodpecker Cider.

The basic menu is a little bit of everything, in the burgers-salads-sandwiches vein. Half-pound burgers start at $4.95 with fries and cole slaw. From there, you can add any of a dozen other toppings for 25-50 cents each, including roasted garlic or red wine cheddar. Other sandwiches range from grilled chicken breast to blackened tuna on pita bread, each $5.75. Mr. C gave this a try, and found it moist and tasty.

It wouldn't be Chicago without a couple of pizzas, but McDunna's gives them a twist for the nouvelle crowd—pesto with sun-dried tomatoes, and vegetarian with grilled eggplant. Both are $5.75, sized for one or two people. There is a separate version of the menu for lunch, on which everything is priced at $2.99. Oh, and speaking of Italian food, Tuesday is spaghetti and garlic bread night—all you can eat for a mere $1.99. Pig out!

Java Jive
- 909 W. School St., Chicago; (312) 549-3500

Among Chicago's multitude of coffeehouses, this Wrigleyville joint gets Mr. C's vote for its extensive (not expensive) food menu and for the free live music offered every night. You may hear anything from jazz to traditional Irish folk music, in solos or du-

ets; but even a couple of players makes such a lively difference. The musicians gratefully accept tips, but otherwise there is no cover charge for the music.

The food, meanwhile, is quite good. There are half a dozen interesting sandwiches to choose from. Mr. C's friend had the "Avocado Jive" ($4.95), and was delighted by the sheer size of this sandwich—thick wedges of avocado, plus tomato, cream cheese, and onion on hearty pumpernickel bread. "Jive Turkey," a dollar more, is made with real hand-sliced meat—not pressed from the deli. And for something different on the salad scene, try one topped with roquefort dressing and pecans ($4.00).

Desserts, of course, are wonderful. Chocolate praline cake ($3.00) is one of many choices that change daily, listed on a large blackboard. It's dark and moist, topped with sticky praline syrup and nuts—and a mighty large piece, too. Java Jive is open daily until midnight.

Johnny Rockets, The Original Hamburger
- 2530 N. Clark St., Chicago; (312) 472-6191
- 901 N. Rush St., Chicago; (312) 337-3900
- One Schaumburg Place, Schaumburg; (708) 240-1900

Okay, so the menu is limited at Johnny Rockets, but this national chain's food and prices will make you think that you've been transported back in time to the 1950's. That's not unique in Chicago, of course—but Johnny Rockets can take you there for less than certain other trendy retro-cafes.

Hamburger is the basic language spoken here. The "Original Burger," starting at $3.35, is topped with all the necessaries: Lettuce, tomato, mustard, pickle, mayo, relish, and chopped onion. For a quarter more, you can add Johnny's cheddar cheese and "red, red sauce." Chili and bacon will add still more to the ticket, yet will still keep the burger under $5.

Hamburger haters can find something for themselves here, like an egg salad sandwich ($2.45), the ever-popular BLT ($3.55), and a grilled cheese sandwich ($2.65). Throw some fries on the side for $1.45; better yet, try their chili fries for $2.75.

Johnny Rockets' "famous" malts and shakes are $2.95. For dessert, apple pie is $1.65; served a la mode, it's $2.40. It ain't like mom's, but it's not bad. Basically, this is fast food with a bit more character than all your McChains, with its counter and stools, and sparkling white tile motif—an idealized, "Happy Days" kinda joint. Johnny Rockets also stays open until 2:00 a.m. on weekends.

Leona's
- 3215 N. Sheffield Ave., Chicago; (312) 327-8861
- 6935 N. Sheridan Ave., Chicago; (312) 764-5757
- 1936 W. Augusta Blvd., Chicago; (312) 292-4300
- 1419 W. Taylor St., Chicago; (312) 850-2222
- 848 W. Madison St., Oak Park; (708) 445-0101.

Family-run (and darn proud of it) since 1950, Leona's has grown into a Chicagoland chain serving almost 50,000 people a week. A Mr. C warning: Not all of the entrees are under $10, but the pizza and the weekday lunch buffet can't be beat for great values in food.

The above-mentioned buffet includes your choice of turkey (a whole bird is out on the table for carving), boneless chicken breast, fried eggplant, meatballs, four kinds of pizza, super-fresh broccoli and zucchini, onion rings, and a slew of pasta and regular salads. Desserts, like cheesecake, brownie-bottom chocolate cake, and a slew of cookies and truffle-like treats are included in the tab. The whole shabang, all you can eat, is a reasonable $8.95. It's served from 11:30 a.m. until 2:00 p.m., weekdays only.

If you're not feeling that Bacchanalian, opt for a sandwich—and this is no short-changing compromise.

Mr. C can't put into words just how huge the chicken Parmesan sandwich is; it's comparable to a football (in size only). At $4.45, it's a great deal, loaded with marinara and provolone. $1.50 more gets you "broccoli slaw," fresh fruit, or Leona's homemade Italian cookies, plus a side of pasta, fries, pesto veggies, or salad. Tummy-stuffing indeed!

Of course, what would an Italian restaurant (or, in Chicago, *any* restaurant) be without pizza? Here, they come with a mind-boggling choice of 26 toppings—everything from turkey breast and giardiniera peppers to zucchini and soy cheese. A small thin-crust pie is $6.75; pan is $7.25 and stuffed is $8.50. Homemade pesto shrimp pie is a specialty, starting at $10.95 for the individual size.

Don't forget dessert if you can hack it. *Tiramisu* is $3.25, homemade cannoli are $2.25 each, and a dozen of those famous Italian cookies goes for $2.75.

Leona's has a promotional deal: Visit all five locations (with a tab of $20 or more), and they'll give you a free dinner for two. Ask for a "Road Rally Challenge" form, to which they will attach a sticker at each place.

Mamasita's
- 2665 N. Clark St., Chicago; (312) 975-1190

Sure, there's Mexican food on every block of Clark Street. What's special about this one? The food is wonderful, the prices are low, and the portions are enormous. No bigger than your average taco stand, Mamasita's makes the most of its space, giving it the feel of a small and cozy restaurant. There is an open kitchen and a take-out counter at the door, but if you're dining in, you get full table service.

Like a restaurant, a basket of warm tortilla chips and salsa are placed on the table as you arrive. The menu is pretty simple. Tacos are $1.80, quesadillas are $4.00, and burritos are $4.25. Big, bigger, biggest. Choose what goes inside, whether chicken, steak, beans, vegetables, or a combination, and...*Olé*! You'll get a delicious, freshly-cooked meal for almost no money.

There are a few other choices, like a three fajita plate for $5.75, or a taco salad for $5.50 with chicken, steak, or veggies. It's all homemade on the premises, using fresh ingredients and no lard. There is also no liquor license, but you are welcome to bring your own. Or, wash the food down with mango, papaya, or pineapple juice ($1.00).

Melrose Diner
- 3233 N. Broadway, Chicago; (312) 327-2060
- 930 W. Belmont Ave., Chicago; (312) 404-7901

The clear intent at the Melrose Diner is to overwhelm you. It's a big, slick, suburban-palace kind of place, where the waitress mothers you and calls you "honey." Food is brought out in big portions, with everything on the side. Unfortunately, mom isn't in the kitchen—the food doesn't always live up to its promise.

The menu covers every cuisine known to modern man. From the basic burger and fries to something called "Chicken Vesuvio" (does that mean it makes you erupt with heartburn?), from a hundred breakfasts to steaks and seafood, it's a classic diner smorgasbord.

Those breakfasts are fun, by the way. Cheese blintzes with fruit are $4.95; same price for banana pancakes with chocolate chips. Mmmm. Moving on to lunch (though you can have breakfast anytime), there are dozens of salads, soups, and sandwiches. Get this—a turkey melt sandwich on a croissant, with a cup of soup to start, a basket of bread, French fries, cole slaw, a wedge of melon, and a big pickle—all for $5.95! The soups are good, but the sandwich isn't made with fresh turkey...that's the kind of place we're talking here.

Daily specials, of which there are about thirty, all include soup or salad, and a simple dessert (y'know, bread pudding or ice cream). All of these meals are priced under $10, some as low as $4.95 (for chicken riganati, with rice and potato). Again, you may find any mix of globe-trotting options, like veal parmigiana with spaghetti, chicken fajitas, London broil, crabmeat-stuffed trout, or pepper steak over rice (all of which happen to be priced at $6.95), and many others. If you can, do save room for the real desserts, big and laden with calories, on display in lighted glass cases, of course.

So, if you want to just plain stuff yourself, and you're not too fussy, the Melrose could be what you're looking for. One other winning feature, in true diner fashion: They're open 24 hours, every day of the week.

Metropolis Rotisseria
- 924 W. Armitage Ave., Chicago; (312) 868-9000

Restaurants like Metropolis are among the better things to come from the yuppie revolution—fast food that's actually made with real, fresh ingredients and a measure of creativity. Made to be eaten in their own attractive setting or taken home. Not as cheap as McBurgers, but still a great value.

Metropolis specializes in rotisserie-cooked chicken and—this being Chicago—pizza. Are there *any* restaurants in Chicago that don't serve whatever "...and pizza"? Anyway. A half-chicken, golden brown and yummy, costs just $4.25; it comes with a yogurt-garlic sauce and whole-grain bread. Add two side dishes and make a full meal out of it for $7.25, choosing from real mashed potatoes, polenta, pasta salad, Greek salad, white bean stew, and many more.

They offer a sandwich version for $4.75, among others; here, the menu begins to lean toward the Mediterranean. The "Tuscan" ($4.50) combines roasted tomatoes, sweet peppers, onions, and pesto on crunchy bread, with a side of cole slaw. Which brings us back to the pizzas. You can have pan pizza by the slice, packed with veggies, for $2.25. But try the ten-inch thin crust pie for just $6.95, topped with things like chicken, spinach, mushrooms, and garlic; or with sauteed onions, blue cheese, and walnuts. Call it nouvelle Italian.

The restaurant's decor is another Italian pedigree—white tile walls livened by a color scheme of turquoise, goldenrod, and other American southwestern hues. Order at the counter and bring your food to a table—or, sit at the window counter and watch the world walk by. They also deliver in the evenings. Open daily until 9:30 p.m.

Moti Mahal
- 1031 W. Belmont Ave., Chicago; (312) 348-4393
- 2525 W. Devon Ave., Chicago; (312) 262-2080

Moti Mahal is perhaps the king (or should that be rajah?) of Devon's many Indian restaurants, having spawned this busy Lake View location as well. Both are extremely popular for their daily lunch buffets, in which you can heap your plate with food for only $5.95. The buffet is offered from 11:30 a.m. to 3:30 p.m. every day of the week.

The extremely humble decor, lack of signs identifying each buffet item, and the long, communal dining tables make Moti feel almost like a soup kitchen; unattentive service, marked by a paucity of English, doesn't improve the atmosphere any. Why then, do so many people eat here on an almost-daily basis? Because the food is wonderful, of course—and cheap.

The buffet is really rather small, but offers just enough variety to give you some interesting choices. Appetizers include wonderful nan bread, a slightly spicy vegetable soup, and pakoras, deep-fried patties filled with vegetables. Grab a pile of saffron rice, and top it with things like sag paneer—cooked spinach with cheese (who says all Indian food has to be spicy?), or aloo gobhi, a sort of potato and cauliflower stew. You'll probably find tandoori baked chicken, your basic; but try the chicken tikka

masala—an absolutely yummy dish in a creamy tomato sauce that's out of this world.

Sodas, coffees, and teas are not included in the buffet price; and you're welcome to bring your own beer or wine, with no corkage fee. Remember, "BYO" places invariably charge less for their food! The regular menu, by the way, is also very inexpensive. Only the big combination platters, enough for two people to share, top $10—no single item approaches this. The "Moti Mahal Mix," for instance, gives you tandoori chicken, chicken tikka, lamb kebabs, lamb curry, lentil stew, mixed vegetables, nan bread and rice—all for just $11.95. The menu is available during buffet hours, too. Forget about ambiance....go for the food.

Muskie's Hamburgers
- 963 W. Belmont Ave., Chicago; (312) 477-1880

Located right below the Avalon nightclub at Sheffield, Muskie's is just a hop away from the Belmont "el" stop on the Howard line. If you like oldies on the radio, red-glitter vinyl on your chairs, and burgers, dogs, and seafood on your plate, this is the place.

Even if you've had enough of the 1950's diner theme, give Muskie's a try—it's an interesting mix of trendy and true-life. The stainless steel of the grill extends to the ceiling in a starburst pattern, all of which is kept spotless; the James Dean wall pictures are balanced by potted ficus plants. Drifters and yuppies sit side-by-side while listening to Patsy Cline, Ritchie Valens, and Buddy Holly on the juke box.

As for the food, their 1/3-pound charcoal-grilled burgers are just $3.00. There are also chili dogs at $2.30 each, pork chop sandwiches for $2.95, and fish sandwiches for $2.65. Add an order of hand-cut French fries for 89 cents. Muskies also has a selection of vegetarian choices (talk about "back to the future"): An overstuffed hummus sandwich in pita bread, with tons of onion, sprouts, and cucumber, is good eats for a paltry $2.50.

Muskie's is open from 11 to 11 daily. Delivery is available for a nominal charge.

My Pie

- 2417 N. Clark St., Chicago; (312) 929-3380

Actually, the big sign out front reads, "My π," which means they must specialize in pun pizza. What are they trying to tell us? That the cook is a math major? That these pizzas cannot be evenly divided? Maybe. But don't let that deter you from trying these fine deep dish creations. And no matter how large or small your dining party, there's a size you can divide with nothing left over. The pizzas are baked to a crunchy finish in a deep pan which is brought to the table (thin pizzas are also available).

The basic pies start at $4.45 for the "midget" size, just two slices' worth; they range up to $11.25 for a large, which indeed it is. Add as many other ingredients as you like; sausage, garlic, Canadian bacon, and many more, about a dollar each. Or, go for the "My Pie Special," which has mushrooms, onions, peppers, and either sausage or pepperoni. These range from $7.25 to $15.95, which may seem a bit pricey; but don't forget, you could feed half of Chicago with one of these.

Pizza isn't the only thing on the menu, either. Pasta dinners, like spinach fettucine Alfredo, are all $5.45. There are burgers, salads, and homemade soups. Also, lots of appetizer/snacks, including spicy Buffalo wings ($3.95) and a stuffed garlic bread made with cheese and real garlic ($2.75). A large salad bar is not only well-stocked with vegetables and fruits, but also pasta and slices of cheese and pepperoni—make a meal of it, or add it to your pizza. In fact, the weekday lunch special offers all you can eat—soup, salad, and pizza—for just $5.25.

Beer and wine are served, including beer by the pitcher, making this a good place for large groups; the restaurant itself, despite its small doorfront, is gigantic on the inside. It's also a good place for families, with a kids' menu, pitchers of soda, and video games. Service can be slow, since everything is baked to order, but the atmosphere is boisterous and comfortable. Especially nice on a cold winter's eve is the large, open fireplace in the center of the room.

Nakayoshi Sushi

- 919 W. Belmont Ave., Chicago; (312) 929-9333

It's difficult to find inexpensive sushi, for obvious reasons: It's seafood, and it's trendy. Nevertheless, Mr. C did find Nakayoshi—a no-frills, no-atmosphere BYOB with a basic menu that's the real McCoy. Or is that mako? Anyway, it's definitely a place where you can have a satisfying meal for under $10, which of course is Mr. Cheap's culinary mission.

For the most part, your sushi and sashimi choices are limited to a handful of combination platters, which range in price from $7.00 to $8.50. You cannot order a la carte, but evidently that's what keeps the costs down—and the prices too. The platters do give you plenty of fish; the one Mr. C's companion ordered included two pieces each of tuna and shrimp, along with yellowtail, salmon, mackerel, and octopus. It certainly got this sushi lover's seal of approval (no pun intended there). All platters come with rice and a peppy green horseradish sauce.

For non-sushi fans, Nakayoshi also serves a good variety of other traditional Japanese dinners. There are hefty bowls of soup with soba or udon noodles, and your choice of meats and veggies, all under $5 and hard to finish; and several teriyaki dinners, like mackerel or chicken (each $5.80) and steak ($6.25). You can't go far wrong here—it's good stuff.

Mainly a lunch and early dinner place, Nakayoshi is open from noon until only 9:00 or so. They're also closed on Wednesdays.

The Original Pancake House

- 22 E. Bellevue Place, Chicago;
  (312) 642-7917
- 10437 S. Western Ave, Chicago;
  (312) 445-6100
- 1517 E. Hyde Park Blvd., Chicago;
  (312) 288-2322
- 2020 N. Lincoln Park West,
  Chicago; (312) 929-8130
- 700 E. 87th Ave., Chicago; (312)
  874-0010

Many other suburban locations
Proudly located across the street from
the fancy-shmancy Meridien Hotel,
this charming, warm and homey eatery—part of a chain based in Portland, Oregon—wins Mr. C's award
for friendliest and most efficient staff
in town.

Even though the folks at OPH
are obsessively preoccupied with
high quality, the breakfast-all-day
meals here won't budge your budget
too much. You'll be stuffed after a
ham and cheese omelette, served
with three buttermilk pancakes, all
for $5.95. The pancakes are extra-
smooth and fluffy, thanks to a special
sourdough yeast made especially for
the House.

You can also beat the breakfast
blahs here by ordering something out
of the ordinary. Ever tried coconut
pancakes ($4.50)? Ever heard of
them? Or, how about Hawaiian pancakes, topped with pineapple and
tropical syrup ($4.25). Get back to na-
ture with OPH's old-fashioned oats,
served with cream, for $1.60. And
their trademark coffee, brought to
you topped with whipping cream if
you wish, is 90 cents. Potato pancakes are served with apple sauce
and sour cream for $4.25. The spuds
are imported all the way from Idaho,
and their lingonberries (another sweet
pancake option) have come even further—from Sweden.

The Original Pancake House
does not accept credit cards, which is
one way they keep their prices down.

Pastafina

- 921 W. Belmont Ave., Chicago;
  (312) 528-4499

Simply by walking next door from

Nakayoshi (see listing above), you
can travel halfway across the world.
Pastafina is a light and airy cafe, all
in white, serving homemade Italian
pastas and sandwiches with a nouvelle flair. Start off with a hearty
bowl of soup, like cream of broccoli,
for $2.25; it comes with a slab of gar-
lic bread.

At lunchtime, you can move on
to one of a half-dozen sandwiches—
such as chicken caprese ($4.25),
grilled chicken breast topped with
mozzarella, tomato, and a pesto
sauce. The grilled vegetable sandwich ($3.95) is a mix of zucchini,
eggplant, peppers, onion, and again,
tomato and mozzarella. These are all
served on fresh, crunchy Italian rolls;
and you can add gnocchi or angel
hair pasta on the side for just two dollars more. Soup/salad and soup/sand-
wich combos are also available, each
around $5.

The pasta side works off a fixed
menu, from which you select your
own combination of noodles and
sauces at a couple of different price
scales Choose from angel hair, linguine, fettucine, or gnocchi, in egg or
spinach pastas, for $6.50; top them
with marinara, alfredo, or gorgonzola
or pesto sauce. For $7.25, you can
choose from filled pastas including
tortellini and ravioli. There are also a
few other entrees available, like linguine with littleneck clams in a light
clam sauce ($8.95).

Refrigerated glass cases of cold
pasta salads make Pastafina a popular
place for carry-out meals as well, especially at lunchtime. It's one of
those places where, as Mr. C's friend
noted, everything looks good.

Penny's Noodle Shop

- 3400 N. Sheffield Ave., Chicago;
  (312) 281-8222

If you're a visitor to Chicago,
chances are someone will insist that
"you *have* to eat at Penny's Noodles." If you live here, no doubt you
already know. Penny's is a fabulous
and popular little cafe around the corner from Wrigley Field (but don't
even *think* about getting in before the

game). It serves up a mix of dishes from several Asian cuisines that are wholesome, filling, and just plain cheap. If you can manage to get a table, you can stuff yourself for well under $10—and that's what Mr. C likes to hear.

Start off with one of half a dozen appetizers, like Thai spring rolls ($3.50). Unlike the tiny deep-fried finger rolls you may expect, this is a single, soft log served cold and filled with tofu, cucumber, bean sprouts, and egg. For one person, it could almost be an entree; for two or three, there's plenty to share.

The noodle dishes themselves range from pad Thai ($4.75) to barbecued pork ($3.85)—thick slices on top of a heap of bean sprouts, egg noodles, greens, cilantro, and ground peanuts. It's served in a deep bowl (especially good if you're chopstick skills aren't up to par), and you can have it as a soup, or without broth. The same option is yours with sliced beef or chicken ($3.85) or pork and shrimp wontons ($4.25). In fact, nothing on the menu costs over $5 (for lad nar, stir-fried vegetables with chicken or beef over crisp rice noodles). Gotta love it.

The surprising thing is that these dishes are hard to finish—you'd hardly expect that from little chopped-up things in a bowl. It's the noodles, of course, that do it; gee, it's healthy, too. Penny's has tables outside during the warm months, which helps with the crunch for tables. Getting seated during peak dining hours can be tough. Penny's opens at noon, and is closed on Mondays.

Pequod's Pizza

- 2201 N. Clybourn Ave., Chicago; (312) 327-1512
- 8520 Fernald Ave., Morton Grove; (708) 470-9161

The staff at Pequod's get really ticked off when people complain that their pizza is overdone. It may look burnt, but that's because the baking process has "carmelized" the cheese, turning it dark. This makes for a distinctly different, brick oven flavor.

The price is right, too, especially with great value lunch specials. So don't complain, just dig in!

Situated on the corner of Clybourn and Webster, Pequod's is really a thinly disguised college-age sports bar, imitating Gino's graffiti and Christmas-light idea. The graffiti can border on the rude side, and Polaroids of tanked-up regulars adorn the walls, so you probably won't want to bring the kids. Gino's it certainly ain't but then again, the pizza is good and you probably won't have to wait in line here.

For appetizers, a tremendous bowl of French fries is $2.00, and a good-sized order of garlic bread is just $1.35 (get it with cheese on top, 50 cents extra). In keeping with the restaurant's nautical theme, the bread is served on a whale-shaped cutting board. Thin crust pizzas are priced at $5.50, $6.95, and $10; deep dish pies go for $6.75, $8.25, and $9.85 (these are a tad smaller than the thin crust versions).

On weekdays, they offer the lunch special of a 7" pan pizza with one topping, plus soda or draft beer, all for $2.95. Now, *that's* a deal.

Not in the mood for pizza? Try mostaccioli marinara for $5.25; or the Pequod salad, with cheese, green peppers, onion, mushrooms, pepperoncinis, carrots, black olives, tomato, and pepperoni—just $3.75. A meatball sandwich is only $3.50, as are the Italian beef or sausage sandwiches. The famous Eli's Cheesecake is the only dessert offering, available plain or in all its indulgent varieties: Amaretto with almonds, chocolate carmel pecan, and chocolate chip.

Pequod's is open from 11 a.m. until 2 a.m. on weekdays, Saturdays from 12 noon until 2 a.m., and Sundays from noon to midnight. Delivery service is available, too.

Red Lion Pub

- 2446 N. Lincoln Ave., Chicago; (312) 348-2695

Along with the Duke of Perth (see listing above), the Red Lion brings a touch of jolly old England to Lincoln

Park. And even more so than the Duke, this place really feels like an authentic Brit pub—dark and crowded (especially in the evenings), with well-worn wooden tables, and walls crammed with decorative knick-knacks. The front room is mainly a bar area, with some tables; a more proper dining room is to the back.

So, grab a pint of genuine Whitbread Ale or Young's Lager ($3, but remember, it's a pint), and have a lunch or dinner of true pub food. Unlike an actual pub, the waiter comes around to take your order—evidently, Americans want only so much authenticity—but at least the gentleman takes the orders without writing them down. Now, *that's* English, practiced all the way up to the finest restaurants on the Strand.

Start off with some sausage rolls ($2.95), or beans on toast ($3.25, or $4.25 with a poached egg on top). Speaking of sausage, that's what is meant by "Bangers and Mash" ($5.95), a plate of sausage and mashed potatoes. If you think the name has to do with a rude epithet, you're right—that's the Brits for you. Mr. C enjoyed the very crispy batter on his fish and chips ($6.25), three large pieces of fish with terrific steak fries. Malt vinegar is served with the chips, by the way, another authentic touch. And the Ploughman's Lunch—bread, cheese, and fruit—is healthy as well as cheap at $4.25.

Shepherd's pie, and steak and kidney pie (each $6.50) round out the English part of the menu, all of which seems to be done with genuine Anglo spirit. Now, you can get burgers, sandwiches, and salads here too, though why anyone would come in to such a place for a burger is not really worth exploring. Suffice it to say, if you can't afford a vacation in old Blighty, the Red Lion will do very well for a quick trans-Atlantic trip.

Rocky Mountain Bagel Company
- 2154 N. Halsted St., Chicago; (312) 248-2154

Bagels from the hills? Who ever heard of a Jewish cowboy? Well, if there are any, chances are they'd stop in here to get some grub—choosing from more than a dozen unusual sandwiches available on fourteen different bagel varieties. They all have cutesy names too, like "Telluride Triple." This combines dill havarti, provolone, and muenster cheeses, topped with a mound of vegetables, all for $3.00. The "Colorado River Run" has nova lox (so *that's* where it comes from!) on cream cheese with more veggies—and, at $4.95, it's the most expensive thing on the entire menu. Most sandwiches run about $3.50. This is Mr. C's kind of place!

But even at cheap prices, RMBC pledges to use top-quality ingredients, with everything made to order. They also make their own blended cream cheeses, like chive, strawberry, and cinnamon raisin. And the bagel choices go far beyond your basic plain, onion and poppy—how about a cheddar bagel? Or banana nut, blueberry, and even chocolate chip? Try 'em out, pardner.

Daily specials are offered, like smoked turkey with any cheese, veggies, chips, and a drink for $4.50. The atmosphere is a pleasant variation on fast food—order at the counter, and sit at a high table on bar stools. Works by local artists adorn the walls, and bright colors abound.

Shiroi Hana Japanese Restaurant
- 3242 N. Clark St., Chicago; (312) 477-1652

Make your visit to a Cubs game more exotic—instead of the usual hot dog before or after a game, consider a crab stick, $1 a pop; such other Asian delicacies as quail eggs, 40 cents apiece; and, of course, sushi.

At Shiroi Hana, just a few blocks from the ballpark, you can select your own mix of sushi rolls without sinking your budget. Since everything here is sold individually, you won't end up dawdling over a plate laden with California rolls, as some sushi restaurants will force you to do.

A single California roll at Shiroi is just $3; a tuna (tekka) roll is just $2.75. Ume rolls (plum paste) are just $2.50 each, as are the flavored gourd and pickled radish rolls. Sea eel and cucumber rolls are $3 each. You can also make up your own combinations by ordering eight large rolls (futomaki) for $7.50, or $4.00 for a half-order.

The restaurant also offers plain old sushi in a dozen different varieties. Tuna, yellow tail, Norwegian salmon, octopus, sea eel, fresh water eel, squid, mackerel, giant clam, abalone, salmon, shrimp, crab, smelt, sea urchin, and salmon roe are all priced from $1.30-$2.00 each.

Shiroi Hana is open for lunch Monday through Saturday from noon to 2:30 p.m. Dinner is served from 5:00 Monday through Saturday, closing at 10:00 p.m. on weekdays, and 10:30 on Fridays and Saturdays. Sunday hours, for dinner only, are from 4:30 until 9:30 p.m.

Siam Delight
- 2540 N. Clark St., Chicago; (312) 404-7200

This restaurant is a delight, serving up super-cheap Thai food in the heart of Lincoln Park West. Yes, that's not unique—there must be such a place on just about every other block in the area—but this one is a fine example. It's small and intimate, with just a handful of tables covered in pink linen and a mellow atmosphere. Service is with a smile, nothing on the menu is over $4.95, and the food is delicious.

Start off with crispy egg rolls; these are filled with chicken, along with the usual vegetables. An order of four is only $2.50. Vegetarian fans may want to try the fried tofu ($1.95) instead—served with ground peanuts over the top and sweet and sour sauce. In fact, though, since everything here is cooked to order, you can request just about anything on the menu to be made without meat.

Siam's soups are equally cheap and tasty. Shrimp tom yum (hot & sour soup) is $3.50, while the chicken version is $2.75. A spicy coconut milk soup (tom kha kai), laced with chicken, cabbage, and peppers, is $3.50.

Mr. C went with chicken masaman curry ($4.75) for a main dish, a yellow curry with just a bit of zing to it. Unlike the treatment at most other restaurants, this came as more of a soup than a plate; but if that makes you think it's not enough for a meal, guess again. With a mound of boiled rice on the side for mixing in, this was hard to finish.

Among other entrees: Curry fried rice is only $4.50 with chicken or beef, and $4.75 with shrimp. Pepper steak—done up as a kind of Oriental pot roast, with tomatoes, garlic, and thick gravy—is $4.50; same price for the ever-popular pad Thai. Add a tiny but tasty side order of cucumber salad for another fifty cents.

Finish off with a cup of Thai iced coffee ($1.25) or a fruit shake ($1.50). Siam Delight is open seven days a week, but is closed Tuesday until dinner. It's open from 11:00 in the morning until 10:00 in the evening on weekdays, and until 11:00 p.m. on weekends. Delivery is available.

Star of India
- 3204 N. Sheffield Ave., Chicago; (312) 525-2100

The scuttlebutt along Belmont is that this new restaurant, just around the corner on Sheffield from the venerable Moti Mahal, is the new hot spot for those cheap, pig-out Indian lunch buffets. The reason, as they have proudly announced in the window, is that they have lured away Moti's main chef for themselves. Still, there are many who maintain their allegiance to Moti Mahal (see listing above). Take your pick; you can't go far wrong.

Right off, you can see that Star of India certainly has a more pleasant atmosphere than the Lake View Moti. Red-check tablecloths, hanging plants and lots of windows give it a lighter, almost country-style interior. And as far as the menu is concerned, it seems the chef literally took everything with him when he left. The two menus are almost identical. Tandoori chicken, at $8.50 for a whole bird and $5.00 for a half, is even prefaced by exactly the same description ("Our tandoori food is marinated in a special masala...").

If there are any differences in the prices, it seems that Star of India checks in just a bit higher on certain items. Moti's "Fish Curry," cooked in tomato and coconut cream, is $7.25;

at Star, the very same entree is called "Fish Tikka Masala" and is priced at $7.95. And the special combination platters feature identical foods and prices at both joints. Needless to say, Star also offers its lunch buffet every day from 11:30 to 3:30, also at $5.95 per person. One other significant difference is that Star stays open later, until midnight, on Fridays and Saturdays. Otherwise, it closes at 10:00, as Moti does, seven nights a week.

NEAR NORTH
(including Gold Coast, Old Town, River North, Streeterville)

Andy's
- 11 E. Hubbard St., Chicago; (312) 642-6805

This popular restaurant/bar, just across the river from the Loop, is as well-known for its live jazz music as for its food. It deserves equal billing for both. For bargain hunters, lunch is really the best time to come here. Every weekday from noon until 2:30, live jazz with no cover charge accompanies your meal. Mondays and Tuesdays feature solo piano, but sidemen are added as the week goes on, leading to a lively quintet on Fridays. For more details about the music, see the separate listing in the "Entertainment" section.

Mr. C frequently points out that bar food is cheap food; yet, this is no little smoke-filled dive. The handsome wooden interior is large, with a central bar at the door and then a big dining room filled with tables. And the air, even with all those business folks at lunch, is surprisingly non-smoky. Anyway, getting to the food, there is a wide range of hot and cold sandwiches, which come as full plates with French fries and cole slaw. Half-pound hamburgers are $5.50; the reuben is $5.95, as is a

veal bratwurst sandwich. Some of these babies are a challenge to get your mitts around—and to finish off.

Other options include salads and pizzas. A chicken pasta salad platter is $5.95, nice and big; deep-dish pizzas range from $7.50 to $9.50, depending on the size. Split 'em and you can eat really cheap. But then, you can even get a half-slab of barbecued ribs, again with fries and cole slaw, plus a soup or salad appetizer, all for $7.95—very good indeed!

Dinners are a bit pricier for much the same menu, but not necessarily. The pizzas are priced the same as lunch, and the sandwiches only go up a dollar or two. Andy's also has a children's menu, by the way, with deals like a hot dog, fries, and soda for $3.95. Good for tourist families wandering around the area—though, tucked into the shadows of the Michigan Avenue overpass, Andy's can't get a lot of passersby. It's more the kind of place you know about and introduce friends to.

Au Marché
- 437 N. Clark St., Chicago; (312) 321-0551

While Mr. C is generally wary of restaurants which offer catering (often tantamount to putting a neon sign out reading, "This place is expensive!"), this is, as the French would certainly agree, un bon marché—a good deal. Why pay the price for such "scenes" as Michael Jordan's and other nearby power-tie, schmooze-fest eateries, when you can go around the corner to this trendy, yet low-key cafe and deli? The menu items are innovative without being expensive, and since it's just counter service, you won't even need to tip—an added bonus that Mr. C and his readers always appreciate.

The immaculate Au Marché features hardwood floors and walls covered with a series of black and white photographs by a local artist known only as Seroni. Lit by mini track lights, these combine with the large streetside window to create an airy, cheerfully pleasant atmosphere. Combine this with healthy cuisine, and you'll head back to work both sated and relaxed—with a wallet that's not empty!

Raspberry/blueberry and strawberry/blueberry lemonades are simply heavenly, and cost not much more than a soda. Sandwiches can be ordered with sides of crispy, colorful veggies—carrots, red- skinned potatoes, and green beans—steamed just right. Mr. C enjoyed the tuna salad sandwich, which has not only celery chunks mixed in, but also fresh lingonberries for a tangy taste. It's served on rosemary bread, with a side of broccoli, for $4.25. Same price for a turkey sandwich with provolone cheese on seven-grain bread.

Deli specialties and prepared foods can be purchased by the pound to take home, and they're yummy. Some of these are priced rather exorbitantly, but you can always order individual-sized servings. Hummus is $6 a pound, which is comparable to grocery stores, and fresher; but lemon asparagus, at $7 a pound, could be made for a third that price at home. Stick to the chicken al fresco and turkey cashew crunch, which are about $2 for a single-sized serving. Au Marché is open weekdays only,

from 7:30 in the morning until 5:00 in the afternoon.

Billy Goat Tavern and Grill

- 430 N. Michigan Ave., Chicago; (312) 222-1525
- 309 W. Washington St., Chicago; (312) 899-1873

Well, no discussion of cheap dining in Chicago would be complete without a mention of these cut-rate charcuteries. Is there anyone who *doesn't* know by now that this is the birthplace of John Belushi's famous cry, "Chizbugger, chizbugger, chizbugger....No fries—*cheeps*!...." So the legend is told and retold—including here at the Billy Goat itself. Hey, they're proud of it.

Those cheeseburgers are $2.30 each, flat and greasy. If you're feeling particularly brave, go for the double at $3.55. And by the way, you can get fries, for another buck. The BG also has breakfast specials each morning, most around $2-$3. A ham and cheese omelette, for instance, goes for $2.95. Let's face it, sometimes cheap is cheap; the place is certainly not going to win any awards for health food. Especially when you consider that a full bar is positioned directly across from the grill—somehow, an odd sight, at least during the day. But it all makes for a nice, divey hangout that's popular with the working crowd.

Boogies Diner

- 923 N. Rush St., Chicago; (312) 915-0555

If you enjoy the nostalgic 1950's atmosphere of Ed Debevic's, but don't want to camp out overnight just to get a good spot in that loooooooonnnng line, you may want to try Boogie's instead.

"Eat Heavy Dress Cool" is their motto (it even appears in their phone book listing). Gary Busey, Daryl Hannah, and Kriss Kross have all done so. Sharon Stone, the story goes, had jeans delivered to her from the clothing boutique downstairs when her luggage got lost. Despite the ritzy guests, the atmosphere is definitely down-to-earth. Rock music blares almost as loudly as the Hard Rock Cafe's, running the gamut from the Everly Brothers to Joan Jett.

The food is all-American diner fare. The basic hamburger is $5.95, a bit pricey, but it's served with mashed potatoes or curly fries and it's a huge, super-stuffing sandwich. A separate order of the curly fries is $2.25, which gets you what they describe as a "mountain," definitely enough for two people. A similar order of beer-battered onion rings are $2.95.

Daily soup specials are hearty enough to get by on their own. Mr. C particularly enjoyed the spinach tortellini soup, which is $1.95 for a cup and $2.95 for a bowl. Turkey vegetable rice soup is always on hand, priced the same as the special.

Other diner classics include mac-n-cheese for $5.50 and a cold meatloaf sandwich for $6.50. Milkshakes are the drink of choice here, and not just in your generic chocolate, vanilla and strawberry flavors; how about peanut butter, coffee, raspberry, and banana. They may cost more than other milkshakes, at $3.25 a pop, but they're thick with ice cream, and available malted at no extra charge.

If you're not stuffed before it's dessert time, try the black cow ($2.65) or the homemade chocolate layer cake ($3.25, or a la mode for $4.25). Sundaes and banana splits run about $4, but a miniature sundae is just $1.75.

Yes, you can find food like this for less. Boogie's subscribes to the notion that bigger is better—both in prices *and* portions. Well, this is the Gold Coast...and relatively speaking, this ain't bad for the area. They do offer a patronage card, which may save you some dough if you come in here a lot. Buy five meals, get your card punched each time, and you'll get one meal free. Boogie's is open daily from 10 a.m. to 10 p.m., Fridays and Saturdays until 11 p.m., and Sundays from 11 a.m. to 8 p.m.

The CHIC Cafe
- 361 W. Chestnut St., Chicago; (312) 944-0882

You wouldn't guess from the name, but this is actually a school dining room. Ugh—why would anyone recommend such a place in a restaurant guide? Well, before you ponder images of warmed-over gruel and stale jello, let Mr. C add one important point: *This* school is the Cooking and Hospitality Institute of Chicago. Ahhhhhhh.

In fact, Mr. C is about to turn you on to the most inexpensive gourmet meal you may ever eat. For a fixed price of $10, these students—who will doubtless go on to cook in many of Chicagoland's finest restaurants—serve you a very fancy three-course lunch. The menu changes every day, offering two or three choices in each course of appetizer, soup or salad, and entree. It's always different, and always wonderful—elegant food in a casual setting.

Start off with something like grilled scallops in pear salsa, or peppered goat cheese in phyllo dough, topped with a liqueur sauce. Your second course might be a "Tuscan bread salad," a basic and very fresh salad of mixed greens, or a bowl of cold strawberry mango soup.

For the main course, your choices may include such delicacies as grilled catfish in basquaise sauce, served with rice and a fennel-vegetable compote; or, chicken cacciatore with spinach pasta and grilled fresh vegetables. The cafe may even spruce up a basic Mexican dish, like pork and green onion enchiladas, served with black bean and corn salsa and a stuffed sweet potato on the side—a far cry from El Torito!

There are some pretty fancy desserts on hand too, but alas, these cost $3.00 extra. For that matter, you may order a la carte from the menu—though Mr. C heartily recommends the package deal to get the full experience and the best value. Lunch is served here Mondays through Fridays, with one seating at noon only; beginning in January of 1994, they

MR. CHEAP'S PICKS
Near North—River
North, Streeterville

✔ **Au Marché**—Elegant, light French foods at even lighter prices.

✔ **The CHIC Cafe**—A gourmet cooking school opens its doors for upscale dining at bargain-basement prices.

✔ **Dick's Last Resort**—Not so cheap, unless you go for their late-night menu, from 12:30 to 3:30 a.m. Night owls rejoice!

✔ **Pizzeria Uno/Pizzeria Due**—Where it all began! The seats of the deep dish pizza empire.

✔ **P.K.'s Cafe**—Home cooking, cheap, for the business suit *and* coverall sets.

---

do expect to add Saturday and Sunday lunches at 12:30. No alcohol is served, but you are welcome to bring your own. The cafe itself is quite attractive, in an industrial-chic sort of way, with mauve walls and ficus trees underneath shiny ductwork. It only holds about ninety people, and so reservations are recommended (and required for groups). Tipping, by the way, is welcomed by these hardworking chefs-in-training; all tips are donated to the institute's scholarship fund.

The Corner Bakery
- 210 S. Canal St., Union Station, Chicago; (312) 441-0821
- 516 N. Clark St., Chicago, (312) 644-8100

A bakery with more than just sweets, the Corner Bakery's Union Station branch is a favorite among harried Loop office workers who gobble down their lunches in five minutes or less (not required, of course). At either location, the portions are good-sized, and the help is extremely friendly without being overbearing— even during lunch and dinner rushes. And all the baked goods are really made on the premises.

While the regular bakery items can thin your wallet (a loaf of chocolate cherry bread is $6.50), this is a good spot for lunch or breakfast with a number of different salads and sandwiches offered daily. Wheat berry salad, made with two kinds of peppers, is $3.50 for a small, $5.95 for a large. Curry chicken salad, with grapes and parsley is $3.85 and $6.95; and a hefty tuna salad sandwich with sprouts, on olive bread, is $4.50.

For snacks, desserts, or whatever, the Corner's popular pretzel rolls are just 75 cents each, and giant fudge brownies sprinkled with confectioner's sugar are $1.50.

The Union Station location is open Monday through Friday, from 6 a.m. to 10 p.m., on Saturday 8 a.m. to 8 p.m., on Sunday 8 a.m. to 7 p.m. Hours on Clark Street are Monday through Friday, 7 a.m. to 10 p.m., Saturday 7:30 a.m. to 11 p.m., and Sunday 8 a.m. to 9 p.m.

Dao Thai Restaurant
- 105 E. Ontario St., Chicago; (312) 664-9600

Mr. C is always on the lookout for good, cheap food in otherwise expensive parts of town. Here's a perfect example. Just a block in from Michgan Avenue, tucked in with ritzy hotels and shops, is a clean, cozy restaurant where almost nothing on the menu is priced over $6.00. And the food is really good.

Dao has a large selection of traditional Thai foods, from spring roll appetizers ($3.50) and soups (hot and sour, with shrimp, $2.75) to good ol' pad Thai ($4.75) and many other entrees. Half a dozen hot and cold salads are all around $5, such as bean thread salad—boiled clear noodles in a tangy coconut milk sauce, with bits of chicken, shrimp and vegetables mixed in.

Dinners include such tasty, good-sized platters as cashew chicken, mixed with pea pods, peppers, dried chili peppers, and pineapple; oyster beef, stir-fried with mushrooms, onions, ginger, and oyster sauce; and "Spicy crazy noodles," rice noodles mixed with prawn, chicken, vegetables, and chopped chili peppers. Only the roast duck, the steamed curried catfish (each $6.95) and fried whole red snapper (market price) go above the average price of $4-$6 per dish.

The restaurant makes a point of being helpful to particular diets, using vegetable oil for cooking and offering to substitute tofu in meat dishes for vegetarians. Beer and wine are served, along with cocktails. The atmosphere tends toward the noisy, bustling side, in what is pretty much a no-frills setting; but for good food at these prices, no one seems to mind.

Dick's Last Resort
- 435 E. Illinois St., Chicago; (312) 836-7870

You can escape to this "resort" by going only as far as the North Pier Festival Market. With patrons arriving on foot and by boat, this lakefront indoor/outdoor spot certainly has a yacht-club feeling to it. That's where the resemblance ends, though, at this extremely casual restaurant.

In fact, Mr. C wonders if the waiters and waitresses at Dick's Last Resort have to pass a surliness test before being hired. If you're not assertive or quick with witty remarks, well, be prepared to have your ego bruised! Actually, they're friendly enough, but mock-mockery has been cultivated as the house style.

You may also be wondering if a touristy-looking joint in a touristy location can be cheap; the answer is a definitive "yes and no." The dinner menu in its entirety, as well as Sunday brunch ($12.95 for adults, $5.95 for children) sail out of range on Mr. C's radar—though they're still good values, considering the enormous portions served. If you do go for brunch, you won't have to eat again until Wednesday at the earliest.

Still, you can experience this resort on a bargain-hunter's budget by going at a particular time: Late at night. Dick's after-hours menu merges dinner and breakfast together, and prices them affordably. Two eggs, any way you want them (assuming your server is in a good mood), with "spuds" and a biscuit on the side, are just $2.95. Good deal. A ham steak and eggs are $4.95, as are "Disaster" omelettes, available in any combination of mushrooms, cheese, or ham.

During the wee hours, Dick's famous pizza is not available, for reasons not clear to Mr. C; but you can get "Yuppie fried mozzarella sticks" (there's that attitude again) for $3.95, cheeseburgers for $4.25, and a giant plate of crispy chicken tenders for $5.95. Lots of folks also like to reel in the $6.95 steak sandwich. For dessert: Pecan pie, cheesecake with strawberries, and chocolate mousse pie are a reasonable $2.25 a slice each.

The atmosphere at Dick's is bustling, and the music is loud; nighttimes frequently feature live rhythm and blues bands. And, believe it or not, gospel groups raise the roof during Sunday brunch.

The wisecracking wait staff must also have to pass a night-owl skills test, since the after-midnight menu is offered from 12:30 a.m. until 3:30 a.m. on Fridays, and until 4:30 a.m. on Saturdays. Of course, that really means Saturdays and Sundays—but if you already knew that, you've passed the test yourself.

Ed Debevic's
- 640 N. Wells St., Chicago; (312) 664-1707
- 660 W. Lake Cook Rd., Deerfield; (708) 945-3242.

"Make up your mind!!" yelled a waiter to a hapless booth of dawdling teenagers. Regulars continued to sip their coffee, unconcerned, while uninitiated tourists whipped their heads around to investigate the cause of the outburst. They might have been forewarned that this is a quirky place by the sign that reads, "No shoes, no shirt, no pants, no service." This is Ed Debevic's, where the the customers eat good ol' American food on the cheap while being entertained by verbally abusive waiters and waitresses.

The crowd (there's *always* a crowd) consists of families with rambunctious kids, bachelor businessmen looking for a close-as-you-can-get-to-home-cooked meal, couples on dates, and the aforementioned tourists. They are served primarily by out-of-work actors, who pay the rent by slinging hash here (something Mr. C can appreciate from personal experience). Their dramatics may be more at home on the stage, but no one seems to mind. You're just as likely to be called "honey" or "sweetie" in between their histrionic outbursts.

Mr. C digresses. On to the food! As another of Ed's many signs proclaims, "If you can find a better diner, eat there." Choosing to eat here is easy—*getting in* is hard. If you do stay here, you can grab a juicy hamburger for $4.30; not as cheap as some places, but huge and served with onion and tomato. Add a pile of French fries for $1.95, easily enough for two people to share. Homemade "Windy City Chili" is $2.30 a cup. The truly deluxe plate of "Mile High Meatloaf" comes with potatoes, a choice of vegetables, bread, and another choice of soup, cole slaw, or salad...all for $4.95. Mom never made it so good! Other deluxe choices include chicken pot pie and chicken fried steak. Mom probably never made those, period. Mr. C enjoyed a similar roast turkey deluxe platter for $5.95.

There are always daily specials, including desserts. On Mr. C's visit, he loved the special peach cobbler ($2.95)—homemade and yummy. All of the pies, such as Oreo, coconut and apple, are always homemade, and reasonably priced indeed at $1.95 and up. For those who are sweet-toothed but small of stomach, Ed's also sells "The world's smallest hot fudge sundae," squeezed into something barely larger than a shot glass, for a suitably miniscule 49 cents.

Modeled after the All-American diners of the 1950's, Ed's is a proud recipient of the "Good Coffee Award" from the Coffee Brewing Association of America. The volume of the restaurant requires java to be made almost constantly, if not more often. There is also a full bar, serving cocktails, beer and reasonably priced wines. And try Ed Debevic's own beer, "aged in the bottle," $2.50 a pop.

Ed's now accepts credit cards—something unpracticed in years past. They serve until 11:00 p.m. on weeknights, and to 1:00 a.m. on weekends.

Edwardo's Natural Pizza Restaurant

- 1212 N. Dearborn St., Chicago; (312) 337-4490
- 521 S. Dearborn St., Chicago; (312) 939-3366
- 1321 E. 57th St., Chicago, (312) 241-7960

Many other suburban locations
Despite its yuppie exterior and award-winning pizza, Edwardo's is not all that expensive, especially if you take advantage of their terrific lunch buffet. But you can split a pizza, order an individual salad and a soda at any hour, and still only spend $6 or so.

Now, about that buffet. It costs just $4.95 per person. First, fill up at the salad bar with fresh greens and tomatoes, multicolored rotini in a nutty pesto sauce, thick cantaloupe wedges, and tangy poppyseed dressing. Then, choose from four different pizzas (two with a whole-wheat crust, including their wonderfully tasty spinach pie), baked ziti, and other entrees. Don't forget frozen glacee or chocolate cake for dessert. This incredible deal is offered weekdays from 11:30 a.m. until 3 p.m., with a $6.49 dinner version offered daily from 5-9 p.m. The main difference between the two buffets is that the dinner buffet offers stuffed pizza while the lunch buffet does not.

If you're not in the mood for the

buffet, the appetizer menu has great garlic bread for $1.75 (slather it with mozzarella for 50 cents extra), or a Caesar salad for $2.95. Stuffed pizzas start at $9.35 for a regular size mozzarella, which itself can be enough to share. Prices go on to $14.75 for a basic large pie, higher with extra toppings; but it serves four or five people. Thin crust pizzas run up to $19 for the large Edwardo's special, and a whole wheat crust is 75 cents extra for either style pizza. Other types of pies include vegetarian, with mushrooms, peppers and onions; pesto pizza, and several more. Desserts are on the rich side, with a slice of blueberry cheesecake about $3.

Edwardo's also offers delivery (not free) to limited areas.

Foodlife

- Water Tower Place, 835 N. Michigan Ave., Chicago; (312) 335-3663

What is Mr. Cheap doing in a place like this? A Gold Coast shopping mall anchored by Marshall Field's on one side and Lord & Taylor on the other? Eating, that's what. Believe it or don't—the trendy Foodlife dining area on the mezzanine level is a relatively cheap place for tourists and shoppers to cool their jets. Certainly, it's unique and worth a look; you can eat very well here and still stay under Mr. C's budget of $10 per person. It sure puts the McChain food courts to shame.

Okay, this place is as much a concept as a restaurant. Signs overhead read, "Be kind. Eat true. It's now." Whatever that means. Foodlife is a Disneyland of dining, with food stands for about a dozen cuisines from around the globe, each festooned with the appropriate decor. World-beat music offers gentle rhythms to smooth out the otherwise bustling environs; in all, it feels like you've traveled to some foreign marketplace. When you arrive at the entrance to Foodlife, you are greeted and ushered to a table with instructions on the law of the land—"This is your table; feel free to walk around,

MR. CHEAP'S PICKS
Near North—Gold Coast

- ✔ **Foodlife**—How can such trendy, "concept" dining be so inexpensive? A most unusual place.
- ✔ **Third Coast Coffee House**—Get these popular pastries directly from the source. Full meals, too, and all inexpensive.

decide what you'd like to eat...as long as this blue card is showing, no one will take your table...." You are also given your own "passport," a temporary credit card enabling you to visit as many booths as you wish, putting together any kind of meal, and pay for the whole thing at the end.

Needless to say, there are as many folks wandering around with a sort of bewildered look on their faces, as there are regulars who have the system down. The professional crowd makes lunch here a big business, although Foodlife is open for dinner until 10:00 p.m. (there is a movie theater in the mall, too).

The food can be as fancy as the surroundings, although there are enough of the basics for any taste or age group. The "Roadhouse" stand, for example, has good burgers from $3.50; an Italian food booth nearby allows you to mix and match from several spaghettis and sauces at $4.95 for the plate. And, for $2.75, try a hefty slice of sweet fennel sausage pizza.

At "Mother Earth Grains," though, Mr. C tried a platter of acorn squash stuffed with vegetables and angel hair pasta, with baked cheese over the top. This included a side dish (red beans and rice, Cuban black beans, etc.), all for $4.75, and all delicious. The Mexican place around the corner, along with quesadillas, offered as its special of the day a hunk of pan-blackened cod in pineapple salsa, with rice and beans, for a somewhat pricier $6.50 (about as expensive as any entree gets here). The same price at "Some Dim Sum" gets you a mountainous shrimp and vegetable salad plate.

What to drink with all this? Take your pick from an espresso bar, a juice bar, or a good selection of beers and wines. And for $1.60, you can get a large soda cup which you can use for endless refills. There are also soups, salads, breads, and of course, desserts.

While Foodlife doesn't quite qualify as a "No-Tip" restaurant, you don't have to leave anything on the table—a surcharge of only 6% is added to your bill, and you may elect not to pay it if you wish. However, Mr. C found the service to be among the most polite he's ever seen. As he heard one food server say to an obvious first-timer, "Just relax and enjoy the ride!"

Gino's East

- 160 E. Superior St., Chicago; (312) 943-1124
- 164 E. Superior St., Chicago (carry-out only); (312) 988-4200

And other suburban locations

Not to be confused with the similarly dark and artsy-graffitied Gino's on Rush Street (a mistake only a tourist could make—don't be fooled!), this famous Streeterville landmark can actually be a cheap place to dine. The carry-out side of the operation is the real deal; it sells Gino's "mini-pizzas" at all times, while the main restaurant only offers them during weekday lunch. You can even save the tip.

These wonderful little creations are just $3.75 for the regular variety, or $4.25 with sausage; other topping specials change daily, including lots of unusual vegetarian choices. A cup of thick minestrone will go nicely with your pie at $1.50.

Small or medium pizzas ($7.75 and $9.75, respectively) can also be a bargain, if you split them with someone. They're so stuffed with good ingredients that you'll have plenty to share—or leftovers to take home—unless you arrive here absolutely famished.

If, for some odd reason, you feel like skipping the pizza for a hot Italian beef or sausage sandwich, you'll shell out only $4.95 for either one. Or go for something lighter, like a turkey salad plate for $4.25.

Desserts are not available for carry-out, but in the restaurant you can finish off your meal with tortoni or spumoni, $1.50 each; cannoli go for $1.75, and lemon ice is $1.95.

Delivery is also available. Another nice feature at Gino's is the fact that you can pre-order your pizzas by calling the restaurant half an hour before you plan to arrive.

Hard Rock Cafe

- 63 W. Ontario St., Chicago; (312) 943-2252

If you want to pay for atmosphere as much as for food, this is the place. The food is quite good and very filling, but as everyone knows, that's not what the place is all about. It's about the decor. Two dining floors are packed with t-shirts, autographed guitars, platinum and gold records and other doo-dads from the likes of Madonna, the Pretenders, Fleetwood Mac, the Beatles, and Bo Diddley. They're also packed with customers, mainly tourists, at all times. There's no escaping the high-decibel music on either level, so prepare for a party-hearty atmosphere; but the "Love All—Serve All" service is super.

A 1/3 pound turkey burger comes with thick-cut steak fries and a side salad for $5.95, not too shabby at all. A tub-size grilled chicken breast salad is $6.95. The tuna salad sandwich ($6.50) is uniquely crunchy, thanks to the mixed-in water chestnuts; it also comes with fries and salad.

Desserts are where they get ya. New-York style cheesecake is a bit rich for Mr. C at $3.75 a slice. A coffee float will set you back $2.95. Liquor and sodas, of course, are

similarly inflated (in price, that is).
The Hard Rock is open seven days a
week, serving until 11:30 or 12:00
midnight.

Ishtar Inn
- 615 N. Wells St., Chicago; (312)
  587-0721

If you're like Mr. C, and the name of
this place reminds you of that famous
flop of a movie with Warren Beatty
and Dustin Hoffman, don't worry.
The food here is no turkey. In fact,
the specialty of the house is Assyrian
cuisine (y'know, Middle Eastern),
making this newcomer a fine, inexpensive River North dining option.

No simple falafel joint, Ishtar is
a proper restaurant, with white linen
tablecloths, potted plants, and tapestry carpeting for decor. Ancient
Assyrians gaze down upon you from
wall murals, while their modern-day
descendants serve you dinners like
zinde d'erba ($8), broiled lamb shank
cooked in spices, nice and tender.
Dolmeh ($8.50) is the traditional
grape leaves, stuffed here with rice
and your choice of ground lamb,
beef, or chicken. And cornish hen is
charcoal broiled in a tasty house mari-
nade. It's also $8; there are several en-
trees which go over Mr. C's $10
limit, but don't forget that all dinners
include rice, salad, and pita bread.

There are also vegetarian entrees, which are even better deals; the
vegetarian combo, with hummus,
tabouleh, baba ganouj, falafel, and
salad, is just $6.75. And you can get
sandwich versions of most items, for
about $3-$4 each. Finish off with a
piece of baklava ($1.50) and dark
Assyrian coffee ($1.75), strong
enough to knock Starbucks for a loop.

Jacob Bros. Bagels
- 58 E. Randolph St., Chicago; (312)
  368-1180
- 53 W. Jackson Blvd., Chicago;
  (312) 922-BAGL (2245)
- 50 E. Chicago Ave., Chicago; (312)
  664-0026

With two locations tucked inside the
Loop and one to the north, you can
stop in here for a snack on the run or
a quick meal. The prices, meanwhile,

are nice and cheap—hardly what
you'd expect from the fancy gold lettering on the door or the yuppified
mauve and ivory color scheme.

Choose from 17 different types
of bagels, from the standard ingredients to flavors like cheese and honey-
oat bran. Bagels are all 50 cents
each; slathered with various blends of
terrific cream cheese, shipped in
from Vermont, they go for $1.40.

Lunch items include pasta salad
for 95 cents. Real deli-style sandwiches are all around $3.25; among
the good picks are chicken salad,
tuna, turkey, ham, Havarti cheese and
kosher salami. Add a side order of
fresh couscous salad for 90 cents
more. There are several Middle Eastern items on the menu, in fact; take
home a half pound of hummus for
$2.65. Half a pound of their cream
cheese or lox spread is about $2.50.
Mr. C found the fruit salad, though,
to be laden with that bitter-tasting sul-
fate flavor preservative.

Many of the "dessert" choices,
while good, are geared to the ascetic:
Oatmeal raisin bars, carrot-raisin
bread, or zucchini bread. But don't
worry—you can eschew the healthy
for the sinful route and grab a rich
brownie for $1, and a good cup of
coffee for just 70 cents.

An obvious commuter stop, Jacob Bros. Bagels is open from 6:30
a.m. to 6:00 p.m. weekdays, and 10-3
on Saturdays.

Johnny Rockets, The Original Hamburger
- 2530 N. Clark St., Chicago; (312)
  472-6191
- 901 N. Rush St., Chicago; (312)
  337-3900
- One Schaumburg Place,
  Schaumburg; (708) 240-1900

Okay, so the menu is limited at
Johnny Rockets, but this national
chain's food and prices will make
you think that you've been transported back in time to the 1950's.
That's not unique in Chicago, of
course—but Johnny Rockets can take
you there for less than certain other
trendy retro-cafes.

Hamburger is the basic language spoken here. The "Original Burger," starting at $3.35, is topped with all the necessaries: Lettuce, tomato, mustard, pickle, mayo, relish, and chopped onion. For a quarter more, you can add Johnny's cheddar cheese and "red, red sauce." Chili and bacon will add still more to the ticket, yet will still keep the burger under $5.

Hamburger haters can find something for themselves here, like an egg salad sandwich ($2.45), the ever-popular BLT ($3.55), and a grilled cheese sandwich ($2.65). Throw some fries on the side for $1.45; better yet, try their chili fries for $2.75.

Johnny Rockets' "famous" malts and shakes are $2.95. For dessert, apple pie is $1.65; served a la mode, it's $2.40. It ain't like mom's, but it's not bad. Basically, this is fast food with a bit more character than all your McChains, with its counter and stools, and sparkling white tile motif—an idealized, "Happy Days" kinda joint. Johnny Rockets also stays open until 2:00 a.m. on weekends.

Lo-Cal Zone
- 912 N. Rush St. Chicago; (312) 943-9060

While the front door of Lo-Cal Zone sports the word FAT with the familiar red circle-and-slash symbol over it, don't run away for fear of tasteless, boring food. This teeny-tiny purple-painted health food haven specializes in such traditional junk food as burritos, fajitas, and even soft-serve ice cream.

Just opened in 1989, the Zone's motto is "Eat here, your body will love it." Your wallet won't complain, either. The aforementioned burritos are about $4.25 each; Mr. C particularly enjoyed the turkey and pepper combination, one of over ten different varieties. Fat-free, dairy-free mini-pizzas made with soy cheese are just $2.65 (and only 160 calories) each; a lo-cal tuna sandwich is $4.15.

Lo-Cal Zone is also a smoke-free zone.

Open from 11:00 a.m. to 10:30 p.m. Mondays through Thursdays, 'til 11 Fridays, midnight Saturdays and 9:00 p.m. Sundays.

Melvin B's Truck Stop Cafe and Beer Garden
- 1114 N. State St., Chicago; (312) 751-9897

An unusual spot for the ritzy Gold Coast neighborhood, Melvin B's attracts a hip, but young, crowd. College-age seems to be the norm, especially from Wednesday through the weekend, when the place really packs 'em in. The walls of its atmospheric, hunter-green interior are lined with political posters from campaigns of years gone by. Hmm...is that one for Richard Nixon intended as a decoration or a dart board in such a traditionally Democratic town?

No matter. Melvin's bar food isn't politics-as-usual either, with such offerings as a hearty chicken pot pie for $6.95. Hamburgers are served with a rah-ther trendy basil herb dressing (don't forget where you are) and Saratoga chips, for $5.95. Plenty of good beers on tap, of course.

Melvin B's is open from 11:00 a.m. for lunch; it stays open until 2:00 a.m. on weekdays, and 3:00 a.m. on Saturdays. The huge front beer garden of the title closes up a bit earlier, probably to spare the neighbors—11:00 weeknights, and midnight on Saturdays.

Michigan Avenue Hot Dogs
- 111 E. Ontario St., Chicago; (312) 335-9393.

A busy Near North fixture, recently under new management, Michigan Avenue Hot Dogs is actually tucked into a narrow storefront just a few steps off of Michigan—a seemingly odd neighbor for those glitzy shops, or perhaps the perfect antidote. It caters to folks in a hurry as well as those who prefer to sit down while eating. People do, you know.

Not only do you get served quickly here, but you won't have to tip (unless you want to, of course). The prices are certainly right. And an added bonus is that the place is very—and Mr. C means *very*—clean. No ordinary hot dog stand, this.

The *specialty du maison* is the "Chicago Dog," with all the fixings—celery salt, onions, chili peppers, name your poison—for just $1.69. There are plenty of other varieties, too; but, in spite of the name, coming here does not only mean going to the dogs. The menu is filled out by such choices as a fried fish sandwich ($1.99), a bacon, egg, and cheese sandwich ($1.79), and cheese pizza by the slice ($1.39). Burger lovers will love the $2.59 price for a single-patty, $4.09 for the double.

Complete your gourmet meal with French fries for 99 cents, or a garden salad for $2.59. Chef's salads are also available, for $4.19. And a quart(!) of soda to wash it all down is $1.19.

M.A.H.D. offers delivery and is open every day of the week. Monday through Thursday hours are from 7 a.m.-7 p.m.; Fridays and Saturdays from 7 a.m. until 9 p.m., and Sundays 9 a.m. until 6 p.m.

The Original Pancake House
- 22 E. Bellevue Place, Chicago; (312) 642-7917
- 10437 S. Western Ave, Chicago; (312) 445-6100
- 1517 E. Hyde Park Blvd., Chicago; (312) 288-2322
- 2020 N. Lincoln Park West, Chicago; (312) 929-8130
- 700 E. 87th Ave., Chicago; (312) 874-0010

Many other suburban locations
Proudly located across the street from the fancy-shmancy Meridien Hotel, this charming, warm, and homey eatery—part of a chain based in Portland, Oregon—wins Mr. C's award for friendliest and most efficient staff in town.

Even though the folks at OPH are obsessively preoccupied with high quality, the breakfast-all-day meals here won't budge your budget too much. You'll be stuffed after a ham and cheese omelette, served with three buttermilk pancakes, all for $5.95. The pancakes are extra-smooth and fluffy, thanks to a special sourdough yeast made especially for the House.

You can also beat the breakfast blahs here by ordering something out of the ordinary. Ever tried coconut pancakes ($4.50)? Ever heard of them? Or, how about Hawaiian pancakes, topped with pineapple and tropical syrup ($4.25). Get back to nature with OPH's old-fashioned oats, served with cream, for $1.60. And their trademark coffee, brought to you topped with whipping cream if you wish, is 90 cents. Potato pancakes are served with apple sauce and sour cream for $4.25. The spuds are imported all the way from Idaho, and their lingonberries (another sweet pancake option) have come even further—from Sweden.

The Original Pancake House does not accept credit cards, which is one way they keep their prices down.

Pizzeria Uno
- 29 E. Ohio St., Chicago; (312) 321-1000

Pizzeria Due
- 619 N. Wabash Ave., Chicago; (312) 943-2400

To call these restaurants a Chicago legend, as the creators of deep-dish pizza, is by now an understatement. Especially since they've undertaken a nationwide expansion which, in some cities, seems to have put an Uno's on every other block. Fortunately, Mssrs. Sewell and company haven't messed with the original recipes, and these two establishments remain pleasant and inexpensive dining options in the touristy Near North area.

They both share an identical menu and prices, by the way; the only appreciable difference between the two is size. Due is the larger of the pair, a rambling warren of cozy and intimate rooms. It also offers an outdoor patio on the second floor, a particularly nice option on a warm summer evening. Speaking of which, Due stays open later—until about 2:30 a.m. most nights, compared to 1:00 a.m. at Uno.

There, the disparities end. At either place, you get the same great pizza, from just $3.85 for an individual cheese pie up to $17.95 for a large-size "Numero Uno" packed with sausage, pepperoni, mushrooms, onions, peppers, and extra cheese. You could probably live off this for a month. In between, there are two other sizes and a zillion combinations of ingredients for you to mix and match. And there are plenty of good beers to wash it down with, as well as wines and a full bar.

Meanwhile, you're not limited to pies here—try a plate of angel hair pasta in marinara sauce, with a side salad and garlic bread, all for just $4.95. Add meatballs, and it's $6.95. Soups, salads, and sandwiches round out the bill of fare, all reasonably priced. And their express lunches, offering an individual pizza with your choice of soup or salad for $4.95, can't be beat. It's served up super-quick on weekdays from 11:30 a.m. to 3:00 p.m.

P.K.'s Cafe
- 659 N. State St., Chicago; (312) 266-8114

"Excellent food at reasonable prices," proclaims the menu at this neighborhood eatery, a Mr. C dream-come-true. During lunch and dinner rushes, the carry-out order phone rings as soon as they put it down, and a line of hungry patrons winds out the door. Yet, no matter how crazy it gets here, you'll still be served quickly. Siskel and Ebert gave the place two thumbs up, as seen in autographed pictures hanging on the wall; and you *know* how hard it is for them to agree on anything.

The restaurant's location, amidst the Near North hotel district, may seem a bit unlikely. So does the mix of construction workers, men in three-piece suits, and students who all frequent the joint. Side by side at the counter, they don't mind asking one another to pass the salt or ketchup for their $2.25 hamburgers or their 79 cent French fries. The "American croissant" (basically a gussied-up cheeseburger), comes with those fries all for a neat $2.80.

Mr. C heartily recommends P.K.'s homemade chicken alphabet soup, chock full of big chunks of carrots; a bowl sells for a delectable $1.16. This is also one of the few good places in the downtown area to get cheap seafood and fish—like broiled rainbow trout for just $4.95, with soup or salad, potato, rolls and butter. And that's a la carte—with the vegetable of the day, the meal is just $1 more! P.K.'s lighter offerings include stuffed avocado with shrimp salad for $3.95, and stuffed cantaloupe with tuna or chicken salad for $3.75. Oh, and for those who follow this sort of thing, it's also one of the few places which still dispenses RC Cola.

Breakfast is served all day—one of Mr. C's favorite features. The omelettes, fluffy and enormous, are actually a popular lunch item. A plain cheese omelette sells for $3.05. A plate of butt steak and eggs goes for $5.15. The cafe opens bright and early at 5:30 a.m. seven days a week, and remains open until 7:30 p.m. on weekdays. Saturdays, they close up shop at 6:30 p.m.; Sundays, at 4:00.

Reza's Restaurant
- 432 W. Ontario St., Chicago; (312) 664-4500
- 5255 N. Clark St., Chicago; (312) 561-1898

A longtime Middle Eastern favorite in Andersonville, Reza's has been serving up incredibly large portions of Persian specialties at surprisingly low prices for years. Many folks call it one of the best deals in town. Now, they've opened a second location in River North. It's even larger and flashier than the handsome original, with outdoor tables for *al fresco* dining on a quiet stretch of Ontario Street. The new spot doubles as a brewery, dominated by huge copper vats behind the bar.

Both locations feature the same menu. Start off with one of two dozen appetizers, many of which are vegetarian—and nearly all of which are around $3 each. Falafel, of course, is a must; but try the vegetable casserole ($3.50), a blend of zucchini, eggplant, carrots, green peppers, and scallions baked in a tomato sauce and served over rice. Mmmmmmm.

Entrees divide mainly into two types: Stews and skewers. Both, again, come in gigantic proportions. Mr. C opted for what is simply called "The Combo" ($7.95): One skewer of char-broiled filet mignon and one skewer of marinated grilled chicken, separated by a mountain of dill flavored rice. Each skewer was big enough to be an entree in itself—a footlong strip of meat, juicy and delicious. And none of your "beef, tomato, pepper, onion, beef..." skewer; each one was all meat, and the vegetables came in a third strip on the side. It was all too much to finish, and tasted just as good the next day.

Mr. C's dining companion chose a bowl of "khoresht ghormeh sabzi" ($5.95—and don't worry, you can order any item by number). This is a savory soup of ground beef, kidney beans, chopped onions, and greens, all spiked with tangy lemon juice and other spices. The vast bowl was accompanied by another mound of rice (white, this time); and if you think this can't be enough by itself, think again. Scrumptious and filling.

There are plenty of seafood and vegetarian dishes on the large menu; with the exception of some seafood orders, almost every entree is priced under $10. And if you have room for dessert, try a strong cup of coffee and a piece of the homemade baklava (only 95¢) or zoulbia (75¢), a deep-fried pastry made without sugar.

The downtown Reza's is clearly designed to be a showplace, a trendy spot to see and be seen among the galleries of River North. During Mr. C's visit, alas, the brewing operation was not yet up and running; no doubt it will only add to the spectacle, and yield up some potent potables. In the meantime, there is an extensive beer and wine list. The service here is like that of a fancy hotel—including valet parking, something you certainly won't find at many of the establishments in this book! In all, it's a place where you can really impress someone—a date, a client, or whomever—without spending a fortune.

River North Cafe
- 750 N. Franklin St., Chicago; (312) 642-6633

Sitting as it does underneath the Chicago Avenue "el" station, the River North Cafe is a surprisingly pleasant place to stop in for a quick bite or a good cup of cappuccino. It's really sort of a cross between a coffeehouse and a sandwich shop; mixed with a heavy dose of humor born, perhaps, out of the regular rumble of trains.

Hefty sandwiches are a specialty here, with a full array of deli choices. Chomp down on their pastrami or corned beef (each $4.75), made with one-third of a pound of meat on thick-sliced bakery breads. For a bit more, the specialty sandwiches (all $5.95) offer unique combinations like the "Feta-Compli"—roasted red peppers, feta cheese, ham, lettuce, and tomato. The "Macintosh" combines slices of two kinds of apples with ham and cheese. And "Surf and Turf" here means tuna salad and bacon (there's that sense of humor) with avocado, lettuce, and tomato. These come with a side order of potato salad, cole slaw, or bok choy salad—now, that's different.

Salads are big and interesting too, if a bit high in price; most are $6.50 a bowl. But with choices like lemon chicken salad, smoked turkey and pasta, and the recently introduced "Tex-Mex Beef"—roast beef with peppers, cilantro and salsa, and homemade corn bread on the side— you may just find these well worth it.

Speaking of Tex-Mex, River North makes its own chili ($3.95 a bowl), soups, and baked stuffed potatoes. There is also a daily special hot meal, like stuffed green peppers with garlic bread, always $4.95.

Of course, you could skip all this and go for the sweets, from flavored coffees and iced teas to kahlua brownies and peanut butter pie. These, quite frankly, are a bit pricey, but yummy all the same. River North Cafe is open during breakfast and lunch hours only, closing at 5:30 p.m. and all day Sunday.

Rock 'N Roll McDonald's

- 600 N. Clark St., Chicago; (312) 664-7940

Mr. C has a rule—he does not write about fast-food chains. After all, you certainly don't need him to tell you about Mickey D's. He also knows that rules are made to be broken, and this is the place to do it.

Can't wait an hour to see the rock memorabilia at the Hard Rock across the street? Jam into this McDonald's instead. It's always crowded, yet there never seems to be a line to get in. The music, an endless supply of teeny-boppers' greatest hits, is every bit as loud (and fun) as that of its neighbor. Wander around as best you can; there's plenty to take in.

Prices are a tad higher than in a regular McDonald's, but that's because this one has life-size plaster of Paris replicas of John, Paul, George, and Ringo walking down Abbey Road. Marilyn and Elvis also figure prominently, as do 1960's Corvettes—including a full-size model, complete with joyriders. Not to mention mirror balls revolving from the ceiling, and one of those amusement park photo booths.

Open 24 hours Thursday, Friday, and Saturday, and from 6 a.m. to 3 a.m. the rest of the week. A word of caution, though: The neighborhood can get a bit rough in the wee hours of the morning. Mr. C advises that you stick to day or evening times when eating here.

The Third Coast Coffee House and Wine Bar

- 1260 N. Dearborn St., Chicago; (312) 649-0730

The Third Coast really makes waves with its funky atmosphere and great prices. Ostensibly just a coffee shop, catering to the Parcheesi/Ouija board-playing crowd, they actually serve breakfast, lunch, and dinner. You'll find Third Coast muffins and munchies in many other coffee shops in the city, but of course the prices are cheapest here at the source.

The Third Coast also beats out other coffeehouses with its atmosphere. Old-fashioned metal milk-crates, worn, circa-1940's ice skates, antique model airplanes, and cases of footballs and baseball gloves from decades past decorate the entire restaurant. Shaded light sconces keep the room mellow, even during the busy evening hours. And the cozy marble-topped tables and the blue cushioned chairs make this place perfect for a hot game of Trivial Pursuit.

In the morning, open your eyes with their homemade scones ($1.75), available in blueberry, chocolate, raspberry, and currant. Muffins, $1.50 each, are truly enormous and will keep you stuffed until lunch. These come in such flavors as lemon poppyseed, cranberry, and blueberry. Other breakfast items include fresh fruit salad ($3.50) and granola with milk ($2.75, also available with fruit for 50 cents more, or with fruit and yogurt for 75 cents more).

Moving on to lunch and dinner: A very filling and spicy hummos plate, with veggies and warmed pita bread goes for $4.50, and a simple order of salsa and tortilla chips is a bargain at $1.50. On the fancier side, have a fresh Niçoise salad for $5.95, or a smoked turkey sandwich for $5.50. Vegetarian chili and other soups are $1.95 per cup, and $2.95 for a bowl.

On tap at Third Coast, you'll find Heineken, Amstel, Guinness, Leinenkugel's and Paulner Weiss. For your caffeine fix, espresso is $1.50 and cafe au lait is $1.75—or try the delightful iced raspberry coffee for $2.75. Tuesdays through Saturdays, Third Coast stays open twenty-four hours; Sundays and Mondays, they close at midnight.

Timothy O'Toole's

- 622 N. Fairbanks Court, Chicago; (312) 642-0700

Tourists and just plain regular folks who find themselves among the pricey environs of Streeterville may want to check out this casual, pub-style joint. It's hidden away underneath the corner of Fairbanks and Ontario, with an entrance tucked in amongst more trendy cafes; but downstairs, you'll find a cavernous restaurant with a large central bar area, pool tables, TV sets with the obligatory ball games, and more. The dining tables are set apart from the bar, giving them a bit of, shall we say, aesthetic distance.

The menu is just as big as the room, with a wide variety of pub grub. Nibble your way through the afternoon or evening with all the classic appetizers, from Buffalo wings ($4.95 for a pound of them, on a bed of French fries!) to potato skins (same price) or a basket of fried zucchini, mushrooms and onion rings for $3.95.

Soups, salads, and sandwiches are all here, though the salads are priced a bit higher than they could be. Burgers, chicken sandwiches, reubens and the like are all priced around $6, served with fries and cole slaw.

The real bargains, though, are the dinner entrees—nearly two dozen choices, many in the $6-$8 price range. Fish and chips are $5.95; same price for a plate of baked mostaccioli; chicken or beef chimichangas are $6.95; and a barbecued whole (!) chicken dinner, with potato or rice and garlic bread, is just $7.95—that's nothing to flap at. For $9.95, you can even get a half-chicken and half-rack of ribs combo.

Oh, and each day there's a special deal, like lasagna with garlic bread for $2.99 (not a typo), or "Wings, wings, wings" for 25 cents apiece. There is, of course, a fine selection of beers and other libations to help you with the pig-out; plenty of good drafts and bottles, including Guinness, Samuel Adams, Wild Boar, and Sierra Nevada Pale Ale. Mr. C often points out that where there's booze, there's cheap food; this is a perfect example.

West Egg Cafe & Rotisserie
- 620 N. Fairbanks Ct., Chicago; (312) 280-8366

- West Egg on State, 1139 N. State St., Chicago; (312) 951-7900
- West Egg on Monroe, 525 W. Monroe St., Chicago; (312) 454-9939, (takeout line, 454-0652)

You don't have to be rich as Gatsby to eat at the West Egg. They serve breakfast, lunch, and dinner, in hefty portions at reasonable prices. Ingredients are all super-fresh, too—and what they do with them gets rather creative.

Breakfast is served all day long. Start off with fresh-squeezed orange or grapefruit juice for $1.35. Omelettes come with an English muffin and potatoes or tomato slices, priced from $5 for your basic cheese version to $6 for the "Bacado," which is stuffed with bacon, guacamole, Jack cheese, and a side of salsa. *Olé*! The clever "breakfast salad" is actually layers of granola, yogurt, fruit, and nuts in a parfait glass, served with a homemade muffin for $4.95. Plain granola topped with beautiful blueberries or sweet strawberries is just $2.95, and the California Crepe, with broccoli, cheese, avocado, mushrooms, and eggs stuffed inside, is $5.95. You can even create your own breakfast, and add sides of potatoes for $1, an English muffin for 75 cents or a bowl of yogurt for $2.25.

The West Egg's wit continues into the lunch menu. Try the "Coop de Ville" ($6.75), a marinated chicken breast covered with bacon, avocado and melted cheese on a kaiser roll; or the "Creole Chicadee" ($6.25), all-white chicken meat grilled with fiery-hot sauce, plus lettuce, tomato, and Cajun mayonnaise. On the lighter side, Cobb and shrimp salads are each $6.95, and a crunchy taco salad is $5.95.

More standard fare includes a whopping half-pound burger for $4.95, and the Sicilian version of the New Orleans poor boy sandwich (grilled eggplant, zucchini, mushrooms, onions, and tomato on top of spinach, with a basil-pesto sauce and melted Montery Jack cheese) for $6.25. Most lunch dishes are served with a side salad and potatoes.

Be sure to watch for specials of the day. There's often a $4.95 dinner special, such as barbecued ribs, or chicken fajitas; these are especially popular with the after-work crowd that hangs out at the bar. If you're looking for a quieter spot to eat, there's also a sunken dining room with handsomely spotless hardwood floors.

The West Eggers are a bit snitty about substitutions—the place just gets too busy. They won't even give you separate checks, so don't bother asking. Another no-no is cigar or pipe smoking, though; you'll be able to breathe easy during your meal. And insomniacs can egg each other into staying until the wee hours; West Egg is open from 6:30 a.m. until midnight, Monday through Thursday. It's also open all the way through from 6:30 Friday morning until midnight on Sunday. That's no yolk!

SOUTH SIDE
(including Bridgeport, Chinatown, Hyde Park)

Ann Sather
- 929 W. Belmont Ave., Chicago; (312) 348-2378
- 5207 N. Clark St., Chicago; (312) 271-6677
- 1329 E. 57th St., Chicago; (312) 947-9323

For true-blue Swedish dining, a significant part of Chicago's heritage, this famous restaurant has it all. The original Ann Sather in Lake View was formerly a funeral home, but you can't tell now with the way that they have it decorated. Well, the chairs and tables *are* black, but the restaurant is warmed up by a crystal chandelier, stained glass windows, and red and gold trim.

The food will warm you up, too, with goodies like three-egg omelettes for $4.75, whether filled with peaches, cheddar cheese, broccoli, ham, or several other choices. Or, try one with crab, spinach, and sour cream for $6.25. And if you're watching your cholesterol, you can have any omelette made with just egg whites. Other breakfast "musts" at Ann Sather are their heavenly homemade cinnamon rolls (two for $1.50), and Swedish limpa rye bread, made tangy with anise seeds ($1).

Breakfast is served all day, while both the lunch and dinner menus start at 11 a.m. (who could eat dinner at that hour?) On the lunch menu, three Swedish pancakes are $4.25 (ice cream and strawberries are extra), grilled cheese and tomato sandwiches are $3.95, the veggie burger is $4.95 (both sandwiches served with cole slaw), and the Caesar chicken tortellini salad is $6.95. Add a cup of homemade soup to any salad or sandwich order for just $1 extra.

For big appetites, Ann Sather offers a long list of dinners under $10, complete with appetizer, two side dishes, dessert, and beverage. They're also available as "lite" meals, in smaller portions with just the side dishes and drink. The roast duck dinner is $9.50 ($7.50 in the lite version); chicken croquettes are $8.50 ($6.50 lite); and baked meat loaf is $8.95 ($6.95 lite).

Several beers are available; though, for a true Scandinavian experience, you may want to try the potent Swedish glogg ($3.50)—a mixture of spiced sherry, red wine, and brandy, with almonds and raisins, served warm. For those not wishing to be knocked out, one dollar gets you a bottomless cup of coffee, or Darjeeling tea.

By the way, you can take home a dozen of those famous cinnamon rolls or muffins for $6, or a loaf of their limpa bread for $3.75.

The Lake View restaurant is open from 7 a.m. until 11 p.m. Thursday through Sunday, and until midnight on Friday and Saturday. The Andersonville branch is open daily from 7 a.m until 10 p.m.; while the Hyde Park location, near the University of Chicago campus, is open from 7 a.m. only until 3 p.m. daily.

Cedars of Lebanon

- 1618 E. 53rd St., Chicago; (312) 324-8959

Further proof of the fascinating mix of cultures in Hyde Park, Cedars is a fairly upscale-looking restaurant serving Middle Eastern food at great prices. The interior is all freshly done in business-world pink and mauve, with natural blond wood (well, veneer, really) tables and chairs in its two large rooms. You *will* notice the smell of cooking oil as soon as you walk in the door; it can be somewhat overpowering, but the folks here assure their patrons that they only use pure vegetable oil, with no animal fats. Also, they serve no pork products.

What do they serve? All the standards for chicken, lamb, and beef, along with vegetarian dishes, in many varieties. Try the turkey shawarma—that's the one you always see being slow-grilled on a spit, made from ground meat and spices, though it's usually lamb or beef (those are here, too). Any one is $7.75, and all dinners include soup or a salad. Kastalata ($8.85) is charcoal-broiled lamb chops, served with roasted potatoes, carrots, and peas. And the fatet makdoos ($7.50) is sauteed eggplant and tomato, mixed with peppers, and onions, with pine nuts over the top.

Just about everything is also available as either a sandwich or an appetizer, in the $3-$4 range. Other apps include spinach or oregano pies ($1.50) and freshly made hummus ($2.75), again with pine nuts. For dessert, baklava is only a dollar a slice—and that's as low as it gets, folks. They do a big take-out business, too.

Edwardo's Natural Pizza Restaurant

- 1212 N. Dearborn St., Chicago; (312) 337-4490
- 521 S. Dearborn St., Chicago; (312) 939-3366
- 1321 E. 57th St., Chicago (312) 241-7960

Many other suburban locations
Despite its yuppie exterior and award-winning pizza, Edwardo's is not all that expensive, especially if you take advantage of their terrific lunch buffet. But you can split a pizza, order an individual salad and a soda at any hour, and still only spend $6 or so.

Now, about that buffet. It costs just $4.95 per person. First, fill up at the salad bar with fresh greens and tomatoes, multicolored rotini in a nutty pesto sauce, thick cantaloupe wedges and tangy poppyseed dressing. Then, choose from four different pizzas (two with a whole-wheat crust, including their wonderfully tasty spinach pie), baked ziti, and other entrees. Don't forget frozen glacee or chocolate cake for dessert. This incredible deal is offered weekdays from 11:30 a.m. until 3 p.m., with a $6.49 dinner version offered daily from 5-9 p.m. The main difference between the two buffets is that the dinner buffet offers stuffed pizza while the lunch buffet does not.

If you're not in the mood for the buffet, the appetizer menu has great garlic bread for $1.75 (slather it with mozzarella for 50 cents extra), or a Caesar salad for $2.95. Stuffed pizzas start at $9.35 for a regular size mozzarella, which itself can be enough to share. Prices go on to $14.75 for a basic large pie, higher with extra toppings; but it serves four or five people. Thin crust pizzas run up to $19 for the large Edwardo's special, and a whole wheat crust is 75 cents extra for either style pizza. Other types of pies include vegetarian, with mushrooms, peppers and onions; pesto pizza, and several more. Desserts are on the rich side, with a slice of blueberry cheesecake about $3.

Edwardo's also offers delivery (not free) to limited areas.

Glass Dome Hickory Pit
- 2801 S. Halsted St., Chicago; (312) 842-7600

Hickory Pit?? Hickory *Castle* would be more like it. Man, is this place huge! From humble beginnings over fifty years ago, the Beninato family has created a colossus big enough to feed a sellout crowd at nearby Comiskey Park. And, spinning a variation on the nickname for another famous ballpark, they call this "The House that Ribs Built." It's a combination restaurant and banquet facility, doing a steady business in both.

Surprisingly, then, ribs actually make up a small portion of the equally giant menu. The basic platter of barbecued baby back ribs is $11.95; slightly over Mr. C's $10 limit, but worth it considering the size of the portions here. All dinners also include a salad or soup (go for the homemade minestrone), a baked potato or French fries, and bread—so it really works out to quite a lot for your money. And you can get an even larger order for $13.95.

Of course, there are plenty of chicken entrees, too; the barbecued chicken dinner is just $7.95, and you can get a combination platter of chicken and ribs for $9.95. But, being an Italian restaurant in an Italian neighborhood, the menu doesn't stop there. They cook up plenty of good, cheap pasta dishes, like spaghetti marinara ($5.95) and linguine in white clam sauce ($6.95). And a strip steak parmesan dinner, with pasta, is just $9.95. Plenty of sandwiches, too, such as barbecued beef or Italian sausage on toasted garlic bread for $4.50.

Glass Dome has lots of beers to wash this all down, as well as a full bar. And they are fully equipped to prepare anything on the menu for take-out, whether you want dinner for one or enough to get a party rolling.

Medici
- 1327 S. 57th St., Chicago; (312) 667-7394
- 5211 S. Harper Court, Chicago; (312) 667-4008
- 2850 N. Sheridan Rd., Chicago; (312) 929-7300

Medici sure has the college business sewn up. Not only do they have two restaurants in Hyde Park for the U of C crowd, but they also run the campus pub—which, for all practical purposes, the 57th Street branch may as well be anyway. It's also the cheapest of the lot, a real collegiate hangout kind of place, well-known for its burgers and deep-dish pizza. The latter start at just $3.85 for a basic seven-inch pie, going up to $11.75 for a fourteen-incher. In suitably downscale fashion, their pizza with the works is called the "Garbage Pie," ranging from $6.55 to $20.35. It includes beef, sausage, pepperoni, Canadian bacon, mushrooms, peppers, and onions. Good luck.

The burgers are serious too—big, juicy half-pounders served up with good, thin French fries for just $4.90. Again, there are a dozen or so toppings which can be added on, including bleu cheese, chili, black olives, etc. The rather unusual "Stroganoff burger" is $6.00.

The menu goes on to a smattering of dinner entrees, such as basic pasta dishes (all under $6); barbecued chicken, with fries and salad, for $3.85; and a homemade lamb stew for $4.25. In the other direction, a large bowl of spinach salad mixes in veggies, bacon, and hard-boiled eggs for $5.25; and sandwiches are all in the $3-$6 range, with fries (or potato salad, if you prefer).

Clearly, comfort food is the order of the day here—and that means desserts are just as important. Along with several rather pricey (but good) homemade cakes and pies, the bread pudding weighs in (heavily) as a popular choice for $2.25, topped with whipped cream. Malt milk shakes ($2.90), in several flavors, are good here too; and they serve you that metal container with the extra stuff in it—always a good touch.

The large, near-campus Medici has a very comfortable feel, with exposed brick walls and well-worn wooden booths. Open all the way up to the second floor, the central part of the room is light and airy by day. The area toward the rear, including the restrooms, attempts to raise graffiti to an art form. Frankly, it doesn't work. Upstairs, there are more tables, and an outdoor patio which is probably better for evenings than steamy summer days.

Medici is experimenting with its menus at the other locations, and at the time of this writing, the Harper Court branch has become more upscale (read: expensive). It also has more of a formal restaurant feel to it—Mr. C prefers the pubby ambiance and lower prices of 57th Street.

The Original Pancake House

- 22 E. Bellevue Place, Chicago; (312) 642-7917
- 10437 S. Western Ave, Chicago; (312) 445-6100
- 1517 E. Hyde Park Blvd., Chicago; (312) 288-2322
- 2020 N. Lincoln Park West, Chicago; (312) 929-8130
- 700 E. 87th Ave., Chicago; (312) 874-0010

Many other suburban locations
Proudly located across the street from the fancy-shmancy Meridien Hotel, this charming, warm, and homey eatery—part of a chain based in Portland, Oregon—wins Mr. C's award for friendliest and most efficient staff in town.

Even though the folks at OPH are obsessively preoccupied with high quality, the breakfast-all-day meals here won't budge your budget too much. You'll be stuffed after a ham and cheese omelette, served with three buttermilk pancakes, all for $5.95. The pancakes are extra-smooth and fluffy, thanks to a special sourdough yeast made especially for the House.

You can also beat the breakfast blahs here by ordering something out of the ordinary. Ever tried coconut pancakes ($4.50)? Ever heard of them? Or, how about Hawaiian pancakes, topped with pineapple and tropical syrup ($4.25). Get back to nature with OPH's old-fashioned oats,

---

MR. CHEAP'S PICKS
South Side

✔ **Glass Dome Hickory Pit**—Huge servings of great barbecued chicken and ribs, not too far from Comiskey Park.

✔ **Medici**—A pair of Hyde Park hangouts (Mr. C prefers the funkier joint on 57th) with great burgers, pizzas and malteds.

✔ **Three Happiness**—For the authentic Chinatown experience, try to get into the smaller, original shop—as opposed to the newer behemoth across the street.

✔ **Valois Cafeteria**—In Hyde Park, this gritty old coffee shop has some of the best food at the lowest prices you may ever see.

---

served with cream, for $1.60. And their trademark coffee, brought to you topped with whipping cream if you wish, is 90 cents. Potato pancakes are served with apple sauce and sour cream for $4.25. The spuds are imported all the way from Idaho, and their lingonberries (another sweet pancake option) have come even further—from Sweden.

The Original Pancake House does not accept credit cards, which is one way they keep their prices down.

Pauline's New Lung Fung

- 2200 S. Wentworth Ave., Chicago; (312) 225-5050

At the corner of Wentworth and Cermak in Chinatown, you could almost miss this rather dingy-looking eatery. The years have taken their toll on whatever decor it may have ever had. But, while the look of the place remains unchanged, the ownership—as the name implies—is another story. Pauline herself takes a hands-on approach, and the revamped menu offers large portions at small prices.

Start your meal with a plate of beef-filled pot stickers, something not often found in a Chinese restaurant; you get half a dozen for $3.25. Alas, the good variety of soups, at $4.95 for small and $6.95 for large, are somewhat pricey.

Rice dishes are a better bet. In that style which blends two nationalities, you can find shrimp with scrambled eggs over rice for $5.95, or minced beef with eggs and peas for $4.95. And you can't go wrong with the combination fried rice ($6.95), laced with chicken, shrimp, and pork—there's plenty for everyone at the table.

There are plenty of Cantonese staples, such as egg foo young and chow mein, in the $6-$8 range. Mr. C enjoyed barbecued pork chow mein ($7.25), which featured rather salty and pungent hunks of meat. And the place is well-reputed for its "sizzling" beef and chicken dishes, both $7.95, made with plenty of ginger.

Service is friendly and even helpful if you want a recommendation when ordering. In fact, you may even get some whether you request help or not. That's part of the fun.

Three Happiness

- 209 W. Cermak Rd., Chicago; (312) 842-1964
- 2130 S. Wentworth Ave., Chicago; (312) 791-1228

You've got two ways to enjoy Three Happiness. Facing each other across the main intersection of Chinatown are the original, no-frills location and its large, banquet hall offspring. Either way, the food is the same wonderful, oft-recommended stuff.

The difference comes down to atmosphere. Mr. C prefers the cozy, bustling original; that is, if you can get in. It's a popular place, with a small counter, several booths, and a few tables that are practically in the booths themselves. The menu seems gigantic for such a small place; an endless array of beef, pork, seafood, chicken, chow mein, and rice casseroles.

The house style is Cantonese, and everything that Mr. C and his dining companions sampled was delicious and served in generous portions. Chicken in black bean and garlic sauce ($6.75) was terrific, as was a simple platter of crisply stir-fried mixed vegetables ($5.50).

Chow mein dishes, mostly in the $6-$8 range, come with your choice of pan-fried wide noodles or thin rice noodles. Noodle soups, though, are an even better bargain; try a hearty beef stew with noodles for just $4.00, or roast duck with wontons and noodles for $6.00.

The zillions of rice dishes are also especially good deals. Beef and broccoli over rice is just $4.75; curried shrimp on rice is $5.95. Can't do much better than that for shrimp, folks. And for something unusual, the rice casserole made with duck, sausage, and cured pork ($7.25) is almost like a Chinese paella.

Both 3H's, by the way, serve dim sum daily. Have a pot of tea, and sample a wide assortment of nibbles from the cart. It's a popular brunch option, too. Dim sum is served from 10:00 a.m. until 2:00 weekdays, and 3:00 on Saturday and Sunday.

Across the street, the newer, two-story restaurant is more like an entertainment complex. The first level is a dark cocktail bar, which frequently features Asian karaoke music for ambiance. The dining rooms are upstairs; they have a distinctly suburban feel, including a well-dressed maitre d' to seat you. The place is cavernous and mellow, good for a quiet meal—which, as you would guess, is slightly more expensive (but not much; less than a dollar higher per entree). It's all very attractive, but again, you sort of miss the cheerfully busy atmosphere. Still, how many restaurants can give you such a choice?

Tulpe Restaurant

- 2447 W. 69th St. (Lithuanian Plaza Court), Chicago; (312) 925-1123

Tucked away on the South Side is a tiny pocket of Eastern Europe—a small but proud neighborhood of

Lithuanian folks (not unlike the country itself). They've even had this stretch of 69th Street renamed for their homeland. Once you find it, a couple of blocks in from Western Avenue, look carefully and you'll also find the unassuming doorway of Tulpe. It's a small and simple homestyle restaurant serving the hearty cuisine of the old country.

Tulpe looks more like a coffee shop, with a lunch counter front and center and tables to the sides. There are no menus—just a black felt letter board on the wall, listing about a dozen platters, nearly all of which are priced under $6.00. Your tour starts off with a bowl of Lithuanian beet soup ($1.40), enough to put a dent in any appetite by itself; move along, though, to something like veal stroganoff ($5.40) or the chicken leg dinner ($5.95). Or, perhaps you'd like to try thuringer ($5.00), the tasty variation on pork sausage from this part of the world.

All dinners come with side orders of mashed potatoes and the vegetables of the day. You may also opt to go instead with breakfasty items, like a hefty stack of pancakes ($5.00) or various egg dishes. Service comes with a smile and an accent; guess that's what they call old world charm. One of Mr. C's companions also commented on the absolute spotlessness of the place—you can even see it in the kitchen. That's clearly where the pride comes in.

Valois Cafeteria
- 1518 E. 53rd St., Chicago; (312) 667-0647

Ah, they don't make cafeterias like this anymore. Too bad. Stepping into this Hyde Park shop is like going back to an earlier time in this century, when you could get a full meal for a few bucks and eat it in a no-frills atmosphere that was still, somehow, comfortable. Ed Debevic could learn a thing or two from Valois; so, for that matter, could McDonalds, et al.

Okay, enough waxing philosophi-

cal. On to the chow. The sign at Valois reads, "SEE YOUR FOOD," which is just what you'll do. As you walk along the glass counter, the friendly cooks will grab whatever catches your eye (and stomach) and heap it all onto a plate. Be forewarned, this is not going to be health food. It's hearty, stick-to-your-arteries stuff, with more than a touch of down home cooking. Given the mixed ethnicity of Hyde Park, this is just right.

The price is right, too. Mr. C enjoyed a baked half chicken, with mashed potatoes and gravy, biscuits and coffee, all for—get ready—$4.25. Yow! All right, it wasn't the largest bird you ever saw, but there was plenty of juicy meat and crispy skin. The taters were real, and those biscuits may be the very best Mr. C has ever tasted—freshly browned from the oven, crumbly and buttery sweet inside. Even the coffee was delicious, and it's only 40 cents a cup—take that, Starbucks.

Among the other choices on this particular visit (some items change daily) were barbecued ribs ($3.95), a hot pork sandwich with gravy ($3.25), a turkey version of the same ($2.90), and even a New York strip steak for $5.95. Add extra vegetables for 70 cents. Of course, you can always get a plain ol' burger (for $1.50!), a grilled cheese sandwich ($1.40), various cold sandwiches for $2-$3, or a chef's salad ($2.45). Now, that's what these things ought to cost!

Meanwhile, you'll be eating with the most ethnically-correct crowd to have ever broken bread together. African-Americans in dashikis, old Jewish men in baseball caps, yuppies in shirts and ties, they all hang out here. The room itself is cozy, with its ceiling fans and recently redone furniture. This is cheap eats at its best. Open every day from six in the morning for breakfast, until nine in the evening.

WEST OF TOWN
(including Bucktown, Greek Town, Polish Village, West Loop, Wicker Park)

Busy Bee Restaurant
- 1546 N. Damen Ave., Chicago; (312) 772-4433

A neighborhood "secret" that has actually been featured in a 1991 National Geographic article on Chicago's ethnic mix, this Polish deli packs them in day and night. Owner Sophie Madej, who came to Chicago in 1951, has become a legend in her own time with the Bee, where you can watch pierogi being rolled out in the kitchen, hang out over coffee, and even buy your lottery ticket before you leave.

The restaurant is divided into two parts; the long, rectangular counter favored by cops and students, and the adjacent dining table area. Old photos lining the wood-paneled walls show the Busy Bee in bygone days; it seems that not much has really changed.

Breakfast, which starts at 6 a.m., is super-cheap. Three fried eggs are $2.50, and Polish ham with two fried eggs is $3.00. The Busy Bee Omelette, with green peppers, onions, mushrooms, ham, and tomatoes, is $4.50. All of these include fried potatoes, toast, butter, and jelly. Try the plain wheatcakes for $2.25, or $3.50 with ham. The coffee is wonderful—and only 65 cents a cup.

Lunch and dinner specialties include the BB's award-winning hot meatloaf sandwich, served with mashed potatoes, gravy and vegetable of the day, all for a ridiculously low $3.25; and those pierogi, dumplings filled with meat, cheese, turkey, potato, or sauerkraut, served with sour cream or apple sauce, for $4. Complete dinners will sure keep you busy—to the main dish, these add soup and salad, potatoes, vegetable, dessert, and coffee or tea. The hearty stuffed cabbage dinner is $5.50, while spaghetti with meat sauce is $5.25. The chicken liver dinner, $5.75, is very popular too.

The BB has a full bar, and in the dining room, you can get their special drink—the Busy Bee Stinger—which is made with brandy, white creme de menthe, and a dash of *krupnick* for what they call "a touch of honey." Desserts are priced right; cheesecake, pound cake, rice pudding, and chocolate pudding are all only $1 each.

Free parking is available in the rear, but most people arrive via the "el"—the Damen station is literally just a couple of yards away—or on foot, since there's still plenty of Polish presence in this changing neighborhood.

Cafe Du Midi
- 2118 N. Damen Ave., Chicago; (312) 235-MIDI (6434)

A fancy—but not as pricey as it *could* be—Bucktown bistro, Cafe du Midi is a fantastic spot for lunch. With its bright aqua facade and red doors, and the wrought-iron mini-Eiffel Tower in the garden, it sure looks like it's out of Mr. C's range; but, at lunch, a couple can dine here for under $20 easily. Specials change daily, so call ahead to see what they're whipping up. It also gets crowded after noon, so it may be a good idea to make reservations, which are accepted for lunch and dinner.

Appetizers like the tomato basil soup ($3) and the arugula-black bean salad ($4) are popular. Soup du jour is $2.50, and the pate maison is $3.50. Mr. C's guests liked the salade nicoise ($4.50), and the fluffy shii-take mushroom omelette, served with shredded fried potato strips ($6.50). Mr. C loved the grilled chicken, served with mostaccioli and mush-rooms and green beans ($7.50). All entrees are served with bread and a salad.

Other Parisian palate pleasers in-clude mussels provencale with rice ($6), and fried bay scallops with ca-per mayonnaise and vegetables for $6.50. Anyone not in ze mood for haute cuisine can go with the unique "antipasto sandwich," or a grilled bur-ger topped with bleu, Swiss or goat cheese; both are priced at $5.

Quaff these down with Norman-die sparkling cider for $3 a glass, or a $10 bottle of Georges du Boeuf wine. The tempting desserts, should you have any room left, include brandied cherries with chocolate sauce and ice cream for $4, and mango sorbet for $3.50.

Of course, nobody's perfect, and Mr. C does have two tiny gripes about Cafe du Midi: The water glasses are just tooooooo small, and the espresso machine makes a racket that can probably be heard all the way to the Loop, rendering conversa-tion all but impossible during its brewings. *C'est la vie.*

Dinners do rise above Mr. C's price range; but again, you can man-age to have a very chic and afford-able meal during the day. Lunch is served at Cafe du Midi from 11:30 a.m. to 2:30 p.m.

Cappuccino Alfredo
- 1509 W. Taylor St., Chicago; (312) 243-1177

Mr. C came here in search of some-thing he has found in so many other cities: Little Italy. Surprisingly, there doesn't really seem to be one in this town of ethnic neighborhoods. You know, a gritty, bustling place where the streets are lined with great restau-rants and cafes, bakeries and butch-ers, and mothers shouting "Anthonyyyyyyy!" as their little boys dart through the crowds. Evidently, Little Italy has up and gone to the

'burbs. What remains is this quiet and handsome stretch of Taylor Street, which does have a few nice restaurants, including this ultra-mod-ern cafe.

In appearance, Cappuccino Al-fredo has more to do with the modern Europe than the old world; this long and narrow room features spare white walls decorated with art deco prints and dashes of neon lighting. The food, however, is definitely the good old stuff, with a few nouvelle touches mixed in. The restaurant is proud of its standards for fresh ingre-dients and courteous service.

It's a light and simple menu of a few pastas, sandwiches, and salads—and of course, desserts and coffees. Begin with an appetizer of home-made soup, which changes daily, or a fresh garden salad. Spaghetti or mo-staccioli with meat sauce is just $3.75, served with crusty bread and butter. They also serve up a different pasta special every day. Sandwiches include focaccia, made with cold cuts, lettuce, and tomato, for $3.95; or a smaller turkey breast "focaccina" for $2.75. Char-broiled chicken breast or rib-eye steak sandwiches are $3.45 and $4.95, respectively.

These light meals will probably leave you with a bit of room for Al-fredo's desserts, which are a good enough reason to stop in by them-selves. Homemade *tiramisu* ($2.75) or cannoli ($1.75) are perfect with a cup of—what else?—cappuccino, caffe latté, or espresso. You may have these hot or cold, and in a nod to the Seattle-based coffee rage, they can add in gourmet flavorings as well. The old country meets the new in this chic and cozy eatery. Open daily from 9 a.m. to 10:30 at night, and Sundays from noon to 9.

The Corner Bakery
- 210 S. Canal St., Union Station, Chicago; (312) 441-0821
- 516 N. Clark St., Chicago, (312) 644-8100

A bakery with more than just sweets, the Corner Bakery's Union Station branch is a favorite among harried

Loop office workers who gobble down their lunches in five minutes or less (not required, of course). At either location, the portions are good-sized, and the help is extremely friendly without being overbearing—even during lunch and dinner rushes. And all the baked goods are really made on the premises.

While the regular bakery items can thin your wallet (a loaf of chocolate cherry bread is $6.50), this is a good spot for lunch or breakfast with a number of different salads and sandwiches offered daily. Wheat berry salad, made with two kinds of peppers, is $3.50 for a small, $5.95 for a large. Curry chicken salad, with grapes and parsley is $3.85 and $6.95; and a hefty tuna salad sandwich with sprouts, on olive bread, is $4.50.

For snacks, desserts, or whatever, the Corner's popular pretzel rolls are just 75 cents each, and giant fudge brownies sprinkled with confectioner's sugar are $1.50.

The Union Station location is open Monday through Friday, from 6 a.m. to 10 p.m., on Saturday 8 a.m. to 8 p.m., on Sunday 8 a.m. to 7 p.m. Hours on Clark Street are Monday through Friday, 7 a.m. to 10 p.m., Saturday 7:30 a.m. to 11 p.m., and Sunday 8 a.m. to 9 p.m.

Dixie Que
- 2001 W. Fullerton Ave., Chicago; (312) 252-5600

Is this place a hoot or *what*? Dixie Que is like a Bucktown Hard Rock Cafe, without the tourists. Elvis is the patron saint here, and if he did come back from the great beyond, why would he bother with that diner in Indiana? His songs are blasting on the jukebox, the walls are lined with old advertisements from the deep South (plus signs like "Save Water—Drink Beer"), and the menu is packed with every food that's ever been barbecued—and some that have never been before.

In fact, a recent promotion offered $10 gift certificates to anyone shouting "Elvis Lives!" at the moment their check arrived.

MR. CHEAP'S PICKS
West of Town

✔ **Lou Mitchell's**—The ever-popular diner packs 'em in and fills 'em up with great, cheap food—and fast.

✔ **Manny's Coffee Shop**—A coupla blocks south of Lou's, this time-warp of a deli is like a quick visit to the old-world neighborhood of New York's Lower East Side.

✔ **Wishbone Restaurants**—These down-home yuppie joints can be hard to get into, but are worth the wait.

Burgers and sandwiches, of course, are a major part of the territory. Charcoaled half-pound burgers start at $5.50 and go up from there, depending on extras like smoked cheddar cheese or "Tennesee mustard slaw." They all come with regular slaw, great crispy French fries and a side of barbecue sauce. For something more unusual, go with the butterfly pork chop sandwich ($6.50, with fries), topped with sauce and hot onions. It's juicy, delicious and appropriately messy.

Dinners are a bit pricier, but just as good. Kentucky bourbon chicken ($8.95) comes with fries and "apple raisin beans." The catfish basket ($7.95) consists of fried fillets in a cornmeal batter. The menu tops out at $13.95 for a full slab of barbecued ribs, nearly two pounds' worth; but you can get a half-slab for $8.95, with the aforementioned trimmings. Mr. C's friend tried "BBQ Spaghetti" ($6.95); such an odd idea, and yet so simple. Why have we never heard of this before? It's tasty, and comes with chopped beef brisket mixed in for a filling meal.

The restaurant rambles and

sprawls all over the place, inside and out. During the summer months, they use an outdoor patio built onto the parking lot; they need the space, but we don't need the fumes. There's also an outdoor stage, where rockabilly musicians hold forth on weekends. Inside, you'll find "The LARGE Bar," which is actually so tiny that it would be easier to put the room inside the bottles. They know this, of course; it's all part of the fun.

There are some good beers to wash the food down with, including Samuel Adams from Boston and something called "Blackened Voo-Doo" made by Dixie (Beer, not Que). It's good, but at $3.50 a bottle, you won't want to Doo many of them.

Dixie Que does a substantial carry-out business, especially at lunchtime, when they offer a number of low-priced specials. The restaurant stays open until 1:00 a.m. on weekends, 11:00 p.m. on weeknights.

Earwax Cafe
- 1564 N. Milwaukee Ave., Chicago; (312) 772-4019

It is certain that nowhere, throughout the annals of time, has anyone ever considered putting these two words together before. Yet here we have them, improbably describing this grunge-rock-meets-nouvelle-cuisine spot in Wicker Park. It is truly a place of odd pairings, being both a restaurant and a record store all in one.

The main room is a large and airy cafe, with a lengthy bar running along one side, and big storefront windows. Have a bowl of feta cheese gazpacho for $3.25, or a marinated mushroom salad with peppers, olives, carrots, and French bread, for $4.95. Or, go for one of their hearty sandwiches, like the chimayo chicken sandwich, with chicken marinated in chili powder and lime juice, sitting on that crusty French bread with Monterey jack cheese and fresh tomato. It's served with tortilla chips and salsa for $5.25.

The desserts here are amazing. Try a slice of white chocolate cheese-cake, espresso torte, or chocolate banana torte, with any of a zillion coffees and teas. Priced between $3-$4, their desserts are not cheap, but worth it. If you're on a tight budget, maybe you should skip right to these.

Meanwhile, through the restaurant to the rear, you'll come to the record shop, which stocks lots of used cassettes and CDs. Tapes go from $1.99 to $10, while most CDs are in the $6-$10 range; most are $9. Every style of music is mixed into one alphabetical hodgepodge, where Tom Petty, Ray Charles, Shawn Colvin, and David Sanborn are all thrown together. Perhaps they prefer it that way—though it does make searching for a particular title more difficult. Think of it as a serendipitous experience, a good way to approach this entire wacky place.

Galans
- 2210 W. Chicago Ave., Chicago; (312) 292-1000

Well to the west of downtown, the stretch of Chicago Avenue between Damen and Western is the heart of the neighborhood known as Ukrainian Village. These folks are as proud of their national heritage as any such group; there is even a Ukrainian National Museum and a Ukrainian Institute of Contemporary Art within the same few blocks. And if this district can be said to have a culinary heart, it would have to be Galans.

It's a surprisingly big and modern restaurant, as geared to banquets and groups as to individual diners. The cooking is hearty, in the old-world style, of course; not unlike that of Chicago's many Polish restaurants, though with its own distinctive variations. And while it can get expensive here, there are plenty of things on the large menu that stay within Mr. C's price range.

Varenyky, which bear a strong resemblance to pierogies, make a good start. For $4.25 you get half a dozen boiled dumplings, filled with cheese, meat, potato, and sauerkraut, topped with butter and bits of bacon (no one said this was going to be health food). The combo plate appetizer ($3.25) is another fine introduction: A cabbage roll, stuffed mushrooms, spinach varenyky and sausage. Think of it as Ukrainian tapas. And of course, you should try the borscht—$1.50 for a cup of beet soup made with shredded cabbage and meat (which not everyone puts in!).

Most of the entrees are at or above Mr. C's $10 limit, but there are a few you could easily go for—and remember, the portions here are certainly filling. Holubtsi ($6.25) are cabbages filled with meat and rice in a tomato sauce, served with potatoes. Bigos ($5.95) is a sort of stew, with chunks of sausage, beef, and potatoes mixed into a heap of sauerkraut. And try the stuffed kartoplyanyk ($8.95), a Galans original, which is a sort of variation on a theme: A huge potato pancake filled with ground, seasoned beef and covered with gravy.

You may also want to consider the "Kozak Feast," a prix-fixe dinner which gives you borscht and salad, varenyky, potato pancake, sausage, a skewer of beef and pork, dessert, and coffee with liqueur—all for $15.95. Again, above the limit, but a great value overall.

On the lighter (?) side, there are sandwiches, including corned beef, reuben, and a hamburger that actually has ham mixed in with the beef; all come with French fries and cole slaw, and are priced from $3.50-$4.95. Galans also offers weekday lunch specials, from 11:30 to 4:00, like chicken paprika with boiled dumplings ($4.95) or roast pork with mushrooms, potatoes, and gravy ($3.95).

Galans has a wine list, and offers several of its own unique cocktails. Friday and Saturday evenings feature live entertainment, usually folk and popular music from the old country. Come to think of it, maybe they should just make this the Ukrainian museum.

Greek Islands
- 200 S. Halsted St., Chicago; (312) 782-9855

- 300 E. 22nd St., Lombard; (708) 932-4545

One of the largest and best-known spots along Greek Town's restaurant strip, Greek Islands manages to be showy and reasonably priced at the same time. Yes, there's a lot done here for the benefit of the tourists; but then, unless you're Greek yourself, it's bound to seem that way anyhow. Enjoy the ride.

After all, you're probably going to have to ask the waiter to pronounce half of the items on the menu. Can you say "bardouniotiko" convincingly? Thought not. It's worth the attempt, though, to get this tasty casserole of chicken, onions, feta cheese, and tomato sauce. Much easier to say, and equally worth it, is their braised lamb, in a thick lemony sauce, for $7.50; or Grecian-style shrimp, $8.95, served over rice. Most dinners also include potatoes on the side.

Adding to the festivities is the popular appetizer, saganaki ($2.95). It's a creamy, sharp cheese which is brought to your table, then set ablaze with the cry, "Opaa!" This phrase appears to be Greek for "Don't worry! You're safe, but I've just singed the hair of someone at the next table!" It's also the kind of showpiece which leads more diners to order "that flaming thing," which explains why the traditionally impassioned cry of "Opaa!" is delivered with less fire than the cheese itself.

For other traditional Greek delicacies, consider ordering the combination plate, which gives you a chance to try roast lamb, stuffed grape leaves, mousaka, meatballs, and mixed vegetables—quite a lot, all for $7.25. Greek Islands also has larger, stuff-yourself versions, which they call family-style dinners, for $10.95 per person; these include appetizers, salad, entrees, side orders, dessert, and coffee—not a bad deal at all.

There are many other very affordable entrees, such as pan-fried Greek sausage with rice or potato, and the ever-popular gyros—ground, marinated lamb and beef, slow-roasted on a spit (you can see them turning in the central, open kitchen). These dinners are each priced at $6.95. And bakalao ($7.25) is none other than deep-fried cod fillets, alias fish and chips without the chips; instead, you get a wonderful creamy garlic sauce.

Greek Islands has wines by the glass or bottle, several of which are around $10 a bottle; decent prices on domestic and imported beers as well. So, in spite of the theatrical nature of the restaurant, it's all quite affordable—and an attractive, festive place for a big meal out with a group. Even if you all live right in town.

Home Bakery Delicatessen and Restaurant

• 2931 N. Milwaukee Ave., Chicago; (312) 252-3708

One of the treasures of Polish Village, Home Bakery is as high on value as it is low on aesthetics—but nobody's complaining. Only in this neighborhood can you completely stuff yourself on huge size-servings of pierogi, borscht and potato pancakes and other entrees and still spend only $5.00; and Home Bakery is among the best of the Milwaukee Avenue bunch.

Heavy accents sometimes make the waitresses difficult to understand, but they're very friendly and make you feel right at home. It's hard to choose from the listings on the four-page menu, but many items are only available on certain days of the week, making your decision a little easier.

The breakfast choices are nondescript, like oatmeal and milk ($1.79) or a Denver omelette ($3.29). For lunch, try a Rubinski sandwich on rye for $3.99 (corned beef with Swiss cheese, cole slaw, lettuce, and sauerkraut—y'know, *Rubinski*, get it?). It includes French fries. The classic Polish sausage sandwich with sauerkraut is $2.79, available hot or fresh.

Entrees are offered a la carte with potato, rice, or dumplings, hot vegetables and a Polish salad—yes, that's a la carte—or as complete dinners with soup and dessert added in. The "Hunter's Stew," for instance, is $3.19 a la carte and $4.19 as a dinner; cheese blintzes are $3.99 and $4.99 respectively. Viennar schnitzel is $6.59 and $7.59, and herring with oil, vinegar or sour cream is $3.59 or $4.59. You can also stay light by choosing from the many homemade soups (like beef tripe, chicken noodle, and white borscht), priced at $1.39 to $2.79.

Mr. C was just stuffed after the potato pancake dinner. It came with terrific borscht (full of chunky beets and potatoes), a good size salad, mixed vegetables, and chocolate cake—all for just 4.69!

The Home Bakery has a liquor license, offering dozens of imported beers, as well as wine and champagne.

Before leaving for your own home, pick up some of the very sweet pastries called *bezy moregi*, made entirely with sugar and eggs, for 40 cents a pop. Or, maybe some apricot cookies, sweet rolls, or tortes. Tasty butter cookies, one of very few items not baked in-house, are $3.99 a pound (available for some reason in pumpkin and Santa Claus shapes, even in the middle of summer—hmm, maybe that's why they're cheap).

An entire cheesecake is $2.99, as is a good-sized lemon roll cake. Super-fresh baguettes and loaves of bread cost about a dollar each, while dinner rolls are $2.99 a pound.

Both the restaurant and bakery are open from 8:00 a.m. to 9:00 p.m. daily, and on Sundays from 9 a.m. to 9 p.m.

Joe's Fisheries

• 1438 W. Cortland St., Chicago; (312) 278-8990

Since 1922, Joe's Fisheries has been a little bit of Cape Cod on the Chicago River. Well, perhaps that's a bit too rosy; in any case, these folks are proud to say they catch their own fish (in the lake, not the river) which they sell fresh, for you to cook at home, or fried up and ready to eat in their bright, modern shanty.

You can even see their two fishing boats, moored by midday behind the shop, which is situated right on the water beside the Cortland Street Bridge. Finding your way here by car or foot, though, can be trickier; it's just across the river from Clybourn, and not far from the Kennedy's Armitage exit.

Nibble on a half-pound of fried jumbo shrimp for $5; Joe's claims to have created this particular treatment. Fried scallops are $6 for half a pound, and "fish chips"—chunks of Alaskan whitefish—are $2.40. Okay...they don't catch everything they serve here. Anyway, for a dollar more, you can add French fries or cajun rice, plus cole slaw and crackers, and make a full meal out of any item.

Joe's also serves fresh steamed shrimp. An order of twenty medium-sized shrimp, with all the fixings, is just $6.09 (for "peel 'n eat") or $7.09 (for "ready to eat"). Why the extra nine cents, who knows? Add a bowl of seafood gumbo or Boston clam chowder for $3.68. And Joe's makes its own smoked fish—$4.75 a pound for lake trout or whitefish, among others.

This is a family operation, taking real care with the food (frying in cottonseed oil, smoking with natural hardwoods). It's good, fresh, and filling; and if you can't get away to one of the coasts, this can be a quick and cheap substitute.

Leo's Lunchroom
- 1809 W. Division St., Chicago; (312) 276-6509

It may sound like an old greasy spoon for truck drivers, and at first glance, it may even look like one; but Leo's Lunchroom is actually part of the young, artsy rebirth of Wicker Park. It puts a hip spin on traditional diner food, without touching traditional diner prices. As a result, Leo's has become a grungy hot spot in what still looks like the middle of nowhere.

From good ol' grilled cheese ($3) made on whole wheat bread, to hot pastrami on rye with scallions and cream cheese ($4.75), Leo's will fill you up cheaply. Try the chili, regular or vegetarian, just $1.95 a cup; or the big, fresh julienne salad with ham, turkey, cheddar and Swiss cheese, tomatoes, cucumbers, mushrooms, eggs, and onions—all for $4.75.

Everything here gets a modern, homestyle touch. Corned beef hash ($4.25) isn't your average, ground up mystery; you get diced chunks of tasty beef, mixed with sauteed potato, with two eggs done any style over the top. And daily specials offer even more artistic touches, like their "Southwestern French Toast"—in which flour tortillas are given the French toast treatment, filled with sweet ricotta cheese, and topped with fresh raspberries, all for $4.25. Speaking of breakfast, the biscuits, and gravy (just $2.50) can't be beat. It's only served on weekends.

There is an outdoor split-level patio in the back, which helps with crowd control when weather permits. But then, you miss the exciting decor, best seen from the lunch counter—a haywire collage of pictures from seemingly every TV show known to man, including autographed pictures of some of the celebs who've found their way to this downscale scene. Leo's is open every day but Monday, from 8:00 a.m. to 10:00 p.m.

Leona's
- 3215 N. Sheffield Ave., Chicago; (312) 327-8861
- 6935 N. Sheridan Ave., Chicago; (312) 764-5757
- 1936 W. Augusta Blvd., Chicago; (312) 292-4300
- 1419 W. Taylor St., Chicago; (312) 850-2222
- 848 W. Madison St., Oak Park; (708) 445-0101.

Family-run (and darn proud of it) since 1950, Leona's has grown into a Chicagoland chain serving almost 50,000 people a week. A Mr. C warning: Not all of the entrees are under $10, but the pizza and the weekday lunch buffet can't be beat for great values in food.

The above-mentioned buffet includes your choice of turkey (a whole bird is out on the table for carving), boneless chicken breast, fried eggplant, meatballs, four kinds of pizza, super-fresh broccoli and zucchini, onion rings, and a slew of pasta and regular salads. Desserts, like cheesecake, brownie-bottom chocolate cake, and a slew of cookies and truffle-like treats are included in the tab. The whole shabang, all you can eat, is a reasonable $8.95. It's served from 11:30 a.m. until 2:00 p.m., weekdays only.

If you're not feeling that Bacchanalian, opt for a sandwich—and this is no short-changing compromise. Mr. C can't put into words just how huge the chicken parmesan sandwich is; it's comparable to a football (in size only). At $4.45, it's a great deal, loaded with marinara and provolone. $1.50 more gets you "broccoli slaw," fresh fruit, or Leona's homemade Italian cookies, plus a side of pasta, fries, pesto veggies or salad. Tummy-stuffing indeed!

Of course, what would an Italian restaurant (or, in Chicago, *any* restaurant) be without pizza? Here, they come with a mind-boggling choice of 26 toppings—everything from turkey breast and giardiniera peppers to zucchini and soy cheese. A small thin-crust pie is $6.75; pan is $7.25 and stuffed is $8.50. Homemade pesto shrimp pie is a specialty, starting at $10.95 for the individual size.

Don't forget dessert if you can hack it. *Tiramisu* is $3.25, homemade cannoli are $2.25 each, and a dozen of those famous Italian cookies goes for $2.75.

Leona's has a promotional deal: Visit all five locations (with a tab of $20 or more), and they'll give you a free dinner for two. Ask for a "Road Rally Challenge" form, to which they will attach a sticker at each place.

Lou Mitchell's

● 565 W. Jackson Blvd., Chicago; (312) 939-6800

Chivalry is not dead! Lou Mitchell's, a popular diner just west of the Loop since 1923, offers a box of Milk Duds to any lady who has to wait in line for a seat. Prepare to go ahead and lose a few fillings, since at any time of day you're apt to find a winding line. But the queue moves quickly, and any wait you may need to endure will surely be worth it.

USA Today has recommended Lou Mitchell's, and Bisquick named the place one of the top 25 "neighborhood eateries" in the country. To these kudos, Mr. C adds his humble nod. The crowd is diverse; businesspeople, families, travelers from the nearby Union Station and Greyhound bus terminal. They line up under the kelly-green-and-white-striped awning, with its neon sign showing an exuberant chef rolling out dough. They come for Lou's amazingly quick service, cheap prices, and delicious food that's hearty, but won't send you running for the bottle of Pepto.

Breakfast is served all day long. Cinnamon raisin bread, baked daily on the premises, is sliced extra thick. A giant mound of hash browns, fried in real butter, is just $1.25; the popular (and gigantic) fresh fruit salad goes for $2.75. Malted waffles, a neat idea, are served with real maple syrup for just $3.10. A steady supply of marmalade and jam are kept in silver bowls on the tables and countertop. The omelettes all cost $5 or more, but the price is easily justified by their size and fluffiness.

Lunch and dinner specials change daily, but the most expensive item on the permanent menu is the deluxe albacore tuna salad sandwich. For all of $5.85, it's a hefty handful, garnished with tomato and cheddar, and served with both French fries and cole slaw. Other popular classics include beefburgers for $2.95, BLTs for $2.35, and real sliced turkey sandwiches for $4.15.

If you opt to skip dessert, you should be hit over the head with that neon rolling pin. They're all homemade. Lou's chocolate chip cookies are loaded with chips and big pecan pieces and the pound cake is extra buttery, while the pie of the day sells for just $1.60 a slice—a bargain in itself. If you're too full for dessert after your meal, you can always order something to take home with you; not just the desserts, but perhaps a loaf of Greek bread ($3.25) or raisin bread ($4.50) too.

Service here could be classified as obsessive-compulsive; sugar, salt and pepper shakers are constantly refilled to the brim, and counters constantly being wiped down. Mr. C wonders if the coffee cups are equipped with some state-of-the-art sensory device, for the moment his cup got to half full, there was a waiter or waitress offering to refill it.

If the weather's good, tables are set up on the brick front patio. There's a minimum order of $1 per person at Lou's, and no credit cards or checks are accepted; this helps keep costs, and prices, down. On the other hand, the restaurant does offer one hour of free parking right across the street.

Manny's Coffee Shop and Deli
- 1141 S. Jefferson St., Chicago; (312) 939-2855

Mr. C felt like he had been transported to the Lower East Side of New York when he dropped into Manny's, the home of good old fashioned corned beef sandwiches, chicken soup, and other Jewish delicacies. It's a cafeteria, which means forget about decor; in fact, it looks like it hasn't been updated since the early 1960's. The same appears true for some of the patrons, who spread themselves around the two large dining rooms.

Ambiance aside, the food here may be as close as Chicago gets to real Old World Jewish noshery. Corned beef is the traditional yardstick, and it measures up well; $5.20 gets you a hefty handful that will take a while to finish, and even longer to let go of your ribs. All the other hot sandwiches are here: Brisket of beef, pastrami, tongue, reuben, all between $5-$6. On the cold side, try the chopped liver sandwich

($3.50) or nova lox with cream cheese ($5.95).

Hot dishes include things like meatloaf and baked half-chicken (each $5.85), beef stew ($6.10), and more, along with a half-dozen daily specials. These never change, sure and steady as the old man sipping tea in the booth next to you. Tuesdays always offer stuffed cabbage ($6.30); Wednesdays, count on chicken pot pie ($4.75); Fridays, gefilte fish ($3.65)—something for every day of the week except Sunday, when the place is closed.

And don't forget the daily side dishes, like overcooked spaghetti (how else should it be?) or kasha and bowties. Any day, you can add things like knishes or crispy potato pancakes on the side, too. Chicken soup is always on the menu, $1.85 a bowl, whether filled with matzo balls, kreplach, noodles, or rice.

It all ranges from decent to very good, with the occasional klunker—but then, why would you come to a place like this and order salisbury steak anyway? Stick with the corned beef. Oh, and don't bother with the desserts, either—they're just never any good at delis like this. Unless you like rubbery jello or goopy rice pudding. Maybe the cheesecake...

No need to worry about a tip, and you pay on your way out. At the cash register, you'll see another old-time touch—the glass counter displaying cigars, candy and sundries for sale. No one is ever quite sure exactly what sundries are, but they are available here. By the way, you can park across the street in the Chernin's Shoes lot, get your ticket validated here, and pay only a dollar. A breakfast and lunch kind of place, Manny's closes at 4:00.

Monday's Restaurants
- 19 E. Jackson Blvd., Chicago; (312) 408-1120
- 75 W. Harrison St., Chicago; (312) 663-3647
- 120 S. Riverside Plaza, Chicago; (312) 372-9866

- 203 N. LaSalle St., Chicago; (312) 629-0444

Monday's Restaurants are best categorized as neighborhood bar/eateries, but they stand out from the crowd with their super-friendly service and unusual menu items. Start your weekend off right with their Sunday brunch, or try breakfast, lunch, or dinner any day of the week.

Some items are basic, like the big Belgian waffles ($3.50); but real maple syrup and whipped butter make it special. Other offbeat offerings include "Ka-Ya-Na" ($4.95), which is scrambled eggs with tomato, onion, and feta cheese mixed in, European style, plus a muffin, or toast.

Several omelettes are on the menu, all under $5.00; go for the zucchini—made with Swiss cheese and onions—or the crabmeat. All of these dishes come with fried potatoes, muffin or toast and jelly. Or, try nova lox and three eggs for $5.95. That Sunday brunch is $9.95, but well worth it for those with hearty appetites. It's an elaborate, all-you-can eat buffet of eggs, salmon, fresh fruit, breads, and other fixings.

Lunches and dinners are just as reasonably priced. Even at dinnertime, nothing on the menu tops $6.95, including burgers, ribs, and "evvvvvvvvverything," as one of the waiters here put it. Mondays also has a full liquor license, and a separate bar area. Dinner is only available, however, until about 8:00—after that, the place is strictly a bar.

All the Monday's branches have similar, though not identical, menus and decor. The Harrison location has funky splatter-painted floors, glow-in-the-dark steps from the bar area to the raised dining floor, and big, comfy green vinyl booths. It must have been a converted warehouse, with its super-high ceiling; but neon stars, hanging lights, and the raised television sets combine for more of a wacky nightclub effect.

MR. CHEAP'S PICKS
West of Town—Ethnic
neighborhoods

✔ **Busy Bee Restaurant**—In this Polish diner, watch the pierogi being rolled out and stuffed on the counter. Then watch the people being rolled out, stuffed, through the front door.

✔ **Galans**—The culinary consulate of the Ukrainian Village.

✔ **Greek Islands**—Dining in this Greektown palace is more like being part of a big show. Yes, it's touristy, but fun and not outrageously priced.

✔ **Leona's on Taylor**—If you're looking for Little Italy, it said *arrivederci* years ago. But you can still eat heartily at this branch of the attractive, moderately priced pizza restaurants.

NeeCee's Deli

- 1600 N. Milwaukee Ave, Chicago; (312) 772-4677

Here's a hip little Wicker Park deli, decorated in a yellow and aqua southwestern motif, serving up top-notch sandwiches and salads. It attracts a youngish crowd of artists and related folk, its walls lined with lots of gallery notices. A fine place for a hangout, it stays open 'til 4 a.m. on weekends in the summer (a bonus which may or may not extend into the fall and winter months, depending on the stamina of the counter help). If you do visit, all bleary-eyed, at that time of morning: Please be careful to not walk smack dab into the mammoth fig tree growing in the middle of the place. It's so big, you may not even notice it—possibly a case of missing the tree for the florist?

Horticulture aside, head to the counter for a 70 cent pot pie to go, or cucumber-onion salad for $4 a pound. Or, pull up a table and get to work on one of Neecee's huge sandwiches, made on thick-cut fresh breads. The "Coyote Club" is a hefty handful of ham, salami, turkey, and swiss, served with cole slaw, potato chips and pickle, all for $5.50. Many others are interesting variations on familiar ideas, like the grilled cheese ($3.99), made with feta, cheddar, and tomato.

There are some hot dishes as well, like meat loaf and potatoes with a garden salad for $5.99; vegetarian or meat chili, $2.99 a bowl. Neecee's also has a limited selection of bottled beers.

The desserts, by the way, are worth a trip by themselves; there is always a variety of fresh cakes, pies, and pastries, all $2 apiece. Linger over a slice of chocolate raspberry cake with a cup of gourmet coffee.

Neecee's is a good bet for brunch, with a $4.99 deal which gives you a choice of omelettes, blintzes, potato pancakes, French toast or a bagel and lox plate. To that, add a buffet of juice and coffee, muffins, scones, pastries, and a variety of fruit and pasta salads. The brunch is served Saturdays from 10 a.m. until 5 p.m. (for you terminally late-sleepers), and on Sundays from 11 to 3.

Orbit
- 2948-54 N. Milwaukee Ave., Chicago; (312) 342-1515

Undoubtedly the heavy hitter of the Polish restaurants along Milwaukee, Orbit is a combination restaurant, banquet facility, and entertainment center taking up several storefronts. Speaking of heavy, you may take up a block or two yourself after one of these hearty meals. But oy, is it good stuff, and cheap.

Start off with a plateful of pierogies for $4.25, tasty dumplings filled with such things as ground meat, potato, sweet cheese, or sauerkraut. Move on to the stuffed pork dinner ($5.95), thin breaded cutlets rolled up with rice and creamy sauce

inside, gravy over the top and your choice of potato on the side. It's all tender and yummy. Same price for a beef cutlet dinner; and even less for the stuffed cabbage plate—can you imagine a filling meal for just $4.50?

Higher up on the price scale, chicken Kiev is a still-reasonable $8.25, and a variety of steak dinners are in the $9-$13 range. Newcomers to this style of cooking may wish to try the "Polish Assortment" platter ($9.50), which includes pierogies, kielbasa with sauerkraut, cheese blintzes, and more. Hey, no one said this was health food.

It doesn't seem possible that anyone could have room left for dessert, but Orbit does have things like good old-fashioned cheesecake, and a hefty three-scoop banana split for $4.95. Good luck. Those blintzes, by the way, also make a good dessert—and are equally popular at breakfast. This is definitely a good place to stoke up in the morning.

Orbit also has a fully-stocked bar, and in fact there is a separate entertainment room with a dance floor. On weekends, the air is as filled with lively Polish old-country music as it is with the aroma of its home-cooked food.

Red Apple Restaurants
- 3121 N. Milwaukee Ave., Chicago; (312) 588-5781
- 6474 N. Milwaukee Ave., Chicago; (312) 763-3407

This pair of Apples is another of the many opportunities for you to polish off your appetite in the Polish family style. Meals at the Red Apple are easy to describe; everything comes off the central buffet, which costs $6 per person. This not only includes your entree and side dishes, but also bread, coffee, and dessert! Well, that is, if you want jello for dessert. If you prefer cake, from the adjacent bakery, that's $1.50 extra.

Still, you can really stuff yourself here without unstuffing your wallet. Choose from such Polski delicacies as kielbasa with sauerkraut, meatballs, pierogies with various meat and cheese fillings, stuffed cabbage, blintzes, and more. The bread, of course, is freshly made in the bakery too. Not much more to say—the decor is clean and modern, the food is wonderful and definitely cheap, considering how much you can have. What else could anyone ask?

Carry-out dinners can be ordered for $5.50 or $6.50 per person, depending on your choice of entree; and be sure to check out that bakery/deli next door for more great food to take home.

Uncle Mike's Place
● 1700 W. Grand Ave., Chicago; (312) 226-5318

If you can't get into the popular and trendy Wishbone down the block (see below), you may want to try Uncle Mike's instead. It has some of the same kind of food, with less of a distinctive touch; not to mention a more upscale atmosphere and fewer crowds.

Like the Wishbone, they also only serve breakfast and lunch. You won't go hungry after chowing down on their "Old Fashioned Farm Breakfast"—three eggs scrambled with ham, onion, peppers, and potato, with cheese melted over the top, all for $3.95. Biscuits and gravy are $2.75; and just $3.75 gets you a pork chop with eggs, home fries and toast. They also have a large selection of waffles and pancakes with various toppings from fruit to chocolate chips, starting around $2.50.

On the lunch side, Mr. C enjoyed a huge salad plate of several mixed greens, avocado and other veggies, cheese, and strips of grilled chicken on top for $5.25. "Southern-style" catfish sandwiches are $3.95; and a chopped steak sandwich, on toasted garlic bread, was $3.75. To this, and most other sandwiches, you can add fries and cole slaw for a dollar more.

On the down side: Service can be a problem. Mr. C is willing to give the benefit of the doubt to the waitress who first brought out the wrong order, and then seemed to forget to bring back any order at all. Maybe it was a bad day. The food, when it arrived, was worth the wait. It is a pleasant place, a modern industrial look with vent ducts and an original pressed-tin ceiling painted over in bold colors.

Urbus Orbis
● 1934 W. North Ave., Chicago; (312) 252-4446

This combination bookstore, coffee shop, and artists' hangout-cum-studio has been open for four years and caters to the tattoo/nose ring/laundromat? What's a laundromat? crowd. Tucked into a dreary corner of Bucktown near the Wicker Park line, it's a truly interesting place for lunch, dinner, or just dessert. You never know if the caffeine fiend at the neighboring table is sketching you or not. And it's open til the wee hours of the a.m. for you nocturnal folk.

The magazine and the book choices reveal much about the lives of the regulars here at Urbus. *Chicago Actor* and *Skeptical Enquirer* can be found in the magazine racks, along with books like *How to Manage the Non-Profit Organization*. Miniature Madagascar palm trees line Urbus's window sills, while a large exposed pipe runs the length of the cafe. The espresso bar's long green counter has high chairs that look like they were swiped from the Salvation Army.

It's hard to tell if the waiters and waitresses are angst-ridden, hung over or generally struck with severe cases of lassitude, but the quality of the food more than compensates for the service. The vegetarian lasagne, at $5, is served with salad (don't leave this place without trying their smooth raspberry dressing!) and fresh bread (seven-grain, millet, onion dill, or dark rye). Though the oregano on the lasagne was laid on with a heavy hand, the dish itself, loaded with spinach, was delicious.

Other good choices here are the spanikopita (yes, they're big on spinach here), served with the same salad and bread deal, for $5, and a tofu

MR. CHEAP'S PICKS
West of Town—Bucktown and Wicker Park

✔ **Cafe du Midi**—Lunch is not *tres* expensive at this romantic bistro.

✔ **Dixie Que**—Cramped and crazy, this barbecue joint is possibly the place where Elvis *should* reappear.

✔ **Joe's Fisheries**—A fresh fish stand tucked into the heart of a Midwestern city? Ay-yup.

✔ **Leo's Lunchroom**—Aggressively hip, this downscale diner serves up huge portions of traditional and creative comfort food.

melt with a choice of cheddar, Swiss, or asiago cheese for $4.25. There are daily specials, too, like chicken pot pie for $4.75.

Salads here are substantial—made with broccoli and both red leaf and iceberg lettuce and (you guessed it!) spinach. The lemonade is fresh and Urbus even sells iced chocolate. Both go for $1.50, a bit much, but worth it. Tea comes in herbal, black, or green varieties for $1.25 a pop. You can also BYOB, but you will be charged a $2 per person corkage fee.

Desserts are often brought in from nearby bakeries, such as Judy's and Fresh Starts. "Chocolate Sin Cake" sells for $3.75, and sour cream apple pie (yum), for $3.25. Other odd and delicious choices include blueberry-nectarine pie ($3.50), melon with mangoes and blueberries ($3.25), and *tiramisu*, the dessert that mystified Tom Hanks in *Sleepless in Seattle*. These folks know it's made with layers of cinnamon, cream filling, and coffee liqueur, all of which goes for $3.75.

Urbus Orbis is open Monday through Thursday from 9 a.m. until midnight, Fridays and Saturdays 'til 1 a.m., and Sundays from 10 a.m. to midnight. Good place for breakfast, too—try "Eggs Espresso" with cheddar or feta cheese for $3, or sip a hot cuppa with a nice, big muffin (bran or sour cream-based, brought in from a local bakery) for $1.95.

West Egg Cafe & Rotisserie
- 620 N. Fairbanks Ct., Chicago; (312) 280-8366
- West Egg on State, 1139 N. State St., Chicago; (312) 951-7900
- West Egg on Monroe, 525 W. Monroe St., Chicago; (312) 454-9939, (takeout line, 454-0652)

You don't have to be rich as Gatsby to eat at the West Egg. They serve breakfast, lunch and dinner, in hefty portions at reasonable prices. Ingredients are all super-fresh, too—and what they do with them gets rather creative.

Breakfast is served all day long. Start off with fresh-squeezed orange or grapefruit juice for $1.35. Omelettes come with an English muffin and potatoes or tomato slices, priced from $5 for your basic cheese version to $6 for the "Bacado," which is stuffed with bacon, guacamole, Jack cheese and a side of salsa. *Olé!* The clever "breakfast salad" is actually layers of granola, yogurt, fruit, and nuts in a parfait glass, served with a homemade muffin for $4.95. Plain granola topped with beautiful blueberries or sweet strawberries is just $2.95, and the California Crepe, with broccoli, cheese, avocado, mushrooms, and eggs stuffed inside, is $5.95. You can even create your own breakfast, and add sides of potatoes for $1, an English muffin for 75 cents or a bowl of yogurt for $2.25.

The West Egg's wit continues into the lunch menu. Try the "Coop de Ville" ($6.75), a marinated chicken breast covered with bacon, avocado, and melted cheese on a kaiser roll; or the "Creole Chicadee" ($6.25), all-white chicken meat grilled with fiery-hot sauce, plus lettuce, tomato, and Cajun mayonnaise. On the lighter side, Cobb and shrimp salads are each $6.95, and a crunchy taco salad is $5.95.

More standard fare includes a whopping half-pound burger for $4.95, and the Sicilian version of the New Orleans poor boy sandwich (grilled eggplant, zucchini, mushrooms, onions, and tomato on top of spinach, with a basil-pesto sauce and melted Montery Jack cheese) for $6.25. Most lunch dishes are served with a side salad and potatoes.

Be sure to watch for specials of the day. There's often a $4.95 dinner special, such as barbecued ribs, or chicken fajitas; these are especially popular with the after-work crowd that hangs out at the bar. If you're looking for a quieter spot to eat, there's also a sunken dining room with handsomely spotless hardwood floors.

The West Eggers are a bit snitty about substitutions—the place just gets too busy. They won't even give you separate checks, so don't bother asking. Another no-no is cigar or pipe smoking, though; you'll be able to breathe easy during your meal. And insomniacs can egg each other into staying until the wee hours; West Egg is open from 6:30 a.m. until midnight, Monday through Thursday. It's also open all the way through from 6:30 Friday morning until midnight on Sunday. That's no yolk!

Wishbone Restaurant
- 1800 W. Grand Ave., Chicago; (312) 829-3597
- 1001 W. Washington Blvd., Chicago; (312) 850-2553

This place *must* be hip. You have to drive a long way from almost anywhere, the area is drab and industrial (and *that's* being kind), they don't take reservations, and yet—especially for weekend brunch—you can't get in. What are they doing right? The food, of course. It's homemade, scrumptious, and cheap. Rustle up a plate of black-eyed peas and rice, with a sauce of melted cheese, scallions, and tomato over the top, with salad and a hunk of cornbread, all for

$4.75. Add grilled ham or chicken, and the total comes to $5.95. Get the picture?

Down home cookin' is the order of the day at the Wishbone. Blackened chicken breast, with rice, cornbread, and a vegetable of the day, is just $6.25, as is the baked bone-in-ham platter or barbecued pork. Jambalaya with shrimp is $5.95. Burgers and sandwiches complete the menu, along with the occasionally exotic special, such as chicken and shrimp etoufee. You can order a la carte; or, for one dollar extra, add your choice of sides like peppered green beans, corn chowder, couscous, or fruit salad.

Mr. C particularly enjoyed an order of bean cakes, slightly spicy, made with potato, black-eyed peas, and chunks of carrot. Vegetarians will be happy here, with things like stuffed acorn squash and eggplant parmigiana. There is a full liquor license, featuring Southern brews like Dixie Beer. For dessert, finish with a slice of sweet potato pie ($2) or peach cobbler ($2.25).

Wishbone also serves breakfast—heaping omelette plates topped with homemade biscuits for around $4. The place opens up at 7:00 on weekday mornings, an hour later on weekends. At the other end of the day, food is served until 11:00 p.m. Tuesdays through Saturdays; on Monday nights, they switch to a cafeteria (tip-free!) arrangement, serving from 5:00 to 8:30 p.m. only. By the way, the restaurant accepts cash only—a way of keeping costs and prices down.

Yep, it's good, all right. All you have to do is get in. On weekends, that can mean groups of folks lounging around on the sidewalk outside; there doesn't seem to be much of a system to it. The decidedly small and humble restaurants consist of a handful of tables, a counter, some local art on the walls, and a young crowd. The original outpost on Grand Avenue serves only breakfast, lunch, and brunch; for dinners, check out the newer location on Washington.

HOTELS AND LODGING

Always on the lookout for a bargain, Mr. C has tried to wade through the tricky waters of the hotel biz to find rooms where you can stay for around $100 a night or less. These waters are tricky because hotel rates ebb and flow faster than the lock between the Chicago River and Lake Michigan. And don't forget that taxes are always going to be added on top of any quoted price. Below, then, are the results of his not-necessarily scientific survey.

Three important tips: First of all, you should always, *always* ask about discounts. Remember: No hotel room ever has only one price. Take advantage of any discounts you can—including corporate, AAA, military, American Association of Retired Persons, and others. Furthermore, if you're going to be in town long enough, ask about weekly rates.

Tip number two: Some of the older establishments, while luxurious-sounding and seemingly out of Mr. C's price range, may offer a relatively inexpensive rate when compared to newer places like the Hilton. How? Because of things like their mortgages being all paid up, allowing them to pass the savings along to you.

Finally, Chicago is convention central. If you're planning to stay in a hotel, motel, or bed and breakfast, be sure to make reservations—and make them *early*. Convention business also means that many rooms are empty come Friday, so you can get a great weekend package deal at almost any hotel in the city. Even ritzier places like the Westin may run under $100 a night with one of these deals.

The Avenue Motel

- 1154 S. Michigan Ave., Chicago, IL 60605; (312) 427-8200 or 1-800-621-4196

The AAA-approved Avenue is your basic budget motel, located right on Grant Park. Its rooms are decorated in earth tones and are slightly cramped, but they all include color televisions. Some have up to three extra lounge chairs and desk. Single and double rooms run about $50-$65, a true bargain considering the Avenue's location near many of the city's main attractions and a short walk away from the subway.

The Avenue also offers an inexpensive restaurant, with friendly waitresses serving breakfast, lunch and dinner daily. Some of them seem to have been doing so for, shall we say, a good long time.

As with the Best Western (below), you will be right near exciting cultural activities like free summer concerts in Grant Park, the Art Institute, and the Auditorium Theatre; at night, though, South Michigan can get kinda scary, so do take care (in other words, take cabs).

Bed & Breakfast Chicago

- P.O. Box 14088, Chicago, IL 60614; (312) 951-0085.

This is not a place to stay, but rather dozens of such places all around Chicagoland. Mr. C hardly has to tell you what a B & B is; but you'll certainly be interested to know of the diversity of lodgings in which this agency can set you up. It can be the traditional inn, where you'll come down to breakfast each morning and compare sightseeing notes with fellow tourists. It can also be as simple as a "room to let" in someone's private home. Since these can be booked for any length of time, they can make a great temporary base of operations for anyone staying in the city for work or pleasure, or perhaps trying Chicago on for size before moving here.

Most important of all, the price range may surprise you. Some rooms can rent for as little as $50 a night, depending of course upon the season; that can be half the cost of hotel rooms in the same areas, even popular locales such as Lincoln Park. And remember, the price includes breakfast and that homey touch—two things you *definitely* won't find at a budget motel. The roster is ever-changing, so call the agency and see what's available; they'll describe each setting in detail, and make all the arrangements for you. They have a fax number, too: (312) 649-9243.

Best Western Grant Park
- 1100 S. Michigan Ave., Chicago, IL 60605; (312) 922-2900 or 1-800-528-1234

This 172-room hotel is often the choice of school groups and European tourists, since it's located right near the Art Institute, Shedd Aquarium, Adler Planetarium, and the Field Museum. It's just a few blocks south of the Loop, and close to the charm of Printer's Row shops and restaurants. McCormick Place is also just a short bus ride to the south, so convention-goers also make a point of booking this hotel (sometimes many months in advance).

For about $40-$60 a night, your stay will include an outdoor pool and a small exercise room, with a Mexican restaurant adjacent to the hotel (although Mr. C would recommend packing antacid if you plan on eating there). Valet parking is provided. Free coffee and tea are continuously available in the lobby, and a limited supply of free newspapers are given

---

MR. CHEAP'S PICKS
Hotels and Lodging

✔ **Bed and Breakfast Chicago**—Call these folks to find inexpensive alternatives to hotel rooms.

✔ **Chicago International Hostel**—A clean place to stay for $13 a night—if you don't mind sharing facilities with fellow travelers.

✔ **Comfort Inn**—Sure, it's a chain, but it's really *nice* and super-conveniently located in Park West.

✔ **Lenox House Suites**—You'd be surprised how affordable a small suite can be in this luxurious hotel. A good mid-price budget option.

---

out each weekday morning.

For its price and location, this is a great pick if you're in town to see the sights. It's two blocks away from the Roosevelt stop on the Howard-Dan Ryan subway line, and taxis pass through the area frequently. A word of caution: Though you're still on Michigan Avenue, the neighborhood is far enough away from the Magnificent Mile to get a bit rough at night, so do be careful. Another drawback is that the front desk is sorely understaffed, allowing phone calls to ring and ring and ring. But if your trip is short and you don't like lines at check-in and check-out, the Best Western is a good bet.

Bismarck Hotel
- 171 W. Randolph St., Chicago, IL 60601; (312) 236-0123 or 1-800-643-1500

Located right in the Loop, the Bismarck is all you'd need a hotel to be—convenient to transportation, shopping, restaurants, and attractions like the Sears Tower. It's a good-sized hotel, with over 500 rooms, but the staff is still quite helpful. Bus service directly to the airports is provided on a regular schedule, and the "el" is only a block away.

The Bismarck is well-known for its super package deals; be sure to call for the latest offerings. One package includes breakfast in the hotel's Walnut Room, cocktails in the lounge, dinner, and tickets to the theater—all for under $100 a person per night. Other packages are centered around the city's various summer music festivals and the "Taste of Chicago," running as low as $78 a person—definitely worth checking out.

There's no pool, but kids won't complain with lakefront beaches close by, the Shedd Aquarium just a short bus ride away (no, you can't swim there, but you get the point), and opportunities to run around and play in Grant Park.

The Blackstone Hotel

- 636 S. Michigan Ave., Chicago, IL 60605; (312) 427-4300 or 1-800-622-6330

The eighty-year-old Blackstone, located on Michigan Avenue across from the Buckingham Fountain in Grant Park, is a venerable Chicago classic—reminiscent of the town's grand old days. It's listed on the National Register of Historic Places, and is famous for being the site where, during the 1920 Republican National Convention, a group of senators broke a deadlock and agreed to nominate Warren Harding for president. Teddy Roosevelt also stayed here, among other notable politicians.

The hotel is also known for contributing to the city's cultural scene. Joe Segal's Jazz Showcase, located off the lobby, is one of Chicago's premier jazz venues (alas, it's not necessarily cheap). It regularly presents such masters as Wynton Marsalis and Oscar Peterson; over the years, Dizzy Gillespie, Duke Ellington, and Charlie Parker have all played here. Elsewhere inside the hotel is the Mayfair Theater, currently home to the long-running comic whodunnit *Shear Madness*. Blues clubs on State Street, and the newly gentrified Burnham Park-Printer's Row area, are just a few blocks away.

The Blackstone is ornately decorated with crystal chandeliers and beautiful marble floors. Its suites with lakefront views cost as much as $260 a night. But some doubles may only cost about $100, with weekend rates as low as $70 a room. And your AAA or AARP discounts may reduce prices further, to about $55—a great deal for this elegant, action-packed hotel so close to the Loop and the Art Institute.

The Congress Parkway, which becomes the Eisenhower Expressway, is right around the corner. And the Blackstone is one of the city's few pet-friendly hotels (though they will charge you), another nod to older, more genteel times.

Chicago International Hostel

- 6318 N. Winthrop Ave., Chicago IL 60640; (312) 262-1011

For the truly ascetic, a hostel is the way to save big money while traveling. What many folks don't realize, though, is that you don't have to be a foreigner to stay in one. For a mere $13 a night, you can stay at the Chicago International Hostel, well uptown on the North Side. It's especially important to reserve early here, since the hostel is often booked months in advance by foreign travelers and adventurous students.

The hostel is located a block away from the Loyola University stop on the Howard-Dan Ryan "el." There's not much to do in the neighborhood, but Lincoln Park is not far away; and it's just a 25-minute ride on the train to get downtown. The front desk clerks will be happy to suggest places for you to visit, same as in any hotel.

The amenities aren't spectacular, as you'd expect from a hostel, but towels and linens are provided. The hostel is open from 7 to 10 a.m. and 4 p.m. to midnight only. In between, they figure, you'll be galavanting about the town. That midnight curfew is strictly in effect all week, but on Friday and Saturday nights, doors open again at 2 a.m. to let stragglers back in. If you arrive back at the hostel after midnight during the week, or after the 2 a.m. "last chance" on weekends, you're probably going to have to wait until 7 a.m. when the doors open again to be let inside. Tough as all that sounds, most people who stay here have no trouble complying.

Payment may only be made in cash, money order, or traveler's check—no personal checks or credit cards are ever accepted. Hostels certainly aren't the choice for everyone, but if you live the simple life, they can sure save you a lot of money. This will free up more of your financial resources to be spent on shopping, sightseeing, restaurants, Cubs games, or whatever your reason is for coming to Chicago in the first place.

Comfort Inn

- 601 W. Diversey Pkwy., Chicago, IL 60614; (312) 348-2810 or 1-800-221-2222

This national chain offers great value for the money, and this branch—very conveniently located on Diversey, in the Lincoln Park area, not far from the lake—certainly doesn't disappoint. The lobby, as well as the motel's 74 rooms, are beautifully decorated with tasteful paintings, oak furnishings, and dramatic drapery. This is a good place to choose if you want to have an in-town weekend getaway without breaking your budget.

Free continental breakfast is provided, to please both earlybirds and late risers—it runs from 6:30 a.m. until noon. Meanwhile, there's no shortage of restaurant choices outside the Inn (many of which are profiled in this book), with the eclectic offerings of Lincoln Avenue and Clark Street a short walk away. Lincoln Park Zoo is around the corner, and Wrigley Field is not far in the other direction. All of this is only a short ride from downtown.

Rates here vary widely, depending on the type of room you want.

You could opt for a suite (with Jacuzzi) for a whopping $175 a night, but a small double is $60 for one person or $65 for two, with the larger queen-doubles available at $87 and $92, respectively. A room with two double beds is $100.

Security in the Comfort Inn is exceptional, too, with lobby areas carefully monitored by screen.

Hotel Lincoln

- 1816 N. Clark St., Chicago, IL 60614; (312) 664-3040 or 1-800-426-1816

The Hotel Lincoln is a great place to consider whether you're bringing the whole family, or looking to get away from it all. Located in a residential area half a block south of the Lincoln Park Zoo and Conservatory, with the North Avenue beach right outside, this place is a great bargain. Gold Coast shops are close by (though few of them are cheap), yet the hotel feels removed from the noise of downtown. Clark Street buses run all day long, taking you south to the Loop or north to Lincoln Park and beyond.

Rooms range in price from $54-$64 for a double, with the higher rate prevailing on the weekends. Some rooms have refrigerators and radios, and there's an inexpensive restaurant as well as a dry cleaners, laundry room, and convenience store inside the hotel. Rooms are comfortably sized, although the staff recommends that families who want to stay together in one room book one of their mini-suites, which run about $120 on the weekends.

There are only 90 rooms in this older, European-style hotel, so be sure to call for reservations early.

Lenox House Suites

- 616 N. Rush St., Chicago, IL 60611; (312) 337-1000 or 1-800-44-LENOX

This spacious 330-room hotel is located in the heart of the Gold Coast, just a block from the Magnificent Mile; at first glance, it would appear to be a place that Mr. C would have to skip. Yet, rooms in this self-described "small hotel" don't go much over $100. For all the conveniences provided and super location, its value is hard to beat for business or pleasure travel.

All of the rooms here are suites, categorized into studios, juniors, and deluxe executive arrangements. A studio can run only $74 a night, and that comes with two queen-size beds. Weekend rates and corporate discounts are offered, and small group rates can also be easily arranged.

Every suite has a kitchen area, which includes a coffee maker; juice, mineral water, and newspapers are provided free. The bathrooms are outfitted with hair dryers, too. Valet and concierge services are available, and both a coffee shop and moderately-priced restaurant are located on street level.

Perhaps the best feature of the hotel, though, is that you won't have to deal with throngs of convention-eers crowding the lobby and restaurant. The Lenox has a small reception area, and meeting facilities for up to only 42 people. These, combined with its small size, almost guarantee you a relaxed, comfortable stay.

Ohio House Motel

- 600 N. LaSalle St., Chicago IL, 60610; (312) 943-6000

This AAA-approved motel in the heart of the Near North area is a good bet for family travelers. The Hard Rock Cafe, Rock 'n Roll McDonalds, Ed Debevic's, and Michael Jordan's restaurants are all within walking distance, as is the subway and the bustle of Michigan Avenue and its shops. Free parking is another bonus—although the front desk is honest enough to admit that the lot may fill up, meaning you'll have to fend for yourself.

The decor is more utilitarian than fancy—it may bring back memories of the Brady Bunch—but the mo-

tel's prices are equally retro, at about $54 a night for a single or $61 for a double before taxes. The motel's five-booth coffee shop has received accolades from the *Chicago Sun-Times* for its huge pancake, sausage, and egg breakfast, which costs only $3.

The motel is near the entrance to the Eisenhower Expressway, and the neighborhood can be boisterous; but security is good, with the switchboard remaining open 24 hours a day. All rooms are air-conditioned, with color television and radio.

River North Hotel

- 125 W. Ohio Street, Chicago, IL 60610; (312) 467-0800 or 1-800-528-1234

If you really want to be in the middle of all the action, pick the River North Hotel, located on the corner of LaSalle. Nightclubs and super shopping are all within walking distance; the Museum of Contemporary Art and the Terra Museum are nearby, as are the restaurants and entertainment of North Pier.

The Loop is about six blocks to the south, making this hotel a favorite of business travelers who want a convenient location without having to pay through the nose for it. The hotel is a rarity in the area, since parking is free, including free in-and-out privileges.

Other perks at the River North Hotel are its indoor pool and fitness room, fitted out with plenty of equipment. Cable television with HBO is also provided. Continental breakfast is included in the room price. That price, for most rooms, is around $90, with AARP discounts available. Children under 18 stay for free when sharing a room with a parent. Weekend rate packages can run as low as $63 a night, but must be reserved in advance.

INDEX

ALPHABETICAL INDEX

SUBJECT INDEX